A First Course in Quantitative Finance

This new and exciting book offers a fresh approach to quantitative finance and utilizes novel new features, including stereoscopic images which permit 3D visualization of complex subjects without the need for additional tools.

Offering an integrated approach to the subject, *A First Course in Quantitative Finance* introduces students to the architecture of complete financial markets before exploring the concepts and models of modern portfolio theory, derivative pricing, and fixed-income products in both complete and incomplete market settings. Subjects are organized throughout in a way that encourages a gradual and parallel learning process of both the economic concepts and their mathematical descriptions, framed by additional perspectives from classical utility theory, financial economics, and behavioral finance.

Suitable for postgraduate students studying courses in quantitative finance, financial engineering, and financial econometrics as part of an economics, finance, econometric, or mathematics program, this book contains all necessary theoretical and mathematical concepts and numerical methods, as well as the necessary programming code for porting algorithms onto a computer.

Professor Dr. Thomas Mazzoni has lectured at the University of Hagen and the Dortmund Business School and is now based at the University of Greifswald, Germany, where he received the 2014 award for excellence in teaching and outstanding dedication.

A First Course in Quantitative Finance

THOMAS MAZZONI

University of Greifswald

CAMBRIDGE
UNIVERSITY PRESS

University Printing House, Cambridge CB2 8BS, United Kingdom

One Liberty Plaza, 20th Floor, New York, NY 10006, USA

477 Williamstown Road, Port Melbourne, VIC 3207, Australia

314-321, 3rd Floor, Plot 3, Splendor Forum, Jasola District Centre, New Delhi - 110025, India

79 Anson Road, #06-04/06, Singapore 079906

Cambridge University Press is part of the University of Cambridge.

It furthers the University's mission by disseminating knowledge in the pursuit of education, learning and research at the highest international levels of excellence.

www.cambridge.org
Information on this title: www.cambridge.org/9781108419574
DOI: 10.1017/9781108303606

First published 2018

A catalogue record for this publication is available from the British Library

ISBN 978-1-108-41957-4 Hardback
ISBN 978-1-108-41143-1 Paperback

Contents

Part II   Financial Markets and Portfolio Theory   77

1 Introduction

Modern financial markets have come a long way from ancient bartering. They are highly interconnected, the information is very dense, and reaction to external events is almost instantaneous. Even though organized markets have existed for a very long time, this level of sophistication was not realized before the second half of the last century. The reason is that sufficient computing power and broadband internet coverage is necessary to allow a market to become a global organic structure. It is not surprising that such a self-organizing structure reveals new rules like for example the no arbitrage principle. What is surprising is that not only the rules, but also the purpose of the whole market seems to have changed. Nowadays, one of the primary objectives of an operational and liquid financial market is risk transfer. There are highly sophisticated instruments like options, swaps, and so forth, designed to decouple all sorts of risks from the underlying contract, and trade them separately. That way market participants can realize their individually desired level of insurance by simply trading the risk. Such a market is certainly not dominated by gambling or speculation, as suggested by the news from time to time, but indeed obeys some very fundamental and deep mathematical principles and is best analyzed using tools from probability theory, econometrics, and engineering.

Unfortunately the required mathematical machinery is not part of the regular education of economists. So the better part of this fascinating field is often reserved to trained mathematicians, physicists, and statisticians. The tragedy is that economists have much to contribute, because they are usually the only ones trained in the economic background and the appropriate way of thinking. It is not easy to bridge the gap, because often economists and mathematicians speak a very different language. Nevertheless, the fundamental structures and principles generally possess more than one representation. They can be proved mathematically, described geometrically, and be understood economically. It is thus the goal of this book to navigate through the equivalent descriptions, avoiding unnecessary technicalities, to provide an unobstructed view on those deep and elegant principles, governing modern financial markets.

About This Book

This book consists of four parts and an appendix, containing a short introduction to complex analysis. Part I provides some basics in probability theory, vector spaces, and utility theory, with strong reference to the geometrical view. The emphasis of those chapters is not on a fully rigorous exposition of measure theory or *Hilbert*-spaces, but on intuitive notation, visualization, and association with familiar concepts like length and geometric forms. Part II deals with the fundamental structure of financial markets, the no arbitrage principle, and classical portfolio theory. A large number of scientists in this field received the Noble Prize for their pioneering work. Models like the capital asset pricing model (CAPM) and the arbitrage pricing theory (APT) are still cornerstones of portfolio management and asset pricing. Furthermore, some of the most famous puzzles in economic theory are discussed. In Part III, the reader enters the world of derivative pricing. There is no doubt that this area is one of the mathematically most intense in quantitative finance. The high level of sophistication is due to the fact that prices of derivative contracts depend on future prices of one or more underlying securities. Such an underlying may as well be another derivative contract. It is also in this area that one experiences the consequences of incomplete markets very distinctly. Thus, approaches to derivative pricing in incomplete markets are also discussed extensively. Finally, Part IV is devoted to fixed-income markets and their derivatives. This is in some way the supreme discipline of quantitative finance. In ordinary derivative pricing, the fundamental quantities are prices of underlying securities, which can be understood as single zero-dimensional objects. In pricing fixed-income derivatives, the fundamental quantities are the yield or forward curve, respectively. They are one-dimensional objects in this geometric view. That makes life considerably more complicated, but also more exciting.

This book is meant as an undergraduate introduction to quantitative finance. It is based on a series of lectures I have given at the University of Greifswald since 2012. In teaching economics students I learned very rapidly that it is of vital importance to provide a basis for the simultaneous development of technical skills and substantial concepts. Much of the necessary mathematical framework is therefore developed along the way to allow the reader to make herself acquainted with the theoretical background step by step.

To support this process, there are lots of short exercises called "quick calculations." Here is an example: Suppose we are talking about the binomial formulas you know from high school, in particular the third one

$$(a + b)(a - b) = a^2 - b^2. \tag{1.1}$$

Now it's your turn.

Quick calculation 1.1   Show that 899 is not a prime number.

If you are looking for factors by trial and error, this surely will be no quick calculation and you are on the wrong track. At least you missed something, in this case that $899 = 30^2 - 1^2$, and thus 31 and 29 have to be factors.

There are also more intense exercises at the end of each chapter. Their level of difficulty is varying and you should not feel bad if you cannot solve them all without stealing a glance at the solutions. Some of them are designed to train you in explicit computations. Others provide additional depth and background information on some topics in the respective chapter, and still others push the concepts discussed a little bit further, to give you a sneak preview of what is to come.

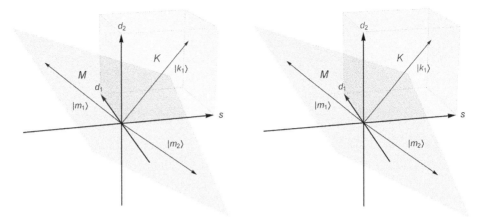

Fig. 1.1 🆔 Stereoscopic image – Space of arbitrage opportunities K and complete market M

In a highly technical field like quantitative finance, it is often unavoidable that we work with three-dimensional figures and graphs. To preserve the spatial perception, these graphics are provided as stereoscopic images. You can visualize them without 3D-glasses or other fancy tools. All it takes is a little getting used to. Whenever you see the 🆔 icon in a caption, it means that the figure is a stereoscopic image. Figure 1.1 is such an image; I borrowed it from a later chapter. At first sight, you will hardly recognize any difference between the two graphs, and you can retrieve all the information from either one of them. But if you follow the subsequent steps, you can explore the third dimension:

1. Slightly increase your usual reading distance and concentrate on the center between the two images, while pretending to look straight through the book, focusing on an imaginary distant point. You will see both images moving towards each other and finally merging.
2. If you have achieved perfect alignment, you will see one image at the center and two peripheral ghost images, that your brain partially blends out. Try to keep the alignment, while refocusing your vision to see the details sharply.
3. If you have difficulties keeping the alignment, try to increase the distance to about half a meter until you get a feeling for it. Don't tilt your head or it is all over.

Your brain is probably not used to controlling ocular alignment and lens accommodation independently, so it may take a little bit of practice, but it is real fun. So give it a try.

My goal in writing this book was to make the sometimes strange, but always fascinating world of modern financial markets accessible to undergraduate students with a little bit of mathematical and statistical background. Needless to say that quantitative finance is such an extensive field that this first course can barely scratch the surface. But the really fundamental principles are not that hard to grasp and exploring them is like a journey through a century of most elegant ideas. So I hope you enjoy it.

Part I Technical Basics

2 | A Primer on Probability

Virtually all decisions we make are subject to a more or less large amount of uncertainty. The mathematical language of uncertainty is probability. This short introduction is intended to equip the reader with a conceptual understanding of the most important ideas with respect to quantitative finance. It is by no means an exhaustive treatment of this subject. Furthermore, a basic familiarity with the most fundamental principles of statistics is assumed.

2.1 Probability and Measure

The mathematical laboratory for random experiments is called probability space. Its first constituent is the set of elementary states of the world $\Omega = \{\omega_1, \omega_2, \ldots\}$ which may or may not realize. The set Ω may as well be an uncountable domain such as a subset of $\mathbb{R}$. The elements $\omega_1, \omega_2, \ldots$ are merely labels for upcoming states of the world which are distinguishable to us in a certain sense. For example imagine tossing a coin. Apart from the very unusual case of staying on the edge, the coin will eventually come to rest either heads up or tails up. In this sense these two states of the world are distinguishable to us and we may want to label them as

$$\Omega = \{H, T\}. \tag{2.1}$$

It is tempting to identify Ω with the set of events which describes the outcome of the random experiment of tossing the coin. However this is not quite true, because not all possible outcomes are contained in Ω, but only those of a certain elementary kind. For example the events "Heads or Tails" or "neither Heads nor Tails" are not contained in Ω. This observation immediately raises the question of what we mean exactly when we are talking of an event? An event is a set of elementary states of the world, for each of which we can tell with certainty whether or not it has realized after the random experiment is over. This is seen very easily by considering the throw of a die. There are six elementary states of the world we can distinguish by reading off the number on the top side after the die has come to rest. We can label these six states by $\Omega = \{1, \ldots, 6\}$. The outcome of throwing an even number for example, corresponds to the event

$$A = \{2, 4, 6\}, \tag{2.2}$$

which means the event of throwing a two, a four, or a six. For each state of the world in A we can tell by reading off the number on the top side of the die, if it has realized or not. Therefore, we can eventually answer the question if A has happened or not with certainty.

There are many more events that can be assembled from elementary states of the world. For example one may want to observe if the number thrown is smaller or equal to three. Which events have to be considered and are there rules for constructing such events? It turns out that there are strict rules by which events are collected in order to guarantee consistent answers for all possible outcomes. A family $\mathcal{F}$ of sets (events) $A, A_1, A_2, \ldots$ is called a σ-algebra, if it satisfies the following conditions

1. $\mathcal{F}$ is nonempty,

2. if $A \in \mathcal{F}$ then $A^C \in \mathcal{F}$,   (2.3)

3. if $A_1, A_2, \ldots \in \mathcal{F}$ then $\bigcup_{n=1}^{\infty} A_n \in \mathcal{F}$.

In (2.3), A^C is the complement of A, which contains all elements of Ω that are not in A. These rules for σ-algebras have some interesting consequences. First of all, $\mathcal{F}$ is not empty, which means there has to be at least one event $A \in \mathcal{F}$. The second rule now immediately implies that $A^C \in \mathcal{F}$, too, and by the third rule $A \cup A^C = \Omega \in \mathcal{F}$. But if Ω is in $\mathcal{F}$, then $\Omega^C = \emptyset$ is also in $\mathcal{F}$ by rule two. Therefore, the smallest possible σ-algebra is $\mathcal{F} = \{\emptyset, \Omega\}$. Another interesting consequence is that for $A_1, A_2, \ldots \in \mathcal{F}$ the intersection $\bigcap_{n=1}^{\infty} A_n$ is also in $\mathcal{F}$. This is an immediate consequence of De Morgan's rule

$$\bigcap_{n=1}^{\infty} A_n = \left(\bigcup_{n=1}^{\infty} A_n^C \right)^C .$$ (2.4)

Quick calculation 2.1 Verify that for $A_1, A_2 \in \mathcal{F}$ the intersection $A_1 \cap A_2$ is also in $\mathcal{F}$.

The pair $(\Omega, \mathcal{F})$ is called a measurable space. The question of how such a space is constructed generally boils down to the question of how to construct $\mathcal{F}$. The smallest possible σ-algebra $\mathcal{F} = \{\emptyset, \Omega\}$ has not enough structure to be of any practical interest. For countable and even for countably infinite Ω one may choose the power set, indicated by 2^{Ω}, which is the family of all possible subsets of Ω that can be constructed. There are $2^{\#\Omega}$ possible subsets, where the symbol # means "number of elements in"; thus the name power set. However, for uncountably infinite sets like $\Omega = \mathbb{R}$ for example, the power set is too large. Instead one uses the σ-algebra, which is generated by all open intervals (a, b) in $\mathbb{R}$ with $a \leq b$, the so-called *Borel-σ-algebra* $\mathcal{B}(\mathbb{R})$. Due to the rules for σ-algebras (2.3), it contains much more than only open intervals. For example the closed intervals, generated by

$$\bigcap_{n=1}^{\infty} \left(a - \frac{1}{n}, b + \frac{1}{n} \right) = [a, b],$$ (2.5)

and sets like $(a, b)^C = (-\infty, a] \cup [b, \infty)$ are also in $\mathcal{B}(\mathbb{R})$. We could have even chosen the closed or half open intervals in the first place. Roughly speaking, all sets that can be generated from open, half open, or closed intervals in a constructive way are in the *Borel-σ-algebra*, but surprisingly, it is still not too large.

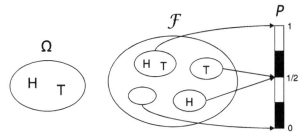

Fig. 2.1 Probability space as mathematical model for a fair coin toss

This discussion opens another interesting possibility, namely that σ-algebras may be generated. Again consider the throw of a die, where all that matters to us is if the number on the top side is even or odd after the die has settled down. Letting again $\Omega = \{1, \ldots, 6\}$, the σ-algebra generated by this (hypothetical) process is

$$\mathcal{F} = \{\emptyset, \{2, 4, 6\}, \{1, 3, 5\}, \Omega\}. \tag{2.6}$$

Quick calculation 2.2 Verify that $\mathcal{F}$ is indeed a valid σ-algebra.

A general statement is that the σ-algebra generated by the event A is $\mathcal{F} = \{\emptyset, A, A^C, \Omega\}$, or shorthand $\mathcal{F} = \sigma(A)$. It is easy to see that this σ-algebra is indeed the smallest one containing A.

A function $\mu : \mathcal{F} \to \mathbb{R}_0^+$, with the properties

1. $\mu(\emptyset) = 0$,

2. $\mu\left(\bigcup\limits_{n=1}^{\infty} A_n\right) = \sum\limits_{n=1}^{\infty} \mu(A_n)$, for $A_1, A_2, \ldots \in \mathcal{F}$ and $A_i \cap A_j = \emptyset$ for $i \neq j$, $\qquad$ (2.7)

is called a measure on $(\Omega, \mathcal{F})$. The triple $(\Omega, \mathcal{F}, \mu)$ is called a measure space. The concept of measure is the most natural concept of length, assigned to all sets in the σ-algebra. This becomes immediately clear by considering the measurable space $(\mathbb{R}, \mathcal{B})$, with the *Borel*-$\sigma$-algebra, generated by say the half open intervals $(a, b]$ with $a \leq b$, and choosing the *Lebesgue*-measure $\mu((a, b]) = b - a$.[1] In case of probability theory one assigns the overall length $\mu(\Omega) = 1$ to Ω. The associated measure is called probability and is abbreviated $P(A)$ for $A \in \mathcal{F}$. Furthermore, the triple $(\Omega, \mathcal{F}, P)$ is called probability space. Figure 2.1 illustrates the construction of the whole probability space for the (fair) coin toss experiment.

There is much more to say about probability spaces and measures than may yet appear. Measure theory is a very rich and subtle branch of mathematics. Nonetheless, most roads inevitably lead to highly technical concepts, barely accessible to

---

[1] Technically, the measure cannot be established on $\mathcal{B}$ directly, it has to be assigned on the semiring $\mathcal{I} = \{(a, b] : a, b \in \mathbb{R} \text{ and } a \leq b\}$. Afterwards, it can be extended to $\mathcal{B} = \sigma(\mathcal{I})$, which is the *Borel*-$\sigma$-algebra.

non-mathematicians. To progress in understanding the fundamental principles of financial markets they are a "nice to have" but not a key requirement at this point.

2.2   Filtrations and the Flow of Information

In practice most of the time we are dealing not with isolated random experiments, but with processes that we observe from time to time, like the quotes of some preferred stock. Sometimes our expectations may be confirmed, other times we may be surprised by a totally unexpected development. We are observing a stochastic process, piece by piece revealing information over time. How is this flow of information incorporated in the static model of a probability space? Imagine tossing a coin two times in succession. We can label the elementary outcomes of this random experiment

$$\Omega = \{(H, H), (H, T), (T, H), (T, T)\}. \tag{2.8}$$

Now, invent a counting variable t, which keeps track of how many times the coin was tossed already. Obviously, this counting variable can take the values $t \in \{0, 1, 2\}$. We can now ask, what is the σ-algebra $\mathcal{F}_t$ that is generated by the coin tossing process at stage (time) t? At $t = 0$ nothing has happened and all we can say at this time is that one of the four possible states of the world will realize with certainty. Therefore, the σ-algebra at $t = 0$ is

$$\mathcal{F}_0 = \{\emptyset, \Omega\}. \tag{2.9}$$

Now imagine, the first toss comes out heads. We can now infer that one of the outcomes $(H, \cdot)$ will realize with certainty and $(T, \cdot)$ is no longer possible. Even though we do not yet have complete information, in the language of probability we can already say that the event $A = \{(H, H), (H, T)\}$ has happened at time $t = 1$. Remember that event A states that either (H, H) or (H, T) will realize eventually, which is obviously true if the first toss was heads. An exactly analogous argument holds if the first toss comes out tails, $B = \{(T, H), (T, T)\}$. Taking events A and B, and adding all required unions and complements, one obtains the largest possible σ-algebra at $t = 1$,

$$\mathcal{F}_1 = \{\emptyset, \{(H, H), (H, T)\}, \{(T, H), (T, T)\}, \Omega\}. \tag{2.10}$$

By comparing $\mathcal{F}_0$ and $\mathcal{F}_1$ it becomes clear how information flows. The finer the partition of the σ-algebra, the more information is revealed by the history of the process. Another important and by no means accidental fact is that $\mathcal{F}_0 \subset \mathcal{F}_1$. It indicates that no past information will ever be forgotten.

Now let's consider the final toss of the coin. After this terminal stage is completed, we know the possible outcomes of the entire experiment in maximum detail. We are now able to say if for example the event $\{(T, T)\}$, or the event $\{(H, T)\}$ has happened or not. Thus the family $\mathcal{F}_2$ has the finest possible partition structure. Of course for $\mathcal{F}_2$ to be a σ-algebra, we have also to consider all possible unions and complements. If one neatly adds all required sets, which is a tedious but not a difficult task, the resulting σ-algebra is the power set of Ω,

$$\mathcal{F}_2 = 2^\Omega = \{\emptyset, \{(H, H)\}, \{(H, T)\}, \dots, \{(H, T), (T, H), (T, T)\}, \Omega\}. \tag{2.11}$$

That is to say that every bit of information one can possibly learn about this process is revealed at $t = 2$. The ascending sequence of σ-algebras $\mathcal{F}_t$, with $\mathcal{F}_0 \subseteq \mathcal{F}_t \subseteq \mathcal{F}$, is called a filtration. If a filtration is generated by successively observing the particular outcomes of a process like the coin toss, it is called the natural filtration of that process. However, since the σ-algebra generated by a particular event is the smallest one, containing the generating event, the terminal σ-algebra of such a natural filtration is usually smaller than the power set of Ω.

Quick calculation 2.3 Convince yourself that the natural filtration $\mathcal{F}_2$, generated by observing the events $A_1 = \{(H, H), (H, T)\}$ and $A_2 = \{(H, T)\}$, has only eight elements.

2.3   Conditional Probability and Independence

Consider the probability space $(\Omega, \mathcal{F}, P)$ and an event $A \in \mathcal{F}$ with $P(A) > 0$. Now define

$$\mathcal{F}_A = \{A \cap B : B \in \mathcal{F}\}, \tag{2.12}$$

the family of all intersections of A with every event in $\mathcal{F}$. Then $\mathcal{F}_A$ is itself a σ-algebra on A and the pair $(A, \mathcal{F}_A)$ is a measurable space. Proving this statement is not very hard, so it seems more beneficial to illustrate it in an example.

Example 2.1

Consider a measurable space $(\Omega, \mathcal{F})$ for a six sided die, with $\Omega = \{1, \dots, 6\}$ and $\mathcal{F} = 2^\Omega$. Let $A = \{2, 4, 6\}$ be the event of throwing an even number. Which events are contained in $\mathcal{F}_A$ and why is it a σ-algebra on A?

Solution
Intersecting A with all other events in $\mathcal{F}$ generates the following family of sets

$$\mathcal{F}_A = \{\emptyset, \{2\}, \{4\}, \{6\}, \{2, 4\}, \{2, 6\}, \{4, 6\}, A\}.$$

But $\mathcal{F}_A$ is the power set of A and thus it has to be a σ-algebra on A.

In case of $P(A) > 0$, the probability measure $P(B|A)$ is called the conditional probability of B given A, and is defined as

$$P(B|A) = \frac{P(B \cap A)}{P(A)}. \tag{2.13}$$

The triple $(A, \mathcal{F}_A, P(\cdot|A))$ forms a new measure space or more precisely a new probability space, which is again illustrated in an example.

Example 2.2

Take the measurable space $(\Omega, \mathcal{F})$ for the six sided die of Example 2.1 and equip it with the probability measure

$$P(B) = \frac{\#B}{6},$$

for all $B \in \mathcal{F}$. Now, as before, pick the particular event $A = \{2, 4, 6\}$ of throwing an even number. What are the conditional probabilities of $P(A|A)$, $P(\{2\}|A)$, and $P(\{5\}|A)$?

Solution

First observe that under the original probability measure

$$P(A) = \frac{3}{6} = \frac{1}{2}.$$

One thus obtains

$$P(A|A) = \frac{P(A \cap A)}{P(A)} = \frac{P(A)}{P(A)} = 1,$$

$$P(\{2\}|A) = \frac{P(\{2\} \cap A)}{P(A)} = \frac{P(\{2\})}{P(A)} = \frac{\frac{1}{6}}{\frac{1}{2}} = \frac{1}{3},$$

$$P(\{5\}|A) = \frac{P(\{5\} \cap A)}{P(A)} = \frac{P(\emptyset)}{P(A)} = \frac{0}{\frac{1}{2}} = 0.$$

An immediate corollary to the definition of conditional probability (2.13) is Bayes' rule. Because $P(B \cap A) = P(A \cap B)$, we have

$$P(B|A) = \frac{P(A|B)P(B)}{P(A)} = \frac{P(A|B)P(B)}{P(A|B)P(B) + P(A|B^C)P(B^C)}. \tag{2.14}$$

The last equality holds, because $B \cap B^C = \emptyset$ and $B \cup B^C = \Omega$.

Quick calculation 2.4 Prove this statement by using the additivity property of measures (2.7) on page 9.

Independence is another extremely important concept in probability theory. It means that by observing one event, one is not able to learn anything about another event. This is best understood by recalling that probability is in the first place a measure of length. Geometrically, the concept equivalent to independence is orthogonality. Consider two intervals A and B, situated on different axes, orthogonal to each other,

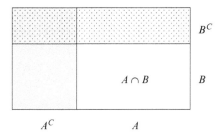

Fig. 2.2 Intervals on orthogonal axes

see Figure 2.2. In this case, the *Lebesgue*-measure for the rectangle $A \cap B$ is the product of the lengths of each side, $\mu(A \cap B) = \mu(A)\mu(B)$, which is of course the area. In complete analogy two events A and B are said to be independent, if

$$P(A \cap B) = P(A)P(B) \tag{2.15}$$

holds. But what does it mean that we can learn nothing about a particular event from observing another event? First, let's take a look at an example where independence fails. Again consider the six sided die and take $A = \{2, 4, 6\}$ to be the event of throwing an even number. Suppose you cannot observe the outcome, but somebody tells you that the number thrown is less than or equal to three. In other words, the event $B = \{1, 2, 3\}$ has happened. It is immediately clear, that you learn something from the information that B has happened because there is only one even number in B but two odd ones. If the die is fair, you would a priori have expected event A to happen roughly half the times you throw the die. Now you still do not know if A has happened or not, but in this situation you would expect it to happen only one third of the times. We can quantify this result by using the formal probability space of Example 2.2 for the fair die, and calculating the conditional probability

$$P(A|B) = \frac{P(A \cap B)}{P(B)} = \frac{P(\{2\})}{P(B)} = \frac{1}{3}, \tag{2.16}$$

which is precisely what we claimed it to be.

Quick calculation 2.5 Confirm the last equality in (2.16).

In particular, $\frac{1}{6} = P(A \cap B) \neq P(A)P(B) = \frac{1}{2} \cdot \frac{1}{2}$, which confirms that A and B are not independent events. If on the other hand B is the event of throwing a number smaller than or equal to two, $B = \{1, 2\}$, we do not learn anything from the information that B has happened or has not happened. We would still expect to see an even number in roughly half the times we throw the die. In this case, we can confirm that

$$\frac{1}{6} = P(A \cap B) = P(A)P(B) = \frac{1}{2} \cdot \frac{1}{3}, \tag{2.17}$$

which means that A and B are indeed independent. An additional consequence of independence is that the conditional probability of an event collapses to the unconditional one,

$$P(A|B) = \frac{P(A \cap B)}{P(B)} = \frac{P(A)P(B)}{P(B)} = P(A). \qquad (2.18)$$

Quick calculation 2.6 Show that for the six sided die, the events of throwing an even number and throwing a number less than or equal to four are also independent.

2.4   Random Variables and Stochastic Processes

Our discussion of probability spaces up to this point was by no means exhaustive. For example, measure theory comes with its own theory of integration, called the *Lebesgue*-integral, which is conceptually very different from the *Riemann*-integral taught in high school. Whereas the *Lebesgue*-integral is easier to manipulate on a technical level, it is much harder to evaluate than the *Riemann*-integral, where one can use the fundamental theorem of calculus. Fortunately, except for some exotic functions, the results of both integrals coincide, so that we can establish a link between both worlds. The situation is exactly the same in case of the whole probability space. As we have seen, it is a very rigorous and elegant model for random experiments, but it is also very hard to calculate concrete results. Luckily, there exists a link to map the measurable space $(\Omega, \mathcal{F})$ onto another measurable space[2] $(E, \mathcal{B})$, equipped with a distribution function F, induced by the original probability measure P. This link is established by a random variable or a stochastic process, respectively.

The designation random variable is a misnomer, because it really is a function $X: \Omega \rightarrow E$, mapping a particular state of the world onto a number. For example in the coin toss experiment, one could easily define the following random variable

$$X(\omega) = \begin{cases} 1 & \text{for } \omega = H, \\ 0 & \text{for } \omega = T. \end{cases} \qquad (2.19)$$

Note that the link established by (2.19) is only meaningful, if for every set $B \in \mathcal{B}$, there is also a $X^{-1}(B) \in \mathcal{F}$, where the inverse mapping of the random variable X is defined by

$$X^{-1}(B) = \{\omega \in \Omega : X(\omega) \in B\}, \qquad (2.20)$$

the set of all states ω, in which $X(\omega)$ belongs to B. If this condition holds, $X(\omega)$ is also more precisely called a "measurable function." This condition is trivially fulfilled in the above example, because (2.19) is a one-to-one mapping. A nontrivial example, emphasizing the usefulness of this transformation, is the following:

---

[2] Usually E is a subset of $\mathbb{R}$, whereas $\mathcal{B}$ is the corresponding *Borel-σ*-algebra. For countable E, $\mathcal{B}$ may be chosen as the power set of E.

Example 2.3

Imagine tossing a coin N times, where each trial is independent of the previous one. Assume that heads is up with probability p and tails with $1 - p$. We are now interested in the probability of getting exactly k times heads.

Solution in the original probability space

Doing it by the book, first we have to set up a sample space

$$\Omega = \{(H, H, \ldots), (T, H, \ldots), \ldots, (T, T, \ldots)\}.$$

Ω has already 2^N elements. Because the sample space is countable, we may choose $\mathcal{F} = 2^\Omega$. Now we have to assign a probability to each event in $\mathcal{F}$. Because the tosses are independent, we can assign the probability

$$P(\{\omega\}) = p^{\#H(\omega)}(1 - p)^{\#T(\omega)}$$

to each elementary event $\{\omega\}$, where in slight abuse of notation $\#H(\omega)$ and $\#T(\omega)$ means "number of heads/tails in ω," respectively. But an arbitrary event $A \in \mathcal{F}$ is a union of those elementary events. Because they are all distinct, we have by the additivity property of measures

$$P(A) = \sum_{\omega \in A} P(\{\omega\}).$$

This assigning of probabilities has to be exercised for all possible events in $\mathcal{F}$. Think of it as laying out all events in $\mathcal{F}$ on a large table and attaching a flag to each of them, labeled with the associated probability. Now we have to look for a very special event in $\mathcal{F}$, containing all sample points with exactly k times H and $N - k$ times T, and no others. Because $\mathcal{F} = 2^\Omega$, this event has to be present somewhere on the table. Once we have identified it, we can finally read off the probability from its flag and we are done. What a mess.

Solution in the transformed probability space

Define the random variable $X : \Omega \to E$, where $E = \{0, 1, \ldots, N\}$, and

$$X(\omega) = \#H(\omega).$$

We do not even have to look at the new σ-algebra $\mathcal{B}$, because we are solely interested in the event $B = \{k\}$, which only contains one elementary sample point. We further know that each ω in $X^{-1}(B)$ has probability $P(\{\omega\}) = p^k(1 - p)^{N-k}$. All we have to do is to count the number of these pre-images to obtain the so-called probability mass function

$$f(k) = P(X = k) = \binom{N}{k} p^k (1 - p)^{N-k},$$

where $\binom{N}{k} = \frac{N!}{k!(N-k)!}$ is the number of possible permutations of k heads in N trials.

We can even go one step further and ask what is the probability of at most k times heads in N trials? We then obtain the distribution function of the random variable X

$$F(k) = P(X \le k) = \sum_{n=0}^{k} \binom{N}{n} p^n (1-p)^{N-n}, \qquad (2.21)$$

which is of course the binomial distribution. Obtaining this probability distribution in the original probability space would have certainly been a very cumbersome business.

The realization of a random variable X itself can generate a σ-algebra $\mathcal{B} = \sigma(X)$, which induces another σ-algebra in the original probability space via X^{-1} as in (2.20). This completes the link in both directions. Indeed the same argument can be refined a little bit more. If one observes a whole family of random variables $X_t(\omega)$, labeled by a continuous or discrete index set $0 \le t \le T$, there is also a family of σ-algebras $\mathcal{F}_t$ induced by X_t^{-1} in the original probability space. But this is nothing else than the concept of filtrations. The family of random variables $X_t(\omega)$ is called a stochastic process. If the filtration $\mathcal{F}_t$ is generated by the process X_t, it is called the natural filtration of this process. If the process X_t is measurable with respect to $\mathcal{F}_t$, it is called "adapted" to this σ-algebra. An important example of a stochastic process in finance is the following:

Example 2.4

The stochastic process W_t, characterized by the properties

1. $W_0 = 0$

2. W_t has independent increments

3. $W_t - W_s \sim N(0, t-s)$ for $0 \le s < t$

is called the *Wiener*-process (or *Brown*ian motion). It is an important part of the famous *Black–Scholes*-theory of option pricing.

Explanation

First observe that the process W_t is specified completely in terms of its distribution function. $N(0, t-s)$ represents the normal distribution with expectation value 0 and variance $t-s$. For any given time interval $t-s$, W is a continuous random variable with probability density function[3]

$$f(w) = \frac{1}{\sqrt{2\pi(t-s)}} e^{-\frac{1}{2}\frac{w^2}{t-s}},$$

---

[3] We will at a later time occasionally label the probability density function by p or q to refer to the associated probability measure.

which is the continuous analogue of the probability mass function of the discrete random variable X in Example 2.3. The corresponding distribution function is obtained not by summation, but by integration

$$F(w) = \int_{-\infty}^{w} f(x)dx.$$

A further subtlety of continuous random variables, originating from the uncountable nature of the sample space Ω, is that a singular point has probability zero. This is immediately obvious, since

$$P(w_1 \le W \le w_2) = \int_{w_1}^{w_2} f(x)dx = F(w_2) - F(w_1),$$

and for $w_1 = w_2$, the integral collapses to zero. The best we can do is to calculate the probability for the small interval $[w, w + dw]$, which is $f(w)dw$.

A technical consequence of this somewhat peculiar feature of uncountable sample spaces is that there are nonempty sets with probability measure zero. These sets have by no means to be small. If $\Omega = \mathbb{R}$ and $\mathcal{F} = \mathcal{B}(\mathbb{R})$, then the whole set $\mathbb{Q}$ of rational numbers has probability zero. Such a set is called a null set. A probability space is called complete, if all subsets of null sets are elements of $\mathcal{F}$. Fortunately, it is always possible to include all these subsets, but because most statements exclusively concern events with probability larger than zero, one indicates this restriction by appending the phrase "almost surely." For example the *Wiener*-process has almost surely continuous but non-differentiable trajectories (paths), which means that this property is at most violated by events with probability zero.

2.5   Moments of Random Variables

There are some probability distributions of particular importance in finance. We have seen two of them, the binomial distribution in Example 2.3, and the normal distribution in Example 2.4. While the distribution function is fully sufficient to define the properties of a random variable, it is usually not very descriptive. Moments are additional concepts to characterize some particular features. The first moment of a random variable X is its expectation value $m_1 = E[X]$. It is defined in the discrete/continuous case as

$$E[X] = \sum_{n} x_n f(x_n) \quad \text{or} \quad E[X] = \int x f(x)dx, \tag{2.22}$$

respectively, provided that a density function for a continuous random variable exists, which is usually the case. The expectation value is best thought of as the center of probability mass. It is by no means always the "expected" value, as seen in Figure 2.3. Both

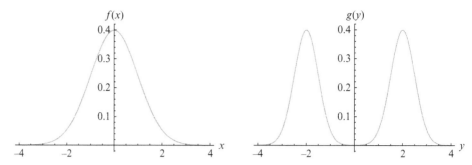

Fig. 2.3 Probability density functions $f(x)$ and $g(y)$ of two random variables X and Y with $E[X] = E[Y] = 0$

random variables X and Y have expectation zero, but one would certainly not expect a value of Y to realize in the vicinity of zero.

To obtain the expectation value of a binomially distributed random variable $X \sim B(p, N)$, we can either use (2.22), or remember that a single coin is tossed N times independently, and each toss has expectation value $p = 1 \cdot p + 0 \cdot (1 - p)$. Thus, the expectation value of N trials is

$$E[X] = N \cdot p. \tag{2.23}$$

Now consider another random variable Y, which is normally distributed, $Y \sim N(\mu, \sigma^2)$. To calculate its expectation value, we have to evaluate the integral

$$E[Y] = \int_{-\infty}^{\infty} y \cdot \frac{1}{\sqrt{2\pi\sigma^2}} e^{-\frac{1}{2}\left(\frac{y-\mu}{\sigma}\right)^2} dy. \tag{2.24}$$

To this end let's first make the substitution $z = \frac{y-\mu}{\sigma}$, which makes $dy = \sigma dz$ and leaves the boundary of integration unchanged, and define

$$\phi(z) = \frac{1}{\sqrt{2\pi}} e^{-\frac{1}{2}z^2}, \tag{2.25}$$

which is the probability density function of a standard normally distributed random variable $Z \sim N(0, 1)$. With these substitutions one obtains

$$E[Y] = \mu \int_{-\infty}^{\infty} \phi(z)dz + \sigma \int_{-\infty}^{\infty} z \cdot \phi(z)dz. \tag{2.26}$$

The first integral in (2.26) is equal to one, because it simply adds up all probabilities. The second integral is zero. To see that, observe that $z \cdot \phi(z) = -\phi'(z)$ and

$$\int_{-\infty}^{\infty} -\phi'(z)dz = -\phi(z)\Big|_{-\infty}^{\infty} = 0. \tag{2.27}$$

Hence, the desired expectation value is

$$E[Y] = \mu. \tag{2.28}$$

Whereas the expectation value is defined as the first raw moment, the second moment is usually understood as a central moment, which means a moment around the expectation value, called the variance, $M_2 = \text{Var}[X]$. It is defined as

$$\text{Var}[X] = E[(X - E[X])^2] = E[X^2] - E[X]^2. \tag{2.29}$$

The second equality follows from the fact that $E[E[X]] = E[X]$, and that the expectation value is a linear functional, $E[aX + bY] = aE[X] + bE[Y]$ for $a, b \in \mathbb{R}$.

Quick calculation 2.7 Confirm that the second equality in (2.29) indeed holds.

The positive root of the variance is called standard deviation, $\text{StD}[X] = \sqrt{\text{Var}[X]}$. Variance and standard deviation are measures of dispersion around the mean (center of probability mass). For binomially distributed X and normally distributed Y the variance is given here without proof

$$\text{Var}[X] = N \cdot p(1 - p) \quad \text{and} \quad \text{Var}[Y] = \sigma^2. \tag{2.30}$$

It is very convenient that the first two moments of a normal distribution coincide with its parameters. In fact the whole moment structure of a normal distribution is determined by the parameters μ and σ. Evaluating the necessary integrals yields

$$M_k = \int_{-\infty}^{\infty} (y - \mu)^k \cdot \frac{1}{\sqrt{2\pi\sigma^2}} e^{-\frac{1}{2}\left(\frac{y-\mu}{\sigma}\right)^2} dy = \begin{cases} 0 & \text{for odd } k, \\ (k - 1)!!\sigma^k & \text{for even } k, \end{cases} \tag{2.31}$$

for $k \geq 1$, where $k!! = k \cdot (k - 2)!!$ and $1!! = 1$. Obviously, all odd moments vanish for normally distributed random variables. This is due to the symmetry of the distribution around μ. Odd moments are exclusively related to asymmetries of the distribution. For example the (standardized) third moment is called the "skewness" of the distribution. Even moments are related to the proportion of probability mass located in the tails of the distribution. The more massive the tails, the higher the likelihood for extreme events. The (standardized) fourth moment is called the "kurtosis" and is 3 in case of a normal distribution. Most financial return time series show a dramatically higher kurtosis of 6 to 9, which indicates a more heavy tailed distribution than the normal.

A closely related concept is that of mixed moments. The most prominent representative of this class is the covariance. For two random variables X and Y, the covariance is defined as

$$\text{Cov}[X, Y] = E[(X - E[X])(Y - E[Y])] = E[XY] - E[X]E[Y]. \tag{2.32}$$

Quick calculation 2.8 Verify the second equality in (2.32), again by using the linearity of expectations.

Covariance is a linear measure of dependence between two random variables X and Y, because the expectation value is a linear functional. Generally, if two random variables have covariance zero this does not mean they are independent!

Example 2.5

Consider two random variables $X \sim N(0, 1)$ and $Y = X^2$. Obviously, X and Y are highly dependent but what is their covariance?

Solution

Recall that for $\mu = 0$, central moments and raw moments are identical, $M_k = m_k$. Applying (2.31) and (2.32) then yields

$$\text{Cov}[X, Y] = E[XY] - E[X]E[Y] = E[X^3] - E[X]E[X^2] = 0 + 0 \cdot 1 = 0.$$

If on the other hand two random variables are independent, their covariance is guaranteed to vanish. The only exceptional case is when both random variables are normally distributed. Only in this case are independence and vanishing covariance equivalent statements. The normal distribution is therefore very special.

Often it is more intuitive to use a kind of standardized measure of linear dependence called correlation. This is not a new concept by itself, but merely a rescaled version of the covariance, defined by

$$\rho_{XY} = \frac{\text{Cov}[X, Y]}{\sqrt{\text{Var}[X]\text{Var}[Y]}}. \tag{2.33}$$

Conveniently the range of the correlation coefficient is $-1 \le \rho_{XY} \le 1$. Thus, one may express the linear dependence of two random variables in terms of positive or negative percentage value. Covariance and correlation are in one-to-one correspondence, therefore the term "uncorrelated" may be used interchangeably to also mean zero covariance.

2.6   Characteristic Function and *Fourier*-Transform

The characteristic function of a random variable is essentially the *Fourier*-transform[4] of its probability density function (or its probability mass function in the discrete case)

---

[4] There is no genuine definition of a *Fourier*-transform. Most commonly, the *Fourier*-transform of an arbitrary function $f: \mathbb{R} \to \mathbb{R}$ is defined as

$$\hat{f}(u) = \frac{1}{(2\pi)^{1-a}} \int_{-\infty}^{\infty} e^{-iux} f(x)dx,$$

$$\varphi(u) = \int_{-\infty}^{\infty} e^{iux} f(x) dx = E[e^{iuX}]. \quad (2.34)$$

The letter i represents the imaginary unit, $i = \sqrt{-1}$. If you are not familiar with complex numbers, you can go over the basics in Appendix A. The characteristic function naturally comes in handy, if one tries to add independent random variables. Recall the example of a fair die. Clearly, the probability for getting any number between one and six is the same, namely $f(n) = P(X = n) = \frac{1}{6}$ for $n = 1, \ldots, 6$ and zero for any other number. But now imagine rolling two fair dice, without gluing them together or interfering in any other way. What is the probability of throwing snake eyes? Well, if both dice are fair and independent we simply multiply the probabilities of the single events,

$$g(2) = P(X_1 = 1, X_2 = 1) = f(1) \cdot f(1) = \frac{1}{36}. \quad (2.35)$$

But what is the probability of throwing a seven? There are several possibilities of ending up with a seven. For example the first die could show a one and the second a six, or the first roll was a two and the second a five. We have to carefully add up all possibilities of getting a total sum of seven pips. The general solution to this problem is

$$g(k) = \sum_{n=1}^{6} f(n) \cdot f(k - n), \quad (2.36)$$

for $k = 2, \ldots, 12$. The operation in (2.36) is called "folding" and it is the correct method for adding two independent random variables. Nevertheless, folding is usually a very inconvenient way of conducting this calculation. The characteristic function offers a much more efficient alternative. It is a general feature of *Fourier*-transforms that the operation of folding in the initial space translates to the operation of multiplication in *Fourier*-space. Let $X_1, \ldots, X_N$ be N independent, not necessarily identically distributed random variables with characteristic functions $\varphi_n(u)$ for $n = 1, \ldots, N$, then

$$X = \sum_{n=1}^{N} X_n \quad \Leftrightarrow \quad \varphi(u) = \prod_{n=1}^{N} \varphi_n(u), \quad (2.37)$$

and the probability density function of the sum X is obtained by inverse transforming its characteristic function

$$f(x) = \frac{1}{2\pi} \int_{-\infty}^{\infty} e^{-iux} \varphi(u) du. \quad (2.38)$$

---

and its inverse transformation is

$$f(x) = \frac{1}{(2\pi)^a} \int_{-\infty}^{\infty} e^{iux} \hat{f}(u) du,$$

with a usually chosen to be 1 or $\frac{1}{2}$, and $i = \sqrt{-1}$. In (2.34) and (2.38), the role of the original and the inverse transformation is interchanged. Nevertheless, we simply call it the *Fourier*-transform hereafter.

Let's look at some examples and tie up some loose ends.

Example 2.6

Consider the N times consecutively conducted coin toss experiment of Example 2.3. Each single toss is represented by a random variable X_n, with

$$X_n(\omega) = \begin{cases} 1 & \text{for } \omega = H, \\ 0 & \text{for } \omega = T. \end{cases}$$

What is the probability mass function of the sum $X = X_1 + \cdots + X_N$, representing the total number of "Heads" in the whole sequence?

Solution

First calculate the characteristic function of the single toss random variable X_n,

$$\varphi_n(u) = E[e^{iuX_n}] = e^{iu\cdot1}p + e^{iu\cdot0}(1-p).$$

Note that in the discrete case the integral (2.34) reduces to a sum. All "copies" of X_n are identical, thus the characteristic function of X is

$$\varphi(u) = \varphi_n^N(u) = \left(e^{iu}p + (1-p)\right)^N.$$

Using the binomial theorem, one can expand the last expression into a sum

$$\varphi(u) = \sum_{n=0}^{N} \binom{N}{n} e^{iun} p^n (1-p)^{N-n} = \sum_{n=0}^{N} e^{iun} f(n),$$

which is immediately identified as the expectation value $E[e^{iuX}]$ with respect to the binomial distribution with probability mass function

$$f(n) = \binom{N}{n} p^n (1-p)^{N-n}.$$

In Example 2.6 it was not even necessary to calculate the inverse transformation because we were able to read off the resulting distribution from the characteristic function.

As a second example, let's show that a finite sum of independently normally distributed random variables is still normally distributed. To this end, we first compute the characteristic function of a standard normally distributed random variable, which is indeed the only tricky part. Let $Z \sim N(0,1)$, then

$$\begin{aligned} \varphi_Z(u) &= \int_{-\infty}^{\infty} e^{iuz} \frac{1}{\sqrt{2\pi}} e^{-\frac{1}{2}z^2} dz \\ &= \int_{-\infty}^{\infty} \frac{1}{\sqrt{2\pi}} e^{-\frac{1}{2}(z-iu)^2 - \frac{1}{2}u^2} dz \\ &= e^{-\frac{1}{2}u^2} \int_{-\infty}^{\infty} \frac{1}{\sqrt{2\pi}} e^{-\frac{1}{2}(z-iu)^2} dz, \end{aligned} \tag{2.39}$$

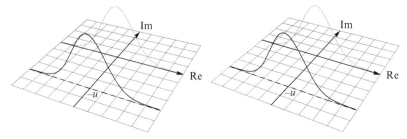

Fig. 2.4 **3D** Standard normal probability density function on a complex line parallel to the real axis

where we completed the (imaginary) square in going from the first line to the second line. The question is, what is the integral in the third line? The correct answer is, it is a complex line integral. To see this, make the substitution $\zeta = z - iu$ to obtain

$$\int_{-iu-\infty}^{-iu+\infty} \frac{1}{\sqrt{2\pi}} e^{-\frac{1}{2}\zeta^2} d\zeta = 1. \tag{2.40}$$

To see heuristically why the value of this integral is one, we have to recall that the complex line along which the integral is evaluated is parallel to the real line, which means it does not vary in the imaginary direction; see Figure 2.4. Therefore, the area under the curve is not affected by shifting the whole density function in the imaginary direction of the complex plane. The characteristic function of a standard normally distributed random variable Z is thus

$$\varphi_Z(u) = e^{-\frac{1}{2}u^2}. \tag{2.41}$$

Obtaining the characteristic function of a random variable $X \sim N(\mu, \sigma^2)$ is now an easy task using that $X = \sigma Z + \mu$ holds.

Quick calculation 2.9 Verify that X has expectation value μ and variance σ^2.

Indeed we get

$$\varphi_X(u) = E[e^{iu(\sigma Z+\mu)}] = e^{iu\mu} E[e^{iu\sigma Z}] = e^{iu\mu} \varphi_Z(u\sigma)$$
$$= \exp\left(iu\mu - \tfrac{1}{2}u^2\sigma^2\right). \tag{2.42}$$

Example 2.7

Consider a sum of N independent and not necessarily identically normally distributed random variables $X_n \sim N(\mu_n, \sigma_n^2)$ for $n = 1, \ldots, N$. How is the sum $X = X_1 + \cdots + X_N$ distributed?

Solution

To sum up all X_ns, we have to multiply their characteristic functions

$$\varphi(u) = \prod_{n=1}^{N} \varphi_n(u) = \exp\left(iu \sum_{n=1}^{N} \mu_n - \frac{1}{2} u^2 \sum_{n=1}^{N} \sigma_n^2 \right).$$

From this, we can immediately conclude that $X \sim N(\mu, \sigma^2)$, with

$$\mu = \sum_{n=1}^{N} \mu_n \quad \text{and} \quad \sigma^2 = \sum_{n=1}^{N} \sigma_n^2.$$

Generally, large sums of independent and identically distributed random variables tend to be normally distributed, even if their genuine distribution is far from normal. This peculiar fact is at the heart of the central limit theorem of statistics.

2.7   Further Reading

There are lots of introductory texts on probability theory and statistics. In the context of quantitative finance there is an exceptionally well written textbook by Patrick Roger (2010), available for free at www.bookboon.com. There is also a very accessible and comprehensive book by Sheldon Ross (2010). To tackle the subtleties of measure theory and *Lebesgue*-integration technically, Rudin (1976, chap. 11) is a good starting point and Shreve (2004b, chap. 1) contains a remarkably clear exposition. For a concise but illuminating introduction to measure theory and probability in finance see Bingham and Kiesel (2004, chap. 2). A rigorous, but still largely comprehensible treatment of the whole subject is found in Shiryaev (1996).

2.8   Problems

2.1 Consider the simplified version of a wheel of fortune, given in Figure 2.5. Create a complete probability space as a model for one turn of the wheel. Assume that the wheel is fair in the same idealized way as the die is usually assumed to be.

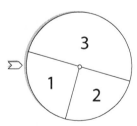

Fig. 2.5 Simplified wheel of fortune with three possible outcomes

2.2 Calculate the natural filtration in the wheel of fortune example of problem 2.1, generated by the outcome $A = \{2\}$. Does $\mathcal{F}_1 = 2^{\Omega}$ hold?

2.3 Consider rolling a fair die, with $X(\omega)$ as the number of pips and the event A of throwing an even number. Show that the conditional expectation, given A, is greater than the unconditional expectation.

2.4 Again consider the die example of Problem 2.3. Show that the property

$$E[X] = E[E[X|A]]$$

holds for A being the event of throwing an even number.

2.5 A theorem by Kolmogorov (see Arnold, 1974, p. 24) states that every stochastic process $X(t)$, which satisfies the inequality

$$E[|X(t) - X(s)|^a] \leq c|t - s|^{1+b},$$

for $t > s$ and a particular set of numbers $a, b, c > 0$, has almost surely continuous paths. Show that the *Wiener*-process meets this condition. Use the moment structure of normally distributed random variables (2.31) on page 19.

2.6 Assume $N \sim \text{Poi}(\lambda)$ is a *Poisson*-distributed random variable with probability mass function

$$f(n) = e^{-\lambda} \frac{\lambda^n}{n!},$$

for $n \in \mathbb{N}_0$. Consider a random variable X, with

$$X = \sum_{n=0}^{N} X_n,$$

where X_n are independent and identically distributed random variables. Prove that the relation

$$\varphi(u) = \exp[\lambda(\varphi_n(u) - 1)]$$

holds for the characteristic functions of X and X_n. Use the one-to-one correspondence of conditional probability and conditional distribution functions.

3 Vector Spaces

The architecture of financial markets and most parts of portfolio theory are best understood in the language of vector spaces. The treatment of this subject is usually either
standard, in terms of a concise introduction into linear algebra, or highly technical, with
mathematical rigor. The objective of this introduction is to build some broader geometric
intuition by not exclusively relying on traditional concepts, but by incorporating modern
ideas, for example from differential geometry.

3.1 Real Vector Spaces

First of all, a vector space is a collection of abstract objects called vectors. A vector space cannot exist on its own, it needs a supporting structure in terms of another
mathematical object, called a field. Typical vector spaces are generated by the fields
of real numbers $\mathbb{R}$ or complex numbers $\mathbb{C}$. The purpose of the field is to provide basic
algebraic structure in the form of rules for addition and multiplication. Besides that,
some special elements, like the identity element of addition and multiplication and the
inverse element of addition are needed. The detailed requirements are not that important here; the baseline is that the field provides the necessary toolbox for calculations
in the associated vector space.

We will most of the time be concerned with real vector spaces, so how is such a space
constructed? Let's first define a new class of (abstract) objects $|\cdot\rangle$, which are elements
of a real vector space, if they fulfill two conditions:

$$
\begin{aligned}
&\text{1. Homogeneity of degree one:}\\
&\quad \alpha|a\rangle = |b\rangle \text{ for } \alpha \in \mathbb{R},\\
&\text{2. Additivity:}\\
&\quad |a\rangle + |b\rangle = |c\rangle.
\end{aligned}
\tag{3.1}
$$

What (3.1) says is that if you can multiply an object $|\cdot\rangle$ with a number, or more pre-
cisely with an element of the field, to obtain a new object of the same class, and if you
can add two such objects to obtain a new one, then all objects in this class are elements
of a vector space. The labels a, b, and c are merely identifiers to distinguish different
elements of the vector space. The condition imposed by (3.1) is called linearity, so every
vector space is linear. Paul Dirac, a great pioneer of quantum mechanics, who invented
this notation, called an object $|\cdot\rangle$ a ket-vector, for reasons that will become clear later.

Quick calculation 3.1 Convince yourself that $\mathbb{R}$ itself is a real vector space.

So the question is, what is a vector and how can it be represented? The answer to the second part of the question depends on the vector space we are talking about and on the concrete rules for addition and multiplication with a scalar. Let's look at an example.

Example 3.1

In the *Euclid*ean vector space $\mathbb{R}^3$, a vector $|a\rangle$ is defined as a column of three real numbers

$$|a\rangle = \begin{pmatrix} a_1 \\ a_2 \\ a_3 \end{pmatrix}.$$

This definition by itself does not create a vector space.

Explanation

We need to explain the operations of adding two vectors and multiplying a vector with a scalar appropriately. So define

$$\alpha|a\rangle = \begin{pmatrix} \alpha \cdot a_1 \\ \alpha \cdot a_2 \\ \alpha \cdot a_3 \end{pmatrix} \quad \text{and} \quad |a\rangle + |b\rangle = \begin{pmatrix} a_1 + b_1 \\ a_2 + b_2 \\ a_3 + b_3 \end{pmatrix},$$

again with $\alpha \in \mathbb{R}$. Now, every object $|\cdot\rangle$ is an element of the vector space $\mathbb{R}^3$.

To demonstrate the full generality of the definition of vector spaces let's look at another, completely different example of a real vector space.

Example 3.2

The real polynomials of degree N

$$|p\rangle = \sum_{n=0}^{N} p_n x^n$$

also form a vector space over $\mathbb{R}$.

Proof

Verify that addition of two polynomials and multiplication with a scalar works out correctly with the common rules of algebra:

$$\alpha|p\rangle = \sum_{n=0}^{N} (\alpha \cdot p_n) x^n \quad \text{and} \quad |p\rangle + |q\rangle = \sum_{n=0}^{N} (p_n + q_n) x^n.$$

Both operations create new polynomials of the same degree. Thus, polynomials of degree N also form a real vector space.

Furthermore, the last example demonstrates the necessity of the underlying algebraic structure of the field $\mathbb{R}$ in a very transparent way. However, it is important to realize that both examples are merely manifestations of the more abstract and fundamental object $|\cdot\rangle$.

In finite dimensional vector spaces, a vector can be thought of as a geometrical object that can be represented in a coordinate system. In linear algebra, vectors are represented as arrows. Take the real vector space $\mathbb{R}^2$, the plane. The vector

$$|a\rangle = \begin{pmatrix} a_1 \\ a_2 \end{pmatrix} = \begin{pmatrix} 1 \\ 1 \end{pmatrix} \tag{3.2}$$

is represented by an arrow from the origin to the Cartesian coordinate pair (a_1, a_2), see Figure 3.1 left. The geometric object $|a\rangle$ itself is invariant, whereas its representation depends on the chosen coordinate system. If we change the coordinate system for example into polar coordinates, by the transformation rule

$$\begin{aligned} a_1 &= r\cos\theta \\ a_2 &= r\sin\theta, \end{aligned} \tag{3.3}$$

we obtain a different representation of the same fundamental object $|a\rangle$. Solving (3.3) for r and θ yields

$$|a\rangle = \begin{pmatrix} r \\ \theta \end{pmatrix} = \begin{pmatrix} \sqrt{2} \\ \frac{\pi}{4} \end{pmatrix}. \tag{3.4}$$

As you can see in Figure 3.1 right, the vector itself, which means the arrow, is invariant, but the coordinate representation has clearly changed.

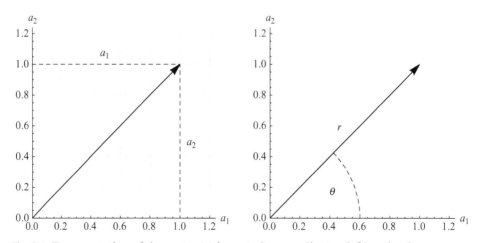

Fig. 3.1 Representation of the vector $|a\rangle$ in cartesian coordinates (left) and polar coordinates (right)

Quick calculation 3.2 Verify that the polar representation (3.4) of $|a\rangle$ is correct by solving (3.3) for r and θ.

It remains to show what the basic operations in such a vector space, namely multiplication with a scalar and addition of vectors, correspond to in geometrical language. To this end let's return to a vector in $\mathbb{R}^2$ in cartesian coordinates, say

$$|a\rangle = \begin{pmatrix} 2 \\ 2 \end{pmatrix}, \tag{3.5}$$

and multiply it with a real number $\alpha = \frac{3}{2}$. The new coordinates are obtained in complete analogy to Example 3.1 by multiplying every entry of the column with α. Figure 3.2 left shows the result of this operation. The original vector $|a\rangle$ is simply scaled in length by the factor $\alpha = \frac{3}{2}$. Note that for $\alpha < 1$, the magnitude of the vector would shrink and for $\alpha < 0$ it would point in the opposite direction, which means into the negative quadrant of the coordinate system. Now let's add two vectors, for example

$$|a\rangle = \begin{pmatrix} \frac{1}{2} \\ 2 \end{pmatrix} \quad \text{and} \quad |b\rangle = \begin{pmatrix} 2 \\ \frac{1}{2} \end{pmatrix}. \tag{3.6}$$

The coordinates of the resulting vector $|c\rangle$ are again obtained in complete analogy to Example 3.1 by adding the respective components of $|a\rangle$ and $|b\rangle$. The procedure is illustrated in Figure 3.2 right. Geometrically, addition of two vectors means spanning a parallelogram by mutually attaching one vector to the tip of the other and taking the transversal distance from the origin to the tips of the shifted vectors as the resulting vector. This rule is known as the parallelogram rule of vector addition.

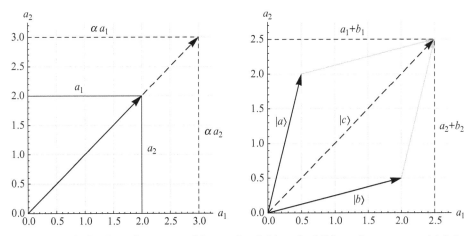

Fig. 3.2 Multiplication of a vector with a scalar (left) and addition of two vectors (right)

You might notice that there is no subtraction defined for vectors. So how do we subtract a vector from another vector? The answer is simple, multiply the vector to be subtracted with $\alpha = -1$ and add,

$$|a\rangle - |b\rangle = |a\rangle + (-1 \cdot |b\rangle). \tag{3.7}$$

Note that multiplying with a scalar and adding of vectors is a simple and efficient business in the Cartesian coordinate representation, but the fundamental geometrical operations are scaling and the parallelogram rule. To see this, convince yourself that scaling in polar coordinates looks different from scaling in cartesian coordinates

$$\alpha|a\rangle = \begin{pmatrix} \alpha\, a_1 \\ \alpha\, a_2 \end{pmatrix} = \begin{pmatrix} \alpha\, r \\ \theta \end{pmatrix}. \tag{3.8}$$

Quick calculation 3.3   Confirm this result by using the transformation rule (3.3).

Geometric operations are the fundamental ones because they are independent of a particular coordinate system. Algebraic operations are always coupled to a specific coordinate frame. Without reference to the chosen representation, algebraic manipulations are meaningless. Fortunately, in finance we work exclusively in Cartesian coordinates, so that we have access to efficient algebraic tools for manipulating vectors.

3.2   Dual Vector Space and Inner Product

Every vector space has a kind of undisclosed twin, a dual vector space, which is in one-to-one correspondence with the original one. Mathematicians call this relation isomorphic, which means that both vector spaces have the same structural properties (they look like twins), and there is a unique connection between any element of the original vector space and a corresponding element in the dual vector space. At this point we need another bit of notation to describe elements of the dual vector space. This is necessary, because only by observing how these objects behave under certain operations, we could never tell if they belong to the original or the dual vector space. So let's define a new class of objects $\langle \cdot |$, and call them co-vectors, bra-vectors or just forms. Let's look at an example to see what they are.

Example 3.3

Once again take the *Euclid*ean vector space $\mathbb{R}^3$. A form $\langle a|$ is defined as a row of three real numbers

$$\langle a| = \begin{pmatrix} a_1 & a_2 & a_3 \end{pmatrix}.$$

In linear algebra, this object is also called a row-vector for the obvious reasons.

Transposition

Departing from a vector $|a\rangle$, the operation of finding the corresponding form $\langle a|$ is called transposition. Transposition means interchanging rows and columns. A vector

$|a\rangle$ in $\mathbb{R}^3$ is an array with one column and three rows, whereas a form $\langle a|$ is an array with three columns and one row.

The mechanism for going from a vector to the corresponding form is by no means always transposition. In fact every vector space comes with its own connection to its dual vector space, depending on the generating field and the nature of the objects it is populated with.

Example 3.4

The complex numbers themselves constitute a vector space over $\mathbb{C}$. A vector and its corresponding form are given by

$$|z\rangle = z = x + iy,$$
$$\langle z| = z^* = x - iy.$$

Complex conjugation

In this case, the connection between original and dual vector space is called complex conjugation and is essentially a sign change of the imaginary part.

Let's return to the geometric representation in real vector spaces. How should a form be represented? Not by an arrow, but by a sequence of oriented surfaces. Orientation is crucial, because vectors also carry information about their orientation in terms of their representation as arrows. The second bit of information a vector carries, is its magnitude. This translates into the spacing between the surfaces of the form. Figure 3.3 gives an example, where $\langle b| = 2\langle a|$. Observe the inverse proportionality. If a vector is scaled

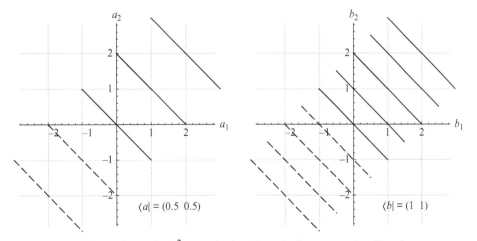

Fig. 3.3 Two different forms in $\mathbb{R}^2$ – Dashed surfaces indicate negative direction

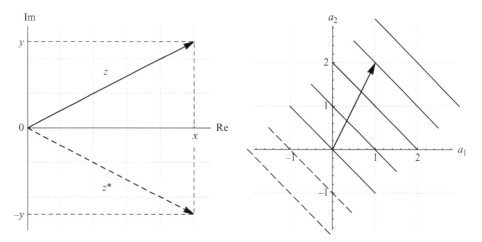

Fig. 3.4 Conjugated pair of complex numbers (left) and inner product in real vector space (right)

with a factor $\alpha > 1$, its length increases. In the case of a form, the spacing between surfaces shrinks, which means the surfaces become denser. Figure 3.3 is only a truncated representation of the respective forms. Technically, the sequence of surfaces extends to infinity in both the transversal and the longitudinal direction. This is not a problem because all relevant information is contained in the spacing and the orientation.

All operations we have seen so far, namely multiplication with a scalar and addition of two vectors, remain valid for forms. But one might wonder if there is a definition of multiplication of vectors and forms? Indeed there is more than one concept of multiplication. The most natural one is the inner product. We will define it as the product of a form and a vector and write it as $\langle a|b\rangle$.[1] Note that in *Dirac*-terminology a bra-vector next to a ket-vector forms a bra-ket. The immediate question is, what kind of result do we get out of the *Dirac*-bracket? Let's try to gain some intuition. We know from Example 3.4 that the complex numbers form a complex vector space. We also know that in this vector space, a form is the complex conjugate of another complex number. Thus, in this special case we know how to perform the inner product. Moreover, multiplying a vector with its corresponding form yields

$$\langle z|z\rangle = z^*z = (x - iy)(x + iy) = x^2 + y^2. \tag{3.9}$$

This is by Pythagoras' theorem the squared length of the vector $|z\rangle$ in the complex plane, see Figure 3.4 left. First of all, length is a scalar, and thus the inner product is also sometimes called the scalar product. But length is also one of the fundamental properties of a vector. From this we can conclude that the inner product has something to do with the basic geometrical properties of vectors and forms. The correct concept

---

[1] To be completely rigorous, the inner product has to be defined as a bilinear mapping $\langle \cdot | \cdot \rangle : V \times V \to \mathbb{R}$ for two elements of a real vector space V, not as a product between one element of V and one element of its dual vector space. We will skip this kind of technicality, because our somewhat simplified definition works just fine in computing the inner product.

of multiplying a form and a vector in a real vector space is counting the number of surfaces of the form, pierced by the respective vector, which is a purely geometrical issue. This principle is illustrated in Figure 3.4 right, where we have multiplied a form $\langle a|$ and a vector $|b\rangle$ in $\mathbb{R}^2$, with

$$\langle a| = \begin{pmatrix} 1 & 1 \end{pmatrix} \quad \text{and} \quad |b\rangle = \begin{pmatrix} 1 \\ 2 \end{pmatrix}. \tag{3.10}$$

The result of this operation is $\langle a|b\rangle = 3$, which is the number of surfaces, pierced by the vector. How can this result be obtained from the coordinate representation in a real vector space $\mathbb{R}^N$? Let's try the following definition

$$\langle a|b\rangle = \sum_{n=1}^{N} a_n b_n. \tag{3.11}$$

Quick calculation 3.4 Show that this definition gives the correct answer for (3.10) in $\mathbb{R}^2$.

More generally, an inner product $\langle \cdot | \cdot \rangle$ in a real vector space is defined by the following properties:

1. Bilinearity:
   $\langle \cdot | \cdot \rangle$ is linear (3.1) in both of its arguments,
2. Symmetry:
   $\langle a|b\rangle = \langle b|a\rangle$,
3. Positive definiteness:
   $\langle a|a\rangle > 0$ for $|a\rangle \neq |0\rangle$,

(3.12)

with the null-vector $|0\rangle$ being a vector with length zero.

Quick calculation 3.5 Verify that definition (3.11) fulfills these requirements.

Every operation that complies with the conditions (3.12) in a given real vector space is an inner product. Here is another example.

Example 3.5

Consider the vector space of real polynomials of degree N in the interval $[a, b] \in \mathbb{R}$. The inner product is given by

$$\langle p|q\rangle = \int_{a}^{b} p(x)q(x)dx.$$

Proof

Clearly the integral is symmetric and linear in both functions. As for positive definiteness, we have

$$\langle p|p \rangle = \int_a^b \left(\sum_{n=0}^N p_n x^n \right)^2 dx,$$

which is guaranteed to be positive, as long as there exists at least one coefficient $p_n \neq 0$, which means $|p\rangle \neq |0\rangle$.

Note that not every vector space has to be equipped with an inner product. A N-dimensional real vector space with inner product is called *Euclid*ean vector space $\mathbb{R}^N$. Under some additional conditions, this concept can be extended to the limit $N \to \infty$ in which case the vector space is called a *Hilbert*-space.

3.3   Dimensionality, Basis, and Subspaces

We occasionally referred to dimensions of a vector space. Presumably you have an intuitive understanding of dimensionality already, but how does this translate into the language of vector spaces? Let's first explore some of the wrong ideas. Because a vector in $\mathbb{R}^N$ is represented by a column with N rows, we could simply count rows of vectors to determine the number of dimensions. But something seems to be not quite right with this idea, because a vector is a geometrical object and a column of numbers is just one possible representation. So we would like a somewhat more fundamental definition of dimensionality. A more geometrical approach to the problem might be to count the spacial dimensions required to draw a vector or a form. Figures 3.5 and 3.6 show some vectors and forms in $\mathbb{R}^3$, but realize that they are printed on the two-dimensional surface of this page. So this idea seems strange, because it mixes properties of the vector space with properties of the ambient space, onto which elements of the vector space are projected.

The correct answer begins with a question: How many vectors are required to construct an arbitrary new vector? Because vectors are elements of a linear space, we know that a linear combination of two or more such objects is also a vector

$$\alpha|a\rangle + \beta|b\rangle = |c\rangle, \tag{3.13}$$

with $\alpha, \beta \in \mathbb{R}$. The idea is illustrated in Figure 3.7 left for $\mathbb{R}^2$. But there is a subtlety. Let's focus for the moment on $\mathbb{R}^2$. Not every pair of vectors is appropriate to construct an arbitrary new one. Take the vectors

$$|a\rangle = \begin{pmatrix} -1 \\ 1 \end{pmatrix} \quad \text{and} \quad |b\rangle = \begin{pmatrix} 1 \\ -1 \end{pmatrix} \tag{3.14}$$

and construct from them a third vector $|c\rangle$ by linear combination of $|a\rangle$ and $|b\rangle$ as in (3.13). Because $|b\rangle = -1 \cdot |a\rangle$, we get in this case

$$|c\rangle = (\alpha - \beta)|a\rangle. \tag{3.15}$$

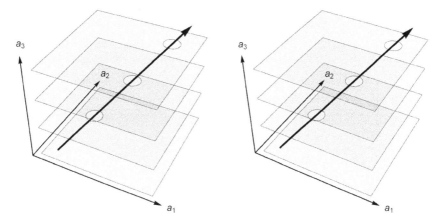

Fig. 3.5 3D Inner product in $\mathbb{R}^3$ – Vector piercing form in the positive direction

The situation is illustrated in Figure 3.7 right. The new vector $|c\rangle$ is really only a scaled version of $|a\rangle$. The cause of this kind of problem is that $|b\rangle$ is a scaled version of $|a\rangle$ in the first place, and so we cannot expect to get a completely new vector out of a linear combination of $|a\rangle$ and $|b\rangle$. If this is the case, one calls $|a\rangle$ and $|b\rangle$ linearly dependent, which really means that they are scaled versions of one another. To construct an arbitrary vector in $\mathbb{R}^2$ by linear combination, one needs two linearly independent vectors like in Figure 3.7 left. This idea can be generalized easily to other vector spaces and we call the number of linearly independent vectors, required to generate an arbitrary new vector, the dimension of that vector space.

In the two-dimensional case of Figure 3.7 we used the vectors $|a\rangle$ and $|b\rangle$ to construct a new vector. Such a set of linearly independent vectors is called a basis of the vector space. We are free to choose any basis, but there is a particularly well suited one, associated with our preferred Cartesian coordinate system. This is the so-called orthonormal basis. The term orthonormal combines two features, orthogonality and

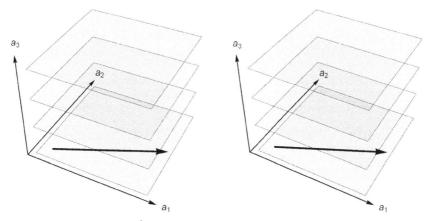

Fig. 3.6 3D Inner product in $\mathbb{R}^3$ – Vector and form are orthogonal

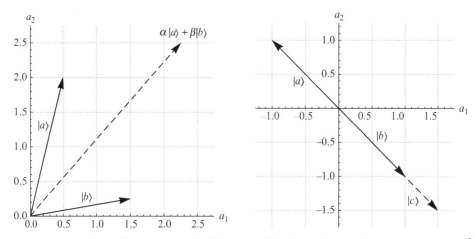

Fig. 3.7 Generation of a new vector by linear combination (left) and linear subspace of $\mathbb{R}^2$ (right)

normalization. What does orthogonality mean? Geometrically, two vectors $|a\rangle$ and $|b\rangle$ are orthogonal, if they form a 90° angle. This translates in vector space formalism to the requirement that the inner product between a corresponding form and the remaining vector vanishes,

$$\langle a|b\rangle = 0. \tag{3.16}$$

This situation is illustrated in Figure 3.6, where the form points into the a_3-direction, whereas the vector lives in the a_1-a_2-plane. The number of surfaces, pierced by the vector is zero. It is easily seen that every vector in the a_1-a_2-plane is orthogonal to this form. Normalization simply means that a vector $|a\rangle$ has unit length, or equivalently

$$\langle a|a\rangle = 1. \tag{3.17}$$

If we combine both properties, we can define a new object $|e_n\rangle$, which points exactly into the a_n-direction, with unit length. In coordinate representation, this vector would be a column, with zeros everywhere, except in the n-th row, where it is one. We call $|e_n\rangle$ the n-th basis vector of the orthonormal basis. Because of orthogonality, we can summarize all information about the basis in a very neat way,

$$\langle e_m|e_n\rangle = \delta_{mn} \quad \text{with} \quad \delta_{mn} = \begin{cases} 1 & \text{if } m = n, \\ 0 & \text{if } m \neq n. \end{cases} \tag{3.18}$$

δ_{mn} is called the *Kronecker*-delta. We can now expand an arbitrary vector in $\mathbb{R}^N$ in terms of its orthonormal basis vectors

$$|a\rangle = \sum_{n=1}^{N} a_n|e_n\rangle. \tag{3.19}$$

Quick calculation 3.6   Verify (3.19) for an arbitrary vector in $\mathbb{R}^3$.

Of course all things said up to this point apply in complete analogy to forms. We are now in a position to understand the definition of the inner product given in (3.11) much better

$$\langle a|b\rangle = \sum_{m=1}^{N}\sum_{n=1}^{N} a_m b_n \langle e_m|e_n\rangle = \sum_{n=1}^{N} a_n b_n, \tag{3.20}$$

where we have used (3.18) in the final step. Note that the notion of an orthonormal basis is by no means unique.

Example 3.6

Consider the *Euclid*ean vector space $\mathbb{R}^2$. The vectors

$$|a\rangle = \frac{1}{\sqrt{2}}\begin{pmatrix} -1 \\ 1 \end{pmatrix} \quad \text{and} \quad |b\rangle = \frac{1}{\sqrt{2}}\begin{pmatrix} 1 \\ 1 \end{pmatrix}$$

form a complete orthonormal basis.

Proof

Both vectors are orthogonal and of unit length

$$\langle a|b\rangle = \frac{1}{2}(-1+1) = 0 \quad \text{and} \quad \langle a|a\rangle = \langle b|b\rangle = \frac{1}{2}(1+1) = 1.$$

Thus, they form an orthonormal basis of the vector space $\mathbb{R}^2$.

The only issue left to discuss is the concept of linear subspaces. Imagine we do not use the complete set of N basis vectors to construct new vectors, but restrict ourselves to $K < N$ basis vectors. These vectors span a K-dimensional linear subspace inside the original vector space. We have already seen such linear subspaces. In Figure 3.7 right there is a one-dimensional linear subspace generated by the basis vector $|a\rangle$. The original vector space is two-dimensional, a plane, and the linear subspace is one-dimensional, a line. The vector in Figure 3.6 lives in the a_1-a_2-plane, which is a two-dimensional linear subspace of the three-dimensional vector space. Most vector spaces contain a large, possibly infinite number of linear subspaces. The same is also true for the associated dual vector spaces.

3.4   Functionals and Operators

Functionals and operators are mappings. A functional maps an element of a given vector space onto an element of its field, which means a number. An operator maps an element of a vector space onto another element of not necessarily the same vector space. Think of functionals and operators as machines into which you throw a vector and a number is ejected in case of the functional, or another vector in case of the operator, respectively. Let's first take a look at functionals.

Example 3.7

Consider the vector space of normally distributed random variables. We will subsequently prove that they indeed form a real vector space! The expectation value of $X \sim N(\mu, \sigma^2)$,

$$E[X] = \int_{-\infty}^{\infty} x \cdot \frac{1}{\sqrt{2\pi\sigma^2}} e^{-\frac{1}{2}\left(\frac{x-\mu}{\sigma}\right)^2} dx = \mu$$

is a linear functional.

Proof

We have already shown in Example 2.7 on page 23 that a sum of normally distributed random variables is also normally distributed. From definition (2.34) on page 21 we see immediately that αX has the characteristic function $\varphi_X(\alpha u)$ for $\alpha \in \mathbb{R}$. We can therefore conclude that $\alpha X \sim N(\alpha\mu, \alpha^2\sigma^2)$, and hence normally distributed random variables form a real vector space. Because $\mu \in \mathbb{R}$, $E[X]$ is a functional. From the rules of integration, it follows even for arbitrary distributed random variables that

$$E[\alpha X] = \alpha E[X] \quad \text{and} \quad E[X+Y] = E[X] + E[Y].$$

Thus, the expectation value is a linear functional.

Quick calculation 3.7 Prove that the variance is not a linear functional.

There is a theorem about linear functionals that is of paramount importance. It is called the *Riesz*-representation-theorem. Essentially it states that every linear functional can be represented as an inner product.[2] This means that for every vector $|a\rangle$ and linear functional L, there exists a unique form $\langle l|$, such that

$$L[|a\rangle] = \langle l|a\rangle. \tag{3.21}$$

Because a vector may itself be a function, it is customary to put the argument of a functional in square brackets to distinguish it from a function. As long as we are interested exclusively in linear functionals, there is really not much more we need to know at the moment, thanks to the *Riesz*-representation theorem.

As in the case of functionals, we are mainly interested in linear operators. In fact, we have seen linear operations before. Scaling an arbitrary vector by a factor α is an

[2] Formally, the set of all linear functionals on a given vector space constitutes the associated dual vector space in the first place. The notion of forms is thus a consequence of the *Riesz*-representation-theorem.

example of a linear operation; squaring its length would be a nonlinear operation. So what is an operator? It is an object, placed next to a vector space element on which it is supposed to operate. It is a convention that an operator always acts to the right. So we could have an equation of the form

$$M|a\rangle = |b\rangle, \tag{3.22}$$

where the operator M acts on the vector $|a\rangle$ to generate a new vector $|b\rangle$. The operator itself is another abstract element, whose concrete representation depends on the vector space we are talking about. A linear operator in $\mathbb{R}^N$ is a $K \times N$ array, called a matrix

$$M = \begin{pmatrix} m_{11} & m_{12} & \cdots & m_{1N} \\ m_{21} & m_{22} & \cdots & m_{2N} \\ \vdots & \vdots & \ddots & \vdots \\ m_{K1} & m_{K2} & \cdots & m_{KN} \end{pmatrix}. \tag{3.23}$$

You can think of a matrix as a list, assembling several vectors or forms, according to whether you look column by column or row by row at it,

$$M = \left(\uparrow \uparrow \uparrow \uparrow \uparrow \right) = \left(\vert\vert\vert\vert\vert\vert\vert\vert \right). \tag{3.24}$$

Hence, in calculating the vector $|b\rangle$ in (3.22), we have to perform inner products of $|a\rangle$ with every form that is contained in M, and to organize the results in a column, just as the forms were organized in M. In $\mathbb{R}^N$, the components of $|b\rangle$ are thus given by

$$b_k = \sum_{n=1}^{N} m_{kn} a_n, \tag{3.25}$$

for $k = 1, \ldots, K$. Matrices themselves form a real vector space sometimes called $\mathbb{R}^{K \times N}$, but this is another story.

Quick calculation 3.8 How does addition and multiplication with a scalar have to be defined in order to make matrices a vector space?

Let's look at a special class of operators $M : \mathbb{R}^N \to \mathbb{R}^N$, called square matrices. They are special in that they have precisely as many vectors contained in them, as they have forms. In other words, they map a vector onto another vector of the same vector space. For illustration purposes we will restrict ourselves to the *Euclidean* vector space $\mathbb{R}^2$.

Example 3.8

The scaling operator

$$M_\alpha = \begin{pmatrix} \alpha & 0 \\ 0 & \alpha \end{pmatrix}$$

scales every vector it acts on by the factor α.

Proof

Perform the componentwise algebra

$$|b\rangle = M_\alpha |a\rangle = \begin{pmatrix} \alpha & 0 \\ 0 & \alpha \end{pmatrix} \begin{pmatrix} a_1 \\ a_2 \end{pmatrix} = \begin{pmatrix} \alpha \, a_1 \\ \alpha \, a_2 \end{pmatrix} = \alpha |a\rangle.$$

See Figure 3.8 left for an illustration.

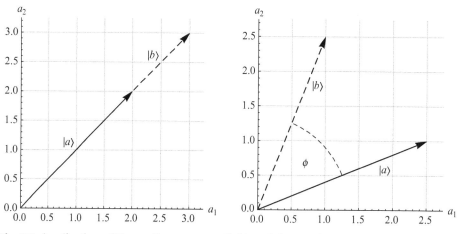

Fig. 3.8 Application of the scaling-operator (left) and the rotation-operator from the SO(2) group (right)

Example 3.9

There is a special orthogonal (SO) group of operators that rotate a vector without changing its length. The SO(2) matrix is given by

$$M_\phi = \begin{pmatrix} \cos\phi & -\sin\phi \\ \sin\phi & \cos\phi \end{pmatrix}.$$

Proof

This one is a little harder to prove. The effect of M_ϕ is seen most clearly under the polar coordinate transformation $a_1 = r\cos\theta$ and $a_2 = r\sin\theta$:

$$M_\phi |a\rangle = \begin{pmatrix} r\cos\theta\cos\phi - r\sin\theta\sin\phi \\ r\cos\theta\sin\phi + r\sin\theta\cos\phi \end{pmatrix} = \begin{pmatrix} r\cos(\theta+\phi) \\ r\sin(\theta+\phi) \end{pmatrix}.$$

In the last step, we have used the trigonometric addition formulas for sine and cosine. Figure 3.8 right illustrates the effect of M_ϕ.

Quick calculation 3.9 Show that both vectors contained in M_ϕ are orthonormal. Use the universal identity $\cos^2\phi + \sin^2\phi = 1$.

There are two other classes of operators worth discussing for a moment. They correspond to the operation of reflection in an axis and projection into a linear subspace.

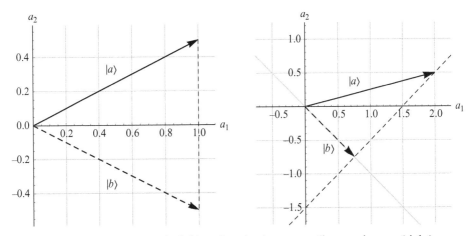

Fig. 3.9 Reflection in the a_1-axis (left) and projection onto a linear subspace (right)

Example 3.10

The reflection in the a_1-axis is governed by the reflection operator

$$R = \begin{pmatrix} 1 & 0 \\ 0 & -1 \end{pmatrix}.$$

Proof

It is easy to see that

$$R|a\rangle = \begin{pmatrix} 1 & 0 \\ 0 & -1 \end{pmatrix}\begin{pmatrix} a_1 \\ a_2 \end{pmatrix} = \begin{pmatrix} a_1 \\ -a_2 \end{pmatrix}$$

corresponds to a reflection in the a_1-axis, see Figure 3.9 left.

Quick calculation 3.10 What does the operator for reflection in the a_2-axis look like?

Example 3.11

The operator

$$P = \begin{pmatrix} \frac{1}{2} & -\frac{1}{2} \\ -\frac{1}{2} & \frac{1}{2} \end{pmatrix}$$

projects an arbitrary vector onto the linear subspace $a_2 = -a_1$.

Proof

The componentwise multiplication yields

$$|b\rangle = P|a\rangle = \begin{pmatrix} \frac{1}{2} & -\frac{1}{2} \\ -\frac{1}{2} & \frac{1}{2} \end{pmatrix}\begin{pmatrix} a_1 \\ a_2 \end{pmatrix} = \frac{1}{2}\begin{pmatrix} a_1 - a_2 \\ -a_1 + a_2 \end{pmatrix} = \begin{pmatrix} b_1 \\ -b_1 \end{pmatrix},$$

which is obviously the demanded subspace, see Figure 3.9 right.

Quick calculation 3.11 Convince yourself that the vectors contained in the projection operator are linearly dependent and that $P^2 = P$ holds.

Let's conclude this paragraph with a few remarks on operators, mapping from one vector space into another one. From the componentwise definition of the matrix-vector product (3.25), it is obvious that in general a $K \times N$ matrix, acting on an N-dimensional vector, generates a K-dimensional vector. But let's look at a completely different example:

Example 3.12

The differential operator, acting on an element $|p\rangle$ of the vector space of real polynomials of degree N, generates an element $|q\rangle$ of the vector space of real polynomials of degree $N - 1$.

Proof

The rules of calculus yield

$$\frac{d}{dx}|p\rangle = \frac{d}{dx} \sum_{n=0}^{N} p_n x^n = \sum_{n=1}^{N} n p_n x^{n-1} = \sum_{n=0}^{N-1} q_n x^n = |q\rangle,$$

with $q_n = (n+1)p_{n+1}$.

Note that because the field $\mathbb{R}$ forms itself a real vector space, a functional is also a special kind of operator.

3.5   Adjoint and Inverse Operators

As emphasized before, it is a convention that operators always act to the right, which means they act on vectors. But what if one wants an operator to act on a form

$$\langle a|M = \langle b|, \tag{3.26}$$

or in other words, to act to the left? We can use the isomorphic structure of the dual vector space to translate a form-problem into a vector-problem. But in the process the operator itself is also transformed, because it now has to act on vectors and no longer on forms. Problem (3.26) has the vector space equivalent

$$M^\dagger|a\rangle = |b\rangle, \tag{3.27}$$

where $M^\dagger$ is called the adjoint operator to M. What adjoining an operator means concretely, depends on the properties of the respective vector space.

Example 3.13

Again consider the *Euclid*ean vector space. The adjoint operator $M^\dagger$ is obtained from M by transposition, which means interchanging the row and column index of every matrix entry.

Proof

The bracket $\langle a|M|b\rangle$ is a scalar and thus the equality

$$\langle a|M|b\rangle = \langle b|M^\dagger|a\rangle$$

has to hold, for arbitrary $\langle a|$ and $|b\rangle$. By the rules of vector/matrix products, this equation reads componentwise

$$\sum_{n=1}^{N}\sum_{k=1}^{K} a_n m_{nk} b_k = \sum_{k=1}^{K}\sum_{n=1}^{N} b_k m_{kn}^{\dagger} a_n = \sum_{n=1}^{N}\sum_{k=1}^{K} a_n m_{kn}^{\dagger} b_k.$$

In the last step, we have only rearranged factors. We can immediately conclude that $m_{kn}^{\dagger} = m_{nk}$ has to hold, but this is the definition of transposition.

In finite dimensional complex vector spaces, adjoining an operator means transposition and complex conjugation. There are other important examples of operators and their adjoint counterparts, like the *Fokker–Planck*-operator and the *Kolmogorov*-backward-operator, but we will discuss them in detail at some later time.

There is also the notion of an inverse operator. This concept is intimately related to the so-called identity operator I, which has the property

$$I|a\rangle = |a\rangle. \tag{3.28}$$

If for an arbitrary operator M, there exists another operator M^{-1}, such that

$$M^{-1} M = I \tag{3.29}$$

holds, then M^{-1} is called the inverse operator to M. Note that such an inverse operator does not have to exist. In *Euclid*ean vector spaces the inverse operator of a square matrix is usually the inverse matrix. But for the projection-matrix in Example 3.11, there exists no inverse matrix, because the vectors contained in M are not linearly independent. Another problem occurs, when the operator is not a square matrix.

Example 3.14

Let M be a $K \times N$ matrix, with $K \geq N$ and linearly independent vectors contained in M. Then the inverse operator is given by the *Moore–Penrose*-inverse

$$M^{-1} = (M^{\dagger} M)^{-1} M^{\dagger}.$$

Proof

Because M contains linearly independent vectors, $M^{\dagger} M$ is an invertible square matrix. The result

$$(M^{\dagger} M)^{-1} M^{\dagger} M = I$$

follows immediately.

Let's look at another example from time series analysis. A stationary *Markov*-process, also called AR(1)-process, is usually written as

$$x_t = \phi x_{t-1} + \epsilon_t, \tag{3.30}$$

with $|\phi| < 1$. This process has an alternative representation.

Example 3.15

Define the backshift operator B, with the property $Bx_t = x_{t-1}$. Note that $B^2 x_t = Bx_{t-1} = x_{t-2}$ and so on. Then the stationary AR(1)-process can be written as

$$x_t = \sum_{k=0}^{\infty} \phi^k \epsilon_{t-k},$$

which is known as the MA(∞)-representation.

Proof

Rewrite the AR(1)-process (3.30) using the backshift operator $(1 - \phi B)x_t = \epsilon_t$ and apply the following algebraic manipulations

$$x_t = \frac{1}{1 - \phi B}\epsilon_t = \sum_{k=0}^{\infty} \phi^k B^k \epsilon_t = \sum_{k=0}^{\infty} \phi^k \epsilon_{t-k},$$

where we have used the geometric series result $\sum_{k=0}^{\infty} z^k = \frac{1}{1-z}$, for $|z| < 1$.

Sometimes problems are easier to solve by using the inverse operator, if it can be computed. But there is no general pattern, and often the inverse operator can only be approximated.

3.6   Eigenvalue Problems

Eigenvalue problems come in many guises, so it is extremely useful to understand their nature. We begin by stating the problem and then discussing its meaning and implications. The generic eigenvalue problem is

$$M|v\rangle = \lambda|v\rangle. \tag{3.31}$$

M is an arbitrary operator, $|v\rangle$ is called an eigenvector of M, and λ its associated eigenvalue. First of all, there is an ambiguity in the eigenvalue problem. If we scale the eigenvector $|v\rangle \to \alpha|v\rangle$, (3.31) is still true.

Quick calculation 3.12 Convince yourself that the last statement is indeed correct.

Because of this, it is customary to scale eigenvectors to unit length. But what is really unique about eigenvectors is that they geometrically point exactly into the intrinsic directions of the operator. To see what this means look at an example in $\mathbb{R}^2$.

Example 3.16

Look at the symmetric $\mathbb{R}^2$ operator-matrix

$$L = \begin{pmatrix} 1 & \frac{2}{3} \\ \frac{2}{3} & 2 \end{pmatrix}.$$

If this operator acts on a typical vector, say

$$|a\rangle = \begin{pmatrix} 2 \\ \frac{1}{2} \end{pmatrix},$$

what it usually does is to scale and rotate this vector, see Figure 3.10 left.

Eigenvalues and eigenvectors

There are two solutions to the eigenvalue problem in this case,

$$\lambda_1 = \frac{7}{3} \text{ and } |v_1\rangle = \frac{1}{\sqrt{5}} \begin{pmatrix} 1 \\ 2 \end{pmatrix} \quad \text{as well as} \quad \lambda_2 = \frac{2}{3} \text{ and } |v_2\rangle = \frac{1}{\sqrt{5}} \begin{pmatrix} -2 \\ 1 \end{pmatrix}.$$

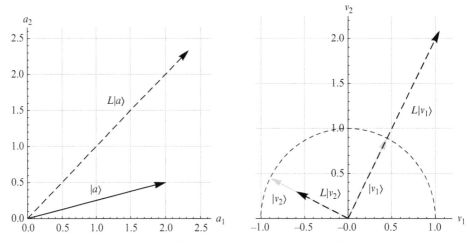

Fig. 3.10 Operator L acting on arbitrary vector $|a\rangle$ (left) and on eigenvectors $|v_1\rangle$ and $|v_2\rangle$ (right)

If L acts on one of these eigenvectors, they are not rotated, but only scaled. Furthermore, the amount of scaling of each eigenvector is given by the associated eigenvalue. This is illustrated for both eigenvectors in Figure 3.10 right.

Quick calculation 3.13   Check that the eigenvectors in Example 3.16 are orthonormal.

Generally, if M is not symmetric, eigenvalues and eigenvectors can be complex, even if the operator itself is real. In this case the above picture does not hold that easily. Further complications occur, if not all eigenvalues are distinct. Fortunately, most of the time we are dealing with situations where such kinds of problems do not emerge.

We will learn more about the eigenvalue problem in the next section. At this point let's have a look at another guise.

Example 3.17

Take the vector space of differentiable real functions $f: \mathbb{R} \to \mathbb{R}$. What is the eigenvector, or better yet the eigenfunction of the differential operator $\frac{d}{dx}$?

Solution
The eigenvalue problem in this case is

$$\frac{d}{dx} v(x) = \lambda v(x).$$

It is easily seen that $v(x) = e^{\lambda x}$ fulfills the eigenvalue equation and is thus an eigenfunction of the differential operator.

3.7   Linear Algebra

Linear algebra deals exclusively with *Euclid*ean vector spaces. In this context some things simplify and we can define some special operations. All operators are real matrices and adjoining an operator always means transposition. This fact is often emphasized by writing

$$M^\dagger = M', \tag{3.32}$$

which we will also do from now on. This simplification is usually extended to the notion of vectors and forms. The following, slightly abusive notation is standard

$$|a\rangle = a \quad \text{and} \quad \langle a| = a'. \tag{3.33}$$

However, we will not adopt this one, because it mixes two completely separate classes of objects. A form $\langle a|$ is an element of the dual vector space of $\mathbb{R}^N$, but a' is a $1 \times N$ matrix, which makes it an element of the vector space $\mathbb{R}^{1 \times N}$, even though the way we represent vectors, forms, and matrices in an *Euclid*ean vector space does not suggest this distinction. Let's first discuss some properties of square matrices.

3.7.1 Symmetry

A N-dimensional square matrix M is called symmetric, if

$$M' = M \tag{3.34}$$

holds. Every square matrix can be decomposed into a symmetric part M^+ and an antisymmetric part M^-, by

$$M = M^+ + M^- = \frac{1}{2}(M + M') + \frac{1}{2}(M - M'). \tag{3.35}$$

Quick calculation 3.14 Verify that (3.35) is always true.

Symmetric matrices play an important role in finance. For example, covariance matrices are always symmetric.

3.7.2 Definiteness

A square matrix is called positive definite, if

$$\langle a|M|a \rangle > 0 \tag{3.36}$$

holds for arbitrary, nonzero $|a\rangle \in \mathbb{R}^N$. (3.36) is called a quadratic form. For symmetric matrices, this statement is equivalent to the requirement that all eigenvalues have to be greater than zero.

Example 3.18

The symmetric matrix

$$L = \begin{pmatrix} 1 & \frac{2}{3} \\ \frac{2}{3} & 2 \end{pmatrix}$$

from Example 3.16 has eigenvalues

$$\lambda_1 = \frac{7}{3} \quad \text{and} \quad \lambda_2 = \frac{2}{3}.$$

Conclusion

The matrix L, or more precisely the quadratic form $\langle a|L|a \rangle$, with arbitrary $|a\rangle$, is positive definite.

If the quadratic form is greater than or equal to zero, it is called positive semidefinite. The analogous definition holds for negative definiteness or semidefiniteness, respectively. If the quadratic form is none of these, it is called indefinite. Covariance matrices are always positive definite.

3.7.3   Determinant

The determinant is a functional of a square matrix. Geometrically it is the (oriented) volume of the parallelepiped, spanned by the vectors contained in M. It can be calculated recursively by Laplace's formula

$$\det[M] = \sum_{n=1}^{N}(-1)^{k+n}m_{kn}M_{kn} = \sum_{k=1}^{N}(-1)^{k+n}m_{kn}M_{kn}, \tag{3.37}$$

with the minor M_{kn}, which is the determinant of the $(N-1) \times (N-1)$ matrix, obtained by removing the k-th row and the n-th column of M. For a 1×1 matrix the determinant is $\det[M] = m_{11}$. This recursive calculation is usually done by a computer. However, for $M \in \mathbb{R}^{2\times2}$, the computation is easy

$$\det[M] = m_{11}m_{22} - m_{12}m_{21}. \tag{3.38}$$

Quick calculation 3.15 Check that this result complies with Laplace's formula (3.37).

If the determinant is zero, the matrix is called singular, which means that it cannot be inverted.[3] The determinant is also the product of all eigenvalues of M. Thus, a zero eigenvalue means equivalently that the matrix is singular.

The determinant is not a linear functional. Indeed we have for $A, B \in \mathbb{R}^{N\times N}$

$$\det[\alpha A] = \alpha^N \det[A] \quad \text{and} \quad \det[A+B] \neq \det[A] + \det[B]. \tag{3.39}$$

But there are some other rules for determinants that frequently come in handy

1. Product of matrices:
$\det[AB] = \det[A] \cdot \det[B]$,
2. Inverse matrix:
$\det[A^{-1}] = \frac{1}{\det[A]}$,
3. Transposed matrix:
$\det[A'] = \det[A]$.

$$\tag{3.40}$$

There is one important remark to the product rule. Even though the product of determinants does obviously commute, because the determinant is a number, the matrix product is generally not commutative,

---

[3] There is nevertheless a unique *Moore–Penrose*-inverse, similar to the one encountered in Example 3.14 on page 44, designed to preserve ceratin properties of an inverse matrix.

$$AB \neq BA. \tag{3.41}$$

This is obvious for non-square matrices, because the dimensional interface between both of them has to comply with the rules of inner products. But it is also true for square matrices of the same dimension. It even holds true, if A and B are symmetric

$$AB = (B'A')' = (BA)', \tag{3.42}$$

because the product AB is not necessarily symmetric. In (3.42) we have used an immediate consequence of matrix multiplication and transposition in the first step and symmetry of A and B in the second.

Quick calculation 3.16 Show that $(AB)' = B'A'$ for $A, B \in \mathbb{R}^{N \times N}$.

3.7.4   Inverse Matrix

The inverse of a square matrix M does only exist if the matrix is non-singular, $\det[M] \neq 0$. Think of this requirement as the matrix analogue of the prohibition of division by zero. To find the inverse matrix M^{-1}, one has to solve the linear system of equations

$$M^{-1}M = MM^{-1} = I, \tag{3.43}$$

where the identity operator I is called the identity matrix

$$I = \begin{pmatrix} 1 & 0 & \dots & 0 \\ 0 & 1 & \dots & 0 \\ \vdots & \vdots & \ddots & \vdots \\ 0 & 0 & \dots & 1 \end{pmatrix} \tag{3.44}$$

in linear algebra. Unfortunately, solving this system of equations requires special algorithms like *Gauss–Jordan*-elimination, that are best implemented on a computer. In $N = 2$ dimensions however, there is an easy formula for calculating the inverse matrix,

$$M^{-1} = \frac{1}{\det[M]} \begin{pmatrix} m_{22} & -m_{12} \\ -m_{21} & m_{11} \end{pmatrix}. \tag{3.45}$$

Note that the entries in the principal diagonal are interchanged, whereas the secondary diagonal only gets a minus sign. Having a definition of an inverse matrix allows us to manipulate linear systems of equations algebraically.

Example 3.19

Consider the solution of the following system of equations

$$M|a\rangle = |b\rangle \Big| \rightarrow \cdot M^{-1} \quad \Leftrightarrow \quad |a\rangle = M^{-1}|b\rangle.$$

Explanation

We have multiplied both sides of the original equation with M^{-1} from the left side, indicated by the little arrow. Remember, in matrix algebra, we have to be careful from which side to multiply. On the left hand side we get the identity matrix, which is like a factor of one in ordinary algebra. Thus, we have already solved for $|a\rangle$.

Furthermore, for invertible and equally dimensioned matrices A and B, we have the useful relation

$$(AB)^{-1} = B^{-1}A^{-1}. \tag{3.46}$$

Quick calculation 3.17   Use (3.43) to prove that $M'^{-1} = (M^{-1})'$.

3.7.5   Eigenvalue Problem

Doing some algebra on the eigenvalue problem (3.31) on page 45, one obtains the equivalent representation

$$(M - \lambda I)|v\rangle = |0\rangle, \tag{3.47}$$

where $|0\rangle$ is the null-vector, a column where every entry equals zero.

Quick calculation 3.18   Verify that (3.47) is equivalent to $M|v\rangle = \lambda|v\rangle$.

If there were an inverse matrix $(M - \lambda I)^{-1}$, then we could solve (3.47) immediately and we would obtain the trivial solution $|v\rangle = |0\rangle$. But we are interested in nontrivial solutions. Thus, we have to require that $(M - \lambda I)$ is singular, or in other words

$$\det[M - \lambda I] = 0. \tag{3.48}$$

The determinant in (3.48) is a polynomial of degree N, called the characteristic polynomial of M. It has N roots, which are the eigenvalues of M. Knowing the eigenvalues, one can substitute them into (3.47) and solve for the eigenvectors.

Example 3.20

Again consider the matrix

$$L = \begin{pmatrix} 1 & \frac{2}{3} \\ \frac{2}{3} & 2 \end{pmatrix}$$

of Example 3.16. What is the largest eigenvalue and its associated eigenvector?

Solution

First, compute the characteristic polynomial

$$\det \left[\begin{pmatrix} 1 & \frac{2}{3} \\ \frac{2}{3} & 2 \end{pmatrix} - \lambda \begin{pmatrix} 1 & 0 \\ 0 & 1 \end{pmatrix} \right] = \det \left[\begin{pmatrix} 1 - \lambda & \frac{2}{3} \\ \frac{2}{3} & 2 - \lambda \end{pmatrix} \right] = (1 - \lambda)(2 - \lambda) - \frac{4}{9}.$$

It is immediately obvious that $\lambda = \frac{7}{3}$ and $\lambda = \frac{2}{3}$ are roots of the characteristic polynomial. Substituting the larger eigenvalue into (3.47) yields

$$\begin{pmatrix} -\frac{4}{3} & \frac{2}{3} \\ \frac{2}{3} & -\frac{1}{3} \end{pmatrix} \begin{pmatrix} v_1 \\ v_2 \end{pmatrix} = \begin{pmatrix} 0 \\ 0 \end{pmatrix},$$

which are two redundant equations for v_1 and v_2. We can again immediately conclude that $2v_1 = v_2$ has to hold. Remember that eigenvectors are only determined by their direction, not by their magnitude. Thus, we can write

$$|v\rangle = \alpha \begin{pmatrix} 1 \\ 2 \end{pmatrix},$$

where the scale factor $\alpha = \frac{1}{\sqrt{5}}$ makes $|v\rangle$ normalized.

Quick calculation 3.19 Compute the eigenvector associated with $\lambda = \frac{2}{3}$.

If we arrange all eigenvectors columnwise in a matrix V, and additionally arrange the eigenvalues $\lambda_1, \ldots, \lambda_N$ in a diagonal matrix

$$\Lambda = \begin{pmatrix} \lambda_1 & 0 & \cdots & 0 \\ 0 & \lambda_2 & \cdots & 0 \\ \vdots & \vdots & \ddots & \vdots \\ 0 & 0 & \cdots & \lambda_N \end{pmatrix}, \tag{3.49}$$

we can restate the complete eigenvalue problem in a very economic way

$$MV = V\Lambda. \tag{3.50}$$

If M is not degenerate, the inverse matrix of V exists, and by multiplying with V^{-1} from the right, we obtain what is called the eigenvalue decomposition

$$M = V\Lambda V^{-1}.\tag{3.51}$$

Note that generally, eigenvalues and eigenvectors may be complex and not orthogonal. However, if L is a real symmetric matrix, like a covariance matrix, it has a complete set of real eigenvalues and eigenvectors. Furthermore, all eigenvectors associated with different eigenvalues are orthogonal. From this we can immediately conclude that

$$V'V = I \quad \Leftrightarrow \quad V' = V^{-1}.\tag{3.52}$$

We then obtain the so-called spectral decomposition of the real symmetric matrix L

$$L = V\Lambda V'.\tag{3.53}$$

Spectral decomposition is the key idea behind principal component analysis, an important tool in dimensionality reduction.

3.8   Vector Differential Calculus

Another important issue is vector calculus. In finance, there are often situations where an objective functional has to be optimized, and thus differentiated with respect to a vector. There are basically three cases of interest, which occur frequently in the framework of modern portfolio theory. The simplest case has the form

$$F = \langle a|b \rangle.\tag{3.54}$$

Generally, it does not matter if we differentiate with respect to a vector or a form, because $\langle a|b \rangle = \langle b|a \rangle$. I like to differentiate with respect to the form, because the result is a vector, but this is personal taste. If we differentiate (3.54) with respect to either one, we obtain in complete analogy to ordinary calculus

$$\frac{\delta F}{\delta \langle a|} = |b \rangle \quad \text{and} \quad \frac{\delta F}{\delta |a \rangle} = \langle b|,\tag{3.55}$$

where the symbol δ was used to distinguish the functional derivative from the ordinary derivative. You can always check the functional derivative componentwise,

$$F = \sum_{n=1}^{N} a_n b_n \quad \text{and} \quad \frac{\delta F}{\delta \langle a|} = \begin{pmatrix} \frac{\partial F}{\partial a_1} \\ \vdots \\ \frac{\partial F}{\partial a_N} \end{pmatrix} = \begin{pmatrix} b_1 \\ \vdots \\ b_N \end{pmatrix}.\tag{3.56}$$

The derivative with respect to the vector $|a\rangle$ is simply defined the other way around, as a form.

Quick calculation 3.20 What is the derivative of $\langle a|M|b\rangle$ with respect to $|a\rangle$? The correct answer is not $\langle b|M!$ Can you see why?

The next more interesting case is the simple quadratic form

$$G = \langle a|a\rangle. \tag{3.57}$$

Again, in complete analogy with ordinary differential calculus, the functional derivative is

$$\frac{\delta G}{\delta\langle a|} = 2|a\rangle. \tag{3.58}$$

The same analogy holds for the derivative with respect to the vector $|a\rangle$. Let's now look at a general quadratic form

$$H = \langle a|M|a\rangle. \tag{3.59}$$

At this point, you might expect that the derivative with respect to $\langle a|$ is $2M|a\rangle$, but this is not generally correct. To see where this idea goes wrong, we have to think about the relation of the derivative with respect to both the form $\langle a|$ and the vector $|a\rangle$. If we label our initial guess $\frac{\delta H}{\delta\langle a|} \stackrel{?}{=} 2M|a\rangle = |\delta\rangle$, then we would certainly expect that $\frac{\delta H}{\delta|a\rangle}$ turns out to be the corresponding form $\langle\delta|$. To check that more thoroughly, decompose M into its symmetric and antisymmetric part as in (3.35) on page 48, and realize that $(M^+)' = M^+$ and $(M^-)' = -M^-$ holds.

Quick calculation 3.21 Verify the last statement.

Now let's see what the functional derivative with respect to a vector $|\delta_V\rangle$ and with respect to a form $\langle\delta_F|$ look like under our preliminary differentiation rule,

$$\begin{aligned}|\delta_V\rangle &= 2M^+|a\rangle + 2M^-|a\rangle\\ \langle\delta_F| &= 2\langle a|M^+ + 2\langle a|M^-.\end{aligned} \tag{3.60}$$

Next, transpose $\langle\delta_F|$, to see whether it is indeed the corresponding form to $|\delta_V\rangle$

$$\begin{aligned}|\delta_F\rangle &= 2(M^+)'|a\rangle + 2(M^-)'|a\rangle\\ &= 2M^+|a\rangle - 2M^-|a\rangle.\end{aligned} \tag{3.61}$$

Comparing this result with the first equation in (3.60), we conclude that $\langle\delta_F|$ does not correspond to $|\delta_V\rangle$. Thus, our initial definition of the functional derivative was obviously incorrect. Closer inspection reveals both the cause and the cure for this. The correct definition is

$$\frac{\delta H}{\delta\langle a|} = 2M^+|a\rangle = (M + M')|a\rangle. \tag{3.62}$$

Table 3.1 Functional derivatives

F	$\frac{\delta F}{\delta\langle a|}$	$\frac{\delta F}{\delta|a\rangle}$
$\alpha\langle a|b\rangle$	$\alpha|b\rangle$	$\alpha\langle b|$
$\alpha\langle a|a\rangle$	$2\alpha|a\rangle$	$2\alpha\langle a|$
$\alpha\langle a|M|b\rangle$	$\alpha M|b\rangle$	$\alpha\langle b|M'$
$\alpha\langle b|M|a\rangle$	$\alpha M'|b\rangle$	$\alpha\langle b|M$
$\alpha\langle a|M|a\rangle$	$\alpha(M+M')|a\rangle$	$\alpha\langle a|(M+M')$

Note that for symmetric M this result simplifies to our initial guess $2M|a\rangle$, so we were not completely wrong in the first place. Table 3.1 summarizes all basic rules for differentiation with respect to a form or a vector, respectively.

3.9 Multivariate Normal Distribution

The probability density function of a multivariate normal random variable is a generalization of the univariate one. Let $|X\rangle$ be a N-dimensional vector of joint normal random variables, then the probability density function is

$$f(x_1,\ldots,x_N) = \frac{1}{\sqrt{(2\pi)^N \det\Sigma}}\exp\left(-\frac{1}{2}\langle v|\Sigma^{-1}|v\rangle\right),\tag{3.63}$$

where $\langle v| = \langle x| - \langle\mu|$, with the form of expectation values $\langle\mu| = \begin{pmatrix}\mu_1 & \cdots & \mu_N\end{pmatrix}$, and Σ is the covariance matrix with the following structure

$$\Sigma = \begin{pmatrix} \sigma_1^2 & \sigma_{12} & \cdots & \sigma_{1N} \\ \sigma_{12} & \sigma_2^2 & \cdots & \sigma_{2N} \\ \vdots & \vdots & \ddots & \vdots \\ \sigma_{1N} & \sigma_{2N} & \cdots & \sigma_N^2 \end{pmatrix},\tag{3.64}$$

where $\sigma_n^2 = \mathrm{Var}[X_n]$, and $\sigma_{mn} = \mathrm{Cov}[X_m, X_n]$. Obviously, Σ is a symmetric matrix, $\Sigma' = \Sigma$, because $\mathrm{Cov}[X_m, X_n] = \mathrm{Cov}[X_n, X_m]$.

Quick calculation 3.22   Verify the last statement.

Sometimes the term $\det\Sigma$ is called the generalized variance, because $\sqrt{\det\Sigma}$ is connected to the volume of the variance ellipsoid, generated by

$$\langle v|\Sigma^{-1}|v\rangle = \text{const.}\tag{3.65}$$

Figures 3.11 and 3.12 show bivariate normal probability density functions, where both random variables have mean zero and variance one, but different correlation structure.

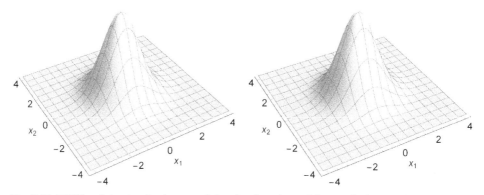

Fig. 3.11 3D Bivariate standard normal density function with correlation $\rho = 0$

An important property of multivariate normal distributions is that all marginal distributions (conditionally or unconditionally) are also normal. This means geometrically that no matter from which direction (the x_1-perspective or the x_2-perspective) you look at Figure 3.11 or 3.12, you will always see a univariate normal marginal density function. This property cumulates in an important theorem of multivariate statistics, sometimes referred to as the normal correlation theorem (see for example Mardia et al., 2003, theorem 3.2.4):

Theorem 3.1 (Normal correlation) *Let* $|X\rangle$ *be a compound vector of joint normally distributed random vectors* $|X_1\rangle$ *and* $|X_2\rangle$, *with moments*

$$E[|X\rangle] = \begin{bmatrix} |\mu_1\rangle \\ |\mu_2\rangle \end{bmatrix} \quad \text{and} \quad \text{Var}[|X\rangle] = \begin{bmatrix} \Sigma_{11} & \Sigma_{12} \\ \Sigma_{21} & \Sigma_{22} \end{bmatrix}.$$

The distribution of $|X_1\rangle$, *conditional on the information* $\mathcal{F}_{X_2}$, *generated by observing* $|X_2\rangle = |x_2\rangle$, *is also normal with moments*

$$E[|X_1\rangle | \mathcal{F}_{X_2}] = |\mu_1\rangle + \Sigma_{12}\Sigma_{22}^{-1}|v_2\rangle,$$

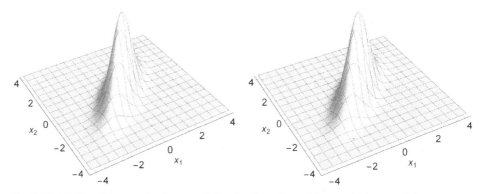

Fig. 3.12 3D Bivariate standard normal density function with correlation $\rho = 0.8$

where $|v_2\rangle = |x_2\rangle - |\mu_2\rangle$, *and*

$$\mathrm{Var}[|X_1\rangle|\mathcal{F}_{X_2}] = \Sigma_{11} - \Sigma_{12}\Sigma_{22}^{-1}\Sigma_{21}.$$

The same holds true for the distribution of $|X_2\rangle$, *conditional on* $\mathcal{F}_{X_1}$, *with the obvious interchange of subscripts.*

For a proof of Theorem 3.1 see Mardia et al. (2003, sect. 3.2). Note that generally $\Sigma_{12} \neq \Sigma_{21}$, but $\Sigma_{12} = \Sigma_{21}'$.

Quick calculation 3.23   Can you see why?

Another useful property of multivariate normal distributions is that they are preserved under affine transformations. Suppose $|X\rangle$ is a N-dimensional $N(|\mu\rangle, \Sigma)$-distributed random vector. Let A be a $K \times N$ matrix and $|b\rangle$ a K-dimensional vector. The new random vector

$$|Y\rangle = A|X\rangle + |b\rangle \tag{3.66}$$

is also normally distributed with moments

$$E[|Y\rangle] = A|\mu\rangle + |b\rangle \quad \text{and} \quad \mathrm{Var}[|Y\rangle] = A\Sigma A'. \tag{3.67}$$

Observe that $|Y\rangle$ is a K-dimensional random vector, where K might be larger than, smaller than, or equal to N. But this also means that $\mathrm{Var}[|Y\rangle]$ has to be a $K \times K$ matrix. Thus, there is only one possible way to translate the square from univariate statistics into a matrix product in multivariate statistics,

$$\mathrm{Var}[Y] = a^2\mathrm{Var}[X] \quad \leftrightarrow \quad \mathrm{Var}[|Y\rangle] = A\mathrm{Var}[|X\rangle]A'. \tag{3.68}$$

3.10   Further Reading

The amount of linear algebra needed in finance is well manageable. There are many suitable textbooks on different levels. A very good introduction from the perspective of image processing is Farin and Hansford (2005). Also a comprehensive introduction is the four volumes of Leif Mejlbro (2009), available for free at www.bookboon.com. A more rigorous treatment can be found in Kostrikin and Manin (1997). To get a handle on representation ideas from differential geometry used here, see Misner et al. (1973, chap. 2). For a concise introduction to *Hilbert*-spaces see Brockwell and Davis (2006, chap. 2). A very comprehensive and helpful textbook about vector/matrix differential calculus is Magnus and Neudecker (2007). For a rigorous introduction to multivariate normal distribution theory see Mardia et al. (2003, chap. 3).

3.11   Problems

3.1 Consider the hyperbolic coordinate transformation

$$a_1 = \rho \cosh \phi$$
$$a_2 = \rho \sinh \phi,$$

limited to the coordinate wedge $a_1 > 0$ and $-a_1 < a_2 < a_1$, see Figure 3.13. How does the operation of scaling a vector affect the hyperbolic radius ρ and the hyperbolic angle ϕ? Use the fact that $\cosh^2 \phi - \sinh^2 \phi = 1$ holds.

3.2 The outer product of a vector $|a\rangle$ and a form $\langle b|$ is defined as

$$|a\rangle\langle b| = \begin{pmatrix} a_1 b_1 & a_1 b_2 & \dots & a_1 b_N \\ a_2 b_1 & a_2 b_2 & \dots & a_2 b_N \\ \vdots & \vdots & \ddots & \vdots \\ a_K b_1 & a_K b_2 & \dots & a_K b_N \end{pmatrix}.$$

Show that the sum of outer products over a complete set of orthonormal basis vectors with the corresponding set of orthonormal basis forms is the identity operator,

$$\sum_{n=1}^{N} |e_n\rangle\langle e_n| = I.$$

3.3 Show that the outer products $|e_k\rangle\langle e_n|$ for $k, n = 1, 2$ form a complete basis of the vector space $\mathbb{R}^{2\times2}$.

3.4 Consider the complex vector space of periodic functions in the interval $[0, 2\pi]$. Show that the exponential *Fourier*-functions

$$|\psi_n\rangle = \frac{1}{\sqrt{2\pi}} e^{inx},$$

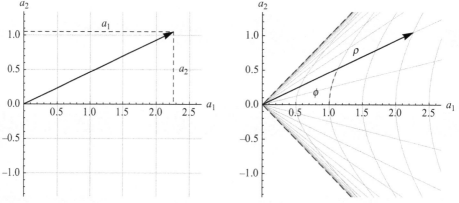

Fig. 3.13 Representation of a vector $|a\rangle$ in Cartesian coordinates (left) and hyperbolic coordinates (right)

for $n \in \mathbb{Z}$, form an orthonormal basis. Use Euler's formula

$$e^{i\omega} = \cos \omega + i \sin \omega$$

in the process and remember to complex conjugate in going from vectors to forms. This is a tough one.

3.5 The trace of a square matrix is a linear functional, defined as the sum of its principal diagonal elements,

$$\text{tr}\,[M] = \sum_{n=1}^{N} m_{nn}.$$

A further property of the trace is $\text{tr}\,[AB] = \text{tr}\,[BA]$, for suitable matrices A and B. Show that for the square matrix M the following property holds

$$\text{tr}\,[M] = \sum_{n=1}^{N} \lambda_n,$$

which means that the trace is also the sum of all eigenvalues.

3.6 The matrix exponential of a square matrix M is defined in terms of its *Taylor*-series

$$e^M = \sum_{k=0}^{\infty} \frac{M^k}{k!}.$$

Prove that an alternative representation is the following:

$$e^M = V e^\Lambda V^{-1} \quad \text{with} \quad e^\Lambda = \begin{pmatrix} e^{\lambda_1} & \cdots & 0 \\ \vdots & \ddots & \vdots \\ 0 & \cdots & e^{\lambda_N} \end{pmatrix}.$$

3.7 One of the most prominent tools in statistics is linear regression. It can be stated as a linear vector model

$$|y\rangle = X|\beta\rangle + |\epsilon\rangle,$$

where $|y\rangle$ contains the observed manifestations of the response variable, the matrix X contains the so-called regressors, $|\beta\rangle$ is a parameter vector to be estimated, and $|\epsilon\rangle$ is a vector of uncorrelated random fluctuations. Show that by minimizing the square error functional $F = \langle\epsilon|\epsilon\rangle$ with respect to $\langle\beta|$, the so-called least-squares estimator

$$|\hat{\beta}\rangle = (X'X)^{-1} X'|y\rangle$$

is obtained. Remember that the chain rule of differentiation has to be obeyed in vector calculus also. This may again be a tough one.

3.8 Take the two-dimensional random vector $|X\rangle$ to be normally distributed with covariance matrix

$$\Sigma = \begin{pmatrix} \sigma_1^2 & \sigma_{12} \\ \sigma_{12} & \sigma_2^2 \end{pmatrix}.$$

What is the variance of $Y = \langle 1|X\rangle$, with $\langle 1| = \begin{pmatrix} 1 & 1 \end{pmatrix}$, and what does this correspond to?

4 Utility Theory

Economic behavior is mainly considered a particular kind of rational decision making. To be more precise, it is assumed that agents maximize their personal felicity, with respect to economic variables like consumption or wealth, in a consistent and predictable manner. The purpose of utility theory is to provide a mathematical framework, in which rational behavior can be analyzed and consistently explained.

4.1 Lotteries

The term lottery refers to the roots of game theory, to gambling. In the modern language of probability theory, it is a concept that collects information about a random variable and a specific probability distribution function, attached to it. Consider a discrete random variable $W:\Omega \to \mathcal{W}$ that assigns to every possible state of the world a specific wealth, $W(\omega_n) = w_n$, measured in monetary units. A lottery is a list of all probability masses associated with the different realizations w_n of the random variable W,

$$L(W) = (f(w_1), \ldots, f(w_N)). \tag{4.1}$$

Because the probability mass function $f(w_n)$ is in one-to-one correspondence with the probability measure P of the underlying probability space $(\Omega, \mathcal{F}, P)$, it is customary to simplify the notation to

$$L = (p_1, \ldots, p_N), \tag{4.2}$$

where we also suppressed the reference to the random variable. This concept is more versatile than it looks at first sight.

Example 4.1

Suppose you want to grant a credit to only one of two customers. You expect different redemption profiles:

Customer 1:
- Full repayment of $16 with $p = \frac{1}{2}$
- Complete default with $1 - p = \frac{1}{2}$

Customer 2:
- Full repayment of $16 with $q = \frac{1}{10}$
- Partial recovery of $4 with $1 - q = \frac{9}{10}$

Which lotteries correspond to the two alternatives?

Solution

First of all, there are three states of the world: "default," "partial recovery," and "full repayment." These are mapped by W onto $\mathcal{W} = \{0, 4, 16\}$. The two lotteries then correspond to the different probability measures P and Q

$$L_1 = \left(\frac{1}{2}, 0, \frac{1}{2}\right) \quad \text{and} \quad L_2 = \left(0, \frac{9}{10}, \frac{1}{10}\right).$$

There is also a notion of compound lotteries. Let L_1 and L_2 be two lotteries, with respect to the random variable W, and π a probability, associated with another random variable X. The new lottery

$$L = \pi L_1 + (1 - \pi)L_2 \quad \text{with} \quad \pi_n = \pi p_n + (1 - \pi)q_n \qquad (4.3)$$

is called a compound lottery. Compound lotteries are based on the independence of W and X. This is why the probabilities multiply.

Quick calculation 4.1 Assume you decide the credit assignment in Example 4.1 by tossing a fair coin. What is the compound lottery?

4.2   Preference Relations and Expected Utility

Given several risky alternatives, you might prefer one over another or you might be indifferent between two lotteries. The personal attitude of an agent towards any such pair of lotteries is described by so-called preference relations:

$$
\begin{array}{lll}
L_1 > L_2 & \leftrightarrow & L_1 \text{ is better then } L_2, \\
L_1 \geq L_2 & \leftrightarrow & L_1 \text{ is at least as good as } L_2, \\
L_1 \sim L_2 & \leftrightarrow & \text{indifference between } L_1 \text{ and } L_2.
\end{array}
\qquad (4.4)
$$

Note that $L_1 \geq L_2$ and simultaneously $L_1 \leq L_2$ implies $L_1 \sim L_2$. Preference relations provide access to an ordering of different lotteries, but realize that not every such order would qualify as rational.

Example 4.2

Imagine you witness a common decision problem in a shoe shop. A customer has difficulties in deciding between a black pair of shoes, a red pair, and a brown pair.

After observing the scene for a while, you arrive at the conclusion that the preference relations of the poor soul have to be

"black" > "red"   and   "brown" > "black"   and   "red" > "brown".

You see the problem?

Explanation

Such a case of circular preferences is called non-transitive. A non-transitive preference structure surely renders any kind of rational ordering impossible. Remarkably, rumor has it that about 50% of all shoe shop customers seem to face this kind of decision problem.

So the natural question arises under which conditions can a rational preference order be achieved. Or put another way, is there a set of rules, such that a preference order, if obeying these rules, can be called rational in a sensible way? The answer is yes, and such a set of rules was stipulated by John von Neumann and Oskar Morgenstern, two great pioneers of game theory. They postulated four conditions, known as the axioms of expected utility theory:

$$
\begin{aligned}
&\text{Axiom 1:} \quad \text{Completeness} \\
&\qquad\qquad \text{Either } L_1 \geq L_2,\ L_1 \leq L_2,\ \text{or both } (L_1 \sim L_2). \\[4pt]
&\text{Axiom 2:} \quad \text{Transitivity} \\
&\qquad\qquad \text{If } L_1 \geq L \text{ and } L \geq L_2,\ \text{then } L_1 \geq L_2. \\[4pt]
&\text{Axiom 3:} \quad \text{Continuity} \\
&\qquad\qquad \text{For } L_1 \geq L \geq L_2 \text{ and some probability } \pi, \\
&\qquad\qquad L \sim \pi L_1 + (1 - \pi)L_2 \text{ holds.} \\[4pt]
&\text{Axiom 4:} \quad \text{Independence} \\
&\qquad\qquad \text{For } L_1 \sim L_2 \text{ and any probability } \pi, \\
&\qquad\qquad \pi L_1 + (1 - \pi)L \sim \pi L_2 + (1 - \pi)L \text{ holds.}
\end{aligned}
\tag{4.5}
$$

Axiom 1 ensures that every two lotteries can be pairwise related to each other. This is an obvious requirement. Axiom 2 rules out circular preferences as in Example 4.2. The true meaning of Axiom 3 is not immediately evident; it rules out lexicographical preferences. This is a highly technical issue, just think of it as a mechanism for adding linear and smooth transitions between different preference levels. Axiom 4 prevents any preference relation from bias due to mixing with another lottery. The last axiom has been subject to intense discussion. A slight modification leads to Yaari's dual theory of choice (Yaari, 1987), which is an alternative decision system that is very popular in actuarial science.

Von Neumann and Morgenstern were able to prove a remarkable fact: If the axioms (4.5) hold, then there exists a real function $u : \mathcal{W} \to \mathbb{R}$, such that for L_1 and L_2 the equivalence

$$
L_1 \gtrsim L_2 \quad \Leftrightarrow \quad \sum_{n=1}^{N} u(w_n)p_n \geq \sum_{n=1}^{N} u(w_n)q_n
\tag{4.6}
$$

holds. $u(w)$ is called the utility function. The functional

$$U[L] = E[u(W)] = \sum_{n=1}^{N} u(w_n)p_n \tag{4.7}$$

is called the *von Neumann–Morgenstern*-utility or expected utility. It is indeed a functional, because it is the expectation value of a function of W.

With expected utility we are now in a position to compare whole lotteries in a quantitative way. This is progress, because we no longer need an extensive list of pairwise preference relations of an agent. Instead a neat table of numbers, one for each lottery, suffices. But keep in mind that expected utility is not a global entity. Every rational agent comes with her own utility function $u(w)$, which is a kind of utility kernel of the *von Neumann–Morgenstern*-functional $U[L]$. Furthermore, there is an ambiguity in the utility function. Take the affine transformation

$$v(w) = au(w) + b, \tag{4.8}$$

with $a, b \in \mathbb{R}$ and $a > 0$. Then the preference order, generated by $U[L]$ and $V[L]$ is identical. For all practical purposes this ambiguity is an advantage, because it creates additional degrees of freedom in scaling and translation of $u(w)$.

Example 4.3

Stick to the credit alternatives in Example 4.1. If you had the utility function $u(w) = \sqrt{w}$, how would you decide?

Solution
Calculating the expected utility yields

$$U[L_1] = 0 \cdot \frac{1}{2} + 2 \cdot 0 + 4 \cdot \frac{1}{2} = 2$$
$$U[L_2] = 0 \cdot 0 + 2 \cdot \frac{9}{10} + 4 \cdot \frac{1}{10} = \frac{11}{5}.$$

Thus, you would prefer to give the loan to customer two.

4.3   Risk Aversion

Let's consider a rather extreme situation. Imagine, someone offers you participation in a one shot coin flip game for your whole wealth. Call the sum of all your possessions V, then the alternatives of participating and not participating in the game can be summarized by $\mathcal{W} = \{0, V, 2V\}$, and the lotteries

$$L_1 = \left(\frac{1}{2}, 0, \frac{1}{2}\right) \quad \text{and} \quad L_2 = (0, 1, 0). \tag{4.9}$$

Would you consider participation in that game? I suppose not. The reason is that agents are usually risk averse. The consequences of losing everything you own are far more shocking than doubling your wealth would be beneficial. Let's ask a somewhat strange question. What if you were solely interested in terminal wealth, no matter what risks are associated with a specific lottery, which means $U[L] = E[W]$? In this case, we can immediately conclude

$$U[L_1] = 0 \cdot \frac{1}{2} + 2V \cdot \frac{1}{2} = V \cdot 1 = U[L_2] \quad \Leftrightarrow \quad L_1 \sim L_2. \tag{4.10}$$

You would be indifferent between participating and not participating in the coin flip game. But this is a special case of expected utility (4.7) with utility function $u(w) = w$, see Figure 4.1 left.

Quick calculation 4.2 Convince yourself that the last statement is true.

Because the risk dimension is completely ignored, the utility function $u(w) = w$ is said to belong to a risk-neutral agent. We can reverse the logic of this conclusion to conjecture that risk attitude has to be encoded in the shape of the utility function. Let's push this idea a little bit further and ask, what sensible shape should a generic utility function have? First of all, more is better than less and thus the slope of $u(w)$ should be positive. But what about the marginal utility? Does \$1000 increase your utility if you already own \$10 million in the same way as if you own \$200? Suppose not, at least you should not draw more utility from the additional \$1000 if you are a

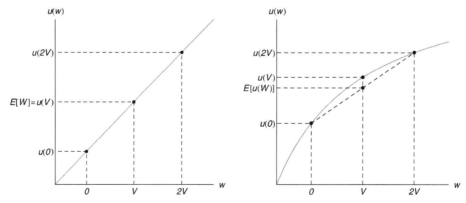

Fig. 4.1 Risk-neutral utility function $u(w) = w$ (left) and concave utility function $u(w) = \frac{2w}{1+2w}$ (right)

millionaire already. That is to say that the increase in marginal utility should not be positive. We can summarize these requirements formally

$$\frac{du}{dw} > 0 \quad \text{and} \quad \frac{d^2u}{dw^2} \leq 0. \tag{4.11}$$

If a utility function obeys (4.11), it is called concave. If the second inequality holds strictly, it is called strictly concave. A risk-averse agent has a strictly concave utility function. Let's see if we can build some intuition for the last claim. Figure 4.1 right shows such a concave utility function. It is easy to see that in this case the condition

$$u(E[W]) \geq E[u(W)] \tag{4.12}$$

holds strictly. Equation (4.12) is known as Jensen's inequality for concave functions. If $u(w)$ is strictly concave, the inequality also holds strictly. Jensen's inequality merely describes what we loosely defined as risk aversion, namely the asymmetric gain or loss in utility of a symmetric gain or loss in wealth.

Quick calculation 4.3   Verify that for $u(w) = w$ equality has to hold in (4.12).

We can now understand better, why we were reluctant about participating in the coin flip game. The gain in utility from winning is not as high as the loss of utility, if the unfavorable outcome occurs. Thus, the expected utility over all outcomes of the game is lower than our current utility. We therefore refuse participation and call the reason risk aversion.

4.4   Measures of Risk Aversion

There is a useful measure of the degree of risk aversion an agent exhibits. It was suggested independently by John Pratt (1964) and Kenneth Arrow (1965), and it is called the absolute risk aversion (ARA)

$$\text{ARA}(w) = -\frac{u''(w)}{u'(w)}, \tag{4.13}$$

where we have used u' and u'' as shorthand for the first and second derivative of u with respect to its argument. For concave utility functions, the restriction $u''(w) \leq 0 < u'(w)$ holds and thus $\text{ARA}(w) \geq 0$, where equality holds for the risk-neutral agent.

There is another version of the *Pratt–Arrow*-measure, scaling risk aversion by the current level of wealth of an individual agent. It is called relative risk aversion (RRA)

$$\mathrm{RRA}(w) = -\frac{w \cdot u''(w)}{u'(w)}. \tag{4.14}$$

For $w > 0$, the condition $\mathrm{RRA}(w) \geq 0$ is also satisfied for concave utility functions. Both coefficients sum up the properties of a given utility function in a neat way.

Example 4.4

Consider Bernoulli's utility function

$$u(w) = \log w.$$

What are the *Pratt–Arrow*-coefficients and what do they mean?

Solution
Calculating the derivatives of $\log w$ yields

$$\mathrm{ARA}(w) = \frac{1}{w} \quad \text{and} \quad \mathrm{RRA}(w) = 1.$$

Obviously, absolute risk aversion decreases with increasing levels of wealth. This is intuitively sensible; think of gaining or losing $1000 if you are either poor or already a millionaire. Relative risk aversion tells us that absolute risk aversion decreases proportionally to the increase in wealth, with a constant proportionality factor of one.

4.5   Certainty Equivalent and Risk Premium

Let's ask the following question: Offered the participation in our coin flip lottery, is there a particular wealth level w^*, such that

$$E[u(W)] = u(w^*)? \tag{4.15}$$

In fact there is and its existence is an immediate consequence of the continuity axiom.

Quick calculation 4.4 Can you see why?

The wealth level w^* is called the certainty equivalent for obvious reasons. Let's try to find out a bit more about it. For a risk-averse agent, we have from Jensen's inequality and (4.15)

$$u(E[W]) > E[u(W)] = u(w^*). \tag{4.16}$$

Furthermore, because the utility function is strictly monotonic increasing in its argument,

$$E[W] > w^* \qquad (4.17)$$

has to hold. In other words, the certainty equivalent wealth level is lower than the expected wealth of the lottery. The risk-averse agent is willing to give up some wealth to avoid uncertainty. The difference between expected wealth and the certainty equivalent is called the risk premium π,

$$E[W] = w^* + \pi. \qquad (4.18)$$

Figure 4.2 illustrates the certainty equivalent and the risk premium for the coin flip example. Of course both concepts are not limited to symmetric lotteries with only two random outcomes, but are completely general.

It is often the case that random fluctuations are rather small and the random variable can be expressed in terms of its expectation value, plus a small random error,

$$W = \mu + \epsilon, \qquad (4.19)$$

with $E[\epsilon] = 0$ and $\mathrm{Var}[\epsilon] = \sigma^2$. If the random error ϵ is small compared to the expectation value μ, then the risk premium will also be small, and we can use the approximation

$$\pi \approx \frac{1}{2} \mathrm{ARA}(\mu)\sigma^2. \qquad (4.20)$$

It is a nice exercise to prove (4.20). From the definition of the risk premium and the certainty equivalent, we have $w^* = \mu - \pi$ and

$$E[u(W)] = u(w^*) = u(\mu - \pi). \qquad (4.21)$$

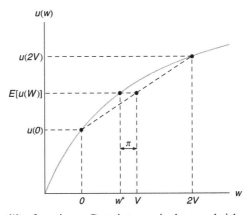

Fig. 4.2 Risk-averse utility function – Certainty equivalent and risk premium

We will now *Taylor*-expand both sides of (4.21) around μ and equate the results. Let's start with the left hand side

$$E[u(W)] = u(\mu) + u'(\mu)E[\epsilon] + \tfrac{1}{2}u''(\mu)E[\epsilon^2] + O(\epsilon^3)$$
$$\approx u(\mu) + \tfrac{1}{2}u''(\mu)\sigma^2. \tag{4.22}$$

Note that if ϵ is distributed symmetrically, then $E[\epsilon^3] = 0$ and the approximation is exact up to order $O(\epsilon^4)$.

Quick calculation 4.5 What is the fourth order expansion term if $\epsilon \sim N(0, \sigma^2)$?

Expanding the right hand side of (4.21), we restrict ourselves to a linear approximation, because π is expected to be small so that terms of order $O(\pi^2)$ can be neglected. We obtain

$$u(\mu - \pi) \approx u(\mu) - u'(\mu)\pi. \tag{4.23}$$

Equating (4.22) and (4.23), and solving for π yields

$$\pi \approx -\frac{1}{2}\frac{u''(\mu)}{u'(\mu)}\sigma^2 = \frac{1}{2}\mathrm{ARA}(\mu)\sigma^2, \tag{4.24}$$

which is the desired result.

4.6   Classes of Utility Functions

There are several standard classes of utility functions we will briefly discuss in this section, along with some of their characteristic properties. Often utility functions are categorized by their relation to the *Pratt–Arrow*-measure of risk aversion.

4.6.1   Constant Absolute Risk Aversion (CARA)

There is one class of utility functions, also referred to as exponential utility, that experiences no shift in absolute risk aversion, no matter how small or large the wealth w becomes. It has the generic form

$$u(w) = -e^{-\alpha w}. \tag{4.25}$$

Remember that utility functions are only uniquely determined up to an affine transformation. Thus, scaling or translating (4.25) makes no difference and we omit the additional parameters. Exponential utility is very pleasant from a mathematical point of view. For example, realize that the n-th derivative of (4.25) is

$$u^{(n)}(w) = (-\alpha)^n u(w). \tag{4.26}$$

Thus, the *Pratt–Arrow*-coefficients can be computed easily,

$$\mathrm{ARA}(w) = \frac{\alpha^2 u(w)}{\alpha u(w)} = \alpha \quad \text{and} \quad \mathrm{RRA}(w) = \alpha w. \tag{4.27}$$

Now the name of this class of utility functions makes perfect sense. Observe that we pay for the simple analytic form in terms of questionable economic implications. In Example 4.4 we advanced the sensible economic argument that absolute risk aversion should decrease with increasing wealth. The CARA-class fails in this regard. Nevertheless, it may be a good local approximation of the true utility function.

4.6.2   Hyperbolic Absolute Risk Aversion (HARA)

A utility function belongs to the HARA-class, if its absolute risk aversion has the form

$$\text{ARA}(w) = -\frac{u''(w)}{u'(w)} = \frac{1}{aw + b},$$

(4.28)

for $a, b \in \mathbb{R}$ and $a > 0$. Equation (4.28) is a second order differential equation in $u(w)$. Thus, we can expect the general solution to have two arbitrary constants, corresponding to the freedom of scaling and translation. A particular solution to the problem is

$$u(w) = \frac{(w + \beta)^{1-\gamma} - 1}{1 - \gamma}.$$

(4.29)

Quick calculation 4.6   Verify that this solution fulfills (4.28) with $a = \frac{1}{\gamma}$ and $b = \frac{\beta}{\gamma}$.

Computing the derivatives of (4.29) with respect to w, one obtains

$$\text{ARA}(w) = \frac{\gamma}{w + \beta} \quad \text{and} \quad \text{RRA}(w) = \frac{\gamma w}{w + \beta}.$$

(4.30)

Quick calculation 4.7   Convince yourself that (4.30) is consistent with our economic intuition.

There is a special case, when $\beta = 0$, that is often called constant relative risk aversion (CRRA), because the *Pratt–Arrow*-coefficient becomes

$$\text{RRA}(w) = \gamma.$$

(4.31)

HARA-utility is the dominant paradigm in economics. It is on the one hand flexible enough to accommodate many standard assumptions, and on the other hand sufficiently tractable, to allow analytical solutions for a large number of problems.

4.6.3   Quadratic Utility

Quadratic utility is really only a local approximation to the true, but most of the time unknown utility function. It has the simple form

$$u(w) = -(\eta - w)^2,$$

(4.32)

where η is called the bliss point, and (4.32) does only make sense for $w < \eta$.

Quick calculation 4.8   Can you see why?

The *Pratt–Arrow*-measures are easily computed as

$$\text{ARA}(w) = \frac{1}{\eta - w} \quad \text{and} \quad \text{RRA}(w) = \frac{w}{\eta - w}. \tag{4.33}$$

Because absolute risk aversion increases as wealth increases towards the bliss point, we can conclude that quadratic utility has a false built-in economic mechanism. However, it tells us something about the attitude of economic agents towards expected wealth and uncertainty; see Problem 4.6 at the end of this chapter.

4.7   Constrained Optimization

Frequently, we have to optimize an objective function, like for example a utility function, with respect to some restrictions, like budget constraints or something similar. This is usually done with Lagrange's method, which is an ingenious trick to translate a constrained optimization problem in given dimensions into a higher-dimensional unconstrained problem. This is profound progress, because dimensionality is much easier to handle than constraints.

Suppose there are two different consumer goods and we want to maximize our utility function $u(c_1, c_2)$, where c_1 and c_2 are the quantities of both commodities to be consumed. Because we do not have unlimited funds, we are subject to a budget constraint $h(c_1, c_2)$ of some kind. If our current wealth is w, we have to solve the problem

$$\max_{c_1, c_2} u(c_1, c_2) \quad \text{subject to} \quad h(c_1, c_2) = w. \tag{4.34}$$

Lagrange's trick is to invent a new function, the *Lagrange*-function

$$\mathcal{L}(c_1, c_2, \lambda) = u(c_1, c_2) + \lambda(w - h(c_1, c_2)), \tag{4.35}$$

that can instead be analyzed without constraints. The only price to pay is that we have an additional variable λ, called the *Lagrange*-multiplier. So let's see if we can understand why this marvelous trick works.

First of all, let's be a little more specific about the utility function and the budget constraint. Suppose we have

$$u(c_1, c_2) = \sqrt{c_1 c_2} \quad \text{and} \quad h(c_1, c_2) = p_1 c_1 + p_2 c_2, \tag{4.36}$$

with commodity prices p_1 and p_2.

Quick calculation 4.9   Verify that the utility function is of the HARA-type.

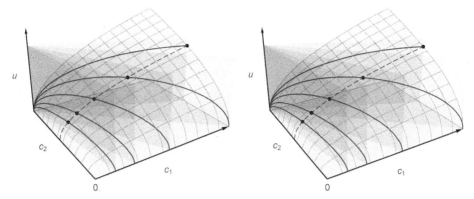

Fig. 4.3 3D Utility maximization problem with different budget constraint slices

The linear budget constraint in (4.36) is typical for economic problems. What it says is that we have no volume discount of any kind. Figure 4.3 illustrates this optimization problem for different budget constraint slices. Lagrange's method is by no means limited to linear constraints. Indeed it can easily deal with several nonlinear constraints, but for every additional one, we get another *Lagrange*-multiplier. The key in understanding the *Lagrange*-formalism is the gradient. For an arbitrary function $f(x_1, \ldots, x_N)$ it is defined by

$$\nabla f = \left(\frac{\partial f}{\partial x_1} \quad \cdots \quad \frac{\partial f}{\partial x_N} \right). \tag{4.37}$$

In differential geometry, the gradient is the archetypical form (co-vector). You should recognize that this expression is identical with the functional derivative with respect to a vector. In this case, the utility function would represent a nonlinear functional of the consumption vector $|c\rangle$. But on the other hand, we could understand the budget constraint as linear functional

$$h[|c\rangle] = \langle p|c \rangle. \tag{4.38}$$

Therefore, we can immediately conclude that $\nabla h = \langle p|$. Figure 4.4 shows a curve of constant utility and the budged constraint for the functions (4.36). Furthermore, the gradients of $u(c_1, c_2)$ at the specific intersection points are indicated. Utility increases the more we proceed to the top right corner. That is why the situation in the left illustration is not optimal. A higher level of utility can still be attained without leaving the budget constraint. In Figure 4.4 right, the utility maximum is realized, because we cannot shift the utility curve any further in the "north-east" direction, without detaching it from the budget constraint. To declutter the illustration, we have not indicated the gradient of $h(c_1, c_2)$, but its corresponding vector $|p\rangle$ instead. The information contained in it, with respect to direction and magnitude, is the same, only the graphical representation changes. There is one crucial and by no means accidental fact to be observed: In the optimum, both gradients point exactly in the same direction. To make this observation even more precise: The gradients are perfectly aligned at the optimum, but they do

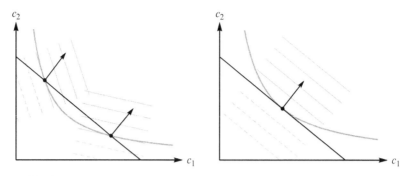

Fig. 4.4 Utility isoquants (gray) and budget constraint (black) – Suboptimal solution with misaligned gradients (left) and utility maximum with aligned gradients (right)

not necessarily have the same magnitude. This is a necessary first order condition for an optimum in the constrained problem (4.34). In our specific case (4.36), it is quite obvious from Figure 4.3 that this condition is also sufficient, because there are no minima or saddle points to worry about in each particular budget constraint slice.

Let's return to the *Lagrange*-function and analyze its first order conditions a little bit. For an unconstrained optimization problem, it is necessary that the gradient in the optimum vanishes. This is the analogue of a vanishing derivative for functions of one variable. So let's see what we get componentwise

$$\frac{\partial \mathcal{L}}{\partial c_n} = \frac{\partial u}{\partial c_n} - \lambda \frac{\partial h}{\partial c_n} \overset{!}{=} 0, \tag{4.39}$$

for $n = 1, 2$. If we rearrange and accumulate the components into a form, we get

$$\nabla u \overset{!}{=} \lambda \cdot \nabla h. \tag{4.40}$$

This is precisely the necessary condition we observed earlier, namely that the gradients have to coincide, up to a scale factor. This scale factor is the *Lagrange*-multiplier λ.

Quick calculation 4.10 Compute the specific form of ∇u for (4.36).

But we still have one more condition from the *Lagrange*-function

$$\frac{\partial \mathcal{L}}{\partial \lambda} = w - h(c_1, c_2) \overset{!}{=} 0. \tag{4.41}$$

Obviously, this one reproduces the original constraint as necessary condition for an admissible optimum

$$h(c_1, c_2) \overset{!}{=} w. \tag{4.42}$$

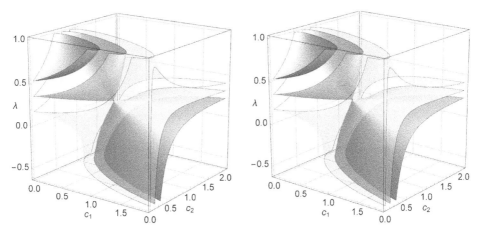

Fig. 4.5 **3D** *Lagrange*ian contour shells with four-dimensional saddlepoint in the mid shell

Now we can see exactly why Lagrange's trick works. The function $\mathcal{L}(c_1, c_2, \lambda)$ is chosen in such a way that

$$\nabla\mathcal{L} \stackrel{!}{=} \langle 0| \qquad (4.43)$$

reproduces all necessary conditions for an optimum in the original constrained problem. To emphasize it once more, even though we focused on a rather simple example to explain the *Lagrange*-formalism, the method is completely general and all arguments carry over to such general situations.

There is however one important subtlety. The first order condition (4.43) does not correspond to an optimum in the *Lagrange*-function, but to a saddlepoint. In our toy example (4.36), this is easily seen for vanishing commodity inputs

$$\mathcal{L}(0, 0, \lambda) = \lambda w. \qquad (4.44)$$

For $w > 0$, the *Lagrange*-function is not bounded, but there are stationary points, where the gradient vanishes. The situation is illustrated in Figure 4.5 for $p_1 = 1$, $p_2 = 2$, and $w = 2$. Because a four-dimensional graph cannot be plotted directly, different surface shells of constant function value are drawn, where the *Lagrange*-function increases in going from the outer to the inner shells. The saddlepoint is located on the mid shell, where the entire surface contracts to a single point. To decide whether or not this point constitutes a minimum or maximum in the original constrained optimization problem, one may analyze the bordered *Hess*ian of the *Lagrange*-problem (for details see Chiang and Wainwright, 2004, sect. 12.3). Fortunately, the structure of common problems in economics and finance often determines the nature of the stationary point beforehand. In our example it was immediately obvious that the first order conditions can only be associated with a maximum in the utility function, because $u(c_1, c_2)$ is monotonically increasing in both arguments, and solely limited by the budget constraint.

4.8   Further Reading

The classical reference to this subject is von Neumann and Morgenstern (1953). A comprehensive introduction is provided in Resnik (1987). Alternative decision theories have been advanced among others by Kahneman and Tversky (1979); Machina (1982); Quiggin (1982), and Yaari (1987). Measures of risk aversion were introduced by Pratt (1964) and Arrow (1965). For known paradoxes of expected utility, see for example Allais (1953); Ellsberg (1961), or Rabin (2000). A comprehensive introduction to optimization techniques in economics and finance is Chiang and Wainwright (2004).

4.9   Problems

4.1 The St. Petersburg paradox is a coin flip game, where a fair coin is tossed successively, until heads occurs. If the first toss is heads, you win \$1. If the first one is tails and the second one is heads, you win \$2. If the first heads occurs in the third toss, you win \$4 and so forth. The amount of money you win is doubled with each coin flip you survive. In the eighteenth century it was believed that the fair price for participating in such a game would be the expected wealth you gain. Show that the expectation value of the St. Petersburg game is infinite.

4.2 Daniel Bernoulli was the first to suggest a kind of expected utility of wealth as a solution to the St. Petersburg paradox of Problem 4.1. He used logarithmic utility

$$u(w) = \log w.$$

Show that the expected utility of the St. Petersburg game is indeed finite and that the certainty equivalent is $w^* = \$2$. Use that

$$\sum_{n=0}^{\infty} \frac{n}{2^n} = 2.$$

4.3 Suppose you own wealth w and you are facing a potential loss l that may occur with probability p. There is an insurance company that offers protection against an arbitrary loss η at an actuarial fair price $p\eta$. Assume you are risk averse; which amount η^* would you insure under expected utility maximization?

4.4 For the special class of utility functions $u(w) = w - be^{-aw}$, with $a, b > 0$, Bell (1988) suggested another measure of risk aversion. For this class, expected utility takes the form

$$E[u(W)] = E[W] - bE[e^{-aw}]$$
$$= E[W] - be^{-aE[W]} \cdot E\left[e^{-a(W-E[W])}\right],$$

where the product on the right hand side contains a scaling factor $be^{-aE[W]}$ and Bell's risk aversion term. Show that

$$E\left[e^{-a(W-E[W])}\right]$$

does not only take the variance into account, but all higher central moments M_k of the probability distribution of W.

4.5 Show that hyperbolic absolute risk aversion with $\beta = 0$, in the limit $\gamma \to 1$ specializes to Bernoulli's logarithmic utility.

4.6 Assume the random variable W has expectation value $E[W] = \mu$ and variance $Var[W] = \sigma^2$. Mean variance analysis postulates that expected utility increases with increasing μ, and decreases with increasing σ^2. Show that quadratic utility coincides with these postulates.

4.7 Assume that the commodity prices in the optimization problem (4.34) with (4.36) are $p_1 = 1$ and $p_2 = 2$. Show that in the optimum $u(c_1^*, c_2^*) = \frac{w}{\sqrt{8}}$ holds.

Part II Financial Markets and Portfolio Theory

5 Architecture of Financial Markets

In this chapter, financial markets are analyzed in the simplest possible setup. Refinements and extensions, to align the theory better with reality, are possible in many ways and often straightforward. But at this point they would be an obstruction in recognizing the fundamental rules of financial markets. It is only on this blueprint that we see the origin of some very deep principles, like the duality between replication and risk-neutral probabilities, easily.

5.1 The *Arrow–Debreu*-World

Originally, Arrow and Debreu (1954) were concerned with optimal allocation problems in an economy with N consumption goods c_n, where $n = 1, \ldots, N$. We will modify this idea by looking at one consumption good, but in different states of the world ω_n. To emphasize this view, we write slightly abusively c_ω, for $\omega = 1, \ldots, \Omega$. The remaining framework is the following:

- There are only two periods of time, $t = 0$ which is today, and $t = T$ which is sometime in the future.

- Consumption today, c_0, is certain.

- Consumption in the future, c_ω, is random and depends on the state $\omega = 1, \ldots, \Omega$, to be realized.

- The agent is equipped with an initial endowment w (wealth) at time $t = 0$.

- There are no frictions like taxes, trading costs, etc.

Accumulating consumption in all different states into a consumption vector $|c\rangle$, the *Arrow–Debreu*-problem becomes maximizing the expected utility $U[C]$, under the wealth constraint

$$c_0 + \sum_{\omega=1}^{\Omega} \psi_\omega c_\omega = c_0 + \langle \psi | c \rangle = w. \tag{5.1}$$

If we were talking about the original allocation problem in a world with N different commodities, ψ_n would be the price of good n in units of c_0. In our modified framework, ψ_ω is the price of consuming one unit of the single good in state ω. Because today we have no idea if state ω will realize in the future or not, ψ_ω is more precisely the price of a claim to one unit of consumption in state ω. The form $\langle \psi |$ is called the state price bra-vector or the state price form.

Solving a constraint optimization problem of this kind is usually done with Lagrange's method. We then obtain the augmented problem

$$\max_{c_0,\dots,c_\Omega} U[C] + \lambda\left(w - c_0 - \sum_{\omega=1}^{\Omega} \psi_\omega c_\omega\right), \tag{5.2}$$

with the auxiliary *Lagrange*-multiplier λ. From equating the derivatives with respect to the consumption variables to zero, we get two different kinds of first order conditions,

$$\frac{\partial U}{\partial c_0} = \lambda \quad \text{and} \quad \frac{\partial U}{\partial c_\omega} = \lambda\psi_\omega, \tag{5.3}$$

from which we can conclude that

$$\psi_\omega = \frac{\partial U/\partial c_\omega}{\partial U/\partial c_0} \tag{5.4}$$

has to hold for $\omega = 1,\dots,\Omega$. This statement is completely general and, to see what it means, we have to specify the *von Neumann–Morgenstern*-utility functional. A most popular choice is a time separable version like

$$U[C] = u(c_0) + e^{-\rho T}\sum_{\omega=1}^{\Omega} u(c_\omega)p_\omega. \tag{5.5}$$

The functional is called time separable, because in differentiating (5.5) with respect to c_0 and c_ω, there will be no mixed terms from different times. The factor $e^{-\rho T}$, for $\rho > 0$ mimics impatience of the agent. She would prefer to reach a given consumption level today, rather than in the future. Put another way around, agents need an extra incentive to postpone consumption into the future, because who knows if they will still be alive and healthy to enjoy it? Using (5.5), we can compute the state price (5.4) explicitly,

$$\psi_\omega = e^{-\rho T}p_\omega\frac{u'(c_\omega)}{u'(c_0)} = -\text{MRS}, \tag{5.6}$$

where MRS is the marginal rate of substitution.

Quick calculation 5.1 Verify the first equality in (5.6).

The marginal rate of substitution is the exchange relationship between c_0 and c_ω, if we hold all other consumptions fixed; see Figure 5.1. To obtain the MRS, we have to compute the total differential of U and set it equal to zero,

$$dU = u'(c_0)dc_0 + e^{-\rho T}p_\omega u'(c_\omega)dc_\omega \overset{!}{=} 0. \tag{5.7}$$

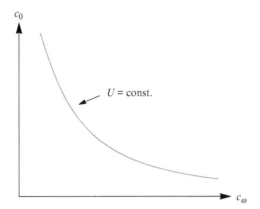

Fig. 5.1 Marginal rate of substitution (MRS) of c_0 and c_ω – All other consumptions fixed

Rearranging terms yields the desired result

$$\frac{dc_0}{dc_\omega} = -e^{-\rho T} p_\omega \frac{u'(c_\omega)}{u'(c_0)} = \text{MRS}. \tag{5.8}$$

The MRS is negative, because you have to give up some consumption today to gain something in state ω in the future, and at the same time keep your expected utility constant. The marginal rate of substitution tells you how much it would cost to trade one unit of consumption in state ω for today's consumption, measured in c_0 units. Thus, the state price ψ_ω is the price of one additional unit of c_ω, in terms of c_0 units, leaving everything else unchanged. Note that it is proportional to the probability of state ω, to the ratio of marginal utilities of c_ω and c_0, and inversely proportional to impatience of the agent.

5.2   The Portfolio Selection Problem

Let's now take a look at a financial market economy. Suppose there are N securities, $S_1, \ldots, S_N$, with different payoffs in different states of the world. We can summarize all this information in a payoff matrix

$$D = \begin{pmatrix} d_{11} & d_{12} & \cdots & d_{1N} \\ d_{21} & d_{22} & \cdots & d_{2N} \\ \vdots & \vdots & \ddots & \vdots \\ d_{\Omega 1} & d_{\Omega 2} & \cdots & d_{\Omega N} \end{pmatrix}, \tag{5.9}$$

where $d_{\omega n}$ is the payoff of security n in state ω, in c_0 consumption units. The payoff-matrix collects all securities column by column, and all possible states of the world row by row. Assume you can invest at time $t = 0$ in security S_n at a price s_n. You are then entitled to a payoff $d_{\omega n}$ at time $t = T$. All security prices are collected in the form $\langle s|$. Recognize the pattern, all prices are forms. You are allowed to buy or even sell arbitrary fractions of all traded securities at $t = 0$. The number θ_n, positive or negative, records the quantity of security S_n you hold. All information of this kind is assembled in the portfolio vector $|\theta\rangle$. The first consequence of this construction is

$$D|\theta\rangle = \begin{pmatrix} d_{11} & \cdots & d_{1N} \\ \vdots & \ddots & \vdots \\ d_{\Omega 1} & \cdots & d_{\Omega N} \end{pmatrix} \begin{pmatrix} \theta_1 \\ \vdots \\ \theta_N \end{pmatrix} = \begin{pmatrix} c_1 \\ \vdots \\ c_\Omega \end{pmatrix} = |c\rangle. \tag{5.10}$$

As you can see, securities are instruments for shifting consumption from period $t = 0$ to period $t = T$ and adjusting your desired consumption profile.

Now we have a new optimization problem. We still maximize expected utility, but now the wealth constraint has the form

$$c_0 + \sum_{n=1}^{N} s_n \theta_n = c_0 + \langle s|\theta\rangle = w. \tag{5.11}$$

This new problem has a known solution, if there is a state price form $\langle\psi|$, such that

$$\langle s| = \langle\psi|D \tag{5.12}$$

holds. To see this, plug (5.12) into the wealth constraint and use (5.10)

$$c_0 + \langle s|\theta\rangle = c_0 + \langle\psi|D|\theta\rangle = c_0 + \langle\psi|c\rangle = w, \tag{5.13}$$

and we are right back in the *Arrow–Debreu*-world. This is a quite remarkable result. The question is, under which conditions does it hold? The key to the answer is Equation (5.12). There has to be a unique solution for $\langle\psi|$ for the whole chain of arguments to hold. A necessary condition for such a solution to exist, is that the financial market, summarized by D, contains a full set of Ω linearly independent securities. In this case DD' is invertible and we obtain

$$\langle\psi| = \langle s|D'(DD')^{-1}. \tag{5.14}$$

Quick calculation 5.2   Confirm the last equation.

Such a market is called complete, because every possible payoff is attainable by a linear combination of traded securities, which means a portfolio. Notice that a complete market alone does not guarantee the existence of a state price form. Thus we have to check, whether or not the potential solution (5.14) indeed satisfies (5.12).

Example 5.1

Consider the following financial market

$$D = \begin{pmatrix} 1 & 3 & 2 \\ 2 & 0 & 4 \end{pmatrix} \quad \text{and} \quad \langle s| = \begin{pmatrix} 1 & 2 & 2 \end{pmatrix}.$$

What is the state price form $\langle\psi|$ if there is one?

Solution

The first and second security are linearly independent, therefore the market is complete. The following building blocks are required in the computation of $\langle\psi|$,

$$\langle s|D' = \begin{pmatrix} 11 & 10 \end{pmatrix} \quad \text{and} \quad (DD')^{-1} = \frac{1}{180}\begin{pmatrix} 20 & -10 \\ -10 & 14 \end{pmatrix}.$$

The potential state price form is then obtained by

$$\langle\psi| = \langle s|D'(DD')^{-1} = \frac{1}{180}\begin{pmatrix} 11 & 10 \end{pmatrix}\begin{pmatrix} 20 & -10 \\ -10 & 14 \end{pmatrix} = \frac{1}{180}\begin{pmatrix} 120 & 30 \end{pmatrix} = \begin{pmatrix} \frac{2}{3} & \frac{1}{6} \end{pmatrix}.$$

It remains to check, whether or not $\langle\psi|$ solves (5.2),

$$\langle\psi|D = \begin{pmatrix} \frac{2}{3} & \frac{1}{6} \end{pmatrix}\begin{pmatrix} 1 & 3 & 2 \\ 2 & 0 & 4 \end{pmatrix} = \begin{pmatrix} 1 & 2 & 2 \end{pmatrix} = \langle s|.$$

Thus, $\langle\psi|$ is the desired state price form.

Quick calculation 5.3 Verify the intermediate results in Example 5.1.

5.3   Preference-Free Results

All results derived so far depend on individual preferences and utilities of economic agents. Recall that the state prices are negative marginal rates of substitution, which depend on marginal utility. In this section we will see a far more powerful machinery, leading to completely preference-free results in complete financial markets. But first, we need an additional bit of notation. For two N-dimensional vectors, $|a\rangle$ and $|b\rangle$, define the following relations:

$$
\begin{aligned}
|a\rangle \geq |b\rangle &\quad\leftrightarrow\quad \text{for all } n, a_n \geq b_n \text{ holds,} \\
|a\rangle > |b\rangle &\quad\leftrightarrow\quad |a\rangle \geq |b\rangle, \text{ and } a_n > b_n \text{ for at least one } n, \\
|a\rangle \gg |b\rangle &\quad\leftrightarrow\quad \text{for all } n, a_n > b_n \text{ holds.}
\end{aligned}
\tag{5.15}
$$

Of course, the same relations apply to forms. Now we are in a position to formulate the portfolio selection problem in a more efficient fashion and to define the notion of arbitrage precisely. The portfolio selection problem can be restated in the compressed form

$$|C\rangle = \begin{bmatrix} c_0 \\ |c\rangle \end{bmatrix} = \begin{bmatrix} w \\ |0\rangle \end{bmatrix} + \begin{bmatrix} -\langle s| \\ D \end{bmatrix}|\theta\rangle, \tag{5.16}$$

where [...] indicates a compound vector or a compound matrix, respectively. This notation may look intimidating but it is quite efficient. You can do the algebra with compound entities just as if they were ordinary vectors and matrices, with scalar coefficients. That is the power of linearity.

Quick calculation 5.4   Verify that the portfolio selection problem and its wealth constraint is summarized in (5.16).

Imagine now, we held a portfolio $|\theta\rangle$ and did a slight modification to obtain a new portfolio $|\theta^*\rangle = |\theta\rangle + |\eta\rangle$. Then our overall change in consumption would be

$$|C^*\rangle - |C\rangle = \begin{bmatrix} -\langle s| \\ D \end{bmatrix} |\eta\rangle. \tag{5.17}$$

We call this change in overall consumption an arbitrage opportunity, if

$$\begin{bmatrix} -\langle s| \\ D \end{bmatrix} |\eta\rangle > |0\rangle \tag{5.18}$$

holds. The portfolio $|\eta\rangle$ offers something for nothing. Either the portfolio costs nothing today, but pays off a positive amount in at least one state of the world, or it has a negative price today, but nonnegative payoffs in the future. Therefore, an arbitrage opportunity is something like a free lunch.

At this point, we make only two structural assumptions about financial markets. First, more is better than less, and second, there is no free lunch. The following theorem is one of the most profound statements in financial economics.

Theorem 5.1 (Fundamental theorem of asset pricing) *The following statements about security prices $\langle s|$ and payoffs D are equivalent*:

1. *There are no arbitrage opportunities,*

$$\nexists |\eta\rangle : \begin{bmatrix} -\langle s| \\ D \end{bmatrix} |\eta\rangle > |0\rangle.$$

2. *There is a strictly positive state price form,*

$$\exists \langle \psi| \gg \langle 0| : \langle s| = \langle \psi|D.$$

3. *There is an agent with strictly monotonic increasing preferences U, who realizes an optimum in the portfolio selection problem.*

We will prove Theorem 5.1 by showing that the chain $1 \Rightarrow 2 \Rightarrow 3 \Rightarrow 1$ holds (cf. Dybvig and Ross, 2003). Proving the first implication is the toughest link in the chain. The major part of the theoretical work on this was done by Harrison and Kreps (1979). To follow their line of very sophisticated reasoning, we need another theorem about linear separation of closed cones that can be found in Duffie (2001, appendix B).

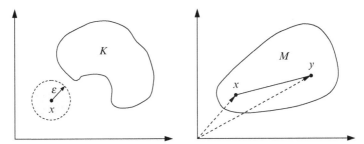

Fig. 5.2 Bounded set of points with ε-vicinity of point x (left) and convex set of points (right)

Theorem 5.2 (Separating hyperplane theorem for closed cones) *Suppose M and K are closed convex cones in $\mathbb{R}^N$ that intersect precisely at zero. If K does not contain a linear subspace other than $\{0\}$, then there is a nonzero linear functional L, such that $L[m] < L[k]$, for each m in M and each nonzero k in K.*

We have to explain some of the technical terms in Theorem 5.2 in more detail, before we can proceed.

Closedness

Recall that the coordinate representation of a vector $|k\rangle$ marks a point k in $\mathbb{R}^N$. A set of points K is closed, if for every point x outside of K, there is an $\varepsilon > 0$, such that the interior of the x-centered sphere with radius ε is outside of K, too. The concept is illustrated in Figure 5.2 left. A line or a plane are examples of closed sets of points. Here is a counterexample:

Example 5.2

The interval $K = [0, 1)$ is not a closed set of points.

Proof

Pick the point $x = 1$. In this case the sphere with radius ε is the interval $[1 - \varepsilon, 1 + \varepsilon]$. Now choose a point in the interior of that sphere, say $y = 1 - \frac{\varepsilon}{2}$. You can immediately see that there is no $\varepsilon > 0$, such that $y \notin [0, 1)$.

Convexity

A set of points M is called convex, if for two arbitrary points x and y in M, every linear combination

$$\lambda x + (1 - \lambda)y, \tag{5.19}$$

with $0 < \lambda < 1$ is also in M. What this means is that every point on the line connecting x and y has to be in M, too; see Figure 5.2 right.

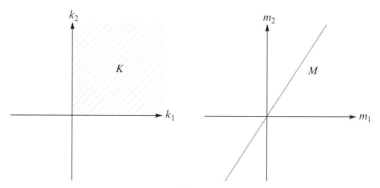

Fig. 5.3 Different closed convex cones in $\mathbb{R}^2$ – Closed half-space (left) and linear subspace (right)

Quick calculation 5.5   Convince yourself that the set K in Figure 5.2 left is not convex.

Closed convex cones

A set of points K is a closed convex cone, if it is closed and convex, and if for every point k in K, αk is also in K, for $\alpha \geq 0$. There are two basic types of closed convex cones we are interested in, closed half-spaces and linear subspaces. An example of a closed half-space is a set of points K, generated by all vectors satisfying $|k\rangle \geq |0\rangle$,

$$K = \left\{ k \in \mathbb{R}^N : |k\rangle \geq |0\rangle \right\}. \tag{5.20}$$

This is the positive orthant; see Figure 5.3 left for an example in $\mathbb{R}^2$. Note that K does not contain any linear subspaces, which are lines or planes that extend to infinity in every direction, with exception of the linear subspace $\{0\}$, which is merely a point. Another example of a convex cone is the set of points generated by projecting an arbitrary vector in $\mathbb{R}^N$ onto a linear subspace,

$$M = \left\{ m : |m\rangle = P|\eta\rangle, \ \eta \in \mathbb{R}^N \right\}, \tag{5.21}$$

where P is a projection matrix. An $\mathbb{R}^2$ example is given in Figure 5.3 right, where we used the projection matrix

$$P = \begin{pmatrix} 3 & -3 \\ 2 & -2 \end{pmatrix}. \tag{5.22}$$

Quick calculation 5.6   Check that both examples satisfy the required conditions for closed convex cones.

We are now in a position to apply Theorem 5.2 to prove the first implication of the fundamental theorem of asset pricing. We will track our steps graphically in $\mathbb{R}^3$, whereas the analytical results are independent of the dimensionality of the vector space.

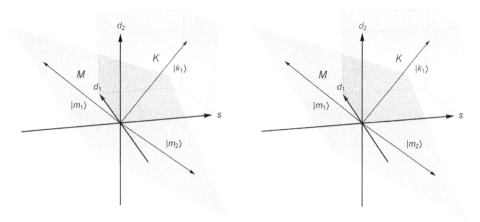

Fig. 5.4 **3D** Fundamental theorem of asset pricing – Convex cones K and M intersecting at zero

1 implies 2:
Let's first define the set of points generated by the prices and payoffs of all traded securities in the market

$$M = \left\{ m : |m\rangle = \begin{bmatrix} -\langle s| \\ D \end{bmatrix} |\eta\rangle, \ \eta \in \mathbb{R}^N \right\}. \tag{5.23}$$

The points m span a linear space in $\mathbb{R}^{\Omega+1}$.

Quick calculation 5.7 Why is M a linear space? Remember what linearity means.

If there is no arbitrage, then according to the fundamental theorem, M intersects the half-space K, defined by

$$K = \left\{ k \in \mathbb{R}^{\Omega+1} : |k\rangle \geq |0\rangle \right\}, \tag{5.24}$$

only at zero, $M \cap K = \{0\}$. Because of this, M has to be a linear subspace of $\mathbb{R}^{\Omega+1}$, which means a (hyper-) plane. The situation is illustrated in Figure 5.4. Every point $m \in M$ represents an arbitrage free configuration of security price and state contingent pay-offs. Every nonzero point $k \in K$ means an arbitrage opportunity. Note that we satisfy precisely the conditions of the separating hyperplane theorem, so let's use it.

   The separating hyperplane theorem ensures that there is a linear functional L, such that $L[m] < L[k]$ for every $m \in M$ and nonzero $k \in K$. We know from the *Riesz*-representation theorem that a linear functional for every vector in the plane M is given by the inner product with a form. But which form is the right one? Let's focus on the two bits of information a form carries, its orientation and its magnitude. The form has to be oriented in a way, such that its inner product with every vector $|m\rangle$ is smaller than the inner product with every nonzero vector $|k\rangle$. There are some vectors drawn in Figure 5.4 to illustrate the situation. On the one hand, for very tiny vectors, pointing into K, the inner product can be very small. On the other hand, M is a linear subspace,

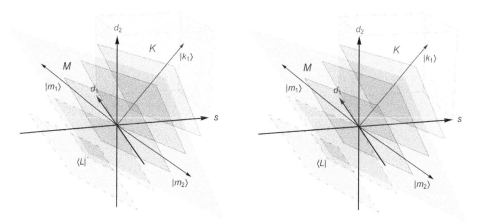

Fig. 5.5 **3D** Fundamental theorem of asset pricing – Convex cones K and M and coplanar form $\langle L|$

which means, if there is a vector $|m\rangle$, then there is also a vector $-|m\rangle$ and infinitely many scaled versions of them. For all those vectors, the inner product with the desired form has to be smaller than the one with a small vector $|k\rangle$. If you think it through thoroughly, there is only one possible solution. The desired form $\langle L|$ has to be coplanar with the plane M. In this case it is orthogonal to every vector $|m\rangle$, which means the inner product is always zero, and it has to point into the direction of K, so that the inner product with every vector $|k\rangle > |0\rangle$ is positive; see Figure 5.5.

We succeeded in determining the orientation of $\langle L|$, but there is still one degree of freedom left, its magnitude. It is easy to see in Figure 5.5, that all arguments we have put forward so far hold independently of the spacing of $\langle L|$. But we can use this ambiguity in a very smart way. We know that the inner product of every vector in the linear subspace M with any scaled version of $\langle L|$ has to vanish,

$$\alpha\langle L|\begin{bmatrix} -\langle s| \\ D \end{bmatrix}|\eta\rangle = \alpha\begin{bmatrix} l_0 & \langle l| \end{bmatrix}\begin{bmatrix} -\langle s| \\ D \end{bmatrix}|\eta\rangle = 0, \qquad (5.25)$$

where we simply partitioned the form $\langle L|$ into $\begin{bmatrix} l_0 & \langle l| \end{bmatrix}$. Now set $\alpha = \frac{1}{l_0}$ and call the form $\frac{1}{l_0}\langle l| = \langle\psi|$. We then obtain

$$\begin{bmatrix} 1 & \langle\psi| \end{bmatrix}\begin{bmatrix} -\langle s| \\ D \end{bmatrix}|\eta\rangle = 0. \qquad (5.26)$$

But (5.26) has to hold for arbitrary vectors $|\eta\rangle$, in particular for $|\eta\rangle \gg |0\rangle$ or $|\eta\rangle \ll |0\rangle$. Thus, we can conclude that

$$\begin{bmatrix} 1 & \langle\psi| \end{bmatrix}\begin{bmatrix} -\langle s| \\ D \end{bmatrix} = \langle 0| \qquad (5.27)$$

has to hold. Expanding and rearranging (5.27) yields

$$\langle s| = \langle\psi|D. \qquad (5.28)$$

We are not finished yet. The fundamental theorem claims additionally that the state price form $\langle\psi|$ is strictly positive. That's where the second part of the separating hyperplane theorem comes in. It ensures that

$$\begin{bmatrix} 1 & \langle\psi| \end{bmatrix} |k\rangle > 0, \tag{5.29}$$

for every vector $|k\rangle > |0\rangle$ in $\mathbb{R}^{\Omega+1}$. Remember what $|k\rangle > |0\rangle$ means. $|k\rangle$ is easily allowed to have Ω zeros and only one positive coefficient. But we do not know which one is the positive one. Thus, to guarantee that (5.29) holds, we must have

$$\langle\psi| \gg \langle 0|. \tag{5.30}$$

This concludes the proof of the first implication of the fundamental theorem. The remaining steps are much easier.

2 implies 3:
We show by construction that a strictly positive state price form implies the existence of an agent with strictly increasing preferences, who realizes an optimum in the portfolio selection problem. Suppose an agent has expected utility $U = \begin{bmatrix} 1 & \langle\psi| \end{bmatrix} |C\rangle$. Such preferences are clearly strictly monotonic increasing in every component of $|C\rangle$. From (5.16) and (5.28), we have

$$\begin{aligned} U &= \begin{bmatrix} 1 & \langle\psi| \end{bmatrix}\left(\begin{bmatrix} w \\ |0\rangle \end{bmatrix} + \begin{bmatrix} -\langle s| \\ D \end{bmatrix}|\theta\rangle\right) \\ &= w + \left(-\langle s| + \langle\psi|D\right)|\theta\rangle \\ &= w + \langle 0|\theta\rangle = w. \end{aligned} \tag{5.31}$$

We cannot increase utility at all by forming or changing portfolios and thus, (5.31) is already an optimum, no matter which portfolio $|\theta^*\rangle$ the agent holds. This concludes the proof of the second implication.

3 implies 1:
The final step is rather trivial. If there is an agent with strictly increasing preferences, realizing an optimum by holding a portfolio $|\theta^*\rangle$, then there cannot be arbitrage opportunities. An arbitrage would increase the agent's expected utility, but $|\theta^*\rangle$ is already a maximum. Therefore, we can conclude that there are no arbitrage opportunities. This argument confirms the last implication and completes the proof.

5.4   *Pareto*-Optimal Allocation and the Representative Agent

The fundamental theorem of asset pricing is a completely general statement. It holds, no matter if the market is complete or incomplete. It even holds for infinite dimensional vector spaces.[1] Complete markets are very attractive from an analytical point of view,

---

[1] The structural consequences of the theorem even remain valid in more general function spaces, where the separating hyperplane theorem is no longer applicable. In this case the *Hahn–Banach*-theorem has to be used (Delbaen and Schachermayer, 1994)

because they guarantee that certain results from equilibrium allocation theory hold. In this section, we look at a financial economy with M agents. The first important result is the analogue of the first welfare theorem in economics:

Theorem 5.3 (Equilibrium allocation) *Consider an M-agents financial economy, with equilibrium portfolio holdings* $|\theta_1^*\rangle, \ldots, |\theta_M^*\rangle$. *If the market is complete, then the allocation of consumption is Pareto-optimal.*

The first thing you should realize is that the absence of arbitrage opportunities is a necessary condition for equilibrium. If there were arbitrage opportunities left in the market, agents would surely exploit them and thus the market would not be in equilibrium. Of course the opposite is not true, absence of arbitrage does not automatically imply equilibrium of the financial market. However, because we have assumed equilibrium in Theorem 5.3, we can be sure that the market is free of arbitrage opportunities. We will now prove the theorem by contradiction.

A consumption allocation is *Pareto*-optimal, if there is no other allocation, in which no agent realizes less consumption at any time and in any state, but at least one agent consumes more, either at time $t = 0$ or in some state at time $t = T$. We will assume, that it is possible for at least one agent to increase consumption and subsequently show that this assumption contradicts the constraints of the optimization problem. So let's assume, there is a collection of portfolios $|\theta_m\rangle$, for $m = 1, \ldots, M$, such that

$$\sum_{m=1}^{M}\left(c_{0m} + \langle s|\theta_m\rangle\right) > \sum_{m=1}^{M}\left(c_{0m}^* + \langle s|\theta_m^*\rangle\right). \tag{5.32}$$

Let's start by manipulating the right hand side of (5.32). We will use the fact that $|\theta_m^*\rangle$ are equilibrium portfolios and thus

$$\sum_{m=1}^{M}|\theta_m^*\rangle = |0\rangle \tag{5.33}$$

has to hold, because in equilibrium we have market clearing. One then obtains

$$\sum_{m=1}^{M}\left(c_{0m}^* + \langle s|\theta_m^*\rangle\right) = \sum_{m=1}^{M}c_{0m}^* + \langle s|\sum_{m=1}^{M}|\theta_m^*\rangle = \sum_{m=1}^{M}c_{0m}^* = W, \tag{5.34}$$

overall consumption equals the total wealth W in the economy, measured in c_0 units. Now let's take a closer look at the left hand side of (5.32). Because the market is arbitrage free and complete, there is a unique state price form, such that

$$\sum_{m=1}^{M}\left(c_{0m} + \langle s|\theta_m\rangle\right) = \sum_{m=1}^{M}\left(c_{0m} + \langle\psi|D|\theta_m\rangle\right) = \sum_{m=1}^{M}\left(c_{0m} + \langle\psi|c_m\rangle\right). \tag{5.35}$$

Combining these results yields

$$\sum_{m=1}^{M}\left(c_{0m} + \sum_{\omega=1}^{\Omega}\psi_\omega c_{\omega m}\right) > \sum_{m=1}^{M}w_m = W, \tag{5.36}$$

which violates the wealth constraint of at least one agent in the *Arrow–Debreu*-problem. Thus, our assumption leads to a contradiction and we can conclude that the original allocation, generated by $|\theta_1^*\rangle, \ldots, |\theta_M^*\rangle$, is *Pareto*-optimal.

Another important feature of complete markets, at least as long as they are frictionless, is the existence of a representative agent (Constantinides, 1982). We will start by briefly reviewing the optimization problem of a single agent in the *Arrow–Debreu*-world. In our multi-agent economy, each single agent has to maximize expected utility, subject to individual wealth constraints. Thus, agent m's problem is

$$\max_{|C_m\rangle} U_m[C_m] \quad \text{subject to} \quad \begin{bmatrix} 1 & \langle \psi| \end{bmatrix} |C_m\rangle = w_m. \tag{5.37}$$

We further assume that the *von Neumann–Morgenstern*-utility functional is the time separable version (5.5) on page 80, and all agents are risk averse. These assumptions are in fact unnecessarily restrictive, but they ensure that the first order conditions of the constraint maximization problem are sufficient. Following the *Lagrange*-formalism, we get agent m's first order condition

$$\frac{\delta U_m}{\delta |C_m\rangle} - \lambda_m \begin{bmatrix} 1 & \langle \psi| \end{bmatrix} \overset{!}{=} \langle 0|, \tag{5.38}$$

and after trivial rearrangement

$$\frac{\delta U_m}{\delta |C_m\rangle} = \lambda_m^* \begin{bmatrix} 1 & \langle \psi| \end{bmatrix}. \tag{5.39}$$

Recognize that λ_m^* is always positive, because it represents agent m's marginal utility of consumption at $t = 0$.

Quick calculation 5.8 Provide a formal argument for the last statement.

Now let's turn to the whole financial economy. Define a candidate for the so-called social welfare functional

$$U[C] = \sum_{m=1}^{M} \frac{1}{\lambda_m^*} U_m[C_m] \tag{5.40}$$

to be maximized with respect to an aggregated wealth constraint,

$$\max_{|C_1\rangle, \ldots, |C_M\rangle} U[C] \quad \text{subject to} \quad \sum_{m=1}^{M} \begin{bmatrix} 1 & \langle \psi| \end{bmatrix} |C_m\rangle = W, \tag{5.41}$$

with $W = \sum_{m=1}^{M} w_m$. It turns out that this is the right guess. Because all λ_m^* are positive, first order conditions are still sufficient.

Quick calculation 5.9 Write the *Lagrange*-function of problem (5.41).

From the *Lagrange*-formalism we now have M first order conditions of the form

$$\frac{1}{\lambda_m^*} \frac{\delta U}{\delta |C_m\rangle} - \lambda \Big[1 \quad \langle \psi | \Big] \stackrel{!}{=} \langle 0 |. \tag{5.42}$$

There is a unique solution to this problem, if we can find one single λ^*, satisfying all M first order conditions (5.42). To this end, use the individual requirement (5.39) for a utility maximum of agent m, to obtain the aggregated first order condition

$$(1 - \lambda^*) \Big[1 \quad \langle \psi | \Big] = \langle 0 |. \tag{5.43}$$

Now it is clear that $\lambda^* = 1$ solves them all. This means that the social welfare functional (5.40) can be understood as the expected utility functional of some representative agent.

Quick calculation 5.10   Show that $U[C] = \sum_{m=1}^{M} \frac{\alpha}{\lambda_m^*} U_m[C_m]$, with $\alpha > 0$, is also an admissible social welfare functional.

Maximizing a social welfare functional results in a *Pareto*-optimal allocation. The converse is also true, if the allocation is *Pareto*-optimal, then a representative agent has realized a maximum in an aggregated expected utility functional (see Hens and Rieger, 2010, p. 190). Large parts of financial economics rely heavily on the analysis of representative agents. At least it makes life a lot easier in many situations.

5.5   Market Completeness and Replicating Portfolios

Complete markets have another pleasant property; the state price form is unique. We will learn later, why uniqueness of state prices does not survive when markets are incomplete. At the moment let's focus on a concrete consequence of this fact: In a complete market, every payoff can be replicated by a portfolio of traded securities. This principle is often stated equivalently as every payoff is attainable. If there is no arbitrage, the price of the replicating portfolio has to be equal to the price of the security it replicates. Otherwise you could sell one short and buy the other, and make a riskless profit.

Let's start the discussion at our initial definition of completeness. We found earlier that a security market is complete, if D contains a full set of Ω linearly independent securities. This means technically, we can pick any set of Ω linearly independent securities we like, and use them as basis for the payoff space. Let's call this collection D^* and the associated security prices $\langle s^* |$. Of course all implications of the fundamental theorem of asset pricing have to hold for this special collection of securities, too, in particular

$$\langle s^* | = \langle \psi | D^*. \tag{5.44}$$

Now let's ask a few very interesting questions. First of all, what is the price of a security S_ω with payoff $|e_\omega\rangle$, which means one c_0-unit in state ω, and zero otherwise? Obviously, for the replicating portfolio we must have $|e_\omega\rangle = D^*|\theta_\omega\rangle$. Because D^* is an invertible square matrix, we obtain

$$|\theta_\omega\rangle = D^{*-1}|e_\omega\rangle. \tag{5.45}$$

But what is the price of this portfolio? It is of course the price of each basis-security times its quantity, $\langle s^*|\theta_\omega\rangle$. So let's put the pieces together,

$$\langle s^*|\theta_\omega\rangle = \langle\psi|D^*D^{*-1}|e_\omega\rangle = \langle\psi|e_\omega\rangle = \psi_\omega. \tag{5.46}$$

Isn't that nice? S_ω is called an *Arrow–Debreu*-security. The payoffs of all *Arrow–Debreu*-securities form an orthonormal basis of the payoff space and the state price form collects the associated *Arrow–Debreu*-prices.

Here is another interesting question. What is the price of a security B_0, with payoff $|1\rangle$, which means a payoff of one c_0-unit in every possible state of the world? Following our own footsteps, we obtain

$$\langle s^*|\theta_0\rangle = \langle\psi|1\rangle = \sum_{\omega=1}^{\Omega} \psi_\omega. \tag{5.47}$$

This one seems to be a little more intricate. Think about what it means, if a security pays off one c_0-unit, no matter what state of the world will be realized. It means that we are dealing with a riskless security. To be a little more precise, B_0 is a riskless zero-coupon bond. But we know that today's price of such a security has to be $(1+r)^{-1}$, where r is the risk-free rate of return from $t=0$ to $t=T$. Thus we can conclude that

$$r = \frac{1}{\sum_{\omega=1}^{\Omega} \psi_\omega} - 1. \tag{5.48}$$

Quick calculation 5.11   Verify the last equation.

Obviously, an arbitrage free and complete market determines a risk-free interest rate. This fact is true, whether a zero-coupon bond is traded or not. In the latter case, r is called a shadow risk-free interest rate.

In a complete market, we can replicate arbitrary payoffs, and in the process assign unique arbitrage free prices to the respective securities. Here is an example:

Example 5.3

Consider the financial market, determined by the payoff matrix and security price form

$$D = \begin{pmatrix} 1 & 4 & 2 \\ 2 & 0 & 4 \end{pmatrix} \quad \text{and} \quad \langle s| = \begin{pmatrix} 1 & 2 & 2 \end{pmatrix}.$$

There is a new security S_4 introduced into the market, with payoff vector

$$|d_4\rangle = \begin{pmatrix} 3 \\ 2 \end{pmatrix}.$$

How can S_4 be replicated and what is its arbitrage free price?

Solution

It is easy to see that the first two payoff vectors in D are linearly independent. We can thus use them as a basis

$$D^* = \begin{pmatrix} 1 & 4 \\ 2 & 0 \end{pmatrix}.$$

From this, we immediately conclude that

$$|\theta_4\rangle = \begin{pmatrix} 1 \\ \frac{1}{2} \end{pmatrix}$$

solves the problem $|d_4\rangle = D^*|\theta_4\rangle$. The fair price of security S_4 is thus

$$s_4 = \langle s^*|\theta_4\rangle = \begin{pmatrix} 1 & 2 \end{pmatrix}\begin{pmatrix} 1 \\ \frac{1}{2} \end{pmatrix} = 2.$$

Because we can pick a basis arbitrarily, there is more than one replicating portfolio. But all of them have to have the same price, otherwise an arbitrage opportunity would be present.

Quick calculation 5.12 Verify that using the second and third security in Example 5.3 as a basis, results in a different replicating portfolio, but in the same price for S_4.

Here comes the big question: What if the market is incomplete? To answer this one, we have to go back to the fundamental theorem of asset pricing. More precisely, to the linear subspace, spanned by all possible arbitrage free configurations of security prices and payoffs

$$M = \left\{ m : |m\rangle = \begin{bmatrix} -\langle s| \\ D \end{bmatrix}|\eta\rangle, \ \eta \in \mathbb{R}^N \right\}. \tag{5.49}$$

If the market is complete, M is an Ω-dimensional linear subspace of $\mathbb{R}^{\Omega+1}$, like in Figure 5.4 on page 87. If the market is incomplete, M is a linear subspace of lower dimension. The situation is illustrated in Figure 5.6. Here, M is a one-dimensional linear subspace, a line, in which all payoffs are situated. The separating hyperplane theorem guarantees the existence of a form, orthogonal to every vector in M, but it does not guarantee its uniqueness. Indeed, there is a continuum of forms, compatible with the consequences of the separating hyperplane theorem. Two of them are indicated in Figure 5.7. What are the implications of this ambiguity? First of all,

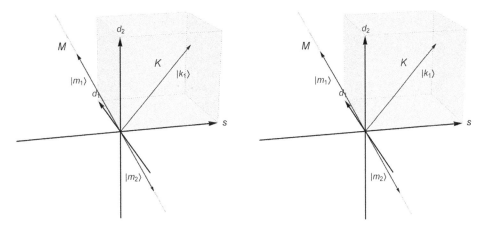

Fig. 5.6 3D Incomplete market – Dimension of subspace M is smaller than Ω

we have

$$\langle L| = \begin{bmatrix} 1 & \langle \psi| \end{bmatrix} \tag{5.50}$$

and thus, the state price form itself is not unique. But that is to say, the price of an arbitrary security is not unique, because the relation

$$s_n = \langle \psi | d_n \rangle \tag{5.51}$$

still holds. The truly remarkable fact is that all those different prices are fair, in that they do not allow arbitrage opportunities. You may be puzzled about the last statement. How can there be two different prices for the same security, but no arbitrage opportunity? If you think it through, there are not only two possible prices, but a whole continuum of prices, as there is a continuum of possible linear functionals and state price forms. You can observe the consequences in real markets, which are doubtlessly

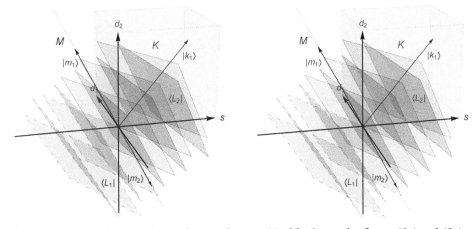

Fig. 5.7 3D Incomplete market – Linear subspace M with alternative forms $\langle L_1|$ and $\langle L_2|$

incomplete, in form of bid–offer spreads. Now you recognize how arbitrage is prevented, despite a whole interval of fair prices. You have to buy at the highest fair price, but can sell only at the lowest fair price.

We can summarize the major consequences of market incompleteness in two statements. First, the state price form is not unique and thus, there is more than one arbitrage free security price. Second, because there is no complete basis contained in D, we cannot find a replicating portfolio for an arbitrary security S_n. The last statement is often expressed equivalently by observing that not all payoffs are attainable. Perfect replication is thus an exclusive feature of complete markets. On the other hand, every security with non-attainable payoff and observable price, traded in an incomplete market, adds an additional dimension to the linear subspace M and thus, brings the market closer to completeness.

5.6　Martingale Measures and Duality

We are now heading towards a duality that is at the heart of quantitative finance. It will reveal its full potential in derivative pricing, but it is built deep into the structure of financial markets. We have already seen some of its building blocks. So essentially, there is only one new ingredient, the notion of martingales. The term martingale originates from horse racing. In probability theory, a martingale describes a fair game. A stochastic process X_t is called a martingale, if

$$E[X_{t+s}|\mathcal{F}_t] = X_t \tag{5.52}$$

holds, for $s \geq 0$. Of course we assumed that X_t is adapted to the filtration $\mathcal{F}_t$, but that is not the point here. What (5.52) says is that the best prediction for the value the random variable X may take tomorrow, is the value observed today. In other words, a martingale is completely unpredictable.

A duality is understood as a different but completely equivalent formal description of a certain issue. In a manner of speaking dual theories represent two sides of one coin. In our case, the coin is the state price form, and we have already seen one side, replication. In a complete market, the state price form is unique, and we can price any state contingent security with known payoff $|d_n\rangle$ by a replicating portfolio $|\theta_n\rangle$,

$$s_n = \langle s^*|\theta_n\rangle = \langle \psi|d_n\rangle. \tag{5.53}$$

We have also seen that replicating a zero-coupon bond B_0 gives rise to a (shadow) risk-free rate of return

$$1 + r = \frac{1}{\sum_{\omega=1}^{\Omega} \psi_\omega}. \tag{5.54}$$

Let's define a new quantity q_ω, with

$$q_\omega = \frac{\psi_\omega}{\sum_{k=1}^{\Omega} \psi_k} \tag{5.55}$$

and analyze it a little bit. Obviously, $q_\omega > 0$ holds for $\omega = 1, \ldots, \Omega$, because all state prices ψ_ω are positive. Furthermore, we have

$$\sum_{\omega=1}^{\Omega} q_\omega = 1. \qquad (5.56)$$

Does that remind you of something? The quantities q_ω have precisely the properties we would expect from a discrete set of probabilities. Let's go one step further. Divide and multiply the right hand side of (5.53) by (5.54) and use (5.55)

$$s_n = \frac{1}{1+r} \sum_{\omega=1}^{\Omega} d_{\omega n} q_\omega = \frac{1}{1+r} E^Q[d_n]. \qquad (5.57)$$

Quick calculation 5.13   Verify the first equality in (5.57).

The probability measure Q, under which the expectation value in (5.57) is taken, is called an equivalent martingale measure. The expectation value of the future payoff under the measure Q is the value of the security today, apart from a discounting factor. Hence the name. It is also called a risk-neutral probability measure, because only the risk-neutral agent would ignore utility and focus only on the expected payoff.

What happens, if the market is incomplete? We know replication breaks down and securities have no longer unique arbitrage free prices. If pricing under the equivalent martingale measure represents a genuine duality, we can expect trouble. The definition of q_ω in (5.55) provides the key. The qs are normalized versions of the state prices, and if state prices are not unique, neither are the qs. This means, in incomplete markets, we can expect a continuum of equivalent martingale measures. The old problem in a new guise.

5.7   Further Reading

The starting point of the discussion in this chapter is the classic competitive equilibrium of Arrow and Debreu (1954). A concise review can be found in Dybvig and Ross (2003); a comprehensive source is Lengwiler (2004). Original work about the fundamental theorem of asset pricing and equivalent martingale measures is due to Harrison and Kreps (1979) and Harrison and Pliska (1981). A technical exposition including multi-period extensions is found in Elliott and Kopp (2005, chap. 3). A full scale mathematical treatment of the whole subject is provided in Duffie (2003), as well as in Delbaen and Schachermayer (2006). A financial economics' perspective can be found in Cochrane (2005).

5.8   Problems

5.1 Assume that *von Neumann–Morgenstern*-utility is a time separable functional of the form

$$U[C] = u(c_0) + e^{-\rho T} \sum_{\omega=1}^{\Omega} u(c_\omega)p_\omega.$$

Show that the price of an arbitrary security can be written as expectation value

$$s_n = E[Md_n],$$

where the random variable M is called the stochastic discount factor (SDF), and is given by

$$M = e^{-\rho T} \frac{u'(C)}{u'(c_0)}.$$

5.2 Use a zero-coupon bond to show that the expectation value of the stochastic discount factor in Problem 5.1 is

$$E[M] = \frac{1}{1+r}.$$

5.3 Show that the risk premium of a security with state contingent payoff $|d_n\rangle$ is given by $\mathrm{Cov}[M, d_n]$. Use the relation

$$\mathrm{Cov}[X, Y] = E[XY] - E[X]E[Y]$$

in the process.

5.4 Consider the payoff matrix

$$D = \begin{pmatrix} 1 & 2 & 3 \\ 1 & 1 & 4 \end{pmatrix}.$$

Check if the financial market is complete, and whether or not any cyclical permutation of the security price form

$$\langle s| = \begin{pmatrix} 1 & 2 & 3 \end{pmatrix}$$

results in an arbitrage free market.

5.5 Imagine a financial market with one zero-coupon bond and one stock. The risk-free rate of interest over one period of time is $r = 25\%$ and the initial value of the stock is $S_0 = \$10$. There are two possible states of the world at $t = 1$, say "up" and "down," and the stock takes values

$$S_1(\omega) = \begin{cases} 15 & \text{if } \omega = \uparrow \\ 5 & \text{if } \omega = \downarrow. \end{cases}$$

Now a call option on the stock is introduced into the market. Its payoff function is

$$C_1 = \max(S_1 - K, 0),$$

with exercise price $K = \$13$. Compute the risk-neutral probabilities and the fair price C_0 of the derivative contract.

5.6 Consider the same financial market as in Problem 5.5. Imagine at $t = 0$ an agent forms the portfolio

$$\Pi_0 = \frac{1}{5} S_0 - C_0.$$

What is the payoff Π_1 of this portfolio and which security does it replicate? Can you derive the fair price C_0 from the replicating portfolio?

6 Modern Portfolio Theory

Modern portfolio theory (MPT) is mainly due to Harry Markowitz (1952, 1959), who received the Nobel Prize in Economics 1990 for his pioneering work. What is remarkable about MPT is that it is conceptually easy to grasp, because it is deeply embedded in the *Gaussian* world of distributions, but at the same time it reveals completely general and important principles, like the consequences of diversification. Those principles remain true, even in highly sophisticated market models like APT.

6.1 The *Gaussian* Framework

It may sound strange to call the work of Markowitz "modern" portfolio theory nowadays, since it is more than 60 years old. Nevertheless, because of its fundamental nature it deserves at least the attribute "classical." We will keep on calling it modern portfolio theory (MPT), where the letter M could interchangeably stand for Markowitz. MPT is concerned with the analysis of returns of risky assets over intermediate- and long-term horizons. It focuses on the first two moments of the return distribution, the mean μ and the variance σ^2. It is worthwhile to demonstrate that both the long-term nature of returns and the limiting moment condition, each by itself, leads inevitably to a *Gaussian* framework.

As for the term structure, it is always possible, to decompose a long-term return into a sum of short-term returns. If the short-term is not too short, returns can be assumed independent or at least uncorrelated, and thus, due to the central limit theorem, large sums of them tend to be normally distributed. That sounds almost too good to be true, so let's see how it actually works. Assume that we partition a given time interval into N smaller subintervals. Let these subintervals be such that we can assume the short-term returns R_n independent and identically distributed with say $E[R_n] = 0$ and $\text{Var}[R_n] = \frac{1}{N}$ for $n = 1, \ldots, N$. We can always do an affine transformation on R_n to obtain these conditions, so there is no harm done. Now let's ask, how the sum

$$R = \sum_{n=1}^{N} R_n \tag{6.1}$$

is distributed? We know that the characteristic function $\varphi(u)$ of R has to be the product of all characteristic functions of R_n, which are all the same, because all short-term returns are identically distributed. Therefore, we have

$$\varphi(u) = \varphi_n^N(u). \tag{6.2}$$

So what is the characteristic function $\varphi_n(u)$ of R_n? Recall the definition (2.34) on page 21 of the characteristic function

$$\varphi_n(u) = E[e^{iuR_n}] = E\left[1 + iuR_n + \frac{1}{2}i^2u^2R_n^2 + \cdots\right]$$
$$\approx 1 - \frac{1}{2}u^2\frac{1}{N}, \tag{6.3}$$

where we simply *Taylor*-expanded the complex exponential and neglected terms of higher order than $O(N^{-1})$, because we want N to grow large.

Quick calculation 6.1 Can you see why $E[R_n^2] = \text{Var}[R_n]$?

In the limit $N \to \infty$ we obtain

$$\lim_{N\to\infty} \varphi(u) = \lim_{N\to\infty}\left(1 - \frac{\frac{1}{2}u^2}{N}\right)^N = e^{-\frac{1}{2}u^2}, \tag{6.4}$$

which is immediately identified as the characteristic function of a standard normal random variable. We have used the very restrictive assumption of independent returns, to prove the central limit theorem in a simple way. It indeed holds for merely uncorrelated returns, too (see Billingsley, 1995, theorem 35.11).

If we accept the central limit argument, then focusing on the mean and variance is absolutely justified, because the normal distribution is completely determined by its first two moments. If we however reject it, there is another chain of arguments, also leading to a *Gauss*ian framework. This one is a little more subtle. Suppose you have no idea, what the utility function of a representative agent looks like. So use quadratic utility as a local approximation. The *von Neumann–Morgenstern*-functional then becomes

$$U[R] = E[-(\eta - R)^2] = -E[\eta^2 - 2\eta R + R^2]$$
$$= -\eta^2 + 2\eta\mu - \sigma^2 - \mu^2 \tag{6.5}$$
$$= -(\eta - \mu)^2 - \sigma^2.$$

The bliss point η is a parameter of the quadratic utility function and carries no information about the return distribution. The only relevant parameters left are μ and σ^2, the mean and the variance. That was the easy part. Now that we are stuck with the first two moments, we have to show that the best guess we can make about the unknown probability distribution of R is a *Gauss*ian. To do this, we need a concept from information theory, the entropy functional

$$S[X] = -\int f(x)\log f(x)dx, \tag{6.6}$$

where $f(x)$ is the unknown probability density function, yet to be determined. For a discussion on information and entropy see Bernardo and Smith (2000, sect. 2.7). Roughly speaking, entropy is a measure for the absence of information. What we are looking for is a probability distribution, incorporating solely the existence of a finite expectation value and a finite variance, and nothing more. In other words, we are looking for the maximum entropy distribution, given a finite mean and variance.

Our formal starting point is the vector space of real random variables with finite first and second moments, $L^2(\Omega, \mathcal{F}, P)$. The L stands for "Lebesgue" here, not for a linear functional. But first we have to explain what it means, to differentiate a functional with respect to a specific coefficient of a vector, or with respect to a function at a specific point, respectively. Let's first take a look at the more intuitive case of $\mathbb{R}^N$. The functional derivative with respect to a vector $|a\rangle$ is a form,

$$\frac{\eth L}{\eth |a\rangle} = \langle \eth L|. \tag{6.7}$$

If we want to differentiate with respect to a specific component, say a_m, we have to use the chain rule

$$\frac{\partial L}{\partial a_m} = \langle \eth L|\partial_m a\rangle, \tag{6.8}$$

where we have used the shorthand notation $|\partial_m a\rangle$ for the vector with components $\frac{\partial a_n}{\partial a_m}$. Obviously, $\frac{\partial a_n}{\partial a_m} = \delta_{nm}$ and hence $|\partial_m a\rangle = |e_m\rangle$. We then obtain

$$\frac{\partial L}{\partial a_m} = \langle \eth L|e_m\rangle = \sum_{n=1}^{N} \eth L_n \delta_{nm} = \eth L_m. \tag{6.9}$$

Now let's look at the function space L^2. The function $f(x)$ can be thought of as an infinite collection of numbers, namely function values, one for each possible value of x. To push this analogy a little bit further, imagine $|f\rangle$ as a column vector with infinitely many components. We want to differentiate a functional with respect to one of them, say $f(y)$. We have then in complete analogy

$$\frac{\partial L}{\partial f(y)} = \langle \eth L|e(y)\rangle = \int \eth L(x)\delta(x-y)dx = \eth L(y), \tag{6.10}$$

where Dirac's delta function $\delta(x-y)$ is the continuous analogue of the *Kronecker*-delta δ_{nm} (3.18) on page 36. Let's not worry too much about the delta function at this point, we will come back to it later. In fact, the last equality in (6.10) gives a correct definition. Let's see how this works in a simple example.

Example 6.1

Consider the vector space $L^2(\Omega, \mathcal{F}, P)$ of real random variables with finite variance. Assume you know that realizations of the random variable X can only occur in the interval $[a, b]$. What is the maximum entropy distribution of X?

Solution

To find the desired distribution, we have to maximize the entropy functional under the normalization constraint,

$$\max_{f(y)} S[X] \quad \text{subject to} \quad \int_a^b f(x)dx = 1.$$

This is done using Lagrange's method. The computation of the first order condition with respect to $f(y)$ is given here in full detail

$$\frac{\partial \mathcal{L}}{\partial f(y)} = -\int_a^b \frac{\delta(f(x)\log f(x))}{\delta f(x)} \cdot \delta(x-y)dx - \lambda \int_a^b \frac{\delta f(x)}{\delta f(x)} \cdot \delta(x-y)dx$$

$$= -\int_a^b (\log f(x) + 1)\delta(x-y)dx - \lambda \int_a^b \delta(x-y)dx$$

$$= -\log f(y) - 1 - \lambda \overset{!}{=} 0,$$

where $\mathcal{L}$ is the *Lagrange*-function. The δ-notation has been used a bit sloppily here, to indicate that the derivative is with respect to the entire function $f(x)$. After trivial algebraic manipulations one obtains

$$f(y) = e^{-(1+\lambda)} = c,$$

where c is a constant, not yet determined. We have now to consider the normalization condition, reproduced by the second first order condition with respect to λ

$$\int_a^b f(y)dy = \int_a^b c\,dy = cy\Big|_a^b = c(b-a) \overset{!}{=} 1,$$

from which we immediately conclude that $c = \frac{1}{b-a}$. Thus, X is uniformly distributed in the interval $[a, b]$, with density function

$$f(y) = \frac{1}{b-a}.$$

This is a very intuitive result, because there was no more initial information than the possible range of realizations. Don't worry about the variable name y here, it is only a label. We could as well rename it back to x, to clean up the notation.

Now let's return to the original question. What is the maximum entropy distribution, given the first two moments are defined? Except for the normalization constraint, we have two additional constraints in the optimization problem,

$$\int_{-\infty}^{\infty} xf(x)dx = \mu \quad \text{and} \quad \int_{-\infty}^{\infty} x^2 f(x)dx = \sigma^2 + \mu^2. \tag{6.11}$$

Quick calculation 6.2 Confirm that the second constraint is equivalent to $\text{Var}[X] = \sigma^2$.

Collecting all terms in a *Lagrange*-function as in Example 6.1, we obtain the first order condition

$$\frac{\partial \mathcal{L}}{\partial f(y)} = -\log f(y) - (1 + \lambda_0) - \lambda_1 y - \lambda_2 y^2 \overset{!}{=} 0. \tag{6.12}$$

Quick calculation 6.3 Verify this first order condition.

Rearranging terms and exponentiating both sides of the equation yields

$$f(y) = ce^{-(\lambda_1 y + \lambda_2 y^2)} \quad \text{with} \quad c = e^{-(1+\lambda_0)}. \tag{6.13}$$

To determine the unknown constant c, we have to use the normalization constraint. But now we run into a problem. There is no way to integrate the exponential with our usual tricks like substitution or integration by parts. The good news is, it can be done by squaring the integral and changing coordinates. The solution of this so-called *Gauss*ian integral is

$$\int_{-\infty}^{\infty} e^{-(\lambda_1 y + \lambda_2 y^2)} dy = \sqrt{\frac{\pi}{\lambda_2}} \exp\left(\frac{\lambda_1^2}{4\lambda_2}\right) = \frac{1}{c} \quad \text{for} \quad \lambda_2 > 0, \tag{6.14}$$

see Gradshteyn and Ryzhik (2007, p. 337). We are on the right track. Using this result, we obtain

$$f(y) = \sqrt{\frac{\lambda_2}{\pi}} \exp\left(-\frac{\lambda_1^2}{4\lambda_2} - \lambda_1 y - \lambda_2 y^2\right) = \sqrt{\frac{\lambda_2}{\pi}} \exp\left(-\lambda_2 \left(y + \frac{\lambda_1}{2\lambda_2}\right)^2\right). \tag{6.15}$$

Now it is time for an educated guess. We will assume certain expressions for the remaining *Lagrange*-multipliers and check afterwards that they satisfy the constraints. Take

$$\lambda_1 = -\frac{\mu}{\sigma^2} \quad \text{and} \quad \lambda_2 = \frac{1}{2\sigma^2}. \tag{6.16}$$

We can already see that the requirement $\lambda_2 > 0$ from the solution of the *Gauss*ian integral (6.14) is satisfied. From (6.15) we get

$$f(y) = \frac{1}{\sqrt{2\pi\sigma^2}} e^{-\frac{(y-\mu)^2}{2\sigma^2}}, \tag{6.17}$$

the normal probability density function. It is immediately clear that the remaining moment constraints are satisfied and we are done.

The normal distribution assumption in modern portfolio theory is by no means a matter of convenience, but has a strong theoretical rationale. We are lucky, because the normal distribution has very pleasant properties, allowing many analytical results. Leaving this path, there are very few results to be obtained without approximations or numerical computations.

6.2   Mean-Variance Analysis

In the *Markowitz*-world, portfolios are entirely described by their expected returns and variances. A given portfolio is said to dominate another one, if its μ-σ-configuration results in a higher level of utility for every possible risk-averse agent. But what are the general characteristics of a curve of constant utility? If we are not allowed to specify a particular utility function beforehand, we can *Taylor*-expand the expected utility functional

$$U[R] = E[u(R)] = u(\mu) + u'(\mu)E[(R - \mu)] + \frac{1}{2}u''(\mu)E[(R - \mu)^2] + \cdots$$
$$\approx u(\mu) + \frac{1}{2}u''(\mu)\sigma^2. \tag{6.18}$$

If we multiply and divide the second order expansion term by $u'(\mu)$, we can write (6.18) in a more transparent way

$$U[R] \approx u(\mu) - \frac{1}{2}u'(\mu)\mathrm{ARA}(\mu)\sigma^2 \approx u(\mu) - u'(\mu)\pi, \tag{6.19}$$

where π is the risk premium, see (4.20) on page 67. We did a lot of approximating here, but we always kept second order terms, because risk aversion is encoded in the second derivative of an agent's utility function. Therefore, we can be sure that we did not lose any characteristic features. The risk premium π is guaranteed to be an increasing function of σ^2, with $\pi = 0$ for $\sigma^2 = 0$, as long as the agent is risk averse.

Quick calculation 6.4 Verify that the risk premium for CARA-utility is $\pi \approx \frac{1}{2}\alpha\sigma^2$.

We now have enough information to sketch the generic shape of the utility functional; see Figure 6.1. As you can see, the projections of all curves of constant utility U onto the μ-σ-plane are convex. This projection is illustrated in Figure 6.2 and it is called a μ-σ-diagram.

Quick calculation 6.5 What does the curve of constant utility for a risk-neutral agent look like in the μ-σ-diagram? It is not a diagonal line!

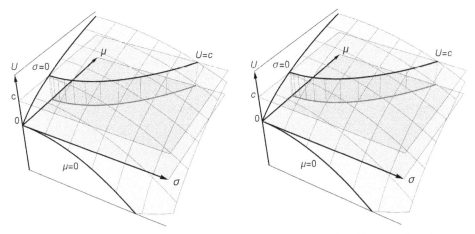

Fig. 6.1 **3D** Mean-variance analysis – Approximation of a generic utility functional

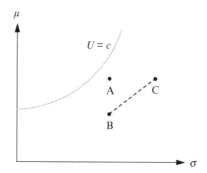

Fig. 6.2 Mean-variance analysis – μ-σ-diagram with curve of constant utility and several securities

The degree of convexity depends on the individual utility function, but since u is strictly concave for any risk-averse agent, the curves $U = $ const. have to remain strictly convex. This allows for a fundamental statement about securities or portfolios of securities according to their positions in the μ-σ-diagram. The concept is called μ-σ-dominance or sometimes stochastic dominance of zeroth order. A security A is said to dominate a security B, if one of the following three conditions hold:

$$
\begin{aligned}
&1.\ \mu_A > \mu_B \quad \text{and} \quad \sigma_A = \sigma_B, \\
&2.\ \mu_A = \mu_B \quad \text{and} \quad \sigma_A < \sigma_B, \\
&3.\ \mu_A > \mu_B \quad \text{and} \quad \sigma_A < \sigma_B.
\end{aligned}
\tag{6.20}
$$

There are three securities indicated in the μ-σ-diagram in Figure 6.2. We can say a lot about their dominance relationships. Security A dominates security B because the first condition in (6.20) holds. Security A also dominates C, because of condition two. But securities B and C have no dominance relationship. Note that A also dominates every hypothetical portfolio of securities, situated on the line connecting B and C, because of condition three. You might expect that those hypothetical portfolios are linear combinations of B and C, but this is not true in general. We will see why in a moment. First let's explain what it means to add securities in a little more detail.

Assume the price of a portfolio P of securities $S_1, \ldots, S_N$, say at time $t = 0$, is

$$
p_0 = \langle s_0 | \theta \rangle = \sum_{n=1}^{N} s_{0n} \theta_n.
\tag{6.21}
$$

Then the return of portfolio P between $t = 0$ and $t = 1$ can be written as

$$
\begin{aligned}
r_P &= \frac{p_1 - p_0}{p_0} = \frac{1}{p_0} \sum_{n=1}^{N} (s_{1n} - s_{0n}) \cdot \theta_n = \sum_{n=1}^{N} \frac{s_{1n} - s_{0n}}{s_{0n}} \cdot \frac{s_{0n} \theta_n}{\langle s_0 | \theta \rangle} \\
&= \sum_{n=1}^{N} r_n w_n = \langle r | w \rangle,
\end{aligned}
\tag{6.22}
$$

with $\langle 1 | w \rangle = 1$, and w_n is the fraction of the total portfolio value at $t = 0$, that is due to the position in S_n. We have assumed in (6.22) that security prices at $t = 0$ and at $t = 1$ are known and thus, returns are deterministic. We indicated this fact by using small letters. Generally, returns are random variables or more precisely, multivariate normally distributed random variables in MPT. A multivariate normally distributed vector (or form) of random variables $\langle R|$ is completely determined by its expectation vector (form)

$$\langle \mu| = \left(\mu_1 \ \mu_2 \ \ldots \ \mu_N \right), \tag{6.23}$$

and its covariance matrix

$$\Sigma = \begin{pmatrix} \sigma_1^2 & \sigma_{12} & \ldots & \sigma_{1N} \\ \sigma_{12} & \sigma_2^2 & \ldots & \sigma_{2N} \\ \vdots & \vdots & \ddots & \vdots \\ \sigma_{1N} & \sigma_{2N} & \ldots & \sigma_N^2 \end{pmatrix}, \tag{6.24}$$

where $\sigma_n^2 = \text{Var}[R_n]$ and $\sigma_{nm} = \sigma_{mn} = \text{Cov}[R_n, R_m]$. If we now form a portfolio $P = \langle S|\theta \rangle$, then the expectation value and variance of its return is given by

$$\mu_P = \langle \mu|w \rangle \quad \text{and} \quad \sigma_P^2 = \langle w|\Sigma|w \rangle. \tag{6.25}$$

Can you see how efficient vector notation is here? Now let's focus on a portfolio composed of only two risky securities, A and B. We call the portfolio weights w and $1 - w$ and require for the moment that $0 \le w \le 1$, which means no short selling is permitted. We get for the expectation value and variance of the portfolio

$$\begin{aligned} \mu_P &= w\mu_A + (1 - w)\mu_B \\ \sigma_P^2 &= w^2\sigma_A^2 + 2w(1 - w)\rho_{AB}\sigma_A\sigma_B + (1 - w)^2\sigma_B^2, \end{aligned} \tag{6.26}$$

where we have used that $\text{Cov}[X, Y] = \rho_{XY} \sqrt{\text{Var}[X]\text{Var}[Y]}$, see (2.33) on page 20, and $-1 \le \rho_{XY} \le 1$ is the correlation coefficient.

Quick calculation 6.6 Confirm (6.26) by using (6.25).

We are interested in the location of the possible portfolios in the μ-σ-diagram for different values of ρ_{AB}. The three natural choices $\rho_{AB} = 1$, $\rho_{AB} = 0$, and $\rho_{AB} = -1$ are illustrated in Figure 6.3 left and it is worthwhile to elaborate on them a bit further.

Perfect correlation:
For $\rho_{AB} = 1$ securities A and B are also called perfectly correlated. In this case we see from (6.26) that the standard deviation of the portfolio becomes

$$\sigma_P = \sqrt{(w\sigma_A + (1 - w)\sigma_B)^2} = w\sigma_A + (1 - w)\sigma_B, \tag{6.27}$$

where we have used the binomial theorem. In this case the resulting portfolio is indeed located on the line, connecting A and B in the μ-σ-diagram, because μ_P as well as σ_P are linear combinations of the corresponding quantities of A and B.

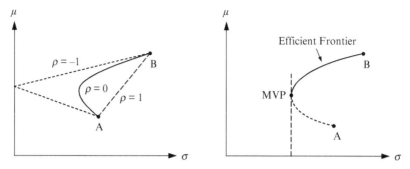

Fig. 6.3 Portfolio of two risky assets with different correlation (left) and minimum variance portfolio (right)

Zero correlation:
If $\rho_{AB} = 0$, securities A and B are called uncorrelated. The standard deviation of the portfolio is

$$\sigma_P = \sqrt{w^2\sigma_A^2 + (1-w)^2\sigma_B^2}. \tag{6.28}$$

In this case, one can find portfolios with smaller standard deviation than either of the original securities. This is the first glimpse of the very important concept of diversification. It can be shown in a rather tedious computation that all possible combinations of A and B lie on a hyperbola in the μ-σ-diagram.

Perfect anti-correlation:
The securities A and B are said to be anti-correlated or perfectly negative correlated, if $\rho_{AB} = -1$. This case is special in that it creates a portfolio with no risk. In other words, the return of such a portfolio would be the (shadow) risk-free rate. In a real world scenario it is highly unlikely to find two perfectly negative correlated securities. Nevertheless, let's compute the weights of the risk-free portfolio. The necessary condition is that the standard deviation vanishes,

$$\sigma_P = w\sigma_A - (1-w)\sigma_B \overset{!}{=} 0. \tag{6.29}$$

This problem is easily solved and one obtains

$$w^* = \frac{\sigma_B}{\sigma_A + \sigma_B}. \tag{6.30}$$

Quick calculation 6.7 Verify this result.

Generally, most of the time the correlation of assets is weakly positive, but even a correlation of $\rho = 0.5$ turns out to be beneficial if we want to reduce the risk of a portfolio. The situation is sketched schematically in Figure 6.3 right. Assume you start with 100% of security B in your portfolio and you want to reduce risk. As you increase the proportion of security A, your standard deviation will decrease, and also your expected return. Nothing comes without a price. You will finally get to a point, where the standard deviation cannot be reduced any further. This portfolio is called the minimum variance portfolio (MVP). Note that on your way down from B to MVP, all portfolios you constructed were not dominated by any other portfolio. This is why the upper branch of the curve is called the efficient frontier. If you increase the proportion of A beyond the MVP, your standard deviation will increase again, but the expected return continues to decrease. All portfolios on the lower branch are dominated by portfolios on the upper branch with smaller or identical standard deviation. Therefore, you would not want to hold one of these lower branch portfolios.

6.3 The Minimum Variance Portfolio

Let's first consider the familiar situation of two risky assets, A and B, before proceeding to the general case. First realize that the minimum variance portfolio (MVP) is of course at the same time the portfolio with the smallest standard deviation, because variance is the square of the standard deviation. If ρ_{AB} is not known beforehand, we have

$$\sigma_P^2 = w^2 \sigma_A^2 + 2w(1-w)\rho_{AB}\sigma_A\sigma_B + (1-w)^2\sigma_B^2. \tag{6.31}$$

This is what we have to minimize, without constraints. Additionally, we will no longer require $0 \leq w \leq 1$, which means short selling is permitted from here on. As a matter of convenience, we will actually minimize $\frac{1}{2}\sigma_P^2$; you will see why in a moment. The necessary first order condition for a minimum is

$$\frac{1}{2}\frac{d\sigma_P^2}{dw} = w\sigma_A^2 + (1-w)\rho_{AB}\sigma_A\sigma_B - w\rho_{AB}\sigma_A\sigma_B - (1-w)\sigma_B^2 \overset{!}{=} 0. \tag{6.32}$$

There it is, no additional factors of 2. Because we allowed short selling, the hyperbola of possible portfolio configurations extends to infinity in the σ-direction, but has only one minimum. So the first order condition is sufficient. Solving (6.32) yields

$$w_{\text{MVP}} = \frac{\sigma_B^2 - \rho_{AB}\sigma_A\sigma_B}{\sigma_A^2 + \sigma_B^2 - 2\rho_{AB}\sigma_A\sigma_B}. \tag{6.33}$$

Quick calculation 6.8 Confirm this result.

That was a neat calculation. But in passing to larger portfolios, we have first to examine what we are up against. Which portfolio combinations are possible if there are N assets? And what does the efficient frontier look like?

You can see most easily what is going on for $N > 2$ risky securities graphically. Figure 6.4 left shows the situation for $N = 4$ assets. You may for example assemble two portfolios, one containing only A and B, and the other containing only C and D. Of course you are also allowed to mix these two portfolios, and there is a continuum of such mixtures. You could have just as well assembled different portfolios, say

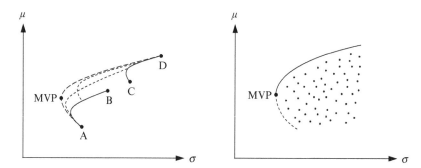

Fig. 6.4 Possible portfolio combinations for $N > 2$ risky assets

from A and C, and from B and D, and mixed those. If you exhaust all possibilities for assembling and mixing portfolios, you obtain a new curve of variance efficient portfolio combinations, including all assets. An even more tedious calculation shows that this curve is a hyperbola, too. In fact this property carries over to the case of arbitrary N, where we will see much easier why this is the case. So the situation in the N-security world is conceptually no more difficult than for two securities; see Figure 6.4 right. The only difference is that not every admissible portfolio with a fixed expected return has the smallest possible variance, but only those portfolios located on the variance efficient hyperbola.

To find the minimum variance portfolio in a N-security world, we have to solve the constrained optimization problem

$$\min_{\langle w|} \frac{1}{2} \langle w|\Sigma|w\rangle \quad \text{subject to} \quad \langle 1|w\rangle = 1. \tag{6.34}$$

Quick calculation 6.9 Write the *Lagrange*-function for this optimization problem.

We obtain two first order conditions, which are sufficient, because we are still looking for a minimum in a hyperbola that extends to infinity in the σ-direction. The first condition is

$$\frac{\delta\mathcal{L}}{\delta\langle w|} = \Sigma|w\rangle - \lambda|1\rangle \overset{!}{=} |0\rangle, \tag{6.35}$$

from which we immediately obtain

$$|w^*\rangle = \lambda\Sigma^{-1}|1\rangle. \tag{6.36}$$

The second first order condition reproduces the normalization constraint

$$\frac{\partial\mathcal{L}}{\partial\lambda} = 1 - \langle 1|w\rangle \overset{!}{=} 0. \tag{6.37}$$

Using this condition with (6.36), one obtains

$$1 = \langle 1|w^*\rangle = \lambda\langle 1|\Sigma^{-1}|1\rangle. \tag{6.38}$$

Note that $\langle 1|\Sigma^{-1}|1\rangle$ is a scalar and we have a solution for λ,

$$\lambda = \frac{1}{\langle 1|\Sigma^{-1}|1\rangle}. \tag{6.39}$$

Putting (6.36) and (6.39) together, the solution to the optimization problem is

$$|w_{\text{MVP}}\rangle = \frac{\Sigma^{-1}|1\rangle}{\langle 1|\Sigma^{-1}|1\rangle}. \tag{6.40}$$

Obviously, the *Lagrange*-multiplier is only a normalizing factor, which is perfectly sensible considering the nature of the constraint. Let's look at an example:

Example 6.2

Consider the situation with $N = 2$ securities. What is the vector of portfolio weights $|w^*\rangle$ of the minimum variance portfolio?

Solution
For $N = 2$ we have

$$\Sigma = \begin{pmatrix} \sigma_1^2 & \rho\sigma_1\sigma_2 \\ \rho\sigma_1\sigma_2 & \sigma_2^2 \end{pmatrix} \quad \Rightarrow \quad \Sigma^{-1} = \frac{1}{\det\Sigma}\begin{pmatrix} \sigma_2^2 & -\rho\sigma_1\sigma_2 \\ -\rho\sigma_1\sigma_2 & \sigma_1^2 \end{pmatrix},$$

and further

$$\Sigma^{-1}|1\rangle = \frac{1}{\det\Sigma}\begin{pmatrix} \sigma_2^2 - \rho\sigma_1\sigma_2 \\ \sigma_1^2 - \rho\sigma_1\sigma_2 \end{pmatrix} \quad \text{and} \quad \langle 1|\Sigma^{-1}|1\rangle = \frac{1}{\det\Sigma}(\sigma_1^2 + \sigma_2^2 - 2\rho\sigma_1\sigma_2).$$

We thus obtain the MVP-weights

$$w_1^* = \frac{\sigma_2^2 - \rho\sigma_1\sigma_2}{\sigma_1^2 + \sigma_2^2 - 2\rho\sigma_1\sigma_2} \quad \text{and} \quad w_2^* = \frac{\sigma_1^2 - \rho\sigma_1\sigma_2}{\sigma_1^2 + \sigma_2^2 - 2\rho\sigma_1\sigma_2},$$

which is exactly our earlier result (6.33).

Quick calculation 6.10 Show that the variance of the MVP is given by $\sigma_{\text{MVP}}^2 = \frac{1}{\langle 1|\Sigma^{-1}|1\rangle}$.

6.4   Variance Efficient Portfolios

A portfolio with expected return μ_P is called variance efficient, if there is no other portfolio with the same expected return, but smaller variance. Note that variance efficient portfolios are not necessarily μ-σ-dominant.

Quick calculation 6.11 Can you see why?

To find the weights of an arbitrary variance efficient portfolio, we have to impose an additional constraint. To be a little more precise, we have to minimize the variance under the condition that the expected return is μ_P and of course that all weights sum to one. The proper *Lagrange*-function has the form

$$\mathcal{L} = \frac{1}{2}\langle w|\Sigma|w\rangle + \lambda_1(\mu_P - \langle \mu|w\rangle) + \lambda_2(1 - \langle 1|w\rangle). \tag{6.41}$$

From the first order conditions, which are still sufficient, we can extract the required vector of portfolio weights

$$|w^*\rangle = \lambda_1 \Sigma^{-1}|\mu\rangle + \lambda_2 \Sigma^{-1}|1\rangle. \tag{6.42}$$

Quick calculation 6.12   Verify this result by deriving the respective first order condition.

From the constraints, we get another pair of first order conditions that is needed in order to solve for the *Lagrange*-multipliers. The result is a system of two linear equations

$$\langle \mu|w^*\rangle = \mu_p = \lambda_1 \underbrace{\langle \mu|\Sigma^{-1}|\mu\rangle}_{a} + \lambda_2 \underbrace{\langle \mu|\Sigma^{-1}|1\rangle}_{b}$$

$$\langle 1|w^*\rangle = 1 = \lambda_1 \underbrace{\langle 1|\Sigma^{-1}|\mu\rangle}_{b} + \lambda_2 \underbrace{\langle 1|\Sigma^{-1}|1\rangle}_{c}, \tag{6.43}$$

which can be written more efficiently as

$$\begin{pmatrix} \mu_P \\ 1 \end{pmatrix} = \begin{pmatrix} a & b \\ b & c \end{pmatrix}\begin{pmatrix} \lambda_1 \\ \lambda_2 \end{pmatrix}. \tag{6.44}$$

Solving this vector equation is not difficult and one obtains the *Lagrange*-multipliers

$$\lambda_1 = \frac{c\mu_P - b}{ac - b^2} \quad \text{and} \quad \lambda_2 = \frac{a - b\mu_P}{ac - b^2}. \tag{6.45}$$

Quick calculation 6.13   Verify this result.

Plugging (6.45) into (6.42) yields

$$|w_P\rangle = \Sigma^{-1}\frac{(c\mu_P - b)|\mu\rangle + (a - b\mu_P)|1\rangle}{ac - b^2}, \tag{6.46}$$

with

$$a = \langle \mu|\Sigma^{-1}|\mu\rangle, \quad b = \langle \mu|\Sigma^{-1}|1\rangle, \quad \text{and} \quad c = \langle 1|\Sigma^{-1}|1\rangle. \tag{6.47}$$

Note one very important point: The expected portfolio return μ_P goes linear into (6.46). That means, if we know two portfolios on the hyperbola of variance efficient portfolios, then we can construct other variance efficient portfolios from them. This fact is summarized in the following theorem:

Theorem 6.1 (Two-fund separation) *Let μ_1 and μ_2 be the expected returns of two variance efficient portfolios with weights $|w_1\rangle$ and $|w_2\rangle$. The portfolio P with expected return $\mu_P = \lambda\mu_1 + (1 - \lambda)\mu_2$ for $\lambda \in \mathbb{R}$ is also variance efficient, if its weights are given by*

$$|w_P\rangle = \lambda|w_1\rangle + (1 - \lambda)|w_2\rangle.$$

Quick calculation 6.14 Prove the theorem by plugging $\mu_P = \lambda\mu_1 + (1 - \lambda)\mu_2$ into (6.46).

What Theorem 6.1 means is that we do not have to solve a constrained optimization problem for every point on the variance efficient frontier. We only have to do it twice. With two solutions, we can reconstruct the entire curve. And remember, the MVP was already one solution.

In the present problem we know the expected return of the portfolio, because we fixed μ_P in the constraint. But how large is its variance? According to our formula, we must have

$$\sigma_P^2 = \langle w_P|\Sigma|w_P\rangle = \frac{c\mu_P^2 - 2b\mu_P + a}{ac - b^2}. \tag{6.48}$$

It is an instructive exercise to verify (6.48), but it is not necessarily a quick calculation. However, we can finally see why the variance efficient portfolios are indeed located on a hyperbola. The general equation for a hyperbola in the μ-σ-space is

$$\frac{\sigma^2}{\alpha^2} - \frac{(\mu - \gamma)^2}{\beta^2} = 1. \tag{6.49}$$

Comparing (6.48) and (6.49), we see that we only have to complete the square, rearrange terms, and make the correct identifications for α, β, and γ. Thus, everything we claimed so far regarding sufficiency of first order conditions, was well justified.

6.5   Optimal Portfolios and Diversification

Until now, we have not chosen a particular portfolio maximizing an agent's utility functional of any kind. All we have done is to narrow down the possible candidates. What we have found so far is that an optimal portfolio has to lie on the efficient frontier, which is the upper branch of the hyperbola of variance efficient portfolios. But that is very good news, because the efficient frontier is a concave function of σ and we know that for any risk-averse agent, curves of constant utility have to be convex. This immediately implies that we find our optimal portfolio in the point where one particular

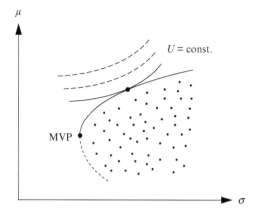

Fig. 6.5 Utility maximizing portfolio for risk-averse agent

utility curve is tangential to the efficient frontier; see Figure 6.5. All we have to do now is to make the *von Neumann–Morgenstern*-utility functional concrete. In MPT, risk is due to the variance of returns. Thus, it is a common assumption that the risk premium is proportional to the variance. Under this assumption the following equality holds

$$E[R] = E[u(R)] + \pi = U[R] + \frac{\alpha}{2}\text{Var}[R], \qquad (6.50)$$

where $\frac{\alpha}{2}$ is an agent specific constant of proportionality. We have thus in our μ-σ-world a one parameter family of utility functionals

$$U_\alpha[R] = \mu - \frac{\alpha}{2}\sigma^2, \qquad (6.51)$$

characterizing the risk aversion of an individual agent by the magnitude of α. To find an optimal portfolio for an agent with given risk aversion α, we have to solve the following optimization problem

$$\max_{|w\rangle} U_\alpha[R_P] \quad \text{subject to} \quad \langle 1|w\rangle = 1. \qquad (6.52)$$

That does not look too bad. The first order condition for a maximum with respect to $\langle w|$ is

$$\frac{\delta\mathcal{L}}{\delta\langle w|} = |\mu\rangle - \alpha\Sigma|w\rangle - \lambda|1\rangle \stackrel{!}{=} |0\rangle, \qquad (6.53)$$

from which we obtain

$$|w^*\rangle = \Sigma^{-1}\frac{|\mu\rangle - \lambda|1\rangle}{\alpha}. \qquad (6.54)$$

Using the normalization constraint, we get an equation for the *Lagrange*-multiplier

$$1 = \langle 1|w^*\rangle = \frac{b - \lambda c}{\alpha}, \qquad (6.55)$$

where we adopted the shorthand notation $b = \langle 1|\Sigma^{-1}|\mu\rangle$ and $c = \langle 1|\Sigma^{-1}|1\rangle$ from (6.47). Solving for λ yields

$$\lambda = \frac{b - \alpha}{c}. \qquad (6.56)$$

Plugging this result into (6.54) yields the desired weights

$$|w_\alpha\rangle = \Sigma^{-1}\left(\frac{1}{\alpha}|\mu\rangle + \frac{1}{c}\left(1 - \frac{b}{\alpha}\right)|1\rangle\right),\tag{6.57}$$

with

$$b = \langle 1|\Sigma^{-1}|\mu\rangle \quad \text{and} \quad c = \langle 1|\Sigma^{-1}|1\rangle.\tag{6.58}$$

Quick calculation 6.15 Verify Equation (6.57).

Up to this point, we have not discussed the effects of diversification in much detail. In fact, we will not be able to understand it thoroughly, until we can distinguish systematic and idiosyncratic risk. But for the moment we can build some intuition, to understand why every optimal portfolio has to be an optimally diversified portfolio. Let's do some calculations in the simplest possible setup. Assume there are N securities, each one of them with expected return $E[R_n] = \mu$ and variance $\text{Var}[R_n] = \sigma^2$, and all returns are uncorrelated. In this framework, all securities are located at the same point in the μ-σ-diagram. You might now argue that in this case it is pointless to build a portfolio, because all securities have identical expected returns and variances. Let's take a somewhat closer look at this argument. All securities have the same μ and σ^2, true, but they are not identical. To see what that means, assemble a simple portfolio, where the weights are all the same, $w_n = \frac{1}{N}$. This portfolio has expected return

$$E[R_P] = \sum_{n=1}^{N}\frac{1}{N}E[R_n] = \frac{1}{N}\sum_{n=1}^{N}\mu = \mu.\tag{6.59}$$

That is not a big surprise. But look what happens to the variance of the portfolio

$$\text{Var}[R_P] = \sum_{n=1}^{N}\frac{1}{N^2}\text{Var}[R_n] = \frac{1}{N^2}\sum_{n=1}^{N}\sigma^2 = \frac{\sigma^2}{N}.\tag{6.60}$$

This portfolio clearly dominates every single security, because its standard deviation is reduced by a factor of $\frac{1}{\sqrt{N}}$. Now you might argue that if this is correct, then the variance of a portfolio has to tend to zero for large enough N. Unfortunately, this is not the case, but for the moment the discussion of that issue has to be postponed.

6.6   Tobin's Separation Theorem and the Market Portfolio

In our current framework, every agent with risk aversion α has her own optimal portfolio with individual composition of securities. This view changed dramatically as Tobin (1958) brought a new player into the game, the risk-free return R_0. Note, that the risk-free rate of return is not a random variable, at least not for now. The uppercase letter notation is only to keep things consistent and to interpret it as the return of the riskless

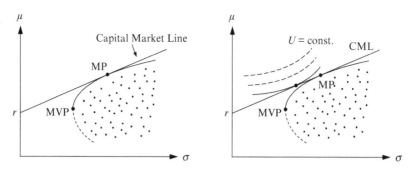

Fig. 6.6 Capital market line and market portfolio (left) with optimal portfolio (right)

zeroth security B_0, with $E[R_0] = r$ and $\mathrm{Var}[R_0] = 0$. Why does this additional security shake things up that violently? Let's see what Tobin's separation principle claims:

Theorem 6.2 (Tobin's separation theorem) *If agents are allowed to borrow or lend at a risk-free rate r, then the optimal portfolio for every risk-averse agent is a particular linear combination of the risk-free security B_0 and the so-called market portfolio (MP), whereas the composition of the market portfolio is the same for every agent.*

Let's see if we can first understand this graphically. In Figure 6.6 the market portfolio (MP) is indicated as the tangential point of the efficient frontier and a straight line with μ-intercept r. This straight line, connecting r and MP, is called the capital market line (CML). Why has this to be the right picture? Remember that the curves of constant utility are convex. Therefore, the steeper the slope of the capital market line, the higher the utility level an agent can achieve. But the capital market line has to intersect the efficient frontier at least at one point, to provide a linear combination with a variance efficient portfolio. The only possible conclusion is that the capital market line has to be tangent to the efficient frontier. Because of this, the market portfolio is also called the tangential portfolio. It is now also obvious, why every agent bases her investment decision on the same portfolio, because the market portfolio is the only remaining efficient portfolio of risky assets. All other variance efficient portfolios are dominated by portfolios on the capital market line. The agent's individual risk aversion merely determines the mixing point on that line.

Having straightened things out, it is time to compute the weights of the market portfolio. This is a surprisingly simple task, not at all requiring constrained optimization. The key observation is that the market portfolio weights do not change relative to one another, because the composition of the market portfolio stays the same for all agents. Let's proceed in two steps. First, locate an arbitrary portfolio on the capital market line, and second, shift this portfolio by setting the weight w_0 of the risk-free bond B_0 to zero. First things first. Because we are looking for an arbitrary portfolio on the capital market line, we can choose an arbitrary risk aversion parameter α. So let's choose $\alpha = 1$ for convenience. The corresponding utility functional is

$$U_1[R_P] = w_0 r + \langle \mu | w \rangle - \frac{1}{2} \langle w | \Sigma | w \rangle. \tag{6.61}$$

The clever trick is now to circumvent the normalization constraint by realizing that

$$w_0 = 1 - \langle 1|w \rangle \qquad (6.62)$$

has to hold. Using this relation, the normalization is built into the optimization problem just as in the case of two securities, where we have used w and $1 - w$ for the weights. One obtains the first order condition

$$\frac{\delta U_1}{\delta \langle w|} = -r|1\rangle + |\mu\rangle - \Sigma|w\rangle \overset{!}{=} |0\rangle, \qquad (6.63)$$

which is solved by

$$|w^*\rangle = \Sigma^{-1}(|\mu\rangle - r|1\rangle). \qquad (6.64)$$

Here comes the second step. For $w_0 = 0$ it follows from (6.62) that $\langle 1|w^*\rangle = 1$ has to hold. But the weights are unchanged relative to one another, they are merely scaled. Thus, the market portfolio weights have to be given by

$$|w_{\mathrm{MP}}\rangle = \frac{\Sigma^{-1}(|\mu\rangle - r|1\rangle)}{\langle 1|\Sigma^{-1}(|\mu\rangle - r|1\rangle)}. \qquad (6.65)$$

We are not finished yet. Now that we know the location of the market portfolio on the efficient frontier, we can compute the agent's optimal portfolio. Tobin's separation theorem states that the desired portfolio is a linear combination of B_0 and the market portfolio. Thus, the portfolio return has to be

$$R_P = (1 - \lambda)R_0 + \lambda R_{\mathrm{MP}}, \qquad (6.66)$$

for $\lambda \geq 0$. It is an easy exercise to compute the expected return of this portfolio,

$$\mu_P = (1 - \lambda)r + \lambda \mu_{\mathrm{MP}}. \qquad (6.67)$$

As for the variance, recall that $\mathrm{Cov}[X, Y] = \rho_{XY}\sigma_X\sigma_Y$ and $\mathrm{Var}[R_0] = 0$. The calculation is then straightforward,

$$\begin{aligned} \sigma_P^2 &= (1 - \lambda)^2\sigma_0^2 + 2(1 - \lambda)\lambda\rho_{0,\mathrm{MP}}\sigma_0\sigma_{\mathrm{MP}} + \lambda^2\sigma_{\mathrm{MP}}^2 \\ &= \lambda^2\sigma_{\mathrm{MP}}^2. \end{aligned} \qquad (6.68)$$

Now using the simplified *von Neumann–Morgenstern*-utility functional

$$U_\alpha[R_P] = (1 - \lambda)r + \lambda\mu_{\mathrm{MP}} - \frac{\alpha}{2}\lambda^2\sigma_{\mathrm{MP}}^2, \qquad (6.69)$$

the unconstrained maximization is with respect to λ only.

Quick calculation 6.16 Write the first order condition for this problem.

Using our standard optimization routine one obtains the solution

$$\lambda_\alpha = \frac{1}{\alpha} \frac{\mu_{\mathrm{MP}} - r}{\sigma_{\mathrm{MP}}^2}. \tag{6.70}$$

Equation (6.70) makes perfect sense. The larger the risk aversion α, the smaller the proportion of the market portfolio the agent is willing to hold. The same is true for the variance σ_{MP}^2, which is a measure for the risk involved. If the excess return $\mu_{\mathrm{MP}} - r$ grows larger, the agent is willing to hold a larger proportion of the market portfolio.

There is an extra bonus that goes along with the calculation of the market portfolio. Since it is very easy to compute the minimum variance portfolio, we can give a parametrized version of the efficient frontier in terms of the respective portfolio weights

$$\begin{aligned}
|w_\gamma\rangle &= (1 - \gamma)|w_{\mathrm{MVP}}\rangle + \gamma|w_{\mathrm{MP}}\rangle \\
&= \Sigma^{-1}\left((1 - \gamma)\frac{|1\rangle}{c} + \gamma\frac{|\mu\rangle - r|1\rangle}{b - rc}\right),
\end{aligned} \tag{6.71}$$

for $\gamma \geq 0$, with

$$b = \langle 1|\Sigma^{-1}|\mu\rangle \quad \text{and} \quad c = \langle 1|\Sigma^{-1}|1\rangle. \tag{6.72}$$

In deriving this result, the two-fund separation theorem on page 113 was used.

Tobin's separation theorem provides a mechanism to decouple the portfolio selection problem from the investment decision problem. The market portfolio is always the same for every agent. Only the proportions held in the risky portfolio and the risk-free security differ between agents. This makes life a lot easier for financial advisors. They do not have to assemble individual portfolios for all their clients, but can rely on only one market portfolio. Usually a proxy, like the S&P 500 for example, is used instead of a genuine market portfolio, because such a portfolio would have to incorporate all assets, even non tradable ones, which is of course impossible.

6.7   Further Reading

A very instructive source is the classical book by Markowitz (1959), and also the original work of Tobin (1958). A non-technical introduction is Estrada (2005). A concise review is provided in Hens and Rieger (2010, chap. 3). For a compressed technical treatment see Janssen et al. (2009, chap. 17). A detailed and carefully written exposition of the whole subject is Elton et al. (2010). For the impact of real market imperfections, like short-selling restrictions for example, see Kan and Smith (2008). A very refreshing discussion of the scientific legacy of modern portfolio theory is Fabozzi et al. (2002).

6.8   Problems

6.1 Think of a world without the opportunity of risk-free borrowing or lending. You can only hold money, which means saving is permitted, or invest in a portfolio of risky assets. Show that in this world the market portfolio is given by

$$|w_{MP}\rangle = \frac{\Sigma^{-1}|\mu\rangle}{\langle 1|\Sigma^{-1}|\mu\rangle}.$$

6.2 Which expected return would an agent in the world of Problem 6.1 require to hold the market portfolio, if her risk aversion is $\alpha = 1$?

6.3 Assume there are different risk-free rates for borrowing and lending, and $R_0^b > R_0^l$. Sketch the capital market curve graphically and explain what happens to the tangential portfolio.

6.4 For a random variable $X \sim N(\mu, \sigma^2)$, the probability of realizing a value x outside the range $\mu \pm 2\sigma$ is roughly 5%. What proportion of the market portfolio should an agent hold, if she is willing to accept a nominal loss with no more than 2.5% probability? Assume that there is a riskless security and the risk-free rate of return is r.

6.5 Assume there are two security funds, one based on corporate bonds B, and the other on stocks S, with $\mu_B < \mu_S$, $\sigma_B < \sigma_S$, and $\rho_{BS} = 0$. Construct a market portfolio out of these two funds, assuming a risk-free rate of return r, and compute the weights w_B^* and w_S^*.

7 CAPM and APT

The capital asset pricing model (CAPM) is a major breakthrough in applying theoretical principles from modern portfolio theory in a real market environment. It is still in use, although in the meantime a more sophisticated model, the arbitrage pricing theory (APT), has become available. Even though both models look like close relatives, their underlying assumptions are very different. Indeed, the APT operates under such general conditions that it is able to generate a whole family of market models.

7.1 Empirical Problems with MPT

We have seen in the last chapter, how everything falls into place in modern portfolio theory. How can there possibly be problems, severe enough to disqualify it for practical application? The answer has to do with the statistical properties of the quantities required by the MPT. It was implicitly assumed that the expectation vector $|\mu\rangle$ and the covariance matrix Σ of a random vector of returns $|R\rangle$ is known. This assumption, as innocent as it looks, is the source of all the problems. In reality these quantities have to be estimated. So let's assume, you have recorded a time series of returns $|r_1\rangle, \ldots, |r_T\rangle$. How would you estimate $|\mu\rangle$ and Σ? The simplest possibility is to use the maximum-likelihood estimators

$$|\hat{\mu}\rangle = \frac{1}{T}\sum_{t=1}^{T}|r_t\rangle \quad \text{and} \quad \hat{\Sigma} = \frac{1}{T}\sum_{t=1}^{T}|r_t\rangle\langle r_t| - |\hat{\mu}\rangle\langle\hat{\mu}|, \tag{7.1}$$

where $|\cdot\rangle\langle\cdot|$ is the outer product, defined by

$$|a\rangle\langle a| = \begin{pmatrix} a_1 a_1 & a_1 a_2 & \cdots & a_1 a_N \\ a_2 a_1 & a_2 a_2 & \cdots & a_2 a_N \\ \vdots & \vdots & \ddots & \vdots \\ a_N a_1 & a_N a_2 & \cdots & a_N a_N \end{pmatrix}. \tag{7.2}$$

For $\hat{\Sigma}$ to be positive definite, there have to be at least $T = N$ linearly independent observations $|r_t\rangle$. You might think now that does not sound too bad altogether. But remember that MPT was tailored for middle- or long-term horizons, where returns can be safely assumed normally distributed. And now think for example only of those stocks contained within the S&P 500 index. If the return horizon is one year, we need at least 500 years of data, to get an admissible estimate for the covariance matrix Σ.

Another way to see the estimation problem of MPT is to count the number of free parameters to be estimated. There are N estimates for the expected returns μ_n, for $n = 1, \ldots, N$. The covariance matrix has N rows and N columns, but not all entries σ_{mn} are free parameters. Because Σ is symmetric, only the upper $(n \geq m)$ or lower $(n \leq m)$ triangle is unrestricted. Altogether there are $\frac{N(N+1)}{2}$ free parameters contained in Σ. The total number of free parameters β to be estimated in the MPT-world with N assets is

$$\#\beta = \frac{N(N+3)}{2}. \tag{7.3}$$

Quick calculation 7.1 Confirm the total number of free parameters.

In the case of the S&P 500 index, we are dealing with a total of 125 750 free parameters. You see the problem. On the other hand, as we will see, the CAPM characterizes the entire market by only N beta-factors. Furthermore, the data requirements are dramatically reduced and well inside empirical range.

7.2   The Capital Asset Pricing Model (CAPM)

Let's start our discussion with some properties of the capital market line (CML). The slope of the CML is obviously

$$m = \frac{\mu_{MP} - r}{\sigma_{MP}}, \tag{7.4}$$

as illustrated in Figure 7.1 left. Because all efficient portfolios are located on the capital market line, we can write an equation, relating the expected return of an arbitrary efficient portfolio P to its risk, expressed in terms of its standard deviation,

$$\mu_P = r + m\sigma_P = r + \frac{\mu_{MP} - r}{\sigma_{MP}}\sigma_P. \tag{7.5}$$

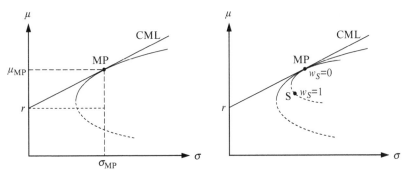

Fig. 7.1 Slope of the capital market line (left) and market portfolio mixed with stock (right)

The slope m is called the market price of risk, because it indicates with how much extra expected return the agent has to be compensated for taking one additional unit of risk, measured in σ-units.

Now let's build a portfolio P by taking an arbitrary stock S, and mixing it with the market portfolio MP. What is the expected return and the standard deviation of this portfolio? A straightforward calculation yields

$$\mu_P = w_S \mu_S + (1 - w_S)\mu_{MP}$$
$$\sigma_P = \sqrt{w_S^2 \sigma_S^2 + 2w_S(1 - w_S)\sigma_{S,MP} + (1 - w_S)^2 \sigma_{MP}^2},\qquad (7.6)$$

where the shorthand notation $\sigma_{S,MP} = \mathrm{Cov}[R_S, R_{MP}]$ was used. For reasons that become clear shortly, we also need the derivative of (7.6) with respect to w_S,

$$\frac{\partial \mu_P}{\partial w_S} = \mu_S - \mu_{MP}$$
$$\frac{\partial \sigma_P}{\partial w_S} = \frac{w_S \sigma_S^2 + (1 - 2w_S)\sigma_{S,MP} - (1 - w_S)\sigma_{MP}^2}{\sigma_P}.\qquad (7.7)$$

Now it is crucial to realize that for the weight $w_S = 0$ the portfolio P is nothing else than the market portfolio and furthermore, the slope of μ_P at $w_S = 0$ is m,

$$\left.\frac{d\mu_P}{d\sigma_P}\right|_{w_S=0} = m,\qquad (7.8)$$

see also Figure 7.1 right. If the moments of R_S and R_{MP} are fixed, we have $d\mu_P = \frac{\partial \mu_P}{\partial w_S} dw_S$ and $d\sigma_P = \frac{\partial \sigma_P}{\partial w_S} dw_S$. Now, everything falls into place and we have

$$m = \left.\frac{\partial \mu_P/\partial w_S}{\partial \sigma_P/\partial w_S}\right|_{w_S=0},\qquad (7.9)$$

or a little bit more detailed using (7.7)

$$\frac{\mu_{MP} - r}{\sigma_{MP}} = \frac{\mu_S - \mu_{MP}}{\sigma_{S,MP} - \sigma_{MP}^2} \cdot \sqrt{\sigma_{MP}^2}.\qquad (7.10)$$

Quick calculation 7.2 Verify the last equation for $w_S = 0$.

Rearranging terms in (7.10), one obtains

$$\mu_S = (\mu_{MP} - r)\left(\frac{\sigma_{S,MP}}{\sigma_{MP}^2} - 1\right) + \mu_{MP}.\qquad (7.11)$$

Renaming the ratio $\frac{\sigma_{S,MP}}{\sigma_{MP}^2} = \beta_S$ and expanding the associated bracket, yields the CAPM equation

$$\mu_S = r + \beta_S(\mu_{MP} - r)\qquad (7.12)$$

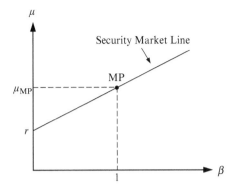

Fig. 7.2 Mean-beta-diagram with market portfolio and security market line (SML)

of Sharpe (1964), Lintner (1965), and Mossin (1966). Let's first calculate a few special βs to get a feeling for the new model. For example let's investigate the β for the risk-free security

$$\beta_0 = \frac{\sigma_{0,\mathrm{MP}}}{\sigma_{\mathrm{MP}}^2} = \frac{\rho_{0,\mathrm{MP}}\sigma_0\sigma_{\mathrm{MP}}}{\sigma_{\mathrm{MP}}^2} = 0, \tag{7.13}$$

where we used that $\sigma_0 = 0$. Next, let's calculate the β of the market portfolio itself,

$$\beta_{\mathrm{MP}} = \frac{\sigma_{\mathrm{MP},\mathrm{MP}}}{\sigma_{\mathrm{MP}}^2} = \frac{\sigma_{\mathrm{MP}}^2}{\sigma_{\mathrm{MP}}^2} = 1. \tag{7.14}$$

We have from (7.12) that μ_S as a function of β_S is a line with μ-intercept r and slope $\mu_{\mathrm{MP}} - r$. We can thus draw a μ-β-diagram as in Figure 7.2. The straight line, connecting r and MP, is called the security market line (SML). It maps the available securities along their respective β-risk, relative to the market portfolio. To understand the last statement completely, we have to investigate the connection between the beta-factors and the so-called market risk.

The capital asset pricing model (7.12) is a statement about the expectation value of the random return of security S. We certainly expect it to occur on average over many realized returns of this security, but we do not expect it to be a precise prediction of the next realization. Instead we can explicitly include a random error, to obtain the more realistic model

$$R_S = R_0 + \beta_S(R_{\mathrm{MP}} - R_0) + \epsilon_S, \tag{7.15}$$

with $E[\epsilon_S] = 0$ and $\mathrm{Var}[\epsilon_S] = \sigma_\epsilon^2$.

Quick calculation 7.3   Check that the expectation of (7.15) is the CAPM-equation.

It is further assumed that the individual random error ϵ_S is not correlated with R_{MP}. We can now calculate the variance of R_S,

$$\mathrm{Var}[R_S] = \beta_S^2\sigma_{\mathrm{MP}}^2 + \sigma_\epsilon^2. \tag{7.16}$$

Obviously, there are two sources of risk, contributing to the overall variability of R_S, the market or systematic risk, represented by $\beta_S^2 \sigma_{\mathrm{MP}}^2$, and a specific or idiosyncratic risk σ_ϵ^2, exclusively related to the security S. Note that only the systematic risk is compensated in terms of extra expected return in the CAPM (7.12). Idiosyncratic risk is not accounted for.

To see the implication for a portfolio, we have to understand first how the beta of a portfolio is calculated. Recall that the return of the portfolio P is

$$R_P = \sum_{n=1}^{N} w_n R_n, \tag{7.17}$$

where R_n is the random return of security S_n, and all weights add up to one. The beta-factor is universally defined as the covariance of the respective random return with the return of the market portfolio, divided by the variance of the market portfolio. Using that the covariance is linear in both of its arguments, one obtains

$$\beta_P = \frac{\mathrm{Cov}[R_P, R_{\mathrm{MP}}]}{\mathrm{Var}[R_{\mathrm{MP}}]} = \sum_{n=1}^{N} w_n \frac{\mathrm{Cov}[R_n, R_{\mathrm{MP}}]}{\mathrm{Var}[R_{\mathrm{MP}}]} = \sum_{n=1}^{N} w_n \beta_n. \tag{7.18}$$

That is, the beta of a portfolio is the weighted sum of all security-betas in the portfolio.

Quick calculation 7.4 Verify that covariances are linear in each argument.

This is a very convenient result and it enables us to finally conclude the discussion of diversification.

We earlier conducted a calculation that suggested that the risk in large portfolios in the limit may be diversified away completely. At that point we had no access to the concepts of systematic and idiosyncratic risk. Now let's finally finish the discussion in the same framework. We earlier assumed that there are N securities with identical expectation value and variance. This translates into every security having the same beta-factor β and identical idiosyncratic variance σ_ϵ^2. As before, choosing equal weights $w_n = \frac{1}{N}$, the expected return of the portfolio is given by the CAPM-equation

$$E[R_P] = r + \sum_{n=1}^{N} \frac{1}{N}\beta \cdot (\mu_{\mathrm{MP}} - r) = r + \beta(\mu_{\mathrm{MP}} - r). \tag{7.19}$$

There is no surprise, that the portfolio has the same expected return as each particular security. But now let's calculate the variance of the portfolio

$$\mathrm{Var}[R_P] = \beta^2 \sigma_{\mathrm{MP}}^2 + \frac{1}{N^2}\sum_{n=1}^{N} \sigma_\epsilon^2 = \beta^2 \sigma_{\mathrm{MP}}^2 + \frac{\sigma_\epsilon^2}{N}. \tag{7.20}$$

In the limit $N \to \infty$ the idiosyncratic risk is diversified away, whereas the systematic risk is non-diversifiable. This is the reason why systematic risk is compensated by expected return but idiosyncratic risk is not. In a manner of speaking, the market expects every agent to only participate in terms of already optimally diversified portfolios. Agents holding single securities or small portfolios are not fully compensated for the risk they take. That is why everyone you hear of making a fortune by trading a small collection of risky securities was probably a good deal more lucky than other market participants. Of course you rarely hear of the poor dogs losing every dollar with a similar strategy.

7.3 Estimating Betas from Market Data

One of the greatest victories of the CAPM is the dramatically reduced hunger for empirical data. We have seen that modern portfolio theory requires a huge amount of data to estimate the covariance matrix of all traded securities. In other words, MPT tries to establish mutual relations between all asset returns. The CAPM does so only between the securities and the market portfolio. The trick is to identify an index like the S&P 500 or the DAX as proxy for the respective market portfolio. In this setup, linear regression is the vehicle to generate estimates for the beta-factors. Linear regression is the working horse of statistics and econometrics. It is based on the linear model

$$Y = \alpha + \beta X + \epsilon, \tag{7.21}$$

where Y is called the response variable, X is the regressor, and ϵ is a random error with known distribution, usually assumed *Gauss*ian. The parameters α and β are the ones to be estimated from the data. Regression analysis requires some technical conditions like stationarity and homogeneity of errors, which are usually satisfied in the context of long-term returns. So we do not bother with any of these at this point. Instead we ask the question: How is regression analysis used to produce estimates for α and β?

Assume, you have an observation series of the response variable y_t, and also of the regression variable x_t for $t = 1, \ldots, T$. Indexing by t suggests that we have time series data, but regression analysis also applies to cross-sectional data. We can organize these observations in vector/matrix form

$$|y\rangle = X|\beta\rangle + |\epsilon\rangle, \tag{7.22}$$

where

$$|y\rangle = \begin{pmatrix} y_1 \\ \vdots \\ y_T \end{pmatrix}, \quad X = \begin{pmatrix} 1 & x_1 \\ \vdots & \vdots \\ 1 & x_T \end{pmatrix}, \quad |\beta\rangle = \begin{pmatrix} \alpha \\ \beta \end{pmatrix}, \quad |\epsilon\rangle = \begin{pmatrix} \epsilon_1 \\ \vdots \\ \epsilon_T \end{pmatrix}. \tag{7.23}$$

Quick calculation 7.5 Verify that (7.22) and (7.23) reproduce the linear model (7.21) for every $t = 1, \ldots, T$.

The notation is a bit ambiguous here, because in (7.22) X represents a data matrix, whereas in (7.21) X is a random regression variable, but it is difficult to argue with tradition. We certainly do not expect the real data to obey an exact linear relationship, which would mean $\epsilon_t = 0$ for all $t = 1, \ldots, T$. Instead we are interested in the best possible linear fit in the least-squares sense. That is, we have to minimize the total square error

$$\sum_{t=1}^{T} \epsilon_t^2 = \langle \epsilon | \epsilon \rangle = ((\langle y | - \langle \beta | X')(| y \rangle - X | \beta \rangle). \tag{7.24}$$

There are two important things to note here: The total square error constitutes a functional $F = \langle \epsilon | \epsilon \rangle$ to be minimized with respect to $\langle \beta |$, and the optimization problem is a convex one. Thus, the necessary and sufficient condition for a minimum is

$$\frac{\delta F}{\delta \langle \beta |} = -2X'(| y \rangle - X | \beta \rangle) \overset{!}{=} |0\rangle. \tag{7.25}$$

The $-X'$ term is due to the chain rule of differentiation.

Quick calculation 7.6 Confirm the functional derivative.

Rearranging (7.25) yields

$$X' X | \hat{\beta} \rangle = X' | y \rangle, \tag{7.26}$$

where we have adopted the common hat-notation for an estimator in statistics. Assuming that $X'X$ is invertible, we can multiply both sides with $(X'X)^{-1}$ from the left to obtain the desired least-squares estimator

$$|\hat{\beta}\rangle = (X'X)^{-1} X' | y \rangle. \tag{7.27}$$

Inverting $X'X$ is usually not a problem. The necessary condition is that X contains at least as many linearly independent observations as there are parameters to be estimated. In most situations there are many more observations than parameters. Under fairly mild conditions, the least-squares estimator is the best linear unbiased estimator available, and it is easy to compute. We can now state an estimated version of the linear model (7.21)

$$\hat{Y} = \hat{\alpha} + \hat{\beta} X + \epsilon, \tag{7.28}$$

where $\hat{Y}$ is the best possible model for Y we can find.

To apply least-squares estimation in the context of the CAPM, in order to estimate the beta-factor of a particular security S, set

$$y_t = r_{S,t} - r \quad \text{and} \quad x_t = r_{\text{MP},t} - r, \tag{7.29}$$

where the realized values of the respective returns are again indicated by small letters. If the CAPM is right, the estimator $\hat{\alpha}$ should be minute. In portfolio management, this estimator is called Jensen's alpha. We will discuss it in more detail in the next chapter.

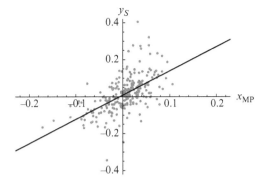

Fig. 7.3 Regression of monthly excess returns of S&P 500 (x_{MP}) on Microsoft (y_S) from 1993 to 2013

Instead, let's state the resulting linear relationship between the excess returns of security S and the market portfolio explicitly,

$$\hat{r}_S - r = \hat{\alpha}_S + \hat{\beta}_S(r_{MP} - r). \tag{7.30}$$

Let's look at a neat example.

Example 7.1

The regression relationship (7.30) was estimated for monthly return data of the Microsoft stock between 1993 and 2013. The S&P 500 index was used as proxy for the market portfolio, and the risk-free rate of return over one month was assumed $r = 0.25\%$, which means a 3% annual interest rate.

Results

The resulting estimates for the parameters α_S and β_S are

$$\hat{\alpha}_S = 8.37 \cdot 10^{-3} \quad \text{and} \quad \hat{\beta}_S = 1.31.$$

The data points (x_t, y_t) and the resulting regression line are shown in Figure 7.3. As expected, the estimate for α_S is small, even though monthly periods are probably not long enough to remove all short-term artifacts in the return series. The estimate of β_S indicates that the systematic risk, inherent in the Microsoft stock, is higher than the risk of the market portfolio.

Now that we have a regression relation at hand, we have immediate access to all consequences of the CAPM. But how do we use it to make predictions about returns of specific securities or portfolios? Assume we have used the information $\mathcal{F}_T$ to estimate the beta-factor of security S. We can take our advanced stochastic model (7.15) on page 123, replace β_S by the estimate $\hat{\beta}_S$, and take conditional expectations on both sides to obtain the prediction formula

$$E[R_{S,T+1}|\mathcal{F}_T] = r + \hat{\beta}_S(\mu_{\text{MP}} - r). \qquad (7.31)$$

This equation needs some explanation. First of all, the expectation value of the random error vanishes conditionally and unconditionally, $E[\epsilon_{T+1}] = 0$. We have further implicitly assumed that we can learn nothing about the expected market portfolio return $R_{\text{MP},T+1}$ from the information $\mathcal{F}_T$, and thus $E[R_{\text{MP},T+1}|\mathcal{F}_T] = E[R_{\text{MP},T+1}] = \mu_{\text{MP}}$. This is always true, if returns are indeed independent and identically distributed, as we usually assume. Of course we do not know μ_{MP} either, so we have to estimate it from the available return data or use some economically motivated guess. The estimate $\hat{\beta}_S$ is known at time T, and is hence treated like a constant.

Equation (7.31) looks different from the original CAPM equation (7.12) on page 122. To show the connection between them we have to use the law of iterated expectations

$$E\left[E[R_{S,T+1}|\mathcal{F}_T]\right] = E[R_{S,T+1}] = \mu_S, \qquad (7.32)$$

and the fact that the estimate $\hat{\beta}_S$ is unbiased, which means $E[\hat{\beta}_S] = \beta_S$. The unconditional expectation is with respect to the information $\mathcal{F}_0$. Thus, the law of iterated expectations says that at time $t = 0$, the expected future prediction you may make at any later time $t = T$, has to equal the prediction you can make today, at time $t = 0$. This is because from today's point of view, you have to predict the available information at time T as well, and so you expect the predicted prediction to be consistent with your current prediction. Taking unconditional expectations on both sides of (7.31) yields

$$\mu_S = r + \beta_S(\mu_{\text{MP}} - r). \qquad (7.33)$$

We can thus conclude that in some way the CAPM is the expectation of (7.31). This insight has a powerful dark side. We have to accept that the conditional expectation $E[R_{S,T+1}|\mathcal{F}_T]$, as well as the estimator $\hat{\beta}_S$ are random variables, with their own distributions. We have already implicitly made this assumption in claiming that $\hat{\beta}_S$ is an unbiased estimator.

Quick calculation 7.7 Can you see why?

To understand these subtleties thoroughly, we have to consider by no means trivial statistical issues. But for assessing the consequences of the CAPM, if it comes in touch with real data, this is both necessary and rewarding.

7.4   Statistical Issues of Regression Analysis and Inference

In order to assess the quality of a prediction based on observation data, it is worthwhile to take a closer look at some statistical properties of estimators and regression analysis. Many inferential conclusions are extremely subtle and it is easy to lose track of the substantial concepts. To avoid confusion this section provides information about relevant topics in structured blocks. We start with some diagnostic tools, then move on to the properties of the relevant estimators, and finally discuss the consequences of estimated beta-factors in the CAPM.

7.4.1   Coefficient of Determination

It seems like a good starting point to ask how accurate the linear fit, provided by regression analysis, actually is. If the regressor provides no information about the response variable, then the whole CAPM is nothing more than an interesting theoretical exercise. The influence of the regressor is usually assessed by the coefficient of determination R^2. It indicates the proportion of variability of the response variable that is explained by the linear regression. That was the easy part. Understanding how it is constructed is the difficult one. Again assume that we have a vector of observations of both the response variable and the regressor. The arithmetic mean of the response variable is

$$\bar{y} = \frac{1}{T} \sum_{t=1}^{T} y_t = \frac{1}{T}\langle 1|y\rangle. \tag{7.34}$$

To turn $|y\rangle$ into a vector of deviations from its mean, we can write

$$|y\rangle - \bar{y}|1\rangle = |y\rangle - \frac{1}{T}|1\rangle\langle 1|y\rangle = M_0|y\rangle, \tag{7.35}$$

where the centering matrix M_0, defined by

$$M_0 = I - \frac{1}{T}|1\rangle\langle 1|, \tag{7.36}$$

turns the observations into deviations from the mean. The matrix M_0 has two useful, and more or less obvious properties. It is symmetric, $M_0 = M_0'$, and it is idempotent, which means that $M_0^2 = M_0$ (see for example Greene, 2003, sect. A.2.8). We will use it shortly to construct sums of squares.

    If the regression parameters are estimated via least-squares, we can write the following decomposition

$$|y\rangle = |\hat{y}\rangle + |e\rangle, \tag{7.37}$$

with $|\hat{y}\rangle = X|\hat{\beta}\rangle$ and the vector of residuals $|e\rangle = |y\rangle - |\hat{y}\rangle$. The residuals are estimates for the realizations of the random error. Note one important fact: By the first order condition of the least-squares estimator (7.25), we have

$$X'(|y\rangle - X|\hat{\beta}\rangle) = X'|e\rangle = |0\rangle. \tag{7.38}$$

But the first row of X' entirely consists of ones and thus, we have $\langle 1|e\rangle = 0$, the residuals sum to zero, and $M_0|e\rangle = |e\rangle$. Now multiply (7.37) with the centering matrix to obtain deviations from the mean

$$M_0|y\rangle = M_0 X|\hat{\beta}\rangle + |e\rangle. \tag{7.39}$$

To obtain the sums of squares, simply square both sides, and use that M_0 is symmetric and idempotent, which means $M_0' M_0 = M_0$,

$$\langle y|M_0|y\rangle = \langle\hat{\beta}|X' M_0 X|\hat{\beta}\rangle + \langle e|e\rangle. \tag{7.40}$$

The cross-terms on the right hand side vanish, because $\langle\hat{\beta}|X' M_0|e\rangle = 0$.

Quick calculation 7.8   Verify the last statement.

The relationship (7.40) is often written in a somewhat less formal way as

$$\text{SST} = \text{SSE} + \text{SSR}, \tag{7.41}$$

where SST stands for "sum of squares total," SSE for "sum of squares explained," and SSR for "sum of squares residual." The coefficient of determination is defined as the ratio of the sum of squares explained and the sum of squares total,

$$R^2 = \frac{\text{SSE}}{\text{SST}} = 1 - \frac{\text{SSR}}{\text{SST}} = 1 - \frac{\langle e|e\rangle}{\langle y|M_0|y\rangle}. \tag{7.42}$$

In Example 7.1 we conducted a linear regression of the S&P 500 returns on the Microsoft stock returns. Calculating the coefficient of determination in this example yields $R^2 = 35\%$. This means that 35% of the variability of the returns of Microsoft is explained by the changes in the returns of the index. On the other hand, 65% of the total variability is due to idiosyncratic random fluctuations. We now begin to see, why it is not easy to test the predictions of the CAPM empirically.

7.4.2   Confidence Intervals

As mentioned before, parameter estimates are themselves random variables, because they are functions of a particular realization of other random variables. We will only consider unbiased estimators that generate at least asymptotically normally distributed estimates. We can then ask the question: What is the probability that the true parameter β, which we do not know, is covered by the symmetric interval $\hat{\beta} \pm z_k \sigma_\beta$, for arbitrary z_k? This is an easy question, because for a normally distributed random variable, we have

$$P\left(-z_{1-\frac{\gamma}{2}} \leq \frac{\hat{\beta} - \beta}{\sigma_\beta} \leq z_{1-\frac{\gamma}{2}}\right) = 1 - \gamma, \tag{7.43}$$

where $z_k = \Phi^{-1}(k)$ is the quantile function of the standard normal distribution. Now we can conclude that the random interval $\hat{\beta} \pm z_{1-\frac{\gamma}{2}}\sigma_\beta$ covers the true unknown parameter with probability $1 - \gamma$. This probability is also called confidence level and is most frequently chosen to be $1 - \gamma = 95\%$. The corresponding standard normal quantile is $z_{0.975} = 1.96$, and the critical values of the resulting confidence interval $[c_l, c_u]$ are $c_{u/l} = \hat{\beta} \pm 1.96\sigma_\beta$.

Now let's look at the least-squares estimator $|\hat{\beta}\rangle$. First let's check that it is unbiased and normally distributed. From the definition of $|\hat{\beta}\rangle$, we have

$$
\begin{aligned}
|\hat{\beta}\rangle &= (X'X)^{-1}X'|y\rangle = (X'X)^{-1}X'(X|\beta\rangle + |\epsilon\rangle) \\
&= |\beta\rangle + (X'X)^{-1}X'|\epsilon\rangle.
\end{aligned}
\tag{7.44}
$$

Define the σ-algebra $\mathcal{R}_T$, generated by the historical observations of the regression variable x_t for $t = 1, \ldots, T$. Then it is easy to see that conditional on $\mathcal{R}_T$, the estimator $|\hat{\beta}\rangle$ is an affine transformation of $|\epsilon\rangle$. If the random vector of errors is normally distributed, then $|\hat{\beta}\rangle$ is normal, too.[1] Furthermore, because $|\epsilon\rangle$ is assumed uncorrelated with the data, we can even take unconditional expectations to obtain

$$
E[|\hat{\beta}\rangle] = |\beta\rangle.
\tag{7.45}
$$

Because the variance of $|\hat{\beta}\rangle$ depends on the history of the regression variable, we have to condition on $\mathcal{R}_T$ to obtain

$$
\text{Var}[|\hat{\beta}\rangle|\mathcal{R}_T] = (X'X)^{-1}X'\text{Var}[|\epsilon\rangle]X(X'X)^{-1}.
\tag{7.46}
$$

But we have assumed the random errors uncorrelated with everything else, especially with themselves, and so $\text{Var}[|\epsilon\rangle] = \sigma_\epsilon^2 I$. Plugging this into (7.46), one obtains

$$
\text{Var}[|\hat{\beta}\rangle|\mathcal{R}_T] = \sigma_\epsilon^2(X'X)^{-1}.
\tag{7.47}
$$

The only problem with (7.47) is that we do not know σ_ϵ^2. We have to estimate it from the data, too. An unbiased estimator is

$$
\hat{\sigma}_\epsilon^2 = \frac{1}{T-2}\sum_{t=1}^{T} e_t^2 = \frac{1}{T-2}\langle e|e\rangle.
\tag{7.48}
$$

To understand the factor $\frac{1}{T-2}$, realize that there would be no residual, if we had only two observations. Because there are two parameters, the least-squares fit would be exact in this case. Only if we have three or more linearly independent observations, is the fit not exact. Therefore, there are really only $T - 2$ free equations. The number 2 is called the degrees of freedom. The same thing happens if we estimate a sample variance. Because we have to estimate the mean first, we lose one equation and the correction factor is $\frac{1}{T-1}$.

---

[1] Even if $|\epsilon\rangle$ is not normally distributed, $|\hat{\beta}\rangle$ is still asymptotically normal under fairly mild conditions, see Greene (2003, chap. 5).

In a general multiple regression framework with Q parameters, like in the arbitrage pricing theory (APT), the correction factor will be $\frac{1}{T-Q}$.

The conditional covariance matrix of the least-squares estimate in Example 7.1 is

$$\text{Var}[|\hat{\beta}_S\rangle|\mathcal{R}_T] = 10^{-3} \cdot \begin{pmatrix} 0.026 & -0.046 \\ -0.046 & 13.453 \end{pmatrix}. \tag{7.49}$$

From this, we can construct confidence intervals for the particular estimates $\hat{\alpha}_S$ and $\hat{\beta}_S$ by using the diagonal entries in (7.49). But because we have used an estimate of σ_ϵ^2, the distribution of $|\hat{\beta}_S\rangle$, conditional on the regression data, is no longer *Gaussian*. Luckily, it is still asymptotically normal, so that we can use the standard normal quantile $z_{1-\frac{\gamma}{2}}$, if T is large enough.[2] We have used 20 years of monthly data in Example 7.1, so there should be no problem. On a confidence level of $1-\gamma = 95\%$, one obtains

$$\hat{\alpha}_S: c_{u/l} = 8.37 \cdot 10^{-3} \pm 9.99 \cdot 10^{-3} \quad \text{and} \quad \hat{\beta}_S: c_{u/l} = 1.31 \pm 0.23. \tag{7.50}$$

At a 95% confidence level, the interval around $\hat{\alpha}_S$ covers the parameter value $\alpha_S = 0$, as predicted by the CAPM. That is a reassuring result. At the same confidence level, we can conclude that the Microsoft stock is indeed riskier than the market portfolio, because $\beta_S = 1$ is outside the confidence interval. The second statement is a lot stronger than the first one, because the statistical error is only $\gamma = 5\%$. In the first case, we do not know the error, all we can say is that it is less than or equal to $1-\gamma = 95\%$.

7.4.3   Confidence Bands

There are two quantities, for which we can compute confidence bands, in order to assess the situation. The first one is the regression line

$$\hat{y}(x) = \hat{\alpha} + \hat{\beta}x = \begin{pmatrix} 1 & x \end{pmatrix}|\hat{\beta}\rangle, \tag{7.51}$$

which is also the expectation value of $\hat{Y}$, conditional on the realization $X = x$ of the regression variable.

Quick calculation 7.9 Check that by reviewing (7.28) on page 126.

The second quantity of interest is the conditional random variable $\hat{Y}(x) = \hat{y}(x) + \epsilon$ itself.

Conditional on the history of the regression variable, the variance of the estimated parameter vector $|\hat{\beta}\rangle$ according to (7.47) is $\sigma_\epsilon^2(X'X)^{-1}$. Thus, we can compute the conditional variance of the estimated regression line as a function of x,

$$\text{Var}[\hat{y}(x)|\mathcal{R}_T] = \sigma_\epsilon^2 \begin{pmatrix} 1 & x \end{pmatrix}(X'X)^{-1}\begin{pmatrix} 1 \\ x \end{pmatrix}. \tag{7.52}$$

---

[2] The exact distribution is Student's t-distribution, with $T-2$ degrees of freedom. For $T>30$, this one virtually coincides with the normal distribution.

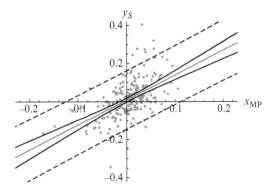

Fig. 7.4 95%-confidence bands for regression line and conditional estimate of the response variable in the Microsoft/S&P 500 Example 7.1

If we take the square root of (7.52), we can compute a confidence interval around $\hat{y}(x)$. This is indicated in Figure 7.4 as the narrow gray shaded area between the 95% critical boundary functions, for the data of Example 7.1. Of course, the variance of ϵ had to be estimated again by $\hat{\sigma}_\epsilon^2$, and thus, the distribution of $\hat{y}_S(x_{MP})$ for any given x_{MP} is only approximately normal. But in our large sample, we do not have to worry about that. You can see nicely that for $x_{MP} = 0$, the confidence area covers $y_S = 0$, confirming the CAPM's prediction, as already discussed at the end of the last section on confidence intervals.

Computing the variance of $\hat{Y}(x) = \hat{y}(x) + \epsilon$ is now an easy task. Because ϵ is uncorrelated with everything else, there are no covariance terms and thus, one obtains

$$\mathrm{Var}[\,\hat{Y}(x)|\mathcal{R}_T] = \mathrm{Var}[\hat{y}(x)|\mathcal{R}_T] + \sigma_\epsilon^2. \tag{7.53}$$

That is, the variance of the estimate $\hat{y}(x)$ is simply augmented by σ_ϵ^2, to account for the uncertainty introduced by the random error ϵ. Taking the square root of (7.53), a confidence band for $\hat{Y}(x)$, conditional on the regression variable taking the value $X = x$, can be computed. The respective band for the data of Example 7.1 is indicated in Figure 7.4 as the area between the two dashed curves. Those curves are the critical boundaries for a confidence level of 95%. This band is considerably broader than the one for the regression line. That is because in Example 7.1, the idiosyncratic error contributed roughly two thirds of the overall variability of the response variable. Therefore, the variance (7.53) is dominated by the σ_ϵ^2 term, which of course again had to be replaced by the appropriate estimate.

7.4.4   Predictions of the CAPM

We have already computed the expected return of an arbitrary security S in the next period, (7.31) on page 128, conditional on the information available today, $\mathcal{F}_T$.

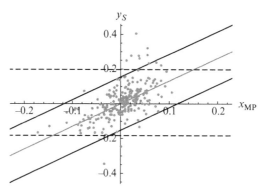

Fig. 7.5 95%-confidence interval for predicted stock return (dashed) and 95%-confidence band for the conditional expected return (shaded area) in the Microsoft/S&P 500 Example 7.1

Now let's assess this prediction. We can easily calculate the conditional variance of $R_{S,T+1}$,

$$\text{Var}[R_{S,T+1}|\mathcal{F}_T] = \hat{\beta}_S^2 \sigma_{\text{MP}}^2 + \sigma_\epsilon^2. \tag{7.54}$$

So by taking the square root, we can compute a confidence interval of the CAPM-prediction. Of course, the variances σ_{MP}^2 and σ_ϵ^2 are not known and have to be estimated. That renders the conditional return estimator again only asymptotically normal. If we compute all this for the monthly Microsoft/S&P 500 data of Example 7.1, we obtain on the 95% confidence level

$$c_{u/l} = 0.7\% \pm 19\%. \tag{7.55}$$

The confidence interval is indicated in Figure 7.5 by the dashed boundaries. That is a tremendously large interval compared to the small expected return. More generally, the problem is said to be subject to a very low signal to noise ratio. In this situation it is a difficult task to make useful statements about the small quantity that is subject to such large noisy fluctuations. This is one source of the problems encountered in trying to verify the CAPM empirically. As it stands today, more than 50 years later, there are still no conclusive statistical results to support acceptance or rejection of the model.

The strength of the CAPM, however, lies in its conditional nature. If we assume for the moment that we can prematurely observe or, more realistically, reliably predict $R_{\text{MP},T+1}$, then we can compute the distribution of $R_{S,T+1}$ with respect to the larger information $\mathcal{F}_X$, generated by additionally conditioning on the market portfolio return. In this case the conditional moments are

$$E[R_{S,T+1}|\mathcal{F}_X] = r + \hat{\beta}_S(r_{\text{MP},T+1} - r) \quad \text{and} \quad \text{Var}[R_{S,T+1}|\mathcal{F}_X] = \sigma_\epsilon^2. \tag{7.56}$$

This is incredibly useful in stress-testing, when the return $r_{\text{MP},T+1}$ is set to some catastrophic level, in order to see what kind of stock or portfolio return is to be expected in such a scenario.

For Example 7.1, the respective 95%-confidence band is indicated as the shaded area in Figure 7.5. This band has still a width of roughly 30.7%, because the dominant contribution to the overall variability of $R_{S,T+1}$ comes from the idiosyncratic variance σ_ϵ^2. But more importantly, the fact that the regression line is tilted means that we can learn something from observing, or better yet adequately predicting the market portfolio return. Once realizing this fact, we can hope to find better models, explaining a larger proportion of the variance of the response variable, to narrow down the interval in which the next stock return is expected. The framework for constructing such models is introduced in the subsequent section.

7.5   The Arbitrage Pricing Theory (APT)

The arbitrage pricing theory (APT) of Ross (1976) and Roll and Ross (1980) looks much like a simple extension of the CAPM. It is in fact a kind of multi-factor version

$$\mu_S = r + \sum_{q=1}^{Q} \lambda_{S,q}(\mu_{F_q} - r). \tag{7.57}$$

It is even used in the same way as the CAPM, but it is based on an entirely different set of assumptions. The different theoretical foundation is what makes the APT an extremely powerful instrument. The CAPM can be understood as one possible version of the arbitrage pricing theory, and thus, much of the criticism associated with some restrictive assumptions, is wiped out in one stroke. But, as we shall see, despite its similarity with the CAPM, the APT is a completely different beast.

The natural starting point is the classical linear factor analytic model of statistics

$$R_S - \mu_S = \sum_{q=1}^{Q} \lambda_{S,q} F_q + \epsilon_S, \tag{7.58}$$

where the factors F_q are independent random variables with zero mean and covariance $\text{Cov}[F_p, F_q] = \delta_{pq}$. The error term ϵ_S is again assumed uncorrelated with everything else. The coefficients $\lambda_{S,q}$ are traditionally called factor loadings, but they play the same role as multiple regression coefficients. The purpose of the linear factor model is to give the variability of R_S more structure, or in other words, to explain a greater proportion of the variability of the random return of security S, by considering Q latent factors. As it turns out, this model has to be modified to allow for an asymptotically arbitrage free security market. But for the moment we will pretend that (7.58) was true until we can see, which restrictions have to be altered. Assume we have a large security market, with

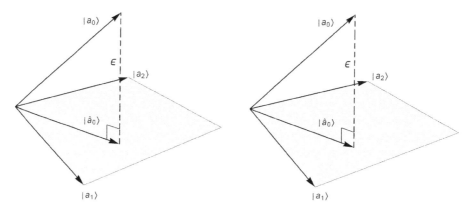

Fig. 7.6 **3D** Orthogonal projection of the vector $|a_0\rangle$ into the a_1-a_2-plane

$n = 1, \ldots, N$ securities. The factor analytic model of this market can be written most efficiently as

$$|R\rangle = |\mu\rangle + \Lambda|F\rangle + |\epsilon\rangle, \tag{7.59}$$

with

$$|R\rangle = \begin{pmatrix} R_1 \\ \vdots \\ R_N \end{pmatrix}, \quad |\mu\rangle = \begin{pmatrix} \mu_1 \\ \vdots \\ \mu_N \end{pmatrix}, \quad \Lambda = \begin{pmatrix} \lambda_{1,1} & \cdots & \lambda_{1,Q} \\ \vdots & \ddots & \vdots \\ \lambda_{N,1} & \cdots & \lambda_{N,Q} \end{pmatrix}, \quad |F\rangle = \begin{pmatrix} F_1 \\ \vdots \\ F_Q \end{pmatrix}, \quad |\epsilon\rangle = \begin{pmatrix} \epsilon_1 \\ \vdots \\ \epsilon_N \end{pmatrix}. \tag{7.60}$$

We will leave it that way for now and turn to a special portfolio that we can assemble in such a market, the so-called projection portfolio.

We have already discussed the *Riesz*-representation theorem, which is of great importance in the theory of vector spaces. There is another very important theorem, called the projection theorem. Take a look at Figure 7.6. There is a plane, call it the a_1-a_2-plane, spanned by the vectors $|a_1\rangle$ and $|a_2\rangle$, and another vector $|a_0\rangle$, not situated in the a_1-a_2-plane. But we can always project the vector $|a_0\rangle$ into that plane. Unfortunately, there are infinitely many perfectly valid projections from which we can choose. We are interested in one particular projection, the so-called orthogonal projection, indicated by the small square in Figure 7.6. Let's call the vector obtained by this particular projection $|\hat{a}_0\rangle$. Clearly, $|\hat{a}_0\rangle$ can be represented as a linear combination of the form

$$|\hat{a}_0\rangle = \beta_1|a_1\rangle + \beta_2|a_2\rangle = \sum_{q=1}^{2} \beta_q|a_q\rangle, \tag{7.61}$$

because by definition, the projection of $|a_0\rangle$ lives in the a_1-a_2-plane. Actually, we can formulate this fact more generally as

$$|\hat{a}_0\rangle = \sum_{q=1}^{Q} \beta_q|a_q\rangle = A|\beta\rangle, \tag{7.62}$$

with

$$A = \begin{bmatrix} |a_1\rangle \ldots |a_Q\rangle \end{bmatrix} \quad \text{and} \quad |\beta\rangle = \begin{pmatrix} \beta_1 \\ \vdots \\ \beta_Q \end{pmatrix}. \tag{7.63}$$

As we can already understand geometrically, $|\hat{a}_0\rangle$ is the orthogonal projection of $|a_0\rangle$ into the a_1-...-a_Q-hyperplane, if the distance, or equivalently the squared distance, between the tip of $|a_0\rangle$ and the tip of $|\hat{a}_0\rangle$ becomes minimal. This distance is called ϵ in Figure 7.6. Actually, ϵ is the length of the vector $|\epsilon\rangle = |a_0\rangle - A|\beta\rangle$. That means, we are facing the problem of choosing a vector $|\beta\rangle$, to minimize the squared length

$$\langle \epsilon | \epsilon \rangle = ((\langle a_0| - \langle \beta | A')(|a_0\rangle - A|\beta\rangle)). \tag{7.64}$$

But we already solved this least-squares problem in (7.27) on page 126, and we found

$$|\hat{\beta}\rangle = (A'A)^{-1} A' |a_0\rangle. \tag{7.65}$$

Thus, we can conclude that the orthogonal projection is obtained by choosing the linear combination

$$|\hat{a}_0\rangle = A|\hat{\beta}\rangle = A(A'A)^{-1} A' |a_0\rangle = B|a_0\rangle, \tag{7.66}$$

where $B = A(A'A)^{-1} A'$ is called the orthogonal projection matrix, or the projector for short. The projector has some special properties, which are easy to prove. For example, it is symmetric, $B' = B$, and it is idempotent, $B^2 = B$.

Quick calculation 7.10 Show that B is symmetric and idempotent.

Returning to our initial setup of the factor analytic model (7.59), the first step is to assemble a projection portfolio $|\theta\rangle$, such that $|\mu\rangle = |\hat{\mu}\rangle + |\theta\rangle$ holds; see Figure 7.7. Using

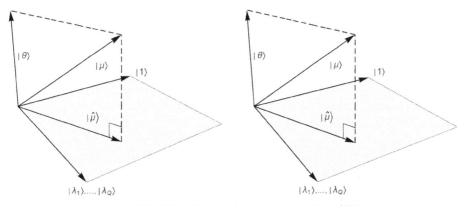

Fig. 7.7 **3D** Projection portfolio $|\theta\rangle$ orthogonal to $|\lambda_1\rangle, \ldots, |\lambda_Q\rangle$ and $|1\rangle$

the projector B, this portfolio is

$$|\theta\rangle = (I - B)|\mu\rangle, \tag{7.67}$$

where again $B = A(A'A)^{-1}A'$, and

$$A = \left[|1\rangle \quad |\lambda_1\rangle \quad \ldots \quad |\lambda_Q\rangle\right] = \left[|1\rangle \quad \Lambda\right]. \tag{7.68}$$

Observe that the form $\langle\theta|$ is orthogonal to every vector in A, and of course to $|\hat\mu\rangle$; see again Figure 7.7. In particular we have

$$\langle\theta|\mu\rangle = \langle\theta|\theta\rangle + \langle\theta|\hat\mu\rangle = \langle\theta|\theta\rangle. \tag{7.69}$$

Quick calculation 7.11 Prove the second equality in (7.69) by using that B is idempotent.

Now suppose, we have an arbitrarily scaled version of the projection portfolio, $\alpha|\theta\rangle$, with $\alpha > 0$. Combining this scaled portfolio with our factor analytic model for the return process, $R_P = \alpha\langle\theta|R\rangle$, we obtain

$$\begin{aligned}
R_P &= \alpha\langle\theta|\mu\rangle + \alpha\langle\theta|\Lambda|F\rangle + \alpha\langle\theta|\epsilon\rangle \\
&= \alpha\langle\theta|\theta\rangle + \alpha\langle\theta|\epsilon\rangle.
\end{aligned} \tag{7.70}$$

With this equation for the returns of the scaled projection portfolio we are now ready to conduct an asymptotic analysis in the limit of very large markets. Following Shiryaev (1999, sect. 2d), we set the scale factor to

$$\alpha = \langle\theta|\theta\rangle^{-\frac{2}{3}}. \tag{7.71}$$

For large portfolios, $N \to \infty$, we obtain the expected return

$$E[R_P] = \langle\theta|\theta\rangle^{\frac{1}{3}} = \sqrt[3]{\sum_{n=1}^{N} \theta_n^2} \xrightarrow{N\to\infty} \infty. \tag{7.72}$$

That is good news; as long as we are able to form portfolios that are sufficiently large, there is obviously no limit to the expected return we can hope for. But we surely expect that there is a catch somewhere. So let's check what the variance of our scaled projection portfolio is:

$$\mathrm{Var}[R_P] = \alpha^2\langle\theta|\Sigma_\epsilon|\theta\rangle = \langle\theta|\theta\rangle^{-\frac{4}{3}} \sum_{n=1}^{N} \theta_n^2 \sigma_{\epsilon_n}^2, \tag{7.73}$$

where Σ_ϵ is the diagonal matrix of variances of the idiosyncratic errors. We do not know the magnitude of the variance of each individual error, but we can bound it from above by taking the largest one

$$\mathrm{Var}[R_P] \le \frac{1}{\sqrt[3]{\sum_{n=1}^{N} \theta_n^2}} \max_n(\sigma_{\epsilon_n}^2) \xrightarrow{N\to\infty} 0. \tag{7.74}$$

This is an amazing result, because in the limit $N \to \infty$, we seem to realize an infinite return almost surely. What would this magical portfolio cost? We can assume without loss of generality that we start with normalized prices for all securities, $s_n = 1$ for $n = 1, \ldots, N$. In this case, the price of the projection portfolio is

$$\langle s|\theta \rangle = \langle 1|\theta \rangle = 0, \tag{7.75}$$

because the portfolio $|\theta\rangle$ is orthogonal to the form $\langle 1|$. The scaling factor does not change anything. To summarize the situation, we have constructed a portfolio that does not cost anything, but in the limit $N \to \infty$ generates infinite returns almost surely. Such a constellation is called an asymptotic arbitrage opportunity (Kabanov and Kramkov, 1998). Clearly, we would expect an efficient market not to support such arbitrage opportunities. But where did things go wrong? If we recap our steps, we have to conclude that the only possible way out is to require that

$$\lim_{N \to \infty} \langle \theta|\theta \rangle = \lim_{N \to \infty} \sum_{n=1}^{N} \theta_n^2 < \infty. \tag{7.76}$$

But what are the implications of this requirement? First, recall the definition of the projection portfolio and the orthogonal projection matrix,

$$|\theta\rangle = (I - B)|\mu\rangle = |\mu\rangle - A|\hat{\beta}\rangle, \tag{7.77}$$

where $|\hat{\beta}\rangle = (A'A)^{-1}A'|\mu\rangle$. Now let's decompose the linear combination $A|\hat{\beta}\rangle$,

$$|\theta\rangle = |\mu\rangle - \hat{\beta}_0|1\rangle - \sum_{q=1}^{Q} \hat{\beta}_q|\lambda_q\rangle. \tag{7.78}$$

Finally, let's rewrite condition (7.76) in another form

$$\lim_{N \to \infty} \sum_{n=1}^{N} \theta_n^2 = \lim_{N \to \infty} \sum_{n=1}^{N} \left(\mu_n - \hat{\beta}_0 - \sum_{q=1}^{Q} \hat{\beta}_q \lambda_{n,q} \right)^2 < \infty. \tag{7.79}$$

For (7.79) to be true, the square bracket has to be zero for most values of n. Put another way, the square bracket is only allowed to be different from zero for a finite number of securities. Because in the limit $N \to \infty$, a finite number of particular securities does not make any difference, the consequence of requirement (7.79) is

$$\mu_n = \hat{\beta}_0 + \sum_{q=1}^{Q} \hat{\beta}_q \lambda_{n,q}, \tag{7.80}$$

for almost all $n \leq N$. All that remains to do is to identify the $\hat{\beta}$-coefficients. Suppose, we are looking at a risk-free security B_0. In this case the latent factors do not influence the expected return. In other words, the loadings vanish, $\lambda_{0,q} = 0$ for $q = 1, \ldots, Q$, and $\mu_0 = \hat{\beta}_0$. This immediately identifies $\hat{\beta}_0$ with the risk-free interest rate r, and (7.80) becomes

$$\mu_n = r + \sum_{q=1}^{Q} \hat{\beta}_q \lambda_{n,q}. \tag{7.81}$$

Now let's see what happens, if we look at a particular factor F_p. In this case, we have $\lambda_{F_p,q} = \delta_{pq}$, and $\mu_{F_p} = r + \hat{\beta}_p$, because the loading for the p-th factor is of course one, and all other loadings vanish. But from this we can conclude that $\hat{\beta}_q = \mu_{F_q} - r$ for all $q = 1, \dots, Q$. Thus, Equation (7.81) becomes

$$\mu_n = r + \sum_{q=1}^{Q} \lambda_{n,q}(\mu_{F_q} - r). \tag{7.82}$$

This relation has to hold for almost all securities $n \leq N$, in particular for the arbitrary security S, in which case we have recovered the APT-equation (7.57) on page 135.

What does our analysis tell us about the factor analytic model from which we departed initially? We have to modify this model in two respects. The obvious modification is to discard the overall expectation vector $|\mu\rangle$ and instead to allow for factor specific expectations $\mu_{F_q} \neq 0$. This is an immediately evident consequence of the structure of (7.82). The second modification is not quite so obvious. Recall that the form $\langle\theta|$, associated with the projection portfolio (7.67), is orthogonal to every loading vector $|\lambda_q\rangle$, for $q = 1, \dots, Q$. Therefore, all results remain unchanged if we allow for oblique factors, which means that the factors F_q may have mutual correlation structure. But that is pretty much everything the APT tells us about the latent factors. It does neither provide information about what they are, nor how many of them to include. Nevertheless, working with the APT is no more difficult than working with the CAPM, which is why the APT is very popular with practitioners.

7.6   Comparing CAPM and APT

Using CAPM and APT makes them appear like close relatives. Analyzing their foundations reveals fundamental differences. But let's first look at the similarities in their application. We have seen that the β-coefficient of a risky security in the framework of the CAPM can be estimated by linear regression. The λs in the APT can be estimated by multiple linear regression

$$|y\rangle = X|\lambda\rangle + |\epsilon\rangle, \tag{7.83}$$

where

$$|y\rangle = \begin{pmatrix} y_1 \\ \vdots \\ y_T \end{pmatrix}, \quad X = \begin{pmatrix} 1 & x_{1,1} & \dots & x_{Q,1} \\ \vdots & \vdots & & \vdots \\ 1 & x_{1,T} & \dots & x_{Q,T} \end{pmatrix}, \quad |\lambda\rangle = \begin{pmatrix} \lambda_0 \\ \vdots \\ \lambda_Q \end{pmatrix}, \quad |\epsilon\rangle = \begin{pmatrix} \epsilon_1 \\ \vdots \\ \epsilon_T \end{pmatrix}. \tag{7.84}$$

If we identify the realized values of the response variable and the regressors, as we did before, with

$$y_t = r_{S,t} - r \quad \text{and} \quad x_{q,t} = f_{q,t} - r, \tag{7.85}$$

then we obtain the estimate of the coefficient vector $|\lambda\rangle$ by least-squares,

$$|\hat{\lambda}\rangle = (X'X)^{-1}X'|y\rangle. \tag{7.86}$$

As in case of the CAPM, we certainly expect the estimate $\hat{\lambda}_0$ to be approximately zero, if the APT is correct. Everything we said about the statistical properties still remains valid. From (7.86) we can only tell the difference, because we called the coefficients of the APT λ and not β. This is a very close resemblance.

What about the differences? The CAPM was derived, departing from modern portfolio theory. The framework included multivariate normal and independently distributed returns, the same risk-free interest rate for borrowing and lending, and equilibrium prices of assets. All of these features have been the subject of harsh criticism in the past, although empirical results do not support rejection of the CAPM. The APT on the other hand is based only on the assumption that in very large markets there should not be any arbitrage opportunities. The absence of arbitrage is an extremely general requirement. Realize that in the presence of arbitrage opportunities, there cannot be an equilibrium, because agents would trade in strategies to exploit them, until price adjustments remove these opportunities. But the absence of arbitrage does not require an equilibrium. The bottom line is that APT operates under extremely mild and barely criticizable conditions. On the other hand, its implications only apply to large portfolios and markets. In small markets, APT can be violated quite seriously. The theoretical implications are also far more general than those of the CAPM. The APT merely provides the shape of the relation between latent factors and the security returns. It says neither what they are, nor how many of them are needed. The fact that the CAPM is reproduced as one particular manifestation of the APT, clearly strengthens the theoretical rationale of the CAPM.

7.7 Further Reading

The classical references for the capital asset pricing model (CAPM) are Sharpe (1964), Lintner (1965), and Mossin (1966). For an excellent review including all technical assumptions, see Gatfaoui (2010). For a non-technical discussion of the CAPM see Estrada (2005, chap. 6 & 7). The former source also discusses the three-factor extension of Fama and French (1993, 1996). The original sources for the arbitrage pricing theory (APT) are Ross (1976), and Roll and Ross (1980). A compressed discussion of the concepts involved can be found in Shiryaev (1999, sect. 2d). A very careful and accessible treatment of this subject is Huberman (1982), and also Ingersoll (1987, chap. 7). Statistical and econometrical issues of regression analysis and parameter estimation are treated thoroughly in Greene (2003). For the factor analytic model see Mardia et al. (2003, chap. 8 & 9).

7.8 Problems

7.1 Practitioners often assume that the true yearly β of a security decays towards $\beta_{MP} = 1$ with time. A simple model for such a mean reversion process is

$$\hat{\beta}_{k+1} = \frac{1}{3}\hat{\beta}_k + \frac{2}{3},$$

where $\hat{\beta}_k = E[\beta_{t+k}|\mathcal{F}_t]$. Show that $\hat{\beta}_k$ is given by

$$\hat{\beta}_k = 1 + \left(\frac{1}{3}\right)^k (\hat{\beta}_0 - 1).$$

7.2 Prove that the half life of the difference $\hat{\beta}_0 - \beta_{\mathrm{MP}}$ in Problem 7.1 is

$$k = \frac{\log 2}{\log 3} \approx 0.63$$

years.

7.3 Look at the general mean reversion structure

$$\hat{\beta}_{k+1} = \lambda \hat{\beta}_k + (1 - \lambda),$$

where $0 \leq \lambda \leq 1$ is an arbitrary coefficient. How is λ to be chosen if the intrinsic period is one month, to maintain the term structure of the yearly period model?

7.4 For an arbitrary random variable Y and a σ-algebra $\mathcal{F}_A$, generated by observing some event A, the variance decomposition

$$\mathrm{Var}[Y] = \mathrm{Var}[E[Y|\mathcal{F}_A]] + E[\mathrm{Var}[Y|\mathcal{F}_A]]$$

holds. Show that the unconditional variance of the least-squares estimator $|\hat{\beta}\rangle$ is

$$\mathrm{Var}[|\hat{\beta}\rangle] = \sigma_\epsilon^2 E[(X'X)^{-1}],$$

where X is the usual data matrix, containing a column of ones and the regressors X_t, for $t = 1, \ldots, T$.

7.5 The original three-factor portfolio model of Fama and French (1993, 1996) is formulated in the form

$$R_P = R_0 + \beta_1(R_{\mathrm{MP}} - R_0) + \beta_2 \mathrm{SMB}_P + \beta_3 \mathrm{HML}_P + \epsilon_P,$$

where SMB indicates the market capitalization spread ("small minus big"), and HML is the spread in the book-to-market ratio ("high minus low"). Show that this model is empirically indistinguishable from a three-factor APT-model, if the restriction

$$\alpha = \lambda_0 - r(\lambda_2 + \lambda_3)$$

holds, and $\beta_q = \lambda_q$ for $q = 1, 2, 3$.

7.6 Show that the modified factor model

$$|R\rangle = R_0 \left[|1\rangle \quad -\Lambda\right] |1\rangle + \Lambda|F\rangle + |\epsilon\rangle,$$

with $E[F_q] = \mu_{F_q}$, $\mathrm{Cov}[F_p, F_q] = \sigma_{pq}$, $\mathrm{Cov}[F_q, \epsilon_n] = 0$, $E[\epsilon_n] = 0$, and $\mathrm{Cov}[\epsilon_m, \epsilon_n] = \delta_{mn}\sigma_n^2$, generates the correct APT-equation (7.57).

8 Portfolio Performance and Management

Portfolio performance is usually measured in terms of certain ratios like the *Sharpe-* or the *Treynor*-ratio. But there is much more to this subject than just comparing statistics. There are questions like: What proportion of the available capital should be invested in the risky part of the portfolio? This is a matter of optimal money management. Another important question is how future expectations affect today's optimal portfolio decisions. Those are important issues of portfolio selection and control.

8.1 Portfolio Performance Statistics

Assessing the performance of a portfolio is more than comparing past returns over a given time horizon. Imagine two managers of different mutual funds. Both have realized precisely the same annual returns over the last 10 years, but the first one generated only half the volatility in terms of yearly standard deviation, compared to the second one. Which fund would you buy? Which portfolio manager did the better job? Indeed, due to their risk-averse attitude, most people would prefer the first mutual fund, because they conclude from observation that the same expected return is realized with half the risk exposure. This is of course an educated guess, because we cannot guarantee returns and volatilities of both funds not to evolve in a completely different way in the future. The lesson here is that portfolio statistics are always based on past performance and cannot predict the future development of a portfolio. Nevertheless, they can be helpful in gaining or losing trust in the abilities of the portfolio manager. Subsequently, three of the most commonly used performance statistics are introduced.

8.1.1 Jensen's Alpha

Jensen's alpha (Jensen, 1968) is named after the usual Greek letter for the intercept in the linear regression model. Let's focus on the CAPM for the moment. If we estimate the regression coefficients for the return series of an arbitrary portfolio P, we get an equation of the form

$$\hat{r}_P - r = \hat{\alpha}_P + \hat{\beta}_P(r_{\mathrm{MP}} - r), \tag{8.1}$$

or after rearranging

$$\hat{\alpha}_P = \hat{r}_P - r - \hat{\beta}_P(r_{\mathrm{MP}} - r). \tag{8.2}$$

In the framework of linear regression, Jensen's alpha is most easily computed from the least-squares estimator, $\hat{\alpha}_P = \langle e_1 | \hat{\beta}_P \rangle$, with $\langle e_1 | = (1 \quad 0)$. In the APT-case we would obtain $\hat{\alpha}_P = \langle e_1 | \hat{\lambda}_P \rangle$, with $\langle e_1 |$ extended to the dimension of $|\hat{\lambda}_P \rangle$.

Obviously, $\hat{\alpha}_P$ represents a kind of extra return above the β-weighted excess return, predicted by the CAPM. We can make this point even more transparent by introducing an estimated extra return $\hat{r}_X$, with $\hat{\alpha}_P = \hat{\beta}_P \hat{r}_X$, and substituting in (8.1),

$$\hat{r}_P - r = \hat{\beta}_P (r_{\mathrm{MP}} + \hat{r}_X - r). \tag{8.3}$$

It is disputable, if such an extra return can be achieved permanently. Of course the market portfolio proxy is never an exact and exhaustive representation of the true market portfolio. But usually it is close enough to prevent $\hat{\alpha}_P$ from being significantly different from zero. In his original article, Jensen (1968) analyzed 115 mutual funds in the period from 1945 to 1964. He found that the vast majority generated a negative estimate for α_P, with an average of -1.1% after fees. He only found three funds, with alpha statistically significant greater than zero, on a significance level of 5%. But as Jensen pointed out himself, when analyzing 115 funds with true $\alpha_P = 0$, one would expect five or six of them to generate a significant result on a 5%-level purely by chance.

There is another possible explanation for a positive alpha. Portfolio managers have to specify an index, against which their fund is to be benchmarked. They are not free to choose such an index, because a high percentage of the securities have to be listed in this index. On the other hand, they are free to include a small proportion of foreign securities, possibly from riskier markets. Those are more volatile and if they realize higher returns, the return series generated by the portfolio supports a positive estimate for α_P. Thus, Jensen's alpha is also a measure for the selection success.

8.1.2 *Treynor*-Ratio

Unlike Jensen's alpha, the *Treynor*-ratio (Treynor, 1966) is inextricably linked to the CAPM. To understand Treynor's measure, first observe that the slope of the security market line (SML) with respect to β is

$$\frac{d}{d\beta}\mathrm{SML} = \frac{\mu_{\mathrm{MP}} - r}{\beta_{\mathrm{MP}}} = \mu_{\mathrm{MP}} - r, \tag{8.4}$$

because $\beta_{\mathrm{MP}} = 1$ (see Figure 8.1). We can of course indicate a point (β_P, μ_P) beyond the SML, representing the beta-factor and the expected return of a hypothetical portfolio P. Assume for the moment that such a violation of the CAPM is possible and call the imaginary line from $(0, r)$ through (β_P, μ_P) the portfolio market line (PML). The *Treynor*-ratio is defined as the estimated slope of the PML with respect to β,

$$\mathrm{TR}_P = \frac{\hat{\mu}_P - r}{\hat{\beta}_P}, \tag{8.5}$$

where $\hat{\mu}_P$ is an unconditional estimate of the expected return of the portfolio P. For all practical purposes, $\hat{\beta}_P$ is the least-squares estimate of the portfolio beta, and $\hat{\mu}_P$ is the mean of the observed portfolio returns.

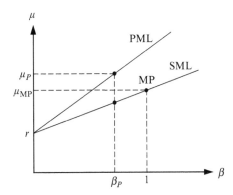

Fig. 8.1 *Treynor*-ratio as slope of the "portfolio market line" in the μ-β-diagram

8.1.3   *Sharpe*-Ratio

The *Sharpe*-ratio (Sharpe, 1966) can be motivated in exactly the same way as the *Treynor*-ratio, but in the μ-σ-diagram, not in the μ-β-diagram. Thus, the *Sharpe*-ratio for an arbitrary portfolio P is

$$\mathrm{SR}_P = \frac{\hat{\mu}_P - r}{\hat{\sigma}_P}, \tag{8.6}$$

where $\hat{\mu}_P$ and $\hat{\sigma}_P$ are the usual sample estimators for the mean and the standard deviation of the portfolio return R_p. The *Sharpe*-ratio is therefore a completely model independent statistic. It also plays an important role in the economic theory of asset pricing, as we shall see.

As pointed out in the last chapter, the confidence bands for predicted returns can be huge compared to the magnitude of the returns themselves. This degree of uncertainty also affects the reliability of coefficients like the *Treynor*- or *Sharpe*-ratio. One should always keep that in mind, before relying on such statistics too heavily.

8.2   Money Management and *Kelly*-Criterion

Money management is a concept often more familiar to professional gamblers than to portfolio managers. For example Long Term Capital Management (LTCM), a hedge fund managed, among others, by two Nobel Prize laureates, crashed in 1998 due to massive liquidity problems. Paul Wilmott (2006b, p. 742) even coined the term Short Term Capital MisManagement (STCMM). This is not the only historical example of a disastrous outcome due to poor money management.

You can see the paramount importance of good money management in a very simple example. Assume, you have to decide which fraction π of your wealth w_0 to invest in a successive coin flip game, where the outcome is in your favor with probability p. You either double the amount of your bet, or you lose your wager, independently in each round all over again. Now assume the odds are extremely in your favor, say $p = 90\%$. Would you put your whole wealth at stake in a repeated game like this? I suppose not. If you repeatedly put 100% of your wealth in jeopardy, the one unfavorable outcome will eventually occur and you lose everything. That much is easy to see. But which fraction π of your wealth should you choose? That is the difficult question. The answer depends on what objective you pursue. If you are interested in maximizing the expected long-term capital growth rate, then the *Kelly*-criterion (Kelly, 1956) gives the right answer. Let's see how this works in our simple coin flip setup.

Example 8.1

Look at the repeated coin flip game with probability p, not necessarily 50%, for the favorable outcome. Which fraction π of the initial wealth w_0 should be invested in each round, to maximize the long-term growth rate?

Solution

First examine what happens in the first round. If you win, your wealth is

$$w_1 = w_0 + \pi w_0 = w_0(1 + \pi).$$

If you lose, your remaining wealth is

$$w_1 = w_0(1 - \pi).$$

It is easy to see that if you have played N successive rounds of the game, and say you won n of those N rounds, your wealth is

$$w_N = w_0(1 + \pi)^n (1 - \pi)^{N-n}.$$

The order in which you win or lose obviously does not make any difference. The average growth g of your capital after N rounds of the game is not given by the arithmetic mean, but by the geometric mean

$$g_N = \sqrt[N]{\frac{w_N}{w_0}} = \sqrt[N]{(1 + \pi)^n (1 - \pi)^{N-n}},$$

or after taking the logarithm on both sides, making it a growth rate

$$\log g_N = \frac{n}{N} \log(1 + \pi) + \left(1 - \frac{n}{N}\right) \log(1 - \pi).$$

Now remember that we are talking about long-term effects and thus, $\lim_{N \to \infty} \frac{n}{N} = p$, and

$$\log g_\infty = p \log(1 + \pi) + (1 - p) \log(1 - \pi).$$

To maximize this quantity, we have to solve the following optimization problem

$$\frac{d}{d\pi} \log g_\infty = \frac{p}{1+\pi} - \frac{1-p}{1-\pi} \overset{!}{=} 0.$$

This is easily solved after applying a few algebraic manipulations, and one obtains

$$\pi^* = 2p - 1,$$

which is the *Kelly*-criterion for the simple coin flip game. It is easily shown that the first order condition is sufficient for $0.5 \leq p \leq 1$. For $p < 0.5$, you simply should not participate in the game.

Quick calculation 8.1 Convince yourself that the *Kelly*-fraction of Example 8.1 is perfectly sensible for the fair coin, $p = 0.5$, and also for the always winning coin, $p = 1$.

Let's now turn to a more realistic scenario. Think of a portfolio P of risky securities. Every day, this portfolio is subject to a randomly driven return process. Let's assume for the moment that daily returns are identically and independently distributed and call the realized return $r_{P,t}$ on day t. Again, starting with an initial wealth w_0 and a fixed fraction π, the wealth at time T is

$$w_T = w_0 \prod_{t=1}^{T} (1 + \pi r_{P,t}). \tag{8.7}$$

Quick calculation 8.2 Convince yourself that (8.7) is correct.

By completely analogous arguments to those presented in Example 8.1, we can calculate the average growth of capital by the geometric mean

$$g_T = \sqrt[T]{\frac{w_T}{w_0}} = \sqrt[T]{\prod_{t=1}^{T} (1 + \pi r_{P,t})}. \tag{8.8}$$

Let's proceed further with our analogy and calculate the average growth rate of the portfolio by taking logarithms

$$\log g_T = \frac{1}{T} \sum_{t=1}^{T} \log(1 + \pi r_{P,t}). \tag{8.9}$$

Now realize that the right hand side of (8.9) is the usual arithmetic mean, and in the limit $T \rightarrow \infty$ we obtain

$$\log g_\infty = E[\log(1 + \pi R_P)]. \tag{8.10}$$

The next step is to *Taylor*-expand the logarithm in (8.10). As usual, we assume that on average daily returns are positive but very small, $E[R_P] = \mu_P \ll 1$, such that $E[R_P^2] \approx \mathrm{Var}[R_P] = \sigma_P^2$ holds. Expanding to second order, one obtains

$$\log g_\infty \approx E\left[\log 1 + \pi R_P - \frac{1}{2}\pi^2 R_P^2\right] \approx \pi\mu_P - \frac{1}{2}\pi^2\sigma_P^2. \qquad (8.11)$$

All that is left to do is to set the derivative of (8.11) with respect to π equal to zero, and to calculate the *Kelly*-fraction for the portfolio problem

$$\pi^* = \frac{\mu_P}{\sigma_P^2}. \qquad (8.12)$$

Quick calculation 8.3　Verify the *Kelly*-criterion (8.12) for the portfolio problem.

Example 8.2

Assume you have the opportunity to invest in a mutual fund that offers an expected return of 5% per year and a standard deviation of 31.63%. Trading is only on a daily basis (250 trading days per year). What is the *Kelly*-fraction and what yearly capital growth rate can you expect?

Solution

The first thing to do is to convert the mean and standard deviation into daily quantities

$$\mu_P = \frac{5\%}{250} = 0.02\% \quad \text{and} \quad \sigma_P = \frac{31.63\%}{\sqrt{250}} = 2\%.$$

From this we get immediately the *Kelly*-fraction

$$\pi^* = \frac{\mu_P}{\sigma_P^2} = \frac{0.02\%}{0.04\%} = \frac{1}{2}.$$

Plugging this ratio into the long-term average growth rate (8.11) yields

$$\log g_\infty^* = \pi^*\mu_P - \frac{1}{2}\pi^{*2}\sigma_P^2 = \frac{\mu_P^2}{2\sigma_P^2} = 0.005\%.$$

Finally, reconverting this growth rate into yearly terms yields an average capital growth rate of 1.25%.

Example 8.2 indicates that the average long-term growth rate of capital is significantly smaller than the expected return of the portfolio. This is partly due to the fraction invested in the fund, which is one half in this case. But there is another effect, best

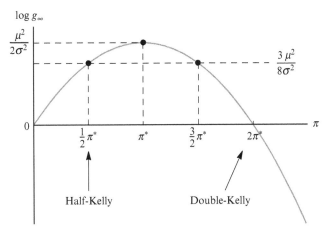

Fig. 8.2 *Kelly*-criterion for the portfolio problem

understood in a heuristic way. Assume you invested an arbitrary amount of money w_0 at time $t = 0$. The return at $t = 1$ is 10% and the return at $t = 2$ is −10%. What does your account look like after the second day? You might be tempted to say it is still w_0, because you realized a loss and a gain in capital of the same magnitude, but this is not correct. The right answer is

$$w_2 = w_0(1 + 0.1)(1 - 0.1) = w_0(1^2 - 0.1^2) = 0.99w_0. \qquad (8.13)$$

You have indeed realized a loss of 1% after the second day. This may seem utterly unfair, but such is life.

It gets even worse. If you plot the average long-term growth rate against the *Kelly*-fraction, as in Figure 8.2, it becomes evident that if you willingly or by accident go beyond double-*Kelly*, you only can expect capital losses. In reality most of the time you do not know the parameters μ_P and σ_P, but have to estimate them from a finite sample of past realizations. Conservative investors therefore often try to invest a half-*Kelly* fraction, because the expected growth rate is still $3\mu_P^2/8\sigma_P^2$, but there is a comfortable margin for error before you enter the danger zone. For investments in ordinary securities or stock indices, the *Kelly*-fraction is most of the time something between one half and one, ruling out all kinds of leveraged strategies.

Finally, returning to our initial discussion of Long Term Capital Management, one may conclude from the analysis of their positions, that they were highly over-leveraged. As pointed out by Wilmott (2006b, p. 741), just their notional position in swaps was $1.25 trillion, which was 5% of the entire market volume at that time, providing a leverage ratio of more than 20:1. It has been estimated that they were committed to about double-*Kelly*.

8.3   Adjusting for Individual Market Views

By now it should be clear that managing a portfolio requires strategic decisions. Maybe the simplest decision of this kind is to choose a buy and hold strategy. This is by no means a dull strategy, because we saw earlier that there is no convincing evidence that managed funds are able to beat their reference index over an extended period of time. Last but not least, this was one of the favorite strategies of the Hungarian stock market wizard André Kostolany. The next more challenging strategy could be to modify the portfolio composition such that in times of bullish market perspectives, the portfolio beta is considerably larger than one, and in bearish periods the beta is smaller than one. With this strategy you should on average participate stronger in market upturns than the index, but weaker in downturns. The problem in both strategies is to decide what the perspective of a single security, or the whole market, respectively, is. This is the point, where individual expectations and beliefs come in. As we shall see, there is a way to combine such individual views in an optimal way with the information the market has provided so far.

The first to consider individual views in the portfolio selection decision were Black and Litterman (1992). Their goal was to improve the estimator for the expected return of an arbitrary asset, provided by an equilibrium model like the CAPM, by incorporating information from individual investors' views. As pointed out by Meucci (2010a), processing the return estimators results in two puzzles with respect to scenario analysis and completely uninformative views. To avoid these kinds of problems, we consider here what is called the market formulation of the *Black–Litterman*-approach by Meucci. This modification is more general and completely consistent.

Departing from a given distribution of an N-dimensional vector of market returns $|R\rangle \sim N(|\mu\rangle, \Sigma)$, assume that an investor has individual views on the future outcome of some of these random returns

$$|V\rangle = P|R\rangle + |\epsilon\rangle, \qquad (8.14)$$

where P is a $K \times N$ "pick"-matrix. The random error $|\epsilon\rangle$ associates uncertainty with the views $|V\rangle$, and is assumed to be independently

$$|\epsilon\rangle \sim N(|0\rangle, \Omega) \qquad (8.15)$$

distributed, where Ω is a $K \times K$ covariance matrix. A convenient choice for Ω is

$$\Omega = \frac{1}{c} P \Sigma P', \qquad (8.16)$$

with c representing an overall confidence parameter. For $c \to 0$, the variance of $|\epsilon\rangle$ grows to infinity, which renders the views completely uninformative, whereas $c \to \infty$ expresses complete confidence, in which case we are in fact doing scenario analysis.

Quick calculation 8.4   Convince yourself that with (8.16), $\Omega = \frac{1}{c}\text{Var}[P|R\rangle]$ holds.

By now you should have two questions about what we have said so far. The first is, what is the pick-matrix exactly and how is it applied to express a particular view? The second is, how does this framework help us at all? So let's answer the first question by an example.

Example 8.3

Assume that there are only four securities relevant to us, and that we have the following views on their future returns

$$\begin{pmatrix} 8\% \\ 2\% \end{pmatrix} = \underbrace{\begin{pmatrix} 1 & 0 & 0 & 0 \\ 0 & 1 & 0 & -1 \end{pmatrix}}_{P} |R\rangle + |\epsilon\rangle.$$

What information is provided by the pick-matrix?

Solution

The first row of P picks only the return of the first security out of $|R\rangle$ and assigns an individual prediction of 8% to its return. The second row picks the difference in returns of the second and the fourth security, and predicts this difference to be 2%. Note that there is no view about the return of the third security, neither absolute, nor relative.

To answer the second question we have to use the concept of conditional distributions. Let $\mathcal{F}_R$ be the σ-algebra, generated by observing the return $|R\rangle = |r\rangle$, and realize that the distribution of $|V\rangle$, conditional on the information $\mathcal{F}_R$, is

$$|V\rangle\big|\mathcal{F}_R \sim N(P|r\rangle, \Omega). \tag{8.17}$$

But this is not the interesting one. What we are looking for is the distribution of $|R\rangle$, conditional on the views to attain a particular value $|V\rangle = |v\rangle$. In Example 8.3, we had $\langle v| = (8\% \quad 2\%)$. The conditional distribution $|R\rangle\big|\mathcal{F}_V$ can be calculated with the help of Bayes' rule. For any two continuous random variables X and Y, the conditional probability density of $X|\mathcal{F}_Y$ is given in shorthand notation by

$$f(x|y) = \frac{f(y|x)f(x)}{f(y)}. \tag{8.18}$$

We know by definition that the distribution of $|R\rangle$ is *Gauss*ian, and also the conditional distribution of $|V\rangle\big|\mathcal{F}_R$ is *Gauss*ian. But the unconditional distribution of $|V\rangle$ is also *Gauss*ian, because $|V\rangle$ is by (8.14) a linear combination of *Gauss*ian random variables. That means, we know all density functions on the right hand side of (8.18) and we can conduct the cumbersome computation of $f(x|y)$.

There is, however, an elegant shortcut to this computation. Realizing that in our case $f(y|x)f(x) = f(y, x)$ is the joint normal probability density of Y and X means that we can apply the normal correlation theorem (Theorem 3.1 on page 56). It states that the conditional distribution of $X|\mathcal{F}_Y$ is also normal with expectation value

$$E[X|\mathcal{F}_Y] = E[X] + \text{Cov}[X, Y]\text{Var}[Y]^{-1}(y - E[Y]), \tag{8.19}$$

and variance

$$\text{Var}[X|\mathcal{F}_Y] = \text{Var}[X] - \text{Cov}[X, Y]\text{Var}[Y]^{-1}\text{Cov}[Y, X]. \tag{8.20}$$

This is a big step in the right direction. We can conclude that the desired distribution of $|R\rangle|\mathcal{F}_V$ is also a *Gauss*ian. We are merely left with the problem of determining $E[|V\rangle]$, $\text{Var}[|V\rangle]$, and $\text{Cov}[|R\rangle, \langle V|]$. The easiest one is the expectation

$$E[|V\rangle] = PE[|R\rangle] + E[|\epsilon\rangle] = P|\mu\rangle. \tag{8.21}$$

Next, let's take a look at the variance of $|V\rangle$, and keep in mind that $|\epsilon\rangle$ is independent of everything else

$$\text{Var}[|V\rangle] = P\text{Var}[|R\rangle]P' + \text{Var}[|\epsilon\rangle] = P\Sigma P' + \Omega. \tag{8.22}$$

Finally, the covariance term is a little tricky. Remember that for arbitrary random variables X and Y the relation $\text{Cov}[X, Y] = E[XY] - E[X]E[Y]$ holds. Thus, one obtains

$$\begin{aligned}
\text{Cov}[|R\rangle, \langle V|] &= E[|R\rangle\langle V|] - E[|R\rangle]E[\langle V|] \\
&= E[|R\rangle\langle R|P' + |R\rangle\langle\epsilon|] - |\mu\rangle\langle\mu|P' \\
&= E[|R\rangle\langle R|]P' - |\mu\rangle\langle\mu|P' \\
&= \Sigma P',
\end{aligned} \tag{8.23}$$

where we again used that $|R\rangle$ and $|\epsilon\rangle$ are independent. We are now able to state the posterior expectation vector and covariance matrix under incorporation of the *Black–Litterman*-views

$$|\mu_{\text{BL}}\rangle = |\mu\rangle + \Sigma P'(P\Sigma P' + \Omega)^{-1}(|v\rangle - P|\mu\rangle), \tag{8.24}$$

and

$$\Sigma_{\text{BL}} = \Sigma - \Sigma P'(P\Sigma P' + \Omega)^{-1}P\Sigma. \tag{8.25}$$

We have used in (8.25) that $\text{Cov}[|V\rangle, \langle R|] = \text{Cov}[|R\rangle, \langle V|]'$.

Quick calculation 8.5 Can you see why this is true?

Blending views with a prior distribution can be embedded perfectly in the framework of modern portfolio theory (MPT). Let's look at an example for this whole process.

Example 8.4

Consider the four stocks of Duke Energy, Lockheed Martin, Microsoft, and Voda-fone. The yearly return distribution is assumed normal, and the expectation vector

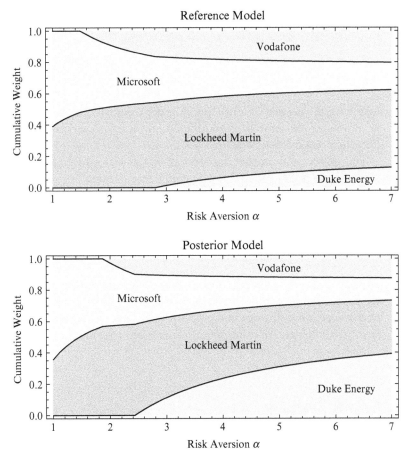

Fig. 8.3 Portfolio composition with (bottom) and without (top) incorporation of *Black–Litterman*-views

and covariance matrix were estimated from data of the years 1993 to 2013,

$$|\mu\rangle = \begin{pmatrix} 10.9\% \\ 14.3\% \\ 23.9\% \\ 17.2\% \end{pmatrix} \quad \text{and} \quad \Sigma = 10^{-2} \cdot \begin{pmatrix} 6.74 & 3.33 & -1.2 & 1.69 \\ 3.33 & 8.51 & -3.1 & -4.8 \\ -1.2 & -3.1 & 20.2 & 13.1 \\ 1.69 & -4.8 & 13.1 & 16.8 \end{pmatrix}.$$

Assume further that utility is represented by the standard parametric family (6.51) from MPT

$$U_\alpha[R_P] = \mu_P - \frac{\alpha}{2}\sigma_P^2.$$

How does the optimal portfolio composition change, if the views of Example 8.3 are incorporated, the confidence parameter is $c = 2$, and short selling is prohibited?

Solution

From (6.57) on page 115 one obtains the optimal portfolio weights

$$|w_\alpha^*\rangle = \Sigma^{-1}\left(\frac{1}{\alpha}|\mu\rangle + \frac{1}{c}\left(1 - \frac{b}{\alpha}\right)|1\rangle\right),$$

with $b = \langle 1|\Sigma^{-1}|\mu\rangle$ and $c = \langle 1|\Sigma^{-1}|1\rangle$. In order to satisfy the short selling constraint, negative weights are set to zero and the optimization is carried out again with respect to the remaining nonzero weights.

The posterior moments, incorporating the views of Example 8.3, are calculated according to (8.24) and (8.25) with confidence parameter $c = 2$. One obtains

$$|\mu_{\text{BL}}\rangle = \begin{pmatrix} 8.97\% \\ 14.7\% \\ 22.5\% \\ 14.3\% \end{pmatrix} \quad \text{and} \quad \Sigma_{\text{BL}} = 10^{-2} \cdot \begin{pmatrix} 2.24 & 1.11 & -0.4 & 0.56 \\ 1.11 & 4.40 & 1.14 & -0.0 \\ -0.4 & 1.14 & 15.2 & 6.54 \\ 0.56 & -0.0 & 6.54 & 7.16 \end{pmatrix}.$$

Figure 8.3 shows the portfolio composition for the prior (reference) model (top) and the posterior model (bottom), incorporating the views. Obviously, for increasing degree of risk aversion α, the optimal proportion of Duke Energy after including the views is larger than before. All other shares are reduced roughly proportional.

8.4 Further Reading

For portfolio performance statistics see the classical papers of Sharpe (1966), Treynor (1966), and Jensen (1968). A gentle introduction to trading strategies based on performance indicators is Reghai (2015, chap. 9). For the *Kelly*-criterion consult the original paper of Kelly (1956), and also the very entertaining chapter "Investment Lessons from Blackjack and Gambling" in Wilmott (2006a, chap. 17). Regarding the incorporation of individual subjective views and optimal blending with a posterior distribution, there exists a vast literature beyond the original work of Black and Litterman (1992); see the papers by Qian and Gorman (2001), Almgren and Chriss (2006), Meucci (2006, 2009, 2010b), and the systematic literature survey therein.

8.5 Problems

8.1 The theoretical information ratio of a portfolio P is defined as

$$\text{IR}_P = \frac{E[R_P - R_{\text{MP}}]}{\sqrt{\text{Var}[R_P - R_{\text{MP}}]}},$$

where R_P is the portfolio return, and R_{MP} is the return on the market portfolio. Show that this ratio can never be larger than the theoretical *Sharpe*-ratio of the market portfolio, if the CAPM holds.

8.2 Assume that you can invest a fraction π of your wealth in a portfolio P that yields a risky return of R_P, and put the other fraction $1 - \pi$ in a bank account, paying the risk-free interest rate R_0. Assume that both expected returns, μ_P and r, are small of order $O(\varepsilon)$, and that terms of order $O(\varepsilon^2)$ can be neglected. What is the optimal *Kelly*-fraction π^* in this case?

8.3 In linear filtering theory, $|\eta\rangle = |v\rangle - P|\mu\rangle$ is called the innovation, and $\Gamma = P\Sigma P' + \Omega$ is the prediction error covariance. The quantity

$$K = \Sigma P' \Gamma^{-1}$$

is called the *Kalman*-filter gain, and the *Kalman*-filter posterior moments are

$$|\mu_{\mathrm{KF}}\rangle = |\mu\rangle + K|\eta\rangle \quad \text{and} \quad \Sigma_{\mathrm{KF}} = \Sigma - K\Gamma K'.$$

Show that this formulation is equivalent to the *Black–Litterman* posterior moments (8.24) and (8.25) on page 152.

8.4 Show that for $\Omega = 0$ and invertible P, the *Black–Litterman* posterior distribution collapses to

$$|\mu_{\mathrm{BL}}\rangle = P^{-1}|v\rangle \quad \text{and} \quad \Sigma_{\mathrm{BL}} = 0.$$

What does invertibility of P mean?

9 Financial Econcomics

In a nutshell, financial economics tries to explain how markets and prices of risky investments evolve. This is an exceedingly difficult task, because expected returns are usually orders of magnitude smaller than the volatility of the investment under consideration. Matters become even worse considering that a serious economic theory of financial returns should also explain the existence and the magnitude of a risk-free interest rate. Attempts to meet these requirements result in some of the most famous puzzles in economic theory, like the equity premium puzzle or the volatility puzzle.

9.1 The Rational Valuation Principle

An important concept in analyzing the evolution of the fair price S_t of a risky security is the fundamental value V_t. Let's focus on an ordinary stock for the moment. In this case, the fundamental value is determined by characteristics of the company like its size, market position, organization, financial structure, and others. The change in the fair price $S_{t+1} - S_t$ from period t to period $t + 1$ is due to immediate changes in the fundamental value $V_{t+1} - V_t$, but also due to dividend payments D_{t+1}. We used upper-case letters here, to emphasize that both the fundamental value, as well as the dividend payments generally are random variables.

The rational expectation hypothesis states that the best prediction of the future value of an arbitrary quantity is the expected value of that quantity, conditional on the present available information. Therefore, the best prediction for the total return R_{t+1} is given by the rational valuation formula (RVF; see Cuthbertson and Nitzsche, 2004, p. 245)

$$E[R_{t+1}|\mathcal{F}_t] = \frac{E[V_{t+1}|\mathcal{F}_t] - V_t + E[D_{t+1}|\mathcal{F}_t]}{V_t}. \tag{9.1}$$

Maybe the most naive assumption one can make is that investors require a fixed expected return $E[R_{t+1}|\mathcal{F}_t] = \mu$, to compensate them for the risk they take when investing in the security. Using this assumption in (9.1), one obtains after a few algebraic manipulations

$$V_t = \delta E[V_{t+1} + D_{t+1}|\mathcal{F}_t], \tag{9.2}$$

with the discounting factor $\delta = \frac{1}{1+\mu}$.

Quick calculation 9.1 Verify Equation (9.2).

To determine what V_t is, let's iterate (9.2) one period into the future

$$V_{t+1} = \delta E[V_{t+2} + D_{t+2}|\mathcal{F}_{t+1}]. \tag{9.3}$$

By the law of iterated expectations, we have

$$E[V_{t+1}|\mathcal{F}_t] = E\left[\delta E[V_{t+2} + D_{t+2}|\mathcal{F}_{t+1}]\big|\mathcal{F}_t\right]$$
$$= \delta E[V_{t+2} + D_{t+2}|\mathcal{F}_t]. \tag{9.4}$$

That is, the best prediction of tomorrow's prediction is today's prediction of the respective value. Plugging (9.4) into (9.2), one obtains

$$V_t = \delta E[D_{t+1} + \delta(D_{t+2} + V_{t+2})|\mathcal{F}_t] \tag{9.5}$$

where we have rearranged the Ds and Vs. The δs can go in or outside the expectation because they are just numbers. We can apply the same argument $T - 1$ times to obtain

$$V_t = \sum_{k=1}^{T} \delta^k E[D_{t+k}|\mathcal{F}_t] + \delta^T E[V_{t+T}|\mathcal{F}_t]. \tag{9.6}$$

Quick calculation 9.2 Convince yourself that the last argument is indeed true.

Another assumption usually made at this point is that the so-called transversality condition is satisfied. It states that the fundamental value remains finite for all times. If this is true, and we let $T \to \infty$, then the last term on the right hand side of (9.6) vanishes, and we obtain for the fundamental value at time t

$$V_t = \sum_{k=1}^{\infty} \delta^k E[D_{t+k}|\mathcal{F}_t]. \tag{9.7}$$

If the price of the stock S_t at time t deviates from the fundamental value V_t, then an investor can take the opposite position to participate in the difference of future income streams and make a profit. Thus, in equilibrium we must have $S_t = V_t$ or

$$S_t = \sum_{k=1}^{\infty} \delta^k E[D_{t+k}|\mathcal{F}_t], \tag{9.8}$$

respectively. The rational valuation formula (9.8) is of little practical use, because we have not specified a stochastic process for D_t yet. So at this point we can conclude nothing more than that the observed stock price should represent a series of discounted future cash flows.

Now let's make a simple educated guess: Assume that the management wants the dividend stream to be as smooth as possible, in order to avoid unnecessary fluctuations in the stock price. Of course this is not always possible, therefore we assume that the dividend process follows a simple random walk

$$D_t = D_{t-1} + \epsilon_t, \tag{9.9}$$

where ϵ_t is a zero expectation random error with variance σ_ϵ^2. This means $E[D_{t+k}|\mathcal{F}_t] = D_t$ for all $k \geq 0$. Using this relation in (9.8) yields the RVF for constant expected dividends

$$S_t = \sum_{k=1}^{\infty} \delta^k D_t = \frac{\delta}{1-\delta} D_t = \frac{D_t}{\mu}. \tag{9.10}$$

Quick calculation 9.3   Verify the last equality in (9.10).

In actuarial science (9.10) is called a perpetuity. You might wonder how the second equality was established. The sum in (9.10) is called an infinite geometric series. Let's first try to calculate a finite version of it. As strange as it might sound, the worst thing you can try in calculating such a series, is to add it up term by term. Let's instead multiply with $\delta^{-1} - 1$

$$(\delta^{-1} - 1) \sum_{k=1}^{K} \delta^k = 1 + \delta + \delta^2 + \cdots + \delta^{K-1}$$
$$\qquad\qquad -\delta - \delta^2 - \cdots - \delta^{K-1} - \delta^K \tag{9.11}$$
$$= 1 - \delta^K.$$

You see how nicely the terms cancel? Dividing both sides by $\delta^{-1} - 1$, we get

$$\sum_{k=1}^{K} \delta^k = \frac{1 - \delta^K}{\delta^{-1} - 1} = \delta \frac{1 - \delta^K}{1 - \delta}, \tag{9.12}$$

and we are nearly done. Remember that $\delta = \frac{1}{1+\mu} < 1$, as long as $\mu > 0$. That is not much of an assumption, because if the expected return on the stock was negative, we would keep our money. Thus, in the limit $K \to \infty$, δ^K tends towards zero, and we get

$$\sum_{k=1}^{\infty} \delta^k = \lim_{K \to \infty} \sum_{k=1}^{K} \delta^k = \frac{\delta}{1 - \delta}. \tag{9.13}$$

There are two interesting consequences of (9.10). The first is that the dividend–price ratio

$$\frac{D_t}{S_t} = \mu \tag{9.14}$$

is constant and equal to the required expected return the investor needs to compensate the risk. The second is that in order for this ratio to remain valid, a 1% change in dividends has to be matched exactly by a 1% change in the stock price in the same direction. In other words, dividends and stock prices have to have exactly the same volatility. We can obviously not expect this to be true, which means we expect μ not really to be a constant. In reality, dividends and stock prices move roughly proportional to each other at best over extended periods of time. In the short and medium term, stock prices are far more volatile than dividends. In fact, they seem to be excessively volatile as pointed out by Shiller (1981).

Another thought might occur to you; stock prices are usually assumed to exhibit an exponential growth. If (9.14) is approximately true in the long term, doesn't that mean that dividends should grow, too? This is exactly the case and pursuing this avenue leads us to Gordon's growth model (Gordon, 1959). Assume that dividends follow an AR(1)-process

$$D_t = (1 + g)D_{t-1} + \epsilon_t, \tag{9.15}$$

where g is the dividend growth rate, and ϵ_t is again a zero mean random error, as in (9.9). Even though g is also introduced as a deterministic and constant parameter, we expect this property not to hold exactly in reality. Calculating the conditional expectation of the dividend now yields

$$E[D_{t+k}|\mathcal{F}_t] = (1 + g)^k D_t, \tag{9.16}$$

for all $k \geq 0$. Using this equation in the rational valuation formula (9.8), yields the RVF for a constant growth rate of dividends

$$S_t = \sum_{k=1}^{\infty} \delta^k (1 + g)^k D_t = \frac{1 + g}{\mu - g} D_t, \tag{9.17}$$

as long as $\mu > g$.

Quick calculation 9.4 Verify the last equality in (9.17).

The condition $\mu > g$ is a necessary requirement for the infinite geometric series in (9.17) to converge, but it is otherwise quite ad hoc.

Quick calculation 9.5 Can you see why this condition is necessary?

Nevertheless, empirical findings indicate that the dividend growth rate is on average indeed much smaller than the growth rate of stock prices.

To see how this can help explain the excessive stock price volatility, let's look at an example.

Example 9.1

Assume that the required expected return is $\mu = 5\%$ and the growth rate of dividends is estimated by the investors to be $g = 3\%$. Now think of bad news about the company coming in, and investors reducing their dividend growth estimation to $g = 2\%$. What happens to the RVF-price of the stock?

Solution

Before the bad news, investors calculated the RVF-price for one stock of the company as

$$S_t = \frac{103\%}{2\%} D_t = 51.5 D_t.$$

After the revision of the dividend growth estimation, the new price calculated by the investors is

$$S_t = \frac{102\%}{3\%} D_t = 34 D_t.$$

Dividing the latter by the former, we see that the stock price has dropped by roughly 34%. This is a considerable amount of extra volatility.

We will return to volatility issues later, but first study another phenomenon observed in stock markets, which is held responsible for occasional market crashes.

9.2   Stock Price Bubbles

You may have listened every now and then to financial economists discussing whether a bubble is currently driving the market or not. More puzzling, if you did not manage to switch to another program in time, you may have witnessed the further discussion of whether or not such a bubble can be detected. This may surprise you, because we have established a theory that connects the rational stock price to the expected dividend stream, which is estimated in a unique way, based on the present available information. There seems to be no way for another phantom process to enter the calculation. Assume for a moment that such a process might exist, or formally

$$S_t = V_t + B_t, \tag{9.18}$$

where $B_t > 0$ (almost surely) is the mysterious bubble contribution, and ask: Can such a process remain undetected? From (9.2) we know that

$$V_t = \delta E[V_{t+1} + D_{t+1} | \mathcal{F}_t]. \tag{9.19}$$

Leading (9.18) one period into the future and plugging into (9.19), one obtains

$$V_t = \delta E[S_{t+1} - B_{t+1} + D_{t+1} | \mathcal{F}_t]. \tag{9.20}$$

Using this result back in (9.18) we get the most illuminating answer

$$S_t = \delta E[S_{t+1} + D_{t+1} | \mathcal{F}_t] + B_t - \delta E[B_{t+1} | \mathcal{F}_t]. \tag{9.21}$$

Imagine now the bubble term is a discounted martingale

$$B_t = \delta^k E[B_{t+k} | \mathcal{F}_t], \tag{9.22}$$

for $k \geq 0$, then only the first term on the right hand side of (9.21) would survive

$$S_t = \delta E[S_{t+1} + D_{t+1}|\mathcal{F}_t].$$ (9.23)

Under rational valuation, you could not distinguish the process S_t from the process V_t and thus you would not be able to tell, if there is a bubble present or not, at least at the beginning. In order for the martingale property (9.22) to hold, the bubble has to have dynamics of the form

$$B_t = (1 + \mu)B_{t-1} + \epsilon_t,$$ (9.24)

where ϵ_t is again a zero mean random error. In the limit $t \to \infty$, B_t tends to infinity with probability one, and because the stock price is the sum of the fundamental value and the bubble, S_t also tends to infinity, thereby violating the transversality condition. An easy way to see this is to assume that dividends follow a random walk, which means they have no growth rate. If at time t a bubble B_t is present, then the expected stock price at a later time $t + k$ is

$$E[S_{t+k}|\mathcal{F}_t] = \frac{D_t}{\mu} + (1 + \mu)^k B_t.$$ (9.25)

That means that the bubble becomes an increasing part of the stock price. Even if there is a positive growth rate of dividends, it is easy to see that the bubble grows faster, because the growth of the fundamental value is connected to expected dividend growth g, whereas the bubble grows with the full expected rate of return $\mu > g$.

Quick calculation 9.6 Use (9.15) and (9.17) to establish this argument formally.

Observe that the occurrence of the bubble in (9.18), even though its persistence under the rational valuation principle can be justified, is not explained by the theory. That is why Cuthbertson and Nitzsche (2004, p. 404) call such a bubble a "deus ex machina."

Furthermore, (9.25) makes clear that over an extended period of time, the price of the stock has to deviate significantly from its fundamental value. You would expect that at some point investors become suspicious, even if they cannot calculate the true fundamental value, because they do not know the dividend driving process with certainty. If this is the case, the bubble specification (9.22) is incomplete, because it does not allow for the bubble to burst. This can be remedied by defining the following bubble process (Blanchard, 1979)

$$B_t = \begin{cases} \frac{1+\mu}{\pi} B_{t-1} & \text{with probability } \pi \\ 0 & \text{with probability } 1 - \pi. \end{cases}$$ (9.26)

Quick calculation 9.7 Verify that this process satisfies the martingale condition (9.22).

There is still no explanation for the formation of a bubble, but at least it can burst now. If we link intuitively the burst probability $1 - \pi$ to the deviation of the stock price from the estimated fundamental value, we can conclude that the bubble will burst eventually, before the stock price grows to infinity. But if we know that the bubble will burst in the future, how is it that it does not burst immediately? After all, the stock price reflects the discounted value of future payments. Obviously, the investment horizon of most agents is short enough to assume that the bubble does not burst until they sell the stock again, so that the bubble really adds value in form of intertemporal price differences.

The bubbles we have analyzed so far are completely exogenous. The problem with that is that we cannot get a handle on a creation mechanism. Froot and Obstfeld (1991) suggested another type of bubble, an intrinsic bubble, immediately linked to the dividend driving process by

$$B_t = cD_t^\lambda. \tag{9.27}$$

The authors do not model the dividend driving process directly, but its logarithm. This is a smart thing to do, because the dividend process is guaranteed to stay nonnegative this way. In the following, the original notation of Froot and Obstfeld (1991) is slightly modified, in order to keep alignment with the formal framework established so far. Assume, the dividend process is of the form

$$\log D_t = \log D_{t-1} + g + \epsilon_t, \tag{9.28}$$

with $\epsilon_t \sim N(0, \sigma_\epsilon^2)$. Of course again, log is the natural logarithm with respect to the basis e. Exponentiating both sides of (9.28) indicates that

$$D_t = D_{t-1}e^{g+\epsilon_t} \tag{9.29}$$

holds. This means, the fluctuations introduced by the random error ϵ_t are not absolute in magnitude, but relatively scaled by the size of D_{t-1}. That seems to be a good thing too, because fluctuations can now be specified relatively as a percentage of the respective quantity. The random variable e^{ϵ_t} is logarithmic normally distributed.

We will often refer to the expectation of a log-normal distributed random variable, so let's discuss that issue a little bit. First of all observe that for an arbitrary random variable $X \sim N(\mu, \sigma^2)$, the following relation always holds

$$E[e^X] = E[e^{\mu+Y}] = e^\mu E[e^Y], \tag{9.30}$$

with $Y \sim N(0, \sigma^2)$. Obviously, we only have to address the case of zero mean random variables, because the mean itself multiplies out of the expectation somehow. Next, *Taylor*-expand e^Y to obtain the series representation

$$E[e^Y] = \sum_{k=0}^\infty \frac{E[Y^k]}{k!}. \tag{9.31}$$

Now remember that there is a recursive relation between the moments of a normally distributed random variable, (2.31) on page 19, which states that all odd moments vanish, and all even moments of order k are $(k-1)!!\sigma^k$. Using this relation in (9.31) the sum can be written as

$$E[e^Y] = \sum_{n=0}^\infty \frac{(2n-1)!!}{(2n)!}\sigma^{2n}, \tag{9.32}$$

with $k = 2n$. Observe that the factorial term in (9.32) can be reexpressed as

$$\frac{(2n-1)!!}{(2n)!} = \frac{1}{(2n)!!} = \frac{1}{2^n n!}. \tag{9.33}$$

Quick calculation 9.8 Confirm the factorial relations established above.

Thus, we finally obtain the desired expectation value

$$E[e^Y] = \sum_{n=0}^{\infty} \frac{1}{n!} \left(\frac{\sigma^2}{2}\right)^n = e^{\frac{\sigma^2}{2}}. \tag{9.34}$$

Quick calculation 9.9 What is the expectation value of e^X?

Returning to the bubble specification (9.27), Froot and Obstfeld (1991) chose the parameter λ to be the positive root of the equation

$$\lambda^2 \frac{\sigma_\epsilon^2}{2} + \lambda g + \log \delta = 0, \tag{9.35}$$

whereas c is a completely free parameter. This choice of λ ensures that the martingale condition (9.22) is satisfied. In detail, we have

$$\begin{aligned} \delta E[B_{t+1}|\mathcal{F}_t] &= \delta E[cD_{t+1}^\lambda|\mathcal{F}_t] \\ &= \delta E[cD_t^\lambda e^{\lambda g + \lambda \epsilon_{t+1}}|\mathcal{F}_t] \\ &= \delta B_t e^{\lambda g + \lambda^2 \frac{\sigma_\epsilon^2}{2}} \\ &= B_t, \end{aligned} \tag{9.36}$$

where we have used (9.35) in the last step.

Quick calculation 9.10 Can you see why $E[e^{\lambda \epsilon_{t+1}}|\mathcal{F}_t] = e^{\lambda^2 \frac{\sigma_\epsilon^2}{2}}$ in (9.36)?

Putting all the pieces together, the rational valuation formula, including an intrinsic bubble is

$$S_t = V_t + B_t = \kappa D_t + cD_t^\lambda, \tag{9.37}$$

with

$$\kappa = \frac{e^{g + \frac{\sigma_\epsilon^2}{2}}}{1 + \mu - e^{g + \frac{\sigma_\epsilon^2}{2}}} \approx \frac{1 + g + \frac{\sigma_\epsilon^2}{2}}{\mu - g - \frac{\sigma_\epsilon^2}{2}}. \tag{9.38}$$

To see this, remember that the fundamental value of the stock, provided the transversality condition holds, is

$$V_t = \sum_{k=1}^{\infty} \delta^k E[D_{t+k}|\mathcal{F}_t] = \sum_{k=1}^{\infty} \delta^k e^{k\left(g + \frac{\sigma_\epsilon^2}{2}\right)} D_t, \tag{9.39}$$

and apply the result for the geometric series.

Quick calculation 9.11 Convince yourself that the result (9.38) is correct.

The approximation in (9.38) holds for small μ, g, and σ_ϵ^2, and reveals a close connection to Gordon's growth model. For $\sigma_\epsilon^2 = 0$, we obtain the already known result. Observe that the parameter c is completely free. If we think of it informally as a quantity that may change over time, in particular from zero to a positive value, we at least have a clue of how a bubble creation mechanism might work.

9.3 Shiller's Volatility Puzzle

By the time Shiller presented his ingenious argument, econometric indications of stock price excess volatility had already been discussed by LeRoy and Porter (1981). What he actually recognized is that there is a way to calculate a perfect foresight price process and subsequently compare this one with the price process under rational expectation. How does such a thing work? Assume you know the stock price at any terminal date T and you have data on dividends over an extended period of time $t = 1, \ldots, T$. Then, according to the rational valuation formula (RVF), the stock price calculated at time t is

$$S_t = \sum_{k=1}^{T-t} \delta^k E[D_{t+k}|\mathcal{F}_t] + \delta^{T-t} E[S_T|\mathcal{F}_t]. \tag{9.40}$$

But because we know the dividends since period $t = 1$ and the terminal stock price, we can calculate the price S_t^* an agent would have computed at any time $t = 0, \ldots, T$, if she had perfect foresight of the future payments

$$S_t^* = \sum_{k=1}^{T-t} \delta^k D_{t+k} + \delta^{T-t} S_T. \tag{9.41}$$

Neglecting the most of the time heavily discounted differences $S_T - E[S_T|\mathcal{F}_t]$, we can write the residual error between the perfect foresight price and the RVF-price as

$$S_t^* - S_t = \sum_{k=1}^{T-t} \delta^k \nu_{t+k}, \tag{9.42}$$

where $\nu_{t+k} = D_{t+k} - E[D_{t+k}|\mathcal{F}_t]$ is the innovation of the dividend process. The problem with this expression is that S_t is usually not a stationary process and thus, moments like the expectation value for example depend on time.

What Shiller (1981) essentially did to fix this problem was to introduce a particular numéraire (detrending factor) that makes the dividend process a martingale. In Gordon's growth model, the dividend process is given by

$$D_t = (1 + g)D_{t-1} + \epsilon_t. \tag{9.43}$$

Shiller defined a new detrended process

$$P_t = \sum_{k=1}^{T-t} \delta^k E\left[\frac{D_{t+k}}{(1 + g)^{t+k-T}}\middle|\mathcal{F}_t\right] + \delta^{T-t} E[P_T|\mathcal{F}_t], \qquad (9.44)$$

where $P_T = S_T$, because the appropriate numéraire to detrend a time T quantity is one. Under the dynamics (9.43), we immediately conclude that the detrended dividend process is a martingale

$$\frac{D_t}{(1 + g)^{t-T}} = E\left[\frac{D_{t+k}}{(1 + g)^{t+k-T}}\middle|\mathcal{F}_t\right]. \qquad (9.45)$$

Quick calculation 9.12 Convince yourself that the last statement is true.

To see that P_t is indeed a process with approximately time independent mean, let the terminal date T grow large compared to the current time t. Then, first of all, we can neglect the last term on the right hand side of (9.44), because of heavy discounting. Next, we can treat the geometric series as an approximately infinite series and use the martingale condition (9.45) to obtain

$$P_t \approx (1 + g)^{T-t} D_t \cdot \frac{\delta}{1 - \delta} = \frac{E[D_T|\mathcal{F}_t]}{\mu}. \qquad (9.46)$$

Using the law of iterated expectations, we obtain

$$E[P_t] \approx \frac{E[D_T]}{\mu}, \qquad (9.47)$$

which is a constant for every t.

In complete analogy, Shiller defined the detrended perfect foresight price process P_t^*, and after subtracting one process from the other, one obtains

$$P_t^* - P_t = \sum_{k=1}^{T-t} \delta^k \omega_{t+k} = \eta_t, \qquad (9.48)$$

where

$$\omega_{t+k} = \frac{D_{t+k}}{(1 + g)^{t+k-T}} - E\left[\frac{D_{t+k}}{(1 + g)^{t+k-T}}\middle|\mathcal{F}_t\right] \qquad (9.49)$$

is the innovation of the detrended dividend process. The zero mean random errors ϵ_t in the dividend process (9.43) were assumed independent of D_t. Thus, the random error η_t, despite a possibly complicated structure, is still an independent innovation. Rearranging (9.48) and taking variances yields

$$\text{Var}[P_t^*] = \text{Var}[P_t] + \text{Var}[\eta_t], \qquad (9.50)$$

from which we can conclude that $\text{Var}[P_t^*] > \text{Var}[P_t]$ has to hold. Figure 9.1 is a reproduction of Shiller's famous illustration, published in 1981 in *The American Economic Review*. He analyzed data for the Standard & Poor's and for the Dow Jones index over

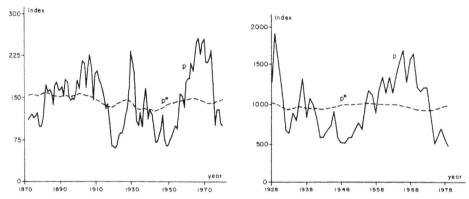

Fig. 9.1 Detrended processes for Standard & Poor's Composite Stock Price Index (left) and Dow Jones Industrial Average (right) – Figures are reproduced from (Shiller, 1981) with permission of the American Economic Association

an extended period of time. Dividends were assigned according to the weight contribution of the corresponding stocks, contained in the respective index. It is immediately evident that the RVF-process P_t is far more volatile than the perfect foresight price process P_t^*. It seems that our analysis finally leads to a dead end.

9.4   Stochastic Discount Factor Models

To understand stochastic discount factor (SDF) models, we have to go back to our discussion of utility functionals and state prices in Chapter 5. We found that a rational agent values consumption in a random future state of the world ω with the marginal rate of substitution (MRS) compared to the present consumption level

$$\psi_\omega = \frac{\partial U/\partial c_\omega}{\partial U/\partial c_0} = -\text{MRS}. \tag{9.51}$$

The state price ψ_ω reflects how much present consumption has to be sacrificed in order to extend the consumption in state ω by one unit, while keeping the overall utility level constant. Most of the time, a time separable *von Neumann–Morgenstern*-utility functional is chosen

$$U[C_t] = u(c_0) + e^{-\rho t} \sum_{\omega=1}^{\Omega} u(c_{t,\omega}) p_\omega, \tag{9.52}$$

where ρ governs the tendency for intertemporal substitution. For large ρ, the agent is very impatient and discounts future utility very heavily. Clearly, for a time separable utility functional of the type (9.52), one obtains the state price

$$\psi_\omega = e^{-\rho t} \frac{u'(c_{t,\omega})}{u'(c_0)} p_\omega, \tag{9.53}$$

where the prime indicates the derivative of the utility function $u(c)$ with respect to its argument, and p_ω is the probability for state ω to occur. Because for simplicity we consider only two periods, all expectations are with respect to the information $\mathcal{F}_0$, and thus we can omit the conditioning argument.

A risky security S is a device to shift consumption from one period to another. If we assume that changes in the fundamental value and dividend payments are incorporated in the price of the security at all times, the fair price from today's perspective should equal

$$S_0 = \langle \psi | S_t \rangle = \sum_{\omega=1}^{\Omega} e^{-\rho t} \frac{u'(c_{t,\omega})}{u'(c_0)} S_{t,\omega} p_\omega = E \left[e^{-\rho t} \frac{u'(C_t)}{u'(c_0)} S_t \right]. \tag{9.54}$$

To simplify matters, define a new random variable

$$M_t = e^{-\rho t} \frac{u'(C_t)}{u'(c_0)}, \tag{9.55}$$

called the stochastic discount factor. Note that M_t is random, because the future consumption C_t is not known initially. Thus, (9.54) simplifies to

$$S_0 = E[M_t S_t]. \tag{9.56}$$

We cannot say much about M_t yet, because we have not specified a particular utility function $u(c)$. But let's see if we can derive some general consequences of the SDF-principle.

First of all, define the gross return of the risky security over the period t as

$$R_S^* = \frac{S_t}{S_0} = 1 + R_S, \tag{9.57}$$

and divide both sides of (9.56) by S_0 to obtain

$$1 = E[M_t R_S^*]. \tag{9.58}$$

Now observe that the stochastic discount factor is the same random variable for all securities, because it is a function of time t consumption only. That means, we can plug every gross return into (9.58) and it nevertheless has to be true. Let's do the exercise with the continuous risk-free gross return $R_0^* = e^{rt}$,

$$1 = E[M_t R_0^*] = E[M_t] e^{rt}. \tag{9.59}$$

Simply rearranging this expression yields an economic explanation of the risk-free discounting factor

$$\frac{1}{R_0^*} = e^{-rt} = E[M_t]. \tag{9.60}$$

That looks like tremendous progress, and it is getting even better. Subtract (9.60) from (9.58) to obtain

$$1 - \frac{1}{R_0^*} = E[M_t(R_S^* - 1)] = E[M_t R_S]. \tag{9.61}$$

Quick calculation 9.13   Verify the last equation.

Now remember from elementary statistics, that the covariance of two random variables X and Y can be written as $\mathrm{Cov}[X, Y] = E[XY] - E[X]E[Y]$. Applying this trick to the right hand side of (9.61) yields

$$1 - \frac{1}{R_0^*} = \mathrm{Cov}[M_t, R_S] + E[M_t]E[R_S]. \tag{9.62}$$

Multiplying both sides by R_0^* and rearranging yields

$$E[R_S] = R_0 - \frac{\mathrm{Cov}[M_t, R_S]}{E[M_t]}. \tag{9.63}$$

Quick calculation 9.14   Confirm that (9.63) is indeed true.

The second term on the right hand side of (9.63) is the risk premium. Don't get fooled by the minus sign. The stochastic discount factor involves marginal utility; see the definition (9.55). If an agent is risk averse, marginal utility decreases with increasing consumption levels. A positive return of security S means additional time t consumption, and thus less marginal utility. Or in other words, we should expect the covariance between M_t and R_S to be negative. The expectation of M_t on the other hand is most certainly positive, because it was already identified as the risk-free discounting factor. The upshot is that the risk premium for an ordinary security is positive, which means we are entitled to expect a higher return than the risk-free rate when investing in a stock. Are there other securities, paying high returns in states with high marginal utility and an expected return below the risk-free rate? Yes there are, but we are used to calling them insurance contracts.

Let's finally see, how the stochastic discount factor framework fits into the rational valuation principle. Define the gross return of the fundamental value of an arbitrary stock as

$$R_{t+1}^* = \frac{V_{t+1} + D_{t+1}}{V_t}. \tag{9.64}$$

Using the conditional relation $E[M_{t+1} R_{t+1}^* | \mathcal{F}_t] = 1$, we can write the time t value as

$$V_t = E[M_{t+1}(V_{t+1} + D_{t+1}) | \mathcal{F}_t]. \tag{9.65}$$

As before, we assume the transversality condition to hold, and iterate (9.65) into the future to obtain

$$V_t = \sum_{k=1}^{\infty} E\left[\prod_{n=1}^{k} M_{t+n} D_{t+k} \middle| \mathcal{F}_t\right]. \tag{9.66}$$

Quick calculation 9.15 Iterate (9.65) one period to confirm the construction.

Finally applying our covariance trick, and recalling that under rational valuation the fundamental value has to equal the price of the stock, we obtain

$$S_t = \sum_{k=1}^{\infty} E\left[\prod_{n=1}^{k} M_{t+n} \middle| \mathcal{F}_t\right] E[D_{t+k}|\mathcal{F}_t] + \sum_{k=1}^{\infty} \text{Cov}\left[\prod_{n=1}^{k} M_{t+n}, D_{t+k} \middle| \mathcal{F}_t\right]. \tag{9.67}$$

Quick calculation 9.16 Convince yourself that (9.67) simplifies exactly to the original RVF (9.8) on page 157, when the stochastic discount factor is deterministic, $M_t = \delta$.

9.5   C-CAPM and *Hansen–Jagannathan*-Bounds

The consumption-based capital asset pricing model (C-CAPM) comes in many guises and is strongly related to the CAPM, if we assume that agents use the market portfolio to shift consumption between periods. Let's take Equation (9.63) and remember that the stochastic discount factor is defined by

$$M_t = e^{-\rho t} \frac{u'(C_t)}{u'(c_0)}. \tag{9.68}$$

We then obtain the consumption-based CAPM equation

$$E[R_S] = R_0 - \frac{\text{Cov}[M_t, R_S]}{E[M_t]} = R_0 - \frac{\text{Cov}[u'(C_t), R_S]}{E[u'(C_t)]}. \tag{9.69}$$

It is now immediately obvious why (9.69) is called the C-CAPM, because it relates the return on the stock S to the marginal utility of consumption at time t. What is its connection to the original CAPM? To get a handle on this, let's first ask what we get for the market portfolio. Replacing R_S by R_{MP} in (9.69) and rearranging yields

$$E[u'(C_t)] = -\frac{\text{Cov}[u'(C_t), R_{\text{MP}}]}{E[R_{\text{MP}}] - R_0}. \tag{9.70}$$

Using (9.70) back in (9.69), we obtain the already more familiar form

$$E[R_S] = R_0 + \frac{\text{Cov}[u'(C_t), R_S]}{\text{Cov}[u'(C_t), R_{\text{MP}}]} (E[R_{\text{MP}}] - R_0). \tag{9.71}$$

We now have to ask, what is the relation of marginal utility and the return of the market portfolio? There is more than one way to obtain a suitable answer (see Cuthbertson and Nitzsche, 2004, sect. 13.2, for four different ways). We will take the short tour here. Let's assume that the unknown utility function $u(c)$ can be sufficiently approximated by the quadratic utility function

$$u(c) = -\frac{(\eta - c)^2}{2}. \tag{9.72}$$

Now remember that the agent has to divide her initial wealth endowment w between time zero consumption c_0 and the proportion invested in the market portfolio, making uncertain time t consumption available, measured in c_0-units. Her budget constraint is thus

$$C_t = (w - c_0)(1 + R_{MP}). \tag{9.73}$$

Calculating marginal utility of the time t consumption C_t under quadratic utility yields

$$u'(C_t) = \eta - C_t = \eta - (w - c_0) - (w - c_0)R_{MP} = a - bR_{MP}, \tag{9.74}$$

with $a = \eta - b$, and $b = w - c_0$. The important point is that the return on the market portfolio is an affine transformation of the marginal utility of consumption. Computing the covariances in (9.71) yields

$$\begin{aligned} \mathrm{Cov}[u'(C_t), R_S] &= -b\,\mathrm{Cov}[R_{MP}, R_S], \\ \mathrm{Cov}[u'(C_t), R_{MP}] &= -b\mathrm{Var}[R_{MP}]. \end{aligned} \tag{9.75}$$

Remember that the quotient of the two covariances in (9.75) is exactly the definition of the beta-coefficient β_S in the original CAPM. We have thus from (9.71)

$$E[R_S] = R_0 + \beta_S(E[R_{MP}] - R_0), \tag{9.76}$$

which is the capital asset pricing model.

We can even examine the relation of marginal utility and the market portfolio a little bit further. Remember that the correlation coefficient between two arbitrary random variables X and Y is defined as

$$\rho = \frac{\mathrm{Cov}[X, Y]}{\sqrt{\mathrm{Var}[X]\mathrm{Var}[Y]}}. \tag{9.77}$$

Correlation is a normalized measure of linear dependence of random variables. So let's calculate the correlation between marginal utility $u'(C_t)$ and the market portfolio return R_{MP},

$$\rho = -\frac{b\mathrm{Var}[R_{MP}]}{\sqrt{b^2\mathrm{Var}[R_{MP}]\mathrm{Var}[R_{MP}]}} = -1. \tag{9.78}$$

Quick calculation 9.17 Confirm the first equality.

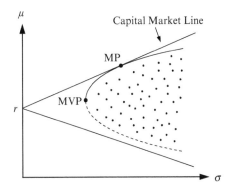

Fig. 9.2 *Hansen–Jagannathan*-bounds in the μ-σ-diagram – Upper leg is the capital market line

Returns on the market portfolio are perfectly negative correlated with marginal utility. Negative correlation was of course to be expected because higher returns coincide with states of higher consumption and thus lower marginal utility of consumption, if the agent is risk averse. The perfect correlation is due to the affine relation of marginal utility and market portfolio returns, because the dependence structure is fully linear.

Quick calculation 9.18 Show that for $X = a + bY$ the correlation of X and Y is $\rho = 1$.

The work of Hansen and Jagannathan (1991) revealed another close connection between the C-CAPM and the original CAPM. This one is particularly important, because it ultimately implies certain empirical predictions. The basic idea is actually straightforward. Rewriting the definition of the correlation coefficient (9.77) in a slightly different way yields

$$\text{Cov}[X, Y] = \rho \sqrt{\text{Var}[X]} \sqrt{\text{Var}[Y]}. \tag{9.79}$$

Using this relation, we can write the C-CAPM equation (9.69) in the following form

$$\frac{E[R_S] - R_0}{\sqrt{\text{Var}[R_S]}} = -\rho \frac{\sqrt{\text{Var}[M_t]}}{E[M_t]}. \tag{9.80}$$

Note that the correlation coefficient is by definition $|\rho| \leq 1$. Therefore, we can formulate an inequality, which is valid for every security S, and in alignment with our earlier notation reads

$$\left| \frac{\mu_S - r}{\sigma_S} \right| \leq \frac{\text{StD}[M_t]}{E[M_t]}, \tag{9.81}$$

where again the standard deviation $\text{StD}[\cdot]$ is the positive root of the variance. Figure 9.2 shows the *Hansen–Jagannathan*-bounds in the μ-σ-diagram. The upper leg is the mean-variance efficient frontier for risky assets (capital market line, CML), whereas the lower leg represents insurance contracts that are perfectly correlated with the stochastic discount factor. For the market portfolio, which is perfectly negative correlated with marginal consumption, and therefore with the stochastic discount factor, we obtain an upper theoretical limit for the *Sharpe*-ratio

$$\text{SR}_{\text{MP}} = \frac{\mu_{\text{MP}} - r}{\sigma_{\text{MP}}} = \frac{\text{StD}[M_t]}{E[M_t]},$$

(9.82)

to be observed in reality, if the respective SDF model is correct.

Quick calculation 9.19 Why are all returns on the CML perfectly negative correlated with the SDF?

9.6   The Equity Premium Puzzle

The equity premium puzzle of Mehra and Prescott (1985) is probably the most prominent puzzle in modern economics. Today it is really understood to consist of two parts, the equity premium puzzle and the risk-free rate puzzle. Each part of the puzzle generates empirical predictions, irreconcilable with the other part. In order to make empirical predictions, we have to specify the stochastic discount factor concretely. Here are the assumptions originally made by Mehra and Prescott:

- Agents have utility functions of the HARA-type, in particular

$$u(c) = \frac{c^{1-\gamma} - 1}{1 - \gamma},$$

  with relative risk aversion $\gamma \geq 0$.
- Agents maximize their lifetime utility successively, according to a time separable *von Neumann–Morgenstern*-utility functional

$$U[C_{t+1}] = u(C_t) + e^{-\rho} E[u(C_{t+1})|\mathcal{F}_t],$$

  depending solely on the consumption stream C_t for $t \in \mathbb{N}_0$.
- Markets are complete.
- There are no frictions like trading costs, etc.

Of course the last two assumptions imply the existence of a representative agent (Constantinides, 1982). The first thing to do is to formulate a model for the historically observed consumption stream. One particularly useful model is the AR(1)-process for the logarithmic consumption

$$c_t = c_{t-1} + g + \epsilon_t,$$

(9.83)

where we followed the widely accepted convention in economics to represent the natural logarithm of a random variable by its lowercase letter. In (9.83), g is the growth rate of the consumption process and $\epsilon_t \sim N(0, \sigma_\epsilon^2)$. It will come in handy to write the consumption growth model in a slightly different form,

$$\Delta c_t = g + \epsilon_t, \tag{9.84}$$

where $\Delta c_t = c_t - c_{t-1}$. Note that (9.84) is a pure noise process, because ϵ_t is not related to the history of the consumption process. Using hyperbolic risk aversion, as assumed by Mehra and Prescott (1985), we can now specify the SDF in a very concrete form

$$M_t = e^{-\rho}\left(\frac{C_t}{C_{t-1}}\right)^{-\gamma} = e^{-\rho - \gamma \Delta c_t}. \tag{9.85}$$

Before we proceed, let's summarize briefly the empirical findings of Mehra and Prescott. Without going into too much detail, they used various time series to calculate inflation adjusted annual returns for the Standard & Poor's Composite Stock Price Index (S&P 500), per capita real consumption growth on non-durable commodities and services and an annual risk-free interest rate proxy from relatively riskless short-term securities like US Treasury bills, in the period of 1889 to 1978. According to this data, the S&P 500 realized an annual average growth rate of $\hat{\mu}_{S\&P} = 6.98\%$, with a standard deviation of $\hat{\sigma}_{S\&P} = 16.54\%$. The average risk-free interest rate was $r = 0.8\%$ p.a. and thus, the average equity premium was $\hat{\mu}_{S\&P} - r = 6.18\%$. Consumption growth rate and standard deviation of the random error in (9.84) were estimated as $\hat{g} = 1.83\%$ and $\hat{\sigma}_\epsilon = 3.57\%$. What do these figures tell us about the agent's risk aversion? First of all, the average *Sharpe*-ratio of the S&P 500 is roughly 37.36%. We can also assume that the Standard & Poor's index is a good proxy for the market portfolio and thus it should be perfectly negative correlated with the SDF. We have thus by (9.82)

$$SR_{S\&P} = 37.36\% = \frac{StD[M_t]}{E[M_t]}. \tag{9.86}$$

In order to complete our calculations we need another standard result from statistics. Consider again the log-normal distributed random variable $Y = e^X$, with $X \sim N(\mu, \sigma^2)$. We already used that $E[Y] = e^{\mu + \frac{1}{2}\sigma^2}$. The variance of Y is given by

$$Var[Y] = (e^{\sigma^2} - 1)e^{2\mu + \sigma^2}. \tag{9.87}$$

Now consider the ratio between the variance and the squared expectation value of such a random variable

$$\frac{Var[Y]}{E[Y]^2} = e^{\sigma^2} - 1 \approx \sigma^2, \tag{9.88}$$

for small variances. The ratio of standard deviation and expectation value is the positive root of (9.88).

According to (9.88), the right hand side of (9.86) is approximately $\gamma \sigma_\epsilon$, because by (9.85) we have $M_t = e^{-\rho - \gamma g - \gamma \epsilon_t}$. Using the estimate obtained from the data and rearranging yields

$$\hat{\gamma} \approx \frac{SR_{S\&P}}{\hat{\sigma}_\epsilon} = 10.47. \tag{9.89}$$

Is this alarmingly high? From experiments on gambles the relative risk aversion was expected to be in the range $3 \leq \gamma \leq 10$. There is a neat self test you can try to determine your own personal relative risk aversion in Cuthbertson and Nitzsche (2004, p. 328). The bottom line is that if your relative risk aversion is too high, sticking to HARA-utility leads to implausible results (see Rabin's paradox, Rabin, 2000). So the question is, is our $\hat{\gamma}$, induced by the observed equity premium, too high? To answer this question, we need a second piece of information provided by the stochastic discount factor framework, that we have not yet extracted. This one leads to what is known as the risk-free rate puzzle.

In (9.60) on page 167, we established the relation between the risk-free gross return and the expectation value of the SDF. For continuous compounding over one period of time, we thus obtain

$$E[M_t|\mathcal{F}_{t-1}] = e^{-r}. \tag{9.90}$$

Because we have now specified the concrete family of utility functions, and we have a stochastic model for the evolution of the consumption stream, we get another equation from (9.85)

$$E[M_t|\mathcal{F}_{t-1}] = e^{-\rho - \gamma g + \frac{1}{2}\gamma^2 \sigma_\epsilon^2}. \tag{9.91}$$

Equating (9.90) and (9.91) one obtains for the risk-free interest rate

$$r = \rho + \gamma g - \frac{1}{2}\gamma^2 \sigma_\epsilon^2 \geq \gamma g - \frac{1}{2}\gamma^2 \sigma_\epsilon^2. \tag{9.92}$$

Using the estimates for γ, g, and σ_ϵ, we have extracted from the data, we can compute a lower bound for the estimate of r,

$$\hat{r} \geq \hat{\gamma}\hat{g} - \frac{1}{2}\hat{\gamma}^2 \hat{\sigma}_\epsilon^2 \approx 12\%. \tag{9.93}$$

This is way too high. Even if we take into account that the risk-free interest rate was averaged by (Mehra and Prescott, 1985). From their data we have $\hat{r} = 0.8\%$, where the estimator is asymptotically normal, with standard deviation

$$\text{StD}[\hat{r}] = 0.6\%. \tag{9.94}$$

There is no way this discrepancy could be explained by random fluctuations. The probability of accidently observing an average rate of $\hat{r} = 0.8\%$ or smaller, like the one in the data, whereas the true risk-free interest rate is indeed $r = 12\%$ is of order $O(10^{-78})$.

Quick calculation 9.20   Can you see how this probability was computed?

This means you would have to wait something like 10^{78} years on average, to see one such weird sample. The age of the entire universe is roughly $1.5 \cdot 10^{10}$ years. You can now appreciate how overwhelmingly improbable such an event would be.

Of course our analysis is based on certain assumptions regarding the utility structure, the consumption stream process, and so forth. It is perfectly possible that relaxing some of those restrictions might work in our favor. But there is still a long way to go and there is no guarantee that modifying the assumptions does not make things worse. Here is one example. We assumed that the market portfolio can be represented by the S&P 500 index and thus, the correlation between the SDF and the return on the index is $\rho = -1$. Empirical findings indicate that the correlation could be substantially smaller, because the S&P 500 is a limited proxy of the real market portfolio. Assume that this correlation was estimated as $\hat{\rho} = -\frac{1}{2}$. Where would it go in the equation? From (9.80) and (9.89) we would conclude that

$$\hat{\gamma} = -\frac{SR_{S\&P}}{\hat{\rho}\hat{\sigma}_\epsilon} = 2\frac{SR_{S\&P}}{\hat{\sigma}_\epsilon} \approx 21. \tag{9.95}$$

Quick calculation 9.21   Confirm this result.

This would make things substantially worse. It has also been questioned, if data reaching more than 100 years into the past is appropriate, because economies and markets have undergone substantial changes due to two world wars and environmental developments in the law and social systems, globalization, technology, etc. Cochrane (2005, sect. 21.1) reports for the New York Stock Exchange index (NYSE) a post-WWII *Sharpe*-ratio of roughly one half. His empirical findings require a relative risk aversion of $\gamma \approx 50$. The corresponding lower bound for the risk-free rate of return is $r \geq 37.5\%$. This is far beyond observation and would cause the economy to collapse because of a massive drop in consumption and investments.

The equity premium puzzle leaves us with two equivalent questions that cannot be answered simultaneously. We can either ask, how can a required moderate relative risk aversion, say in the range $0.5 \leq \gamma \leq 2.5$ generate such a high equity premium as observed in the data, or we can accept a high γ, but are immediately faced with the problem of explaining far too low risk-free interest rates. A number of quite brilliant suggestions have been made since the seminal article of Mehra and Prescott (1985), to resolve the equity premium puzzle. We will discuss one of them in the sequel.

9.7   The *Campbell–Cochrane*-Model

The model of Campbell and Cochrane (1999) resolves the puzzles discussed so far essentially by extending the state space. Until now, we assumed that utility solely depends on the consumption stream. Campbell and Cochrane added another variable, representing a common consumption level all agents in the economy got used to in the recent past. This concept is called habit formation and it generally comes in two flavors. The first one is an individual habit formation, based on becoming adapted to a certain standard of living. Hence, not the absolute levels of consumption dominate the utility function, but the changes with respect to the individual habit level. The second version of habit formation is oriented on the average consumption level of all other agents in the economy. Thus, the stimulus for a given agent is exogenous and is called "keeping up with the Joneses" by Abel (1990). This is the type used by Campbell and Cochrane (1999). In particular they suggested the following utility function

$$u(c, x) = \frac{(c - x)^{1-\gamma} - 1}{1 - \gamma}, \tag{9.96}$$

where the second state variable x represents a common consumption level. There is another useful quantity called the surplus consumption ratio

$$S_t = \frac{C_t - X_t}{C_t} = 1 - \frac{X_t}{C_t}. \tag{9.97}$$

Obviously, the surplus consumption ratio increases with consumption and for $C_t = X_t$, we have $S_t = 0$, which is a very bad state. Let's compute the relative risk aversion of an arbitrary agent with utility function (9.96) and keep in mind that the average consumption level X_t is exogenous for her

$$\mathrm{RRA}(c) = -c \frac{\partial^2 u / \partial c^2}{\partial u / \partial c} = \frac{\gamma}{s}, \tag{9.98}$$

with $s = \frac{c-x}{c}$.

Quick calculation 9.22 Confirm this result.

This is extremely enlightening, because we already get a glimpse of how this mechanism might work. First of all, we may have a small γ, but the surplus ratio s is most likely very small, because it is a relative quantity. Thus, the relative risk aversion may come out large, even if γ is small, because it is divided by a very small number. Second, in times of recession, where S_t decreases and possibly tends to zero, the relative risk aversion becomes very large, and this is precisely what is observed in reality. The only problem is that the whole argument breaks down, if the surplus consumption ratio becomes negative. Campbell and Cochrane (1999) prevented this from happening by making suitable assumptions about the surplus consumption process.

In the following, we again stick to the economic tradition and represent the logarithm of random variables by their lowercase letters. Campbell and Cochrane (1999) also used the AR(1)-model (9.83) for logarithmic consumption $c_t = \log C_t$,

$$c_t = c_{t-1} + g + \epsilon_t, \tag{9.99}$$

with $\epsilon_t \sim N(0, \sigma_\epsilon^2)$. They also assumed that the logarithmic surplus consumption ratio process $s_t = \log S_t$ is a mean reverting process of the kind

$$s_t = (1 - \phi)\bar{s} + \phi s_{t-1} + \lambda(s_{t-1})\epsilon_t. \tag{9.100}$$

That is, the logarithmic surplus process is driven by the same random error as the logarithmic consumption process (random consumption shocks). For $0 \leq \phi < 1$, the process eventually drifts towards its mean reversion level $\bar{s}$, whereas $\lambda(s)$ is called the sensitivity function by Campbell and Cochrane, to be determined in order to satisfy additional model assumptions. The immediate next step is to compute the stochastic discount factor in order to see, if there is an additional contribution, accounting for the large equity premium. A somewhat lengthy calculation yields

$$
\begin{aligned}
M_t &= e^{-\rho} \left(\frac{S_t C_t}{S_{t-1} C_{t-1}} \right)^{-\gamma} = e^{-\rho - \gamma(\Delta c_t + \Delta s_t)} \\
&= \exp\!\left(-\rho - \gamma(g + \epsilon_t) - \gamma((1 - \phi)(\bar{s} - s_{t-1}) + \lambda(s_{t-1})\epsilon_t) \right) \\
&= \exp\!\left(-\rho - \gamma(g + (1 - \phi)(\bar{s} - s_{t-1})) - \gamma(1 + \lambda(s_{t-1}))\epsilon_t \right).
\end{aligned}
\tag{9.101}
$$

Using our log-normal trick (9.88), we obtain for the ratio of the conditional standard deviation and the conditional expectation of the SDF

$$
\frac{\text{StD}[M_t | \mathcal{F}_{t-1}]}{E[M_t | \mathcal{F}_{t-1}]} \approx \gamma \sigma_\epsilon (1 + \lambda(s_{t-1})).
\tag{9.102}
$$

Remember that (9.102) is the *Sharpe*-ratio of the market portfolio we expect to observe, conditional on the information $\mathcal{F}_{t-1}$. And indeed, there is an extra term $\gamma \sigma_\epsilon \lambda(s_{t-1})$, possibly accounting for the high equity premium observed. It all depends on how $\lambda(s)$ is chosen. In order to determine a suitable form of $\lambda(s)$, Campbell and Cochrane imposed three conditions:

- The risk-free interest rate is constant.
- Habit is predetermined at the steady state $s_t = \bar{s}$.
- Habit moves non-negatively with consumption everywhere.

Surprisingly, these conditions are indeed sufficient to determine the sensitivity function

$$
\lambda(s) = \begin{cases} \frac{\sqrt{1 - 2(s - \bar{s})}}{\bar{S}} - 1 & \text{for } s \leq s_{\max} \\ 0 & \text{for } s > s_{\max}, \end{cases}
\tag{9.103}
$$

with $s_{\max} = \bar{s} + \frac{1}{2}(1 - \bar{S}^2)$, and

$$
\bar{S} = \sigma_\epsilon \sqrt{\frac{\gamma}{1 - \phi}}.
\tag{9.104}
$$

We will not go through the entire proof (see the original paper of Campbell and Cochrane, 1999), but let's show that the first condition is indeed satisfied. The risk-free interest rate can be computed from the conditional expectation of the SDF (9.101). In particular for the continuous one period risk-free gross return $R_0^* = e^r$ one obtains

$$
\begin{aligned}
r &= -\log E[M_t | \mathcal{F}_{t-1}] \\
&= \rho + \gamma(g + (1 - \phi)(\bar{s} - s_{t-1})) - \frac{1}{2}\gamma^2 \sigma_\epsilon^2 (1 + \lambda(s_{t-1}))^2 \\
&= \rho + \gamma g - \frac{1}{2}\left(\frac{\gamma}{\bar{S}} \right)^2 \sigma_\epsilon^2 = \rho + \gamma g - \frac{\gamma}{2}(1 - \phi),
\end{aligned}
\tag{9.105}
$$

which is indeed constant.

Quick calculation 9.23 Verify the first and second equality in (9.105).

The big question is, can the large equity premium be explained by the *Campbell–Cochrane*-model, while maintaining a relatively small risk-free interest rate? In their

Table 9.1 Parameters in the *Campbell–Cochrane*-model

Parameter	Variable	Value
Mean consumption growth rate (%)	g	1.89
Standard deviation of consumption growth (%)	σ_ϵ	1.50
Risk-free interest rate (%)	r	0.94
Surplus consumption persistence coefficient	ϕ	0.87
Local utility curvature	γ	2.00

original article, Campbell and Cochrane (1999) chose the model parameters as in Table 9.1. From these figures, we can calculate a steady state surplus consumption ratio of $\bar{S} = 5.88\%$, and a steady state *Sharpe*-ratio of

$$\text{SR}_{\text{MP}}(\bar{s}) = \frac{\gamma \sigma_\epsilon}{\bar{S}} = 0.51, \qquad (9.106)$$

matching more or less exactly the observed *Sharpe*-ratio of the post-WWII NYSE-index data.

But there is much more. In their subsequent paper, Campbell and Cochrane (2000) set up a toy economy with their habit formation model and simulated consumption streams, asset returns, and other quantities. The latter is possible because the price-dividend ratio can be obtained from a functional equation. To understand how this is done, first recall that for the gross return R_t^* of an arbitrary asset

$$1 = E[M_{t+1} R_{t+1}^* | \mathcal{F}_t] \qquad (9.107)$$

holds, and that the gross return on a dividend paying security[1] V is

$$R_{V,t+1}^* = \frac{V_{t+1} + D_{t+1}}{V_t}. \qquad (9.108)$$

Multiplying both sides of (9.107) with $\frac{V_t}{D_t}$, one obtains

$$\frac{V_t}{D_t} = E\left[M_{t+1} \frac{V_{t+1} + D_{t+1}}{D_t} \Big| \mathcal{F}_t \right] = E\left[M_{t+1} \frac{D_{t+1}}{D_t} \left(1 + \frac{V_{t+1}}{D_{t+1}}\right) \Big| \mathcal{F}_t \right]. \qquad (9.109)$$

Quick calculation 9.24 Confirm the last equality in (9.109).

Equation (9.109) is a functional equation for the price-dividend ratio. To make this more transparent, let's write it in a slightly different way and call it the price-dividend function

$$\frac{V}{D}(s_t) = E\left[M_{t+1} \frac{D_{t+1}}{D_t} \left(1 + \frac{V}{D}(s_{t+1})\right) \Big| \mathcal{F}_t \right], \qquad (9.110)$$

---

[1] We use the letter V for the price of a dividend paying security here, in order to avoid confusion with the surplus consumption ratio S.

where the logarithmic surplus consumption ratio s_t is the only state variable for the economy. The objective is now to find a particular function $\frac{V}{D}(s)$ that obeys (9.110). To this end, Campbell and Cochrane assume that the logarithmic dividend process is driven by the same growth factor as consumption

$$d_t = d_{t-1} + g + \eta_t, \tag{9.111}$$

with $d_t = \log D_t$, and that the random error $\eta_t \sim N(0, \sigma_\eta^2)$ is positively correlated with ϵ_t. Now, the conditional expectation can be computed and (9.110) is an equation in the unknown function $\frac{V}{D}(s)$. Campbell and Cochrane solved this functional equation numerically on a grid for the state variable s_t and afterwards interpolated the price–dividend function. Once they obtained this function, they were able to simulate all interesting quantities inside their toy economy.

Campbell and Cochrane (2000) simulated 100 000 months of time series data for their toy economy and used this artificial data to compare the performance of several asset pricing models. Here is what they surprisingly found: Asset pricing models, focusing on the return of a wealth or market portfolio, like the CAPM, perform much better than the C-CAPM pricing method, based on conventional HARA-utility. This is a remarkable result, because the artificial data was generated under the consumption-based habit formation model. Obviously, the CAPM has the edge over the C-CAPM, because its predictions are conditional on the filtration $\mathcal{F}_t$, whereas the utility function

$$u(c) = \frac{c^{1-\gamma} - 1}{1 - \gamma} \tag{9.112}$$

gives rise to an unconditional stochastic discount factor

$$M_t = e^{-\rho} \left(\frac{C_t}{C_{t-1}} \right)^{-\gamma} = e^{-\rho - \gamma g - \gamma \epsilon_t}. \tag{9.113}$$

Campbell and Cochrane do not reject consumption-based asset pricing models in general, but they attribute the poor performance of the C-CAPM to the limitations of the simple parametric form of the utility function.

9.8 Further Reading

There are several comprehensive and accessible textbooks on financial economics like Cochrane (2005), Cuthbertson and Nitzsche (2004), and Lengwiler (2004). The classical references on stock price bubbles are Blanchard (1979) and Froot and Obstfeld (1991). An additional approach to bubbles and crashes, based on herding and critical behavior of complex systems, can be found in Johansen et al. (2000) and Sornette (2003). For the classical paradoxes see Shiller (1981), Mehra and Prescott (1985), and also Weil (1992). To explain the equity premium puzzle, several strategies were suggested. An incomplete list covers generalizing the expected utility functional to disentangle intertemporal substitution and risk aversion (Epstein and Zin, 1989, 1991), habit formation (Constantinides, 1990), incorporating wealth into the utility function

(Bakshi and Chen, 1996), incomplete markets (Constantinides and Duffie, 1996), and habit persistence (Campbell and Cochrane, 1999, 2000).

9.9   Problems

9.1 In adding up an infinite sum, one usually assumes the following two properties to hold

$$\sum_{k=0}^{\infty} s_k = s_0 + \sum_{k=1}^{\infty} s_k \quad \text{and} \quad \sum_{k=0}^{\infty} \alpha s_k = \alpha \sum_{k=0}^{\infty} s_k.$$

Show that using these properties, the surprising result

$$\sum_{k=0}^{\infty} 2^k = -1$$

can be established.

9.2 The rational valuation formula for stochastic discount factor models is

$$S_t = \sum_{k=1}^{\infty} E\left[\prod_{n=1}^{k} M_{t+n} \middle| \mathcal{F}_t \right] E[D_{t+k}|\mathcal{F}_t] + \sum_{k=1}^{\infty} \text{Cov}\left[\prod_{n=1}^{k} M_{t+n}, D_{t+k} \middle| \mathcal{F}_t \right].$$

How does this formula simplify, if the SDF can be assumed conditionally uncorrelated, $\text{Cov}[M_t, M_{t+k}|\mathcal{F}_t] = 0$ for $k \neq 0$?

9.3 Consider an economy at $t = 0$ and $t = T$. Show that under CARA-utility, the stochastic discount factor is

$$M_T = e^{-\rho T - \alpha(C_T - c_0)},$$

if the usual time separable *von Neumann–Morgenstern*-utility functional is assumed.

9.4 The generalized *Epstein–Zin*-utility functional is based on the idea of a discounted certainty equivalent. One possible form is

$$U[C_t] = \left(c_0^{\alpha} + e^{-\rho t} u^{-1} \left(E[u(C_t)] \right)^{\alpha} \right)^{\frac{1}{\alpha}}.$$

Is this functional time separable if the utility function is $u(c) = \sqrt{c}$ and $\alpha = \frac{1}{2}$?

9.5 Show that the interest rate in the *Campbell–Cochrane*-model can be made time dependent of the form

$$r_t = r_0 + B(\bar{s} - s_{t-1})$$

for some fixed r_0, if the steady state surplus consumption ratio is modified to be

$$\bar{S} = \sigma_\epsilon \sqrt{\frac{\gamma}{1 - \phi - \frac{B}{\gamma}}}.$$

What is the fixed steady state rate r_0?

10 Behavioral Finance

Expected utility is a normative theory, which means it explains how agents should behave in order to be perceived as rational decision makers. In fact many deviations from this theoretical blueprint can be observed in reality. This is where psychological influences and mechanisms complement the agent's decision process. Incorporation of such mechanisms paves the road to a descriptive theory of actually observed decision behavior.

10.1 The Efficient Market Hypothesis

Everything we have seen so far points in the direction of efficient markets, in the sense advocated by Fama (1970). To be more precise, Fama analyzed the available theoretical and empirical evidence with respect to three versions of his efficient market hypothesis (EMH). Each version breeds an additional implication, worth discussing briefly. In its weak form, the EMH requires that equilibrium returns are martingales with respect to the information $\mathcal{F}_t$, generated by observing solely the price process of the respective asset. In other words, the sequence of excess returns constitutes a "fair game" with respect to the natural filtration $\mathcal{F}_t$. Since equilibrium returns are ultimately determined by discounting expected utility of future cashflows, weak EMH implies that agents behave sufficiently rationally, such that if the market is cleared, asset prices are aligned with their fundamental values. So the first hypothesis is

$$H_1: \quad \text{weak EMH} \Rightarrow \boxed{\text{rational agents}} + \boxed{S_t = V_t}. \tag{10.1}$$

The second part of the implication is hard to verify. On the one hand, as seen in the last chapter, there may be rational bubbles that cannot be detected, even though it is not clear how they could have originated in an efficient market. On the other hand, this so-called "joint hypothesis problem" requires an equilibrium asset pricing model to test for market inefficiency. But a market is called inefficient, if prices systematically deviate from their equilibrium values, which only can be determined by the model. So if market inefficiencies are observed, either the market is indeed not efficient, or the equilibrium asset pricing model is incorrect, or both.

The second hypothesis is called the semi-strong version of the EMH. It requires the agent to incorporate all publicly available information from news and so forth, not only the information contained in the price process, to determine the fundamental value of an asset. Call this information set $\mathcal{F}_t^P$, then clearly $\mathcal{F}_t^P \supset \mathcal{F}_t$ holds. This requires the rational agent to apply the Bayes' rule to condense the correct posterior distribution out of the current prior distribution and the novel incoming information. So the implication of this hypothesis is

$$H_2: \quad \text{semi-strong EMH} \Rightarrow H_1 + \boxed{\text{Bayes' rule}}. \tag{10.2}$$

If equilibrium returns are martingales with respect to the information $\mathcal{F}_t^P$, too, then all required information is instantaneously stored in the price process of the respective asset. That means it is completely unnecessary to watch CNBC or Bloomberg TV all day, all you have to know is encoded in the history of the price process.

The final hypothesis is the strong version of the EMH. It corresponds to another, yet larger information set $\mathcal{F}_t^I \supset \mathcal{F}_t^P \supset \mathcal{F}_t$, containing all publicly available information plus some insider information, available only to single persons or limited groups of agents. What does it mean if a market is efficient with respect to this information set $\mathcal{F}_t^I$? It does not mean that there is no insider information, it means that this additional information simply does not count. Or in other words, market transparency is that high that only irrelevant information is not revealed to the entire community of market participants. That means

$$H_3: \quad \text{strong EMH} \Rightarrow H_2 + \boxed{\text{full transparency}}. \tag{10.3}$$

What Fama concluded is that there is evidence for occasional violation of strong market efficiency. But theses incidences appear to be rather local phenomena that rarely affect the entire market. On the contrary, the analysis strongly supported the assumption of an at least semi-strong efficient market. So why should these results be challenged? On the one hand, there are anomalies like the equity premium puzzle of Mehra and Prescott (1985). On the other hand, we cannot be sure that the joint hypothesis problem did not create a facsimile of an efficient market. So what we can do is to check the implications of H_1 and H_2 to see if they are in alignment with the behavior of actual decision makers.

Let's proceed backwards and first check if agents follow Bayes' rule, when incorporating new information. There is an outstanding example that has become known as the Harvard Medical School test.

Example 10.1

Casscells et al. (1978) asked 60 people, fourth-year medical students and staff members of Harvard Medical School, the following question: If a test to detect a disease whose prevalence is 1/1000 has a false positive rate of 5%, what is the chance that a person found to have a positive result actually has the disease, assuming that you know nothing about the person's symptoms or signs?

Answers

The estimates varied widely. Nearly half of the test persons answered 95%, incorrectly incorporating the information about the false positive rate. Only 11 out of 60 persons gave the appropriate answer of approximately 2%.

Let's see why 2% is the right answer. Assume that D is the event of contracting the disease, and + is a positive test result. Then the probability of having the disease, conditional on a positive test result is given by Bayes' rule

$$P(D|+) = \frac{P(+|D)P(D)}{P(+)} = \frac{P(+|D)P(D)}{P(+|D)P(D) + P(+|D^C)P(D^C)}. \tag{10.4}$$

Since nothing was said about a false negative rate of the test, we can assume that it is reliable, which means $P(+|D) = 1$. Thus plugging in the numbers, we obtain

$$P(D|+) = \frac{1 \cdot 0.001}{1 \cdot 0.001 + 0.05 \cdot 0.999} \approx \frac{0.001}{0.05} = 2\%. \tag{10.5}$$

Of course we can think of fourth-year medical students and teachers as experts in their field, as well as we might think of participants in a financial market as experts in the field of finance. There is no obvious reason to believe that those agents are better *Bayes*ians. This is a considerable blow for the semi-strong efficient market hypothesis.

Let us now take a look at the second part of the implication of H_1 to check if there is evidence against a weakly efficient market, too. This is a delicate peace of reasoning, because as already emphasized, to detect deviations of asset prices from their fundamental values, we need an equilibrium pricing model, which is already part of the joint hypothesis problem. Put the other way around, we need to check the alignment of prices and fundamental values outside an asset pricing model, if such a thing is possible at all. Surprisingly, it turns out that there are rare occasions, where the market provides sufficient conditions for a model free analysis. Let's look at two particularly striking examples.

Example 10.2

In March 2000, the digital electronics manufacturer 3Com (acquired by Hewlett-Packard in 2010) sold 5% of its subsidiary Palm Inc. in an initial public offering (IPO). 3Com announced that it would spin the remainder of Palm off completely by the end of the year and would provide compensation in the form of 1.5 Palm shares per 3Com share at that time.

Analysis

At the IPO day, Palm closed at $95.06. Because every 3Com share entailed 1.5 Palm shares, this put a lower limit of $142.59 on the 3Com share. In fact, 3Com closed at $81.81, which violates the lower limit by −$60.78. If additionally 3Com's non Palm assets were taken into account, the "stub value" of 3Com shares would have been −$70.77. This mispricing lasted for more than 12 months; see Figure 10.1, taken from Hens and Rieger (2010, p. 163).

There is another very disturbing example of mispricing to be observed when examining so-called "Siamese twin companies."

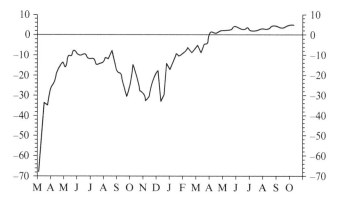

Fig. 10.1 Negative stub value of 3Com after IPO of Palm – Figure is reproduced from Hens and Rieger (2010, p. 163) with permission of Springer

Example 10.3

In 1907, the companies Royal Dutch Petroleum and Shell Transport and Trading merged their interests on a 60:40 basis, while remaining separate legal entities, located in the Netherlands and Great Britain, respectively. Internally, all tax adjusted cash-flows are effectively split in the proportion 60:40 and information about the linkage between the two companies is publicly available. Royal Dutch and Shell are traded liquidly at major exchanges in Europe and the United States.

Analysis

If fundamental value equals asset price, the price for Royal Dutch should be always 1.5 times the price of Shell. In reality, this parity is violated considerably over extended periods of time. Figure 10.2, taken from Froot and Dabora (1999), illustrates the effect.

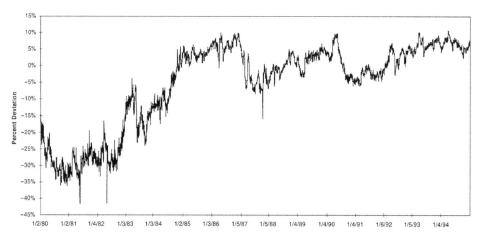

Fig. 10.2 Logarithmic deviations from Royal Dutch/Shell parity – Figure is reproduced from Froot and Dabora (1999) with permission of Elsevier

We can conclude that there is substantial evidence for violations of the equality of asset prices and fundamental values. So if we question the $S_t = V_t$ implication of H_1, we also have to reconsider rationality of agents. This is because our equilibrium asset pricing model was based on the assumption that agents maximize some kind of utility functional, which we in turn called rational behavior. But does that mean that agents behave irrationally? Not necessarily, at least not in the sense we usually use that term. There are indeed systematic decision patterns beyond rationality, leading to alternative decision systems. We will explore two of them in the remainder of this chapter.

10.2   Beyond Rationality

There is a very old paradox challenging one of the axioms of expected utility theory, quite from the start. It is called the *Allais*-paradox (Allais, 1953). It requires people to choose between two lotteries in two different scenarios. There are always three possible outcomes of the lottery in million dollars,

$$W = \{0, 1, 5\}. \tag{10.6}$$

The respective scenarios are:

Scenario 1
- $L_A = (0, 1, 0)$
- $L_B = (0.01, 0.89, 0.1)$

Scenario 2
- $L_A = (0.89, 0.11, 0)$
- $L_B = (0.9, 0, 0.1)$

In scenario 1, people were asked to choose between obtaining a safe amount of one million dollars or taking an additional 10% chance of gaining five million dollars, accompanied by a 1% chance of losing everything. Most people prefer the riskless lottery L_A, because one million dollars is a considerable amount of money and a bird in the hand is worth two in the bush. In scenario 2, people had to choose between an 11% chance of gaining one million dollars and a 10% chance of gaining five million dollars. Because there is not much difference between 10% and 11%, but a considerable difference in the potential gain, people for the most part prefer lottery L_B. But this switch of preferences compromises the independence axiom (4.5) on page 62 of expected utility theory. To see why this is the case, define the new lotteries

$$L_1 = (0, 1, 0), \quad L_2 = (1, 0, 0), \quad \text{and} \quad L_3 = \left(\frac{1}{11}, 0, \frac{10}{11}\right). \tag{10.7}$$

If we choose the probability $\pi = 0.11$, then the lotteries L_A and L_B can be written as compound lotteries

$$L_A = \pi L_1 + (1 - \pi)L_n \quad \text{and} \quad L_B = \pi L_3 + (1 - \pi)L_n \tag{10.8}$$

in both scenarios $n = 1, 2$.

Quick calculation 10.1   Check that this statement is correct.

But if L_A is preferred over L_B in scenario 1, then L_1 is also preferred over L_3. This preference should not depend on the mixing lottery L_n, whatever scenario is considered.

Nevertheless, a flip in the preference order occurs and thus, the independence axiom of expected utility theory is violated.

Even though the effect is clear once L_A and L_B are stated as compound lotteries, it is very hard to explain on a fundamental level. Obviously, the decision maker was distracted from the core problem, and thus did not realize that her preference order was irrational. The mechanism transmitting this distraction is likely to be psychological in nature. Kahneman and Tversky (1981) presented an impressive example of one such psychological mechanism called the **framing effect**. They confronted more than 300 students from Stanford University and the University of British Columbia with what became known as the Asian disease problem.

Example 10.4

One half of the participants were asked the following question: Imagine that the US is preparing for the outbreak of an unusual Asian disease, which is expected to kill 600 people. Two alternative programs to combat the disease have been proposed. Assume that the exact scientific estimate of the consequences of the programs are as follows:

- If program A is adopted, 200 people will be saved.
- If program B is adopted, there is 1/3 probability that 600 people will be saved, and 2/3 probability that no people will be saved.

Which of the two programs would you favor?

Answers

72% of the participants preferred the safe alternative A, only 28% were willing to take the 1/3 chance program B was offering.

Kahneman and Tversky asked the second half of the participants precisely the same question, but this time they phrased the alternative programs in another way.

Example 10.5

Consider the situation in Example 10.4. Now assume that the consequences of the programs are as follows:

- If program A is adopted, 400 people will die.
- If program B is adopted, there is 1/3 probability that nobody will die, and 2/3 probability that 600 people will die.

Which of the two programs would you favor?

Answers

Now only 22% of the participants preferred program A, whereas 78% were willing to take the risky alternative B.

This result is astonishing, because the problem and the consequences are clearly identical in both situations. Yet a large number of decision makers reversed preferences, only because the decision was framed in another way. In the first case, the problem was framed in terms of survivors, or gains. In the second case, the frame was in terms of fatalities, or losses.

There are two lessons to be learned from this observation of actual decision behavior. First, there was no reference to the number of people living in the US at all. Expected utility theory was build around the idea that absolute risk aversion should be linked to the current level of wealth of an individual. The result of the Asian disease problem on the other hand indicates that gains and losses are the relevant quantities in the decision process. Second, agents are obviously risk averse in the domain of gains, but risk seeking in the domain of losses. This in turn implies that gains and losses have to be measured with respect to a specific reference point, where a symmetry breaking occurs. So how did Kahneman and Tversky set this reference point to frame precisely the same consequences in the domain of gains one time, and in the domain of losses the other time? In the first version, the programs were formulated in terms of saved lives in the future, implying that no one has been saved yet, at least not until a program is chosen. Thus, the test persons set their reference point to zero saved lives. But this also means that they accept the 600 threatened persons to be doomed. In the second version, the consequences were phrased in terms of lost lives in the future, again implying that currently no lives have been lost, at least not until a decision is made. So in this case, test persons again chose zero lost lives as a reference point, even though the disease threatens 600 lives. Now it is also clear that Kahneman and Tversky had to split the test subjects into two groups to allow them to establish different views on the 600 threatened lives.

If the conclusion that individuals are risk averse with respect to gains and risk seeking with respect to losses is correct, then why do people participate in organized lotteries and enter into insurance contracts? In the first case, the expected gains from common lotteries are negative, so it seems that in this case the behavior of decision makers is risk seeking. In the second case, insurance contracts provide coverage against low probability events of damage or loss. Usually the insurance premium is not actuarially fair, which means it is clearly higher than the expected loss. So the behavior of decision makers seem to be risk averse in this situation. This is quite the opposite of the behavior observed in the Asian disease problem. So what is the difference between these observations? In the case of the Asian disease, we were dealing with mid-range probabilities, namely 1/3 and 2/3, whereas in the case of organized lotteries and insurance contracts, we are talking about extremely low probability events. Table 10.1 summarizes our observations of actual decision patterns. Kahneman and Tversky (1979) suggested a decision theory explaining this pattern, called prospect theory. We will analyze its elements in the next section, in order to understand how it generates predictions that are in line with the observed decision behavior.

Tversky and Kahneman (1991) report another important fact about gains and losses. They find that when offered a fair coin flip game with a potential gain G and a potential loss L, the ratio G/L for which the game is barely acceptable for an agent is usually higher than 2/1. That means losses loom larger than gains. This principle is called loss aversion and is to be distinguished from risk aversion. Loss aversion means

Table 10.1 Observed decision patterns

	Domain	
	Gains	Losses
Mid-range probabilities	risk averse	risk seeking
Low probabilities	risk seeking	risk averse

that a decision maker fears a loss of certain magnitude more than she values a gain of the same magnitude. Thus, a risk-averse decision maker in expected utility theory is automatically loss averse. But a loss averse decision maker in prospect theory may be risk seeking; see Table 10.1.

10.3　Prospect Theory

In its original form, prospect theory, suggested by Kahneman and Tversky (1979), was a purely descriptive approach to explain actual decision behavior of agents under risk, incorporating the psychological effects we already studied. Even though qualitatively explaining a decision after it was made is important in order to understand the relevant mechanisms, Kahneman and Tversky did much more. They created a quantitative framework to predict how agents will actually decide, which is a much harder task. Their approach has a superficial similarity with expected utility theory, but differs from it considerably with respect to its construction and substantial features. In expected utility theory we encountered a utility function $u : \mathcal{W} \to \mathbb{R}$, mapping the outcome of some random variable into the real numbers. Its existence and properties were the consequences of the four axioms of von Neumann and Morgenstern (4.5) on page 62. Prospect theory has a value function $v : \mathcal{X} \to \mathbb{R}$, doing the same mapping. This time the set of possible realizations is labeled $\mathcal{X}$, to indicate that the random variable X is in terms of gains and losses, and not with respect to an initial wealth. The value function was not derived from a set of axioms, but was designed to accommodate the anomalies observed in actual decision making. Kahneman and Tversky suggested the following form

$$v(x) = \begin{cases} x^\alpha & \text{for } x \geq 0 \\ -\lambda(-x)^\beta & \text{for } x < 0, \end{cases} \tag{10.9}$$

with $0 < \alpha, \beta < 1$, and $\lambda > 1$. The parameters were calibrated in numerous empirical experiments. Kahneman and Tversky found that the values $\alpha = \beta = 0.88$ and $\lambda = 2.25$ reasonably reflect observed decision behavior. The resulting value function is illustrated in Figure 10.3 left. For gains, $x \geq 0$, the value function is concave, indicating

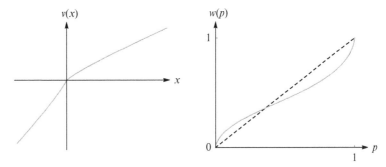

Fig. 10.3 Functions of prospect theory – Value function (left) and probability weighting function (right)

risk-averse behavior of decision makers. In the domain of losses, $x < 0$, it is convex, accommodating risk-seeking behavior of decision makers. Loss aversion is also encoded in the value function. Because $\lambda > 1$, the slope for $x < 0$ is steeper than for $x > 0$ and thus, the reduction in value due to a loss of given magnitude is higher than the increase in value due to a gain of the same magnitude.

Quick calculation 10.2 Verify the last statement for $x = \pm 1$.

What is not explained in terms of the value function is the lottery/insurance puzzle. Kahneman and Tversky came up with a very elegant solution to this problem. They concluded that decision makers presumably have a good intuition for mid-range probabilities, because that is what they face very often in everyday life, but they overestimate small probabilities considerably. This idea was formalized in terms of a suitable probability weighting function. If the true probability is p, then for example the perceived probability weight could be given by

$$w(p) = \frac{p^{\gamma}}{(p^{\gamma} + (1 - p)^{\gamma})^{1/\gamma}}, \tag{10.10}$$

with $\gamma > 0$. The weighting function for $\gamma = 0.65$ is illustrated in Figure 10.3 right.[1] The form of the probability weighting function is by no means completely arbitrary. One

---

[1] Kahneman and Tversky (1992) suggested this functional form, but they defined two versions, $w^+(p)$ and $w^-(p)$ with parameters γ and δ, one for each domain. Their parameter values, determined from experiment, did not differ very much ($\gamma = 0.61$ and $\delta = 0.69$) and thus, it is common practice in finance to define only one weighting function with the arithmetic mean $\gamma = 0.65$.

can assume that decision makers agree on the probabilities of the certain and the impossible event. This requires that

$$w(0) = 0 \quad \text{and} \quad w(1) = 1 \tag{10.11}$$

holds. Furthermore, decision makers are expected to correctly preserve order relations across different probabilities, which means they still know which event has larger probability, even if they have a biased perception of the total magnitude of the respective probabilities. This requires the weighting function to be monotonically increasing in p,

$$\frac{dw}{dp} \geq 0, \tag{10.12}$$

for $0 \leq p \leq 1$.[2]

Now that we know the fundamental building blocks of prospect theory, the value functional can be defined. Assume that a lottery L has N different possible outcomes, collected in the set X, then the value functional is

$$V[L] = \sum_{n=1}^{N} v(x_n) w(p_n). \tag{10.13}$$

This functional can be understood as expectation of the value function with respect to the weighted probability measure $w(P)$. It is used precisely in the same way as the *von Neumann–Morgenstern*-utility functional. If there are two lotteries, L_1 and L_2, with probability measures P and Q, then the equivalence

$$L_1 \gtrsim L_2 \quad \Leftrightarrow \quad \sum_{n=1}^{N} v(x_n) w(p_n) \geq \sum_{n=1}^{N} v(x_n) w(q_n) \tag{10.14}$$

holds.

Prospect theory laid the foundations of behavioral economics and its sub-field behavioral finance. It also had an enormous impact on corporate finance. Because of its psychological roots, it was able to provide a new perspective on agency relations. But there were also problems with the original formulation, both technically and conceptually. Technical difficulties are mostly related to the fact that prospect theory is discontinuous (for details see Hens and Rieger, 2010, sect. 2.4.5). Conceptually, the greatest obstacle is that prospect theory does not respect first order stochastic dominance. These shortcomings were remedied with the formulation of cumulative prospect theory.

---

[2] Remarkably, this property does not hold for the weighting function (10.10) of Kahneman and Tversky for $\gamma \leq 0.278$, as pointed out by Rieger and Wang (2006).

10.4 Cumulative Prospect Theory (CPT)

Let's start our discussion by looking at the definition of first order stochastic dominance.

Theorem 10.1 (First order stochastic dominance) *Let $X, Y : \Omega \to \mathbb{R}$ be two real random variables. Then X dominates Y stochastically to first order, if for all $x \in \mathbb{R}$*

$$P(X > x) \geq P(Y > x)$$

holds, with strict inequality for some x.

Because the probability distribution function of a random variable X is defined as $F_X(x) = P(X \leq x)$, the condition of Theorem 10.1 can alternatively be expressed as

$$F_X(x) \leq F_Y(x). \tag{10.15}$$

Quick calculation 10.3 Give a formal verification of this statement.

Example 10.6

Consider the set $X = \{1, 2, 3\}$ of possible outcomes, and the lotteries

$$L_A = \left(\frac{1}{2}, \frac{1}{2}, 0\right) \quad \text{and} \quad L_B = \left(\frac{1}{2}, 0, \frac{1}{2}\right).$$

Does one of the lotteries dominate the other stochastically to first order?

Solution

It is easy to see that lottery L_B dominates lottery L_A, because the distribution function can be immediately extracted from the lotteries, see Table 10.2. For all x, condition (10.15) holds, and additionally

$$F_B(x) < F_A(x)$$

for $2 \leq x < 3$.

Table 10.2 Distribution functions of lotteries A and B

	$x < 1$	$1 \leq x < 2$	$2 \leq x < 3$	$x \geq 3$
$F_A(x)$	0	1/2	1	1
$F_B(x)$	0	1/2	1/2	1

Now, consider a family of lotteries L_N with possible outcomes in $\mathcal{X}_N$, given by

$$x_n = 1 - \frac{n-1}{N} \tag{10.16}$$

for $n \leq N$, and uniform probabilities

$$p_n = \frac{1}{N}. \tag{10.17}$$

The first member of this family, L_1, is the lottery that provides a sure gain of one unit of currency. The next lottery L_2 is given by

$$L_2 = \left(\frac{1}{2}, \frac{1}{2}\right) \quad \text{on} \quad \mathcal{X}_2 = \left\{1, \frac{1}{2}\right\}. \tag{10.18}$$

It is easy to see that L_1 dominates L_2 stochastically to first order.

Quick calculation 10.4 Sketch the distribution functions of L_1 and L_2.

In fact, L_1 dominates all lotteries L_N for $N > 1$, because none of them can pay off more than one unit of currency and in L_1 this outcome is certain. Unfortunately, in prospect theory one can find an N^*, such that the lotteries L_N with $N \geq N^*$ are preferred over L_1. Let's try to understand why this is the case. Using the value function (10.9) and the probability weighting (10.10) on page 189, we can compute the value functional for L_1 explicitly,

$$V[L_1] = v(1)w(1) = 1. \tag{10.19}$$

For $N > 1$, this computation is not that easy, but we can compute a lower limit. Because $\alpha < 1$ holds, we have $v(x) \geq x$ for positive $x \leq 1$, and thus

$$V[L_N] \geq \sum_{n=1}^{N} x_n w(p_n). \tag{10.20}$$

The next step is to put a lower limit on the probability weighting function

$$w(p) = \frac{p^\gamma}{(p^\gamma + (1-p)^\gamma)^{1/\gamma}}. \tag{10.21}$$

To this end, let's see, for which p the denominator takes its maximum value,

$$\frac{d}{dp}(p^\gamma + (1-p)^\gamma)^{1/\gamma} = \frac{p^{\gamma-1} - (1-p)^{\gamma-1}}{(p^\gamma + (1-p)^\gamma)^{1-1/\gamma}} \overset{!}{=} 0. \tag{10.22}$$

Quick calculation 10.5 Confirm this derivative.

In order for the derivative to vanish, the numerator has to become zero. This is precisely the case for $p^* = \frac{1}{2}$. Thus, we obtain the following lower bound on the probability weight

$$w(p) \geq \frac{p^\gamma}{(2 \cdot 2^{-\gamma})^{1/\gamma}} = 2^{1-1/\gamma} p^\gamma. \tag{10.23}$$

for $\gamma < 1$, as estimated by Kahneman and Tversky. Combining (10.16), (10.17), and (10.23), we can compute a lower limit of the value functional

$$V[L_N] \geq 2^{1-1/\gamma} N^{-\gamma} \sum_{n=1}^{N} \left(1 - \frac{n-1}{N}\right) = 2^{1-1/\gamma} N^{-\gamma} \cdot \frac{N+1}{2}$$
$$= 2^{-1/\gamma} N^{1-\gamma} + 2^{-1/\gamma} N^{-\gamma} \tag{10.24}$$

The second term is negligible if N grows large and thus, we obtain the final inequality

$$V[L_N] \geq 2^{-1/\gamma} N^{1-\gamma}. \tag{10.25}$$

The term on the right hand side of (10.25) is unbounded and thus, there has to exist an N^*, such that

$$V[L_N] \geq 1 = V[L_1] \tag{10.26}$$

for all $N \geq N^*$ and $0 < \gamma < 1$. This proves that prospect theory can make predictions that do not respect first order stochastic dominance.

Violation of first order stochastic dominance was an undesired feature of the theory, because Kahneman and Tversky assumed that there exists a so-called **editing phase**, where the decision maker systematically arranges and analyzes the available alternatives, before the actual decision is made. Unfortunately, the editing phase is not a formalized part of the theory, but it is generally assumed that an economic agent identifies stochastically dominated and thus inferior alternatives. These problems were solved with the formulation of cumulative prospect theory (CPT, Kahneman and Tversky, 1992). The major difference to prospect theory is that probability weighting is now done with respect to the (cumulative) distribution function; hence the name cumulative prospect theory. This results in a new value functional[3]

$$V[L] = \int_{-\infty}^{\infty} v(x) dw(F(x)). \tag{10.27}$$

To see, why this functional respects first order stochastic dominance, let's first manipulate the integral a bit. If the distribution function is invertible, and the weighting function is strictly monotonic increasing and differentiable, which is usually the case,

---

[3] Because originally Kahneman and Tversky defined the weighting functions $w^+(x)$ and $w^-(x)$ separately, they obtained two functionals $V^+[L]$ and $V^-[L]$ on the respective half lines, which, besides some technical conditions, requires a proper rescaling (for details see the appendix of Kahneman and Tversky, 1992).

the integral in (10.27) can be transformed with the help of the substitution $F(x) = u$. The result is

$$V[L] = \int_0^1 v(F^{-1}(u))w'(u)du, \tag{10.28}$$

where $w'(u)$ is the derivative of the weighting function with respect to its argument, and $F^{-1}(u)$ is the quantile function.

Quick calculation 10.6   Confirm this result.

Consider the lotteries L_A and L_B and assume that L_A stochastically dominates L_B to first order. Due to Theorem 10.1 this means $F_A(x) \le F_B(x)$ for all $x \in \mathbb{R}$. But it is not hard to see that this also means

$$F_A^{-1}(u) \ge F_B^{-1}(u). \tag{10.29}$$

Quick calculation 10.7   Make the substitution $F_A(x) = u$ to prove (10.29).

Because $w'(u)$ is a positive function for $u \in [0, 1]$ and $v(x)$ is strictly monotonic increasing, we also have

$$V[L_A] = \int_0^1 v(F_A^{-1}(u))w'(u)du \ge \int_0^1 v(F_B^{-1}(u))w'(u)du = V[L_B]. \tag{10.30}$$

For discrete probability distributions, a related proof can be found in Hens and Rieger (2010, p. 64).

What enhances the appeal of CPT even further is the fact that it can be axiomatized in the same way as expected utility theory. To this end, the independence axiom has to be modified and some care has to be taken of sign changes. The technical details are quite intricate but this was an important breakthrough, finally resulting in the Nobel Prize for Daniel Kahneman in 2002 (sadly Amos Tversky had already died).

10.5   CPT and the Equity Premium Puzzle

The equity premium puzzle of Mehra and Prescott (1985), extensively discussed in Chapter 9, is probably the most prominent conundrum of expected utility theory. In a nutshell, observed equity premia of more than 6% and risk-free interest rates of less than 1% are irreconcilable with a common order of magnitude of risk aversion. We have seen that this puzzle is resolvable within the model of Campbell and Cochrane (1999), if we assume that utility does not only depend on individual consumption, but also on a particular common level of consumption. Apart from a translation, the *Campbell–Cochrane*-utility function was

$$u(c, x) = \frac{(c - x)^{1-\gamma}}{1 - \gamma}, \tag{10.31}$$

where c indicates consumption and x acts as a reference level, against which consumption is measured as gain or loss relative to a common level. Why the reference point may be a substantial ingredient is best understood by looking at the often-quoted anecdote of Paul Samuelson's chat with a colleague. Samuelson asked his colleague, whose name he did not reveal until many years later, if he was willing to accept a fair coin flip gamble, in which he could either win \$200 or lose \$100. After some contemplation the colleague turned his bet down, but announced that he would happily accept 100 such bets. Samuelson (1963) retaliated with his famous publication "Risk and Uncertainty: A Fallacy of Large Numbers," in which he proved that his colleague was acting irrationally.

To understand the argument we have to pay close attention to Samuelson's requirement that for the whole range of wealth levels attainable in such a sequence of coin tosses, one isolated bet should always be unfavorable. Assume we start at the wealth level w_0 and the coin toss leaves us either with w_+ with probability p, or w_- with probability $1 - p$. Because this single bet is unfavorable to us, we can conclude that the certainty equivalent w_0^* is smaller than our initial wealth w_0. Because of the same argument we also have

$$w_+^* < w_+ \quad \text{and} \quad w_-^* < w_-. \tag{10.32}$$

But the decision maker is indifferent between the second stage lotteries and the respective certainty equivalents, and because the experiments in the sequence are independent, it does not matter if she takes the lottery or the certainty equivalent in stage two.

Quick calculation 10.8   Provide a formal argument for this statement.

However, taking $w_{+/-}^*$ in stage two, leaves us with a lottery in stage one, where we either obtain w_+^* with probability p or w_-^* with probability $1 - p$. This lottery is stochastically dominated by the initial isolated lottery, and thus if one rejects the single bet, a double bet should even more be rejected. This argument can be iterated over the whole sequence and is conceptually the core of Samuelson's proof.

However, things change dramatically in the framework of cumulative prospect theory. This can already be seen from the very simplified situation

$$v(x) = \begin{cases} x & \text{for } x \geq 0 \\ 2.5x & \text{for } x < 0 \end{cases} \quad \text{and} \quad w(p) = p, \tag{10.33}$$

where all characteristic effects of prospect theory, with the exception of loss aversion, have been switched off. The decision maker should participate in the lottery L, if $V[L] > 0$, which means that the prospective value is positive.

Quick calculation 10.9   Show that the single bet of Samuelson's fair coin flip gamble is not favorable, but the double bet has already positive prospective value.

So Samuelson's colleague may have been irrational with respect to expected utility theory, but in the light of prospect theory, his answer was perfectly justified. Here is another subtlety. What happens, if the colleague evaluates his gains and losses after every single toss of the coin? In this case, he would reset his reference point after every round of the game. We shall call this an evaluation period of only one round. Why is that a problem? Well, if he does so, he would not participate in the last round of the game, because it would seem unfavorable to him. But knowing that he will actually participate only in 99 rounds would mean he has to refuse participation in round 98, too. That means he would eventually turn down the complete sequence. Only for an evaluation period of at least two rounds, which means he restrains himself from checking the result of every coin flip, does the whole sequence become an attractive investment. The longer the evaluation period, the less severe the risk is perceived. On the other hand, two factors seem to prevent decision makers from taking risky investment opportunities, loss aversion and short evaluation periods. The combination of both is called **myopic loss aversion**.

Can myopic loss aversion explain the equity premium puzzle? This question was analyzed by Benartzi and Thaler (1995). They assumed that market participants act on average according to CPT, with the parameter set determined by Kahneman and Tversky (1992). Under this hypothesis, they conducted historical simulations by drawing random samples with replacement from monthly returns on stocks, bonds, and treasury bills between 1926 and 1990, to answer the question: For which evaluation period will the average market participant be indifferent between holding stocks and bonds? Or in other words, for which evaluation period has the observed equity premium exactly the right magnitude to compensate for the perceived risk associated with stocks? The desired period is the one at which the prospective value of a bond investment equals the prospective value of a stock investment. From their simulation studies, Benartzi and Thaler (1995) discovered a nearly perfectly linear relationship between prospective value and the evaluation period, sketched in Figure 10.4 left. It is easily seen that both lines cross in the vicinity of 12 months, which means that agents have an average evaluation period of about one year. It is hard to believe in a coincidence because an evaluation period of one year is highly plausible. As the authors already

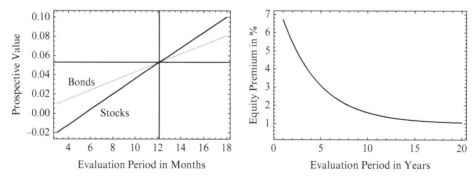

Fig. 10.4 Prospective value (left) and equilibrium equity premium (right) as a function of length of the evaluation period – Schematic illustration of the results of Benartzi and Thaler (1995)

emphasized: "Individual investors file taxes annually, receive their most comprehensive reports from their brokers, mutual funds, and retirement accounts once a year, and institutional investors also take the annual reports most seriously."

Benartzi and Thaler asked another question: How does the equilibrium equity premium change with respect to the evaluation period? This time they used real returns, because the time horizon is considerably longer. The result is a nearly perfectly exponentially decaying function, sketched in Figure 10.4 right. Empirical results, demonstrating such a clear linear or exponential relationship, often point in the direction of a potentially deep and fundamental law. So if decision makers indeed act according to CPT, the exceptionally high observed equity premium could be generated by the short evaluation period of one year. In the long term, investors would require a much lower premium to prefer a stock position over a riskless investment. So it seems that the equity premium puzzle can be resolved in cumulative prospect theory, even though we cannot verify, if this explanation is the right one. Nevertheless, we can now understand much better, why the *Campbell–Cochrane*-model was so successful; namely because it adopted the idea of a variable reference point. Furthermore, it was formulated as a time series model with a natural lag of precisely one year.

10.6 The Price Momentum Effect

From the perspective of standard equilibrium models, one of the most bizarre observations is the price momentum effect, first analyzed by Jegadeesh and Titman (1993). In short, this effect describes the tendency of the best (worst) performing stocks over a three- to twelve-month period to perform well (poorly) over the subsequent period of the same length. This strange effect also does not seem to be limited to the USA, but could be observed in European markets, too (Rouwenhorst, 1998). Jegadeesh and Titman presented an impressive analysis of momentum strategies. They assembled portfolios of the top decile performing stocks, funded by short selling the decile of the poorest performing stocks over the respective period. The composition of their momentum portfolios was adjusted periodically in the same self-financing way. So their strategies did not cost anything, but surprisingly, monthly returns of nearly 1.5% were observed between 1965 and 1989. Subsequent work confirms the persistence of this effect in the more recent past. If markets were efficient, there should not be any statistically significant return on average at all, because a zero net investment should not generate positive payoffs in the future.

Several explanations for this effect have been suggested. A particularly interesting one, referring to prospect theory, is the one of Grinblatt and Han (2005). They assume that there is a fraction of rational decision makers in the market, but also another fraction, behaving only partially rational. To be more precise, they assume that those agents behave consistently with prospect theory and **mental accounting**. In behavioral economics, mental accounting describes the tendency of decision makers to mentally separate the development of different assets and to account for the gains and losses individually. For such a decision maker, there is a clear difference between losing a ticket worth $50, say for a baseball match, and losing the same amount in cash. She has mental accounts for baseball cards and for cash money. If she loses the ticket, she would have to buy a new one, but that would make the ticket cost $100. She might well decide that this is too expensive for seeing a baseball match and will no longer attend it, even though she had not even thought about selling her ticket, if she had lost the $50 in cash instead. That is because cash money and baseball tickets were held in different mental accounts. In finance, mental accounting means that the investor does not aggregate gains and losses on a portfolio level, but accounts them to specific assets. That is a central element in the reasoning of Grinblatt and Han. The rest of their model uses the following slightly simplified framework: Assume that the fundamental value V of an arbitrary stock S follows a random walk

$$V_{t+1} = V_t + \epsilon_{t+1}, \tag{10.34}$$

where ϵ_t is a zero mean random innovation. There is a fraction μ of partially rational (PT) decision makers, and a fraction $1 - \mu$ of entirely rational (EU) decision makers in the market. The excess demand X, generated by both groups is

$$\begin{aligned} X_t^{\text{EU}} &= b(V_t - S_t) \\ X_t^{\text{PT}} &= b((V_t - S_t) + \lambda(R_t - S_t)), \end{aligned} \tag{10.35}$$

with $b, \lambda > 0$, and the time-dependent reference point R_t, which is usually the individual buying price of the stock. In case of market clearing, we must have

$$X_t = \mu X_t^{\text{PT}} + (1 - \mu) X_t^{\text{EU}} = 0. \tag{10.36}$$

Plugging in (10.35) and conducting some algebraic manipulations, one obtains

$$S_t = wV_t + (1 - w)R_t \quad \text{with} \quad w = \frac{1}{1 + \mu\lambda}. \tag{10.37}$$

That means, the observed stock price is a linear combination of the fundamental value and the (average) individual reference point.

Quick calculation 10.10 Verify the last result formally.

The next question is, how does the reference point change with time? Grinblatt and Han assume that it reverts back to the observed stock price,

$$R_{t+1} = \gamma S_t + (1 - \gamma)R_t, \tag{10.38}$$

where $0 < \gamma < 1$ is related to the stock's turnover ratio. Take a minute to appreciate the elegant idea behind this simple formula. Through trading, a large number of stocks change hands. Every time a PT decision maker trades the stock, her reference point is reset to the current price and so, gradually, the average reference point tends to the current price of the stock. Figure 10.5 illustrates the dynamics of the key quantities in the *Grinblatt–Han*-model, simulated over a twelve month period. All quantities start in equilibrium at $100, and then a shock is injected, possibly an unanticipated event

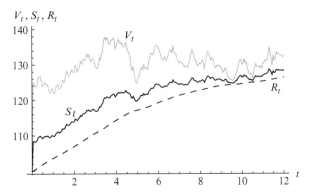

Fig. 10.5 Simulation of fundamental value (gray), stock price (black), and average reference point (dashed) in the *Grinblatt–Han*-model

or information affecting the respective company, pushing the fundamental value of the stock to $125. The shock is partially absorbed in the stock price immediately, but the remaining difference builds up momentum that is released over the next 12 months.

It is also interesting to analyze the expected returns, predicted by the *Grinblatt–Han*-model. Because the random innovation in (10.34) has zero expectation, one obtains

$$E[S_{t+1} - S_t] = (1 - w)\gamma(S_t - R_t) \tag{10.39}$$

for the expected change in stock price.

Quick calculation 10.11   Verify this result.

After dividing by the current price of the stock, the expected return is

$$E\left[\frac{S_{t+1} - S_t}{S_t}\right] = (1 - w)\gamma\frac{S_t - R_t}{S_t}. \tag{10.40}$$

The quotient on the right hand side of (10.40) is called the investor's (percentage) unrealized capital gain. So even if we do not have a reliable equilibrium model, observing large returns may be evidence for an unrealized capital gain, which in turn provides momentum for future returns. This mechanism can easily explain why the momentum strategy of Jegadeesh and Titman worked so well, while under the efficient market hypothesis the very existence of such a mechanism is inexplicable.

10.7   Unifying CPT and Modern Portfolio Theory

Until now, we have seen that prospect theory is able to explain some of the most challenging puzzles in modern financial markets remarkably well. So the big question is, does CPT fit in the framework of modern portfolio theory? This question was thoroughly addressed under different aspects by De Giorgi and Hens (2006). Unfortunately, the answer is no. But the good news is, it can be made compatible with very few modifications. To understand why this is necessary, let's look at some problems of CPT, when it encounters modern portfolio theory.

One of the oldest paradoxes is the one generated by the so-called St. Petersburg game. It is a fair coin flip game, where the payoff depends on the first occurrence of heads in a sequence of trials. If heads occurs in the first toss, the gain is \$1 and the game is over. If the first toss is tails, the game continues and the potential gain is doubled. The game always ends if the coin shows heads for the first time. Thus, the set of elementary states of this game is $\Omega = \mathbb{N}$, and the potential gain X is represented by the random variable

$$X(\omega_n) = 2^{n-1}. \tag{10.41}$$

The actual paradox arises from the fact that in the eighteenth century, the expected gain was considered a fair price for participating in a game of chance. But in case of the St. Petersburg game, the expected gain is

$$E[X] = \sum_{n=1}^{\infty} 2^{n-1} \cdot \frac{1}{2^n} = \frac{1}{2} \sum_{n=1}^{\infty} 1 = \infty. \tag{10.42}$$

Obviously nobody would be willing to pay an infinite amount of money for participation in this game. In 1738, Daniel Bernoulli offered a way out of this paradox. He suggested not to focus on the expected gain, but on the expected utility, induced by the gain. He assumed that the utility of money grows logarithmically, $u(x) = \log x$ and hence, the expected utility was

$$E[u(X)] = \sum_{n=1}^{\infty} \log(2^{n-1}) \frac{1}{2^n} = \log 2 \sum_{n=1}^{\infty} \frac{n-1}{2^n} = \log 2 \cdot \frac{1}{2} \sum_{n=1}^{\infty} \frac{n}{2^n} = \log 2. \tag{10.43}$$

The last equality holds, because for $|x| < 1$, differentiating the standard infinite geometric series yields

$$\frac{d}{dx} \sum_{n=0}^{\infty} x^n = \sum_{n=1}^{\infty} nx^{n-1} = \frac{1}{(1-x)^2}. \tag{10.44}$$

Quick calculation 10.12   Use this relation to verify the last equality in (10.43).

Even though Bernoulli anticipated the idea of expected utility, his solution lacked the axiomatic structure to be introduced more than 200 years later by von Neumann and Morgenstern. Another problem occurred, when the payoff of the St. Petersburg game was modified appropriately. For example, if the gains were represented by the random variable

$$X(\omega_n) = \exp(2^{n-1}), \tag{10.45}$$

the expected *Bernoulli*-utility would still be infinite. A sufficient condition to guarantee finite expected utility, no matter which utility function is used, is to limit the trials to a possibly large, but finite number N. That is to say, we limit the set of "fair" games to those with a finite expectation value. In case of the St. Petersburg game, this expectation is obviously

$$E[X] = \frac{N}{2}. \tag{10.46}$$

Surprisingly, this precaution is generally not sufficient, if we replace the expected utility functional by the prospective value functional of CPT. This was shown by Rieger and Wang (2006), with the help of the probability density function

$$f_q(x) = \begin{cases} 0 & \text{for } x \le 1 \\ (q-1)x^{-q} & \text{for } x > 1, \end{cases} \tag{10.47}$$

with $q > 2$. It is easy to see that the expectation of a random variable with this density function is finite,

$$E[X] = (q-1) \int_1^\infty x^{1-q} dx = \frac{q-1}{q-2} < \infty. \tag{10.48}$$

Quick calculation 10.13 Verify this result.

Note that the probability distribution function and also the quantile function, corresponding to the density (10.47), are available analytically,

$$F_q(x) = 1 - x^{1-q} \quad \text{and} \quad F_q^{-1}(u) = (1-u)^{1/(1-q)}, \tag{10.49}$$

with $x \in [1, \infty)$. Using the standard value and weighting functions (10.9) and (10.10) on pages 188–189, for $0 < \gamma < \alpha < 1$, as estimated by Kahneman and Tversky, it can be shown that there is a $q^* > 2$, such that the prospective value functional

$$V[X] = \int_1^\infty v(x)dw(F_q(x)) = \int_0^1 (1-u)^{\frac{\alpha}{1-q}} w'(u)du \tag{10.50}$$

diverges for $q \to q^*$. Let's see if we can prove this claim. First of all, we have to compute the derivative of the weighting function,

$$w'(u) = \frac{\gamma u^{\gamma-1}}{(u^\gamma + (1-u)^\gamma)^{1/\gamma}} - \frac{u^{2\gamma-1}}{(u^\gamma + (1-u)^\gamma)^{1+1/\gamma}} + \frac{u^\gamma(1-u)^{\gamma-1}}{(u^\gamma + (1-u)^\gamma)^{1+1/\gamma}}. \tag{10.51}$$

We have already shown that the terms in the denominator of (10.51) have a maximum at $u = \frac{1}{2}$. Furthermore it is not hard to see that they achieve their minimum value at $u = 0$ or $u = 1$, respectively. That means, if we use the maximum in the positive terms on the right hand side of (10.51), and the minimum in the negative term, we can bound the derivative of the probability weighting function from below by

$$w'(u) \ge \gamma 2^{1-1/\gamma} u^{\gamma-1} - u^{2\gamma-1} + 2^{\gamma-1/\gamma} u^\gamma (1-u)^{\gamma-1}. \tag{10.52}$$

Using this expression in (10.50), we can represent the lower limit of the value functional as a sum of the generic form

$$\int_0^1 (1-u)^{\frac{\alpha}{1-q}} w'(u)du \ge \sum_{n=1}^3 c_n \int_0^1 (1-u)^{a_n} u^{b_n} du. \tag{10.53}$$

The integrals on the right hand side of (10.53) are immediately identified as beta-functions (see for example Abramowitz and Stegun, 1970, p. 258)

$$B(x, y) = \int_0^1 (1 - t)^{x-1} t^{y-1} dt = \frac{\Gamma(x)\Gamma(y)}{\Gamma(x + y)}, \tag{10.54}$$

for $x, y > 0$, where capital gamma denotes the *Euler-Γ-function*

$$\Gamma(x) = \int_0^\infty t^{x-1} e^{-t} dt. \tag{10.55}$$

The Γ-function diverges to infinity, if its argument tends to zero. Thus, we have to check if one of the terms on the right hand side of (10.53) contains a suitable exponent. It turns out that the first two integrals are finite in any case, but the third one is not. Plugging in the numbers, one obtains

$$\int_0^1 (1 - u)^{\frac{\alpha}{1-q}+\gamma-1} u^\gamma du = \frac{\Gamma\left(\frac{\alpha}{1-q} + \gamma\right)\Gamma(1 + \gamma)}{\Gamma\left(1 + \frac{\alpha}{1-q} + 2\gamma\right)}. \tag{10.56}$$

The argument of the first Γ-function in the numerator becomes zero for

$$q^* = \frac{\alpha}{\gamma} + 1, \tag{10.57}$$

and because $c_3 = 2^{\gamma-1/\gamma} > 0$, the prospective value functional diverges to plus infinity,

$$\lim_{q \to q^*} \int_0^1 (1 - u)^{\frac{\alpha}{1-q}} w'(u) du = \infty, \tag{10.58}$$

if q approaches q^* from below. That means, probability weighting can cause infinite prospective value, even though the expectation value of the associated random variable is finite.

To remedy this problem, De Giorgi and Hens (2006) suggest using the alternative value function

$$v(x) = \begin{cases} \lambda^+(1 - e^{-\alpha x}) & \text{for } x \geq 0 \\ \lambda^-(e^{\alpha x} - 1) & \text{for } x < 0. \end{cases} \tag{10.59}$$

Unlike the original value function (10.9) on page 188, this modified version is bounded. Surprisingly, this is enough to prevent the prospective value functional from becoming infinite. This can be seen from the simple inequality

$$V[X] = \int_{-\infty}^\infty v(x) dw(F(x)) \leq \lambda^+ \int_0^1 dw(u) = \lambda^+, \tag{10.60}$$

where again the substitution $F(x) = u$ was used in the second step. De Giorgi and Hens chose the parameters $\alpha = 0.2$, $\lambda^+ = 6.52$, and $\lambda^- = 14.7$, in order to align their version with the original unbounded value function as closely as possible for small and moderate values of x; see Figure 10.6. In this way, the experimental results of Kahneman and Tversky still remain valid. Note that the quotient $\lambda^-/\lambda^+ \approx 2.25$ is approximately

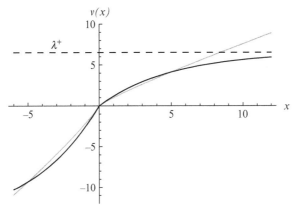

Fig. 10.6 Original CPT value function (gray) and bounded version (black) by De Giorgi and Hens (2006)

equal to the original coefficient of loss aversion, estimated by Kahneman and Tversky (1992).

Unifying prospect theory and modern portfolio theory is still an ongoing process. The existence of a market equilibrium is of paramount importance for the success of such a synthesis. So what happens, if we replace the classical mean-variance functional by an appropriate CPT functional? First of all, we have to consider two features of CPT. On the one hand, it is formulated in terms of gains and losses, not in terms of returns, and on the other hand, gains and losses are measured with respect to an appropriate reference point. If we assume that the current price of a portfolio P of risky assets is X_0, then it is quite natural to stipulate the risk-free capital gains rX_0 as the reference point. Thus, the prospective value functional becomes

$$V[X_P] = \int_{-\infty}^{\infty} v((x-r)X_0)dw(F(x)), \tag{10.61}$$

where now $F(x)$ is the distribution of the portfolio returns R_P. De Giorgi and Hens (2006) show that if there is a market portfolio, with

$$V[X_{\text{MP}}] > 0, \tag{10.62}$$

and short selling is allowed, then the original CPT functional does not permit an equilibrium, because agents would try to infinitely leverage the portfolio. To see this, remember that the capital market line contains all variance efficient portfolios with return

$$R_P = (1 - \lambda)r + \lambda R_{\text{MP}}. \tag{10.63}$$

Even though we have not shown at this point that a CPT decision maker would prefer a variance efficient portfolio, we can confidently make this assumption, because usually the expected return of the market portfolio is higher than the risk-free interest rate, and the CPT decision maker is risk averse in the domain of gains. It is not hard to see that using the original value function (10.9) on page 188 with $\alpha = \beta$, the relation

$$v(\lambda x) = \lambda^{\alpha} v(x) \tag{10.64}$$

holds, for $\lambda > 0$.

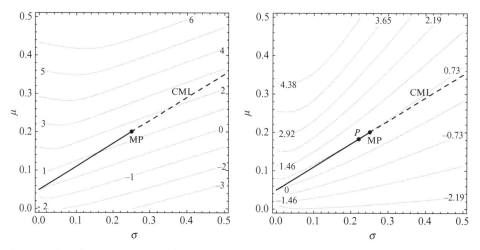

Fig. 10.7 CPT isoquants and capital market line for $X_0 = 20$ – Original value function of Kahneman and Tversky (left) and piecewise exponential version of De Giorgi and Hens (right)

Quick calculation 10.14 Confirm this result.

If $G(x)$ is the distribution function of the market portfolio returns, then, collecting all pieces, we obtain

$$V[X_P] = \int_{-\infty}^{\infty} \lambda^\alpha v((x - r)X_0)dw(G(x)) = \lambda^\alpha V[X_{\mathrm{MP}}]. \qquad (10.65)$$

Because $\alpha > 0$, and we have no short selling constraints, the prospective value of a leveraged position grows without limit for $\lambda \to \infty$. This does not happen, if we use the modified value function (10.59) on page 202, because the factorization argument (10.64) does not apply in this case.

We can analyze the situation a little bit further by assuming that returns are normally distributed, which is the case in classical portfolio theory. After standard normal transformation, the prospective value functional becomes

$$V[X_P] = \int_{-\infty}^{\infty} v((\sigma x + \mu - r)X_0)dw(\Phi(x)). \qquad (10.66)$$

This functional can be evaluated numerically and the resulting isoquants can be illustrated in a μ-σ-diagram. It is not surprising that in this more restrictive setting the infinite leverage problem shows up again; see Figure 10.7 left. Because the isoquants become parallel for large σ, it is advantageous to lever the portfolio without limit, if the slope of the capital market line (CML) is steeper than the slope of the isoquants for $\sigma \to \infty$. If the slope of the CML is shallower, agents exclusively invest in the riskless asset. This leads to another strange effect, called the robustness problem by De Giorgi and Hens (2006). If the slope of the CML is just below the critical point, only the riskless asset is held. But a very small change in the expected return or standard deviation of the market portfolio can increase the slope beyond the critical point. In this situation the demand for the market portfolio immediately jumps to an infinite amount. There is no smooth transition from risk-free to risky portfolio portions, but only a sharp switch. Thus, very small changes in μ, σ, or r can have a tremendous impact on the resulting market configuration. This is certainly not a desirable situation.

It can be shown rigorously, but also be seen from Figure 10.7 right, that these problems do not occur and an equilibrium exists, if the piecewise exponential value function (10.59) is used. The terminal slope of the isoquants increases with increasing level of prospective value. Hence, there is only one isoquant tangent to the capital market line and its tangential point yields the expected return and standard deviation of the agent's equilibrium portfolio P. Even though it seems that this is the end of the story, there is one further subtle point. A necessary requirement for the existence of an equilibrium was the absence of the scaling property (10.64) of the value function. But on the other hand, this scaling property is necessary to proceed from gains to returns without any qualitative changes. Put another way, the equilibrium P indicated in Figure 10.7 right is only valid for an initial investment of $X_0 = \$20$. A decision maker, who wants to invest for example \$1000 would realize a completely different equilibrium portfolio on the capital market line. In principle, this problem can be remedied by individually adjusting the parameters of the value function. But CPT is a descriptive theory of decision making and λ^+, λ^-, and α were chosen to closely resemble the original, empirically estimated value function of Kahneman and Tversky in the experimentally relevant range. So even if CPT is a promising candidate for a realistic theory of decision making in financial markets, there are fundamental questions still to be answered.

10.8   Further Reading

The classical sources are the papers of Kahneman and Tversky (1979, 1992). A concise introduction to prospect theory is found in Hens and Rieger (2010, sect. 2.4). A more comprehensive survey is Barberis and Thaler (2005). There is also a very accessible textbook on behavioral finance by Ackert and Deaves (2010). For a rigorous axiomatic foundation of cumulative prospect theory, see Wakker and Tversky (1993). Explanations for momentum and reversal anomalies were suggested by Barberis et al. (1998), Daniel et al. (2001), and Grinblatt and Han (2005). A full scale formal treatment of CPT equilibrium asset pricing theory is found in De Giorgi et al. (2011).

10.9   Problems

10.1 Consider the following problem presented by Tversky and Kahneman (1983):
Linda is 31 years old, single, outspoken, and very bright. She majored in philosophy. As a student, she was deeply concerned with issues of discrimination

and social justice, and also participated in anti-nuclear demonstrations. Which is more probable?

1. Linda is a bank teller.
2. Linda is a bank teller and is active in the feminist movement.

Most people choose the second answer, but this is a so-called conjunction fallacy. Provide a formal argument why alternative two cannot be more likely than alternative one.

10.2 Prelec (1998) suggested the alternative probability weighting function

$$w(p) = e^{-(-\log p)^\gamma},$$

with $0 < \gamma < 1$. Show that $w(p)$ satisfies the necessary conditions for a weighting function to be admissible.

10.3 Reconsider Problem 10.2 and its solution to show that $w(p)$, like the original weighting function of Kahneman and Tversky, is S-shaped, with concave curvature for small p and convex curvature for large p.

10.4 Birnbaum and Navarrete (1998) analyzed choices between two gambles. One of their decision problems was the following:

Gamble A:
- $12 with prob. 5%
- $14 with prob. 5%
- $96 with prob. 90%

Gamble B:
- $12 with prob. 10%
- $90 with prob. 5%
- $96 with prob. 85%

73% of the test subjects chose gamble B. Provide a fundamental argument why this is a bad choice.

10.5 A random variable X is said to dominate another random variable Y statewise, if

$$X(\omega) \ge Y(\omega)$$

holds, for all $\omega \in \Omega$, with strict inequality for at least one ω. Statewise dominance implies first order stochastic dominance, but the converse is not true. Construct two random variables X and Y on the probability space of a fair coin flip experiment, such that X dominates Y stochastically to first order, but no statewise dominance relation can be established.

Part III Derivatives

11 Forwards, Futures, and Options

We are now entering the world of derivatives. Derivatives are contracts whose value depends on the value of other securities, commodities, rates, or even derivatives themselves; hence their name. They are nowadays traded as highly sophisticated risk transfer instruments in organized markets like the Chicago Board Options Exchange (CBOE) or in secondary over the counter markets (OTC). Valuation of derivatives is at the heart of quantitative finance, and can sometimes be a very challenging task. This chapter is only a gentle warm-up for the techniques to be discussed in the sequel.

11.1 Forward and Future Contracts

Forwards and futures are contracts, which enable an agent to lock in a future price for an arbitrary underlying today. An underlying can be a security, a commodity, an exchange rate, or in principle everything that can be traded. The difference between forward and future contracts is the way they are traded and settled. Forwards are individually "over the counter" (OTC) brokered contracts. Settlement is at expiry or shortly after, usually but not necessarily in cash. A future is a standardized contract that is traded in an organized market. Both sides of the future can be contracted independently with a clearing house as counterparty. To reduce the default risk for the clearing house, the agent has to provide collateral and to agree to daily settlement payments via a margin account. By this procedure, the value of an open contract is reset every day. In a world where the risk-free interest rate is either constant, or a deterministic function of time, forward and future prices have to coincide. In reality, where interest rates themselves are stochastic, both prices diverge because of the different settlement policies. Until further notice, we will assume that the risk-free interest rate is deterministic.

Why would anyone enter into a forward or future contract at all? Let's look at the following example.

Example 11.1

Assume A is a large food retail chain, say in Germany, and B is an agricultural producer in Spain. A would like to buy 50 tons of tomatoes from B next year. B is willing to sell the requested quantity to A, but both operate under a fair amount of risk and effort. The underlying commodity, the 50 tons of tomatoes, does not even exist today. They have to be planted at the beginning of the next year, in order to be ready for harvesting shortly before the contracted delivery date. It is uncertain if there will be enough rain in Spain next year to prevent crop failures, which could drive up the market price of tomatoes or worse, rendering delivery of the full quantity impossible. Last but not least, 50 tons of tomatoes have to be shipped all the way across Europe, to get them from B to A.

Entering a forward contract

Imagine A and B agree to a cash settled forward contract, in which the delivery price and date are fixed. What happens at expiry of this contract? A will buy at the local market in Germany at the market price, prevailing at the delivery date. B will sell in Spain, also at the prevailing market price. Additionally, one party will compensate the other party for the difference between the contracted delivery price and the actual market price. There is no physical delivery, and hence no transportation costs, and no risk regarding the future market price of tomatoes.

You see how efficient the forward contract is? It avoids costly physical delivery and completely removes the uncertainty of next year's price. Now you have a first glimpse of why modern economies vitally depend on a liquid and operational financial market.

There are two questions regarding such a forward contract, we have to answer. The first is, is there a rule to determine the delivery price, such that the contract is fair for both parties? And if there is, how should the delivery price be chosen? The second question is a little more subtle. Recall that the forward contract in Example 11.1 involves the right and the obligation to buy or sell the underlying at the delivery date at a pre-determined price. This right can also be traded, and it thus should have a price itself. How can we determine its fair price? This is our first problem in derivative pricing.

11.2   Bank Account and Forward Price

The concepts we will see in this section are some of the most powerful tools in derivative pricing, because they are completely model independent. As soon as a market is considered liquid enough to prevent arbitrage opportunities (at least on a large scale), these principles have to hold no matter what additional conditions we might have imposed.

Let's first talk about the time value of money. You might have learned already the golden rule of financial mathematics: Never compare two nominal payments at different times. What this means is that the value of money changes with time. How can that be? If you put $100 under your pillow and come back tomorrow, you will still have $100. But this is a particular property of your pillow. If you put $100 into a bank account today and come back tomorrow, you have more than $100, because you earned interest. In a liquid market, everyone puts her money into a bank account. If you find somebody preferring a pillow, offer him yours, then afterwards secretly put the money into your bank account and withdraw it the next day. So she gets her money back and you earn the interest. But that is an arbitrage, isn't it? The question is how does the value of money evolve with time? Let's assume for the moment that interest rates are constant, and call the risk-free interest rate r. If you deposit a certain capital in a bank account B, its value changes proportional to the interest rate, the capital itself, and of course the time of your deposit. Let's write this for very short amounts of time,

$$dB(t) = rB(t)dt, \qquad (11.1)$$

and let's see what we can do with it. Without loss of generality, we can assume that the capital you put into your account at time $t = 0$ was $B(0) = 1$ unit of currency. If you put 100 units of currency there, think of it as 100 distinct accounts, it makes no difference. Next, divide both sides by $B(t)$,

$$\frac{dB(t)}{B(t)} = d\log B(t) = rdt. \qquad (11.2)$$

We can integrate this differential equation easily to obtain

$$\int_0^t d\log B(s) = \log B(t) = rt = r \int_0^t ds. \qquad (11.3)$$

Exponentiating both sides of (11.3) yields

$$B(t) = e^{rt}. \qquad (11.4)$$

On the other hand, it is easy to see that a value of K at time t requires an initial deposit of $e^{-rt}K$, or more precisely $e^{-rt}K$ standard bank accounts, because

$$e^{-rt}KB(t) = K. \qquad (11.5)$$

Here is a little more tricky question: What is the time t value of an amount K at T for $0 < t < T$? By now you will agree that you initially need $e^{-rT}K$ standard accounts. But their value at time t is simply

$$e^{-rT}KB(t) = e^{-r(T-t)}K. \qquad (11.6)$$

Quick calculation 11.1 What is the time T value of a time t deposit of one unit of currency for $t < T$?

Now let us return to our initial problem and answer the first question. How should the delivery price of a forward contract be chosen? Suppose the contract has an ordinary, non dividend paying stock S as underlying. When initiated, neither party should have to pay anything for contracting the delivery price K and delivery date T. Thus, at time $t = 0$ the forward contract has zero value, $F_0(K, T) = 0$. Consider building the following hypothetical portfolio: Enter a forward contract as buyer, short one unit of the underlying, put the earnings from the short selling into your bank account. The position is summarized in Table 11.1. Obviously this portfolio does not cost anything at $t = 0$. But this means, it has to have zero price at $t = T$, too, otherwise we would have

Table 11.1 Forward arbitrage portfolio

Position	Value at $t = 0$	Value at $t = T$
Forward	0	$S_T - K$
Stock	$-S_0$	$-S_T$
Bank account	S_0	$e^{rT}S_0$
Total sum	$S_0 - S_0 = 0$	$e^{rT}S_0 - K$

an arbitrage opportunity, either by holding this portfolio or by shorting it. To rule out such an arbitrage opportunity, the delivery price of the forward contract has to be chosen as

$$K = e^{rT}S_0. \tag{11.7}$$

Except for a constant risk-free interest rate, this argument is completely free of model-based assumptions. We only used a genuine arbitrage argument. Thus, this result is a very strong one and as long as interest rates are deterministic, it holds for the future contract as well.

The second question is, how should a running contract, initiated at some time in the past, be valued? To answer this question, we make use of another luxury the arbitrage free choice of the delivery price provides us with, we build ourselves a time machine. Note that the value of the forward contract at delivery is

$$F_T(K, T) = S_T - K, \tag{11.8}$$

see Table 11.1. All quantities depend on time, even if this is not so obvious for the delivery price. To see this, let's write it in a slightly different form

$$K = e^{-rT}KB(T). \tag{11.9}$$

Quick calculation 11.2 Convince yourself that (11.9) is correct.

So the time t value of the delivery price K is

$$e^{-rT}KB(t) = e^{-r(T-t)}K. \tag{11.10}$$

Of course, what we discussed so thoroughly in terms of our standardized bank account is nothing else but continuous discounting. There is a deeper reason for going through it so rigorously. It has to do with a certain choice of numéraire we will encounter at a later point. At the moment, we simply take the value of the contract at expiry (11.8), and crank the dials of our time machine back to any desired time t. In doing so, we obtain

$$F_t(K, T) = S_t - e^{-r(T-t)}K. \tag{11.11}$$

You have probably learned that something like a time machine cannot work in real life. So let's see if we can understand why our financial time machine works correctly. Fix an arbitrary time $t = \tau$ and assume that you already hold one forward contract, initiated at $t = 0$. Initiate another forward contract with identical delivery date T and delivery price $\mathcal{K}$, and take the opposite side. By definition, entering this contract does not cost you anything and thus, the value of your position has not changed. At expiry of both contracts, your position has the value $\mathcal{K} - K$. But this difference is only a positive or negative amount of currency with time τ value $e^{-r(T-\tau)}(\mathcal{K} - K)$. Now realize that you have to choose the delivery price

$$\mathcal{K} = e^{r(T-\tau)} S_\tau \tag{11.12}$$

in order to prevent arbitrage opportunities. Hence, the present value of your position at $t = \tau$ is

$$F_\tau(K, T) - 0 = S_\tau - e^{-r(T-\tau)} K. \tag{11.13}$$

Because τ is arbitrary, the substitution $\tau \to t$ does the trick.

Quick calculation 11.3 Sketch the arbitrage portfolio for the contract initiated at $t = \tau$.

We can now see why our time machine worked for the forward contract. But the argument behind the derivation is far more general. Whenever the market is free of arbitrage opportunities and you can build a portfolio that costs nothing at one time, it cannot cost anything at any other time. This principle is at the heart of parity relations, which are the strongest conditions we can hope to find in pricing derivatives.

11.3   Options

We learned that risk aversion is expressed in terms of a certain asymmetry in utility between losing or gaining a fixed amount of wealth. That usually holds also for the costs of precautionary measures.

Imagine you were employed at company A of Example 11.1, and you were the person in charge of the tomato deal with B. You are concerned that anything could go wrong and so you decide to enter a forward contract with B. Let's speculate what might happen. First think of the possibility that your precaution was well justified and tomato prices are considerably higher than expected, $S_T > K$. In this case you can relax, because no matter what the price is, your forward contract will provide compensation of the difference between market price and delivery price, and everyone will praise you for your vigilance and your professional skills. But what happens if everything goes well and the tomatoes cost considerably less than expected, $S_T < K$? Everyone will celebrate, because they hope for spectacular profits. Then you have to step in front of the CFO and explain, why your company has to pay $K - S_T$ from a forward contract you entered one year ago. You are lucky if you can keep your job.

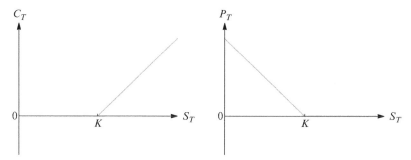

Fig. 11.1 Payoff function of a call option (left) and a put option (right) from the holder's perspective (long position)

An option contract is designed to keep you out of such trouble, by certifying the right but not the obligation to buy (call) or sell (put) the underlying at an exercise price K. At expiry, the value of a call option for example is $S_T - K$, if $S_T > K$, and zero else. If the market price is higher than the contracted exercise price, you would of course exercise the option, because you can buy at K and immediately sell at S_T at the market. Your riskless profit would be the difference $S_T - K$, which is exactly the value of the option at expiry, if $S_T > K$. If $S_T < K$, you would not exercise the option at all, because you can buy cheaper at the market. Therefore, the contract expires worthlessly and its value at time T is zero. We can summarize these arguments by introducing the payoff function of the call option as its intrinsic value at expiry

$$C_T(S_T) = \max(S_T - K, 0) = (S_T - K)^+, \tag{11.14}$$

where we have written the terminal value as a function of the price of the underlying at time T. The right hand side is only a shorthand for the maximum function we will use frequently. Figure 11.1 left illustrates the payoff function from the perspective of the option holder. This position is also called the long position. The person who has written the option is said to be in the short position.

Quick calculation 11.4 What is the payoff function of a forward contract?

If we are in the long position of a put option, then we have the right, but not the obligation, to sell the underlying at the contracted exercise price K. The writer of the option (short position) is under the obligation to buy the underlying from us, if we choose to exercise the option. If the market price of the underlying at expiry is less than the exercise price, $S_T < K$, we can immediately buy in the market at S_T and exercise the option to sell for K to the writer of the contract, providing an instantaneous profit of $K - S_T$. If $S_T > K$, we would of course not exercise the option, because we can earn more money by selling at the market price S_T, rather than at the exercise price K. Thus, the payoff function of the put option has to be

$$P_T(S_T) = \max(K - S_T, 0) = (K - S_T)^+, \tag{11.15}$$

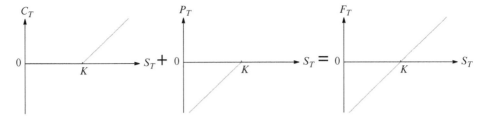

Fig. 11.2 Adding up the payoff functions of a long call and short put with identical exercise price K and expiry date T

where we have used the same shorthand for the maximum function as before. The payoff function is illustrated in Figure 11.1 right.

Quick calculation 11.5 Sketch the payoff function for a short call and short put position.

Let's ask the following question: What payoff function do we get, if we hold one call option and short a put option with identical exercise price and time to expiry? The answer is illustrated in Figure 11.2. Adding both payoff functions results in an exact replication of the payoff function of a forward or future contract. This means that at time T we have

$$C_T - P_T = F_T. \tag{11.16}$$

But recognize that a portfolio of one long call, one short put, and one short forward of this kind has value zero at time T. This means that it must be zero at all times and we can again use our time machine. The resulting identity

$$C_t(K, T) - P_t(K, T) = F_t(K, T) = S_t - e^{-r(T-t)}K \tag{11.17}$$

is called put-call parity. It enables us to immediately find the value of a put option for example, if the corresponding call option is traded. As emphasized before, parity relations do not require model based assumptions, and are thus very powerful.

The most common types of options are called plain vanilla options after a very popular ice cream flavor in the USA. A position in plain vanilla options is characterized by the following features:

Position

- Long: Contract holder with the right to exercise the option.
- Short: Contract writer under the obligation to comply, if the holder exercises.

Option type

- Call: Right to buy the underlying from the writer at the contracted exercise price.
- Put: Right to sell the underlying to the writer at the contracted exercise price.

Exercise right

- European: Option can only be exercised at expiry.
- American: Option can be exercised at any time until expiry.

Of course there is a multiverse of non-vanilla option contracts, called exotics, but vanillas are still the most liquidly traded derivatives in the market.

11.4   Compound Positions and Option Strategies

Plain vanilla options are most versatile in that a desired payoff profile can be generated by combining long and short positions in calls and puts. Furthermore, they are appropriate for manipulating the downside risk or the return characteristics of a given position in the underlying. In this paragraph we will discuss some of the most basic strategies, frequently encountered in the market.

11.4.1   Straddle

A straddle position is often used to hedge against massive up- or downturns of the underlying. Imagine the underlying is a stock, and the respective company is about to report quarterly figures. Often the trading volume drops before such an event, because there are some opposing rumors, but nobody really knows what to expect. In this situation it is likely that the report triggers one of two possible events. Either the figures are good and the price moves up, due to temporal excess demand, or the report is disappointing for the investors and the price drops, because of increasing sales. Either way, a straddle position can provide insurance against the consequences of such an event. It is composed of a long call and a long put, both with identical exercise price K and expiry T,

$$\Pi_{\text{Straddle}} = C(K, T) + P(K, T). \tag{11.18}$$

The corresponding payoff function is illustrated in Figure 11.3 left. From the payoff it is obvious, why the straddle can provide insurance against both outcomes. Of course, such an insurance has its price; note that the straddle contains only long positions.

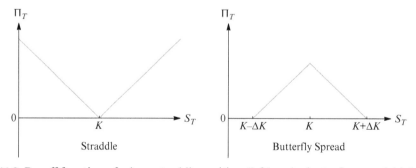

Fig. 11.3 Payoff function of a long straddle position (left) and a butterfly spread (right)

11.4.2   Butterfly Spread

In a certain sense, the butterfly spread is an opposite position to the straddle. It pays off its maximum ΔK, if the price at expiry equals the exercise price K, see Figure 11.3 right. To establish a butterfly spread, one requires call options with three different exercise prices, K, and $K \pm \Delta K$, where $\Delta K > 0$ is arbitrary. The structure of the entire position is

$$\Pi_{\text{Butterfly}} = C(K - \Delta K, T) - 2C(K, T) + C(K + \Delta K, T). \tag{11.19}$$

Because the butterfly spread contains two long and two short positions, it is relatively cheap to enter because

$$C_t(K - \Delta K, T) > C_t(K, T) > C_t(K + \Delta K, T) \tag{11.20}$$

has to hold for every $t < T$. Nevertheless, the butterfly spread has to cost a positive amount of money, $\Pi_t > 0$, because it has a positive payoff in states of the world, in which $K - \Delta K < S_T < K + \Delta K$ holds. Otherwise we would have an arbitrage opportunity.

Quick calculation 11.6   Sketch an arbitrage argument for the price of a butterfly spread to be bounded by $0 \leq \Pi_t \leq e^{-r(T-t)}\Delta K$ for $t \leq T$.

11.4.3   Bull and Bear Spreads

Bull and bear spreads are limited risk positions with two options with the same expiry T, but with different exercise prices $K_2 > K_1$. The difference between both positions is the direction in which the underlying has to evolve, in order to trigger a payoff at expiry. Imagine the current price of an underlying is $K_1 < S_t < K_2$. If it behaves bullish, which means its price rises, the payoff from the bull spread increases, see Figure 11.4 left. The position is established by the simple combination

$$\Pi_{\text{Bull}} = C(K_1, T) - C(K_2, T). \tag{11.21}$$

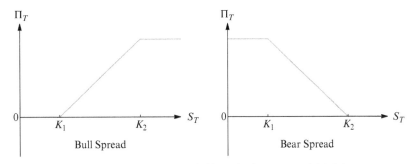

Fig. 11.4 Payoff function of a bull spread (left) and a bear spread (right)

Of course the price of a bull spread is bounded by $0 \leq \Pi_t \leq e^{-r(T-t)}(K_2 - K_1)$ for $t \leq T$. Otherwise we would again have an arbitrage opportunity.

Quick calculation 11.7 Confirm the above mentioned bounds for $S_T < K_1$ and $S_T > K_2$.

The same holds true for the bear spread, because it is merely a mirror image of the bull spread, see Figure 11.4 right. It can be established by combining two put options,

$$\Pi_{\text{Bear}} = P(K_2, T) - P(K_1, T). \tag{11.22}$$

Of course, an investor would hold a bear spread, if she expects the price of the underlying to fall. Such a development is often called bearish, hence the name.

There is another spread strategy an investor can pursue, called a calendar spread. In this case the options involved have the same exercise price K, but different expiries, T_1 and T_2. With this strategy, an investor usually does not speculate on rising or falling prices of the underlying, but on changes in implied volatility. Since we have not treated volatility concepts in detail so far, we will not discuss this position here.

11.4.4   Protective Put Buying

Protective put buying is a strategy to limit the downside risk of a security or portfolio of securities, held by an investor. It works by establishing a so-called floor with the help of a long position in an appropriate put option. Imagine you hold a security with current price S_0, and your investment horizon is T. You can limit the loss potential of this position by buying a put option with expiry T and exercise price $K < S_0$. In case the price of the security falls below the floor, $S_T < K$, the put option provides insurance by paying $K - S_T$ at expiry. Your potential loss from S is therefore bounded by $S_0 - K$. Of course this insurance does not come for free. At $t = 0$ you have to pay the option premium P_0, reducing your expected profits from S. Assume that you have to borrow the money to buy the put option, then the value of your position at any time $0 \leq t \leq T$ is

$$\Pi_t = S_t + P_t(K, T) - e^{rt}P_0. \tag{11.23}$$

In particular at $t = T$, your portfolio is floored by $\Pi_T \geq K - e^{rT}P_0$. This is reassuring, but it comes at the cost of a reduced return, due to the long position in the put option. You can even increase the insurance level of this strategy for example by choosing an option with $K = S_0$. You are then completely shielded from losses in your stock position, but such an at-the-money put option would be fairly expensive. Thus, your stock would have to perform extraordinarily well, just to break even.

11.4.5   Covered Call Writing

Covered call writing is a strategy for manipulating the return profile of a position in a stock or a portfolio. It has no insurance character, but it earns a positive amount of money at the beginning of the investment period. Let's again consider an investment horizon $0 \leq t \leq T$, and a long position in the stock S. Typically writing a call option is a delicate decision, because the potential loss is not bounded.

Quick calculation 11.8 Sketch the payoff function of a short call position.

However, in this case shorting a call is noncritical, because we already own the underlying. If the option holder decides to exercise the option at expiry, we can hand over the stock and receive the exercise price. Of course, we obtain an option premium C_0 at $t = 0$, which we deposit in our bank account in order to earn interest. The whole position at any time t is thus

$$\Pi_t = S_t - C_t(K, T) + e^{rt} C_0. \tag{11.24}$$

For this position to make sense, we have to choose an exercise price $K > S_0$, because eventually our gains are bounded by $\Pi_T \leq K + e^{rT} C_0$ from above. Which means, we sell the possibility of extraordinary high returns for a fixed option premium at $t = 0$. This decision is advantageous in all cases, where $S_T \leq K$, because the option is not exercised. If $S_T > K$ we do not participate further in any winnings, no matter how high they might be. We can decide how much of the potential gains to trade for the initial call premium; the lower K, the higher the premium, but the less we participate in potential gains.

11.5   Arbitrage Bounds on Options

To determine the fair price of a plain vanilla European option, it is in general not sufficient to exploit arbitrage arguments. An exception is the theoretical possibility that the market contains a continuum of call options with all possible exercise prices at any given expiry; see Breeden and Litzenberger (1978). Nevertheless, they will carry us a good part of the way, so let's see what we can learn from them. Consider the problem of pricing a plain vanilla European call with exercise price K and expiry T today, at $t = 0$. We can apply three arbitrage arguments to bound its price from above and below:

1. The price of the call option $C_0(K, T)$ can never exceed the price of the underlying S_0. To see this realize that for the payoff at expiry $(S_T - K)^+ - S_T \leq 0$ holds. Now crank the dials of the time machine back to $t = 0$ to obtain $C_0(K, T) - S_0 \leq 0$. The claim follows immediately.

2. The price of the call option can never be smaller than the price of a corresponding forward contract. To see this, again set up a portfolio of one call and short one forward contract. The payoff is $(S_T - K)^+ - (S_T - K) \geq 0$. Dialing back the time we obtain $C_0(K, T) - S_0 + e^{-rT} K \geq 0$, as required.

3. The price of the call option can never be negative. The argument for this is a fundamental one. The payoff of the call is nonnegative and positive for states of the world, in which $S_T > K$. Thus, the price at $t = 0$ must not be negative by the very definition of an arbitrage opportunity.

Condensing all three arguments into one formula, we can make the following statement about the arbitrage bounds for a European call option

$$(S_0 - e^{-rT}K)^+ \le C_0(K, T) \le S_0. \tag{11.25}$$

Going through a similar set of arguments for a European plain vanilla put option, we arrive at the arbitrage bounds

$$(e^{-rT}K - S_0)^+ \le P_0(K, T) \le e^{-rT}K. \tag{11.26}$$

Quick calculation 11.9 Apply the appropriate arbitrage arguments to confirm (11.26).

That is how far arbitrage considerations can carry us. Unfortunately those bounds are not very tight, which means we have to do much better.

11.6   Further Reading

For the time value of money, see Capinski and Zastawniak (2003, sect. 2.1). Forward and future contracts are introduced very carefully in Hull (2009, chap. 5). In particular, a simple proof for the equality of forward and future prices for constant interest rates is provided in the appendix. For a deeper treatment of this subject, see Cox et al. (1981). A very good introduction to options, parity relations, and option strategies is provided in Hull (2009, chap. 8 & 10), and also in Wilmott (2006a, chap. 2). For arbitrage bounds on options see Hull (2009, chap. 9) and Cox (2010).

11.7   Problems

11.1 Suppose a stock pays a fixed percentage dividend stream q that is continuously reinvested, such that an initial investment S_0 has time T value $e^{qT}S_T$. Construct an arbitrage portfolio for a forward contract and find the delivery price, such that entering the contract does not cost anything.

11.2 An option that pays off one unit of currency at expiry, in case of $S_T \ge K$, and zero else, is called a binary or digital call option. Likewise a binary put option pays one unit of currency, if $S_T < K$ holds, and nothing otherwise. Sketch the payoff function of a binary call and put.

11.3 Establish a parity relation for binary calls and puts by adding their payoff functions and derive a formula for $0 \le t \le T$.

11.4 Consider a modified butterfly position

$$\Pi_{\text{Butterfly}} = C(K_1, T) - a \cdot C(K_2, T) + C(K_3, T),$$

with $K_1 < K_2 < K_3$, and $a > 0$. How is a to be chosen to guarantee a vanishing payoff for $S_T = K_1$ and $S_T = K_3$?

11.5 It is possible to generalize the butterfly position even more to the form

$$\Pi_{\text{Butterfly}} = C(K_1, T) - a \cdot C(K_2, T) + b \cdot C(K_3, T),$$

with $K_1 < K_2 < K_3$, and $a, b > 0$ How are the coefficients a and b to be chosen, to generate a vanishing payoff for $S_T \leq K_1$ and $S_T \geq K_3$?

11.6 Describe the position an investor holds, if she is long in a covered call and short in a protective put, with both options having the same exercise price and time to expiry.

11.7 Assume an investor holds long positions in a covered call and a protective put. Both options have identical expiries and exercise prices. What is the payoff of this combined position at expiry?

12   The Binomial Model

Historically, Cox et al. (1979) introduced their binomial option pricing model after the seminal work of Black and Scholes (1973), and also Merton (1973). Surprisingly, the *Cox–Ross–Rubinstein*-model (CRR) is not a further stage of the *Black–Scholes*-model, but a simplification. Cox et al. engineered an option pricing model, based merely on fundamental algebraic operations, which in a certain limit approaches the *Black–Scholes*-model, but avoids the advanced mathematical machinery. Thus, the CRR-model seems a natural and pedagogical starting point.

12.1   The Coin Flip Universe

Let's start with the very easiest setting of a financial market we can think of. Such a market is characterized by:

- only two discrete points in time, $t = 0$ (today) and $t = T$ (in the future), where trading is possible,
- two possible states of the world at time T, "up" ($\uparrow$) and "down" ($\downarrow$),
- only one stock S with known price at $t = 0$,
- a zero risk-free interest rate,
- no market frictions, trading costs, or short-selling constraints,
- infinite divisibility of assets.

Further assume that the initial price of the stock is $S_0 = 100$ units of currency, and that the states $\omega = \uparrow$ and $\omega = \downarrow$ occur with equal probability $p = \frac{1}{2}$. You can think of this setting as a single time coin flip universe. Observe that in such a market all possible option contracts have European exercise right. The price of the stock at $t = T$ is random, with

$$S_T(\omega) = \begin{cases} 120 & \text{for } \omega = \uparrow \\ 90 & \text{for } \omega = \downarrow. \end{cases} \tag{12.1}$$

The situation is illustrated in Figure 12.1 left. Let us now introduce a call option on the stock S into this market, with an exercise price of $K = 105$. The payoff of this option at expiry T is also random, with

$$C_T(\omega) = \begin{cases} 15 & \text{for } \omega = \uparrow \\ 0 & \text{for } \omega = \downarrow. \end{cases} \tag{12.2}$$

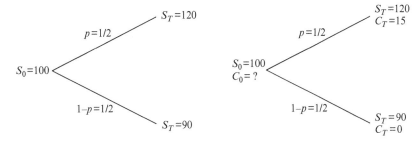

Fig. 12.1 One period binomial option pricing model – Stock market (left) and extended market with one derivative (right)

To be a little more precise, the value of the option at $t = T$ is measurable with respect to the σ-algebra $\mathcal{F}_T$, generated by S_T.

Quick calculation 12.1 What is the σ-algebra $\mathcal{F}_T$?

The possible values of the call option and the underlying are illustrated in Figure 12.1 right. The big question is, what is the fair price of the call option at $t = 0$? You may be tempted to answer $C_0 = 7.5$, because that is the expected payoff at expiry, but that is the wrong idea. In fact there are two ways to figure out the correct price, both completely equivalent. We have already encountered this duality in Chapter 5.

Let's try to build a hedge-portfolio of one call option and short half a stock,

$$\Pi_t = C_t - \frac{1}{2}S_t. \tag{12.3}$$

At this point it is far from clear, why half a unit of the stock should be shorted, so let's think of it as an educated guess for the moment. What is the value of this portfolio at expiry T? Figure 12.2 provides the answer. Obviously, the payoff does not depend on the state of the world at all. If the value of the portfolio at expiry is $\Pi_T = -45$ in all possible states, then the initial value has to be also

$$\Pi_0 = C_0 - 50 = -45. \tag{12.4}$$

From this requirement we can easily conclude that $C_0 = 5$ has to hold. Let's now answer the question of how we made our educated guess in the first place. The whole setup only

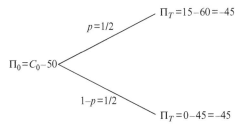

Fig. 12.2 Hedge-portfolio for the call option in the one period binomial model

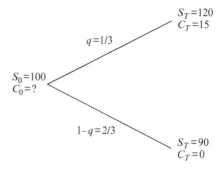

Fig. 12.3 Underlying with call option under the alternative probability measure Q

works, if the payoff at expiry is identical in both states of the world. In other words, we are looking for a hedge-ratio Δ, such that

$$C_T(\uparrow) - \Delta \cdot S_T(\uparrow) = C_T(\downarrow) - \Delta \cdot S_T(\downarrow) \tag{12.5}$$

holds. Rearranging (12.5) yields the desired condition

$$\Delta = \frac{C_T(\uparrow) - C_T(\downarrow)}{S_T(\uparrow) - S_T(\downarrow)} = \frac{\Delta C_T}{\Delta S_T}. \tag{12.6}$$

This hedge-ratio will show up again in a different guise in the *Black–Scholes*-theory. Leave it that way for the moment and let's see how the dual pricing procedure works.

Quick calculation 12.2   Verify that the hedge-ratio in the above toy market is $\Delta = \frac{1}{2}$.

Let's again look at the same option valuation problem, but now, just for fun, choose other probabilities. To avoid confusion, call the alternative probability measure Q, and choose $q = \frac{1}{3}$, as indicated in Figure 12.3. Now, let's make the following observation: Under the probability measure Q, the expected terminal stock price is

$$E^Q[S_T] = \frac{1}{3} \cdot 120 + \frac{2}{3} \cdot 90 = 40 + 60 = 100. \tag{12.7}$$

But that is exactly today's price of the stock, S_0. This means that S_t is a martingale under the alternative probability measure Q. We can emphasize this by including the information set $\mathcal{F}_0$ and writing

$$E^Q[S_T|\mathcal{F}_0] = S_0. \tag{12.8}$$

The deeper meaning of explicitly conditioning on $\mathcal{F}_0$ is that we have to know S_0 to be able to determine the probability q in the first place. We can obtain q by solving

$$S_0 = q \cdot S_T(\uparrow) + (1 - q) \cdot S_T(\downarrow), \tag{12.9}$$

because we can unambiguously tell what value S took at $t = 0$. The key advantage of the martingale measure Q is that it holds for all securities traded in the market. We can check this for the call option

$$E^Q[C_T|\mathcal{F}_0] = \frac{1}{3} \cdot 15 + \frac{2}{3} \cdot 0 = 5 = C_0. \qquad (12.10)$$

Note that once such an equivalent martingale measure is established, it is the same for all contracts that can potentially be traded in the market. In pricing via an arbitrage portfolio, we have to compute an individual hedge-ratio for each contract separately.

12.2   The Multi-Period Binomial Model

We will now relax some of the restrictions we imposed on our coin flip toy market. In particular, we will allow

- multi-period trading at discrete points in time $t = 0, \ldots, T$,
- a nonzero risk-free interest rate r.

Think of this setup as an independently, T times repeated coin flip. The successive prices of the stock S are given by

$$S_{t+1} = \begin{cases} u \cdot S_t & \text{for } \omega_{t+1} = \uparrow \\ d \cdot S_t & \text{for } \omega_{t+1} = \downarrow, \end{cases} \qquad (12.11)$$

see Figure 12.4, where ω_{t+1} is a somewhat sloppy shorthand for all states that are either 'up' or 'down' at $t + 1$. The coefficients u and d are just numbers, yet to be determined. The only requirement is the condition

$$0 < d < 1 + r\Delta t < u, \qquad (12.12)$$

otherwise we would generate an arbitrage opportunity. Note that in this multi-period setting we can by all means have contracts with American exercise right. Figure 12.5 illustrates a two-period version of the so-called binomial tree. We will indicate the

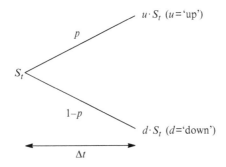

Fig. 12.4 Notational conventions in the binomial model

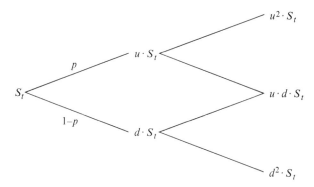

Fig. 12.5 Two-period version of the binomial tree

probabilities only on the first branch, because they remain unchanged for the whole tree. Finally, let's introduce a more efficient notation for the vertices of the tree. Let's call $S_t^{(n)}$ the price of the stock at time t at the n-th ascending vertex, for $t = 1, \ldots, T$ and $n = 0, \ldots, t$; see Figure 12.6. Of course S_0 is only a single vertex and we do not need an additional label. We can now easily see that every vertex in the tree is described by

$$S_t^{(n)} = u^n d^{t-n} S_0. \tag{12.13}$$

Does this remind you of something? It looks almost like a binomial distribution. Indeed S_t is a binomial random variable with probability mass function

$$f_n(S_t) = P(S_t = S_t^{(n)}) = \binom{t}{n} p^n (1 - p)^{t-n}. \tag{12.14}$$

In order to proceed with the binomial model, we have to discuss equivalent martingale measures in a little more detail.

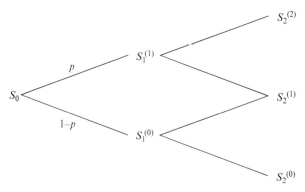

Fig. 12.6 Efficient notation for the two-period version of the binomial tree

What we really need in order to compute security prices, is a traded and strictly positive numéraire quantity N, and associated with it, a certain equivalent probability measure P_N, such that the ratio

$$\frac{S_t}{N_t} = E^{P_N}\left[\frac{S_T}{N_T}\Big|\mathcal{F}_t\right] \tag{12.15}$$

is a martingale under the measure P_N; hence the name equivalent martingale measure. Let's for example choose our bank account as the numéraire,

$$N_t = B(t) = e^{rt}, \tag{12.16}$$

and let's call the martingale measure associated with it Q. We thus have

$$e^{-rt}S_t = E^Q[e^{-rT}S_T|\mathcal{F}_t]. \tag{12.17}$$

Because r is constant and known, it factors out of the conditional expectation and after trivial rearrangements we have

$$S_t = e^{-r(T-t)}E^Q[S_T|\mathcal{F}_t]. \tag{12.18}$$

What the martingale pricing principle says is that under the probability measure Q, the price of every security should equal the discounted expected price in the future, based on today's information. Because only a risk-neutral agent would price a security solely based on its expected payoff, the measure Q is often called the risk-neutral probability measure. Every security, including derivatives, traded in the market, has to obey this relation. The delicate piece of reasoning is to compute this magnificent probability measure. Let's see how this is done in the binomial model.

Traditionally, compounding is done discretely in the binomial model. It mirrors the discrete nature of the model setup. Translating (12.18) into this framework, we can eventually derive the relation

$$\begin{aligned} S_t &= \frac{1}{1+r\Delta t}E^Q[S_{t+1}|\mathcal{F}_t] \\ &= \frac{1}{1+r\Delta t}(q \cdot u \cdot S_t + (1-q)\cdot d \cdot S_t). \end{aligned} \tag{12.19}$$

The stock price S_t cancels out of the equation and after a few rearrangements we obtain

$$q = \frac{1+r\Delta t - d}{u-d}. \tag{12.20}$$

Quick calculation 12.3   Verify this result.

That is a nice and very powerful result. In particular, we are still free to choose u and d, as long as the no-arbitrage condition (12.12) is satisfied. Here are some ideas on choosing u and d that may come in handy. You may want the tree to arrive at the same value after one up and one down turn, or equivalently after one down and one up turn. Let's call such a tree stable. It is easy to see that a stable tree requires the simple condition

$$u \cdot d = 1. \tag{12.21}$$

Quick calculation 12.4 Confirm that a stable tree implies $S_t^{(n)} = S_{t+2}^{(n+1)}$.

You may also want to choose u and d such that the magnitude of volatility of the stock is roughly preserved. There are several possible parametrizations, but a particularly neat choice is

$$u/d = e^{\pm \sigma \sqrt{\Delta t}}. \tag{12.22}$$

Quick calculation 12.5 Convince yourself that this choice is also stable.

Of course we are under no obligation to choose u and d in any predetermined way, as long as we ensure that the no-arbitrage limits (12.12) are respected.

12.3   Valuating a European Call in the Binomial Model

Finally, we get to valuating our first option contract in the binomial model. To keep the notation compact, remember that the probability to occupy the n-th vertex of the tree at time t is given by the binomial distribution, and write for the probability mass function

$$\mathcal{B}_n(q, t) = \binom{t}{n} q^n (1 - q)^{t-n}. \tag{12.23}$$

The payoff function of a European plain vanilla call option is $C_T = (S_T - K)^+$. In the binomial model this function is approximated by the vertices in the terminal time slice T, and we have

$$C_T^{(n)} = (S_T^{(n)} - K)^+ = (u^n d^{T-n} S_0 - K)^+. \tag{12.24}$$

The situation is sketched schematically in Figure 12.7, where a small collection of branches and vertices is indicated. Note that T is not the expiry date of the option, but merely the discrete number of time slices used in the binomial model. At $t = 0$, the time to expiry is $\tau = \Delta t \cdot T$. We can now price the option contract by calculating the discounted expected payoff of the call option under the probability measure Q. We already know how to switch from measure P to measure Q, once we have fixed u and d; see (12.20). Once we know q, the fair value of the call option at $t = 0$ is

$$
\begin{aligned}
C_0 &= \frac{1}{(1 + r\Delta t)^T} E^Q[C_T | \mathcal{F}_0] \\
&= \frac{1}{(1 + r\Delta t)^T} \sum_{n=0}^{T} \mathcal{B}_n(q, T) \cdot C_T^{(n)} \\
&= \frac{1}{(1 + r\Delta t)^T} \sum_{n=0}^{T} \binom{T}{n} q^n (1 - q)^{T-n} \cdot (u^n d^{T-n} S_0 - K)^+.
\end{aligned} \tag{12.25}
$$

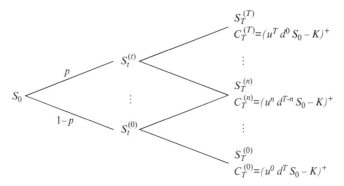

Fig. 12.7 Valuation scheme for a European plain vanilla call option in the binomial model

In principle we are done, because (12.25) is a perfectly explicit formula. But it is not a very efficient one. For all n, such that $S_T^{(n)} \leq K$, the payoff is zero, and computation of the associated sum terms is a waste of time. But we can do better. Let a be the smallest integer, such that

$$u^a d^{T-a} S_0 > K. \tag{12.26}$$

Taking logarithms on both sides and solving for a yields

$$a > \frac{\log(K/S_0) - T \log d}{\log(u/d)}. \tag{12.27}$$

Quick calculation 12.6 Verify this result.

For all $n < a$ the payoff vanishes and the sum terms are zero. For all $n \geq a$ the payoff function is

$$C_T^{(n)} = u^n d^{T-n} S_0 - K. \tag{12.28}$$

The maximum function has disappeared, because by definition of a, the payoff is positive. So we can write the call price as

$$C_0 = S_0 \sum_{n=a}^{T} \binom{T}{n} q^n (1-q)^{T-n} \frac{u^n d^{T-n}}{(1+r\Delta t)^T} - \frac{K}{(1+r\Delta t)^T} \sum_{n=a}^{T} \binom{T}{n} q^n (1-q)^{T-n}. \tag{12.29}$$

There is one more clever move we can make. Focus on the first term on the right hand side of (12.29) and realize that

$$q^n (1-q)^{T-n} \cdot \frac{u^n d^{T-n}}{(1+r\Delta t)^T} = \left(\frac{uq}{1+r\Delta t}\right)^n \cdot \left(\frac{d(1-q)}{1+r\Delta t}\right)^{T-n} \tag{12.30}$$

holds, and define

$$q' = \frac{u}{1+r\Delta t} \cdot q. \tag{12.31}$$

Quick calculation 12.7 Show that the definition of q implies $1 - q' = \frac{d}{1+r\Delta t}(1 - q)$.

Putting all the pieces together, we can now write our first option pricing formula in its most efficient form

$$C_0(K, T) = S_0 \sum_{n=a}^{T} \mathcal{B}_n(q', T) - \frac{K}{(1 + r\Delta t)^T} \sum_{n=a}^{T} \mathcal{B}_n(q, T), \qquad (12.32)$$

with

$$a = \min \left\{ n \in \mathbb{N}_0 : n > \frac{\log(K/S_0) - T\log d}{\log(u/d)} \right\},$$

$$q = \frac{1 + r\Delta t - d}{u - d}, \quad \text{and} \quad q' = \frac{u}{1 + r\Delta t} \cdot q. \qquad (12.33)$$

Let's see how this works in an example.

Example 12.1

To illustrate the whole pricing procedure let's compute the fair value of a European call option with the following features:

- current price of the underlying $S_0 = 100$,
- exercise price $K = 105$,
- time to expiry $\tau = 1$ year,
- annual risk-free interest rate $r = 8\%$.

For the valuation process, we choose $\Delta t = 0.25$, which means that we have $T = \frac{\tau}{\Delta t} = 4$, and $u/d = 1 \pm 0.1$.

Valuation in the binomial model

The first step is the computation of the risk-neutral probability q. Plugging in the given quantities, one obtains

$$q = \frac{1 + r\Delta t - d}{u - d} = \frac{1 + 0.02 - 0.9}{1.1 - 0.9} = 0.6.$$

With this, one can immediately compute $q' = 0.647$. To identify the exercise threshold a, evaluate

$$\frac{\log(K/S_0) - T\log d}{\log(u/d)} = \frac{\log 1.05 - 4\log 0.9}{\log 1.222} = 2.345,$$

from which we can conclude that $a = 3$ is the smallest integer to induce a positive payoff. We have thus the intermediate result

$$C_0(105, 4) = 100 \sum_{n=3}^{4} \mathcal{B}_n(0.647, 4) - \frac{105}{(1 + 0.02)^4} \sum_{n=3}^{4} \mathcal{B}_n(0.6, 4).$$

The computation of the $\mathcal{B}_n$s is according to (12.23). One obtains

$$\mathcal{B}_3(0.647, 4) = 0.3824, \quad \mathcal{B}_4(0.647, 4) = 0.1752,$$

and
$$\mathcal{B}_3(0.6, 4) = 0.3456, \quad \mathcal{B}_4(0.6, 4) = 0.1296.$$

Putting all the pieces together, the fair price of the call option is
$$C_0(105, 4) = 100 \cdot 0.5576 - 97 \cdot 0.4752 = 9.67.$$

Consider another kind of European call option, the binary call. Its payoff function in terms of the vertices in the terminal time slice is

$$C_T^{B^{(n)}} = \theta(S_T^{(n)} - K) = \theta(u^n d^{T-n} S_0 - K), \tag{12.34}$$

where $\theta(x)$ is the *Heaviside-θ-function*, defined by

$$\theta(x) = \begin{cases} 1 & \text{if } x \geq 0 \\ 0 & \text{if } x < 0. \end{cases} \tag{12.35}$$

Observe that for $n < a$, the payoff is still zero, but for $n \geq a$, the payoff is simply one. Thus we can write a very neat option pricing formula for the binary call in the binomial model

$$C_0^B(K, T) = \frac{1}{(1 + r\Delta t)^T} \sum_{n=a}^{T} \mathcal{B}_n(q, T), \tag{12.36}$$

where a and q are to be chosen as in (12.33). That is a spectacularly easy formula, so let's see how the option price is computed in a concrete example.

Example 12.2

To demonstrate the computation of the fair value of a European binary call option, a setup nearly identical to Example 12.1 is used. In particular:

- current price of the underlying $S_0 = 100$,
- exercise price $K = 105$,
- time to expiry $\tau = 1$ year,
- annual risk-free interest rate $r = 10\%$.

The tree structure is again given by $u/d = 1 \pm 0.1$, but this time $\Delta t = 0.5$ is chosen, which means that $T = \frac{\tau}{\Delta t} = 2$.

Valuation in the binomial model

Again, the first step is the computation of the risk-neutral probability q. Using the given quantities, one obtains

$$q = \frac{1 + r\Delta t - d}{u - d} = \frac{1 + 0.05 - 0.9}{1.1 - 0.9} = 0.75.$$

The exercise boundary a, can be found by evaluating

$$\frac{\log(K/S_0) - T\log d}{\log(u/d)} = \frac{\log 1.05 - 2\log 0.9}{\log 1.222} = 1.294,$$

from which one can conclude that $a = 2$ is the smallest integer to be considered. Thus, the desired option value is

$$C_0^B(105, 2) = \frac{1}{(1 + 0.05)^2} \cdot \mathcal{B}_2(0.75, 2) = 0.907 \cdot 0.5625 = 0.51.$$

12.4   Backward Valuation and American Options

Options with American exercise right allow the holder to exercise the option at any time during the lifetime of the contract. This feature causes a far reaching problem, because the value of the contract is no longer entirely determined by its payoff at expiry. To price option contracts with American exercise right, we have first to study an alternative valuation method, called "backward valuation" or "valuation down the tree."

Let's stick to a problem we already know. In Example 12.1, we valued a European plain vanilla call option. Take a closer look at the tree we used to compute the fair option price. This tree is illustrated in Figure 12.8. All stock-vertices have been calculated, and we know the payoff of the option at expiry. That means, we also know the option-vertices in the terminal time slice T. From our martingale pricing principle, we can write

$$
\begin{aligned}
C_{t-1}^{(n)} &= \frac{1}{1 + r\Delta t} E^Q[C_t | \mathcal{F}_{t-1}] \\
&= \frac{1}{1 + r\Delta t} \cdot \left(q \cdot C_t^{(n+1)} + (1 - q) \cdot C_t^{(n)} \right),
\end{aligned}
\tag{12.37}
$$

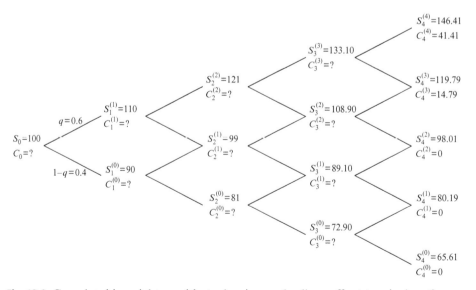

Fig. 12.8 Complete binomial tree with stock prices and call payoffs at terminal vertices

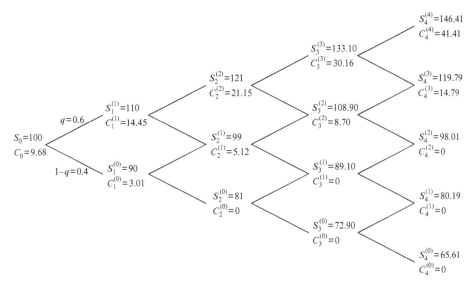

Fig. 12.9 Complete binomial tree with underlying and call option valuated down the tree

and start with $t = T$, working backwards down the tree until we reach $t = 1$. Because S_t is adapted to $\mathcal{F}_t$, the conditional expectation in (12.37) keeps track of the appropriate position in the tree. Put another way, if the process is at vertex n at time $t-1$, there is no way it can reach vertices below n or above $n+1$ in the next time slice t. Thus, only those two vertices contribute to the option value at vertex n at time $t-1$. Because this conditioning argument holds, valuating down the tree is a completely equivalent strategy and should provide identical results. Figure 12.9 shows the entire tree and the resulting option price C_0, generated by this procedure. Comparing the results with Example 12.1, the difference of 0.01 is clearly due to rounding errors.

Unlike European contracts, American options can only be valued down the tree. This is because they involve embedded decisions. In pricing such contracts, we make the possibly restrictive assumption that the option holder will follow an optimal exercise policy. This is the only consistent course of action. Suppose we assume the holder does not exercise optimally, then the value of the contract is reduced and we would sell it cheaper. But then another investor would have an arbitrage opportunity, by entering the appropriate positions and simply exercising optimally. Why is the decision embedded in an American contract so delicate? Of course, the right to exercise the option at any time during the lifetime is a reassuring comfort that will make the contract more valuable. But when exactly should it be exercised, if at all? Once again, from the martingale pricing principle we know that the fair value of the option at time t is the discounted expected value of the option at time $t+1$ under the measure Q. If we observe that immediate exercise would result in a payoff above this value, we should do so. Let's look at a call option first. From the arbitrage bounds (11.25) on page 220 we can write the following inequalities

$$C_t(K, T) \geq (S_t - e^{-r(T-t)}K)^+ \geq (S_t - K)^+, \qquad (12.38)$$

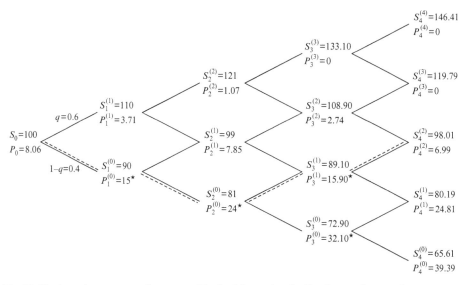

Fig. 12.10 American put option tree – Dashed branches indicating early exercise boundary

for $0 \le t \le T$. The first inequality is a lower bound on the value of the ordinary European call option. The last term on the right hand side of (12.38) is the payoff when immediately exercised. From this it is clear that an American call option should never be exercised before expiry.[1] Consequently, the price of an American and European call option is identical. Using a completely analogous argument and (11.26), we can write inequalities for a put option

$$P_t(K, T) \ge (K - S_t)^+ \ge (e^{-r(T-t)}K - S_t)^+, \tag{12.39}$$

again for $0 \le t \le T$. But this time the price of the European put option is bounded from below by the last term on the right hand side of (12.39). Thus, exercising the put before expiry might as well be advantageous. Therefore, we have to consider the condition

$$
\begin{aligned}
P_{t-1}^{(n)} &= \max\left(\frac{1}{1 + r\Delta t} E^Q[P_t|\mathcal{F}_{t-1}], (K - S_{t-1}^{(n)})^+ \right) \\
&= \max\left(\frac{1}{1 + r\Delta t} \cdot \left(q \cdot P_t^{(n+1)} + (1 - q) \cdot P_t^{(n)} \right), (K - S_{t-1}^{(n)})^+ \right),
\end{aligned}
\tag{12.40}
$$

starting at $t = T$ and working backwards until $t = 1$. It is actually quite remarkable, how easy an American option can be priced in the binomial model. With the exception of a perpetual put, which means an option with infinite time to expiry, there exists no analytical solution in the *Black–Scholes*-framework. But we will worry about that later. For the moment, let's see how the valuation proceeds.

Figure 12.10 illustrates the complete binomial tree for an American put with exactly the same environmental conditions as in Example 12.1. The vertices where early

---

[1] Strictly speaking this is only true as long as the underlying stock does not pay a dividend, or in case of an exchange rate, no foreign interests are earned.

exercise is appropriate are marked with a star. The early exercise boundary is indicated by a second dashed line.

Quick calculation 12.8 Calculate the price for a European put from the result in Example 12.1 and put-call parity. Confirm that the American put option is indeed more valuable.

We can elaborate on our former argument about the higher value of the American put a little more. Imagine you hold such a contract and your exercise policy is very sloppy. Indeed you never exercise early. In this case, you could have chosen a European contract, because you did not plan on taking advantage of your additional early exercise right anyway, and the European contract is cheaper. If you are the one to write the option, there is an extra incentive to make it an American option. You can hope for a buyer to act sloppily and not to exercise optimally. On average, such a buyer will pay too much for the contract.

12.5   Stopping Times and *Snell*-Envelope

A concept intimately related to the valuation of American options is stopping times. A stopping time τ is a $\mathcal{F}_t$-measurable random variable, taking values in an index set $\mathcal{T}$.[2] In the binomial model the index set is $\mathcal{T} = \{0, 1, \ldots, T\}$. A stopping event is usually written $\{\tau = t\}$ or $\{\tau \leq t\}$, but this is only a shorthand for the definition

$$\{\tau \leq t\} = \{\omega \in \Omega : \tau(\omega) \leq t\} \in \mathcal{F}_t, \tag{12.41}$$

for all $t \in \mathcal{T}$. To understand this definition better, look at an example of a stopping time and afterwards at a counterexample.

Example 12.3

Suppose you give your broker the order to sell a stock S you are currently holding, as soon as its price falls below a certain lower limit S_l. Your order is valid for the next four weeks.

Explanation
The time τ your broker triggers the sale of your stock is clearly random, because you do not know when, if at all, the price of the stock will fall below S_l. But at any time $t \in \mathcal{T}$, you know if the stock is already sold or if it is still in your portfolio, because the σ-algebra $\mathcal{F}_t = \sigma(S_t)$ contains the information about the stock price to have fallen below S_l or not.

---

[2] Earlier, we defined τ as the time to expiry. This is again an unfortunate clash of traditional notation. Nevertheless, the potential for confusion is very small, so we continue labeling the stopping time τ in this section.

Such a problem is called a "first passage" problem. Now suppose you try to persuade your broker to take the order to sell your stock for the highest price to be taken over the next four weeks. Would the random time of the sale still be a stopping time? No, because this time τ is not $\mathcal{F}_t$- but only $\mathcal{F}_T$-measurable. Your broker would never take such an order from you. At least as long as she does not know how to deal with lookback options.

We have to examine the requirements of stopping times and their relation to martingales a little bit more closely. Let's ask the question, whether or not we can determine an optimal stopping time to sell a security or liquidate a portfolio. To answer this one, we need the concept of a stopped process and Doob's optional stopping theorem. Let X_t be an $\mathcal{F}_t$-adapted stochastic process, preferably a martingale. Then the stopped process Y_t, with respect to X_t and the stopping time τ, is defined by

$$Y_t = \begin{cases} X_t & \text{if } t < \tau \\ X_\tau & \text{if } t \geq \tau. \end{cases} \tag{12.42}$$

X_t could for example be $e^{-rt}S_t$, where the bank account was used as numéraire. To avoid formal subtleties, we will restrict ourselves to discrete time processes. Of course all results carry over to the continuous time case, with a little bit of extra technical finesse.

Theorem 12.1 (Optional stopping) *Let $\mathcal{T} = \mathbb{N}_0$, X_t a martingale, and τ a stopping time, both with respect to the filtration $\mathcal{F}_t$. If there exists an arbitrary constant c, such that one of the following conditions holds almost surely*

1. $\tau \leq c$,
2. $E[\tau] < \infty$ and $E\left[|X_{t+1} - X_t| \,\big|\, \mathcal{F}_t\right] \leq c$,
3. $|Y_t| \leq c$,

then X_τ is almost surely well-defined and $E[X_\tau | \mathcal{F}_0] = X_0$.

If X_t and τ satisfy the requirements of Theorem 12.1, then Y_t is also an $\mathcal{F}_t$-adapted martingale. To see this, first decompose the stopped process

$$Y_t = X_0 + \sum_{s=1}^{t} \theta(\tau - s)(X_s - X_{s-1}), \tag{12.43}$$

where $\theta(x)$ is again the *Heaviside-θ*-function. If $\tau \geq t$, then all *Heaviside*-factors in the sum are one, and $Y_t = X_t$. If $\tau < t$, then for all $s > \tau$ the *Heaviside*-factors vanish and we have $Y_t = X_\tau$. Because the event $\{\tau \geq t\} = \{\tau \leq t - 1\}^C$ has to be contained already in $\mathcal{F}_{t-1}$, $\theta(\tau - t)$ has to be $\mathcal{F}_{t-1}$-predictable. We can thus write

$$\begin{aligned} E[Y_t - Y_{t-1} | \mathcal{F}_{t-1}] &= E[\theta(\tau - t)(X_t - X_{t-1}) | \mathcal{F}_{t-1}] \\ &= \theta(\tau - t)E[X_t - X_{t-1} | \mathcal{F}_{t-1}] \\ &= 0. \end{aligned} \tag{12.44}$$

Pulling Y_{t-1} out of the expectation and using the law of iterated expectations proves the claim. Because we already agreed on the martingale pricing principle in arbitrage free markets, there seems to be no way to beat the market.

You might have heard from people passionately playing roulette in casinos, with a special system called doubling strategy. They make their bet on say rouge and if they lose, successively double their bet, until they finally win. In the next round they start all over again. Let's investigate, if such a strategy could work. Generously neglecting for the moment that only the house wins if the ball plays out zero, there is a 50% chance of winning and successive trials can be assumed to be independent. The gains from a pure doubling process can be written as

$$X_t = X_{t-1} + 2^{t-1}\epsilon_t \tag{12.45}$$

for $t \in \mathbb{N}$, with $X_0 = 0$ and $\epsilon_t = \pm 1$ with probability $p = \frac{1}{2}$. Clearly such a process is a martingale. Now consider the betting process of the player. In the first round, she bets one dollar. If she wins, she doubles, and her gain is $Y_1 = 1$, and the game starts over again. If she loses, she gets nothing, her gain is $Y_1 = -1$ and she has to bet two dollars in the next round. After say t unfavorable outcomes the poor player's gain is

$$Y_t = -\sum_{s=1}^{t} 2^{s-1} = -\sum_{s=0}^{t-1} 2^s = 1 - 2^t. \tag{12.46}$$

Quick calculation 12.9 Verify the last equation by using geometric series' results.

In the next round the player has to bet 2^t, and if she wins, her gain is exactly $Y_{t+1} = 1$. Obviously, Y_t is a stopped process with respect to X_t and the random stopping time $\tau = \inf\{t : X_t = 1\}$. Furthermore, it seems that we finally managed to beat the martingale and the whole strategy looks like an airtight money machine. We can even calculate, how long the player has to wait on average, before she can start all over again[3]

$$E[\tau] = \sum_{t=1}^{\infty} \frac{t}{2^t} = 2. \tag{12.47}$$

This is all very nice, but we missed an important point from Theorem 12.1. Neither of the three required conditions holds and so X_τ is not a well-defined random process. To see this, realize that our strategy only works, if we are capable of waiting an infinite amount of time and temporarily losing an infinite amount of money, if we have a very unfortunate day.

Quick calculation 12.10 Show that $E[|X_{t+1} - X_t| \,|\, \mathcal{F}_t] = 2^t$ holds.

---

[3] In evaluating the sum, one has to isolate the first term and then do some manipulations

$$\sum_{t=1}^{\infty} \frac{t}{2^t} = \frac{1}{2} + \sum_{t=2}^{\infty} \frac{t}{2^t} = \frac{1}{2} + \sum_{t=1}^{\infty} \frac{t+1}{2^{t+1}} = \frac{1}{2} + \frac{1}{2}\sum_{t=1}^{\infty} \frac{t}{2^t} + \frac{1}{2}\sum_{t=1}^{\infty} \frac{1}{2^t} = 1 + \frac{1}{2}\sum_{t=1}^{\infty} \frac{t}{2^t}.$$

Multiplying the left and right hand side by two and subtracting the sum on both sides does the trick.

In reality, casinos put limits on the bets, in which case the optional stopping theorem holds, Y_t is a martingale, and we are back to square one.

Now let's return to our initial problem of pricing American option contracts. We have now nearly all the machinery required to formalize the concepts involved. We continue our discussion in the discrete time setup of the binomial model. The stochastic process

$$X_t = \begin{cases} \dfrac{P_T}{(1+r\Delta t)^T} & \text{for } t = T \\ \max\left(\dfrac{P_t}{(1+r\Delta t)^t}, E^Q[X_{t+1}|\mathcal{F}_t]\right) & \text{for } t < T, \end{cases} \tag{12.48}$$

with $P_t = (K - S_t)^+$, is called the *Snell*-envelope of the American put option. Apart from discounting, this is exactly what we calculated by backward valuation earlier. The *Snell*-envelope is a Q-super-martingale, satisfying $X_t \geq \frac{P_t}{(1+r\Delta t)^t}$ for all $t \leq T$. By a super-martingale we mean an $\mathcal{F}_t$-adapted process with the property

$$X_t \geq E[X_{t+s}|\mathcal{F}_t], \tag{12.49}$$

for $s \geq 0$. Now you understand the financial engineer's joke that the market is a super-martingale. The *Snell*-envelope is also the smallest super-martingale with this property. To see this, take another Q-super-martingale Z_t, with $Z_t \geq \frac{P_t}{(1+r\Delta t)^t}$ almost surely, for every $t \leq T$. From the definition (12.48), we have that $Z_T \geq X_T$. Taking conditional expectations, we can write

$$Z_{T-1} \geq E^Q[Z_T|\mathcal{F}_{T-1}] \geq E^Q[X_T|\mathcal{F}_{T-1}]. \tag{12.50}$$

We also have that $Z_{T-1} \geq \frac{P_{T-1}}{(1+r\Delta t)^{T-1}}$, which is what we assumed in the first place. It follows immediately that

$$Z_{T-1} \geq \max\left(\frac{P_{T-1}}{(1+r\Delta t)^{T-1}}, E^Q[X_T|\mathcal{F}_{T-1}]\right) = X_{T-1} \tag{12.51}$$

has to hold. This argument can be easily iterated backwards until $t = 0$. In case of the American option, the exercise decision should be made at the first time the *Snell*-envelope hits the floor,

$$\tau^* = \inf\left\{t \in \mathcal{T} : X_t = \frac{P_t}{(1+r\Delta t)^t}\right\}. \tag{12.52}$$

Clearly, τ^* is a stopping time, because the event $\{\tau^* \leq t\}$ is in $\mathcal{F}_t$, and the stopped process

$$Y_t = \begin{cases} X_t & \text{if } t < \tau^* \\ X_{\tau^*} & \text{if } t \geq \tau^* \end{cases} \tag{12.53}$$

is a Q-martingale, by the same chain of arguments we applied before. Furthermore, τ^* solves the problem

$$Y_0 = P_0(K, T) = \sup_{\tau \in \mathcal{T}} E^Q\left[\frac{1}{(1+r\Delta t)^\tau}(K - S_\tau)^+ \middle| \mathcal{F}_0\right]. \tag{12.54}$$

Note that the discounting factor is now inside the expectation. This is because τ is a random variable, too. The representation (12.54) is a little bit deceiving, because we require the *Snell*-envelope to compute the supremum of the expectation value. This problem is essentially an application of the dynamic programming approach of Bellman (1954). This is very abstract and subtle business, so let's see how it works in an actual example.

Example 12.4

Look at the situation illustrated in Figure 12.11. The *Snell*-envelope has already been computed and the process is stopped with respect to the optimal stopping time τ^* as in (12.52). Show that τ^* is indeed a stopping time and compute the fair value of the American option at $t = 0$.

Solution

The optimal stopping vertices are indicated by a star in Figure 12.11. From this we conclude that the random variable τ^* has to be defined by

$$\tau^*(\omega) = \begin{cases} 1 & \text{if } \omega = (\downarrow, \uparrow) \text{ or } \omega = (\downarrow, \downarrow) \\ 2 & \text{if } \omega = (\uparrow, \uparrow) \text{ or } \omega = (\uparrow, \downarrow). \end{cases}$$

We have thus the stopping events

$$\begin{aligned} \{\tau^* \leq 0\} &= \emptyset \in \mathcal{F}_0 \\ \{\tau^* \leq 1\} &= \{(\downarrow, \uparrow), (\downarrow, \downarrow)\} \in \mathcal{F}_1 \\ \{\tau^* \leq 2\} &= \Omega \in \mathcal{F}_2, \end{aligned}$$

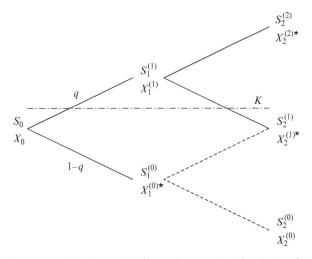

Fig. 12.11 American put option tree – *Snell*-envelope and optimal stopping vertices

and therefore, τ^* is an $\mathcal{F}_t$-adapted stopping time. The paths to the proper stop events are indicated by solid lines in Figure 12.11. All we have to do is compute the expectation value of the stopped process Y_t. That means, we have to average over the payoffs at the τ^*-stopped vertices

$$Y_0 = E^Q \left[\frac{1}{(1+r\Delta t)^{\tau^*}} (K - S_{\tau^*})^+ \Big| \mathcal{F}_0 \right]$$
$$= \frac{1-q}{1+r\Delta t} \cdot (K - S_1^{(0)}) + \frac{q^2}{(1+r\Delta t)^2} \cdot 0 + \frac{q(1-q)}{(1+r\Delta t)^2} \cdot (K - S_2^{(1)}).$$

Of course Y_0 is the desired fair price $P_0(K, T)$.

12.6   Path Dependent Options

Path dependent options can be roughly divided into two classes, weakly and strongly path dependent ones. You could also say those that do not cause trouble in valuating them and the other kind. We will eventually learn how to deal with strongly path dependent options, but the binomial setup is not well suited for this class. Typical examples of weak path dependence are barrier options, whereas Asian options are examples of strong path dependence. We will first talk about barrier options.

Barrier options are so liquidly traded that they are barely considered exotics nowadays. They come in certain flavors, adding extra variety to the standard put-call building blocks. Barrier options have the following characteristics:

Barrier type

- Knockout barrier: The contract expires worthlessly, if the barrier is hit.
- Knockin barrier: The contract does not come into life, before the barrier is hit.

Barrier location

- Upper barrier: The underlying has to cross the barrier from below.
- Lower barrier: The underlying has to cross the barrier from above.

Additionally, a rebate can be granted, if a knockout barrier is hit, so that the contract does not expire completely worthlessly.

Why do we consider barrier options weakly path dependent? Let's focus on a European option for the moment. The payoff does by all means depend on the path the underlying has taken up to expiry. Take for example a knockout call option with upper barrier. If the underlying ends up in the money, but below the barrier, it is not guaranteed that the option pays off anything. It all depends on which path the underlying took. If it hit the barrier during the lifetime of the contract, the option was knocked out, if it did not hit the barrier, the usual payoff is due at expiry. But the important point is that the barrier itself does not depend on the path of the underlying. This fact keeps valuation simple, so that we can use backward valuation, as in the case of American options. Only this time, we have not to track the *Snell*-envelope at each vertex, but

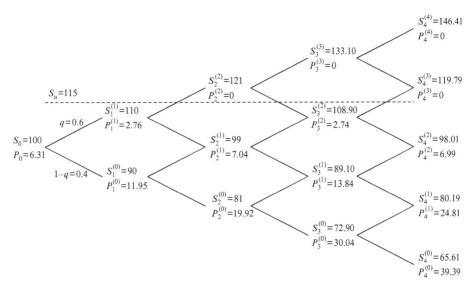

Fig. 12.12 European knockout put option tree – Upper knockout barrier indicated by dashed line

only to check, if the barrier is hit or not. For reasons that will become clear shortly, the subsequent discussion addresses only knockout options.

Imagine you want to floor your portfolio. To this end you can enter a protective put position. But now assume that all goes well, and your portfolio performs extraordinarily favorably. There comes a point, where the floor is no longer needed for insurance. In fact you would probably want to install a new floor, to backup your profits. Unfortunately, you have already paid the option premium for your put. If you had chosen an identical knockout barrier put with an appropriate upper knockout barrier, you would have saved money. Think about it; both contracts have the same payoff function, but the barrier option pays off only in those states of the world, where the underlying has not hit the barrier. Thus, its value has to be smaller than that of the standard put option. Let's see how the valuation procedure works in our familiar setting of Example 12.1, with a European knockout put option with upper knockout barrier $S_u = 115$. Figure 12.12 illustrates the whole tree and the fair option price due to backward valuation. The vertices have to be computed as

$$
P^{(n)}_{t-1} = \begin{cases} \frac{1}{1+r\Delta t} \cdot \left(q \cdot P^{(n+1)}_t + (1-q) \cdot P^{(n)}_t \right) & \text{if } S^{(n)}_{t-1} < S_u \\ 0 & \text{if } S^{(n)}_{t-1} \geq S_u. \end{cases}
\tag{12.55}
$$

Here comes a tricky question: A knockout barrier option is a contract contingent on a security. What is the underlying of a knockin barrier option? Realize that if the knockin barrier is hit, you are left with an ordinary call or put option. That means, the knockin barrier option is an option on another option. One would call such a derivative a second order contract. From the perspective of valuation, this is as bad as if the knockin version were a strongly path dependent option. Luckily, we can work around this problem. Ask yourself the following question: What payoff do you generate, if you hold a knockout barrier option and an identical knockin option, with the same barrier, exercise price, and time to expiry? Correct, you just replicated an ordinary plain vanilla option. If one contract is knocked out, the other knocks in at the same time and you are done with the barrier condition. It does not matter, if we are talking about calls or puts, so let's call the value of the contract V_t. It also does not matter, if there is an upper or lower barrier, so let's call the barrier S_b. We can then formulate a parity relation for barrier options

$$V_t^{\odot}(K, T, S_b) + V_t^{\otimes}(K, T, S_b) = V_t(K, T), \qquad (12.56)$$

where we have used the somewhat neat superscripts $\odot$ for knockin, and $\otimes$ for knock-out. Think of an arrow flying towards you ($\odot \rightarrow$ knockin), or away from you ($\otimes \rightarrow$ knockout). Furthermore, the parity relation (12.56) provides a formal argument for our earlier claim

$$P_t^{\otimes}(K, T, S_u) \leq P_t(K, T). \qquad (12.57)$$

Thus, the fair price of a knockin barrier option can be found by valuating the corresponding knockout and plain vanilla options.

Let's now move on to strongly path dependent options. A standard example of such contracts are Asian options. The characteristic property of Asian contracts is that their payoff function always involves some kind of average over the path of the underlying. As in the case of barrier options, there are several permutations of Asian options. The most basic characteristics are:

Strike type

- Fixed strike: The exercise price is fixed and not affected by the path of the underlying.
- Floating strike: The exercise price itself is calculated by averaging over the path of the underlying.

Averaging method

- Arithmetic average: The average is computed as

$$\bar{S}_T = \frac{1}{T+1} \sum_{t=0}^{T} S_t \quad \text{or} \quad \bar{S}_T = \frac{1}{T} \int_0^T S_t dt.$$

- Geometric average: The average is computed as

$$\bar{S}_T = \sqrt[T+1]{\prod_{t=0}^{T} S_t} \quad \text{or} \quad \bar{S}_T = e^{\frac{1}{T} \int_0^T \log S_t dt}.$$

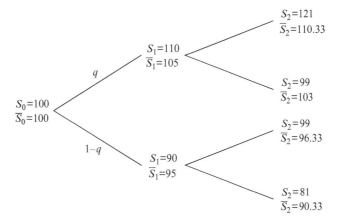

Fig. 12.13 Binomial tree for arithmetic Asian option – Tree grows bushy with 2^t vertices

Thus, an Asian fixed strike call option, with exercise price K and expiry date T has the payoff function

$$C_T^{\yen}(K, T, \bar{S}_T) = (\bar{S}_T - K)^+. \tag{12.58}$$

Obviously, $\bar{S}_0 = S_0$ has to hold, if not specified otherwise. The payoff of the identical floating strike version is

$$C_T^{\yen}(\bar{S}_T, T) = (S_T - \bar{S}_T)^+. \tag{12.59}$$

Now let's see what happens, if we try to price such an option in the binomial model. Figure 12.13 sketches the first two levels of a possible tree. As you immediately see, the problem is that the tree grows bushy, thereby enormously increasing the number of branches and vertices. Until now, our trees generated $t + 1$ vertices in time slice t. A tree for an Asian option obviously generates 2^t vertices in the same time slice. This number grows prohibitively large for computational purposes very rapidly. There is another way to price such contracts, via Monte Carlo simulation. But since it is more reasonable to introduce this method when we have a better model for the price process of the underlying, we will postpone the valuation of strongly path dependent contracts.

12.7 The *Black–Scholes*-Limit of the Binomial Model

The parameters in the binomial model can be chosen such that in the limit $T \to \infty$, the price of an arbitrary option converges to the *Black–Scholes*-price of the contract. The appropriate parametrization and the limit process are elaborated for a European binary call option. The whole procedure is best understood, if executed step-by-step.

Step 1

Write an equation for the lower exercise threshold a. We have from (12.33) on page 230 that

$$a = \min\left\{n \in \mathbb{N}_0 : n > \frac{\log(K/S_0) - T\log d}{\log(u/d)}\right\}. \tag{12.60}$$

This merely means that a is the first nonnegative integer, greater than the ratio in (12.60). We can write an equation by filling up the gap with a new variable $\varepsilon > 0$,

$$\begin{aligned} a &= \frac{\log(K/S_0) - T\log d}{\log(u/d)} + \varepsilon \\ &= \frac{\log(K/S_0) - T\log d + \varepsilon \log(u/d)}{\log(u/d)}. \end{aligned} \tag{12.61}$$

Eventually, in the limit $T \to \infty$, the gap shrinks to zero, which means $\lim_{T\to\infty} \varepsilon = 0$.

Step 2

Compute the moments of the logarithmic return. Because the price of the underlying at vertex n in the terminal time slice T is $S_T^{(n)} = u^n d^{T-n} S_0$, the logarithmic return at the same vertex is given by

$$\begin{aligned} \log\left(S_T^{(n)}/S_0\right) &= n\log u + (T - n)\log d \\ &= n\log(u/d) + T\log d. \end{aligned} \tag{12.62}$$

Observe that in general, the vertex n we end up is the realization of a binomially distributed random variable $N : \Omega \to \{0, 1, \ldots, T\}$. We thus have

$$\begin{aligned} E[\log(S_T/S_0)] &= E[N]\log(u/d) + T\log d \\ &= p \cdot T\log(u/d) + T\log d. \end{aligned} \tag{12.63}$$

From the same consideration, we can compute the variance of the logarithmic return

$$\begin{aligned} \mathrm{Var}[\log(S_T/S_0)] &= \mathrm{Var}[N]\log^2(u/d) \\ &= p(1 - p) \cdot T\log^2(u/d). \end{aligned} \tag{12.64}$$

Step 3

Choose a suitable parametrization. Let again τ denote the time to expiry. We want three conditions to be satisfied:

1. $u \cdot d = 1$ (stable tree),
2. $\lim_{T\to\infty} E[\log(S_T/S_0)] = \mu\tau$,
3. $\lim_{T\to\infty} \mathrm{Var}[\log(S_T/S_0)] = \sigma^2\tau$,

where μ and σ are the expected (annual) logarithmic return and standard deviation of the underlying. Observe that we have three conditions and three unknowns, u, d, and p. Thus, we can satisfy all requirements. Indeed the parametrization

$$u/d = e^{\pm\sigma\sqrt{\frac{\tau}{T}}} \quad \text{and} \quad p = \frac{1}{2} + \frac{\mu}{2\sigma}\sqrt{\frac{\tau}{T}} \tag{12.65}$$

does the trick. Let's prove that for all three conditions:

1. Simply observe that

$$e^{\sigma\sqrt{\frac{\tau}{T}}}e^{-\sigma\sqrt{\frac{\tau}{T}}} = e^0 = 1.$$

2. Plug the parametrization into (12.63) to obtain

$$E[\log(S_T/S_0)] = \left(\left(\tfrac{1}{2} + \tfrac{\mu}{2\sigma}\sqrt{\tfrac{\tau}{T}}\right)\cdot 2\sigma\sqrt{\tfrac{\tau}{T}} - \sigma\sqrt{\tfrac{\tau}{T}}\right)\cdot T$$
$$= \tfrac{\mu}{2\sigma}\sqrt{\tfrac{\tau}{T}}\cdot 2\sigma\sqrt{\tfrac{\tau}{T}}\cdot T = \mu\tau.$$

It is not even necessary to take the limit, because the parametrization is exact for every $T \in \mathbb{N}$.

3. First observe that

$$1 - p = \frac{1}{2} - \frac{\mu}{2\sigma}\sqrt{\frac{\tau}{T}}.$$

One then obtains by using (12.64)

$$\mathrm{Var}[\log(S_T/S_0)] = \left(\frac{1}{4} - \frac{\mu^2}{4\sigma^2}\frac{\tau}{T}\right)\cdot 4\sigma^2\frac{\tau}{T}\cdot T = \sigma^2\tau - \mu^2\frac{\tau^2}{T}.$$

In the limit $T \to \infty$ the last term on the right hand side vanishes and the proof is complete.

Step 4

Make preparations for the application of the central limit theorem. Observe that for a binomial random variable $N \sim B(p, T)$ the central limit theorem ensures that

$$\frac{N - p\cdot T}{\sqrt{p(1-p)\cdot T}} \xrightarrow{D} Z \sim N(0, 1) \tag{12.66}$$

for $T \to \infty$, where the symbol $\xrightarrow{D}$ indicates convergence in distribution. Now plug in a and take the limit

$$\lim_{T\to\infty}\frac{a - p\cdot T}{\sqrt{p(1-p)\cdot T}} = \lim_{T\to\infty}\frac{\log(K/S_0) - T\log d + \varepsilon\log(u/d) - p\cdot T\log(u/d)}{\sqrt{p(1-p)\cdot T\log^2(u/d)}}$$
$$= \frac{\log(K/S_0) - \mu\tau}{\sigma\sqrt{\tau}}. \tag{12.67}$$

Recall that $\varepsilon\log(u/d)$ vanishes automatically in the limit.

Step 5

Compute the risk-neutral probability measure. The logarithmic returns in the *Black–Scholes*-model are normally distributed, $R_S \sim N(\mu\tau, \sigma^2\tau)$. From the martingale pricing principle, we know that

$$S_0 = e^{-r\tau}E^Q[S_0 e^{R_S}|\mathcal{F}_0] \tag{12.68}$$

has to hold. If we evaluate the expectation value under the physical probability measure P, we obtain

$$S_0 = e^{-r\tau} E^P[S_0 e^{R_S}|\mathcal{F}_0] = S_0 e^{-\tau(r-\mu-\frac{1}{2}\sigma^2)}, \tag{12.69}$$

from which we can conclude that in going from P to Q

$$\mu = r - \frac{1}{2}\sigma^2 \tag{12.70}$$

has to hold. Strictly speaking, this conclusion is not yet justified. We have implicitly assumed that the change of measure preserves the normal distribution and only changes its mean. We will back up this claim later in the context of the important *Girsanov*-theorem. However, taking this fact for granted at the moment, we obtain the risk-neutral probability measure

$$q = \frac{1}{2} + \frac{r - \frac{1}{2}\sigma^2}{2\sigma} \sqrt{\frac{\tau}{T}}, \tag{12.71}$$

by substituting (12.70) into (12.65).

Step 6
Apply the central limit theorem. We are now in a position to make the final transition. Recall that in the binomial model the time step is $\Delta t = \frac{\tau}{T}$. We then obtain for the fair price of a European binary call option

$$C_0^B(K,\tau) = \lim_{T\to\infty} \frac{1}{\left(1 + \frac{r\tau}{T}\right)^T} \sum_{n=a}^{T} \mathcal{B}_n(q,T) = e^{-r\tau} \int_a^\infty \phi(z)dz, \tag{12.72}$$

where

$$a = \frac{\log(K/S_0) - \left(r - \frac{1}{2}\sigma^2\right)\tau}{\sigma\sqrt{\tau}} \quad \text{and} \quad \phi(z) = \frac{1}{\sqrt{2\pi}}e^{-\frac{1}{2}z^2}. \tag{12.73}$$

We can finally use the symmetry property of the normal distribution to rewrite the result a little bit,

$$\int_a^\infty \phi(z)dz = \int_{-\infty}^{-a} \phi(z)dz = \Phi(-a). \tag{12.74}$$

Putting all the pieces together, we obtain

$$C_0^B(K,\tau) - e^{-r\tau}\Phi(-a), \tag{12.75}$$

which is precisely the fair price of a European binary call option in the *Black–Scholes*-model.

12.8   Further Reading

Originally, the binomial model was introduced by Cox et al. (1979). A deep and comprehensive treatment is Shreve (2004a). A very accessible and entertaining introduction is provided in Wilmott (2006a, chap. 15). Advanced issues and trinomial tree extensions can be found in Haug (2007, chap. 7). Stopping times and early exercise problems are discussed in Bingham and Kiesel (2004, sect. 3.5 & 3.6). An excellent treatment of American contingent claims is provided in Föllmer and Schied (2011, chap. 6). For dynamic programming issues, see the book by Bellman (1957) in various reprints. An impressive collection of exotic options is provided also in Haug (2007).

12.9   Problems

12.1 Look at the binomial tree in Figure 12.14. Assume that the risk-free interest rate vanishes, $r = 0\%$, and price the European plain vanilla put option by computing the hedge-portfolios $\Pi_1^{(1)}$, $\Pi_1^{(0)}$, and Π_0.

12.2 In Example 12.2 on page 231, a European binary call was valuated with the binomial formula. Price the corresponding put option in the same setting, and check whether or not your result satisfies binary put-call parity.

12.3 Let $\mathcal{F}_t$ be a filtration generated by the stochastic process X_t, and τ a stopping time with respect to X_t. The stopped σ-algebra $\mathcal{F}_\tau$ is defined by

$$\mathcal{F}_\tau = \{A \in \mathcal{F} : A \cap \{\tau \le t\} \in \mathcal{F}_t \text{ for all } t \in \mathcal{T}\}.$$

In fact, $\mathcal{F}_\tau$ is the σ-algebra generated by the realizations of the process X_t at all stopping times, $\mathcal{F}_\tau = \sigma(X_\tau)$. What is the stopped σ-algebra for the process in Example 12.4 on page 239?

12.4 Imagine the stopping time τ is a fixed deterministic time $\tau = s$, with $0 < s < T$. What are the stopping events?

12.5 Show that for the deterministic stopping time of Problem 12.4, the stopped σ-algebra is $\mathcal{F}_\tau = \mathcal{F}_s$.

12.6 Consider the environmental conditions of the standard example 12.1 on page 230 and valuate a knockout call option with upper knockout barrier $S_u = 125$ and American exercise right. Formulate the computation rule for vertex n in time slice t and sketch the binomial tree.

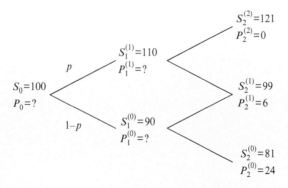

Fig. 12.14 Binomial tree for European plain vanilla put option

12.7 In demonstrating the transition from the binomial model to the *Black–Scholes-*model, the parametrization $u/d = e^{\pm\sigma\sqrt{\Delta t}}$ was chosen in step 3, with $\Delta t = \frac{\tau}{T}$. Show that the martingale principle results in the same risk-neutral probability

$$q = \frac{1}{2} + \frac{r - \frac{1}{2}\sigma^2}{2\sigma} \sqrt{\Delta t},$$

if the u/d-parametrization is *Taylor*-expanded to second order.

13 The *Black–Scholes*-Theory

The option pricing theory of Black and Scholes (1973), and Merton (1973) is undoubtedly one of the most influential and elegant theories in economics. Sadly, Fisher Black died in 1995, before he could receive the Nobel Prize for this achievement, along with Myron Scholes and Robert Merton. The *Black–Scholes*-theory is still a cornerstone of derivative pricing and the starting point for numerous kinds of refinements.

13.1 Geometric *Brown*ian Motion and Itô's Lemma

We have already encountered a very simple model for the price process of a risky security. We called it a coin flip process back in Chapter 12. There we assumed that the price of a security evolves between time t and time $t + \Delta t$ by

$$
S_{t+\Delta t} = \begin{cases} u \cdot S_t & \text{for } \omega = \uparrow \\ d \cdot S_t & \text{for } \omega = \downarrow, \end{cases} \tag{13.1}
$$

with probability p and $1 - p$, respectively. The *Black–Scholes*-theory is based on a far more sophisticated model for the price process of the underlying, called the geometric *Brown*ian motion. It is named after the Scottish botanist Robert Brown, who in 1827 documented a bizarre jittering motion of suspended pollen grain, when observed under his microscope. At that time it was not known that this peculiar motion was delivered by random collisions of molecules in the fluid. At the beginning of the twentieth century, the governing laws of this motion were discovered mainly by Einstein and Perrin. But it took nearly a century to prove the existence of such a process formally in a measure-theoretic framework. This was done in 1923 by Norbert Wiener and therefore, the process is nowadays also called the *Wiener*-process. The *Wiener*-process W_t is defined by three basic properties:

1. $W_0 = 0$,
2. W_t has independent increments, $\qquad\qquad$ (13.2)
3. $W_t - W_s \sim N(0, t - s)$ for $0 \leq s < t$.

From these properties it is impossible to appreciate how strange this process really is. It can be proved that W_t has continuous paths with probability one, but at the same time it is almost surely nowhere differentiable. Because the time increments in the *Black–Scholes*-world are infinitesimal, we have a transition $\Delta t \to dt$, which also extends to the increments of the *Wiener*-process. Thus, we can informally state that dW_t is normally distributed, with

$$E[dW_t] = 0 \quad \text{and} \quad \text{Var}[dW_t] = dt. \tag{13.3}$$

Louis Bachelier (1900), already suggested a model, based on *Brown*ian motion, that in modern language would be written as

$$dS_t = \sigma dW_t, \tag{13.4}$$

in his PhD thesis. Remember that at this time there was no formal concept of a *Wiener*-process. What Bachelier postulated is a simple scaled *Brown*ian motion. The model used by Black and Scholes is the geometric *Brown*ian motion

$$dS_t = \mu S_t dt + \sigma S_t dW_t. \tag{13.5}$$

What is the difference? Apart from the drift term $\mu S_t dt$, *Brown*ian motion implies an absolute level of volatility, whereas geometric *Brown*ian motion generates volatility relative to the price of the security. That is, we can say the annual volatility is 20% or so. Think about it the other way around. If absolute volatility is 50 cents, then the price of the security hardly fluctuates at all, if it currently costs 100 dollars. But if the price is merely one dollar, it is subject to very heavy fluctuations with respect to its absolute value. This somewhat strange behavior is avoided by using the geometric *Brown*ian motion. The additional drift term in (13.5) is the analogue of the riskless interest rate r in the bank account. Of course we assume $\mu > r$, because a security comes with risk to be compensated by a higher expected return.

The object (13.5) is called a stochastic differential equation. This term is a bit awkward, because W_t is not even differentiable. An easy way to get a feeling for what is happening, is to try to calculate its derivative. We can postulate as usual

$$\frac{dW_t}{dt} = \lim_{\Delta t \to 0} \frac{W_{t+\Delta t} - W_t}{\Delta t}. \tag{13.6}$$

What is the expectation value of this? It is still zero, because the increment $W_{t+\Delta t} - W_t$ was defined to have zero expectation. But what about the variance? We get

$$\text{Var}\left[\frac{dW_t}{dt}\right] = \lim_{\Delta t \to 0} \frac{1}{\Delta t^2} \text{Var}[W_{t+\Delta t} - W_t] = \lim_{\Delta t \to 0} \frac{1}{\Delta t} = \infty. \tag{13.7}$$

The smaller we make the increment, the more violent the fluctuations become. In the end the process is too irregular to be differentiable. But because W_t is continuous, at least we can hope for the stochastic differential equation (13.5) to be integrable. That is indeed possible, but not with our standard integral calculus toolbox.

Recall what we did in Chapter 11, to solve for the time t value of the bank account $B(t)$. Initially we had the differential equation $dB(t) = rB(t)dt$. Then we took the logarithm to obtain

$$d\log B(t) = \frac{1}{B(t)} dB(t) = rdt. \tag{13.8}$$

What we applied here is of course the total differential. In fact, the total differential itself is a first order *Taylor*-series expansion. The big question is, why are there no higher order terms? This is the holy secret of calculus. You write dt instead of Δt, if it is so small that you can neglect higher order terms like dt^2 or even $dt^{3/2}$. But you have to keep all terms of order dt. So let's check to what order dW_t contributes. We know from the definition of the *Wiener*-process that

$$E[dW_t^2] = dt \tag{13.9}$$

has to hold. This is merely the variance of the infinitesimal *Wiener*-increment, because $E[dW_t] = 0$. But what is the variance of dW_t^2? Remember that the *Wiener*-increments are independently normally distributed. We have already seen a formula for higher moments of normally distributed random variables, (2.31) on page 19. We thus can write

$$\text{Var}[dW_t^2] = E[dW_t^4] - E[dW_t^2]^2 = 3dt^2 - dt^2 = 2dt^2. \tag{13.10}$$

But orders dt^2 are supposed to be neglected, and thus the variance of dW_t^2 vanishes. We can therefore conclude, at least heuristically, that $dW_t^2 = dt$ has to hold. This also means that the order of dW_t has to be $dt^{1/2}$. Now let us see what we get, if we take the logarithm of the geometric *Brown*ian motion and expand the *Taylor*-series up to second order,

$$
\begin{aligned}
d\log S_t &= \frac{1}{S_t}dS_t - \frac{1}{2}\frac{1}{S_t^2}dS_t^2 \\
&= \mu dt + \sigma dW_t - \frac{1}{2}\left(\mu^2 dt^2 + 2\mu\sigma dt dW_t + \sigma^2 dW_t^2\right) \\
&= \left(\mu - \frac{1}{2}\sigma^2\right)dt + \sigma dW_t.
\end{aligned}
\tag{13.11}
$$

Only the dW_t^2 term of the quadratic contribution survives, because it is of order dt. This contribution provides an adjustment of the drift by $-\frac{1}{2}\sigma^2$ that one would have missed, if one not kept track carefully of the order of dW_t. Now (13.11) is easily integrated, and subsequently exponentiated, to obtain

$$S_t = S_0 e^{(\mu - \frac{1}{2}\sigma^2)t + \sigma W_t}, \tag{13.12}$$

where we have to keep in mind that W_t is a normally distributed random variable with $E[W_t] = 0$ and $\text{Var}[W_t] = t$. Equation (13.12) is called a strong solution to the stochastic differential equation (13.5). There is a most illuminating way to see why the drift adjustment was necessary. Calculate the expectation value of (13.12) and recall that $e^{\sigma W_t}$ is a log-normal distributed random variable,

$$E[S_t] = S_0 e^{(\mu - \frac{1}{2}\sigma^2)t} E[e^{\sigma W_t}] = S_0 e^{(\mu - \frac{1}{2}\sigma^2)t} e^{\frac{1}{2}\sigma^2 t} = S_0 e^{\mu t}. \tag{13.13}$$

You can see that the expected rate of return is indeed μ.

Everything we have motivated in the example of geometric *Brown*ian motion can be made more general and rigorous in terms of the *Itô*-integral. One of the most profound statements of this integration theory is the following theorem:

Theorem 13.1 (Itô's lemma) *Let X_t be a generalized Wiener-process (Itô-process) of the form*

$$dX_t = f(X_t, t)dt + g(X_t, t)dW_t,$$

and $y(x, t)$ a sufficiently smooth function. Then the stochastic process $Y_t = y(X_t, t)$ is also an Itô-process, with

$$dY_t = \left(f(X_t, t)\frac{\partial y}{\partial x} + \frac{\partial y}{\partial t} + \frac{1}{2}g^2(X_t, t)\frac{\partial^2 y}{\partial x^2} \right)dt + g(X_t, t)\frac{\partial y}{\partial x}dW_t,$$

where the partial derivatives are to be evaluated at $x = X_t$.

Itô's lemma is the generalization of the total differential to stochastic differential equations. We have left one open end. As explained, we gained the strong solution (13.12) by (implicitly) applying Itô's lemma. But is there also a weak solution, and what is the difference? There is a weak solution that describes the evolution of the probability density function of the *Itô*-process (13.5). It is governed by a deterministic partial differential equation called the *Fokker–Planck*-equation, but we will postpone its discussion. For the moment let's simply say that a strong solution describes the properties of a particular path, whereas a weak solution describes the properties of the whole process in terms of its probability density.

It should be emphasized again that W_t is not a differentiable process, but it is continuous everywhere, almost surely. Thus, the stochastic differential notation is purely formal and is to be understood in terms of the associated integrals. Therefore, *Itô*-calculus is a theory of integration. We will conclude this section by stating two important properties of the *Itô*-integral, which are really at the heart of Itô's lemma.

Theorem 13.2 (Properties of the *Itô*-integral) *Let $X_t \in L^2(\Omega, \mathcal{F}, P)$ be a stochastic process, adapted to the natural filtration $\mathcal{F}_t$, generated by the Wiener-process W_t. Then the stochastic Itô-integral satisfies*

$$E\left[\int_t^T X_s dW_s \right] = 0$$

for $0 \leq t \leq T$. Because of this property, the Itô-integral is a martingale

$$E\left[\int_0^T X_s dW_s \middle| \mathcal{F}_t \right] = \int_0^t X_s dW_s.$$

Furthermore, for $0 \leq t \leq T$ the Itô-isometry

$$\mathrm{Var}\left[\int_t^T X_s dW_s \right] = E\left[\left(\int_t^T X_s dW_s \right)^2 \right] = E\left[\int_t^T X_s^2 ds \right]$$

holds.

13.2   The *Black–Scholes*-Equation

We are now entering the domain of complete *Black–Scholes*-markets. All unrealistic environmental conditions from the binomial world are relaxed here. We stick only to the following assumptions:

- Continuous trading is possible at any time $t \in \mathbb{R}_0^+$.
- Prices of primitive assets (securities) follow a geometric *Brown*ian motion.
- Security prices are $\mathcal{F}_t$-measureable.
- There are no market frictions, transaction costs, or short-selling constraints.
- Assets are infinitely divisible.

The last two assumptions seem restrictive, but they are not. If the market is liquid, and individual trading volumes are high, transaction costs or indivisibility of a single security is absolutely negligible. In this setup, the value of a derivative contract V, contingent on a security S, is given by the function $V(S, t)$, yet to be determined.[1] So let's try to compute it, using familiar tools. From Itô's lemma, we know the differential of V,

$$dV = \left(\mu S \frac{\partial V}{\partial S} + \frac{\partial V}{\partial t} + \frac{1}{2}\sigma^2 S^2 \frac{\partial^2 V}{\partial S^2} \right) dt + \sigma S \frac{\partial V}{\partial S} dW. \tag{13.14}$$

Now let's try what worked so well before. Build a hedge-portfolio, containing a long position in the derivative and a fractional short position in the underlying

$$\Pi = V - \Delta \cdot S. \tag{13.15}$$

Let's ask an easy question: How does this portfolio change? From (13.14) and the geometric *Brown*ian motion (13.5) we get

$$\begin{aligned} d\Pi &= dV - \Delta \cdot dS \\ &= dV - \Delta \cdot \mu S dt - \Delta \cdot \sigma S dW. \end{aligned} \tag{13.16}$$

Here comes the clever trick Black and Scholes (1973) applied. They chose the hedge-ratio

$$\Delta = \frac{\partial V}{\partial S}. \tag{13.17}$$

Does that remind you of something? Take a look at the hedge-ratio in the binomial model (12.6) on page 224. The ratio (13.17) is an infinitesimal version of it. That is perfectly reconcilable with our intuition of the *Black–Scholes*-model as a certain limit of the binomial model. Let's see which terms cancel by applying (13.17)

$$d\Pi = \frac{\partial V}{\partial t} dt + \frac{1}{2}\sigma^2 S^2 \frac{\partial^2 V}{\partial S^2} dt. \tag{13.18}$$

---

[1] To be completely rigorous, we would have to say that $V(S, t)$ is a sufficiently smooth function and that $V_t = V(S_t, t)$ is the stochastic *Itô*-process of the derivative contract. But let's be deliberately sloppy with the notation, to emphasize the really important aspects.

First of all, the variation of the portfolio no longer depends on the expected rate of return μ of the underlying, but far more important, it is no longer driven by the *Wiener*-process. We have in fact a deterministic rule for the evolution of our hedge-portfolio. But wait, there is already such a rule for a riskless portfolio,

$$d\Pi = r\Pi dt = rVdt - rS\frac{\partial V}{\partial S}dt. \tag{13.19}$$

In order to rule out arbitrage opportunities, the right hand sides of (13.18) and (13.19) have to coincide. After rearranging and dividing by dt, one obtains the famous *Black–Scholes*-equation

$$\frac{\partial V}{\partial t} + rS\frac{\partial V}{\partial S} + \frac{1}{2}\sigma^2 S^2\frac{\partial^2 V}{\partial S^2} - rV = 0. \tag{13.20}$$

Strictly speaking, (13.20) is a second order partial differential equation (PDE), and from this technical perspective it is hard to see why the *Black–Scholes*-PDE is such a powerful device, but it is. The fair price of every asset, tradable in the *Black–Schloes*-world, is governed by (13.20). That is an outrageous statement so let's demonstrate it in a couple of examples.

Example 13.1

Let V be the risk-free bank account

$$V(S, t) = B(t) = e^{rt}.$$

Does it satisfy the *Black–Scholes*-PDE?

Solution

There are no partial derivatives with respect to an underlying S, so the *Black–Scholes*-PDE reduces to

$$\frac{\partial B}{\partial t} - rB = 0.$$

This condition is obviously satisfied.

Here is another one:

Example 13.2

Let V be the risky security S itself

$$V(S, t) = S.$$

Does it satisfy the *Black–Scholes*-PDE?

Solution

In this case, the partial differentials are $\frac{\partial S}{\partial t} = 0$, $\frac{\partial S}{\partial S} = 1$, and $\frac{\partial^2 S}{\partial S^2} = 0$. Thus, the *Black–Scholes*-PDE becomes

$$rS\frac{\partial S}{\partial S} - rS = 0,$$

which is also true.

Let's try something more ambitious. We derived the price of a forward contract in Chapter 11 purely from arbitrage arguments. No model assumptions were involved. So let's take a look at it.

Example 13.3

Let V be the price of a forward contract

$$V(S,t) = F(S,t) = S - e^{-r(T-t)}K.$$

Does it satisfy the *Black–Scholes*-PDE?

Solution

The price of the forward contract has a partial derivative with respect to t and to S, but no second partial derivative with respect to S. Hence, the *Black–Scholes*-PDE becomes

$$\frac{\partial F}{\partial t} + rS\frac{\partial F}{\partial S} - rF = -re^{-r(T-t)}K + rS - rF = 0,$$

which is also satisfied.

At this point you should begin to see how powerful the *Black–Scholes*-PDE indeed is. But proving that prices of assets we already know obey the equation is one thing. Finding the prices of assets we do not know from the equation is the true power of the *Black–Scholes*-framework.

In order to find the price of a derivative, let's say a plain vanilla European call option, we have to require additional conditions to be satisfied. In case of the call option, the additional condition is the payoff function

$$V(S,T) = (S - K)^+. \tag{13.21}$$

If we can find a function $V(S,t)$, satisfying the *Black–Scholes*-PDE and the additional condition (13.21) simultaneously, then we can read off the call price

$$C_t(K,T) = V(S_t,t). \tag{13.22}$$

It all boils down to solving the partial differential equation (13.20) under additional conditions. Can you guess what option price we would obtain, if we can find a function $V(S, t)$, satisfying the *Black–Scholes*-PDE, (13.21), and additionally

$$V(S_u, t) = 0? \tag{13.23}$$

Correct, this is the price of a European barrier call option $C_t^{\otimes}(K, T, S_u)$, with upper knockout barrier S_u.

We will exercise the procedure of deriving the *Black–Scholes*-price of a European binary call option in detail. But first we have to learn a little bit about generalized functions.

13.3   Dirac's δ-Function and Tempered Distributions

A lot of mathematical and engineering applications heavily rely on the δ-function, introduced by Paul Dirac. The problem with this function is that its definition does not fit with the requirements of ordinary functions. The *Dirac*-δ-function is defined by the properties

$$\delta(x) = \begin{cases} \infty & \text{for } x = 0 \\ 0 & \text{for } x \neq 0 \end{cases} \quad \text{and} \quad \int_{-\infty}^{\infty} \delta(x)dx = 1. \tag{13.24}$$

There are two major problems with that. First of all, a function $\delta : \mathbb{R} \to \mathbb{R}$ would require a unique definite value for each element in its domain. This requirement is violated for $x = 0$. Furthermore, $\delta(x)$ is obviously not an integrable function. The old way to deal with these problems is to understand the δ-function as a generalized function or "distribution," defined as the limit of a family of functions (see for example Lighthill, 1980, chap. 2). For example

$$\delta(x) = \lim_{\varepsilon \to 0} \Pi_\varepsilon(x) \quad \text{with} \quad \Pi_\varepsilon(x) = \begin{cases} \frac{1}{\varepsilon} & \text{for } -\frac{\varepsilon}{2} \leq x \leq \frac{\varepsilon}{2} \\ 0 & \text{else.} \end{cases} \tag{13.25}$$

Quick calculation 13.1 Convince yourself that $\phi_\varepsilon(x) = \frac{1}{\sqrt{2\pi\varepsilon^2}} e^{-\frac{1}{2}\left(\frac{x}{\varepsilon}\right)^2}$ is also a representation of the δ-function as $\varepsilon \to 0$.

Figure 13.1 illustrates two different sequences of functions, approaching the δ-function in the limit $\varepsilon \to 0$. The technical term "distribution" is another example of an unfortunate clash of terminology, because it has absolutely nothing to do with probability distributions. The modern, and far more powerful, way is to define $\delta(x)$ in terms of a "pairing" with another so-called test function, which is so well behaved that all the unpleasant properties of the distribution can be rolled over to the test function. To make head or tail out of it, we have to see how it works.

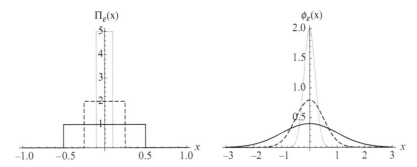

Fig. 13.1 Different limit sequences for the δ-function with $\varepsilon = 1$ (black), $\varepsilon = 0.5$ (dashed), and $\varepsilon = 0.2$ (gray)

Let's start by looking for a very well behaved class of functions to be used as test functions. Call $\varphi(x)$ a rapidly decreasing function, if

    1. $\varphi(x)$ is infinitely differentiable,

    2. for every $m, n \geq 0$, $\displaystyle\lim_{x \to \pm\infty} |x|^m \left| \frac{d^n \varphi(x)}{dx^n} \right| = 0.$ (13.26)

Such functions are also called *Schwartz*-functions. Essentially, (13.26) says that every derivative of $\varphi(x)$ decreases faster than any arbitrary power of x. That seems like a very strong statement, but one reason for choosing this class of test functions is that the probability density function of a normally distributed random variable is such a function. The *Schwartz*-functions form a vector space S, and its dual vector space is called the space of "tempered distributions." Consequently, we want a generalized function $\mathcal{T}(x)$ to be defined by a continuous linear functional in S. We already know what it means for a functional to be linear,

    1. $\langle \mathcal{T} | \alpha \cdot \varphi \rangle = \alpha \cdot \langle \mathcal{T} | \varphi \rangle,$

    2. $\langle \mathcal{T} | \varphi_1 + \varphi_2 \rangle = \langle \mathcal{T} | \varphi_1 \rangle + \langle \mathcal{T} | \varphi_2 \rangle.$ (13.27)

To be a continuous functional means that we have a sequence of test functions $\varphi_n(x)$, such that

$$\lim_{n \to \infty} \varphi_n(x) = \varphi(x) \quad \Rightarrow \quad \lim_{n \to \infty} \langle \mathcal{T} | \varphi_n \rangle = \langle \mathcal{T} | \varphi \rangle. \qquad (13.28)$$

This condition is necessary to preserve certain limit properties. Actually, ensuring (13.28) is the really hard part, but let's not bother with these technical issues. Instead, define the δ-function as such a functional on S by

$$\langle \delta | \varphi \rangle = \varphi(0). \qquad (13.29)$$

To understand the meaning of (13.29), write the functional in a more traditional form

$$\int_{-\infty}^{\infty} \delta(x)\varphi(x)dx = \varphi(0), \qquad (13.30)$$

and recall that $\varphi(x)$ is an arbitrary function in $\mathcal{S}$. In order for (13.30) to be true, $\delta(x)$ can only be allowed to be nonzero in an infinitesimal vicinity of $x = 0$, so that we can pull $\varphi(x)$ at $x = 0$ out of the integral

$$\int_{-\infty}^{\infty} \delta(x)\varphi(x)dx = \varphi(0) \int_{-\infty}^{\infty} \delta(x)dx. \qquad (13.31)$$

But this means that the integral over the δ-function has to equal one. Isn't that ingenious? Let's define another generalized function by such a continuous linear functional

$$\langle \delta_y | \varphi \rangle = \varphi(y). \qquad (13.32)$$

From this definition, we can immediately conclude what $\delta_y(x)$ is, namely

$$\int_{-\infty}^{\infty} \delta_y(x)\varphi(x)dx = \int_{-\infty}^{\infty} \delta(x - y)\varphi(x)dx = \varphi(y), \qquad (13.33)$$

the shifted δ-function. But that is only the tip of the iceberg. To demonstrate the incredible power of the formalism, let's look at two more applications: Derivatives of generalized functions and *Fourier*-transforms.

What does it mean to have a derivative of a distribution? Has the distribution itself to be differentiable? Surprisingly it does not have to be. The lack of differentiability is rolled over to the test function. Let's see how it works. Look at the following functional

$$\langle \tfrac{d}{dx}\mathcal{T} | \varphi \rangle = \int_{-\infty}^{\infty} \tfrac{d}{dx}\mathcal{T}(x)\varphi(x)dx. \qquad (13.34)$$

Using integration by parts, we get most easily

$$\int_{-\infty}^{\infty} \tfrac{d}{dx}\mathcal{T}(x)\varphi(x)dx = \mathcal{T}(x)\varphi(x)\Big|_{-\infty}^{+\infty} - \int_{-\infty}^{\infty} \mathcal{T}(x)\tfrac{d}{dx}\varphi(x)dx. \qquad (13.35)$$

The first term on the right hand side has to vanish because of the defining properties of the test function $\varphi(x)$ at $x = \pm\infty$. Thus, we can immediately conclude that

$$\langle \tfrac{d}{dx}\mathcal{T} | \varphi \rangle = -\langle \mathcal{T} | \tfrac{d}{dx}\varphi \rangle. \qquad (13.36)$$

By completely analogous reasoning, we can infer that the differential operator $D_n = \frac{d^n}{dx^n}$ has an adjoint operator $D_n^{\dagger} = (-1)^n \frac{d^n}{dx^n}$, such that

$$\langle D_n\mathcal{T} | \varphi \rangle = \langle \mathcal{T} | D_n^{\dagger}\varphi \rangle \qquad (13.37)$$

holds. Let's look at two important examples.

Example 13.4

Let $\theta(x)$ be the *Heaviside-θ*-function

$$\theta(x) = \begin{cases} 1 & \text{for } x \geq 0 \\ 0 & \text{for } x < 0, \end{cases}$$

and consider the functional $\langle \frac{d}{dx}\theta | \varphi \rangle$. What distribution is induced by it?

Solution

Follow the formalism (13.36) to obtain

$$\langle \tfrac{d}{dx}\theta | \varphi \rangle = -\langle \theta | \tfrac{d}{dx}\varphi \rangle = -\int_{-\infty}^{\infty} \theta(x)\tfrac{d}{dx}\varphi(x)dx = -\int_0^{\infty} d\varphi(x) = \varphi(0).$$

But $\varphi(0)$ is the result of the pairing with the δ-function, and so we have

$$\langle \tfrac{d}{dx}\theta | \varphi \rangle = \langle \delta | \varphi \rangle.$$

We can thus conclude that $\frac{d}{dx}\theta(x) = \delta(x)$.

Here is another example:

Example 13.5

Take the maximum function $\max(x, 0) = x^+$, and consider the functional

$$\langle \tfrac{d}{dx}x^+ | \varphi \rangle.$$

What distribution is induced by this pairing?

Solution

Again stick to the formalism (13.36) to obtain

$$\langle \tfrac{d}{dx}x^+ | \varphi \rangle = -\langle x^+ | \tfrac{d}{dx}\varphi \rangle = -\int_0^{\infty} x\tfrac{d}{dx}\varphi(x)dx = -x\varphi(x)\Big|_0^{\infty} + \int_0^{\infty} \varphi(x)dx,$$

where we have used integration by parts in the last step. The first term on the right hand side is apparently zero, and the integral can be expressed as

$$\int_0^{\infty} \varphi(x)dx = \int_{-\infty}^{\infty} \theta(x)\varphi(x)dx = \langle \theta | \varphi \rangle.$$

Hence, we find that $\frac{d}{dx}x^+ = \theta(x)$.

Those derivatives are of course only valid, if understood as distributions. They will come in handy at a later time when discussing the *Dupire*-equation.

The class of *Schwartz*-functions has another very pleasing property. It permits unconditional access to the *Fourier*-transform and the inverse *Fourier*-transform.

We will rely heavily on those transformations, when discussing stochastic volatility and *Lévy*-processes. Let's indicate the *Fourier*-transform of a function traditionally by hat-notation. How is the quantity $\hat{\mathcal{T}}(u)$ defined? Again, stick to the formalism,

$$
\begin{aligned}
\langle \hat{\mathcal{T}} | \varphi \rangle &= \int_{-\infty}^{\infty} \int_{-\infty}^{\infty} e^{iux} \mathcal{T}(x) \varphi(u) dx du \\
&= \int_{-\infty}^{\infty} \int_{-\infty}^{\infty} \mathcal{T}(x) e^{iux} \varphi(u) du dx \\
&= \int_{-\infty}^{\infty} \mathcal{T}(x) \hat{\varphi}(x) dx.
\end{aligned}
\tag{13.38}
$$

That is, we have a general rule for the *Fourier*-transform of a distribution

$$
\langle \hat{\mathcal{T}} | \varphi \rangle = \langle \mathcal{T} | \hat{\varphi} \rangle.
\tag{13.39}
$$

So let's find the *Fourier*-transform of the δ-function. We follow our new formalism (13.39) to obtain

$$
\langle \delta | \hat{\varphi} \rangle = \hat{\varphi}(0) = \int_{-\infty}^{\infty} e^{i0x} \varphi(x) dx = \int_{-\infty}^{\infty} 1 \cdot \varphi(x) dx.
\tag{13.40}
$$

Obviously, there is a new pairing induced

$$
\langle \hat{\delta} | \varphi \rangle = \langle 1 | \varphi \rangle,
\tag{13.41}
$$

from which we can conclude that $\hat{\delta}(u) = 1$.

Although the *Schwartz*-functions are a well-suited class of test functions, there are other appropriate classes, on which a distribution like the δ-function can be defined. In everyday life, the background connection to the respective class of test functions is usually brushed under the big carpet, and one writes

$$
f(y) = \int_{-\infty}^{\infty} \delta(x - y) f(x) dx
\tag{13.42}
$$

as defining equation for the *Dirac-δ*-function.

13.4   The Fundamental Solution

Linear partial differential equations, as well as ordinary linear differential equations, obey the principle of superposition. This principle describes the fact that one can generate new solutions to a given problem by adding already known solutions. This should not come as a surprise, because what we call superposition is really at the heart of linearity. How can it be that a differential equation has more than one solution? Remember that such a solution is a function, not a number. Look at the following differential equation

$$
\frac{d^2 x(t)}{dt^2} = -x(t).
\tag{13.43}
$$

Can you guess a function that satisfies this equation? Here is one, $x(t) = \sin t$. Here is another one, $x(t) = \cos t$. Because the differential equation (13.43) is linear, which means it contains no multiplicative terms in $x(t)$, we can add solutions to obtain new ones,

$$x(t) = c_1 \sin t + c_2 \cos t, \tag{13.44}$$

where c_1 and c_2 are arbitrary constants. It is easily checked that (13.44) is also a solution to (13.43).

Quick calculation 13.2 Confirm that $x(t) = e^{it}$, with $i = \sqrt{-1}$, is also a solution.

Now that we understand superposition, let's discuss the concept of an initial value problem. Suppose you deposit a fixed amount of money B_0 in your bank account at $t = 0$. B_0 is only a number, but the time value of the bank account is a function $B(t)$, evolving as

$$\frac{dB(t)}{dt} = r B(t). \tag{13.45}$$

We know at least one solution to that differential equation, $B(t) = e^{rt}$, but there are many others like for example

$$B(t) = ce^{rt}, \tag{13.46}$$

for arbitrary values of c. To single out the desired individual solution, we have to exploit the initial condition $B(0) = B_0$. Evaluating (13.46) at $t = 0$ yields $B(0) = c$, and thus we can conclude that $c = B_0$. Hence, the unique solution to our initial value problem is

$$B(t) = B_0 e^{rt}. \tag{13.47}$$

A partial differential equation like the *Black–Scholes*-equation is a rule for the evolution of a function $V(S, t)$. Its initial value is not a number V_0, but an entire function $V(S, 0)$. And that is where the superposition principle comes in. If we can find a really special solution $V_0(S, t)$ that corresponds to the initial condition $V_0(S, 0) = \delta(S)$, then we can write the initial condition as superposition

$$V(S, 0) = \int_{-\infty}^{\infty} \delta(x - S) V(x, 0) dx = \int_{-\infty}^{\infty} V_0(x - S, 0) V(x, 0) dx. \tag{13.48}$$

Such a solution $V_0(S, t)$ is called a fundamental solution and it is so powerful, because the superposition principle is valid at any time t. We can immediately write the solution to the entire initial value problem

$$V(S, t) = \int_{-\infty}^{\infty} V_0(x - S, t) V(x, 0) dx \tag{13.49}$$

as superposition of the fundamental solution with the initial condition. Thus, our first step should be to look for a fundamental solution of the *Black–Scholes*-PDE.

In order to identify a fundamental solution to the *Black–Scholes*-PDE, we have to do some manipulations. The valuation of a European contract for example is a terminal value problem, which means that we first have to reverse the direction of time to turn it into an initial value problem. Departing from the original *Black–Scholes*-equation

$$\frac{\partial V}{\partial t} + rS\frac{\partial V}{\partial S} + \frac{1}{2}\sigma^2 S^2 \frac{\partial^2 V}{\partial S^2} - rV = 0, \tag{13.50}$$

we will organize the necessary steps in a way that allows us to retrace every manipulation.

Step 1
Eliminate the inhomogeneity in the *Black–Scholes*-PDE. Make the substitution

$$V(S,t) = e^{-r(T-t)}U(S,t). \tag{13.51}$$

This substitution adds an extra term to the time derivative,

$$\frac{\partial V}{\partial t} = rV + e^{-r(T-t)}\frac{\partial U}{\partial t}. \tag{13.52}$$

The partial derivative with respect to S is not affected by (13.51). Thus, one obtains in terms of $U(S,t)$

$$e^{-r(T-t)}\left(\frac{\partial U}{\partial t} + rS\frac{\partial U}{\partial S} + \frac{1}{2}\sigma^2 S^2 \frac{\partial^2 U}{\partial S^2}\right) = 0. \tag{13.53}$$

We can multiply both sides by $e^{r(T-t)}$ to obtain the final form of the *Black–Scholes*-PDE in terms of $U(S,t)$,

$$\frac{\partial U}{\partial t} + rS\frac{\partial U}{\partial S} + \frac{1}{2}\sigma^2 S^2 \frac{\partial^2 U}{\partial S^2} = 0. \tag{13.54}$$

Step 2
Reversing the flow of time. Define the time to expiry

$$\tau = T - t. \tag{13.55}$$

By the chain rule of differentiation, we can compute the partial derivative of U with respect to τ,

$$\frac{\partial U}{\partial \tau} = \frac{\partial U}{\partial t}\frac{dt}{d\tau} = -\frac{\partial U}{\partial t}. \tag{13.56}$$

That leaves us with an initial value problem and the following PDE

$$\frac{\partial U}{\partial \tau} = rS\frac{\partial U}{\partial S} + \frac{1}{2}\sigma^2 S^2 \frac{\partial^2 U}{\partial S^2}. \tag{13.57}$$

Step 3

Proceed to logarithmic prices. Define the log-price

$$x = \log S. \tag{13.58}$$

This transition has consequences for both partial derivatives of U with respect to S. The first derivative becomes

$$\frac{\partial U}{\partial S} = \frac{\partial U}{\partial x}\frac{dx}{dS} = \frac{\partial U}{\partial x}\cdot\frac{1}{S}. \tag{13.59}$$

The second derivative is a little more involved. One obtains

$$\frac{\partial^2 U}{\partial S^2} = \frac{\partial}{\partial S}\left(\frac{\partial U}{\partial x}\cdot\frac{1}{S}\right) = \frac{\partial^2 U}{\partial x^2}\cdot\frac{1}{S^2} - \frac{\partial U}{\partial x}\cdot\frac{1}{S^2}. \tag{13.60}$$

Using these derivatives, one obtains the new PDE

$$\frac{\partial U}{\partial \tau} = \left(r - \frac{1}{2}\sigma^2\right)\frac{\partial U}{\partial x} + \frac{1}{2}\sigma^2\frac{\partial^2 U}{\partial x^2}. \tag{13.61}$$

Step 4

Change variables. Let

$$y = x + \left(r - \frac{1}{2}\sigma^2\right)\tau, \tag{13.62}$$

and define the new function W by

$$U(S,t) = U(e^x, T - \tau) = U(e^{y-(r-\frac{1}{2}\sigma^2)\tau}, T - \tau) = W(y, \tau). \tag{13.63}$$

Under this transformation, the partial derivative with respect to τ changes to

$$\frac{\partial U}{\partial \tau} = \frac{\partial W}{\partial \tau} + \frac{\partial W}{\partial y}\frac{\partial y}{\partial \tau} = \frac{\partial W}{\partial \tau} + \frac{\partial W}{\partial y}\left(r - \frac{1}{2}\sigma^2\right), \tag{13.64}$$

and the partial derivative with respect to x becomes

$$\frac{\partial U}{\partial x} = \frac{\partial W}{\partial y}\frac{\partial y}{\partial x} = \frac{\partial W}{\partial y}. \tag{13.65}$$

It is easy to see that the second partial derivative is also unaltered, $\frac{\partial^2 U}{\partial x^2} = \frac{\partial^2 W}{\partial y^2}$. One thus obtains in terms of the function $W(y, \tau)$

$$\frac{\partial W}{\partial \tau} = \frac{1}{2}\sigma^2\frac{\partial^2 W}{\partial y^2}. \tag{13.66}$$

This partial differential equation also has a special name; it is called the diffusion equation. We can solve this equation easily, using a special trick *Fourier*-transform provides us with.

Suppose you have a sufficiently fast decreasing function $f(x)$, and you are looking for the *Fourier*-transform of its derivative. The definition of the *Fourier*-transform leads the way and one arrives at

$$\int_{-\infty}^{\infty} e^{iux}\frac{d}{dx}f(x)dx = e^{iux}f(x)\Big|_{-\infty}^{+\infty} - iu\int_{-\infty}^{\infty} e^{iux}f(x)dx = -iu\hat{f}(u). \qquad (13.67)$$

The boundary term, generated by the integration by parts, vanishes, because we have assumed $f(x)$ to be sufficiently fast decreasing, or in other words $f^{(n)}(\pm\infty) = 0$, for $n \in \mathbb{N}_0$. Repeating exactly the same argument successively, we can see what happens to arbitrary derivatives under *Fourier*-transform,

$$\frac{d^n}{dx^n}f(x) \longrightarrow (-iu)^n\hat{f}(u). \qquad (13.68)$$

Quick calculation 13.3   Verify (13.68) for $n = 2$.

This relation is instrumental in solving the diffusion equation. In *Fourier*-space, (13.66) reads

$$\frac{\partial}{\partial\tau}\hat{W}(u,\tau) = -\frac{1}{2}u^2\sigma^2\,\hat{W}(u,\tau). \qquad (13.69)$$

This is nothing but an ordinary differential equation. Furthermore, we are looking for a fundamental solution, which means $W_0(y,0) = \delta(y)$. But we have already seen that the *Fourier*-transform of the δ-function is one, and therefore the initial value is $\hat{W}_0(u,0) = 1$. The unique fundamental solution to (13.69) in *Fourier*-space is thus

$$\hat{W}_0(u,\tau) = e^{-\frac{1}{2}u^2\sigma^2\tau}. \qquad (13.70)$$

That should ring an enormous bell. Equation (13.70) is precisely the characteristic function of a normally distributed random variable with zero expectation value and variance $\sigma^2\tau$. This means, the inverse *Fourier*-transform is the probability density function of such a random variable,

$$W_0(y,\tau) = \frac{1}{\sqrt{2\pi\sigma^2\tau}}e^{-\frac{1}{2}\left(\frac{y}{\sigma\sqrt{\tau}}\right)^2}. \qquad (13.71)$$

By retracing our steps, we have the relation $V_0(S,t) = e^{-r\tau}W_0(y,\tau)$, with $\tau = T - t$ and $y = \log S + (r - \frac{1}{2}\sigma^2)(T - t)$. Thus, we have found the desired fundamental solution.

13.5   Binary and Plain Vanilla Option Prices

Now that we know the fundamental solution, we can start computing option prices. The whole procedure is demonstrated for a binary option pair, but the methodology carries over analogously to all analytically solvable option types. The European binary call option has the payoff function $C_T^B(K, T) = \theta(S - K)$.

Quick calculation 13.4 Convince yourself that for $x = \log S$ the payoff function is equivalently formulated as $C_T^B(K, T) = \theta(x - \log K)$.

Using the fundamental solution, one obtains

$$
\begin{aligned}
C_t^B(K, T) &= e^{-r\tau} \int_{-\infty}^{\infty} W_0(x - y, \tau)\theta(x - \log K)dx \\
&= e^{-r\tau} \int_{\log K}^{\infty} W_0(x - y, \tau)dx \\
&= e^{-r\tau} \int_{\log K}^{\infty} \frac{1}{\sqrt{2\pi\sigma^2\tau}} e^{-\frac{1}{2}\left(\frac{x-y}{\sigma\sqrt{\tau}}\right)^2} dx.
\end{aligned}
\tag{13.72}
$$

Now, make the substitution $z = \frac{x-y}{\sigma\sqrt{\tau}}$. Under this transformation, the increment becomes $dx = \sigma\sqrt{\tau}dz$, and one obtains

$$
\begin{aligned}
C_t^B(K, T) &= e^{-r\tau} \int_{\frac{\log K - y}{\sigma\sqrt{\tau}}}^{\infty} \frac{1}{\sqrt{2\pi}} e^{-\frac{1}{2}z^2} dz \\
&= e^{-r\tau} \int_{-\infty}^{\frac{y-\log K}{\sigma\sqrt{\tau}}} \phi(z)dz,
\end{aligned}
\tag{13.73}
$$

where $\phi(z)$ is again the probability density function of a standard normally distributed random variable. In the second equality, we have used the fact that $\phi(z)$ is symmetric around $z = 0$. Retracing all substitutions we have made, the fair price of a European binary call option in the *Black–Scholes*-model is

$$
C_t^B(K, T) = e^{-r(T-t)}\Phi(d),
\tag{13.74}
$$

with

$$
d = \frac{\log(S_t/K) + (r - \frac{1}{2}\sigma^2)(T - t)}{\sigma\sqrt{T - t}},
\tag{13.75}
$$

where $\Phi(x)$ is of course the distribution function of a standard normally distributed random variable. Except for slight notational variations, this is exactly what we already found in the limit of the binomial model, see (12.75) on page 246. To obtain a formula for the binary put option, we can simply use binary put-call parity

$$
C_t^B(K, T) + P_t^B(K, T) = e^{-r(T-t)}.
\tag{13.76}
$$

Quick calculation 13.5 Confirm this parity relation by adding the payoffs.

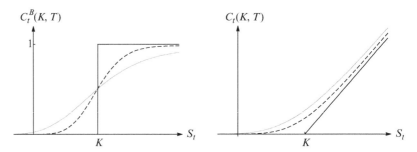

Fig. 13.2 Fair price of European binary call (left) and plain vanilla call (right) – Different times to expiry (gray, dashed, black) in descending order

The resulting price for the binary European put option is

$$P_t^B(K, T) = e^{-r(T-t)}(1 - \Phi(d)) = e^{-r(T-t)}\Phi(-d), \qquad (13.77)$$

with d as in (13.75).

Quick calculation 13.6 Verify that $\Phi(x) = 1 - \Phi(-x)$ holds.

Figure 13.2 left shows the fair price of a European binary call option, as a function of the current price of the underlying, for different times to expiry. The solid black line is the payoff at expiry.

Black and Scholes (1973) derived the analytic formula for a European plain vanilla call option. The steps are analogous to those in the binary case. They obtained for the fair value of that option

$$C_t(K, T) = S_t\Phi(d_1) - e^{-r(T-t)}K\Phi(d_2), \qquad (13.78)$$

with

$$d_1 = \frac{\log(S_t/K) + (r + \frac{1}{2}\sigma^2)(T - t)}{\sigma\sqrt{T-t}} \quad \text{and} \quad d_2 = d_1 - \sigma\sqrt{T-t}. \qquad (13.79)$$

From put-call parity, the fair price for a plain vanilla put option is easily obtained as

$$P_t(K, T) = -S_t\Phi(-d_1) + e^{-r(T-t)}K\Phi(-d_2), \qquad (13.80)$$

with d_1 and d_2 as in (13.79).

Quick calculation 13.7 Verify the last formula from put-call parity.

The fair price of a European plain vanilla call option is illustrated in Figure 13.2 right, for different times to expiry. The solid black line again indicates the payoff function at expiry.

13.6   Simple Extensions of the *Black–Scholes*-Model

The original option pricing formula (13.78) is only valid, if the underlying neither pays dividends, nor causes costs of any kind. But it can be easily extended to cover all kinds of exceptional properties of the underlying. We will discuss the case of a continuous dividend stream in detail, and subsequently extend the basic principle to all kinds of other anomalies.

13.6.1   Continuous Dividend Stream

Suppose the underlying S pays a constant dividend stream q, also called a dividend yield, which is continuously reinvested in the position itself. That is, in every instant dt, the position Δ in S grows by $d\Delta = q\Delta dt$. Let's set up the usual hedge-portfolio $\Pi = V - \Delta \cdot S$ and let's analyze how it changes

$$d\Pi = dV - \Delta \cdot dS - d\Delta \cdot S \\ = dV - \Delta \cdot dS - \Delta \cdot qSdt. \tag{13.81}$$

We have one additional term, due to the reinvestment of the dividend stream. Let's do the same as we did before, namely apply Itô's lemma and choose $\Delta = \frac{\partial V}{\partial S}$ to obtain

$$d\Pi = \frac{\partial V}{\partial t}dt + \frac{1}{2}\sigma^2 S^2 \frac{\partial^2 V}{\partial S^2}dt - qS\frac{\partial V}{\partial S}dt. \tag{13.82}$$

This result is completely analogous to (13.18), except for the additional last term on the right hand side. The change in portfolio value (13.82) does not depend on the *Wiener*-process anymore, and should therefore be related to the riskless interest rate, $d\Pi = r\Pi dt$. Plugging everything in, one obtains a modified *Black–Scholes*-equation

$$\frac{\partial V}{\partial t} + (r - q)S\frac{\partial V}{\partial S} + \frac{1}{2}\sigma^2 S^2 \frac{\partial^2 V}{\partial S^2} - rV = 0. \tag{13.83}$$

Quick calculation 13.8   Confirm that (13.83) is correct.

We have now to repeat our earlier steps, to find a fundamental solution. But we can take a very effective shortcut. Let's execute our former step 1 and substitute $V(S, t) = e^{-r(T-t)}U(S, t)$. This results in the partial differential equation

$$\frac{\partial U}{\partial t} + (r - q)S\frac{\partial U}{\partial S} + \frac{1}{2}\sigma^2 S^2 \frac{\partial^2 U}{\partial S^2} = 0. \tag{13.84}$$

Now invent a "generalized cost-of-carry rate" $b = r - q$, and observe that we only have to make the replacement $r \to b$, to turn the original fundamental solution into the desired solution of the modified *Black–Scholes*-PDE. Exercising the entire computation, one obtains a new generalized *Black–Scholes*-formula for the European plain vanilla call option

$$C_t(K, T) = e^{(b-r)(T-t)} S_t \Phi(d_+) - e^{-r(T-t)} K \Phi(d_-), \tag{13.85}$$

with

$$d_{+/-} = \frac{\log(S_t/K) + (b \pm \frac{1}{2}\sigma^2)(T-t)}{\sigma\sqrt{T-t}}. \tag{13.86}$$

For the non dividend paying underlying, $b = r$ reproduces the original *Black–Scholes*-formula. For $b = r - q$, we obtain the modified formula for the dividend paying underlying. For the sake of completeness, the price of the corresponding put option, obtained from put-call parity is

$$P_t(K, T) = -e^{(b-r)(T-t)} S_t \Phi(-d_+) + e^{-r(T-t)} K \Phi(-d_-). \tag{13.87}$$

Quick calculation 13.9 Confirm that $C_t^B(K, T) = e^{-r(T-t)} \Phi(d_-)$ is the correct generalized formula for a European binary call option.

13.6.2   Options on a Foreign Currency

Suppose the underlying is a foreign currency. The holder of a position Δ in foreign currency receives foreign interest according to $d\Delta = r_f \Delta dt$, with the foreign risk-free interest rate r_f. The changes in the hedge-portfolio in this case become

$$d\Pi = dV - \Delta \cdot dS - \Delta \cdot r_f S dt, \tag{13.88}$$

and we can immediately conclude that the corresponding modified *Black–Scholes*-equation is

$$\frac{\partial V}{\partial t} + (r - r_f) S \frac{\partial V}{\partial S} + \frac{1}{2}\sigma^2 S^2 \frac{\partial^2 V}{\partial S^2} - rV = 0. \tag{13.89}$$

Without further analysis it is obvious that our generalized framework carries over to the case of foreign currencies, with the generalized cost-of-carry rate $b = r - r_f$.

13.6.3   Commodity Options

The underlying does not have to be a security of some sort, it is also common that option contracts are contingent on commodities like copper, gold, wheat, petroleum, and so forth. The primary difference between those two classes of underlyings is that commodities have to be stored. Take gold for example. It has not only to be stored, but it has additionally to be guarded. It is again sensible to assume that the overall storage costs are proportional to the size of the position and the storage period. Suppose the storage costs are funded by the proceeds of trading the associated commodity. Then we can think of storage costs as continuously reducing the position in the commodity, $d\Delta = -c_s \Delta dt$, where c_s is the instantaneous cost rate. This immediately induces another modification of the *Black–Scholes*-equation,

$$\frac{\partial V}{\partial t} + (r + c_s)S\frac{\partial V}{\partial S} + \frac{1}{2}\sigma^2 S^2 \frac{\partial^2 V}{\partial S^2} - rV = 0, \tag{13.90}$$

where this time, the generalized cost-of-carry rate is $b = r + c_s$.

13.6.4   Options on Forwards and Futures

We still consider the case of a deterministic risk-free interest rate. Therefore, the fair delivery or forward price of a forward or future contract, initiated at time t, is given by

$$F_t = e^{r(T_F - t)} S_t, \tag{13.91}$$

where $T_F \geq T$ is the delivery date of the forward or future contract. Define $V(S, t) = U(F, t)$ and let's see how the derivatives change. For the time derivative we get

$$\frac{\partial V}{\partial t} = \frac{\partial U}{\partial t} + \frac{\partial U}{\partial F}\frac{\partial F}{\partial t} = \frac{\partial U}{\partial t} - rF\frac{\partial U}{\partial F}. \tag{13.92}$$

The first derivative with respect to S is also altered. One obtains

$$\frac{\partial V}{\partial S} = \frac{\partial U}{\partial F}\frac{\partial F}{\partial S} = e^{r(T_F - t)}\frac{\partial U}{\partial F}. \tag{13.93}$$

But recall the term in the *Black–Scholes*-equation that contains this first order derivative. This particular term transforms to

$$rS\frac{\partial V}{\partial S} = re^{r(T_F - t)}S\frac{\partial U}{\partial F} = rF\frac{\partial U}{\partial F}. \tag{13.94}$$

Isn't that nice? And it gets even better. From (13.91) we have $\frac{\partial^2 F}{\partial S^2} = 0$, and thus

$$\frac{\partial^2 V}{\partial S^2} = \frac{\partial}{\partial S}\left(\frac{\partial U}{\partial F}\frac{\partial F}{\partial S}\right) = \frac{\partial^2 U}{\partial F^2}\left(\frac{\partial F}{\partial S}\right)^2. \tag{13.95}$$

That makes the second derivative term in the original *Black–Scholes*-equation

$$\frac{1}{2}\sigma^2 S^2 \frac{\partial^2 V}{\partial S^2} = \frac{1}{2}\sigma^2 F^2 \frac{\partial^2 U}{\partial F^2}. \tag{13.96}$$

Table 13.1 Generalized cost-of-carry rates

Underlying	Cost-of-carry rate b
Non dividend paying security	r
Dividend paying security (dividend rate q)	$r - q$
Foreign currency (foreign interest rate r_f)	$r - r_f$
Commodity (storage cost rate c_s)	$r + c_s$
Forward or future contract	0

Hence, the modified *Black–Scholes*-equation, where the underlying is a forward or future contract on a non dividend paying security is

$$\frac{\partial U}{\partial t} + \frac{1}{2}\sigma^2 F^2 \frac{\partial^2 U}{\partial F^2} - rU = 0. \tag{13.97}$$

We can immediately read off that the generalized cost-of-carry rate is $b = 0$. This version is also known as the *Black*-76-model (Black, 1976). Table 13.1 summarizes all extensions to the *Black–Scholes*-model discussed in this section.

13.7 Discrete Dividend Payments

In this section, we will look at the more realistic assumption that dividend payments are to occur at discrete times over the lifetime of the option. We will still assume that the magnitude as well as the time of the dividend payment is known in advance. There are two common manifestations of this restriction. The first is a simple cash dividend D_n, paid at time t_n, for $t < t_n < T$. The second is a fixed discrete dividend yield q_n, that is, the dividend due at t_n is $D_n = q_n S_{t_n}$. We will study the latter alternative first, because it does not require any volatility adjustments.

Let's ask the question: Is the price of the dividend paying security S affected by the discrete dividend payment D_n? To be as precise as possible, call the instant just before the dividend payment t_n^- and the successive instant, where the dividend is already paid t_n^+. Now let's see, what the holder of this security gets out of the transition. We assume heuristically that the time difference between t_n^- and t_n^+ is too small for any appreciable change in the price of the underlying due to random fluctuations. Therefore, the overall value of the position cannot change, and

$$S_{t_n^-} = S_{t_n^+} + D_n \tag{13.98}$$

has to hold. If $D_n = q_n S_{t_n}$, we obtain an explicit expression for the ex-dividend price of the security

$$S_{t_n^+} = (1 - q_n)S_{t_n^-}. \tag{13.99}$$

Table 13.2 Option arbitrage portfolio

Position	Value at t_n^-	Value at t_n^+
Stock	$S_{t_n^-}$	$(1 - q_n)S_{t_n^-}$
Bank account	0	$q_n S_{t_n^-}$
Option	$-\Delta V_{t_n^-}$	$-\Delta V_{t_n^+}$
Total sum	$S_{t_n^-} - \Delta V_{t_n^-} = 0$	$S_{t_n^-} - \Delta V_{t_n^+} = 0$

This means, the price of the dividend paying security jumps during the transition from t_n^- to t_n^+. The magnitude of the jump is exactly the magnitude of the dividend, paid at t_n. Here comes the interesting question: does a derivative, contingent on S, jump, too? Let's answer this one with an arbitrage argument. Suppose an investor holds a dividend paying stock S, just before the payment is due. The position is funded by short selling

$$\Delta = \frac{S_{t_n^-}}{V_{t_n^-}} \tag{13.100}$$

units of a derivative V, contingent on S. If the dividend is of the type (13.99), the overall position of the investor can be summarized as in Table 13.2. We can immediately conclude that $V_{t_n^-} = V_{t_n^+}$ has to hold. This fact implies a "jump condition" in the *Black–Scholes*-equation, namely

$$V(S, t_n^-) = V((1 - q_n)S, t_n^+). \tag{13.101}$$

If you think it through, it is obvious why the security, but not the option, jumps. The holder of the security receives the dividend, but the holder of the option receives nothing. So why should the option value jump?

The principle we just encountered is so general that it applies to any kind of option. In particular, if there are N dividend payments to come during the lifetime of the option, and the discrete dividend yields q_n are known for $n = 1, \ldots, N$, then we can use any formula we already derived with the replacement

$$S_t^q = \prod_{n=1}^{N}(1 - q_n)S_t. \tag{13.102}$$

If $q_n = q$ for all n, (13.102) simplifies to $S_t^q = (1 - q)^N S_t$. Let's look at an example.

Example 13.6

Consider a stock with current price $S_0 = 110$. There is a European call option written on S, with exercise price $K = 100$, expiring at $T = 0.5$. The annual volatility is $\sigma = 20\%$, and the annual risk-free interest rate is $r = 4\%$. How does the value of the call option change, if there are two dividend payments, in two and in five months, to be accounted for? Assume that the dividend yield is fixed at $q = 2\%$.

Solution

Without accounting for dividend payments, the quantities $d_{+/-}$ are

$$d_+ = \frac{\log 1.1 + 0.03}{0.1414} = 0.8862 \quad \text{and} \quad d_- = \frac{\log 1.1 + 0.01}{0.1414} = 0.7448.$$

The *Black–Scholes*-price for the European call is

$$C_0(K, T) = S_0 \Phi(d_+) - e^{-rT} K \Phi(d_-) = 13.69.$$

With two dividend payments to come, we have to adjust the stock price $S_0^q = (1 - q)^2 S_0 = 105.64$. The adjusted quantities $d_{+/-}^q$ are

$$d_+^q = \frac{\log 1.0564 + 0.03}{0.1414} = 0.6002 \quad \text{and} \quad d_-^q = \frac{\log 1.0564 + 0.01}{0.1414} = 0.4587.$$

The *Black–Scholes*-price for the European call on the dividend paying stock is

$$C_0(K, T) = S_0^q \Phi(d_+^q) - e^{-rT} K \Phi(d_-^q) = 10.34.$$

The call option on the dividend paying stock is cheaper than the contract contingent on the non dividend paying stock.

The conclusion that dividend payments should reduce the value of a call option is reasonable, because dividend payments cause an instantaneous reduction of the stock price, driving the option in the less valuable direction.

Quick calculation 13.10 How should the put price behave under dividend payments?

Let's now discuss simple cash dividends. The associated framework is called the "escrowed dividend model" by Haug (2007, chap. 9). Assume that there are N known dividends to come over the remaining lifetime of the option. More precisely, the cash dividend D_n is scheduled at time t_n, for $n = 1, \ldots, N$. The idea of escrowed dividend models is that the current price of the underlying S_t can be split into one risky part S_t^r, and the present value of all future dividend payments

$$S_t = S_t^r + D = S_t^r + \sum_{n=1}^{N} e^{-r(t_n - t)} D_n. \tag{13.103}$$

Of course, we have to assume that the tenor of the dividend payments is $t < t_n < T$ for all n. Only $S_t^r = S_t - D$ goes into the *Black–Scholes*-formula to calculate the fair option price. But in doing so, we miss a subtle and important point. The volatility, fed into the *Black–Scholes*-formula, is usually an estimate, extracted from the history of S, not from the history of S^r. Clearly $S_t^r < S_t$ for $t < t_N$ and thus, the true volatility of S^r has to be greater than the one observed from S. There are several adjustments suggested in the literature, to compensate for the volatility bias. A simple adjustment, very popular with practitioners, is

$$\sigma_{\text{adj.}} = \sigma \frac{S_t}{S_t - D}, \tag{13.104}$$

where D is again the present value of all future dividend payments. This adjustment is clearly a very crude one, because it does not account for the descending magnitude of the bias caused by the dividend tenor. A better adjustment can be found in Haug (2007, p. 369)

$$\sigma_{\text{adj.}}^2 = \frac{\sigma^2}{T-t} \sum_{n=1}^{N+1} \left(\frac{S_t}{S_t - \sum_{k=n}^{N} e^{-r(t_k - t)} D_k} \right)^2 (t_n - t_{n-1}), \tag{13.105}$$

with $t_0 = t$ and $t_{N+1} = T$.

Example 13.7

Look at the setup of Example 13.6, but now assume that the dividend is a cash dividend with $D_1 = D_2 = 2$. What are the volatility adjustments and the *Black–Scholes*-prices?

Solution
First calculate the risky part of the stock price S_0^r

$$S_0^r = S_0 - \sum_{n=1}^{2} e^{-rt_n} D_n = 110 - 2(e^{-0.04 \cdot \frac{2}{12}} + e^{-0.04 \cdot \frac{5}{12}}) = 106.05.$$

The simple volatility adjustment is

$$\sigma_{\text{adj.}} = \sigma \frac{S_0}{S_0^r} = 20.745\%,$$

and the corresponding *Black–Scholes*-price, using S_0^r and $\sigma_{\text{adj.}}$ is

$$C_0(K, T) = 10.82.$$

For the tenor-based adjustment, one obtains

$$\sigma_{\text{adj.}}^2 = \frac{\sigma^2}{T} \left(\left(\frac{S_0}{S_0 - 2(e^{-0.04 \cdot \frac{2}{12}} + e^{-0.04 \cdot \frac{5}{12}})} \right)^2 \frac{2}{12} + \left(\frac{S_0}{S_0 - 2e^{-0.04 \cdot \frac{5}{12}}} \right)^2 \frac{3}{12} + \frac{1}{12} \right)$$

$$= \frac{0.04}{0.5}(0.1793 + 0.2592 + 0.0833) = 0.0417.$$

Taking the positive root yields $\sigma_{\text{adj.}} = 20.421\%$. Plugging this adjusted volatility into the *Black–Scholes*-formula along with S_0^r, one obtains

$$C_0(K, T) = 10.74.$$

Thus, the simple volatility adjustment results in a slight overpricing of the call option.

13.8   American Exercise Right

Options with American exercise right allow the holder to exercise the contract at any time during the lifetime of the option. This is an additional right for the holder that makes the contract usually more valuable, but it also makes the valuation much harder. Indeed, there exist only very few analytical formulas for American options. One special case is the American plain vanilla call option on a non-dividend paying underlying. We have already learned that under no circumstances such an option should be exercised early. Thus, its price coincides with the price of the European contract. Another rare exception, where an analytical solution is available, is the perpetual put option. We will discuss this contract shortly, but let's first think about the more general implications of American exercise right.

Recall that in deriving the *Black–Scholes*-PDE, we set up a hedge-portfolio $\Pi = V - \Delta S$, with a long position in the derivative contract. Using Itô's lemma and plugging in the hedge-ratio $\Delta = \frac{\partial V}{\partial S}$, eliminated the risk, and thus we concluded that the value of the hedge-portfolio has to change according to the risk-free interest rate. Our last step before stating the *Black–Scholes*-equation (13.20) on page 254 was to divide out dt, because it appeared in every single term. Let's go back to this point and slightly rearrange

$$\left(\frac{\partial V}{\partial t} + rS\frac{\partial V}{\partial S} + \frac{1}{2}\sigma^2 S^2 \frac{\partial^2 V}{\partial S^2} \right) dt = rV dt. \tag{13.106}$$

What (13.106) tells us is that if properly hedged, we earn exactly the risk-free interest with our long position in the option contract. In case of an American option, proper hedging is not enough. We have also to exercise optimally. That is, the holder of an American contract cannot earn more than the risk-free interest, but she can very well earn less, if she does not exercise optimally. Thus, the equal to sign in (13.106) has to be replaced by a less than or equal to sign. In doing so, we obtain a more general *Black–Scholes*-equation

$$\frac{\partial V}{\partial t} + rS\frac{\partial V}{\partial S} + \frac{1}{2}\sigma^2 S^2 \frac{\partial^2 V}{\partial S^2} - rV \leq 0. \tag{13.107}$$

European contracts satisfy (13.107), because equality holds for all of them. For American contracts equality only holds as long as the holder follows the optimal exercise policy. Otherwise the left hand side is strictly less than zero. Let's now look at a very special American contract.

A perpetual option is a contract that never expires. You should immediately realize that such a contract can only exist, if equipped with American exercise right. So let's analyze a perpetual American put option. If optimally exercised, the value of this contract is always

$$P_t(K) \geq (K - S_t)^+.$$ (13.108)

During the lifetime, strict inequality should hold, because the contract is to be exercised the first time equality occurs. Assume strict inequality for the moment. This means that the *Black–Scholes*-equation holds with equality. Because the contract is perpetual, the partial derivative with respect to t vanishes,

$$\frac{1}{2}\sigma^2 S^2 \frac{\partial^2 P}{\partial S^2} + rS\frac{\partial P}{\partial S} - rP = 0.$$ (13.109)

But this is only an ordinary differential equation, which makes life much easier. Unfortunately, there is no general theoretical framework for solving differential equations. It is always tinkering with trial and error. Mathematicians have developed very good instincts for making educated guesses about an ansatz that might work. In this case, let's try a power law

$$P = c_1 S^{c_2},$$ (13.110)

where c_1 and c_2 are constants, yet to be determined. Plug this ansatz back into (13.109) and let's see what we get,

$$\frac{1}{2}\sigma^2 c_2(c_2 - 1)c_1 S^{c_2} + r(c_2 - 1)c_1 S^{c_2} = 0.$$ (13.111)

From this we can immediately conclude that both,

$$c_2 = 1 \quad \text{and} \quad c_2 = -\frac{2r}{\sigma^2}$$ (13.112)

satisfy (13.111).

Quick calculation 13.11 Verify the second solution for c_2.

The original differential equation (13.109) is linear and thus, the superposition of two solutions is also a valid solution. Hence, the road leads us to a general solution of the form

$$P = c_0 S + c_1 S^{-\frac{2r}{\sigma^2}}.$$ (13.113)

Even though this might not look like progress, it is. We know that the value of a put option has to tend to zero in the limit $S \to \infty$. Therefore, the first coefficient has to be $c_0 = 0$. So all we have to care about is the constant c_1. To determine this one, we need a more subtle idea. We know that the contract does not depend on time. This means there is one particular S^*, such that the holder has to exercise immediately when approached from above, in order to follow an optimal exercise policy. In other words,

$$P^* = c_1 S^{*-\frac{2r}{\sigma^2}} = K - S^*. \tag{13.114}$$

We can turn this into a definition of c_1 and obtain

$$c_1 = \frac{K - S^*}{S^{*-\frac{2r}{\sigma^2}}}. \tag{13.115}$$

Of course we do not know S^* either, and so it again seems as if we are stuck. But that is not quite correct. Let's eliminate c_1 and write the option value as

$$P = (K - S^*) \left(\frac{S}{S^*} \right)^{-\frac{2r}{\sigma^2}}. \tag{13.116}$$

Because S^* is the optimal exercise price, it gives the contract its maximum value. But that means the derivative of P with respect to S^* has to vanish, and we have

$$\frac{\partial P}{\partial S^*} = -\frac{1}{S^*} \left(\frac{S}{S^*} \right)^{-\frac{2r}{\sigma^2}} \left(S^* - \frac{2r}{\sigma^2} (K - S^*) \right) = 0. \tag{13.117}$$

This condition can only be met, if the second bracket equals zero, and we thus obtain

$$S^* = \frac{K}{1 + \frac{\sigma^2}{2r}}. \tag{13.118}$$

Plugging this result into (13.116), we obtain the value of the American perpetual put option for $S_t \geq S^*$

$$P_t(K) = \frac{\sigma^2 K}{2r + \sigma^2} \left(\frac{K}{S_t(1 + \frac{\sigma^2}{2r})} \right)^{\frac{2r}{\sigma^2}}. \tag{13.119}$$

Observe that at the optimal exercise price S^*, the partial derivative with respect to S is

$$\left. \frac{\partial P}{\partial S} \right|_{S=S^*} = -1 = \frac{\partial (K - S)}{\partial S}. \tag{13.120}$$

This condition is also known as the "smooth-pasting" condition.

Quick calculation 13.12 Verify the first equality in (13.120).

13.9 Discrete Hedging and the Greeks

We have already learned that the *Black–Scholes*-equation is motivated by a hedging argument. More precisely, we assumed that it is possible to adjust a hedge-portfolio continuously, such that it is held risk-free at every instant. The growth rate of such a portfolio was then identified with the risk-free interest rate. In reality continuous hedging is not possible. There is no general rule for discrete hedging. A good hedging strategy depends on all kinds of market imperfections like transaction costs, changes in volatility of the underlying, and so forth. As a result, the risk cannot be fully eliminated by hedging and thus, the option will be offered at a slightly higher price. In fact, we have two different prices for buying and selling an option. If we are the ones to sell the option, we have to choose a "nearly fair" price and take precautions to limit the risk. In this section, we will take a look at some general hedging strategies.

13.9.1 Delta-Hedging

Delta-hedging is not a new concept, it is closely related to what we did when deriving the *Black–Scholes*-PDE. The objective of a delta-hedge is to immunize the portfolio against small changes in the price of the underlying. To this end, one linearizes the change in the value of a derivative with respect to the price of the underlying

$$V(S + \Delta S, t) \approx V(S, t) + \frac{\partial V(S, t)}{\partial S} \Delta S. \tag{13.121}$$

To first order, the change in the value of a derivative is locally proportional to the change in the value of the underlying. The factor of proportionality is called the delta of the option,

$$\Delta = \frac{\partial V}{\partial S}\bigg|_{S=S_t}. \tag{13.122}$$

If the *Black–Scholes*-theory is correct, we can compute the delta immediately from the analytical *Black–Scholes*-formula, if there is one. For the plain vanilla call and put formulas (13.78) and (13.80) on page 266, the delta is surprisingly simple,

$$\Delta_C = \Phi(d_1) \quad \text{and} \quad \Delta_P = \Phi(d_1) - 1. \tag{13.123}$$

The delta of the put option is most easily derived from put-call parity.

Quick calculation 13.13 Confirm Δ_C by differentiating (13.78) with respect to S_t.

How is a delta-hedge achieved in practice? Assume you have a short position in say x options, and you want to hedge against small changes in the price of the underlying.

Then you have to add the quantity $x \cdot \Delta$ of the underlying to immunize your position. The resulting hedge-portfolio is

$$\Pi = -x \cdot V + x \cdot \Delta \cdot S. \tag{13.124}$$

Let's check, if this modification of the position has the desired effect. First, a small change in the portfolio value is given by

$$d\Pi = \frac{\partial \Pi}{\partial V} \frac{\partial V}{\partial S} dS + \frac{\partial \Pi}{\partial S} dS. \tag{13.125}$$

From this we can easily see that the portfolio itself has a delta and plugging in the ingredients from (13.124) yields

$$\Delta_\Pi = \frac{d\Pi}{dS} = -x \cdot \Delta + x \cdot \Delta = 0. \tag{13.126}$$

Thus, the position is called delta-neutral. It is important to realize that a position remains delta-neutral only for a very short amount of time. As soon as the price of the underlying changes, the delta of the option changes, too. As a consequence, the position will no longer be perfectly delta-neutral, see Figure 13.3 for a graphical illustration. There are two more points worth noting. The first one is a mere triviality that becomes important in more sophisticated hedging schemes: the delta of the underlying is one,

$$\Delta_S = \frac{\partial S}{\partial S} = 1. \tag{13.127}$$

Second, because the portfolio Π is a linear combination of say N assets, with respective quantity x_n for $n = 1 \ldots, N$, the delta of the entire portfolio is given by

$$\Delta_\Pi = \sum_{n=1}^{N} x_n \Delta_n. \tag{13.128}$$

13.9.2   Gamma-Hedging

The Greek letter gamma represents the second derivative of a position with respect to the price of the underlying. Because linearity of a portfolio still holds, we obtain

$$\Gamma_\Pi = \frac{d^2\Pi}{dS^2} = \sum_{n=1}^{N} x_n \Gamma_n. \tag{13.129}$$

In particular, it is easy to see that the gamma of the underlying itself vanishes. We have

$$\Gamma_S = \frac{\partial}{\partial S} \Delta_S = \frac{\partial}{\partial S} 1 = 0. \tag{13.130}$$

On the other hand, the gamma for a plain vanilla call or put option can be obtained by differentiating the *Black–Scholes*-formula twice with respect to S_t. From the result

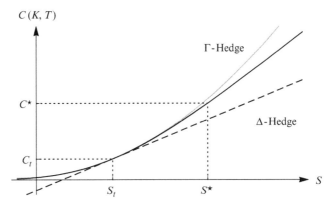

Fig. 13.3 Hedging of a call option position – Delta-hedge (dashed) and gamma-hedge (gray)

for the delta (13.123), we can immediately conclude that the gammas of the call and the put option have to coincide. Computing the second derivative yields

$$\Gamma_C = \Gamma_P = \frac{\phi(d_1)}{S_t \sigma \sqrt{T-t}} \quad \text{with} \quad \phi(z) = \frac{1}{\sqrt{2\pi}} e^{-\frac{1}{2}z^2}. \tag{13.131}$$

A portfolio that is delta- and gamma-neutral is much more robust against changes in the price of the underlying. The reason for that is easily seen from Figure 13.3. The gamma-hedge corresponds to a second order *Taylor*-expansion around the current value S_t of the underlying, whereas the delta-hedge is only a first order expansion. If the price of the underlying changes to S^*, the hedging error is significantly smaller, if the portfolio is delta- and gamma-neutral. But there is a downside. In order to build a delta- and gamma-neutral portfolio, we need a second traded option. How is such a portfolio constructed? Assume you have already a delta-neutral portfolio. Here is a simple recipe for establishing gamma-neutrality:

1. Start with a delta neutral portfolio Π.
2. Add a quantity $x_1 = -\frac{\Gamma_\Pi}{\Gamma_1}$ of another traded option V_1, contingent on the same underlying, to your position. The resulting overall gamma is

$$\Gamma = x_1 \Gamma_1 + \Gamma_\Pi = 0.$$

3. Compute the delta of the overall position

$$\Delta = x_1 \Delta_1 + \Delta_\Pi = x_1 \Delta_1.$$

4. Add a quantity $-\Delta$ of the underlying. The resulting position is delta- and gamma-neutral.

Let's see how this recipe works out in an example.

Table 13.3 Initial position

Position	Delta	Gamma
Portfolio	0	−3000
Option 1	0.6	1.6

Example 13.8

Assume you start with a delta-neutral portfolio and an additional traded option as in Table 13.3. How is the position gamma-neutralized?

Solution

First, the required quantity in option 1 has to be computed

$$x_1 = -\frac{\Gamma_\Pi}{\Gamma_1} = \frac{3000}{1.6} = 1875.$$

Second, the delta of the overall position is

$$\Delta = x_1 \Delta_1 = 1875 \cdot 0.6 = 1125.$$

Thus, 1125 units of the underlying should be shorted to restore delta-neutrality. The new position is summarized in Table 13.4.

13.9.3   Vega-Hedging

Neutralizing small changes in the volatility of the underlying is called vega-hedging. This is a kind of inconsistent concept, because in the *Black–Scholes*-world the underlying is assumed to have a fixed volatility σ. Of course in reality the volatility is neither fixed, nor measurable. Nevertheless, there is strong evidence that the level of variability of the underlying changes with time. Consequently, the partial derivative of the option value with respect to volatility is called vega,

$$\mathcal{V} = \frac{\partial V}{\partial \sigma}, \tag{13.132}$$

Table 13.4 Δ-Γ-neutral position

Position	Delta	Gamma
Portfolio	0	−3000
$1875 \cdot V_1$	+1125	+3000
$-1125 \cdot S$	−1125	0
Total	0	0

Table 13.5 Initial position

Position	Delta	Gamma	Vega
Portfolio	0	−3000	−5000
Option 1	0.6	1.6	2.0
Option 2	0.5	1.3	1.0

which is not a Greek letter at all. Everything we said so far about linearity of positions still holds for the vega of a portfolio. Thus, we can immediately delve into the question of how to construct a delta-, gamma-, and vega-neutral portfolio. This time, we need two additional traded options, V_1 and V_2. Here is the recipe:

1. Again, start with a delta neutral portfolio Π.

2. Solve the linear system of equations

$$x_1\Gamma_1 + x_2\Gamma_2 = -\Gamma_\Pi$$
$$x_1\mathcal{V}_1 + x_2\mathcal{V}_2 = -\mathcal{V}_\Pi$$

   for x_1 and x_2.

3. Add a quantity x_1 of V_1, and x_2 of V_2 to the position, where both options are contingent on the same underlying. The resulting overall position is gamma- and vega-neutral.

4. Compute the delta of the overall position

$$\Delta = x_1\Delta_1 + x_2\Delta_2.$$

5. Add a quantity $-\Delta$ of the underlying. The resulting position is delta-, gamma-, and vega-neutral.

Here again is an example:

Example 13.9

We start again with an already delta-neutral portfolio and two additional traded options as in Table 13.5. How is the position gamma- and vega-neutralized?

Solution

We first have to solve the linear system of equations

$$\begin{pmatrix} 1.6 & 1.3 \\ 2 & 1 \end{pmatrix}\begin{pmatrix} x_1 \\ x_2 \end{pmatrix} = \begin{pmatrix} 3000 \\ 5000 \end{pmatrix}.$$

This is most conveniently accomplished by matrix inversion

$$\begin{pmatrix} x_1 \\ x_2 \end{pmatrix} = \begin{pmatrix} 1.6 & 1.3 \\ 2 & 1 \end{pmatrix}^{-1}\begin{pmatrix} 3000 \\ 5000 \end{pmatrix} = \begin{pmatrix} -1 & 1.3 \\ 2 & -1.6 \end{pmatrix}\begin{pmatrix} 3000 \\ 5000 \end{pmatrix} = \begin{pmatrix} 3500 \\ -2000 \end{pmatrix}.$$

Table 13.6 Δ-Γ-$\mathcal{V}$-neutral position

Position	Delta	Gamma	Vega
Portfolio	0	−3000	−5000
$3500 \cdot V_1$	+2100	+5600	+7000
$-2000 \cdot V_2$	−1000	−2600	−2000
$-1100 \cdot S$	−1100	0	0
Total	0	0	0

Hence, we need an additional long position in 3500 V_1 and a short position in 2000 V_2. The delta of the overall position is now

$$\Delta = 3500 \cdot 0.6 - 2000 \cdot 0.5 = 1100.$$

Thus, we have to short 1100 units of the underlying to restore delta-neutrality. The new position is summarized in Table 13.6.

Of course there are more Greeks and thus, more possible hedging schemes. For example the partial derivative with respect to time is called the theta of an option, and the partial derivative with respect to the risk-free interest rate is called rho. Table 13.7 summarizes the most common Greeks in terms of the generalized *Black–Scholes*-formulas for plain vanilla European call and put options. The generalizing factor $a = e^{(b-r)(T-t)}$ equals one in the standard *Black–Scholes*-model.

Table 13.7 Generalized *Black–Scholes*-Greeks

Name	Symbol	Formula[a]
Delta (call)	$\Delta_C = \frac{\partial C}{\partial S}$	$a\,\Phi(d_+)$
Delta (put)	$\Delta_P = \frac{\partial P}{\partial S}$	$-a\,\Phi(-d_+)$
Gamma	$\Gamma = \frac{\partial^2 V}{\partial S^2}$	$a\,\frac{\phi(d_+)}{S_t\sigma\sqrt{T-t}}$
Vega	$\mathcal{V} = \frac{\partial V}{\partial \sigma}$	$a\,S_t\sqrt{T-t}\,\phi(d_+)$
Theta (call)	$\Theta_C = \frac{\partial C}{\partial t}$	$-a\,S_t\left(\frac{\sigma\phi(d_+)}{2\sqrt{T-t}} + (b-r)\Phi(d_+)\right) - re^{-r(T-t)}K\Phi(d_-)$
Theta (put)	$\Theta_P = \frac{\partial P}{\partial t}$	$-a\,S_t\left(\frac{\sigma\phi(d_+)}{2\sqrt{T-t}} - (b-r)\Phi(-d_+)\right) + re^{-r(T-t)}K\Phi(-d_-)$
Rho (call)	$\rho_C = \frac{\partial C}{\partial r}$	$(T-t)e^{-r(T-t)}K\Phi(d_-)$
Rho (put)	$\rho_P = \frac{\partial P}{\partial r}$	$-(T-t)e^{-r(T-t)}K\Phi(-d_-)$

[a] Note: $d_{+/-}$ as in (13.86), $a = e^{(b-r)(T-t)}$, and generalized cost-of-carry rate b as in Table 13.1.

13.10   Transaction Costs

Except for technical issues, transaction costs are the primary reason why hedging can only be done discretely. This has far reaching consequences as we will see soon. Our analysis will take us to the *Hoggard–Whalley–Wilmott*-equation (Hoggard et al., 1994), which is a nonlinear generalization of the *Black–Scholes*-equation. The very irritating consequence of the nonlinearity of this partial differential equation is that the value of a portfolio is not necessarily the sum of the values of its components. But first we have to study some results for normally distributed random variables.

Assume Z is a standard normally distributed random variable. We are interested in the properties of $|Z|$. Let's first try to evaluate its expectation value

$$
\begin{aligned}
E[|Z|] &= \int_{-\infty}^{\infty} |z| \frac{1}{\sqrt{2\pi}} e^{-\frac{1}{2}z^2} dz \\
&= -\int_{-\infty}^{0} z \frac{1}{\sqrt{2\pi}} e^{-\frac{1}{2}z^2} dz + \int_{0}^{\infty} z \frac{1}{\sqrt{2\pi}} e^{-\frac{1}{2}z^2} dz \\
&= \frac{2}{\sqrt{2\pi}} \int_{0}^{\infty} z e^{-\frac{1}{2}z^2} dz.
\end{aligned}
\tag{13.133}
$$

In the last step we have used the symmetry of the standard normal probability density function around $z = 0$. The final integral in (13.133) is easily solved and yields one. We have thus

$$
E[|Z|] = \sqrt{\frac{2}{\pi}}.
\tag{13.134}
$$

Another expectation we will need is $E[Z|Z|]$. Again, split the integral to obtain

$$
\begin{aligned}
E[Z|Z|] &= \int_{-\infty}^{\infty} z|z| \frac{1}{\sqrt{2\pi}} e^{-\frac{1}{2}z^2} dz \\
&= -\int_{-\infty}^{0} z^2 \frac{1}{\sqrt{2\pi}} e^{-\frac{1}{2}z^2} dz + \int_{0}^{\infty} z^2 \frac{1}{\sqrt{2\pi}} e^{-\frac{1}{2}z^2} dz.
\end{aligned}
\tag{13.135}
$$

Both, z^2 and the standard normal probability density are even functions and thus, both integrals cancel each other. Hence, the result is

$$
E[Z|Z|] = 0.
\tag{13.136}
$$

We are now ready to discuss the derivation of the *Hoggard–Whalley–Wilmott*-equation (see also the appendix to chap. 48 in Wilmott, 2006c).

The starting point, as in the derivation of the *Black–Scholes*-equation, is again the geometric *Brown*ian motion

$$
dS_t = \mu S_t dt + \sigma S_t dW_t.
\tag{13.137}
$$

But this time, we need a discrete analogue, because our continuous hedging argument will not apply. Instead we will use the approximation

$$\Delta S_t = \mu S_t \Delta t + \sigma S_t \sqrt{\Delta t} Z_t, \tag{13.138}$$

with $Z_t \sim N(0, 1)$.

Quick calculation 13.14 Verify that the distributions of ΔW_t and $\sqrt{\Delta t} Z_t$ coincide.

We can set up our usual hedge-portfolio $\Pi = V(S, t) - \Delta \cdot S$, but this time the change after the discrete time interval Δt is

$$\Delta \Pi = V(S + \Delta S, t + \Delta t) - V(S, t) - \Delta \cdot \Delta S. \tag{13.139}$$

The change in the portfolio value can be *Taylor*-expanded to arbitrary order, as long as $V(S, t)$ can be assumed sufficiently smooth. In the case of continuous hedging, we merely had to expand to order dt, but in the discrete case terms of order $\Delta t^{3/2}$ and higher do not vanish. We will nevertheless neglect those higher order terms because they are small, but keep in mind that the results only hold approximately to leading order. We thus obtain

$$\begin{aligned}
\Delta \Pi &= \frac{\partial V}{\partial t} \Delta t + \frac{\partial V}{\partial S} \Delta S + \frac{1}{2} \frac{\partial^2 V}{\partial S^2} \Delta S^2 - \Delta \cdot \Delta S \\
&= \sqrt{\Delta t}\, \sigma SZ \left(\frac{\partial V}{\partial S} - \Delta \right) + \Delta t \left(\frac{\partial V}{\partial t} + \mu S \left(\frac{\partial V}{\partial S} - \Delta \right) + \frac{1}{2} \sigma^2 S^2 Z^2 \frac{\partial^2 V}{\partial S^2} \right).
\end{aligned} \tag{13.140}$$

But (13.140) does not yet contain any transaction costs from hedging. Hoggard et al. (1994) used the assumption of Leland (1985) that transaction costs are proportional to the price of the underlying, κS, where κ is a dimensionless cost factor, and to the quantity ν to be shorted or purchased. Hence the transaction costs are

$$c_{\text{tr}} = \kappa S |\nu|. \tag{13.141}$$

The quantity ν of the underlying to be sold or purchased depends on the change of the option delta over the time interval Δt

$$\begin{aligned}
\nu &= \left. \frac{\partial V}{\partial S} \right|_{S + \Delta S, t + \Delta t} - \left. \frac{\partial V}{\partial S} \right|_{S, t} \\
&\approx \frac{\partial V}{\partial S} + \frac{\partial^2 V}{\partial S^2} \Delta S + \frac{\partial^2 V}{\partial S \partial t} \Delta t - \frac{\partial V}{\partial S}.
\end{aligned} \tag{13.142}$$

We will keep only terms to leading order $\sqrt{\Delta t}$. This can be heuristically justified by the fact that the transactions costs involve the absolute value $|\nu|$, which is defined as the positive root of ν^2. Thus, we approximately obtain

$$|\nu| \approx \sigma S \sqrt{\Delta t} |Z| \left| \frac{\partial^2 V}{\partial S^2} \right|. \tag{13.143}$$

Subtracting the transaction costs from (13.140), the change in the hedge-portfolio value becomes

$$
\Delta \Pi = \sqrt{\Delta t}\, \sigma SZ\left(\frac{\partial V}{\partial S} - \Delta\right) + \Delta t \left(\frac{\partial V}{\partial t} + \mu S\left(\frac{\partial V}{\partial S} - \Delta\right) + \frac{1}{2}\sigma^2 S^2 Z^2 \frac{\partial^2 V}{\partial S^2}\right)
$$
$$
- \sqrt{\Delta t}\, \kappa \sigma S^2 |Z| \left|\frac{\partial^2 V}{\partial S^2}\right|. \tag{13.144}
$$

The next step is to compute the expectation value and the variance of the portfolio changes. We will choose the hedge-ratio to minimize the variance and equate the resulting expectation to the growth rate, induced by the risk-free interest rate. Of course the expected change in the portfolio value is not risk-free, but it has the smallest possible variance. But first let's compute the expectation value

$$
E[\Delta \Pi] = \Delta t \left(\frac{\partial V}{\partial t} + \mu S\left(\frac{\partial V}{\partial S} - \Delta\right) + \frac{1}{2}\sigma^2 S^2 \frac{\partial^2 V}{\partial S^2}\right) - \sqrt{\Delta t}\, \kappa \sigma S^2 \sqrt{\frac{2}{\pi}}\left|\frac{\partial^2 V}{\partial S^2}\right|. \tag{13.145}
$$

We used of course that $E[Z^2] = \text{Var}[Z] = 1$ and (13.134). To compute the variance, remember that for any random variable X, $\text{Var}[X] = E[X^2] - E[X]^2$ holds. Thus, let's compute the expectation of the squared portfolio change. Keep in mind that only terms up to order Δt survive and that $E[Z|Z|] = 0$,

$$
E[\Delta \Pi^2] = \Delta t \left(\sigma^2 S^2 \left(\frac{\partial V}{\partial S} - \Delta\right)^2 + \kappa^2 \sigma^2 S^4 \left(\frac{\partial^2 V}{\partial S^2}\right)^2\right). \tag{13.146}
$$

Quick calculation 13.15 Confirm this equation.

Putting both pieces together, and once again neglecting terms of higher order than Δt, one obtains

$$
\text{Var}[\Delta \Pi] = \Delta t \left(\sigma^2 S^2 \left(\frac{\partial V}{\partial S} - \Delta\right)^2 + \left(1 - \frac{2}{\pi}\right)\kappa^2 \sigma^2 S^4 \left(\frac{\partial^2 V}{\partial S^2}\right)^2\right). \tag{13.147}
$$

From (13.147) it is immediately clear that choosing the familiar hedge-ratio $\Delta = \frac{\partial V}{\partial S}$ minimizes the variance. It is also obvious that the variance collapses to zero, if the cost factor κ is zero. Substituting the minimum-variance hedge-ratio into the expectation (13.145) yields

$$
E[\Delta \Pi] = \Delta t \left(\frac{\partial V}{\partial t} + \frac{1}{2}\sigma^2 S^2 \frac{\partial^2 V}{\partial S^2}\right) - \sqrt{\Delta t}\, \kappa \sigma S^2 \sqrt{\frac{2}{\pi}}\left|\frac{\partial^2 V}{\partial S^2}\right|. \tag{13.148}
$$

If the hedge-portfolio were riskless, it would grow over the interval Δt with the risk-free interest rate

$$
\Delta \Pi = r \Pi \Delta t = r V \Delta t - r S \frac{\partial V}{\partial S} \Delta t. \tag{13.149}
$$

Equating the expected variance-minimal change and the risk-free change of the portfolio, and dividing by Δt, yields the *Hoggard–Whalley–Wilmott*-equation

$$\frac{\partial V}{\partial t} + rS\frac{\partial V}{\partial S} + \frac{1}{2}\sigma^2 S^2 \frac{\partial^2 V}{\partial S^2} - \kappa\sigma S^2 \sqrt{\frac{2}{\pi\Delta t}}\left|\frac{\partial^2 V}{\partial S^2}\right| - rV = 0. \tag{13.150}$$

Comparing (13.150) with the original *Black–Scholes*-PDE, there is an additional term, representing the influence of transaction costs. We can learn a great deal from this correction. First of all, if the cost factor is $\kappa = 0$, we are back in the original *Black–Scholes*-world. Second, for $\kappa > 0$ in the limit $\Delta t \to 0$, the transaction costs become infinitely high, prohibiting quasi-continuous rebalancing of the hedge-portfolio. But there is more. Recall that the gamma of a plain vanilla European contract is always positive,

$$\Gamma = \frac{\partial^2 V}{\partial S^2} = \frac{\phi(d_1)}{S_t\sigma\sqrt{T-t}}, \tag{13.151}$$

with d_1 given in (13.79) on page 266. If we assume that this also holds in the presence of transaction costs, we can abandon the modulus sign and invent a new volatility for the long position in the contract

$$\sigma_{\text{long}}^2 = \sigma^2 - 2\kappa\sigma\sqrt{\frac{2}{\pi\Delta t}}. \tag{13.152}$$

With this new volatility, (13.150) simplifies to

$$\frac{\partial V}{\partial t} + rS\frac{\partial V}{\partial S} + \frac{1}{2}\sigma_{\text{long}}^2 S^2 \frac{\partial^2 V}{\partial S^2} - rV = 0. \tag{13.153}$$

But this is again the original *Black–Scholes*-PDE, with a corrected volatility $\sigma_{\text{long}} < \sigma$. But be careful, there is a very subtle point. If we had assembled the hedge-portfolio the other way around, starting with a short position in the option contract, all signs would have come out the opposite way, with exception of the transaction costs. They would have remained negative. Thus, for the short position in a plain vanilla call or put, we obtain a corrected volatility with opposite sign,

$$\sigma_{\text{short}}^2 = \sigma^2 + 2\kappa\sigma\sqrt{\frac{2}{\pi\Delta t}}. \tag{13.154}$$

The volatility corrections (13.152) and (13.154) are the main results of Leland (1985), but the *Hoggard–Whalley–Wilmott*-equation is far more general. It explains in a very natural way why bid-offer spreads are unavoidable, if perfect hedging is not possible. Let's do one more computation. We can determine the order of magnitude of the spread to be expected, depending on a given transaction cost factor κ. To prepare the computation, *Taylor*-expand the corrected volatility for the short position around $\kappa = 0$

$$\sigma_{\text{short}} \approx \sigma + \kappa\sqrt{\frac{2}{\pi\Delta t}}. \tag{13.155}$$

Quick calculation 13.16 Confirm this linear expansion.

We would expect the bid-offer spread to be roughly twice the difference between the original *Black–Scholes*-price and the one with corrected volatility

$$2(V_{\text{short}} - V) \approx 2\frac{\partial V}{\partial \sigma}(\sigma_{\text{short}} - \sigma). \tag{13.156}$$

Plugging in the vega of a plain vanilla option and using the *Taylor*-expansion (13.155), one obtains

$$\text{spread} \approx \frac{4\kappa S_t \phi(d_1) \sqrt{T - t}}{\sqrt{2\pi\Delta t}}. \tag{13.157}$$

This result again confirms that the bid-offer spread vanishes if transaction costs are zero. But remember that our volatility corrections and the spread approximation only hold for plain vanilla European contracts.

It is now clear, how the nonlinearity of the *Hoggard–Whalley–Wilmott*-equation prevents the portfolio value from being the sum of the value of its components. Because it introduces a bid-offer spread, we have different prices for short and long positions. Suppose you hold a short and a long position in a plain vanilla contract, contingent on the same underlying, with identical exercise price and time to expiry. Clearly the overall value of this position is zero, because no matter what happens, the payoffs will cancel exactly. But if you hedge this position, you lose money because of the bid-offer spread, even though the payoffs will still cancel exactly. You can see most easily that the componentwise value of this position is negative, by realizing that the short position in the plain vanilla contract is more expensive, because after the *Leland*-correction, its volatility is larger than that of the long position. Hence, the sum of both positions is negative, because the more expensive short position comes with a minus sign.

13.11   Merton's Firm Value Model

Merton (1974) used a hidden connection between the financial macrostructure of a firm and option valuation, to introduce an ingenious model for the value of a firm. His idea is the basic component of what is called structural models in credit risk management today. His assumptions look a little coarse-grained but they are also very robust. Here is the framework:

- The firm is only funded by debt D and equity S.
- All debt is in form of a corporate zero-coupon bond $B_0(t, T)$, with principal D, due at time T.
- The value of the firm is the sum of debt and equity, $V_t = S_t + B_0(t, T)$.
- Both V_t and S_t follow a geometric *Brown*ian motion.

When the debt is due, there are only two possible scenarios. Either the firm value is greater than the liabilities, $V_T \geq D$, then the debt is repaid and the remaining assets

Table 13.8 Firm value in Merton's model

Event	Firm value	Liabilities	Equity
No default	$V_T \geq D$	$B_0(T, T) = D$	$S_T = V_T - D$
Default	$V_T < D$	$B_0(T, T) = V_T$	$S_T = 0$

belong to the investors, or the firm value is insufficient to fully repay the debt, $V_T < D$, then there is only a partial redemption and the investors get nothing. In this case the investors are of course not willing to provide additional capital, because creditors would immediately collect their pending debts and so this event represents default. Table 13.8 summarizes the consequences of both scenarios for the value of debt and equity.

Let's see, if we can summarize the value of the equity at the terminal date T in a simple equation

$$S_T = \max(V_T - D, 0) = (V_T - D)^+. \tag{13.158}$$

Does that ring a bell? The value of the equity at time T matches precisely the payoff function of a call option on the firm value with exercise price D. Let's see, what we get for the liabilities

$$B_0(T, T) = \min(D, V_T) = D - (D - V_T)^+. \tag{13.159}$$

Quick calculation 13.17 Convince yourself that the last equality indeed holds.

That is, the liabilities correspond to the debt plus a short position in a plain vanilla put option. The only problem with this identification is that we cannot compute the option value.

To see where the computation fails, let's write the *Black–Scholes*-formula for the value of the equity

$$S_t = V_t \Phi(d_1) - e^{-r(T-t)} D \Phi(d_2), \tag{13.160}$$

with

$$d_{1/2} = \frac{\log(V_t/D) + (r \pm \frac{1}{2}\sigma_V^2)(T - t)}{\sigma_V \sqrt{T - t}}. \tag{13.161}$$

Although we might be able to estimate the parameters of the geometric *Brown*ian motion μ_S and σ_S for the equity, from observing the stock price S_t, the firm value process V_t is unobservable. Thus there are two quantities we do not know, V_t and σ_V. But there is a remedy. Since we can observe the market price of the stock, (13.160) is one equation in two unknowns. If we can find a second equation, we are in business.

Since the firm value follows a geometric *Brown*ian motion, and equity is a derivative, contingent on the firm value, we can apply Itô's lemma,

$$dS = \left(\mu_V V \frac{\partial S}{\partial V} + \frac{\partial S}{\partial t} + \frac{1}{2} \sigma_V^2 V^2 \frac{\partial^2 S}{\partial V^2} \right) dt + \sigma_V V \frac{\partial S}{\partial V} dW_V. \tag{13.162}$$

On the other hand we know that the equity process itself is a geometric *Brown*ian motion

$$dS = \mu_S S dt + \sigma_S S dW_S. \tag{13.163}$$

We not only have two equations for dS, but the distributions of dW_V and dW_S coincide. Thus we can match the terms. Taking the diffusion term yields

$$\sigma_S S = \sigma_V V \frac{\partial S}{\partial V}. \tag{13.164}$$

Finally realize that the partial derivative in (13.164) is the *Black–Scholes*-delta of the call option $\frac{\partial S}{\partial V} = \Phi(d_1)$. This argument is of course valid for every time $0 \leq t \leq T$ and thus, we obtain the second equation

$$\sigma_S S_t = \sigma_V V_t \Phi(d_1), \tag{13.165}$$

with d_1 as in (13.161). This is the second equation in the two unknowns V_t and σ_V. Unfortunately, there is no analytic solution for the desired quantities; they have to be determined numerically. But that is no big deal because the problem is not ill posed.

13.12   Further Reading

The seminal papers of Black and Scholes (1973) and Merton (1973) are at the heart of the subject. There are many well written textbooks, detailing the derivation of the *Black–Scholes*-equation. A small collection is Hull (2009), Neftci (2000), Shreve (2004b), and Wilmott (2006a). For a deeper background in stochastic differential equations and the Itô-integral see Arnold (1974) and Shreve (2004b, chap. 4). For technical details about generalized functions and their *Fourier*-transforms see Rudin (1991, chap. 6 & 7). A comprehensive source for the theory of partial differential equations is Evans (2010). Generalizations of the *Black–Scholes*-formula can be found in Haug (2007, sect. 1.1.6). The subject of discrete dividend payments is treated very accessibly in Haug (2007, chap. 9) and Wilmott (2006a, sect. 8.3). Analytical approximations for the value of American options can be found in Haug (2007, chap. 3). General hedging strategies based on option Greeks are detailed with examples in Hull (2009, chap. 17). For more background information on transaction costs, see Wilmott (2006c, chap. 48). There is also an interesting version of Merton's firm value model provided in Wilmott (2006b, chap. 39).

13.13   Problems

13.1 Use Itô's lemma to show that the forward price

$$F_t = e^{r(T_F - t)} S_t$$

follows the stochastic process

$$dF_t = (\mu - r)F_t dt + \sigma F_t dW_t,$$

if the dynamics of S_t are governed by the geometric *Brown*ian motion (13.5) on page 250.

13.2 The evolution of the bank account is governed by

$$dB(t) = rB(t)dt,$$

which can be understood as geometric *Brown*ian motion with $\sigma = 0$. Manipulate the resulting *Black–Scholes*-equation to show that it is equivalent to the so-called transport equation

$$\frac{\partial U}{\partial t} + r\frac{\partial U}{\partial x} = 0,$$

with the substitution $V(B, t) = e^{-r(T-t)} U(B, t)$ and $x = \log B$.

13.3 Consider the fair price of a European plain vanilla binary contract in the *Black–Scholes*-framework. What is the delta of a binary call and put option?

13.4 Prove that the so-called European put-call symmetry

$$C_t(K, T) = \frac{K}{e^{b(T-t)} S_t} P_t\left(\frac{e^{2b(T-t)} S_t^2}{K}, T\right)$$

holds in the generalized *Black–Scholes*-framework.

13.5 There is another Greek called vanna, defined by the mixed partial derivative

$$\text{vanna} = \frac{\partial^2 V}{\partial S \partial \sigma}.$$

Derive the vanna of a European plain vanilla contract and show that it is identical for both put and call options.

13.6 Derive an explicit formula for the value of the liabilities in the *Merton*-model of the firm value.

14 Exotics in the *Black–Scholes*-Model

Analytic solutions are very rare exceptional cases in derivative pricing. Most of the time, the *Black–Scholes*-equation has to be solved numerically. The strategy for solving the equation depends on the nature of the contract under consideration. There are two major avenues one can take: solving the *Black–Scholes*-PDE with finite difference methods, and Monte Carlo simulation. Both strategies are intimately linked by the duality we already encountered several times. In the *Black–Scholes*-world, the connection is provided explicitly by the *Feynman–Kac*-theorem.

14.1   Finite Difference Methods

The solution of the *Black–Scholes*-PDE is a function $V(S, t)$ that is much like a map of geographic elevation above the S-t-plane. Finite difference techniques represent the S-t-plane by a finite discrete grid, see Figure 14.1. The idea is to solve the respective PDE approximately at the grid points and afterwards, if necessary, to interpolate intermediate values. The method is only approximately exact, because differentials are replaced by finite differences. The order of magnitude of the resulting error depends on how fine- or course-grained we choose our grid. This is also an ideal opportunity to briefly discuss what we mean exactly by the order of magnitude.

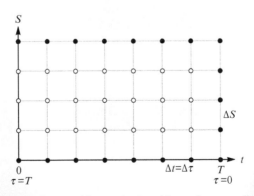

Fig. 14.1 Finite difference scheme with terminal and boundary conditions

The concept is best understood by considering a concrete example. Suppose you *Taylor*-expand the exponential e^x around $x = 0$, but because x is small, you want to indicate that terms of order x^2 are probably negligible. You thus write

$$e^x = 1 + x + O(x^2). \tag{14.1}$$

The symbol O is called the *Landau*-symbol and it represents all terms of order x^2 and higher in (14.1). More precisely, an arbitrary function $f(x)$ is said to be of order $g(x)$, $f(x) \in O(g(x))$, if

$$\lim_{x \to x_0} \frac{f(x)}{g(x)} = c < \infty, \tag{14.2}$$

with c being a constant. We can check this definition in our example. Clearly $x_0 = 0$ and $g(x) = x^2$. The function $f(x)$ is given by all missing terms in the *Taylor*-expansion, that is

$$f(x) = \sum_{k=2}^{\infty} \frac{x^k}{k!}. \tag{14.3}$$

We can now evaluate (14.2),

$$\lim_{x \to 0} \frac{f(x)}{x^2} = \lim_{x \to 0} \left(\frac{1}{2} + \frac{x}{6} + \frac{x^2}{24} + \cdots \right) = \frac{1}{2}. \tag{14.4}$$

So we know that our notation in (14.1) is consistent. But what does the O-term tell us? If we neglect terms that can be represented by a function $f(x)$, then the approximation error we make is $c \cdot g(x)$ for $x \to x_0$. So in our above example, the approximation error for small x is given by

$$e^x - (1 + x) \approx \frac{x^2}{2}. \tag{14.5}$$

There are two important things to note about the *Landau*-symbol. First, nothing changes whether we add or subtract the order term, because we can always change the sign of the constant c. More generally, we can absorb any constant in front of the order term into c. Second, if we have a function $f(x) \in O(x^n)$, then the order of $x^m \cdot f(x)$ is $O(x^{m+n})$.

Let's now turn to the problem of discretizing the *Black–Scholes*-equation. Let's reverse the direction of time by focusing on the time to expiry $\tau = T - t$. The generalized *Black–Scholes*-PDE in terms of τ is

$$\frac{\partial V}{\partial \tau} = bS \frac{\partial V}{\partial S} + \frac{1}{2}\sigma^2 S^2 \frac{\partial^2 V}{\partial S^2} - rV. \tag{14.6}$$

Suppose, we have already established a grid as in Figure 14.1. Then the values of the independent variables at the grid points are $S = n \cdot \Delta S$ for $n = 0, \ldots, N$, and $\tau = m \cdot \Delta \tau$ for $m = 0, \ldots, M = \frac{T}{\Delta \tau}$. We will represent the function values at the grid points by the following notation, analogous to the binomial model of Chapter 12,

$$V(S, \tau) = V(n\Delta S, m\Delta \tau) = V_m^{(n)}. \tag{14.7}$$

Now let's see what we can do with the partial derivatives. Let's first *Taylor*-expand the value of the derivative V around $\tau = m\Delta\tau$,

$$V_{m+1}^{(n)} = V_m^{(n)} + \frac{\partial V}{\partial \tau}\Delta\tau + O(\Delta\tau^2). \tag{14.8}$$

The expansion (14.8) is exact, because all higher order terms are summarized by the *Landau*-symbol. Rearranging and dividing by $\Delta\tau$ yields

$$\frac{\partial V}{\partial \tau} = \frac{V_{m+1}^{(n)} - V_m^{(n)}}{\Delta\tau} + O(\Delta\tau). \tag{14.9}$$

Additionally, we have two partial derivatives of V with respect to S, namely the delta and the gamma of the option. It is perfectly sensible to define the delta exactly the same way as the first order time derivative (14.9), but we can do better. Because we will require the change of delta in computing gamma, we have to involve at least three different grid points. So let's see if we cannot use this extra computational effort to improve the approximation of the first order derivative. We start as before by *Taylor*-expanding V around $S = n\Delta S$, but this time, we do a second order expansion

$$V_m^{(n+1)} = V_m^{(n)} + \frac{\partial V}{\partial S}\Delta S + \frac{1}{2}\frac{\partial^2 V}{\partial S^2}\Delta S^2 + O(\Delta S^3). \tag{14.10}$$

Now let's do the mirror-inverted expansion

$$V_m^{(n-1)} = V_m^{(n)} - \frac{\partial V}{\partial S}\Delta S + \frac{1}{2}\frac{\partial^2 V}{\partial S^2}\Delta S^2 + O(\Delta S^3), \tag{14.11}$$

and subtract (14.11) from (14.10). The result is

$$V_m^{(n+1)} - V_m^{(n-1)} = 2 \cdot \frac{\partial V}{\partial S}\Delta S + O(\Delta S^3). \tag{14.12}$$

Quick calculation 14.1   Can you see why the $O(\Delta S^3)$-term is unaffected?

Slightly rearranging and dividing by ΔS yields

$$\frac{\partial V}{\partial S} = \Delta_m^{(n)} = \frac{V_m^{(n+1)} - V_m^{(n-1)}}{2\Delta S} + O(\Delta S^2). \tag{14.13}$$

We have succeeded in approximating the delta to order ΔS^2, instead of order ΔS, by applying a central difference. Now let's move on to the second order partial derivative. If we add (14.10) and (14.11), we obtain

$$V_m^{(n+1)} + V_m^{(n-1)} = 2V_m^{(n)} + \frac{\partial^2 V}{\partial S^2}\Delta S^2 + O(\Delta S^4). \tag{14.14}$$

The equation is accurate to order ΔS^4, because all ΔS-terms with odd exponents cancel. Dividing by ΔS^2 and rearranging yields

$$\frac{\partial^2 V}{\partial S^2} = \Gamma_m^{(n)} = \frac{V_m^{(n+1)} - 2V_m^{(n)} + V_m^{(n-1)}}{\Delta S^2} + O(\Delta S^2). \tag{14.15}$$

Putting all the pieces together, we obtain a rule for the update of a grid point in a new time slice

$$V_{m+1}^{(n)} = V_m^{(n)} + \Delta \tau \left(bn\Delta S \cdot \Delta_m^{(n)} + \frac{1}{2}\sigma^2 n^2 \Delta S^2 \cdot \Gamma_m^{(n)} - r V_m^{(n)} \right), \tag{14.16}$$

where we have conveniently neglected the truncation error. Note that only the points $V_m^{(n-1)}$, $V_m^{(n)}$, and $V_m^{(n+1)}$ are required to compute the new point $V_{m+1}^{(n)}$. If all points in time slice m are known, then every interior point in time slice $m + 1$ can be computed; see Figure 14.2. The overall approximation error of this scheme will be $O(\Delta \tau, \Delta S^2)$.

You might ask, whether this scheme is stable in that the approximation errors are guaranteed not to be accumulated and critically amplified, no matter what $\Delta \tau$ and ΔS is chosen? The answer is no, the scheme might very well be unstable if we choose the wrong $\Delta \tau$. The necessary condition can be determined in a stability analysis. We will conduct a non-rigorous version of such an analysis. Instability is always due to oscillations in the approximate solution, which are amplified over time. But oscillatory solutions occur only for second order differentials or higher. Remember that the second order ordinary differential equation (13.43) on page 260 had solutions involving sine and cosine. Thus, for analyzing the stability of the finite difference scheme, we have to concern ourselves only with that part of the *Black–Scholes*-PDE that involves second order partial derivatives,

$$\frac{\partial V}{\partial \tau} = \frac{1}{2}\sigma^2 S^2 \frac{\partial^2 V}{\partial S^2}. \tag{14.17}$$

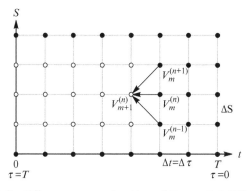

Fig. 14.2 Recursive finite difference approximation of the partial differential equation

For the stability analysis, we will require a discretized version of this equation

$$V^{(n)}_{m+1} = V^{(n)}_m + \frac{\Delta\tau}{2}\sigma^2 n^2 \Delta S^2 \cdot \frac{V^{(n+1)}_m - 2V^{(n)}_m + V^{(n-1)}_m}{\Delta S^2}. \tag{14.18}$$

We are looking for a solution of the form

$$V^{(n)}_m = \alpha^m e^{i\omega n}, \tag{14.19}$$

which is stable, if the absolute value of the amplitude is $|\alpha| \le 1$, because then the oscillations, encoded in the complex exponential, are not amplified over time. Plugging (14.19) into (14.18) yields

$$\alpha^{m+1} e^{i\omega n} = \alpha^m e^{i\omega n} + \Delta\tau\sigma^2 n^2 \cdot \alpha^m e^{i\omega n} \frac{e^{i\omega} + e^{-i\omega} - 2}{2}. \tag{14.20}$$

Using the relation $\cos\omega = \frac{e^{i\omega}+e^{-i\omega}}{2}$ and dividing by $\alpha^m e^{i\omega n}$, one obtains

$$\alpha = 1 + \Delta\tau\sigma^2 n^2 (\cos\omega - 1). \tag{14.21}$$

Because $-1 \le \cos\omega \le 1$, we have the following bounds on α

$$1 - 2\Delta\tau\sigma^2 n^2 \le \alpha \le 1, \tag{14.22}$$

from which we can immediately read off that for $|\alpha| \le 1$, the inequality

$$\Delta\tau\sigma^2 n^2 \le 1 \tag{14.23}$$

has to hold. This condition is most binding for $n = N$ and therefore, we end up with the stability condition

$$\Delta\tau \le \frac{1}{\sigma^2 N^2} = \frac{\Delta S^2}{\sigma^2 S^2_{\max}}, \tag{14.24}$$

where $S_{\max} = N\Delta S$ is the upper boundary of the grid in the spatial direction. Of course there are other schemes that are unconditionally stable. For example the one of Crank and Nicolson (1996), which is the working horse of derivative pricing. Furthermore, it has an overall approximation error of $O(\Delta\tau^2, \Delta S^2)$. But our first order finite difference scheme has its advantages. It is hard to make mistakes in coding and the implementation of American exercise right is straightforward.

We have one issue left out so far: Boundary conditions. We are only able to recursively compute one time slice after another, if we know the values $V^{(0)}_m$ and $V^{(N)}_m$ for $m = 0, \dots, M$ in advance, see again Figure 14.2. Strictly speaking, this is not entirely correct. There are two possible types of boundary conditions we can impose, *Dirichlet*- and *Neumann*-boundary conditions. They are best understood by referring to our earlier ordinary differential equation (13.43)

$$\frac{d^2 x(t)}{dt^2} = -x(t). \tag{14.25}$$

Assume that we are interested in a solution of this equation in the interval $t \in [0, \pi]$. We have seen earlier that there are multiple solutions to this problem, but by imposing

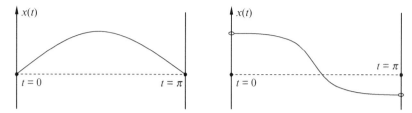

Fig. 14.3 *Dirichlet-* (left) and *Neumann*-boundary conditions (right)

boundary conditions, we can single out a smaller subset. Let's first impose a *Dirichlet*-condition. This condition requires that the value at the boundary is fixed. We impose such a condition on both boundaries, say

$$x(0) = 0 \quad \text{and} \quad x(\pi) = 0, \tag{14.26}$$

see also Figure 14.3 left. It is immediately clear that the boundary conditions (14.26) only allow solutions of the form

$$x(t) = c \sin t, \tag{14.27}$$

even though the value of the constant c is not yet determined. This is similar to the derivative pricing problem, where the fair value of an option can only be determined, when boundary and initial conditions are known. Now let's look into *Neumann*-boundary conditions. In this kind of condition not the value of the function itself is fixed at the boundary, but the value of its first derivative. You can think of such a condition as describing an elastic string, where the ends can move freely along the poles at $t = 0$ and $t = \pi$ in Figure 14.3 right. But the angle between the string and the respective pole at $t = 0$ and $t = \pi$ is fixed by the *Neumann*-condition. If we impose the *Neumann*-boundary conditions

$$x'(0) = 0 \quad \text{and} \quad x'(\pi) = 0 \tag{14.28}$$

on the differential equation (14.25), it is easily seen that we can only have solutions of the form

$$x(t) = c \cos t. \tag{14.29}$$

Of course nothing prevents us from imposing mixed boundary conditions, for example a *Dirichlet*-condition on the lower boundary and a *Neumann*-condition on the upper boundary.

Quick calculation 14.2 Verify that the mixed boundary conditions $x(0) = c_1$ and $x'(\pi) = c_2$ require the solution $x(t) = c_1 \cos t - c_2 \sin t$ of (14.25).

Let's now investigate some boundary conditions for our finite difference scheme. We will give examples for both *Dirichlet-* and *Neumann*-boundary conditions. Let's start with the lower boundary $V_m^{(0)}$ for $m = 0, \ldots, M$. If the derivative under consideration is a call option, then the payoff at expiry is $C_0^{(0)} = 0$. Remember that expiry means $\tau = 0$. But it also stays zero at every time and thus, the *Dirichlet*-boundary condition in this case is

$$C_m^{(0)} = 0, \tag{14.30}$$

for $m = 0, \ldots, M$. More generally, if we investigate the *Black–Scholes*-equation for $S = 0$, we are left with the ordinary differential equation

$$\frac{\partial V}{\partial \tau} = -rV. \tag{14.31}$$

But that is nothing more than saying that the partial derivative of V with respect to S is zero. Of course the second order partial derivative of V with respect to S has to vanish also in this case. So (14.31) is the result of the *Neumann*-condition

$$\left.\frac{\partial V}{\partial S}\right|_{S=0} = 0. \tag{14.32}$$

Using our finite difference approximation (14.9) on the left hand side of (14.31), and slightly rearranging yields

$$V_{m+1}^{(0)} = (1 - r\Delta\tau)V_m^{(0)}. \tag{14.33}$$

This is the *Neumann*-boundary condition at $S = 0$. It holds for most contracts, including call and put options.

An ideal situation for an upper boundary *Dirichlet*-condition is a barrier option with upper knockout barrier. Because the value of the contract turns to zero immediately if the barrier is hit, we have for $S_u = N\Delta S$

$$V_m^{(N)} = 0. \tag{14.34}$$

An ordinary call option can also be equipped with an upper *Dirichlet*-boundary condition. If S is sufficiently larger than the exercise price K, then the option price is approximately equal to the price of a forward contract, $C_t(K, T) \approx S_t - e^{-r(T-t)}K$. Thus, the boundary condition is

$$C_m^{(N)} = N\Delta S - e^{-rm\Delta\tau}K. \tag{14.35}$$

There is a more elegant way that also covers almost all contracts you will encounter. Most contracts have a payoff that becomes linear for large values of S. That means, we have the *Neumann*-boundary conditions

$$\left.\frac{\partial V}{\partial S}\right|_{S \gg K} = \text{const.} \tag{14.36}$$

There is an even more useful consequence of (14.36); the second partial derivative of V with respect to S has to vanish. Assume this holds already for $\Gamma_m^{(N-1)}$, then trivial rearrangements yield the upper boundary condition

$$V_m^{(N)} = 2V_m^{(N-1)} - V_m^{(N-2)}. \tag{14.37}$$

14.2   Numerical Valuation and Coding

Since for all practical purposes numerical computation of option prices is unavoidable, the necessary algorithms are presented in terms of a hopefully intuitive pseudo-code, not referring to any particular programming language. We will use only a minimum of commands: `Set`, `Int`, `Draw`, and `Print`. The `Set`-command fixes parameters we have chosen, usually the upper boundary value $S_{\max}$ and the vertical resolution of the grid N. `Int` returns the integer part of a real number, for example `Int` $\pi = 3$ or `Int` $e = 2$. Note that `Int` always rounds down. `Draw` generates a random number from a specified distribution. For example `Draw` $z \sim N(0,1)$ generates a realization z of a standard normally distributed random variable. This command will be used later in coding Monte Carlo simulations. Finally, the `Print`-command enables the algorithm to generate output.

Besides those simple commands, we will use two structural elements, a simple loop construction and an `If-then` gate. A loop always has the architecture

```
For n = n₀ to N
    ⋮
Next n
```

where the elements to be repeatedly executed (body of the loop) are enclosed by the `For-Next`-marks. The `If-then` gate has always the form

```
If (condition) then (implication).
```

If the condition is true, the implication becomes effective, otherwise nothing happens. There are of course more sophisticated versions of loops and gates, but we want to keep things simple and transparent.

To enhance structural clarity of our code, there are three very useful formatting tricks at our disposal. First, we will separate different structural parts of the algorithm by horizontal lines. Second, we will emphasize loops by indenting the body, and third, we will include comments in the form of non-executable code, indicated by the symbol ▷. The use of such structuring tools is imperative in programming, if you are to have the slightest hope of being able to reconstruct what you have done, when looking at your code at a later time. Furthermore, you may want to design your code so that it is as versatile as possible, in order to use it for many different option types with only minor modifications. In this case, a clear structure and ample use of comments is also enormously helpful.

To see how all this works, consider a very simple example of a plain vanilla European call option. Of course, we can solve this problem analytically, but let's do it anyway and afterwards check the quality of our numerical result.

Box 14.1 Pseudo-code for plain vanilla European call option

Set S_{max}, N	▷ Initialization
$b = r$	▷ Cost-of-carry rate
$\Delta S = S_{max}/N$	
$M = \text{Int}\left(T\sigma^2 S_{max}^2/\Delta S^2\right) + 1$	▷ Stability constraint
$\Delta\tau = T/M$	

For $n = 0$ to N ▷ Initial condition
$$V_0^{(n)} = \max\left(n\Delta S - K, 0\right)$$
Next n

For $m = 1$ to M ▷ Time slices
 For $n = 1$ to $N - 1$ ▷ Interior points
$$\Delta = \left(V_{m-1}^{(n+1)} - V_{m-1}^{(n-1)}\right)/(2\Delta S)$$
$$\Gamma = \left(V_{m-1}^{(n+1)} - 2V_{m-1}^{(n)} + V_{m-1}^{(n-1)}\right)/\Delta S^2$$
$$V_m^{(n)} = V_{m-1}^{(n)} + \Delta\tau\left(bn\Delta S\Delta + \tfrac{1}{2}\sigma^2 n^2 \Delta S^2\Gamma - rV_{m-1}^{(n)}\right)$$
 Next n
$V_m^{(0)} = 0$ ▷ Boundary conditions
$V_m^{(N)} = 2V_m^{(N-1)} - V_m^{(N-2)}$
Next m

Print V_M ▷ Output

Example 14.1

Consider a plain vanilla European call option, contingent on a non-dividend paying stock, with known r, σ, K, and T. What is the fair price of this option at $t = 0$, when valuated numerically?

Solution

The entire pseudo-code for pricing this option is provided in Box 14.1. The algorithm is divided into four parts: initialization, determination of the initial condition, main part, and output of the results. Furthermore, there was a *Dirichlet*-condition imposed at the lower boundary $n = 0$ and a *Neumann*-condition at the upper boundary $n = N$. Finally, the output V_M is shorthand for $V_M^{(n)}$ with $n = 0, \ldots, N$.

To make the problem of Example 14.1 concrete, choose the parameters $r = 5\%$, $\sigma = 20\%$, $K = \$10$, and $T = 1$ year. To start the numerical valuation algorithm, we fix the upper boundary by $S_{max} = \$20$ and the number of grid points in the spatial direction

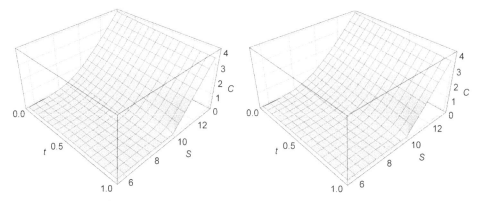

Fig. 14.4 **3D** Numerical solution of the European plain vanilla call valuation problem

$N = 100$. From those values, we immediately find that in order to obey the stability condition (14.24), we have to use $\Delta\tau \leq 2.5 \cdot 10^{-3}$. Figure 14.4 shows the interpolated result of the finite difference approximation over the entire interval $[0, T]$. The surface cannot be distinguished from the one produced by the analytical *Black–Scholes*-formula with the naked eye. To get an impression of the precision of the numerical solution, the difference between the exact and the approximate surface is indicated in Figure 14.5. The spatial spacing ΔS is roughly $O(10^{-1})$. Thus, ΔS^2 has to be $O(10^{-2})$. The error in the time direction can be neglected, because $\Delta\tau$ is $O(10^{-3})$. It is easily seen that the maximal approximation error is within the correct order of magnitude. The rapid increase around the exercise price at expiry is partly due to interpolation and should not be taken too seriously.

Now that we have successfully valuated our first contract numerically, we can move on to the more severe cases, where numerical valuation is not a fancy alternative to the analytic solution, but the only way to determine the fair price of an option.

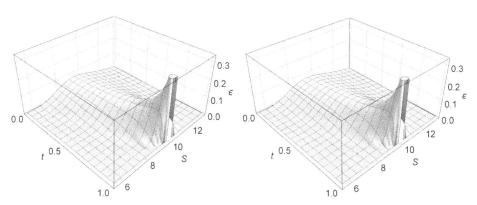

Fig. 14.5 **3D** Approximation error ϵ in percent of the numerical solution for the plain vanilla call option

14.3   Weak Path Dependence and Early Exercise

We have already learned that knockout barrier options are only weakly path dependent. Although there exist analytical formulas for a number of standard barrier contracts (see Haug, 2007, sect. 4.17), we will continue pricing them numerically, mainly for two reasons. First, most barrier options are very sensitive to changes in volatility near the barrier, and since the assumption of a constant volatility of the underlying is a kind of flaw in the *Black–Scholes*-theory, barrier options are usually valuated numerically within local or stochastic volatility models. Second, this class of options are optimal candidates for numerical schemes like our first order finite difference scheme. The reason is that we can easily impose a *Dirichlet*-condition on the knockout boundary. Think for example of the plain vanilla call option we have just valuated. If there were a knockout barrier, say at $S_u = \$15$, we would only have to make two tiny modifications in the pseudo-code, provided in Box 14.1. Naturally, we would have chosen $S_{max} = S_u$, because the value of the contract at $S > S_u$ does not matter anymore, the option is knocked out. The first modification would have affected the initial condition. The code fragment would have changed into

For $n = 0$ to $N - 1$
$\quad V_0^{(n)} = \max{(n \Delta S - K, 0)}$
Next n
$V_0^{(N)} = 0.$

The second modification is even smaller and concerns the upper boundary condition, which simplifies to $V_m^{(N)} = 0$. Everything else in our code remains unchanged. If we run the algorithm, we get the solution for the barrier knockout call indicated in Figure 14.6. Of course, we can immediately compute the fair price for the associated knockin call option from barrier put-call parity (12.56) on page 242. The solution for this option is provided in Figure 14.7. Note that the interpolation is not very accurate around S_u at expiry, because a violent jump in the value of the option occurs at the boundary.

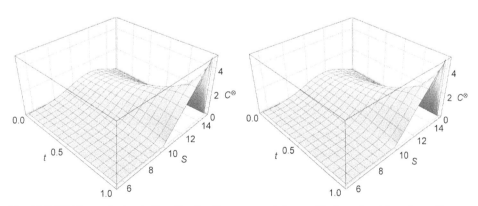

Fig. 14.6 3D Numerical solution for the European plain vanilla knockout barrier call option

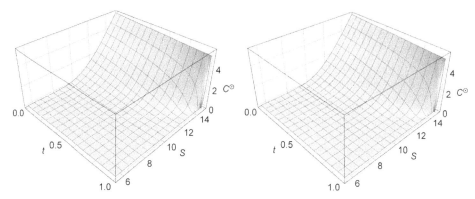

Fig. 14.7 **3D** Numerical solution for the plain vanilla knockin barrier call option from barrier put-call parity

What modifications do we have to make if there is American exercise right? In this case we have to compare the value of the option at every grid point with the value if immediately exercising the contract. The easiest way to accomplish this task is to insert an additional code fragment immediately after the update of the boundary conditions in Box 14.1

For $n = 0$ to N
$$V_m^{(n)} = \max\left(V_m^{(n)}, V_0^{(n)} \right)$$
Next n.

Because $V_0^{(n)}$ is the payoff of the option at grid point n, we do not even need to worry about the particular type of contract we are dealing with. Thus, there is no need for additional modifications for a vast variety of options. Let's take a look at an individually designed contract.

Example 14.2

Consider the contract specified by the term sheet given in Table 14.1. Assume that the annual domestic interest rate r and the volatility of the foreign currency σ is known. How can this option be valuated numerically?

Table 14.1 Option term sheet

Option type:	Knockout call option
Barrier type:	Lower barrier S_l with rebate R
Underlying:	Foreign currency with interest rate r_f
Exercise right:	American
Exercise price:	K
Expiry date:	T

Box 14.2 Pseudo-code for individually contracted option	
Set $S_{\max}, N$	▷ Initialization
$b = r - r_f$	▷ Cost-of-carry rate
$\Delta S = (S_{\max} - S_l)/N$	
$M = \texttt{Int}\left(T\sigma^2 S_{\max}^2/\Delta S^2\right) + 1$	▷ Stability constraint
$\Delta\tau = T/M$	

For $n = 1$ to N	▷ Initial condition
$\quad V_0^{(n)} = \max\left(S_l + n\Delta S - K, 0\right)$	
Next n	
$V_0^{(0)} = R$	▷ Rebate

For $m = 1$ to M	▷ Time slices
$\quad$ For $n = 1$ to $N - 1$	▷ Interior points
$\qquad \Delta = \left(V_{m-1}^{(n+1)} - V_{m-1}^{(n-1)}\right)/(2\Delta S)$	
$\qquad \Gamma = \left(V_{m-1}^{(n+1)} - 2V_{m-1}^{(n)} + V_{m-1}^{(n-1)}\right)/\Delta S^2$	
$\qquad V_m^{(n)} = V_{m-1}^{(n)} + \Delta\tau\left(b(S_l + n\Delta S)\Delta + \frac{1}{2}\sigma^2(S_l + n\Delta S)^2\Gamma - rV_{m-1}^{(n)}\right)$	
$\quad$ Next n	
$\quad V_m^{(0)} = R$	▷ Boundary conditions
$\quad V_m^{(N)} = 2V_m^{(N-1)} - V_m^{(N-2)}$	
$\quad$ For $n = 1$ to N	▷ American exercise
$\qquad V_m^{(n)} = \max\left(V_m^{(n)}, V_0^{(n)}\right)$	
$\quad$ Next n	
Next m	

Print V_M	▷ Output

Solution

The pseudo-code for valuating this contract is provided in Box 14.2. The grid points are now concentrated in the spatial direction between S_l and $S_{\max}$, because the contract is knocked out for $S < S_l$. The lower boundary condition includes the rebate R and there is an additional code fragment, accounting for the American exercise right.

14.4   Girsanov's Theorem

Girsanov's theorem is one of the cornerstones of derivative pricing. We have assumed that the price process of an arbitrary underlying S is governed by the geometric *Brown*ian motion

$$dS_t = \mu S_t dt + \sigma S_t dW_t. \tag{14.38}$$

Of course this process is embedded in a background probability space $(\Omega, \mathcal{F}, P)$, equipped with a filtration $\mathcal{F}_t$, to which S_t is adapted. But this model is with respect to the physical probability measure P. By now we know very well that pricing is governed by another probability measure Q, referred to as the risk-neutral probability measure. Girsanov's theorem tells us how the geometric *Brown*ian motion (14.38) transforms, if W_t is perceived under the risk-neutral measure Q. At first sight this theorem appears cryptic. We will first state it in full generality and afterwards reduce and decipher it step by step.

Theorem 14.1 (Girsanov's theorem) *Let $(\Omega, \mathcal{F}, P)$ be a probability space, equipped with a natural filtration $\mathcal{F}_t$, generated by the Wiener-process W_t for $0 \le t \le T$. If λ_t is a $\mathcal{F}_t$-adapted process, such that*

$$\int_0^T \lambda_s^2 ds < \infty$$

holds almost surely, and the process M_t, defined by

$$M_t = e^{-\int_0^t \lambda_s dW_s - \frac{1}{2}\int_0^t \lambda_s^2 ds},$$

is a martingale, then there exists an equivalent probability measure Q, induced by the Radon–Nikodym-derivative $\frac{dQ}{dP}\big|_{\mathcal{F}_t} = M_t$, such that

$$W_t^Q = W_t + \int_0^t \lambda_s ds$$

is a standard Wiener-process under Q.

Don't get fooled by the fancy terms and integrals. M_t is strongly related to the stochastic discount factor of Chapter 9 and we have

$$E[M_t S_t] = E^Q[S_t]. \tag{14.39}$$

The most delicate piece in Theorem 14.1 is the requirement that M_t is a P-martingale. There is a simple condition which provides sufficient support, but may be too restrictive in some cases.

Theorem 14.2 (*Novikov*-condition) *The process M_t is a P-martingale if*

$$E\left[e^{\frac{1}{2}\int_0^T \lambda_s^2 ds}\right] < \infty$$

holds.

Let's see if we can make head or tail of this. In going from W_t to W_t^Q in Theorem 14.1, there is something added that looks like a risk premium. To see this even clearer, let's rewrite the equation in differential notation

$$dW_t^Q = dW_t + \lambda_t dt. \tag{14.40}$$

We know that in our complete market framework, the risk premium is

$$\lambda = \frac{\mu - r}{\sigma}. \tag{14.41}$$

Quick calculation 14.3 Verify that λ satisfies the *Novikov*-condition.

This is very convenient, because λ is neither a stochastic process, nor time dependent. So we can easily determine how the geometric *Brown*ian motion (14.38) looks under the risk-neutral measure Q, by simply replacing dW_t with $dW_t^Q - \lambda dt$,

$$\begin{aligned} dS_t &= \mu S_t dt + \sigma S_t dW_t^Q - (\mu - r)S_t dt \\ &= r S_t dt + \sigma S_t dW_t^Q. \end{aligned} \tag{14.42}$$

The expected rate of return μ is simply replaced by the risk-free rate of return r under the risk-neutral measure Q. Because under Q, W_t^Q is again $N(0, t)$-distributed, we usually omit the superscript. The even more interesting question is why the *Girsanov*-theorem changes the drift, but leaves the volatility unaltered. This is indeed not an easy one so let's see if we can understand heuristically what is going on.

Once more define a simple random variable X, based on a coin flip experiment, with

$$X(\omega) = \begin{cases} +1 & \text{for } \omega = \uparrow \\ -1 & \text{for } \omega = \downarrow. \end{cases} \tag{14.43}$$

Let the probabilities for the up- and down-state be $p = \frac{1}{2}$ and $1 - p = \frac{1}{2}$. Clearly, we have $E[X] = 0$ and $\text{Var}[X] = 1$.

Quick calculation 14.4 Check that the variance of X is indeed one.

Let X_n for $n = 1, \dots, N$ be identical but independent copies of X and define the new random variable S_n by

$$S_n = \sum_{k=1}^{n} X_k. \tag{14.44}$$

Furthermore, we will give the ratio n/N a new name and call it $t = \frac{n}{N}$. Take a third random variable Z_t, defined by

$$Z_t = \frac{S_n}{\sqrt{N}}, \tag{14.45}$$

and let's analyze this quantity a little bit. It is quite obvious that the expectation value is $E[Z_t] = 0$. But what is the variance? Let's compute it

$$\text{Var}[Z_t] = \frac{1}{N} \cdot n \cdot \text{Var}[X] = \frac{n}{N} = t. \tag{14.46}$$

That is, Z_t has the same first two moments as W_t, for $t \in [0, 1]$. But there is more. Due to the central limit theorem, Z_t converges in distribution to W_t as $N \rightarrow \infty$,

$$Z_t \xrightarrow{D} W_t \sim N(0, t). \tag{14.47}$$

We have now a limit process for the *Wiener*-process for $0 \leq t \leq 1$. Furthermore, because Z_t is a binomial kind of process, it is very easy to manipulate the probability measure and to see what happens in the limit. Define a new probability measure Q by

$$q = \frac{1}{2} + \frac{\varepsilon}{2\sqrt{N}}. \tag{14.48}$$

We have to scale the ε-correction by $N^{-1/2}$ in order to keep the moments of Z_t constant when $N \rightarrow \infty$. Note that the central limit theorem still holds and Z_t approaches a normal distribution. But what are the moments now? Let's first do the computations for X. One obtains the expectation

$$E^Q[X] = 1 \cdot \left(\frac{1}{2} + \frac{\varepsilon}{2\sqrt{N}} \right) - 1 \cdot \left(\frac{1}{2} - \frac{\varepsilon}{2\sqrt{N}} \right) = \frac{\varepsilon}{\sqrt{N}}, \tag{14.49}$$

and the variance

$$\text{Var}^Q[X] = E^Q[X^2] - E^Q[X]^2 = 1 - \frac{\varepsilon^2}{N}. \tag{14.50}$$

It is now straightforward to compute the moments of Z_t,

$$E^Q[Z_t] = \frac{n}{N} \cdot \varepsilon = t \cdot \varepsilon, \tag{14.51}$$

and

$$\text{Var}^Q[Z_t] = \frac{n}{N} \cdot \left(1 - \frac{\varepsilon^2}{N} \right) = t \cdot \left(1 - \frac{\varepsilon^2}{N} \right). \tag{14.52}$$

Taking the limit $N \rightarrow \infty$, we can now see that Z_t approaches a *Brown*ian motion with drift ε under measure Q, because the variance is still

$$\lim_{N \rightarrow \infty} \text{Var}^Q[Z_t] = t. \tag{14.53}$$

This argument shows in a constructive way, why the change of measure under the *Girsanov*-transformation only affects the drift, but leaves the volatility unchanged.

14.5   The *Feynman–Kac*-Formula

The *Feynman–Kac*-theorem is a very general connection between parabolic partial differential equations and stochastic differential equations of the *Itô*-type. It is named after the Nobel laureate Richard Feynman and the Polish mathematician Mark Kac. The theorem is a rigorous proof of Feynman's path integral formalism in the real domain. We will, as in the previous section, first state the theorem and subsequently elaborate on it.

Theorem 14.3 (*Feynman–Kac*-theorem) *Fix the usual probability space* $(\Omega, \mathcal{F}, P)$ *and let* S_t *be a* $\mathcal{F}_t$*-measurable Itô-process of the general kind*

$$dS_t = \mu(S_t, t)dt + \sigma(S_t, t)dW_t.$$

For $0 \le t \le T$, *let* $V(S, t)$ *be a sufficiently smooth function with known terminal function values* $V(S, T)$, *such that*

$$V(S_t, t) = E\left[e^{-\int_t^T r(S_\tau, \tau)d\tau} V(S_T, T) \Big| \mathcal{F}_t\right]$$

holds. Then $V(S, t)$ *satisfies the parabolic partial differential equation*

$$\frac{\partial V}{\partial t} + \mu(S, t)\frac{\partial V}{\partial S} + \frac{1}{2}\sigma^2(S, t)\frac{\partial^2 V}{\partial S^2} - r(S, t)V = 0,$$

subject to the terminal condition $V(S, T)$.

To understand this result, we first have to generalize the concept of an adjoint differential operator. For a simple operator $D_n = \frac{d^n}{dx^n}$, we found earlier that the adjoint operator is $D_n^\dagger = (-1)^n \frac{d^n}{dx^n}$, and for a sufficiently well behaved test function $\varphi(x)$, we have

$$\langle D_n f | \varphi \rangle = \langle f | D_n^\dagger \varphi \rangle. \tag{14.54}$$

Adjoining an operator means of course successive application of integration by parts, because the abstract *Dirac*-bracket of two functions is nothing else than an integral over both components. Now assume we have an operator of the form

$$L(x) = g(x)\frac{d}{dx}. \tag{14.55}$$

Applying our routine of integration by parts, we find

$$\begin{aligned}\langle Lf|\varphi\rangle &= \int_{-\infty}^{\infty} g(x)\frac{df(x)}{dx}\varphi(x)dx \\ &= g(x)f(x)\varphi(x)\Big|_{-\infty}^{+\infty} - \int_{-\infty}^{\infty} f(x)\frac{dg(x)\varphi(x)}{dx}dx \\ &= -\langle f|\frac{d}{dx}g\varphi\rangle,\end{aligned} \tag{14.56}$$

from which we immediately conclude that $L^\dagger(x) = -\frac{d}{dx}g(x)$. Assume, there are two arbitrary operators $L(x)$ and $K(x)$. It is obvious that we can adjoin them successively using integration by parts, that is

$$\langle LKf|\varphi\rangle = \langle Kf|L^\dagger\varphi\rangle = \langle f|K^\dagger L^\dagger\varphi\rangle. \tag{14.57}$$

We can thus conclude that $(LK)^\dagger(x) = K^\dagger L^\dagger(x)$ holds. Of course an analogous statement for an arbitrary sequence of operators is also true. Let's define the operator

$$L_n(x) = g(x)\frac{d^n}{dx^n} = L_1 D_{n-1}(x), \tag{14.58}$$

where again $D_n = \frac{d^n}{dx^n}$. This one obviously has the adjoint operator

$$L_n^\dagger(x) = (-1)^n \frac{d^n}{dx^n}g(x) = D_{n-1}^\dagger L_1^\dagger(x). \tag{14.59}$$

There is another important consequence of the rule for adjoining a sequence of operators. Suppose we apply $L(x)$ successively two times, then we obtain $(L^2)^\dagger(x) = (L^\dagger)^2(x)$ for the adjoint sequence. Of course this statement also holds true for arbitrary exponents. Combining this property with the bilinearity of inner products, we obtain for the exponential of an operator

$$\left(e^{L(x)}\right)^\dagger = \sum_{k=0}^{\infty} \frac{(L^k)^\dagger(x)}{k!} = \sum_{k=0}^{\infty} \frac{(L^\dagger)^k(x)}{k!} = e^{L^\dagger(x)}. \tag{14.60}$$

Quick calculation 14.5   Use the bilinearity of inner products to prove that $(L + K)^\dagger(x) = L^\dagger(x) + K^\dagger(x)$ holds.

Let's now turn to a very special operator, sometimes called the *Kolmogorov-backward-operator*

$$A(S) = rS\frac{\partial}{\partial S} + \frac{1}{2}\sigma^2 S^2 \frac{\partial^2}{\partial S^2}. \tag{14.61}$$

It is also referred to as the infinitesimal generator of the *Itô*-diffusion. Note that using (14.61), we can write the *Black–Scholes*-equation in a very compact form

$$\frac{\partial V}{\partial t} + (A(S) - r)V = 0. \tag{14.62}$$

Not only is (14.62) a neat way to write the *Black–Scholes*-PDE, it almost looks like an ordinary differential equation. If this were the case, we could immediately write the solution

$$V(S, T) = e^{-(A(S)-r)T}V(S, 0). \tag{14.63}$$

Because we do not have an initial value problem, but a terminal value problem, $V(S, T)$ is known, but not $V(S, 0)$. Thus, we should divide both sides by the exponential factor to obtain

$$V(S, 0) = e^{(A(S)-r)T}V(S, T). \tag{14.64}$$

Of course this is a purely formal statement, because we cannot operate on $V(S, T)$ directly with the exponential of an operator. At best, we would have to *Taylor*-expand the exponential and operate with the resulting products of $A(S)$. This would certainly be a very messy business most of the time. But instead, we can do something far more clever. Assume that at $t = 0$, the price of the underlying is $S = S_0$, with $S_0 > 0$. Otherwise, we would not have a valuation problem because the price would not change over time anymore. We can thus write

$$V(S_0, 0) = e^{-rT}\int_0^\infty \left(e^{A(S)T}V(S, T)\right)\delta(S - S_0)dS \tag{14.65}$$

for the price of the derivative at $t = 0$. This already looks similar to a discounted expectation value. But it is also an inner product with an operator $e^{A(S)T}$, operating on the first component. So adjoining this operator, we obtain

$$V(S_0, 0) = e^{-rT} \int_0^\infty V(S, T)\, e^{A^\dagger(S)T}\delta(S - S_0)dS. \tag{14.66}$$

This indeed looks like an expectation and it should do, because the martingale pricing principle tells us that the value of the derivative at $t = 0$ is the discounted expected payoff at $t = T$, under the risk-neutral probability measure Q. Therefore, the second component in the integral has to be the risk-neutral probability density

$$q(S, T) = e^{A^\dagger(S)T}q(S, 0), \tag{14.67}$$

where $q(S, 0) = \delta(S - S_0)$. If this is correct, it is also inevitable that $q(S, t)$ has to satisfy the partial differential equation

$$\frac{\partial}{\partial t}q(S, t) = A^\dagger(S)q(S, t) = -\frac{\partial}{\partial S}rSq(S, t) + \frac{1}{2}\frac{\partial^2}{\partial S^2}\sigma^2 S^2 q(S, t). \tag{14.68}$$

This equation is known as the *Fokker–Planck*-equation and it governs the evolution of the risk-neutral probability density. Its solution is also known as the weak solution to the geometric *Brown*ian motion (14.42) with risk-neutral drift rate r. In the most general case of the *Feynman–Kac*-theorem 14.3, the associated *Fokker–Planck*-equation has the form

$$\frac{\partial}{\partial t}p(S, t) = -\frac{\partial}{\partial S}\mu(S, t)p(S, t) + \frac{1}{2}\frac{\partial^2}{\partial S^2}\sigma^2(S, t)p(S, t), \tag{14.69}$$

with $p(S, 0) = \delta(S - S_0)$. We can now see that conditioning an expectation value on the filtration $\mathcal{F}_t$, generated by the stochastic process S_t, corresponds to a (degenerate) probability density $p(S, t) = \delta(S - S_t)$. We can thus write a semi-general version of the *Feynman–Kac*-formula in two ways

$$V(S_t, t) = e^{-r(T-t)}E^Q[V(S_T, T)|\mathcal{F}_t]$$
$$= e^{-r(T-t)} \int_0^\infty V(S, T)q(S, T)dS, \tag{14.70}$$

with the density $q(S, T)$ provided by the solution of the *Fokker–Planck*-equation, with initial condition $q(S, t) = \delta(S - S_t)$.

Let's conclude this section by calculating the weak solution to the risk-neutral geometric *Brown*ian motion

$$dS_t = rS_t dt + \sigma S_t dW_t. \tag{14.71}$$

To simplify the computation, let $x_t = \log S_t$ be the logarithmic price process and apply Itô's lemma

$$dx_t = \left(rS_t\frac{\partial x}{\partial S} + \frac{1}{2}\sigma^2 S_t^2\frac{\partial^2 x}{\partial S^2}\right)dt + \sigma S_t\frac{\partial x}{\partial S}dW_t$$
$$= \left(r - \frac{1}{2}\sigma^2\right)dt + \sigma dW_t. \tag{14.72}$$

This can be integrated easily, and one obtains

$$x_t = x_0 + \left(r - \frac{1}{2}\sigma^2\right)t + \sigma W_t. \tag{14.73}$$

We can already see that x is normally distributed, with time-dependent expectation value and variance. The probability density function is

$$q_x(x, t) = \frac{1}{\sqrt{2\pi\sigma^2 t}} \exp\left(-\frac{1}{2}\left(\frac{x - x_0 - (r - \frac{1}{2}\sigma^2)t}{\sigma\sqrt{t}}\right)^2\right). \tag{14.74}$$

It is easily checked, even though this is not a quick calculation, that (14.74) satisfies the *Fokker–Planck*-equation

$$\frac{\partial q_x}{\partial t} = -\left(r - \frac{1}{2}\sigma^2\right)\frac{\partial q_x}{\partial x} + \frac{1}{2}\sigma^2\frac{\partial^2 q_x}{\partial x^2}. \tag{14.75}$$

To express the probability density in terms of ordinary stock prices S, we use the fact that the logarithm is a monotone transformation. Thus, all infinitesimal areas under the probability densities have to coincide, and we have

$$q_x(x, t)dx = q_S(S, t)dS \quad \Leftrightarrow \quad q_S(S, t) = q_x(\log S, t)\frac{dx}{dS}. \tag{14.76}$$

Thus, the weak solution to the risk-neutral geometric *Brown*ian motion is

$$q_S(S, t) = \frac{1}{S\sqrt{2\pi\sigma^2 t}} \exp\left(-\frac{1}{2}\left(\frac{\log(S/S_0) - (r - \frac{1}{2}\sigma^2)t}{\sigma\sqrt{t}}\right)^2\right), \tag{14.77}$$

for $S \geq 0$.

14.6   Monte Carlo Simulation

There are generally two ways to use the *Feynman–Kac*-formula (14.70). Either one can use the weak solution to compute the integral numerically, or one can approximate the expectation value by an appropriate average value. The former is essentially what we will do later, when the risk-neutral probability density of more elaborate processes is not known explicitly, but only in terms of its inverse *Fourier*-transform; the latter is the domain of Monte Carlo simulation. The key equation for valuating a given contract with simulation methods is

$$V(S_t, t) = e^{-r(T-t)}E^Q[V(S_T, T)|\mathcal{F}_t] \approx e^{-r(T-t)}\frac{1}{N}\sum_{n=1}^{N} V(S_T^{(n)}, T). \tag{14.78}$$

This equation needs some comment. First of all, Monte Carlo simulation never generates exact results, but you can make the solution as precise as you want, if you are willing to commit enough computational resources. Second, averaging is pathwise, where in (14.78) all N paths start at S_t, but because of the simulated randomness, each one will end at a different value $S_T^{(n)}$. Obviously, we need the strong (pathwise) solution of the geometric *Brown*ian motion to generate the N paths. More precisely, we need the strong solution of the risk-neutral version, because the expectation is under the measure Q. We obtain this version of course by applying the *Girsanov*-transformation to the original geometric *Brown*ian motion under P. We already know that the only effect of the measure change is that the drift μ is replaced by the risk-free interest rate r. Thus, in complete analogy to (13.12) on page 251, the required strong solution is

$$S_t = S_0 e^{(r-\frac{1}{2}\sigma^2)t + \sigma W_t}. \tag{14.79}$$

Because the increments of the *Wiener*-process are independent and $W_0 = 0$, we have

$$W_t - W_s = W_{t-s}, \tag{14.80}$$

for $0 \le s \le t$. This is most convenient, because it allows for an easy conditioning. In the situation of equation (14.78), we would write the strong solution as

$$S_T = S_t e^{(r-\frac{1}{2}\sigma^2)(T-t) + \sigma W_{T-t}}. \tag{14.81}$$

Recall that for computational purposes, it is often more convenient to always use standard normally distributed random variables. We can apply the old scaling trick $W_{t-s} = \sqrt{t-s}\, Z_t$, where $Z_t \sim N(0,1)$. That leaves us with

$$S_T = S_t e^{(r-\frac{1}{2}\sigma^2)(T-t) + \sigma \sqrt{T-t}\, Z_T}. \tag{14.82}$$

To see how valuation with Monte Carlo simulation actually works, let's return to the basic valuation problem of Example 14.1. We can use our analytic result for the value of the European plain vanilla call to assess the quality of the Monte Carlo approximation.

Example 14.3

Assume that today's price of the underlying in the plain vanilla call example 14.1 is S_0. How can this contract be valuated using Monte Carlo simulation?

Solution

The Monte Carlo pseudo-code is provided in Box 14.3. There is only one loop for simulating the outcome of the N independent paths of the risk-neutral geometric *Brown*ian motion.

We have earlier valuated this contract numerically with the ambient parameters $r = 5\%$ $\sigma = 20\%$, $K = \$10$, and $T = 1$ year. In order to do the same via Monte Carlo simulation,

Box 14.3 Pseudo-code for Monte Carlo simulation of a plain vanilla call	
Set N	▷ Initialization
$b = r$	▷ Cost-of-carry rate

For $n = 1$ to N	▷ Path replication
Draw $z \sim N(0, 1)$	▷ Random number generation
$S_T = S_0 \exp\left((b - \tfrac{1}{2}\sigma^2)T + \sigma\sqrt{T}z\right)$	
$V_T^{(n)} = \max(S_T - K, 0)$	▷ Payoff function
Next n	

$V_0 = \exp(-rT) \cdot 1/N \sum_{n=1}^{N} V_T^{(n)}$	
Print V_0	▷ Output

we have additionally to specify the current price of the underlying. Let this price be $S_0 = \$8$. The result will be an estimate $\hat{V}_0$ of the true but unknown price of the derivative V_0. This estimate is itself an asymptotically normally distributed random variable with moments

$$E[\hat{V}_0] = V_0 \quad \text{and} \quad \text{Var}[\hat{V}_0] = \frac{\hat{\sigma}_{V_0}^2}{N}, \tag{14.83}$$

where the sample variance $\hat{\sigma}_{V_0}^2$ is given by

$$\hat{\sigma}_{V_0}^2 = \frac{1}{N-1} \sum_{n=1}^{N} \left(e^{-rT}V_T^{(n)} - \hat{V}_0\right)^2. \tag{14.84}$$

What (14.83) tells us is that the variance goes down by a factor of N, but this also means that the standard deviation goes down only by a factor of $\sqrt{N}$. For illustration purposes, the simulation was conducted with $N = 500$, $N = 1000$, and $N = 5000$ path replications. The probability density functions of the resulting estimates are illustrated in Figure 14.8. The true value of the option, as computed from the *Black–Scholes*-formula, is indicated by a vertical line. It is quite obvious that there is still a substantial amount of variability in the estimate, even if we sample 5000 paths.

Monte Carlo simulation is usually conducted with a lot more replicated paths. Additionally, variance reduction techniques like antithetic-, stratified-, and importance-sampling can be used. We will not pursue this road any further, but an excellent source for background information is Glasserman (2010).

14.7   Strongly Path Dependent Contracts

If the payoff of a derivative contract does not only depend on the path to hit a pre-defined barrier, but on the entire history of the path, we call it strongly path dependent.

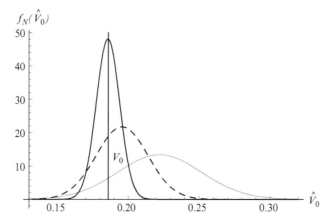

Fig. 14.8 Monte Carlo simulation of European plain vanilla call option price – $N = 500$ (gray), $N = 1000$ (dashed), and $N = 5000$ (black)

Such a contract introduces a new variable into the *Black–Scholes*-equation. To analyze the situation, define the new random process

$$I_t = \int_0^t f(S_\tau, \tau)d\tau, \tag{14.85}$$

with an appropriate function $f(S, t)$, collecting all the relevant path information. What information is relevant, depends on the contract itself. For a continuously averaged arithmetic Asian fixed strike call, we have $f(S, t) = S$ and the payoff becomes

$$V(S, I, T) = \left(\frac{I}{T} - K\right)^+. \tag{14.86}$$

But we could have far more fancy contracts. Imagine an option that pays one unit of currency per time the price of the underlying is above a certain barrier S_u. The function $f(S, t)$, collecting this information over the entire path, would be

$$f(S, t) = \theta(S - S_u), \tag{14.87}$$

the *Heaviside-θ*-function. How is the *Black–Scholes*-equation affected by the additional variable I? Again assuming a geometric *Brown*ian motion as model for the price process of the underlying, we can establish our usual hedge-portfolio and apply Itô's lemma to obtain

$$d\Pi = \left(\frac{\partial V}{\partial t} + \frac{1}{2}\sigma^2 S^2 \frac{\partial^2 V}{\partial S^2}\right)dt + \frac{\partial V}{\partial I}dI + \left(\frac{\partial V}{\partial S} - \Delta\right)dS, \tag{14.88}$$

where we have arranged the equation with respect to the different increments. If we choose the hedge-ratio $\Delta = \frac{\partial V}{\partial S}$, the portfolio is risk-free, because from (14.85) a small change in the process I_t is given by

$$dI_t = f(S_t, t)dt. \tag{14.89}$$

Thus, equating the change in the hedge-portfolio with the growth rate $r\Pi dt$, induced by the risk-free interest rate, and rearranging yields

$$\frac{\partial V}{\partial t} + rS\frac{\partial V}{\partial S} + \frac{1}{2}\sigma^2 S^2 \frac{\partial^2 V}{\partial S^2} + f(S,t)\frac{\partial V}{\partial I} - rV = 0. \tag{14.90}$$

This is a modified version of the *Black–Scholes*-PDE, which has an additional spatial dimension I. In counting dimensions, it is customary to only count the spatial dimensions and so we have a two-dimensional problem. In principle, such a problem can be solved by finite difference methods in a three-dimensional lattice. A collection of appropriate schemes can be found in Wilmott (2006c, chap. 79). But generally, the higher the dimension of the problem, the less appropriate finite difference methods are, because they become exceedingly computationally demanding. We will therefore use Monte Carlo simulation, if the problem is not one-dimensional.

Probably the most prominent examples in the class of strongly path dependent contracts are Asian options. We already learned some characterizations of those contracts in Chapter 12. So let's start our discussion with a surprise. For the continuously averaged geometric fixed strike option with European exercise right, there exists a generalized closed form solution (Kemna and Vorst, 1990). The price of such an Asian call, when written at $t = 0$, is

$$C_0^{\yen}(K, T, S_0) = e^{(b_{\text{adj.}} - r)T} S_0 \Phi(d_+) - e^{-rT} K\Phi(d_-), \tag{14.91}$$

with

$$d_{+/-} = \frac{\log(S_0/K) + (b_{\text{adj.}} \pm \frac{1}{2}\sigma^2_{\text{adj.}})T}{\sigma_{\text{adj.}} \sqrt{T}}, \quad b_{\text{adj.}} = \frac{1}{2}\left(b - \frac{\sigma^2}{6}\right), \text{ and } \sigma_{\text{adj.}} = \frac{\sigma}{\sqrt{3}}. \tag{14.92}$$

For a later time t in the life of the contract, the formulas for the fair price $V_t^{\yen}(K, T, \bar{S}_t)$ become more complex but nevertheless remain completely analytic (see for example Wilmott, 2006b, sect. 25.11). The lucky coincidence that makes this work is that the geometric average of a log-normal distributed random variable is also log-normal distributed. The price for the geometric average fixed strike put is

$$P_0^{\yen}(K, T, S_0) = -e^{(b_{\text{adj.}} - r)T} S_0 \Phi(-d_+) + e^{-rT} K\Phi(-d_-), \tag{14.93}$$

with $d_{+/-}$, $b_{\text{adj.}}$, and $\sigma_{\text{adj.}}$ as in (14.92). That is how far analytical computations will carry us. From here on, we have to completely rely on numerical approximations. So let's start by approximating an individual path of our standard risk-neutral geometric *Brown*ian motion. Such a path S_t for $0 \le t \le T$ is a (almost surely) continuous function of the state variable $\omega \in \Omega$. But that does not help much for any computational purpose. So let's discretize it by

$$S_{t+\Delta t} = S_t e^{(r-\frac{1}{2}\sigma^2)\Delta t + \sigma \sqrt{\Delta t} Z_{t+\Delta t}}, \qquad (14.94)$$

where again Z_t is assumed independently standard normally distributed, $Z_t \sim N(0,1)$. Once we have chosen Δt, we can represent the continuous path by the sequence of discrete values $S_{m\Delta t}$ for $m = 0, \dots, M = \frac{T}{\Delta t}$. That is indeed all we need to run a simulation based numerical pricing algorithm.

Example 14.4

Suppose a fixed strike arithmetic Asian call option with European exercise right has strike price K and expiry date T. The current price S_0 and annual volatility σ of the underlying is known, also the risk-free interest rate r. The underlying pays no dividend. How can this contract be valuated?

Solution

The pseudo-code for this problem is provided in Box 14.4. The only additional fragments are due to the discretization of the path and the computation of the arithmetic average.

From the pseudo-code in Box 14.4 it is obvious that it is hard to make mistakes in setting up a simple Monte Carlo pricing algorithm. This is an important aspect, because

Box 14.4 Pseudo-code for fixed strike arithmetic Asian call

Set N, M	▷ Initialization
$b = r$	▷ Cost-of-carry rate
$\Delta t = T/M$	

For $n = 1$ to N	▷ Path replication
For $m = 1$ to M	▷ Path discretization
Draw $z \sim N(0,1)$	▷ Random number generation
$S_m = S_{m-1} \exp\left((b - \frac{1}{2}\sigma^2)\Delta t + \sigma \sqrt{\Delta t}\, z\right)$	
Next m	
$\bar{S}_T = 1/(M+1) \sum_{m=0}^{M} S_m$	▷ Arithmetic average
$V_T^{(n)} = \max(\bar{S}_T - K, 0)$	▷ Payoff function
Next n	

$V_0 = \exp(-rT) \cdot 1/N \sum_{n=1}^{N} V_T^{(n)}$	
Print V_0	▷ Output

often there is no way to check against analytical references in order to see, if there is an error in the code.

Of course we can have additional barrier conditions within an Asian option. Assume the contract in Example 14.4 would have expired worthlessly, if the underlying had hit the lower knockout barrier S_l during the lifetime of the contract. Then we would have only to insert the fragment

> If $\min(S_0, \ldots, S_M) \leq S_l$ then $V_T^{(n)} = 0$

immediately below the payoff function. You might suspect that we could have valuated barrier options as well via Monte Carlo simulation and that is correct. But since barrier type contracts are so well suited to finite difference schemes, it would have been inefficient. On the other hand American options cannot be dealt with easily in a simulation framework. The reason is that we have to determine the early exercise boundary, as we are progressing backwards in time. But Monte Carlo simulation is a purely forward progressing scheme. There are workarounds like the method of Longstaff and Schwartz (2001) to be discussed in the next section, but valuation of high-dimensional contracts with American exercise right are the most challenging problems in quantitative finance.

There is another common path dependent option type called a lookback option. This kind of option is the dream of every trader, because its payoff depends on the minimum or maximum price of the underlying during the lifetime of the contract. It generally comes in two flavors (fixed and floating):

Strike type

- Fixed strike: The exercise price is fixed and not affected by the path of the underlying. The payoffs are

$$\overleftarrow{C}(K, T, S_{\max}) = (S_{\max} - K)^+ \quad \text{and} \quad \overleftarrow{P}(K, T, S_{\min}) = (K - S_{\min})^+,$$

  where $S_{\max}$ and $S_{\min}$ are the maximum and minimum prices of the underlying over the lifetime of the contract.

- Floating strike: The exercise price itself is given by the maximum $S_{\max}$ or the minimum $S_{\min}$ of the path of the underlying, respectively. The payoffs are

$$\overleftarrow{C}(S_{\min}, T) = S_T - S_{\min} \quad \text{and} \quad \overleftarrow{P}(S_{\max}, T) = S_{\max} - S_T.$$

The path dependence of the lookback option is very clear. It is thus very surprising that explicit formulas exist in the *Black–Scholes*-framework. For the floating strike case they are due to Goldman et al. (1979), and for the fixed strike due to Conze and Viswanathan (1991). The formulas are a little bulky and therefore the reader is referred to Haug (2007, sect. 4.15), where also additional versions of the lookback option can be found. Of course nothing prevents us from valuating a lookback option numerically.

Quick calculation 14.6 How is the pseudo-code in Box 14.4 to be modified, to valuate a European fixed strike lookback call?

14.8   Valuating American Contracts with Monte Carlo

Higher-dimensional contracts can be equipped with American exercise right as well. The problem with this is that we are used to pricing such contracts by Monte Carlo simulation, which builds a path from many small simulated increments. The point is that this construction progresses forward in time. We cannot simulate the path backwards, because we only know the price of the underlying today, not at expiry. To determine the optimal exercise strategy, and hence the fair price of an American contract, we have to compute the *Snell*-envelope, which has to be done recursively backwards in time. If today is time $t = 0$ and the contract under consideration expires at $t = T$, then the *Snell*-envelope is computed by

$$X_t = \begin{cases} e^{-rT} V_T & \text{for } t = T \\ \max\left(e^{-rt} V_t, E^Q[X_{t+\Delta t}|\mathcal{F}_t]\right) & \text{for } t < T, \end{cases} \tag{14.95}$$

with V_t denoting the intrinsic value of the contract at time t. Of course we have assumed implicitly in (14.95) that all paths are simulated in discrete time steps of length Δt. The problem is now very clear. For any given path we obtained by simulation, we have to work backwards in Δt-steps from $t = T$ to $t = 0$ to determine the *Snell*-envelope. But in the process, at every time $t < T$ we need the conditional expectation $E^Q[X_{t+\Delta t}|\mathcal{F}_t]$. We could of course try to approximate it by again forward simulating paths, but note that the expectation has to cover all possible early exercise events of those new paths as well. So this strategy becomes unmanageable very rapidly from a computational point of view.

The idea of Longstaff and Schwartz (2001) is both simple and brilliant. They suggest to generate the required paths independently by simulation and afterwards use cross-sectional information to approximate the required conditional expectation values. To be more precise, they approximate the expectation value at time t by least-squares regression from all paths that are in the money at that time. The resulting approach is called LSM-algorithm (least-squares Monte Carlo) and is best understood by looking at a simplified numerical example.

Example 14.5

Based on the example in Longstaff and Schwartz (2001, sect. 1), valuate an American put option on a non dividend paying stock with current price $S_0 = \$100$, exercise price $K = \$110$, time to expiry $T = 3$ years, and annual risk-free interest rate $r = 6\%$. Assume that $\Delta t = 1$ year and the option is exercisable at times $t = 1, 2, 3$. A total of $N = 8$ simulated paths under the risk-neutral measure Q is provided in Table 14.2.

LSM-Algorithm

The first step is to compute the *Snell*-envelope at expiry

$$X_3 = e^{-3r}(K - S_3)^+$$

Table 14.2 Simulated paths of S_t

Path ω_n	$t=0$	$t=1$	$t=2$	$t=3$
1	100	109	108	134
2	100	116	126	154
3	100	122	107	103
4	100	93	97	92
5	100	111	156	152
6	100	76	77	90
7	100	92	84	101
8	100	88	122	134

for every path ω_n. The result is given in Table 14.3. These cashflows are the pathwise present values of a European put option. If the option is in the money at time $t=2$, the holder has to make the decision whether or not to exercise it immediately or to hold it until $t=3$. To make the right decision, she requires knowledge of the conditional expectation $E^Q[X_3|\mathcal{F}_2]$. This expectation value can be approximated by least-squares regression. The key idea is to formulate a stochastic model of the form

$$X_{t+1} = \sum_{k=0}^{K} \beta_k S_t^k + \epsilon_{t+1}.$$

Note that even though powers of S_t are involved, the stochastic model is still linear in its coefficients. That means one can easily obtain the least-squares estimator

$$|\hat{\beta}\rangle = \begin{pmatrix} \hat{\beta}_0 \\ \vdots \\ \hat{\beta}_K \end{pmatrix}$$

as already elaborated in Chapter 7. In the present example, $K=2$ was chosen and the realizations of the response variable and the regressors are provided in Table 14.4. Only paths that are in the money at $t=2$ are considered in the regression, because only in

Table 14.3 *Snell*-envelope at $t=3$

Path ω_n	$t=1$	$t=2$	$t=3$
1	–	–	0
2	–	–	0
3	–	–	5.85
4	–	–	15.03
5	–	–	0
6	–	–	16.71
7	–	–	7.52
8	–	–	0

Table 14.4 Regression at time $t = 2$

Path ω_n	X_3	S_2	S_2^2
1	0	108	11 664
2	–	–	–
3	5.85	107	11 449
4	15.03	97	9 409
5	–	–	–
6	16.71	77	5 929
7	7.52	84	7 056
8	–	–	–

those states of the world, does the holder have to make an exercise decision at that time. It is not prohibited to include all paths in the regression, but Longstaff and Schwartz found that in this case more regressors are needed to obtain accurate results. In the current regression model for $t = 2$, one obtains

$$E^Q[\hat{X}_3|\mathcal{F}_2] = -94.665 + 2.641 \cdot S_2 - 0.016 \cdot S_2^2.$$

This quantity is the least-squares estimator for the conditional expectation $E^Q[X_3|\mathcal{F}_2]$ and is used as a proxy in the early exercise decision. All required information for this decision at $t = 2$ is now available. The discounted intrinsic values from early exercise and the conditional expectation proxies from least-squares regression are summarized in Table 14.5. From this, one can now easily compute the *Snell*-envelope at $t = 2$; see Table 14.6.

The entries in the last two tables require some explanation. First of all, all values $X_2^{(n)}$, resulting from early exercise, are identified by a star. That has happened in paths 4, 6, and 7. But take a closer look at those paths with negative exercise decision. In path 1, the option is not exercised at $t = 2$, even though it is now in the money and its discounted exercise value is $1.77. That is because the exercise decision is based on comparing the discounted intrinsic value and the conditional expectation of $\hat{X}_3$. The optimal strategy in this case is not to exercise the option early. Of course the terminal

Table 14.5 Exercise decision at $t = 2$

Path ω_n	$e^{-2r}(K - S_2)$	$E^Q[\hat{X}_3|\mathcal{F}_2]$
1	1.77	3.94
2	–	–
3	2.66	4.74
4	11.53	10.97
5	–	–
6	29.27	13.83
7	23.06	14.28
8	–	–

Table 14.6 *Snell*-envelope at $t = 2$

Path ω_n	$t = 1$	$t = 2$	$t = 3$
1	–	0	0
2	–	0	0
3	–	5.85	5.85
4	–	11.53*	15.03
5	–	0	0
6	–	29.27*	16.71
7	–	23.06*	7.52
8	–	0	0

intrinsic value in this path vanishes, so that it had better been exercised at $t = 2$, but this information is not available to the decision maker at that point, because it is not contained in $\mathcal{F}_2$. Only the omniscient observer, running the simulation, knows that. In path 3, the option is also not exercised early, which means the cashflow is still obtained at $t = 3$ and thus, its present value is unchanged. Unlike in path 1, this exercise decision is optimal from both points of view, the one of the option holder, as well as the one of the spectator with complete knowledge.

It is worthwhile to stop for a minute and go back to the binomial model of Chapter 12, in order to understand how the exercise decision is made and the continuation value is generated in the LSM-approach. There is a fundamental difference in the architecture of binomial models and Monte Carlo simulated paths regarding the way they fill the space of potential realizations of the price process of the underlying; see Figure 14.9. In particular, in the binomial model, every node has two successors, and the space of potential prices is swept out systematically. Systematically here means that ascending nodes in every time slice represent ascending prices of the underlying. In a set of simulated paths, every node, except for the zeroth, has only one successor and the paths fill the space of potential prices randomly. These differences have severe implications for the way the early exercise decision is made and the continuation value of

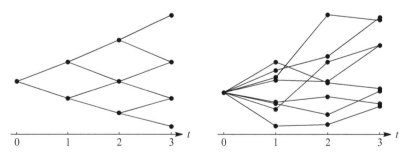

Fig. 14.9 Organization of nodes and edges – Binomial tree (left) and Monte Carlo simulation (right)

Table 14.7 Regression at time $t = 1$

Path ω_n	X_2	S_1	S_1^2
1	0	109	11 881
2	–	–	–
3	–	–	–
4	11.53	93	8 649
5	–	–	–
6	29.27	76	5 776
7	23.06	92	8 464
8	0	88	7 744

the option is generated. For both types of schemes, the *Snell*-envelope in an arbitrary branch has to satisfy

$$X_t^{(n)} = \begin{cases} e^{-rt}(K - S_t^{(n)}) & \text{if option is exercised} \\ E^Q[X_{t+1}|\mathcal{F}_t] & \text{if option is continued} \end{cases}$$

for $t < T$. In the binomial model, the exercise decision is made by directly comparing the discounted value of immediate exercise and the continuation value

$$E^Q[X_{t+1}|\mathcal{F}_t] = q \cdot X_{t+1}^{(n+1)} + (1 - q) \cdot X_{t+1}^{(n)},$$

where q is the risk-neutral probability for entering the upper branch. That is possible, because the binomial tree is organized systematically. A simulated mesh is not organized that way, and hence the LSM-algorithm uses the proxy $E^Q[\hat{X}_{t+1}|\mathcal{F}_t]$ for the exercise decision. Because simulated paths do not branch out, the subsequent node is attained with probability one for $0 < t < T$, and thus the continuation value is

$$E^Q[X_{t+1}|\mathcal{F}_t] = X_{t+1}^{(n)}.$$

That is the reason why in Table 14.6 the terminal value of the *Snell*-envelope is unchanged in all paths, where no early exercise occurs.

Continuing the original example, the next step is to pick out the in-the-money paths at time $t = 1$ and to regress them on X_2; see Table 14.7. The result of the least-squares estimation is

$$E^Q[\hat{X}_2|\mathcal{F}_1] = 191.917 - 3.142 \cdot S_1 + 0.013 \cdot S_1^2.$$

Now all necessary information for the exercise decision at $t = 1$ is available and is summarized in Table 14.8. With exception of path 1, the option is exercised early in all paths that are in the money at time $t = 1$. One can thus finally compute the entire *Snell*-envelope; see Table 14.9. Early exercise is again indicated by a star and occurs in paths 4, 6, 7, and 8 at $t = 1$. Take a closer look at path number 7. In this path, early exercise is recommended at two times, which means $\tau = 1$ and $\tau = 2$ are stopping times. Obviously

Table 14.8 Exercise decision at $t=1$

Path ω_n	$e^{-r}(K-S_1)$	$E^Q[\hat{X}_2|\mathcal{F}_1]$
1	0.94	3.89
2	–	–
3	–	–
4	16.01	12.15
5	–	–
6	32.02	28.21
7	16.95	12.89
8	20.72	16.09

the discounted value of the option is larger, if exercised at $t=2$. Nevertheless, the optimal exercise policy for an American option is associated with the smallest stopping time

$$\tau^* = \inf\{t \in \mathcal{T} : X_t = e^{-rt}(K - S_t)^+\}.$$

Again, defining the stopped process Y_t by

$$Y_t = \begin{cases} X_t & \text{if } t < \tau^* \\ X_{\tau^*} & \text{if } t \geq \tau^* \end{cases}$$

as in Equation (12.53) on page 238, one can easily approximate the value of the American put option by

$$Y_0 = E^Q[Y_3|\mathcal{F}_0] \approx \frac{1}{N} \sum_{n=1}^{N} Y_3^{(n)} = 11.44,$$

because Y_t is a Q-martingale. On the other hand, the price of the corresponding European put option can be obtained from the terminal expectation value of X,

$$E^Q[X_3|\mathcal{F}_0] \approx \frac{1}{N} \sum_{n=1}^{N} X_3^{(n)} = 5.64.$$

Table 14.9 *Snell*-envelope at $t=1$

Path ω_n	$t=1$	$t=2$	$t=3$
1	0	0	0
2	0	0	0
3	5.85	5.85	5.85
4	16.01*	11.53	15.03
5	0	0	0
6	32.02*	29.27	16.71
7	16.95*	23.06	7.52
8	20.72*	0	0

Thus, the right to exercise the option at any time during its lifetime adds substantial value to the contract.

Of course a simple plain vanilla American put option can be valued more efficiently by finite difference methods. But an Asian option with American exercise right would make a perfect candidate for the LSM-algorithm. Its value does not depend exclusively on the price process S_t, but also on the integrated process I_t. Thus, in conducting a least-squares regression up to quadratic order to make the appropriate exercise decision at time t, one would use the stochastic model

$$X_{t+1} = \beta_0 + \beta_1 S_t + \beta_2 I_t + \beta_3 S_t^2 + \beta_4 S_t I_t + \beta_5 I_t^2 + \epsilon_{t+1}. \tag{14.96}$$

There is generally no limit to the order of the polynomials or the number of variables to be included in (14.96), as long as there are enough simulated in-the-money paths to conduct least-squares estimation. Longstaff and Schwartz (2001) even suggest to use orthogonal basis functions as regressors instead of simple powers. In particular they used *Laguerre*-polynomials, which are orthogonal with respect to the weight function e^{-x} in the domain $\mathbb{R}_0^+$. However, their results indicate that the functional form of the regressors is circumstantial.

14.9   Further Reading

A gentle introduction to exotic contracts is Hull (2009, chap. 24). An accessible and very well written treatment of the subject is Wilmott (2006b, part 2). For a comprehensive collection of analytical formulas see Haug (2007). Finite difference schemes frequently used in financial engineering are introduced in Wilmott (2006c, part 6). An authority for Monte Carlo simulation in finance is Glasserman (2010). Girsanov's theorem, generators, and the *Feynman–Kac*-formula are treated in a very comprehensible way in Neftci (2000, chap. 14 & 21). For a more rigorous discussion of the *Girsanov*-transformation see Shiryaev (1999, sect. 7.3b). The connection between path integrals and derivatives is discussed in Baaquie (2004, chap. 5). For Monte Carlo valuation of American options see Glasserman (2010, chap. 8) and the original paper of Longstaff and Schwartz (2001).

14.10   Problems

14.1 Suppose instead of (14.16) on page 294, we had chosen the scheme

$$V_{m+1}^{(n)} = V_m^{(n)} + \Delta\tau \left(bn\Delta S \cdot \Delta_m^{(n)} + \frac{1}{2}\sigma^2 n^2 \Delta S^2 \cdot \Gamma_m^{(n)} - r V_{m+1}^{(n)} \right),$$

where the last term in parenthesis is with respect to time $\tau = (m+1)\Delta\tau$. Prove that this scheme is still explicit and use a martingale argument to show that the stability condition (14.23) on page 295, as well as the additional condition

$$\sigma^2 n \geq b$$

have to hold, in order for the scheme to be consistent.

14.2 A power option is a contract, whose value depends on the payoff $V(S, T)$, with $S = S^\alpha$. Show that the generalized *Black–Scholes*-equation can be expressed in terms of S, with adjusted cost-of-carry rate $b_{\text{adj.}}$ and volatility $\sigma_{\text{adj.}}$.

14.3 Suppose the underlying S follows the standard geometric *Brown*ian motion

$$dS_t = \mu S_t dt + \sigma S_t dW_t.$$

Use the associated *Fokker–Planck*-equation, together with the definition of the probability current

$$F(S, t) = \left(\mu S - \frac{1}{2}\frac{\partial}{\partial S}\sigma^2 S^2 \right) p(S, t),$$

to prove that the probability mass is conserved over time,

$$\frac{\partial}{\partial t} \int_0^\infty p(S, t)dS = \int_0^\infty \frac{\partial}{\partial t} p(S, t)dS = 0.$$

Assume that the probability density function $p(S, t)$ is a sufficiently rapid decreasing function, which is true.

14.4 Monte Carlo simulation approximates an unknown expectation value by an arithmetic mean, computed from a random sample. This mean can be understood as the expectation value with respect to the estimated probability density

$$\hat{f}(x) = \frac{1}{N}\sum_{n=1}^{N} \delta(x - x^{(n)}).$$

Show that for an arbitrary function $h(x)$, the arithmetic mean

$$\hat{h} = \frac{1}{N}\sum_{n=1}^{N} h(x^{(n)})$$

is the exact expectation value with respect to $\hat{f}(x)$, and that $\hat{f}(x)$ itself is an unbiased estimator for the true density $f(x)$.

14.5 An important variance reduction technique in Monte Carlo simulation is importance sampling. The idea behind this concept is to approximate an expectation by a weighted average value

$$\hat{h} = \sum_{n=1}^{N} w_n h(x^{(n)}),$$

where the normalized weights are proportional to the so-called likelihood ratio

$$w_n \propto \frac{f(x^{(n)})}{N \cdot g(x^{(n)})} \quad \text{and} \quad \sum_{n=1}^{N} w_n = 1,$$

and the sampling is conducted with respect to the importance density $g(x)$, not the original density $f(x)$. Show that the expectation of $\hat{h}$ is still unbiased.

14.6 A continuously exponential averaged arithmetic Asian option is a contract, where the average price of the underlying is computed as

$$\bar{S}_t = e^{-\lambda t} S_0 + \lambda \int_0^t e^{-\lambda(t-\tau)} S_\tau d\tau.$$

The parameter $\lambda \geq 0$ is an arbitrary weight factor. Rewrite the averaging condition in differential form and explain the effect of the parameter λ.

14.7 Consider a floating strike version of an exponential arithmetic Asian call (Problem 14.6) with European exercise right, contingent on a forward contract with $T_F > T$. Assume that S_0, T, r, σ, and λ are known. Additionally, the option is knocked out, if $S_{T/2} \leq \bar{S}_{T/2}$ holds. Create a pseudo-code algorithm to valuate this contract at time $t = 0$.

15 Deterministic Volatility

Abandoning the idea of a constant volatility implies a considerable enrichment of the entire concept of derivative pricing. Whereas stochastic volatility naturally leads to incomplete market models, deterministic volatility preserves market completeness. Such models are very popular with practitioners, because they allow for arbitrage free pricing of standard and exotic contracts, with only few exceptions. Nevertheless, they do not unravel the mechanisms of volatility, but only generate a consistent snapshot of the momentary market expectations.

15.1   The Term Structure of Volatility

The simplest possible relaxation of the *Black–Scholes*-assumption of constant volatility is to allow for a deterministic term structure. Going back to the roots, this means that the underlying follows a geometric *Brown*ian motion with time-dependent volatility

$$dS_t = \mu S_t dt + \sigma(t) S_t dW_t. \tag{15.1}$$

To emphasize that $\sigma(t)$ is a deterministic function of time and not a stochastic process, the time variable is expressed explicitly as function argument and not as subscript. *Girsanov*'s theorem is general enough to hold in this situation, and in switching from the physical probability measure P to the risk-neutral measure Q, the drift μ is simply replaced by the risk-free interest rate r, as before. On the other hand, following our earlier hedging argument, the *Black–Scholes*-equation becomes

$$\frac{\partial V}{\partial t} + rS\frac{\partial V}{\partial S} + \frac{1}{2}\sigma^2(t)S\frac{\partial^2 V}{\partial S^2} - rV = 0, \tag{15.2}$$

and the solution for a European plain vanilla call option is

$$C_t(K, T) = S_t \Phi(d_1) - e^{-r(T-t)} K \Phi(d_2), \tag{15.3}$$

with

$$d_1 = \frac{\log(S_t/K) + r(T-t) + \frac{1}{2}\int_t^T \sigma^2(s)ds}{\sqrt{\int_t^T \sigma^2(s)ds}} \quad \text{and} \quad d_2 = d_1 - \sqrt{\int_t^T \sigma^2(s)ds}. \tag{15.4}$$

The resemblance to the original result (13.79) on page 266 is striking. Let us call the volatility $\sigma(t)$, prevailing in our model process (15.1) at time t, the **actual volatility**. We can then ask the question: what volatility would be implied, if we valuate the contract in the standard *Black–Scholes*-framework? Comparing (13.79) and (15.4), we immediately see that this volatility is

$$\sigma_{\text{imp.}}(T) = \sqrt{\frac{1}{T-t} \int_t^T \sigma^2(s)ds}. \tag{15.5}$$

We call this quantity the **implied volatility**. That is, the implied variance is the arithmetic mean over all actual variances. This is a very convenient result, but it does not hold in general. It is only true, if actual volatility is a deterministic function of time and nothing else. We will see at a later point that implied volatility can have a far more intriguing interpretation. The immediate question is: does volatility change over time? If the answer is yes, then the original geometric *Brown*ian motion is an inadequate model for the price process of the underlying. Look at the top row of Figure 15.1, where 20 years of daily prices of the S&P 500 index is indicated on the left. The right side shows an arbitrary simulated path of a geometric *Brown*ian motion, with the same expected growth rate and volatility as found in the data. At first sight it seems to have all the roughness and characteristics of the original price process. It can of course never be a carbon copy of the real process, because it represents only one possible state of the world $\omega \in \Omega$. But in the bottom row of Figure 15.1, the daily returns of both processes are illustrated. Whereas the geometric *Brown*ian motion induces a very homogeneous

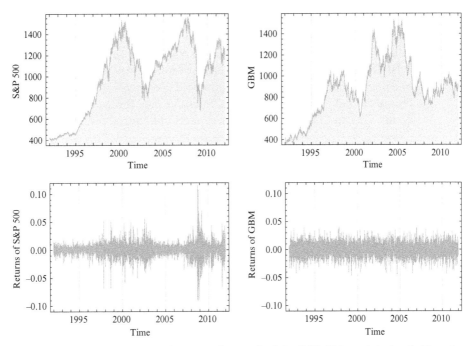

Fig. 15.1 Price process (top) and returns (bottom) of the S&P 500 stock index (left) and simulated geometric *Brown*ian motion (right)

white noise, the empirical result is quite bizarre. Not only does the volatility obviously change over time, but those changes seem to have a certain pattern. There are large segments, where volatility is moderate, and there are clusters, where volatility is exceedingly high. With a little historic background, you can link times with high volatility to financial market distress. There is the 1998 to 2003 segment of increased volatility, corresponding to a series of catastrophic events. In 1998, Russia defaulted on domestic debt and devalued the ruble. In 2000, the so-called dot-com crash occurred as a result of a bursting technology bubble. Finally, the devastating terrorist attack of September 11, 2001 affected financial markets worldwide, cumulating in the 2002 market downturn. In the 2008 to 2012 segment you can see the consequences of the sub-prime crisis and the European sovereign debt crisis. It is very plausible that market risk is higher in times of financial distress, because it becomes very hard to predict what happens next during a crisis. Because risk is linked to volatility, it is clear that we have to abandon the idea of constant volatility, if we are looking for an adequate and realistic model.

The volatility clustering phenomenon has an empirical side effect, called excess kurtosis. The kurtosis of a distribution is the standardized fourth central moment

$$K = E\left[\left(\frac{X - \mu}{\sigma}\right)^4\right] = \frac{M_4}{\sigma^4}. \tag{15.6}$$

Equation (2.31) on page 19 tells us that a normal distribution always has kurtosis $K = 3$. If we estimate the kurtosis in financial return time series with daily or weekly frequency, we observe a much higher kurtosis, probably between six and nine. Of course excess kurtosis does not have to be caused by volatility clustering. It simply indicates that the unconditional distribution is not *Gauss*ian, but a distribution with heavier tails. There is another remarkable pattern encoded in the empirical data of financial time series, called the leverage effect. This effect describes the phenomenon that on average the volatility tomorrow, induced by a negative return today, is larger than the one induced by a positive return of the same magnitude. This effect is indeed found in most financial time series and is understood as additional evidence for the risk-averse attitude of most agents. We can thus state three stylized facts of financial return time series:

- excess kurtosis,
- volatility clustering,
- leverage effect.

It is also true that most financial return series, at least with daily or weekly sampling frequency, correspond to noise processes. That is, apart from a fixed expectation value μ, we cannot predict future returns based on our knowledge of present and past returns. Econometrics has found a quite effective way to deal with those stylized facts, which we will study next.

15.2   GARCH-Models

The abbreviation GARCH stands for Generalized AutoRegressive Conditional Heteroscedasticity. The ingenious idea is due to Robert Engle (1982), who in 2003 received the Nobel Prize in economics for it, even though its generalized form was introduced by Tim Bollerslev (1986), who was Engle's graduate student at that time. Suppose you do not specify the general return distribution, but only the distribution conditional on your present knowledge. That may sound strange so let's see how it is done. Let $x_t = \log S_t$ be the logarithmic (daily) price of an arbitrary security. Then in a GARCH-framework, the dynamics of the logarithmic returns $\Delta x_t = x_t - x_{t-1}$ are given by

$$\Delta x_t = \mu + \epsilon_t = \mu + \sqrt{h_t} z_t, \tag{15.7}$$

where $z_t \sim N(0, 1)$ is independent of everything else. In accordance with tradition in time series analysis, we use small letters for random variables. The trick is that h_t is $\mathcal{F}_{t-1}$-predictable. So conditioning on this information, the logarithmic return Δx_t is normally distributed with expectation μ and variance h_t. We chose the letter h to represent the conditional variance mainly for two reasons. First, h stands for heteroscedasticity and so it automatically refers to the GARCH-model class. Second, even if h_t has no dynamics, we would still have $\sqrt{h_t} \neq \sigma$, because $\sqrt{h_t}$ is naturally scaled on a daily basis, whereas σ is usually the volatility per year. The more interesting question is how the dynamics of h_t are defined. In the simplest possible GARCH-model, the variance tomorrow is explained as a weighted arithmetic mean of the current, the past, and the distant future variance

$$h_{t+1} = \alpha \epsilon_t^2 + \beta h_t + \gamma h_\infty. \tag{15.8}$$

$h_\infty = E[h_t]$ is also called the stationary variance. It is the quantity you can simply estimate by computing the sample variance of all logarithmic returns.[1]

Quick calculation 15.1 Can you see why the entire history of the process contributes in the computation of h_t?

Of course we must have $\alpha, \beta, \gamma \geq 0$ and $\alpha + \beta + \gamma = 1$. It is customary to introduce a new parameter $\omega = \gamma h_\infty$ and to write the GARCH-model as

$$\Delta x_t = \mu + \sqrt{h_t} z_t \tag{15.9}$$

$$h_t = \omega + \alpha \epsilon_{t-1}^2 + \beta h_{t-1}, \tag{15.10}$$

---

[1] We defined the GARCH-model such that it is guaranteed to be stationary and ergodic. The latter property ensures that both the time series and the cross-sectional sample moments converge to the same value. Because z_t is independent and standard normally distributed, we have $\text{Var}[\Delta x_t] = E[h_t z_t^2] = E[h_t]$, and the claim follows immediately. In general, GARCH-models form a much broader class of models. We will exclusively analyze the GARCH(1,1)-member of this class.

where of course $\epsilon_t = \sqrt{h_t} z_t$ with $z_t \sim N(0, 1)$, and the variance equation is now in the typical AR-form. Note that in this parametrization, the stationary variance becomes

$$E[\epsilon_t^2] = h_\infty = \frac{\omega}{1 - \alpha - \beta}. \tag{15.11}$$

Let us elaborate on a particular, quite subtle point. It is easy to see that the distribution of Δx_t, conditional on the information $\mathcal{F}_{t-1}$ is *Gaussian*, because h_t is $\mathcal{F}_{t-1}$-predictable and is thus a known quantity at time t. But the unconditional distribution of Δx_t is far from *Gaussian*. This might be puzzling so let's compute a characteristic and invariant quantity of a normal distribution, we know well: Its kurtosis. To simplify the computation assume that $\beta = 0$, which is the original ARCH-specification of Engle (1982). That makes the stationary variance $E[\epsilon_t^2] = h_\infty = \omega/(1 - \alpha)$. Let's first compute the unconditional fourth moment of Δx_t

$$\begin{aligned}
M_4 = E[\epsilon_t^4] = E[h_t^2]E[z_t^4] &= 3E\left[(\omega + \alpha\epsilon_{t-1}^2)^2\right] \\
&= 3\omega^2 + 6\frac{\alpha\omega^2}{1 - \alpha} + 3\alpha^2 E[\epsilon_{t-1}^4] \\
&= \frac{3\omega^2 + 3\alpha\omega^2}{1 - \alpha} + 3\alpha^2 E[\epsilon_{t-1}^4] \\
&= \frac{3\omega^2(1 + \alpha)}{1 - \alpha} + 3\alpha^2 E[\epsilon_{t-1}^4],
\end{aligned} \tag{15.12}$$

where we used that z_t is independent of everything else and thus the expectations factorize. Because we are looking for the unconditional (stationary) fourth moment, we can use that $M_4 = E[\epsilon_t^4] = E[\epsilon_{t-1}^4]$ and rearrange (15.12) to obtain

$$M_4 = \frac{\omega^2}{(1 - \alpha)^2} \cdot 3\frac{(1 + \alpha)(1 - \alpha)}{1 - 3\alpha^2}, \tag{15.13}$$

where we already organized terms in a convenient way. The kurtosis is $K = M_4/h_\infty^2$, but the first term on the right hand side of (15.13) is already h_∞^2 and thus, we have

$$K = 3\frac{1 - \alpha^2}{1 - 3\alpha^2} \geq 3. \tag{15.14}$$

This is a very neat result, because for $\alpha = 0$ we are back in a *Gaussian* framework with $h_t = \omega$. But for $0 < \alpha < 1/\sqrt{3}$, we have excess kurtosis, as observed in financial time series.

Quick calculation 15.2 Verify that for $K = 9$ we have $\alpha = 1/2$.

One of the most useful properties of GARCH-models is that their expected variance can be computed recursively. Suppose we have fitted a GARCH-model to past return data, with daily frequency. Departing from $t = 0$, what variance do we expect at an arbitrary future day? Let's start by expressing the expected variance at day t in terms of the expected variance at day $t - 1$,

$$
\begin{aligned}
E[h_t] &= \omega + \alpha E[h_{t-1}]E[z_{t-1}^2] + \beta E[h_{t-1}] \\
&= \omega + (\alpha + \beta)E[h_{t-1}],
\end{aligned}
\tag{15.15}
$$

where we have again used the independence of z_t. We can iterate this result backwards right to the beginning to obtain

$$
\begin{aligned}
E[h_t] &= \omega + \omega(\alpha + \beta) + (\alpha + \beta)^2 E[h_{t-2}] \\
&= \omega \sum_{s=0}^{t-1}(\alpha + \beta)^s + (\alpha + \beta)^t h_0.
\end{aligned}
\tag{15.16}
$$

Now recognize that the sum in (15.16) is a geometric series and use the definition of the stationary variance (15.11) to obtain

$$
\begin{aligned}
E[h_t] &= \omega \frac{1 - (\alpha + \beta)^t}{1 - \alpha - \beta} + (\alpha + \beta)^t h_0 \\
&= h_\infty + (\alpha + \beta)^t (h_0 - h_\infty).
\end{aligned}
\tag{15.17}
$$

That is again a very nice result. Because $\alpha + \beta < 1$ has to hold, the initial variance h_0 decays exponentially to the stationary variance h_∞. But we can do even more. Let's compute the average expected variance up to some terminal time T

$$
\begin{aligned}
\frac{1}{T+1} \sum_{t=0}^{T} E[h_t] &= h_\infty + \frac{h_0 - h_\infty}{T+1} \cdot \sum_{t=0}^{T}(\alpha + \beta)^t \\
&= h_\infty + \frac{h_0 - h_\infty}{T+1} \cdot \frac{1 - (\alpha + \beta)^{T+1}}{1 - \alpha - \beta}.
\end{aligned}
\tag{15.18}
$$

Recall that T is measured in days in the GARCH-framework. More precisely, time is measured in trading days. If we assume that one year has 252 trading days, we can use this conversion factor to provide a new GARCH-model based formula for the implied volatility of an option

$$
\sigma_{\text{imp.}}(T) = \sqrt{252 h_\infty + \frac{h_0 - h_\infty}{T + 1/252} \cdot \frac{1 - (\alpha + \beta)^{252T+1}}{1 - \alpha - \beta}},
\tag{15.19}
$$

with h_∞ given by (15.11) and T now measured in years. This is a most convenient way to provide a term structure for the volatility that is realistically supported by empirical data. Unfortunately, there are two problems not yet accounted for. First, we have used the expected GARCH-variance to provide a volatility term structure, but the variance can deviate substantially from its expected value. Second, so far we have said nothing about the leverage effect. There are far more effective ways to apply GARCH-models in option pricing.

15.3 Duan's Option Pricing Model

In 1995, Jin-Chuan Duan came up with an approach for pricing derivatives, solely relying on a GARCH-model. We will discuss the components of this model, namely the GARCH-equations and the equivalent risk-neutral measure, which was called the locally risk-neutral valuation relationship (LRNVR) by Duan, separately. Let's first make an observation about the variance equation (15.10) on page 329.

We have already seen two possible specifications, the original ARCH-version ($\beta = 0$), and its generalization. The ARCH-model was already able to generate excess kurtosis as observed in financial time series, but it cannot account for volatility clustering. The GARCH-version can incorporate this stylized fact, by introducing a dependence on past variances. Both versions cannot account for the leverage effect, because ϵ_{t-1}^2 is completely symmetric with respect to positive and negative random errors of the same magnitude. A surprising side effect of applying Duan's LRNVR-transformation is that the original GARCH-model turns into the nonlinear asymmetric GARCH-specification (NGARCH), introduced by Engle and Ng (1993). In this version the variance has the dynamics

$$h_t = \omega + \alpha \left(\epsilon_{t-1} - \sqrt{h_{t-1}}\gamma \right)^2 + \beta h_{t-1}, \tag{15.20}$$

with $\gamma > 0$ and as usual $\epsilon_{t-1} = \sqrt{h_{t-1}}z_{t-1}$. To see that this specification indeed accounts for the leverage effect, let us compute the covariance between tomorrow's variance h_{t+1} and today's innovation z_t,

$$\begin{aligned} \text{Cov}[h_{t+1}, z_t] = E[h_{t+1}z_t] &= E\left[\left(\omega + \alpha h_t(z_t - \gamma)^2 + \beta h_t \right) z_t \right] \\ &= E[-2\alpha\gamma h_t z_t^2] = -2\alpha\gamma h_\infty, \end{aligned} \tag{15.21}$$

which is clearly negative. So as claimed, a negative innovation today on average causes a larger volatility tomorrow.

Quick calculation 15.3 Prove that in the NGARCH-model $h_\infty = \frac{\omega}{1-\alpha(1+\gamma^2)-\beta}$ holds.

The GARCH-model used by Duan (1995) is a discrete version of the *Itô*-process for $x_t = \log S_t$, where S_t follows the standard geometric *Brown*ian motion,

$$dx_t = \left(\mu - \frac{1}{2}\sigma^2 \right) dt + \sigma dW_t. \tag{15.22}$$

In discretizing this process, Duan made three modifications. First, the time interval was set to $\Delta t = 1$, second, the fixed variance σ^2 was replaced by the GARCH-variance h_t, and third, the expected daily return was expressed as the sum of a daily risk-free return and a risk premium, proportional to the actual volatility, $\mu = r + \lambda \sqrt{h_t}$. The resulting *Duan*-model is thus

$$\Delta x_t = r - \frac{1}{2}h_t + \lambda \sqrt{h_t} + \sqrt{h_t} z_t \qquad (15.23)$$

$$h_t = \omega + \alpha h_{t-1} z_{t-1}^2 + \beta h_{t-1}, \qquad (15.24)$$

where again $z_t \sim N(0, 1)$. Duan concluded that under the risk-neutral measure Q, the risk premium has to vanish, and thus he introduced the locally risk-neutral valuation relation (LRNVR)

$$z_t^Q = z_t + \lambda, \qquad (15.25)$$

which is nothing else than a discrete version of the *Girsanov*-transformation (14.40) on page 304. Because z_t is unconditionally normally distributed, the term "local" refers to the distribution of Δx_t, which is only conditionally normal, given the information $\mathcal{F}_{t-1}$. This is a mere formality, because the conditioning argument holds successively. Under the locally risk-neutral measure Q, the model reads

$$\Delta x_t = r - \frac{1}{2}h_t + \sqrt{h_t} z_t^Q \qquad (15.26)$$

$$h_t = \omega + \alpha h_{t-1}(z_{t-1}^Q - \lambda)^2 + \beta h_{t-1}, \qquad (15.27)$$

where of course $z_t^Q \sim N(0, 1)$ under Q.

Quick calculation 15.4 Show that (15.26) implies $S_{t-1} = e^{-r} E^Q[S_t | \mathcal{F}_{t-1}]$.

What is especially charming in the *Duan*-model, is that the risk premium can be estimated under the physical measure P, and the change to measure Q introduces a leverage effect. It is easy to simulate the price process under Q, once the model is fitted to the available data under P. Thus, an arbitrary derivative can be valuated via Monte Carlo simulation. Figure 15.2 shows one simulated price and return path, driven by a NGARCH-model with parameters fitted to 20 years of S&P 500 data. Compare the characteristics with the real data and the simulated geometric *Brownian* motion in Figure 15.1 on page 327. The NGARCH-model generates much more realistic path characteristics. We nevertheless have to pay a price. Option valuation with GARCH-models is computationally demanding, because we have to use Monte Carlo methods, and we have to keep track of two processes, x_t and h_t. There is a more efficient approach due to Heston and Nandi (1997, 2000), based on an affine class GARCH-model, we will encounter later. Option valuation with GARCH-models is

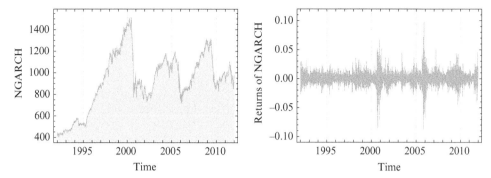

Fig. 15.2 Simulated NGARCH price process (left) and returns (right) – Parameters fitted to S&P 500 data

not mainstream. Although the results are more realistic than in the traditional *Black–Scholes*-framework, they are still not entirely satisfactory. One potential reason for this may be the lack of jumps.

15.4   Local Volatility and the *Dupire*-Equation

What is observed in reality is roughly the following: In the short term vanilla prices show a phenomenon called volatility smile. That means options which are roughly at the money ($S_t = K$), have the lowest implied volatility, whereas options both in the money ($S_t > K$) and out of the money ($S_t < K$) have larger implied volatilities. The criteria for in and out of the money were given for call options here, in case of put options they are reversed. In the long term the volatility smile seems to flatten out and option prices are usually only determined by a skew, where implied volatility is larger when the contract is in the money and smaller if it is out of the money, or vice versa. A typical implied volatility surface is shown in Figure 15.3. In this case the surface was constructed from 466 plain vanilla index options on the "Deutscher Aktienindex" (DAX). The spatial units are provided in terms of inverse logarithmic forward moneyness, where $F_0 = S_0 e^{rT}$ is the forward price of the underlying. The idea of **local volatility** is to find a deterministic function $\sigma_{\text{loc.}}(S, t)$, such that the stochastic process

$$dS_t = \mu S_t dt + \sigma_{\text{loc.}}(S_t, t)S_t dW_t \tag{15.28}$$

induces fair option prices, consistent with the observed implied volatility surface. This is a very subtle idea, even if it seems straightforward. At this point, it is not at all obvious that such a function exists. Furthermore, we have not the slightest clue what local and implied volatility really are in a local volatility setup.

Let's start our discussion with an observation due to Breeden and Litzenberger (1978). Departing from the *Feynman–Kac*-representation for the fair price of a plain vanilla European call option

$$C_t(K, T) = e^{-r(T-t)}E^Q[(S_T - K)^+|\mathcal{F}_t], \tag{15.29}$$

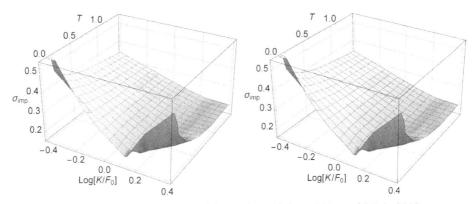

Fig. 15.3 3D Interpolated implied volatility surface of the DAX at mid-July 2012

we can calculate the first derivative with respect to the exercise price K. Even though the payoff function is clearly not differentiable at $S_T = K$, we can confidently assume that the conditional risk-neutral probability density is sufficiently rapidly decreasing, so that we can treat the payoff function as a generalized function. As already shown in Example (13.5) on page 259, the derivative of the maximum function is the *Heaviside-θ-function*, and thus we obtain

$$\frac{\partial C_t}{\partial K} = -e^{-r(T-t)} E^Q[\theta(S_T - K)|\mathcal{F}_t]. \tag{15.30}$$

Applying exactly the same arguments again and differentiating one more time yields

$$\frac{\partial^2 C_t}{\partial K^2} = e^{-r(T-t)} E^Q[\delta(S_T - K)|\mathcal{F}_t]. \tag{15.31}$$

But the expectation over the δ-function is an inner product of the δ-function and the conditional risk-neutral probability density function, $\langle \delta_K | q(T) \rangle = q(K, T)$, and thus we have

$$q(K, T) = e^{r(T-t)} \frac{\partial^2 C_t}{\partial K^2}, \tag{15.32}$$

with initial condition $q(K, t) = \delta(K - S_t)$. Under local volatility, the risk-neutral probability density function has to obey the *Fokker–Planck*-equation

$$\frac{\partial}{\partial T} q(S, T) = -\frac{\partial}{\partial S} rSq(S, T) + \frac{1}{2} \frac{\partial^2}{\partial S^2} \sigma_{\text{loc.}}^2(S, T) S^2 q(S, T)$$
$$= A^\dagger(S, T) q(S, T), \tag{15.33}$$

where

$$A^\dagger(S, T) = -\frac{\partial}{\partial S} rS + \frac{1}{2} \frac{\partial^2}{\partial S^2} \sigma_{\text{loc.}}^2(S, T) S^2 \tag{15.34}$$

is the *Fokker–Planck*-operator, and the initial condition is $q(S, t) = \delta(S - S_t)$. Going back to Equation (15.29) and differentiating with respect to T, one obtains

$$\frac{\partial C_t}{\partial T} = -rC_t + e^{-r(T-t)} \int_0^\infty (S - K)^+ \frac{\partial}{\partial T} q(S, T) dS$$

$$= -rC_t + e^{-r(T-t)} \int_0^\infty (S - K)^+ A^\dagger(S, T) q(S, T) dS \qquad (15.35)$$

$$= -rC_t + e^{-r(T-t)} \int_0^\infty (A(S, T)(S - K)^+) q(S, T) dS,$$

with the *Kolmogorov*-backward-operator

$$A(S, T) = rS \frac{\partial}{\partial S} + \frac{1}{2} \sigma^2_{\text{loc.}}(S, T) S^2 \frac{\partial^2}{\partial S^2}. \qquad (15.36)$$

Using the generalized derivatives $\frac{\partial}{\partial S}(S - K)^+ = \theta(S - K)$ and $\frac{\partial^2}{\partial S^2}(S - K)^+ = \delta(S - K)$, we obtain

$$\frac{\partial C_t}{\partial T} = -rC_t + re^{-r(T-t)} \int_0^\infty S\theta(S - K) q(S, T) ds$$

$$+ \frac{1}{2} \sigma^2_{\text{loc.}}(K, T) K^2 e^{-r(T-t)} q(K, T). \qquad (15.37)$$

Using that the maximum function can be written as $(S - K)^+ = (S - K)\theta(S - K)$, the integral in (15.37) becomes

$$E^Q[S_T \theta(S_T - K)|\mathcal{F}_t] = E^Q[(S_T - K)^+|\mathcal{F}_t] + KE^Q[\theta(S_T - K)|\mathcal{F}_t], \qquad (15.38)$$

where we have switched back to conditional expectations. Now we have to put some pieces together. Remember that $q(K, T) = E^Q[\delta(S_T - K)|\mathcal{F}_t]$, and consider the generalized derivatives (15.30) and (15.31), then we obtain the *Dupire*-equation (Dupire, 1994)

$$\frac{\partial C_t}{\partial T} = -rK \frac{\partial C_t}{\partial K} + \frac{1}{2} \sigma^2_{\text{loc.}}(K, T) K^2 \frac{\partial^2 C_t}{\partial K^2}. \qquad (15.39)$$

The remarkable thing about this equation is that it grants us immediate access to the local volatility surface by simply rearranging. Suppose today is time $t = 0$, then the complete local volatility surface, consistent with all call prices observed today, can be obtained by

$$\sigma_{\text{loc.}}(S, t) = \sqrt{\frac{\left.\frac{\partial C_0}{\partial T}\right|_{T=t} + rS\left.\frac{\partial C_0}{\partial K}\right|_{K=S}}{\frac{1}{2}S^2 \left.\frac{\partial^2 C_0}{\partial K^2}\right|_{K=S}}}. \qquad (15.40)$$

Unfortunately, this relation is of rather limited use. If an option is far in or out of the money, we divide a small number by another very small number, which can cause considerable numerical inaccuracies. What we really want is to express local volatility in terms of implied volatility. But before we come to this point, let's first try to understand what local volatility really is.

The subsequent exposition follows the very elegant argument of Derman and Kani (1998). Suppose the risk-neutral dynamics of the underlying are governed by the stochastic process

$$dS_t = \sigma_{\text{act.}}(S_t, t)S_t dW_t. \tag{15.41}$$

We have set the risk-free interest rate to $r = 0$, because we are solely interested in the volatility. The results are unaffected by this simplification. Actual volatility is a function of the random process S_t, and therefore random itself, but it is still adapted to the filtration $\mathcal{F}_t$, generated by W_t. Formal application of Itô's lemma to the function $(S - K)^+$ at time $t = T$ yields

$$d(S_T - K)^+ = \frac{1}{2}\sigma_{\text{act.}}^2(S_T, T)S_T^2\delta(S_T - K)dT + \sigma_{\text{act.}}(S_T, T)S_T\theta(S_T - K)dW_T. \tag{15.42}$$

Taking conditional expectations and recalling that $C_t(K, T) = E^Q[(S_T - K)^+|\mathcal{F}_t]$ holds for $r = 0$, we can express the dynamics of the call price as

$$dC_t = E^Q\left[\frac{1}{2}\sigma_{\text{act.}}^2(S_T, T)S_T^2\delta(S_T - K)\middle|\mathcal{F}_t\right]dT. \tag{15.43}$$

The conditional expectation of the *Wiener*-term vanishes, because of the defining properties of the *Itô*-integral. Remember that actual volatility is random itself and thus, the expectation is with respect to the joint conditional probability density $q(\sigma^2, S, T)$. This joint density can be factorized into the conditional product $q(\sigma^2|S, T)q(S, T)$ of densities.[2] Now (15.43) can be written as

$$\frac{\partial C_t}{\partial T} = \frac{1}{2}\int_0^\infty E^Q[\sigma_{\text{act.}}^2(S_T, T)|\mathcal{F}_{t\to S}]S^2\delta(S - K)q(S, T)dS$$
$$= \frac{1}{2}E^Q[\sigma_{\text{act.}}^2(S_T, T)|\mathcal{F}_{t\to K}]K^2\frac{\partial^2 C_t}{\partial K^2}, \tag{15.44}$$

where in slight abuse of notation $\mathcal{F}_{t\to K} = \mathcal{F}_t \cap \{S_T = K\}$ represents the information that the joint process starts at $(S_t, \sigma_{\text{act.}}^2(S_t, t))$ at time t and ends at $(K, \cdot)$ at time T. Comparing this result with the *Dupire*-equation (15.39) for $r = 0$, we can immediately conclude that

$$\sigma_{\text{loc.}}^2(K, T) = E^Q[\sigma_{\text{act.}}^2(S_T, T)|\mathcal{F}_{t\to K}] \tag{15.45}$$

has to hold. That is, local variance is the risk-neutral expected actual variance, conditional on the underlying to end up precisely at the money.

---

[2] The notation of conditional densities used here is of course far from rigorous, because conditioning is always with respect to a σ-algebra or an event and furthermore, T is not a random variable at all.

15.5   Implied Volatility and Most Likely Path

There is an easy and a most challenging answer to the question of what implied volatility truly is. Both answers are useful in a certain sense. The easy one is: Implied volatility is what you get, if you plug an observed option price into the *Black–Scholes*-formula and solve for the volatility. This may seem trivial but it is extremely useful in expressing local volatility (15.40), as derived from the *Dupire*-equation, in terms of implied volatility. This is in principle a simple matter, because we only have to use the chain rule. For example the partial derivative of C_0 with respect to the expiry time T becomes

$$\frac{\partial C_0}{\partial T} = \frac{\partial C_{BS}}{\partial T} + \frac{\partial C_{BS}}{\partial \sigma_{imp.}} \frac{\partial \sigma_{imp.}}{\partial T}, \qquad (15.46)$$

where C_{BS} is the *Black–Scholes*-price with respect to $\sigma_{imp.}$. In reality, the computation is extremely tedious and we will only state the final result. The reader is referred for details to Gatheral (2006, p. 11) or van der Kamp (2009, sect. 2.3). For brevity, we drop the subscript "imp." and state the result in terms of K and T

$$\sigma_{loc.}(K, T) = \sqrt{\frac{\sigma^2 + 2\sigma T\left(\frac{\partial \sigma}{\partial T} + rK\frac{\partial \sigma}{\partial K}\right)}{\left(1 + Kd_1 \sqrt{T}\frac{\partial \sigma}{\partial K}\right)^2 + K^2\sigma T\left(\frac{\partial^2 \sigma}{\partial K^2} - d_1\left(\frac{\partial \sigma}{\partial K}\right)^2 \sqrt{T}\right)}}, \qquad (15.47)$$

with

$$d_1 = \frac{\log(S_0/K) + (r + \frac{1}{2}\sigma^2)T}{\sigma \sqrt{T}}. \qquad (15.48)$$

Equipped with this solution, we can in principle use an interpolated implied volatility surface like the one in Figure 15.3, to compute the local volatility at every desired point. If we evaluate (15.47) at $K = S_t$ and $T = t$, the resulting local volatility can be fed straight into a Monte Carlo algorithm to valuate an arbitrary option contract. Of course the partial derivatives depend on the interpolation scheme we use. But that is not a major problem if there are enough traded options. The ultimate problem is that if we come back next week and again fit the implied and local volatility surface, both have changed. That means pricing contracts with forward starting features, like cliquet options for example, with local volatility methods is not a good idea. But besides that, the local volatility surface is a very useful tool for arbitrage free pricing. Now let's move on to the challenging part of the answer.

   As before, we will assume without loss of generality that pricing is conducted at time $t = 0$. Furthermore, because we are again only interested in volatility, we assume the risk-free interest rate $r = 0$ to obtain the risk-neutral dynamics (15.41) of the underlying. The results are again not affected by this simplification. The ideas explored in the rest of this section are due to Gatheral (2006, chap. 3), and were made completely rigorous by a remark of Keller-Ressel and Teichmann (2009). The first step is to define a so-called "forward starting implied volatility," labeled as

$$\sigma_{\text{imp.}}(t, K, T). \tag{15.49}$$

This is the implied volatility we expect to be fed into the *Black–Scholes*-formula to price a plain vanilla contract correctly at time t. We will again rely exclusively on the European call option and because the risk-free interest rate is zero, we have

$$C_0(K, T) = E^Q[(S_T - K)^+] = E^Q\left[E^Q[(S_T - K)^+|\mathcal{F}_t]\right] = E^Q[C_t(K, T)]. \tag{15.50}$$

The unconditional expectation is of course as always with respect to the information $\mathcal{F}_0$. The final risk-neutral expectation in (15.50) is the predicted *Black–Scholes*-price at time t, containing the forward starting implied volatility $\sigma_{\text{imp.}}(t, K, T)$, based on the information available today at $t = 0$. We can assume that the forward starting implied volatility is a smooth function of t, and thus there has to be another deterministic function

$$\sigma^2(t, K, T) = -\frac{\partial}{\partial t}\left(\sigma_{\text{imp.}}^2(t, K, T) \cdot (T - t)\right). \tag{15.51}$$

From this argument, we can see immediately by rearranging and integrating that

$$\sigma_{\text{imp.}}(K, T) = \sigma_{\text{imp.}}(0, K, T) = \sqrt{\frac{1}{T} \int_0^T \sigma^2(t, K, T) dt}. \tag{15.52}$$

This is in complete analogy to the case of volatility with pure term structure (15.5) on page 327. The truly remarkable fact is that $\sigma^2(t, K, T)$ is also deterministic. We will make considerable efforts to determine this key quantity.

In order to conduct the next step, we need the following observation. In the original *Black–Scholes*-model, there is a neat relation between the vega and the gamma of a European plain vanilla option

$$\frac{\partial V_t}{\partial \sigma} = \sigma(T - t)S_t^2 \frac{\partial^2 V_t}{\partial S^2}. \tag{15.53}$$

We used the function $V_t(K, T)$ for the *Black–Scholes*-price to emphasize that this relation holds for call and put options. In our implied volatility framework, however, $\sigma_{\text{imp.}}(t, K, T)$ has a partial derivative with respect to t and we thus obtain

$$\begin{aligned}
\frac{\partial}{\partial t} C_t(K, T) &= \frac{\partial C_t}{\partial t} + \frac{\partial C_t}{\partial \sigma_{\text{imp.}}} \frac{\partial \sigma_{\text{imp.}}}{\partial t} \\
&= -\frac{1}{2}\sigma_{\text{imp.}}^2(t, K, T)S_t^2 \frac{\partial^2 C_t}{\partial S^2} + \sigma_{\text{imp.}}(t, K, T)(T - t)S_t^2 \frac{\partial^2 C_t}{\partial S^2} \cdot \frac{\partial \sigma_{\text{imp.}}}{\partial t} \\
&= -\frac{1}{2}\sigma^2(t, K, T)S_t^2 \frac{\partial^2 C_t}{\partial S^2}, \tag{15.54}
\end{aligned}$$

where we have used (15.51) in the final step. The first term in the second row is due to the *Black–Scholes*-equation for $r = 0$. On the other hand, applying Itô's lemma, we must have

$$C_T(K, T) - C_0(K, T) = \int_0^T \left(\frac{\partial C_t}{\partial S} dS_t + \frac{\partial C_t}{\partial t} dt + \frac{1}{2}\sigma_{\text{act.}}^2(S_t, t)S_t^2 \frac{\partial^2 C_t}{\partial S^2} dt\right). \tag{15.55}$$

Taking expectations on both sides of (15.55) with respect to the risk-neutral probability measure Q, and interchanging the order of integration yields

$$E^Q[(S_T - K)^+] - C_0(K, T) = \frac{1}{2} \int_0^T E^Q \left[\left(\sigma_{\text{act.}}^2(S_t, t) - \sigma^2(t, K, T) \right) S_t^2 \frac{\partial^2 C_t}{\partial S^2} \right] dt. \quad (15.56)$$

The left hand side of (15.56) obviously vanishes, because the risk-free interest rate is zero. But that means that the integral on the right hand side has to vanish, too. Furthermore, because $E^Q[C_t(K, T)] = C_0(K, T)$, we could have chosen any lower bound of integration $t \leq T$. Therefore, it is clear that the integrand itself has to vanish and we obtain

$$\sigma^2(t, K, T) = \frac{E^Q[\sigma_{\text{act.}}^2(S_t, t) S_t^2 \Gamma(S_t, t)]}{E^Q[S_t^2 \Gamma(S_t, t)]}, \quad (15.57)$$

where we have replaced the second derivative of the call price with respect to the price of the underlying by the *Black–Scholes*-gamma, $\frac{\partial^2 C_t}{\partial S^2} = \Gamma(S_t, t)$. Note that in the special case of a pure term structure $\sigma_{\text{act.}}(S_t, t) = \sigma(t)$, we have

$$\sigma^2(t, K, T) = \frac{\sigma^2(t) E^Q[S_t^2 \Gamma(S_t, t)]}{E^Q[S_t^2 \Gamma(S_t, t)]} = \sigma^2(t). \quad (15.58)$$

It is possible to write (15.57) in a more elegant way. Following Lee (2004), we can define a new family of equivalent probability measures G_t by the *Radon–Nikodym*-derivatives

$$\frac{dG_t}{dQ} = \frac{S_t^2 \Gamma(S_t, t)}{E^Q[S_t^2 \Gamma(S_t, t)]}, \quad (15.59)$$

think of it as of a family of stochastic discount factors, to obtain the representation

$$\sigma^2(t, K, T) = E^Q \left[\frac{dG_t}{dQ} \sigma_{\text{act.}}^2(S_t, t) \right] = E^{G_t}[\sigma_{\text{act.}}^2(S_t, t)]. \quad (15.60)$$

We can thus express the implied volatility as an average expectation value, with respect to the family of probability measures G_t,

$$\sigma_{\text{imp.}}(K, T) = \sqrt{\frac{1}{T} \int_0^T E^{G_t}[\sigma_{\text{act.}}^2(S_t, t)] dt}. \quad (15.61)$$

More precisely, implied variance is the average expected actual variance, with respect to a certain time-dependent probability measure G_t. Although the expression (15.61) is exact, it carries very little intuition about what this average really is.

Let's ask what the conditional probability density function, associated with that mysterious measure family G_t is. From (15.59) it is easy to see that the desired density has to be

$$g(\sigma^2, S, t) = \frac{S^2 \Gamma(S, t) q(\sigma^2, S, t)}{E^Q[S^2 \Gamma(S, t)]}, \tag{15.62}$$

where $q(\sigma^2, S, t)$ is the joint risk-neutral probability density, conditional on $\mathcal{F}_0$. We can apply the same conditioning argument as before to factorize the new density $g(\sigma^2, S, t)$ into $q(\sigma^2|S, t)g(S, t)$, with

$$g(S, t) = \frac{S^2 \Gamma(S, t) q(S, t)}{E^Q[S^2 \Gamma(S, t)]}. \tag{15.63}$$

With this factorization, we can go back and reexpress (15.60) as

$$\sigma^2(t, K, T) = \int_0^\infty E^Q[\sigma^2_{\text{act.}}(S_t, t)|\mathcal{F}_{0 \to S}]g(S, t)dS$$
$$= \int_0^\infty \sigma^2_{\text{loc.}}(S, t)g(S, t)dS. \tag{15.64}$$

In the first equality we have again used the notation $\mathcal{F}_{0 \to S}$ to indicate the information that the joint process originates at $(S_0, \sigma^2_{\text{act.}}(S_0, 0))$, and crosses through $(S, \cdot)$ at time t. For the following steps, it is more convenient to switch to logarithmic prices $x_t = \log S_t$. This is not a difficult task, but we have to relabel our functions, at least with a subscript referring to x. However, to avoid notational overload, we will be a bit sloppy at this point and suppress the subscript. We then obtain

$$\sigma^2(t, K, T) = \int_{-\infty}^\infty \sigma^2_{\text{loc.}}(x, t)g(x, t)dx, \tag{15.65}$$

with

$$g(x, t) = \frac{e^{2x}\Gamma(x, t)q(x, t)}{E^Q[e^{2x}\Gamma(x, t)]}. \tag{15.66}$$

Figure 15.4 shows the density function $g(x, t)$ for a standard European call option with fixed volatility. Obviously it is a kind of bridge density. At $t = 0$, the risk-neutral probability density is a δ-function, concentrated at $x_0 = \log S_0$. At $t = T$, the *Black–Scholes*-gamma becomes a δ-function, concentrated at $x_T = \log K$. Furthermore, the density is nearly perfectly symmetric at every time t. This can be used to expand the local volatility in a clever way. Gatheral (2006, p. 30) suggests to expand around the ridge of the bridge density, which is the most likely path $\hat{x}_t$ of the logarithmic price process under the measure G_t. He argues that local volatility does not vary too rapidly over the relevant region of x_t. Thus, a linear *Taylor*-expansion yields

$$\sigma^2(t, K, T) \approx \sigma^2_{\text{loc.}}(\hat{x}_t, t) + \frac{\partial \sigma^2_{\text{loc.}}}{\partial x}\bigg|_{x=\hat{x}_t} \int_{-\infty}^\infty (x - \hat{x}_t)g(x, t)dx$$
$$= \sigma^2_{\text{loc.}}(\hat{x}_t, t) + \frac{\partial \sigma^2_{\text{loc.}}}{\partial x}\bigg|_{x=\hat{x}_t} E^{G_t}[x_t - \hat{x}_t]$$
$$\approx \sigma^2_{\text{loc.}}(\hat{x}_t, t) \tag{15.67}$$

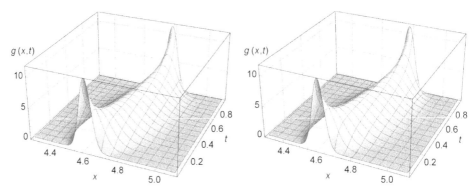

Fig. 15.4 **3D** Bridge density for call option with $S_0 = \$100$, $K = \$120$, $T = 1$ year, $r = 5\%$ and $\sigma = 20\%$

In particular, if we assume that local volatility has negligible curvature at $\hat{x}_t$, the expansion is approximately correct up to third order.

Quick calculation 15.5 Convince yourself that the last argument holds exactly if $g(x, t)$ is symmetric around $\hat{x}_t$.

Using (15.67), we can now express implied volatility in terms of local volatility

$$\sigma_{\text{imp.}}(K, T) \approx \sqrt{\frac{1}{T} \int_0^T \sigma_{\text{loc.}}^2(\hat{x}_t, t)dt}. \qquad (15.68)$$

Thus, implied variance corresponds approximately to the average local variance along the most likely path from $S = S_0$ at $t = 0$, to $S = K$ at $t = T$.

There is one subtle point worth discussing briefly. You might ask yourself what exactly the difference is between a local volatility model with diffusion term $\sigma_{\text{loc.}}(S_t, t)S_t dW_t$ and the more general case with $\sigma_{\text{act.}}(S_t, t)S_t dW_t$? Both volatilities are functions of a random variable, at least so it seems. Local volatility is a deterministic function of S and t, which is supplied with the random price of the underlying S_t at time t. That means, if you know S_t, you need no more information to determine $\sigma_{\text{loc.}}(S_t, t)$. The function $\sigma_{\text{act.}}(S_t, t)$ on the other hand evolves according to the random path of the underlying. It can only be determined if we know the entire path history of S_t, or in other words, we need the full information $\mathcal{F}_t$. Merely given the price S_t at time t, actual volatility generally remains a random variable. A discrete time example for this situation is a GARCH-model. In the next chapter, we will encounter models with stochastic volatility. In this case $\sigma_{\text{act.}}(S_t, t)$ is not only a function of a random variable, but it is a random function itself. Some authors like to express the explicit randomness by writing $\sigma_{\text{act.}}(S_t, t, \omega)$, but since we did not write $S_t(\omega)$ either, we will not do so. The important point is that in this case the volatility at time t cannot be determined by knowing the entire path of S_t. It is indeed not measurable with respect to the information $\mathcal{F}_t$. That is the reason why it is often delicate to handle stochastic volatility models.

15.6   Skew-Based Parametric Representation of the Volatility Surface

In real markets, prices are not observable with arbitrary precision. There are two major obstacles, more or less obvious. The first one is the bid-offer spread and the second one is the fact that securities are not traded in a synchronized way. That is, all prices except the ones just coming in are obsolete. They belong to another volatility surface, prevailing at the particular moment the price was quoted. As a result of this problem Dumas et al. (1998) found that exhausting all pricing information available in a non- or high-parametric way causes overfitting of the volatility surface, and the substantial pricing information is partly lost. Thus, it might be more effective to use a parsimonious parametric model of the volatility surface, and calibrate the few parameters to the available market data. In this section we will discuss the skew-based model suggested by Wilmott (2006c, chap. 50).

Suppose implied volatility is dominated by a nearly linear skew, which is not an unrealistic assumption if the option's time to expiry is not too short. Then a neat model for the implied volatility at $t = 0$ is

$$\sigma_{\text{imp.}}(K, T) = a(T)(K - S_0) + b(T). \tag{15.69}$$

The functions $a(T)$ and $b(T)$ are understood as parameters with a term structure over the different expiry time slices we can observe in the market. Usually, a simple linear interpolation scheme is used to fill the gaps. The information needed to determine $a(T)$ and $b(T)$ is contained in two special positions, an at-the-money straddle and a risk reversal. Let's see how it works.

Recall that the straddle is a long position of one call and one put with identical exercise price and time to expiry, $\Pi_t(K, T) = C_t(K, T) + P_t(K, T)$. The price of such a straddle is observable in the market. Using put-call parity, the price at time $t = 0$ can be expressed exclusively as a function of the call price

$$\Pi_0^{\text{Std}} = 2C_0(K, T) - S_0 + e^{-rT}K. \tag{15.70}$$

Quick calculation 15.6 Confirm this result by using (11.17) on page 215.

After some simple rearrangements we can express the call price in terms of observable quantities

$$C_0(K, T) = \frac{1}{2}\left(\Pi_0^{\text{Std}} + S_0 - e^{-rT}K\right). \tag{15.71}$$

Recall that we are interested in an at-the-money straddle, which means $S_0 = K$. Use the *Black–Scholes*-formula for the call option and divide by S_0 to obtain

$$\Phi(d_1) - e^{-rT}\Phi(d_2) = \frac{1}{2}\left(\frac{\Pi_0^{\text{Std}}}{S_0} + 1 - e^{-rT}\right). \tag{15.72}$$

Because at the money, the implied volatility (15.69) becomes $\sigma_{\text{imp.}}(K, T) = b(T)$, we have

$$d_1 = \frac{(r + \frac{1}{2}b^2(T))\sqrt{T}}{b(T)} \quad \text{and} \quad d_2 = d_1 - b(T)\sqrt{T}. \tag{15.73}$$

We can solve numerically for $b(T)$, because all other quantities in (15.72) are known. If this is done for all available expiry dates T_n, with $n = 1, \ldots, N$, we obtain a term structure $b(T_n)$, and we have gathered half the necessary information to parametrize the implied volatility surface.

The second half of the information comes from a risk reversal. A risk reversal is a long call and short put position entered simultaneously, with identical times to expiry and both options out of the money,

$$\Pi_t(K_1, K_2, T) = C_t(K_2, T) - P_t(K_1, T), \tag{15.74}$$

with $K_1 < S_t < K_2$. If both strikes have the same distance to the current price of the underlying, we can write this position at time $t = 0$ as

$$\Pi_0^{\text{RR}} = C_0(S_0 + \Delta K, T) - P_0(S_0 - \Delta K, T)$$
$$= C_0(S_0 + \Delta K, T) - C_0(S_0 - \Delta K, T) + S_0 - e^{-rT}(S_0 - \Delta K), \tag{15.75}$$

where we have again used put–call parity in the second step. If ΔK is small, and it usually is, we can do a linear *Taylor*-expansion of the call price at the money and obtain

$$\Pi_0^{\text{RR}} - S_0(1 - e^{-rT}) = \Delta K\left(2\frac{\partial C_0}{\partial K}\Big|_{K=S_0} + 2\frac{\partial C_0}{\partial \sigma_{\text{imp.}}}\frac{\partial \sigma_{\text{imp.}}}{\partial K}\Big|_{K=S_0} + e^{-rT}\right)$$
$$= \Delta K\left(e^{-rT}(1 - 2\Phi(d_2)) + 2S_0\sqrt{T}\phi(d_1)a(T)\right), \tag{15.76}$$

with d_1 and d_2 as in (15.73) and as usual $\phi(z) = \frac{1}{\sqrt{2\pi}}e^{-\frac{1}{2}z^2}$. Because $b(T)$ is known from the market price of the straddle, we can solve for $a(T)$ and obtain

$$a(T) = \frac{\Pi_0^{\text{RR}} - S_0(1 - e^{-rT})}{2\Delta K S_0\sqrt{T}\phi(d_1)} - e^{-rT}\frac{1 - 2\Phi(d_2)}{2S_0\sqrt{T}\phi(d_1)}. \tag{15.77}$$

Instead of the whole implied volatility surface, we have now only to interpolate the time-dependent parameters between the different expiry time slices. The choice of an interpolation scheme is highly subjective and there is no correct or optimal method.

In this case most of the time a linear interpolation will be sufficient. We thus obtain for $T_n \leq T < T_{n+1}$

$$a(T) = \lambda(T)a(T_n) + (1 - \lambda(T))a(T_{n+1}), \tag{15.78}$$

with

$$\lambda(T) = \frac{T_{n+1} - T}{T_{n+1} - T_n}. \tag{15.79}$$

Of course the same holds true for $b(T)$ in complete analogy.

The only thing left to do is to write down the partial derivatives that go into the *Dupire*-formula (15.47). With the implied volatility model (15.69) and the definition of $a(T)$ and $b(T)$ we have

$$\frac{\partial \sigma_{\text{imp.}}}{\partial T} = \frac{(a(T_{n+1}) - a(T_n))(K - S_0) + b(T_{n+1}) - b(T_n)}{T_{n+1} - T_n}, \tag{15.80}$$

and

$$\frac{\partial \sigma_{\text{imp.}}}{\partial K} = \frac{a(T_n)(T_{n+1} - T) + a(T_{n+1})(T - T_n)}{T_{n+1} - T_n}, \tag{15.81}$$

for $T_n \leq T < T_{n+1}$. The second partial derivative with respect to K vanishes, $\frac{\partial^2 \sigma_{\text{imp.}}}{\partial K^2} = 0$, due to (15.69).

Quick calculation 15.7 Use (15.78) and (15.79) to confirm the partial derivative $\frac{\partial \sigma_{\text{imp.}}}{\partial K}$.

15.7   *Brown*ian Bridge and GARCH-Parametrization

The *Brown*ian bridge is another important stochastic process in finance. It can be derived from *Brown*ian motion by the following definition

$$B_t = \left(1 - \frac{t}{T}\right)b_0 + W_t - \frac{t}{T}(W_T - b_T), \tag{15.82}$$

where the starting point $B_0 = b_0$ and the endpoint $B_T = b_T$ is fixed, hence the name *Brown*ian bridge. Of course the process requires anticipating knowledge of W_T, but it is otherwise a *Gauss*ian random process between $t = 0$ and $t = T$. Its moments are easily derived from those of the *Brown*ian motion and one obtains

$$E[B_t] = \left(1 - \frac{t}{T}\right)b_0 + \frac{t}{T}b_T \quad \text{and} \quad \text{Var}[B_t] = t - \frac{t^2}{T}. \tag{15.83}$$

Quick calculation 15.8 Use $\text{Cov}[W_s, W_t] = \min(s, t)$ to derive the variance of B_t.

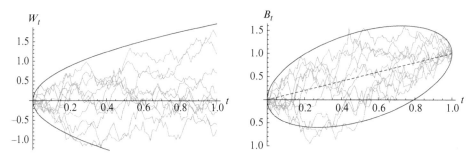

Fig. 15.5 *Brown*ian motion (left) and *Brown*ian bridge (right) with $b_0 = 0$ and $b_1 = 1$

Some simulated paths of a *Brown*ian motion and the corresponding *Brown*ian bridge are illustrated in Figure 15.5. The bridge process is started at $b_0 = 0$ and is forced to end at $b_1 = 1$. Additionally, the 95 % region of the *Gauss*ian path distribution is indicated. It is immediately clear that such a process is a natural candidate if we try to exploit the most likely path relation of local and implied volatility.

The lesson we learned from Duan's GARCH-model for option pricing is that under the local risk-neutral measure, the logarithmic price process $x_t = \log S_t$ has to satisfy

$$x_t = x_{t-1} + r - \frac{1}{2}h_t + \epsilon_t, \tag{15.84}$$

with $\epsilon_t = \sqrt{h_t}z_t$ and $z_t \sim N(0, 1)$. Again, recall that r is the risk-free daily interest rate. For brevity, let's call the logarithmic exercise price $\log K = k$ so that in the GARCH-framework local variance can be written as

$$\sigma_{\text{loc.}}^2(k, T) = E^Q[h_T | \mathcal{F}_{0 \to k}]. \tag{15.85}$$

Our ultimate goal is to compute this expectation value under a bridge process, starting at (x_0, h_0) and terminating at $(k, \cdot)$. To this end, we will give the conditional heteroscedasticity the Q-dynamics

$$h_t = \omega + \alpha(\epsilon_{t-1} - \gamma)^2 + \beta h_{t-1}, \tag{15.86}$$

first proposed by Engle (1990).

Quick calculation 15.9 Can you see why this specification supports volatility clustering and the leverage effect?

The key in engineering a discrete *Brown*ian bridge process is to replace the *Gauss*ian innovation z_t by a conditional *Gauss*ian random variable ζ_t, with

$$E^Q[\zeta_t | \mathcal{F}_{t-1}] = \frac{1}{\sqrt{h_t}}\left(\frac{k - x_{t-1}}{T - (t-1)} - r\right) + \frac{1}{2}\sqrt{h_t}, \tag{15.87}$$

and

$$\text{Var}[\zeta_t] = 1 - \frac{1}{T - (t-1)} = \frac{T-t}{T-(t-1)}. \tag{15.88}$$

Replacing the original random error in (15.84) by $\epsilon_t = \sqrt{h_t}\zeta_t$ generates a bridge process with $E^Q[x_T|\mathcal{F}_0] = k$ and $\text{Var}^Q[x_T|\mathcal{F}_0] = 0$. Let's check that.

As usual, we will call the expectation value with respect to the information $\mathcal{F}_0$ the unconditional expectation and omit the σ-algebra, if there is no potential for confusion. Let's start by computing the unconditional expectation of x_t,

$$E^Q[x_t] = E^Q\left[E^Q[x_t|\mathcal{F}_{t-1}]\right]$$

$$= \frac{1}{T-(t-1)}k + \frac{T-t}{T-(t-1)}E^Q[x_{t-1}]. \tag{15.89}$$

In the first step, we used the law of iterated expectations and in the second step, we plugged the bridge error $\epsilon_t = \sqrt{h_t}\zeta_t$ into (15.84) and used the property (15.87). We have now a recursive formula for the unconditional expectation of x_t. Actually (15.89) is only the first element of the recursive pattern

$$E^Q[x_t] = \frac{n}{T-(t-n)}k + \frac{T-t}{T-(t-n)}E^Q[x_{t-n}], \tag{15.90}$$

for $n \le t$. A proof is straightforward by induction (see Mazzoni, 2015).

Quick calculation 15.10 Confirm this claim by iterating (15.89) once more.

Ultimately, for $n = t$ one obtains after trivial rearrangements

$$E^Q[x_t] = \left(1 - \frac{t}{T}\right)x_0 + \frac{t}{T}k. \tag{15.91}$$

Compare this result to the expectation of the *Brown*ian bridge in (15.83). In particular it is clear that $E^Q[x_T] = k$. But to see that we have really created a bridge process by replacing the innovation z_t by ζ_t, we have to show that the variance of x_T vanishes. To this end, one can use the variance decomposition[3]

$$\text{Var}^Q[x_T] = \text{Var}^Q\left[E^Q[x_T|\mathcal{F}_{T-1}]\right] + E^Q\left[\text{Var}^Q[x_T|\mathcal{F}_{T-1}]\right]$$

$$= \text{Var}^Q[k] + E^Q[h_T \cdot 0] = 0. \tag{15.92}$$

Thus, we have indeed constructed a bridge process and we can emphasize this fact by conditioning on the information $\mathcal{F}_{0 \to k}$.

---

[3] For a random variable X and a σ-algebra $\mathcal{F}_t \supset \mathcal{F}_0$, the relation

$$\text{Var}[X] = \text{Var}[E[X|\mathcal{F}_t]] + E[\text{Var}[X|\mathcal{F}_t]]$$

holds (see for example Greene, 2003, theorem B.4), where unconditional expectations are with respect to $\mathcal{F}_0$.

Our ultimate goal is to determine the expectation $E^Q[h_T|\mathcal{F}_{0\to k}]$, which is the local variance in our GARCH-framework. To accomplish this task it is a useful intermediate step to compute $E^Q[\epsilon_t|\mathcal{F}_{0\to k}]$. From (15.87) we have

$$E^Q[\epsilon_t|\mathcal{F}_{t-1\to k}] = \frac{k - x_{t-1}}{T - (t-1)} - r + \frac{1}{2}h_t. \tag{15.93}$$

Taking conditional expectations with respect to $\mathcal{F}_{0\to k}$ on both sides and using (15.91) yields

$$E^Q[\epsilon_t|\mathcal{F}_{0\to k}] = \frac{k - x_0}{T} - r + \frac{1}{2}E^Q[h_t|\mathcal{F}_{0\to k}]. \tag{15.94}$$

Quick calculation 15.11   Verify the last equation.

Using the GARCH-model (15.86), we are now in a position to compute the expectation of h_t, conditional on $\mathcal{F}_{0\to k}$, which means with respect to the bridge error $\epsilon_t = \sqrt{h_t}\zeta_t$,

$$E^Q[h_t] = \omega + \alpha E^Q\left[(\epsilon_{t-1} - \gamma)^2\right] + \beta E^Q[h_{t-1}]$$

$$= \omega + \alpha \mathrm{Var}^Q[\epsilon_{t-1}] + \alpha\left(E^Q[\epsilon_{t-1}] - \gamma\right)^2 + \beta E^Q[h_{t-1}]. \tag{15.95}$$

The conditioning argument was omitted to simplify the notation. We have further used the old trick $\mathrm{Var}[X] = E[X^2] - E[X]^2$. It is not easy to compute the variance term in (15.95), but we can expect the variance of the conditional expectation (15.93) to be negligible compared to the variance of ϵ_t itself for most $t < T$. Therefore, again using the variance decomposition, we obtain approximately

$$\mathrm{Var}^Q[\epsilon_t] \approx E^Q\left[\mathrm{Var}^Q[\epsilon_t|\mathcal{F}_{t-1\to k}]\right] = E^Q[h_t\mathrm{Var}[\zeta_t]]$$

$$= E^Q[h_t]\frac{T-t}{T-(t-1)} \approx E^Q[h_t]. \tag{15.96}$$

That is, for most $t < T$, the relation between the variance of ϵ_t and the expectation of h_t is approximately the same as in the unbridged case, especially if T is large. We can now start to put the pieces together. Using (15.94) and (15.96), we can reexpress (15.95) as

$$E^Q[h_t] = \omega + \alpha E^Q[h_{t-1}] + \alpha\left(\eta + \frac{1}{2}E^Q[h_{t-1}]\right)^2 + \beta E^Q[h_{t-1}], \tag{15.97}$$

where the quantity $\eta = \frac{k-x_0}{T} - (r + \gamma)$ was introduced, and still all expectations are with respect to the information $\mathcal{F}_{0\to k}$. If we neglect terms of order $O(h_t^2)$ and their expectation, respectively, we obtain the recursive expression

$$E^Q[h_t|\mathcal{F}_{0\to k}] = a + bE^Q[h_{t-1}|\mathcal{F}_{0\to k}], \tag{15.98}$$

with $a = \omega + \alpha\eta^2$ and $b = \alpha(1 + \eta) + \beta$. This expression can be easily iterated backwards and for $t = T$ one obtains

$$E^Q[h_T|\mathcal{F}_{0\to k}] = a\sum_{t=0}^{T-1} b^t + b^T h_0. \tag{15.99}$$

Local volatility in the GARCH-framework is the square root of this expression, where we can additionally use the geometric series representation to simplify the sum on the right hand side

$$\sigma_{\text{loc.}}(k, T) = \sqrt{a \cdot \frac{1 - b^T}{1 - b} + b^T h_0}, \tag{15.100}$$

with

$$a = \omega + \alpha \eta^2, \quad b = \alpha(1 + \eta) + \beta, \quad \text{and} \quad \eta = \frac{k - x_0}{T} - (r + \gamma). \tag{15.101}$$

This expression makes perfect sense if we analyze the limits. For the short term, we have

$$\lim_{T \to 0} \sigma_{\text{loc.}}^2(k, T) = \begin{cases} h_0 & \text{for } k = x_0 \\ \infty & \text{for } k \neq x_0. \end{cases} \tag{15.102}$$

For $|b| < 1$, local volatility is flat in the limit $T \to \infty$, which means, it does not depend on k anymore.

To calibrate this simple model for local volatility to an observed implied volatility surface, we can use Gatheral's most likely path approximation. Assume that the most likely path is roughly a straight line in the (x, t)-plane. This is usually a very reasonable approximation and implied variance becomes

$$\sigma_{\text{imp.}}^2(k, T) = \frac{1}{T} \int_0^T \sigma_{\text{loc.}}^2 \left(\left(1 - \frac{t}{T}\right) x_0 + \frac{t}{T} k, t \right) dt. \tag{15.103}$$

Translating this idea into our GARCH-framework, the straight line approximation leads to the relation

$$\sigma_{\text{imp.}}^2(k, T) = \frac{1}{T + 1} \sum_{t=0}^T \sigma_{\text{loc.}}^2 \left(\left(1 - \frac{t}{T}\right) x_0 + \frac{t}{T} k, t \right). \tag{15.104}$$

Observe two important points. First, the quantity η, as defined in (15.101), is the only component directly depending on k. Second, η as a function of k and T is invariant under the transformation

$$(k, T) \longrightarrow \left(\left(1 - \frac{t}{T}\right) x_0 + \frac{t}{T} k, t \right). \tag{15.105}$$

Quick calculation 15.12 Prove this statement.

Using this fact and the definition of local volatility (15.100), implied variance can be written as

$$
\begin{aligned}
\sigma_{\text{imp.}}^2(k, T) &= \frac{1}{T+1} \sum_{t=0}^{T} a \cdot \frac{1 - b^t}{1 - b} + b^t h_0 \\
&= \frac{a}{1 - b} + \frac{1}{T+1} \left(h_0 - \frac{a}{1 - b} \right) \sum_{t=0}^{T} b^t,
\end{aligned}
\tag{15.106}
$$

with a, b, and η precisely as in (15.101). We can again use the geometric series formula to obtain the implied volatility in a closed form

$$
\sigma_{\text{imp.}}(k, T) = \sqrt{\frac{a}{1 - b} + \frac{1}{T+1} \left(h_0 - \frac{a}{1 - b} \right) \frac{1 - b^{T+1}}{1 - b}},
\tag{15.107}
$$

where a, b, and η are again defined as in (15.101). Note that the same consistency argument as before applies here. In the limits $T \to 0$ and $T \to \infty$, implied and local volatility coincide. The only caveat is again that the parameters of the GARCH-model are scaled with respect to daily trading frequencies, whereas naturally, interest rates, volatilities, and times to expiry are given in years. To synchronize both model frameworks, we assume again that one year has 252 trading days and thus, the converted formulas are

$$
\sigma_{\text{loc.}}(K, T) = \sqrt{252 \left(a \cdot \frac{1 - b^{252T}}{1 - b} + b^{252T} h_0 \right)}
\tag{15.108}
$$

$$
\sigma_{\text{imp.}}(K, T) = \sqrt{\frac{252a}{1 - b} + \frac{1}{T + 1/252} \left(h_0 - \frac{a}{1 - b} \right) \frac{1 - b^{252T+1}}{1 - b}},
\tag{15.109}
$$

with

$$
a = \omega + \alpha \eta^2, \quad b = \alpha(1 + \eta) + \beta, \quad \text{and} \quad \eta = \frac{\log(K/S_0)}{252T} - \left(\frac{r}{252} + \gamma \right).
\tag{15.110}
$$

Because implied volatility is completely explicit, it is extraordinarily easy to fit the model to observed market data. Figure 15.6 shows the implied volatility surface calibrated to the DAX data we used earlier. Compare this surface to the non-parametrically interpolated surface in Figure 15.3 on page 335. All key features, like the decaying short-term smile and the long-term skew, are present. Furthermore, once the implied volatility surface is calibrated, one has immediate and explicit access to local volatility without using a complex formula, involving certain derivatives of the implied volatility.

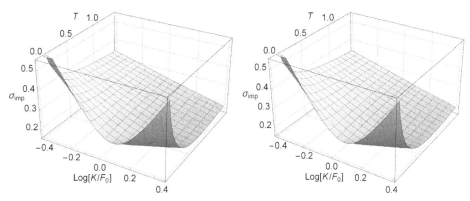

Fig. 15.6 **3D** GARCH-parametrized implied volatility surface based on DAX data of mid-July 2012

15.8 Further Reading

For many concepts introduced in this chapter, the book of Jim Gatheral (2006) is an indispensable source. A compressed analysis of Dupire's work can be found in Ekstrand (2011, chap. 6). A very accessible introduction to deterministic volatility is Wilmott (2006c, chap. 50) and Hull (2012, chap. 10). For GARCH-models see the original work of Engle (1982) and Bollerslev (1986). A well written introduction is Engle (2001). For a technical treatment with multivariate extensions see McNeil et al. (2005, sect. 4.3 & 4.6). The skew-based parametrization of the volatility surface was introduced in Wilmott (2006c, sect. 50.7–50.11).

15.9 Problems

15.1 Assume that actual variance has the mean reverting term structure

$$\frac{d\sigma^2(t)}{dt} = \lambda(\sigma_\infty^2 - \sigma^2(t)),$$

where σ_∞^2 is the stationary variance and $\sigma^2(0) = \sigma_0^2$. What is the implied volatility of an option at time $t = 0$?

15.2 The solution to Problem 15.1 is

$$\sigma_{\text{imp.}}(T) = \sqrt{\sigma_\infty^2 + \frac{1 - e^{-\lambda T}}{\lambda T}(\sigma_0^2 - \sigma_\infty^2)}.$$

Show that this result is consistent in the limit $T \to \infty$ and $T \to 0$.

15.3 Show that the kurtosis in an ordinary GARCH(1,1)-model is

$$K = 3\frac{1 - (\alpha + \beta)^2}{1 - 2\alpha^2 - (\alpha + \beta)^2}.$$

15.4 The *Duan*-model is a modified version of the GARCH-in-mean specification

$$\Delta x_t = \mu + \lambda h_t + \epsilon_t,$$

where again $\epsilon_t = \sqrt{h_t}z_t$, and $z_t \sim N(0, 1)$. Show that under the asymmetric variance dynamics

$$h_t = \omega + \alpha(\epsilon_{t-1} - \gamma)^2 + \beta h_{t-1},$$

the logarithmic return process Δx_t does not constitute a noise process, which means $\mathrm{Cov}[\Delta x_{t+1}, \epsilon_t] \neq 0$.

15.5 The *Heston–Nandi*-model for option pricing (Heston and Nandi, 1997, 2000) is specified as

$$\Delta x_t = r + \lambda h_t + \sqrt{h_t}z_t$$

$$h_t = \omega + \alpha\left(z_{t-1} - \gamma \sqrt{h_{t-1}}\right)^2 + \beta h_{t-1},$$

where z_t is again independent and identically standard normally distributed. In going from probability measure P to Q, the model can be written in unchanged algebraic form but with the substitutions $\lambda \to \lambda^Q$, $z_t \to z_t^Q$, and $\gamma \to \gamma^Q$. What are the modified quantities λ^Q, z_t^Q, and γ^Q?

16 Stochastic Volatility

Stochastic volatility is the door to incomplete market architectures. In such a framework, the fair price of a derivative can no longer be determined uniquely by hedging arguments or switching to a unique equivalent martingale measure. The more realistic properties of stochastic volatility models come at a price. The volatility risk premium has to be determined by calibration, and more sophisticated tools like characteristic functions and the generalized *Fourier*-transform are required.

16.1 The Consequence of Stochastic Volatility

One of the most obvious problems with volatility is that we cannot really specify what it is on a fundamental level. Is it the square root of the average quadratic deviation from the mean? Or is it the magnitude of the range in which say 95% of the logarithmic returns are observed? On the other hand we can clearly say what it is not. It is not a traded security, and hence the generic name incomplete market models, even though this class is much broader. Despite those fundamental concerns, we can take a technical perspective and ask: How can our stochastic model for the price process of the underlying be extended to allow for randomly changing volatility? The answer is by introducing another stochastic process, linked to our original model. A fairly general formulation of such a joint process is

$$dS_t = \mu S_t dt + \sigma_t S_t dW_{1,t} \tag{16.1}$$

$$d\sigma_t = f(S_t, \sigma_t, t)dt + g(S_t, \sigma_t, t)dW_{2,t}, \tag{16.2}$$

where $f(S, \sigma, t)$ and $g(S, \sigma, t)$ are sufficiently smooth functions, not specified yet, and the covariance between the *Wiener*-processes is $\mathrm{Cov}[dW_1, dW_2] = E[dW_1 dW_2] = \rho dt$. Thinking in terms of partial differential equations, any derivative contract is now a function of two spatial variables, $V(S, \sigma, t)$, and Itô's lemma yields the differential

$$dV = \frac{\partial V}{\partial S}dS + \frac{\partial V}{\partial \sigma}d\sigma + \frac{\partial V}{\partial t}dt + \frac{1}{2}\left(\sigma^2 S^2 \frac{\partial^2 V}{\partial S^2} + 2\rho\sigma Sg\frac{\partial^2 V}{\partial S\partial \sigma} + g^2\frac{\partial^2 V}{\partial \sigma^2}\right)dt, \tag{16.3}$$

where the arguments of the function $g(S, \sigma, t)$ were omitted for brevity. The only new element in the *Itô–Taylor*-expansion is the covariance term, resulting from the fact that

$\mathrm{Var}[dW_1 dW_2]$ is of order dt^2. Hence, we can add the heuristic rule $dW_1 dW_2 = \rho dt$ to our informal list for applying Itô's lemma.

If we try to set up a hedge-portfolio, we immediately run into trouble. Because we have two sources of randomness, it is not sufficient to only hedge with the underlying. We need at least one auxiliary contract, contingent on the same underlying, to establish the required portfolio. Assume for the moment that such an auxiliary contract exists and call it $V_a(S, \sigma, t)$. Then our hedge-portfolio has the form

$$\Pi = V - \Delta_1 S - \Delta_2 V_a. \tag{16.4}$$

We have now to follow the usual routine, which means applying Itô's lemma, choosing the hedge-ratios for Δ_1 and Δ_2 properly to eliminate the risk, and equating the resulting differential to the risk-free growth rate of Π. This is a very messy but straightforward computation and the details can be found in Wilmott (2006c, sect. 51.4). The result is that we end up with the equation

$$\frac{\frac{\partial V}{\partial t} + rS\frac{\partial V}{\partial S} + \frac{1}{2}\sigma^2 S^2 \frac{\partial^2 V}{\partial S^2} + \rho\sigma Sg\frac{\partial^2 V}{\partial S \partial \sigma} + \frac{1}{2}g^2\frac{\partial^2 V}{\partial \sigma^2} - rV}{\frac{\partial V}{\partial \sigma}}$$
$$= \frac{\frac{\partial V_a}{\partial t} + rS\frac{\partial V_a}{\partial S} + \frac{1}{2}\sigma^2 S^2 \frac{\partial^2 V_a}{\partial S^2} + \rho\sigma Sg\frac{\partial^2 V_a}{\partial S \partial \sigma} + \frac{1}{2}g^2\frac{\partial^2 V_a}{\partial \sigma^2} - rV_a}{\frac{\partial V_a}{\partial \sigma}}. \tag{16.5}$$

This looks horrible, but the good news is that the left hand side is only a function of V and the right hand side exclusively depends on V_a. Because both contracts have different nonlinear payoffs, we can conclude that each side of the equation separately has to be equal to an unknown function $h(S, \sigma, t)$. For reasons that become clear shortly, it is more convenient to reexpress this function in terms of a linear combination of f, g, and another unknown function λ, $h = \lambda g - f$. We then finally obtain the *Merton–Garman*-equation

$$\frac{\partial V}{\partial t} + rS\frac{\partial V}{\partial S} + (f - \lambda g)\frac{\partial V}{\partial \sigma} + \frac{1}{2}\sigma^2 S^2 \frac{\partial^2 V}{\partial S^2} + \rho\sigma Sg\frac{\partial^2 V}{\partial S \partial \sigma} + \frac{1}{2}g^2\frac{\partial^2 V}{\partial \sigma^2} - rV = 0. \tag{16.6}$$

The unknown function $\lambda(S, \sigma, t)$ is called the market price of volatility risk. What does that mean exactly? Suppose, we indeed build a hedge-portfolio, based only on a position in the option and a short position in the underlying

$$\Pi = V - \Delta S. \tag{16.7}$$

Applying Itô's lemma, we would obtain

$$d\Pi = \left(\frac{\partial V}{\partial t} + \frac{1}{2}\sigma^2 S^2 \frac{\partial^2 V}{\partial S^2} + \rho\sigma Sg\frac{\partial^2 V}{\partial S \partial \sigma} + \frac{1}{2}g^2\frac{\partial^2 V}{\partial \sigma^2}\right)dt$$
$$+ \left(\frac{\partial V}{\partial S} - \Delta\right)dS + \frac{\partial V}{\partial \sigma}d\sigma. \tag{16.8}$$

We can hedge the market risk away by choosing $\Delta = \frac{\partial V}{\partial S}$, but the volatility risk remains. Computing the difference between the stochastic differential of the portfolio and the

Table 16.1 Popular stochastic volatility models

Model	Variable	Drift f	Diffusion g
Hull and White (1987)	$v = \sigma^2$	$f(v) = \theta v$	$g(v) = \alpha v$
Scott (1987)	$y = \log \sigma$	$f(y) = \kappa(\theta - y)$	$g = \alpha$
Stein and Stein (1991)	σ	$f(\sigma) = \kappa(\theta - \sigma)$	$g = \alpha$
Heston (1993)	$v = \sigma^2$	$f(v) = \kappa(\theta - v)$	$g(v) = \alpha \sqrt{v}$
Hagan et al. (2002)	σ	$f = 0$	$g(\sigma) = \alpha \sigma$

risk-free growth rate yields

$$
\begin{aligned}
d\Pi - r\Pi dt &= \left(\frac{\partial V}{\partial t} + rS\frac{\partial V}{\partial S} + f\frac{\partial V}{\partial \sigma} + \frac{1}{2}\sigma^2 S^2 \frac{\partial^2 V}{\partial S^2} + \rho \sigma S g \frac{\partial^2 V}{\partial S \partial \sigma} \right. \\
&\quad \left. + \frac{1}{2}g^2 \frac{\partial^2 V}{\partial \sigma^2} - rV \right) dt + g\frac{\partial V}{\partial \sigma} dW_2 \\
&= g\frac{\partial V}{\partial \sigma}(\lambda dt + dW_2),
\end{aligned}
\tag{16.9}
$$

where we used (16.2) and (16.6). The presence of one unit of volatility risk dW_2 is compensated by an extra return λdt, hence the name market price of volatility risk.

Of course a model in its full generality is not tractable. Thus, the functions f and g have to be specified in a reasonable way, to obtain a suitable model for derivative pricing. It is also possible to model the dynamics of the variance or another nonnegative quantity, instead of volatility. Table 16.1 reviews a small collection of popular stochastic volatility models. Probably the most prominent one is the *Heston*-model, which we will analyze in great detail shortly.

16.2   Characteristic Functions and the Generalized *Fourier*-Transform

We have already learned that characteristic functions are very useful when adding independent random variables. In order to proceed, it is helpful to develop a deeper understanding of the concept of characteristic functions. From the definition

$$
\varphi(u) = E[e^{iuX}] = \int_{-\infty}^{\infty} e^{iux} f(x) dx,
\tag{16.10}
$$

we can see that there is a one-to-one correspondence between the characteristic function and the probability density function of an arbitrary random variable X, provided that the density exists. The integral on the right hand side of (16.10) is also the *Fourier*-transform of the probability density $f(x)$, as mentioned earlier. Let's now open another door, by applying the *Euler*-identity[1]

$$
e^{iuX} = \cos(uX) + i\sin(uX).
\tag{16.11}
$$

---

[1] In case you are not familiar with complex analysis, a brief introduction is provided in Appendix A.

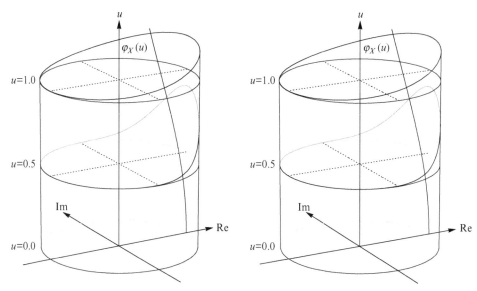

Fig. 16.1 **3D** Characteristic function $\varphi_X(u)$ of $X \sim N(0, 1)$ and distribution of uX, wrapped around the complex unit circle for different u

For any given u, the random variable X is mapped onto the complex unit circle. This fact was used by Epps (1993) to give the characteristic function a geometric meaning. We can see clearly from (16.11) that the distribution of the scaled random variable uX is wrapped around the perimeter of the complex unit circle, and hence the characteristic function is the center of mass of the corresponding "probability density coil"; see Figure 16.1, based on the illustration of Epps (1993, p. 34). It is always bounded, because it is confined to the infinite complex tube with radius one. If the characteristic function itself is absolutely integrable from $u = -\infty$ to $u = \infty$, then the corresponding probability distribution $F(x)$ is absolutely continuous and has a density function $f(x)$. Furthermore, from the trigonometric representation (16.11), we can immediately conclude that

$$\varphi(-u) = \varphi^*(u), \tag{16.12}$$

where $\varphi^*(u)$ is the complex conjugate of the characteristic function.

Quick calculation 16.1 Convince yourself that this statement is true by recalling that cosine is an even function and sine is odd.

An equally important result in applying characteristic functions is the *Fourier-inversion-theorem*. It ensures that the original probability density can be recovered by the inverse transformation

$$f(x) = \frac{1}{2\pi} \int_{-\infty}^{\infty} e^{-iux} \varphi(u) du. \tag{16.13}$$

Now you should be able to see, why absolute integrability of $\varphi(u)$ is a necessary condition for the probability density function to exist. Most of the time we have to compute such integrals numerically. Although we will discuss that issue at a later time, it is nice to derive a better suited representation. Once again, recall the *Euler*-identity (16.11) to realize that the real part of the characteristic function is

$$\text{Re}[\varphi(u)] = \frac{\varphi(u) + \varphi^*(u)}{2}. \tag{16.14}$$

Quick calculation 16.2 Confirm that also $\text{Im}[\varphi(u)] = \frac{\varphi(u)-\varphi^*(u)}{2i}$ holds.

The same holds true of course for e^{iux} itself. Let's now split the inversion integral in (16.13) and use (16.14) to obtain

$$
\begin{aligned}
f(x) &= \frac{1}{2\pi} \int_{-\infty}^{0} e^{-iux} \varphi(u) du + \frac{1}{2\pi} \int_{0}^{\infty} e^{-iux} \varphi(u) du \\
&= \frac{1}{2\pi} \int_{0}^{\infty} e^{iux} \varphi^*(u) du + \frac{1}{2\pi} \int_{0}^{\infty} e^{-iux} \varphi(u) du \\
&= \frac{1}{\pi} \int_{0}^{\infty} \frac{(e^{-iux}\varphi(u))^* + e^{-iux}\varphi(u)}{2} du \\
&= \frac{1}{\pi} \int_{0}^{\infty} \text{Re}\left[e^{-iux}\varphi(u) \right] du.
\end{aligned}
\tag{16.15}
$$

As we will see, this is a far more convenient form for the application of numerical integration schemes.

The generalized *Fourier*-transform, sometimes also called the fundamental transform, uses the complex number z, instead of the real number u, as variable. We thus obtain the generalized characteristic function

$$\varphi(z) = E[e^{izX}] = \int_{-\infty}^{\infty} e^{izx} f(x) dx, \quad z \in S. \tag{16.16}$$

This formula needs some comment. First of all, the generalized characteristic function does not necessarily exist in the entire complex plane. But there is always a so-called strip of regularity S, where it does. A complex function is called regular, if it is single valued and analytic. This is guaranteed by a theorem of Lukacs (1970, theorem 7.1.1), also found in Lewis (2001).

Theorem 16.1 (Strip of regularity) *If a characteristic function $\varphi(z)$ with $z \in \mathbb{C}$ is regular in the neighborhood of $z = 0$, then it is also regular in a horizontal strip S and can be represented in this strip by a Fourier-integral. This strip is either the whole z-plane, or it has one or two horizontal boundary lines. The purely imaginary points on the boundary of the strip of regularity (if this strip is not the whole plane) are singular points of $\varphi(z)$.*

The statement of Theorem 16.1 is fairly general and applies to arbitrary distributions. In particular, we have $\varphi(0) = 1$, because every probability density function has to be normalized.

Quick calculation 16.3 Confirm the last statement with the help of (16.16).

In derivative pricing, we have an additional condition because of the martingale pricing relation. Assume that the stochastic process Y_t is the purely nonsystematic part of the return, and

$$\varphi_s(z) = E^Q[e^{izY_t}|\mathcal{F}_s] \tag{16.17}$$

for $s \leq t$ is its generalized conditional characteristic function under the risk-neutral measure Q. We can then write the price process of the underlying as

$$S_t = S_0 e^{bt + Y_t} = S_0 e^{bt} e^{Y_t}, \tag{16.18}$$

where b is the generalized cost-of-carry rate. Clearly Y_t has to be a Q-martingale with $E^Q[e^{Y_t}] = 1$. But this also means $\varphi_0(-i) = 1$. This gives us a necessary condition for an appropriate return process under the risk-neutral measure Q. A "good" process Y_t satisfies $Y_0 = 0$ and generates a risk-neutral probability density $q_Y(y, t)$, whose conditional characteristic function $\varphi_0(z)$ exists within a strip of regularity $S_Y = \{z = u + iv : v \in (\alpha, \beta)\}$, with $\alpha < -1$ and $\beta > 0$.

The generalized inverse *Fourier*-transform is similar to the ordinary inversion formula (16.13), but the integration is conducted along an arbitrary straight line parallel to the real axis, within the strip of regularity

$$f(x) = \frac{1}{2\pi} \int_{iv-\infty}^{iv+\infty} e^{-izx} \varphi(z) dz, \quad z \in S. \tag{16.19}$$

In most cases, properties of the ordinary *Fourier*-transform also hold for the generalized transform, without any modification.

16.3   The Pricing Formula in *Fourier*-Space

It is not really necessary to use a generalized version of the *Fourier*-transform to obtain a pricing formula in *Fourier*-space; see for example the methods proposed by Heston (1993) or Carr and Madan (1999). But we will follow here the very elegant idea of Lewis (2000), which is modular in a certain sense, because it separates the payoff function and the conditional pricing density. Key to this approach is a theorem that can be found in Lewis (2001, theorem 3.2):

Theorem 16.2 (Option Valuation) *Let $V_0(K, T)$ be the current price of a European-style option with payoff function $V(e^x, \sigma, T) = w(x)$, where $x_t = \log S_t$ is the logarithmic price of the underlying. Assume that $w(x)$ is Fourier-integrable in a strip S_w and bounded for $|x| < \infty$. Let $S_t = S_0 e^{bt + Y_t}$, where e^{Y_t} is a Q-martingale, and assume that Y_T has the analytic* *conditional characteristic function $\varphi_0(z)$, regular in the strip $S_Y = \{z = u + iv : v \in (\alpha, \beta)\}$, where $\alpha < -1$ and $\beta > 0$. If $S_V = S_w \cap S_Y^*$ is not empty, then the option value at time $t = 0$ is given by*

$$V_0(K, T) = \frac{e^{-rT}}{2\pi} \int_{iv-\infty}^{iv+\infty} e^{-iz(\log S_0 + bT)} \varphi_0(-z) \hat{w}(z) dz, \quad z \in S_V = S_w \cap S_Y^*.$$

Moreover, S_V is not empty for the payoff function of a call or put option.

Let's see if we can understand how this formula arises. First of all, we have again adopted the hat notation $\hat{w}(z)$, to indicate the generalized *Fourier*-transform of $w(x)$. Next, from the martingale pricing principle, we know that

$$
\begin{aligned}
V_0(K, T) &= e^{-rT} E^Q[w(x_T)] \\
&= \frac{e^{-rT}}{2\pi} E^Q\left[\int_{iv-\infty}^{iv+\infty} e^{-izx_T} \hat{w}(z) dz \right] \qquad (16.20) \\
&= \frac{e^{-rT}}{2\pi} E^Q\left[\int_{iv-\infty}^{iv+\infty} e^{-iz(\log S_0 + bT)} e^{-iz Y_T} \hat{w}(z) dz \right], \quad z \in S_w.
\end{aligned}
$$

As always, the risk-neutral expectation is conditional on $\mathcal{F}_0$. The next step is to bring the expectation inside the integral, which is only a valid operation, if we can ensure that $E^Q[e^{-iz Y_T}] = \varphi_0(-z)$ exists. This is the case, if $z \in S_Y^*$, but z is already confined to the strip S_w. Hence, the integrand exists and is regular if $z \in S_V = S_w \cap S_Y^*$, with $S_Y^* = \{z = u + iv : v \in (\alpha, \beta)\}$, where now $\alpha < 0$ and $\beta > 1$. We thus obtain the result in Theorem 16.2. Observe that even though the strip condition contains the conjugate strip S_Y^*, $\varphi(-z)$ is not the complex conjugate of the characteristic function $\varphi(z)$, but close to it.

Quick calculation 16.4 Use Euler's identity to show that $\varphi^*(z) = \varphi(-z^*)$ holds.

We still have to verify that the strip S_V is not empty for call and put option payoffs. To this end, let's see what the generalized transforms of these functions are and in which strip they are regular. Start with the call payoff,

$$
\begin{aligned}
\hat{w}(z) &= \int_{-\infty}^{\infty} e^{izx}(e^x - K)^+ dx \\
&= \int_{\log K}^{\infty} e^{izx}(e^x - K) dx \qquad (16.21) \\
&= \left[\frac{e^{(iz+1)x}}{iz + 1} - K\frac{e^{izx}}{iz} \right]_{x=\log K}^{x=\infty}.
\end{aligned}
$$

It is not hard to see that the upper limit only exists, if $\text{Im}[z] > 1$. In this case both exponentials vanish at $x = \infty$ and the result is

$$\hat{w}(z) = -\frac{K^{iz+1}}{z^2 - iz}, \quad z \in S_w, \qquad (16.22)$$

with $S_w = \{z = u + iv : v > 1\}$.

Table 16.2 Standard payoff functions

Financial Claim	Payoff $w(x)$	Transform $\hat{w}(z)$	Regular Strip S_w
Call	$(e^x - K)^+$	$-\dfrac{K^{iz+1}}{z^2 - iz}$	$\text{Im}[z] > 1$
Put	$(K - e^x)^+$	$-\dfrac{K^{iz+1}}{z^2 - iz}$	$\text{Im}[z] < 0$
Binary Call	$\theta(e^x - K)$	$-\dfrac{K^{iz}}{iz}$	$\text{Im}[z] > 0$
Binary Put	$\theta(K - e^x)$	$\dfrac{K^{iz}}{iz}$	$\text{Im}[z] < 0$
Covered Call	$\min(e^x, K)$	$\dfrac{K^{iz+1}}{z^2 - iz}$	$0 < \text{Im}[z] < 1$
Arrow–Debreu	$\delta(e^x - K)$	K^{iz}	entire z-plane

Quick calculation 16.5 Confirm that the payoff transform of a put is regular for $v < 0$.

Interestingly, but not completely surprisingly, the transformed payoff (16.22) is also the result for the put option, but now the strip of regularity is $S_w = \{z = u + iv : v < 0\}$. Both strips intersect the conjugate strip S_Y^* in Theorem 16.2, and thus S_V is not empty. Table 16.2 contains a small collection of transformed payoff functions and their associated strips of regularity.

The formula provided in Theorem 16.2 is not yet an explicit pricing equation, but more a blueprint for the construction of such an equation. Because calibrating a stochastic volatility model is usually done with plain vanilla European call and put options, we will derive the explicit formulas for those contracts. Plugging the call payoff transform (16.22) into the general formula of Theorem 16.2, one obtains

$$C_0(K, T) = -\frac{e^{-rT}K}{2\pi} \int_{iv_0 - \infty}^{iv_0 + \infty} \frac{e^{-izk}\varphi_0(-z)}{z^2 - iz}\,dz, \quad v_0 \in (1, \beta), \tag{16.23}$$

where $k = \log(S_0/K) + bT$ is the forward log-moneyness. The integral in (16.23) is guaranteed to exist, because $S_V = S_w \cap S_Y^* = \{z = u + iv_0 : v_0 \in (1, \beta)\}$ is not empty as long as $\beta > 1$. It is indeed easy to see that the integrand

$$f(z) = \frac{e^{-izk}\varphi_0(-z)}{z(z - i)} \tag{16.24}$$

is regular in the entire strip S_Y^* with exception of the two simple poles at $z = 0$ and $z = i$. Thus, it might be a clever idea to shift the integration contour to $0 < v_1 < 1$, because every appropriate characteristic function has to be regular in this strip. Let $I(v_0)$ be the integral in (16.23). Then we know from Cauchy's residue theorem (Theorem A.4 on page 522) that

$$I(v_1) - I(v_0) = 2\pi i \operatorname*{Res}_{z=i} f. \tag{16.25}$$

This conclusion needs some comment. The situation is illustrated in Figure 16.2. The minus sign results from the counterclockwise orientation of the closed curve. The

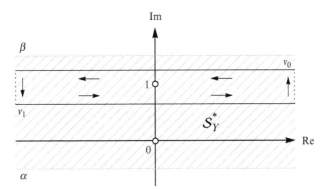

Fig. 16.2 Strip of regularity S^*_Y and simple poles at $z = 0$ and $z = i$ – The integral along the closed curve can be computed with the residue theorem

contributions from the legs at $u = \pm\infty$ are zero and hence, the left hand side of (16.25) contains all correctly oriented contributions to the closed loop. To find the residue at $z = i$, define the function

$$g_1(z) = (z - i)f(z) = \frac{e^{-izk}\varphi_0(-z)}{z}, \tag{16.26}$$

and evaluate it at $z = i$,

$$\operatorname*{Res}_{z=i} f = g_1(i) = \frac{e^k}{i}, \tag{16.27}$$

where again $k = \log(S_0/K) + bT$. Because of the martingale condition under the pricing measure, $\varphi_0(-i) = 1$ holds. Combining (16.23), (16.25), and (16.27), one obtains

$$C_0(K, T) = e^{(b-r)T}S_0 - \frac{e^{-rT}K}{2\pi} \int_{iv_1-\infty}^{iv_1+\infty} \frac{e^{-izk}\varphi_0(-z)}{z^2 - iz}dz, \quad v_1 \in (0, 1). \tag{16.28}$$

This is our preferred integration contour, because we can choose freely a value in the range $0 < v_1 < 1$, without bothering about particular boundaries for different characteristic functions. To make this pricing formula concrete, choose for example $v_1 = \frac{1}{2}$ and make the substitution $z = u + \frac{i}{2}$ to obtain

$$
\begin{aligned}
C_0(K, T) &= e^{(b-r)T}S_0 - \frac{e^{(\frac{b}{2}-r)T}\sqrt{S_0 K}}{2\pi} \int_{-\infty}^{\infty} \frac{e^{-iuk}\varphi_0(-u - \frac{i}{2})}{u^2 + \frac{1}{4}}du \\
&= e^{(b-r)T}S_0 - \frac{e^{(\frac{b}{2}-r)T}\sqrt{S_0 K}}{\pi} \int_0^{\infty} \frac{\operatorname{Re}\left[e^{iuk}\varphi_0(u - \frac{i}{2})\right]}{u^2 + \frac{1}{4}}du.
\end{aligned}
\tag{16.29}
$$

Inside the real part in the second row of (16.29), we have changed the sign of u. That does not change the result, as long as we flip signs in both the phase factor and the characteristic function.

Quick calculation 16.6 Use the fact that $\varphi(z^*) = \varphi^*(-z)$ to convince yourself that this statement is true.

The integral in (16.29) converges more rapidly than a plain *Fourier*-integral, because of the u^2-term in the denominator.

There is another surprising twist. Imagine, we shift the integration contour to $v_2 \in (\alpha, 0)$. In doing so, we pick up an additional residue at $z = 0$. To compute this one, define the function

$$g_2(z) = zf(z) = \frac{e^{-izk}\varphi_0(-z)}{z - i}, \tag{16.30}$$

and evaluate it at $z = 0$,

$$\operatorname*{Res}_{z=0} f = g_2(0) = -\frac{1}{i}. \tag{16.31}$$

By an argument, completely analogous to the one illustrated in Figure 16.2, we can see immediately that

$$I(v_2) - I(v_1) = 2\pi i \operatorname*{Res}_{z=0} f \tag{16.32}$$

has to hold, where we used our previous notation for the integral along a particular contour. Using this condition in (16.28), one obtains

$$C_0(K, T) = e^{(b-r)T}S_0 - e^{-rT}K - \frac{e^{-rT}K}{2\pi} \int_{iv_2-\infty}^{iv_2+\infty} \frac{e^{-izk}\varphi_0(-z)}{z^2 - iz}dz, \quad v_2 \in (\alpha, 0). \tag{16.33}$$

But realizing that the last term in (16.33) is the fair price of the put option $P_0(K, T)$, we have recovered put-call parity in a truly amazing guise. We therefore have

$$P_0(K, T) = e^{-rT}K - \frac{e^{(\frac{b}{2}-r)T}\sqrt{S_0 K}}{\pi} \int_0^\infty \frac{\operatorname{Re}\left[e^{iuk}\varphi_0(u - \frac{i}{2})\right]}{u^2 + \frac{1}{4}}du. \tag{16.34}$$

16.4   The *Heston–Nandi* GARCH-Model

As a prelude to the introduction of the important *Heston*-model for option pricing, let's consider a particular GARCH-model, suggested by Heston and Nandi (1997, 2000). Even though GARCH-models do not truly possess stochastic volatility, we can understand most ideas of the *Heston*-model in the simpler GARCH framework. In particular, we will restrict ourselves to analyzing the simplest possible member of the *Heston–Nandi*-class, which has the form

$$\Delta x_t = r + \lambda h_t + \sqrt{h_t}z_t \tag{16.35}$$

$$h_t = \omega + \alpha\left(z_{t-1} - \gamma\sqrt{h_{t-1}}\right)^2 + \beta h_{t-1}. \tag{16.36}$$

Again, $x_t = \log S_t$ is the logarithmic price process of a non-dividend paying stock and $\Delta x_t = x_t - x_{t-1}$. The random innovation z_t is assumed standard normally distributed. Contrary to the *Duan*-model (15.23) on page 333, the risk premium in (16.35) is assumed proportional to the variance, not to its square root. This is a necessary requirement for the model to belong to the so-called affine class of GARCH-models; we will learn shortly what that means. With the transformations

$$z_t^Q = z_t + \left(\lambda + \frac{1}{2}\right)\sqrt{h_t} \tag{16.37}$$

$$\gamma^Q = \gamma + \lambda + \frac{1}{2}, \tag{16.38}$$

the whole GARCH-model is transferred into the risk-neutral world, by switching from z_t to z_t^Q. After some trivial rearrangements, one obtains

$$\Delta x_t = r - \frac{1}{2}h_t + \sqrt{h_t}z_t^Q \tag{16.39}$$

$$h_t = \omega + \alpha\left(z_{t-1}^Q - \gamma^Q\sqrt{h_{t-1}}\right)^2 + \beta h_{t-1}. \tag{16.40}$$

Quick calculation 16.7 Check that the transformation is algebraically correct.

Now, (16.39) is identical to the first equation of the *Duan*-model (15.26) under the risk-neutral measure Q. Of course in the GARCH-framework we have the luxury to fit the model under the physical measure P and hence, to obtain the risk premium. This is no longer possible for the true stochastic volatility *Heston*-model. But observe that the risk premium does not appear explicitly in (16.39) and (16.40) and thus, the model can be calibrated to the observed option prices without determining the risk premium in the first place.

Let's first bring the whole model into the right form $S_t = S_0 e^{bt + Y_t}$. Because the underlying is a non-dividend paying stock, the generalized cost-of-carry rate is $b = r$ and e^{Y_t} has to be a Q-martingale with $Y_0 = 0$. From (16.39) we conclude that Y_t has to have the dynamics

$$Y_t = Y_{t-1} - \frac{1}{2}h_t + \sqrt{h_t}z_t^Q, \tag{16.41}$$

with h_t given by (16.40), and again $z_t^Q \sim N(0, 1)$ under the pricing measure Q.

Quick calculation 16.8 Show that e^{Y_t} is indeed a Q-martingale by using the law of iterated expectations.

An affine class GARCH-model is defined by a particular form of its characteristic function. Under the risk-neutral measure Q, the conditional characteristic function has to be given by

$$\varphi_t(u) = E^Q[e^{iuY_T}|\mathcal{F}_t] = e^{iuY_t + A_t(u) + B_t(u)h_{t+1}}, \tag{16.42}$$

with $A_T(u) = 0$ and $B_T(u) = 0$. The unknown complex valued functions $A_t(u)$ and $B_t(u)$ are yet to be determined. The key idea in finding these unknown functions is once again the use of the law of iterated expectations. We can use it to write the identity

$$\varphi_{t-1}(u) = E^Q[\varphi_t(u)|\mathcal{F}_{t-1}] = E^Q[e^{iu\,Y_t+A_t(u)+B_t(u)h_{t+1}}|\mathcal{F}_{t-1}]. \tag{16.43}$$

Quick calculation 16.9 Can you see why the first equality is correct?

The next step is to plug in (16.40) and (16.41) for h_{t+1} and Y_t. After applying some algebraic tricks and enduring rather tedious calculations, one ends up with three sorts of terms, simple terms, which are known from the information $\mathcal{F}_{t-1}$, terms which are also known but are multiplied by h_t, and those terms involving z_t and $\sqrt{h_t}$. We can move everything that is known out of the expectation to obtain the schematic expression

$$\varphi_{t-1}(u) = e^{iu\,Y_{t-1}+\cdots+(\ldots)h_t} \cdot E^Q\left[e^{\alpha B_t(u)\left(z_t+\left(\frac{iu}{2\alpha B_t(u)}-\gamma^Q\right)\sqrt{h_t}\right)^2}\Big|\mathcal{F}_{t-1}\right]. \tag{16.44}$$

Observe that z_t is an independent innovation which is not conditional on $\mathcal{F}_{t-1}$, and $\sqrt{h_t}$ is already known. Thus, we can use the simple identity

$$E\left[e^{a(z+b)^2}\right] = e^{-\frac{1}{2}\log(1-2a)+\frac{ab^2}{1-2a}}, \tag{16.45}$$

for arbitrary a and b with $\mathrm{Re}[a] \le \frac{1}{2}$, and standard normally distributed z. The restriction on a becomes in fact never binding. Computing the expectation in (16.44) generates again two types of terms, simple ones and terms multiplying h_t. So after another round of algebraic manipulations, we end up with an expression like

$$\varphi_{t-1}(u) = e^{iu\,Y_{t-1}+\cdots+(\ldots)h_t}. \tag{16.46}$$

Comparing this result with (16.42), we must conclude that we have indeed computed A_{t-1} and B_{t-1}. Recalling that $Y_0 = 0$, the desired conditional characteristic function is

$$\varphi_0(u) = e^{A_0(u)+B_0(u)h_1}, \tag{16.47}$$

with $A_0(u)$ and $B_0(u)$ recursively computed by

$$A_{t-1}(u) = A_t(u) + \omega B_t(u) - \frac{1}{2}\log(1 - 2\alpha B_t(u)) \tag{16.48}$$

$$B_{t-1}(u) = iu\left(\gamma^Q - \frac{1}{2}\right) - \frac{\gamma^{Q2}}{2} + \beta B_t(u) + \frac{\frac{1}{2}(iu-\gamma^Q)^2}{1-2\alpha B_t(u)}, \tag{16.49}$$

and initial function values $A_T(u) = 0$ and $B_T(u) = 0$. We have omitted most of the messy details of the derivation because they are purely technical. The important fact is that knowledge of $\varphi_0(u)$ is enough to price a couple of plain vanilla contracts with the help of the formalism developed earlier in this chapter. Of course we do not yet know how to compute the integrals in (16.29) and (16.34), and we will postpone this discussion, until we have introduced the important stochastic volatility model of Heston (1993).

16.5   The *Heston*-Model

Heston (1993) considered the following model for the dynamics of a non-dividend paying stock

$$dS_t = \mu S_t dt + \sqrt{v_t} S_t dW_{1,t} \tag{16.50}$$

$$dv_t = \kappa(\theta - v_t)dt + \alpha \sqrt{v_t} dW_{2,t}, \tag{16.51}$$

where the covariance between the *Wiener*-processes is $E[dW_1 dW_2] = \rho dt$. The variance equation (16.51) is the *Cox–Ingersoll–Ross*-model (CIR, Cox et al., 1985), also used as short rate model in pricing fixed-income products. If the *Feller*-condition (Feller, 1951)

$$2\kappa\theta \geq \alpha^2 \tag{16.52}$$

is satisfied, the variance process v_t stays positive for all times. Furthermore, it is mean reverting to the equilibrium variance θ, also called the mean reversion level. The parameter κ controls the strength of the pull back to equilibrium and is called the mean reversion speed. Of course, we expect the correlation ρ to be negative, because of the leverage effect observed in real data.

Because there are now two sources of randomness, we need a second risk premium to account for the volatility risk. Precisely as in the *Heston–Nandi* GARCH-model, this risk premium is assumed proportional to the variance, and therefore we must have

$$\lambda(S, v, t) = \frac{\lambda}{\alpha} \sqrt{v} \tag{16.53}$$

in order to get it right after switching to Q. We can find out how the model looks under the risk-neutral measure, by applying the two-dimensional *Girsanov*-transformation

$$\left.\frac{dQ}{dP}\right|_{\mathcal{F}_t} = \exp\left(-\int_0^t \frac{\mu - r}{\sqrt{v_s}} dW_{1,s} - \int_0^t \frac{\lambda}{\alpha} \sqrt{v_s} dW_{2,s} - \frac{1}{2}\int_0^t \frac{(\mu - r)^2}{v_s} + \frac{\lambda^2}{\alpha^2} v_s ds\right). \tag{16.54}$$

This transformation corresponds to switching to the risk-neutral *Wiener*-increments

$$dW_{1,t}^Q = dW_{1,t} + \frac{\mu - r}{\sqrt{v_t}} dt \tag{16.55}$$

$$dW_{2,t}^Q = dW_{2,t} + \frac{\lambda}{\alpha} \sqrt{v_t} dt. \tag{16.56}$$

Quick calculation 16.10   Prove that $\text{Cov}[dW_1^Q, dW_2^Q] = \rho dt$ still holds.

If we use Itô's lemma to switch to log-prices $x_t = \log S_t$ and apply the parameter transformations $\kappa^Q = \kappa + \lambda$ and $\theta^Q = \frac{\kappa\theta}{\kappa+\lambda}$, then the *Heston*-model under the risk-neutral probability measure Q becomes

$$dx_t = \left(r - \frac{1}{2}v_t\right)dt + \sqrt{v_t}dW^Q_{1,t} \tag{16.57}$$

$$dv_t = \kappa^Q(\theta^Q - v_t)dt + \alpha \sqrt{v_t}dW^Q_{2,t}, \tag{16.58}$$

with

$$\kappa^Q = \kappa + \lambda, \quad \theta^Q = \frac{\kappa\theta}{\kappa + \lambda}, \quad \text{and} \quad E[dW^Q_1 dW^Q_2] = \rho dt. \tag{16.59}$$

Quick calculation 16.11   Confirm that this transformation is algebraically correct.

We have again effectively eliminated the volatility risk premium under Q, by introducing the new parameters κ^Q and θ^Q. We can extract the important martingale process Y_t under Q by simply eliminating the drift part, which is due to compounding with the risk-free interest rate r. The result is

$$dY_t = -\frac{1}{2}v_t dt + \sqrt{v_t}dW_{1,t}, \tag{16.60}$$

with (16.58) and (16.59) still unchanged. Observe that the last two steps are completely analogous to (16.39) to (16.41) in the *Heston–Nandi* GARCH-model.

We proceed by making an observation about the characteristic function. Remember that the unconditional expectation is with respect to the trivial σ-algebra $\mathcal{F}_0$. Therefore, by the law of iterated expectations, we must have

$$E^Q[\varphi_t(u)] = E^Q\left[E^Q[e^{iuY_T}|\mathcal{F}_t]|\mathcal{F}_0\right] = \varphi_0(u). \tag{16.61}$$

That means, the expectation of the characteristic function does not vary over time and thus, we must have also

$$E^Q[d\varphi_t(u)] = 0. \tag{16.62}$$

But how do we get an idea of the dynamics of φ? The answer might come as a shock, but φ is a smooth function of Y, v, and t, so we can apply Itô's lemma. The result is

$$d\varphi = \left(-\frac{v}{2}\frac{\partial\varphi}{\partial Y} + \kappa^Q(\theta^Q - v)\frac{\partial\varphi}{\partial v} + \frac{\partial\varphi}{\partial t} + \frac{v}{2}\frac{\partial^2\varphi}{\partial Y^2} + \rho\alpha v\frac{\partial^2\varphi}{\partial Y\partial v} + \frac{1}{2}\alpha^2 v\frac{\partial^2\varphi}{\partial v^2}\right)dt$$
$$+ \sqrt{v}\frac{\partial\varphi}{\partial Y}dW_1 + \alpha\sqrt{v}\frac{\partial\varphi}{\partial v}dW_2, \tag{16.63}$$

where the function arguments t and u were suppressed for notational convenience. It is obvious that if we take the expectation of (16.63), the terms in the second row vanish. But since we know that the expectation of $d\varphi$ is zero, the terms in the bracket, multiplying dt, must also vanish and we obtain

$$\frac{\partial\varphi}{\partial t} - \frac{v}{2}\frac{\partial\varphi}{\partial Y} + \kappa^Q(\theta^Q - v)\frac{\partial\varphi}{\partial v} + \frac{v}{2}\frac{\partial^2\varphi}{\partial Y^2} + \rho\alpha v\frac{\partial^2\varphi}{\partial Y\partial v} + \frac{1}{2}\alpha^2 v\frac{\partial^2\varphi}{\partial v^2} = 0. \qquad (16.64)$$

Now, let us make the educated guess that the characteristic function has the particular form

$$\varphi_t(u) = e^{iuY_t + A(t,u) + B(t,u)v_t}, \qquad (16.65)$$

with the yet unknown functions $A(t, u)$ and $B(t, u)$. Does that remind you of something? If our guess is correct, the *Heston*-model belongs to the same affine model class as the *Heston–Nandi* GARCH-model. Plugging (16.65) into (16.64) and afterwards dividing by φ yields

$$\frac{\partial A}{\partial t} + \kappa^Q\theta^Q B + v\left(\frac{\partial B}{\partial t} - \frac{1}{2}iu - \kappa^Q B - \frac{1}{2}u^2 + iu\rho\alpha B + \frac{1}{2}\alpha^2 B^2\right) = 0. \qquad (16.66)$$

There are two kinds of terms on the left hand side of this equation, simple ones, and those multiplying v. Since v is arbitrary, the terms inside and outside the bracket have to vanish separately. To see this convince yourself that (16.66) has to hold for both, $v = 0$ and $v \neq 0$. Thus, we obtain a system of two separate ordinary differential equations in A and B

$$\frac{\partial A}{\partial t} = -\kappa^Q\theta^Q B(t, u) \qquad (16.67)$$

$$\frac{\partial B}{\partial t} = \frac{1}{2}(iu + u^2) + (\kappa^Q - iu\rho\alpha)B(t, u) - \frac{1}{2}\alpha^2 B^2(t, u). \qquad (16.68)$$

The second one is an equation of the *Riccati*-type. Solving it is a delicate matter. Let's go through it step by step.

First let's simplify (16.68) to a schematic level and suppress the dependence on the variable u temporarily. The basic form is

$$B'(t) = p + qB(t) - rB^2(t), \qquad (16.69)$$

where the prime now indicates the derivative with respect to time. Remember that the coefficients are

$$p = \frac{1}{2}(iu + u^2), \quad q = (\kappa^Q - iu\rho\alpha), \quad \text{and} \quad r = \frac{1}{2}\alpha^2. \qquad (16.70)$$

At the end we will need to retrace our steps. We cannot solve (16.69) directly; we need the auxiliary second order differential equation

$$w''(t) = qw'(t) + prw(t). \qquad (16.71)$$

With the help of (16.71), we can express the solution of our initial *Riccati*-equation as

$$B(t) = \frac{w'(t)}{w(t)} \cdot \frac{1}{r}. \tag{16.72}$$

Quick calculation 16.12 Prove this statement by differentiating both sides of (16.72).

The auxiliary differential equation is a standard problem with the known solution

$$w(t) = c_1 e^{\frac{q+d}{2}t} + c_2 e^{\frac{q-d}{2}t}, \tag{16.73}$$

with

$$d = \sqrt{q^2 + 4pr}. \tag{16.74}$$

The coefficients c_1 and c_2 are not yet determined. Plugging this solution into (16.72), one obtains

$$B(t) = \frac{c_1(q+d)e^{\frac{q+d}{2}t} + c_2(q-d)e^{\frac{q-d}{2}t}}{c_1 e^{\frac{q+d}{2}t} + c_2 e^{\frac{q-d}{2}t}} \cdot \frac{1}{2r}. \tag{16.75}$$

It is now time to make use of the additional information that the final value of $B(t)$ has to be $B(T) = 0$. This means, at time T the numerator of (16.75) has to vanish. This fact enables us to express one unknown coefficient in terms of the other. Concentrating on c_1, one obtains

$$c_1 = -c_2 c e^{-d \cdot T}, \tag{16.76}$$

where the new coefficient c was introduced as

$$c = \frac{q-d}{q+d}. \tag{16.77}$$

Using this new rule for the coefficient c_1, all remaining coefficients c_2 cancel out of the equation and one obtains

$$B(t) = \frac{q-d}{2r} \cdot \frac{e^{\frac{q-d}{2}t} - e^{\frac{q+d}{2}t - d \cdot T}}{e^{\frac{q-d}{2}t} - c e^{\frac{q+d}{2}t - d \cdot T}} = \frac{q-d}{2r} \cdot \frac{1 - e^{-d(T-t)}}{1 - c e^{-d(T-t)}}. \tag{16.78}$$

This is not quite the form originally derived by Heston (1993). We would have obtained the original form by solving for c_2 in (16.76). But as pointed out by Albrecher et al. (2007), this one is preferable for numerical reasons.

Now let's solve for the second function $A(t)$. Integrating (16.67) with $A(T) = 0$ yields

$$A(t) = -\kappa^Q \theta^Q \int_T^t B(s) ds = \frac{\kappa^Q \theta^Q (q-d)}{2r} \int_t^T \frac{1 - e^{-d(T-s)}}{1 - c e^{-d(T-s)}} ds. \tag{16.79}$$

Let's first focus on solving the integral. Make the substitution $x = e^{-d(T-t)}$. This makes the increment $dx = d \cdot e^{d(T-s)}ds = d \cdot x\, ds$, and the integral becomes

$$
\begin{aligned}
\frac{1}{d}\int_{e^{-d(T-t)}}^{1} \frac{1-x}{(1-cx)x}dx &= \frac{1}{d}\int_{e^{-d(T-t)}}^{1}\left(\frac{1}{x} - \frac{1-c}{1-cx}\right)dx \\
&= \frac{1}{d}\left[\log x + \frac{1-c}{c}\log(1-cx)\right]_{x=e^{-d(T-t)}}^{x=1} \\
&= (T-t) - \frac{1-c}{cd}\log\left(\frac{1-ce^{-d(T-t)}}{1-c}\right).
\end{aligned}
\tag{16.80}
$$

Quick calculation 16.13   Verify the first equality.

Remember that $c = \frac{q-d}{q+d}$ and thus, the coefficient in front of the logarithm becomes

$$
\frac{1-c}{cd} = \frac{1 - \frac{q-d}{q+d}}{\frac{q-d}{q+d}d} = \frac{2d}{(q-d)d} = \frac{2}{q-d}.
\tag{16.81}
$$

Putting all the pieces together, one obtains the desired expression

$$
A(t) = \frac{\kappa^Q\theta^Q}{2r}\left((q-d)(T-t) - 2\log\left(\frac{1-ce^{-d(T-t)}}{1-c}\right)\right).
\tag{16.82}
$$

With this last piece, we are able to price options in the stochastic volatility *Heston*-model. All we needed was an expression for the conditional characteristic function of the martingale process Y_t, to feed into our pricing formula (16.29) or (16.34), respectively. This expression is given in the *Heston*-model by

$$
\varphi_0(u) = e^{A(0,u)+B(0,u)v_0},
\tag{16.83}
$$

where

$$
A(t,u) = \frac{\kappa^Q\theta^Q}{\alpha^2}\left((\kappa^Q - iu\rho\alpha - d)(T-t) - 2\log\left(\frac{1-ce^{-d(T-t)}}{1-c}\right)\right)
\tag{16.84}
$$

$$
B(t,u) = \frac{\kappa^Q - iu\rho\alpha - d}{\alpha^2}\cdot\frac{1-e^{-d(T-t)}}{1-ce^{-d(T-t)}},
\tag{16.85}
$$

with

$$
c = \frac{\kappa^Q - iu\rho\alpha - d}{\kappa^Q - iu\rho\alpha + d} \quad \text{and} \quad d = \sqrt{(\kappa^Q - iu\rho\alpha)^2 + \alpha^2(iu + u^2)}.
\tag{16.86}
$$

Of course we have to show that the generalized characteristic function $\varphi_0(z)$ is regular in the complex strip $S_Y = \{z = u + iv : v \in (\alpha,\beta)\}$, with $\alpha < -1$ and $\beta > 0$. This is far from trivial in the *Heston*-model, but the analysis of Lewis (2000, example II on p. 44) shows that it indeed is. So we are ready to go. The only thing missing is a method for computing the integrals in (16.29) and (16.34).

16.6 Inverting the *Fourier*-Transform

There exist numerous methods to invert a *Fourier*-transformation numerically. Some of them, as for example the fast *Fourier*-transform (FFT), are highly sophisticated algorithms, with whole books written about them. We will use a *Gauss*ian quadrature method instead, because it is easy to implement and the integrals in (16.29) and (16.34) converge rapidly. So what is the idea behind a quadrature method? Assume that $f(x)$ is a smooth function that can be approximated sufficiently well by a polynomial of degree $2N - 1$. Then the integral over $f(x)$ with respect to a nonnegative weighting function $w(x)$ can be evaluated exactly with the *Gauss*ian quadrature rule

$$\int f(x)w(x)dx = \sum_{n=1}^{N} w_n f(x_n), \tag{16.87}$$

with properly chosen weights w_n and points x_n, not at all depending on $f(x)$; see for example theorem 3.6.12 in Stoer and Bulirsch (1993, p. 153). But how are these weights and points chosen? Consider dividing $f(x)$ by a very special polynomial $p_N(x)$ of degree N, then one can write

$$f(x) = q(x)p_N(x) + r(x). \tag{16.88}$$

Both the ratio $q(x)$ and the residual $r(x)$ are polynomials of degree not larger than $N - 1$. If the n-th degree polynomials $p_n(x)$, for $n = 0, \dots, N$, form an orthogonal basis with respect to the weighting function $w(x)$, which means $p_0(x) = 1$ and

$$\langle p_n | p_m \rangle_w = \int p_n(x)p_m(x)w(x)dx = 0 \tag{16.89}$$

for $n \neq m$, then $q(x)$ can always be represented as

$$q(x) = \sum_{n=0}^{N-1} q_n p_n(x), \tag{16.90}$$

for some coefficients q_n, and the following equalities hold

$$\langle f | w \rangle = \sum_{n=0}^{N-1} q_n \langle p_n | p_N \rangle_w + \langle r | w \rangle = \langle r | w \rangle. \tag{16.91}$$

But from the quadrature rule (16.87), we must have

$$\sum_{n=1}^{N} w_n f(x_n) = \sum_{n=1}^{N} w_n r(x_n) = \sum_{n=1}^{N} w_n (f(x_n) - q(x_n)p_N(x_n)), \tag{16.92}$$

and thus the quadrature points x_n have to be chosen as the zeros of the polynomial $p_N(x)$. Because of the orthogonality of the polynomials $p_n(x)$ with respect to $w(x)$, the weights are determined by the linear system of equations

$$\sum_{n=1}^{N} w_n p_k(x_n) = \begin{cases} \int w(x)dx & \text{for } k = 0 \\ 0 & \text{for } 1 \leq k < N. \end{cases} \tag{16.93}$$

Quick calculation 16.14 Can you see why this is true?

The fact that quadrature rules are exact as long as $f(x)$ is a polynomial of degree not larger than $2N - 1$ is absolutely remarkable, because it means that we can evaluate an integral over a cubic function by adding just two numbers, provided we know the correct quadrature points and weights.

Let's first focus on an integral over the interval $[-1, 1]$, and take the weighting function $w(x) = \frac{1}{\sqrt{1-x^2}}$. The polynomials orthogonal with respect to this weighting function are the *Gauss–Chebyshev*-polynomials. What is special about them is that their weights and zeros are known explicitly,

$$w_n = \frac{\pi}{N} \quad \text{and} \quad x_n = \cos\left(\frac{2n - 1}{2N}\pi\right). \tag{16.94}$$

What if there is no weighting function in the integrand? This can be remedied and as it turns out, the weight is modified to account for it. Assume there is only the function $f(x)$ to be integrated. Then we can write

$$\int_{-1}^{1} f(x)dx = \int_{-1}^{1} \sqrt{1 - x^2}f(x)w(x)dx = \sum_{n=1}^{N} w_n \sqrt{1 - x_n^2}f(x_n). \tag{16.95}$$

We have thus obtained a corrected weight, and furthermore, recall that the quadrature points are cosine functions. We can thus use the identity $\sin^2 x + \cos^2 x = 1$ to define the new weight

$$w_n = \frac{\pi}{N} \sin\left(\frac{2n - 1}{2N}\pi\right), \tag{16.96}$$

to be used with the quadrature rule

$$\int_{-1}^{1} f(x)dx = \sum_{n=1}^{N} w_n f(x_n), \tag{16.97}$$

where the quadrature points x_n are still given by (16.94), but the weights are due to (16.96). The only thing left to do is to map our original boundaries of integration $[0, u_{max}]$ onto $[-1, 1]$. To achieve this goal, the transformation $u = \frac{u_{max}}{2}x + \frac{u_{max}}{2}$ is applied internally, before the quadrature becomes effective. We then obtain

$$\int_{0}^{u_{max}} f(u)du = \sum_{n=1}^{N} w_n f(u_n), \tag{16.98}$$

with

$$w_n = \frac{\pi u_{max}}{2N} \sin\left(\frac{2n - 1}{2N}\pi\right) \quad \text{and} \quad u_n = \frac{u_{max}}{2}\cos\left(\frac{2n - 1}{2N}\pi\right) + \frac{u_{max}}{2}. \tag{16.99}$$

Quick calculation 16.15 Can you see why the constant factor of the weights has changed?

To apply our quadrature rule, we have to fix the upper bound u_{max} in a suitable way. First observe that the integral in both pricing formulas (16.29) and (16.34) is the same. The integrand is given by

$$f(u) = \frac{\text{Re}\left[e^{iuk}\varphi_0(u - \frac{i}{2})\right]}{u^2 + \frac{1}{4}}. \tag{16.100}$$

We are not looking for a precise expression, but for a simple and robust approximation. Thus, let's assume that the annual volatility is approximately constant and given by σ. Then the conditional characteristic function of the associated martingale process is

$$\varphi_t(u) = e^{iuY_t - \frac{1}{2}(iu+u^2)\sigma^2(T-t)}. \tag{16.101}$$

We have to evaluate this function for $t = 0$ at the point $u - \frac{i}{2}$. The integrand then becomes

$$f(u) = \frac{\text{Re}\left[e^{iuk}e^{-\frac{1}{2}(u^2+\frac{1}{4})\sigma^2 T}\right]}{u^2 + \frac{1}{4}} = e^{-\frac{1}{2}(u^2+\frac{1}{4})\sigma^2 T} \cdot \frac{\cos(uk)}{u^2 + \frac{1}{4}}. \tag{16.102}$$

This is an exponentially decaying function with a damped oscillation superimposed on it. We want to choose u_{max} such that $|f(u_{max})| \leq \varepsilon$ for a small number ε. Observe that the oscillation term in (16.102) is largest for $u = 0$. We can thus estimate the desired upper bound by

$$|f(u_{max})| \leq 4e^{-\frac{1}{2}(u_{max}^2+\frac{1}{4})\sigma^2 T} = \varepsilon. \tag{16.103}$$

Of course this estimate is very conservative, but on the other hand, we can be sure that the error we made in assuming volatility to be constant, is very unlikely to have any effect. Solving (16.103) for u_{max} yields

$$u_{max} = \sqrt{\frac{2 \log \frac{4}{\varepsilon}}{\sigma^2 T} - \frac{1}{4}}. \tag{16.104}$$

To get an impression of how quickly the integrals in the pricing equations converge, let's do a little computation. Let's assume that the annual volatility is $\sigma = 25\%$ and the time to expiry is $T = 1$ year. If we want the approximation error of the integrand to be smaller than $\varepsilon = 10^{-6}$, then the desired upper bound is $u_{max} \approx 22$. This is way smaller than infinity.

We have now all necessary tools for computing option prices within the *Heston*-model. Of course, we first have to calibrate the parameters to a set of observed plain vanilla options. If this is done, we can valuate any exotic contract with European exercise right, by simulating random paths along the risk-neutral dynamics (16.57) to (16.59). But there is another interesting property of the model we can analyze. If we are able to compute the theoretical call price for every combination of moneyness and time to expiry, we can feed those prices back into the *Black–Scholes*-formula to obtain the implied volatility surface. Figure 16.3 shows the result for the *Heston*-model, calibrated to the DAX data of Chapter 15. Compare this figure to the interpolated

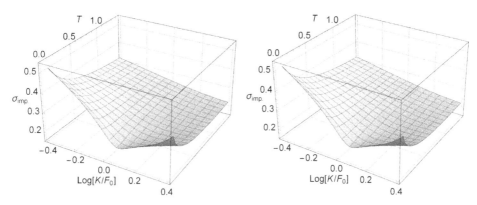

Fig. 16.3 **3D** Implied volatility surface generated by the *Heston*-model calibrated to DAX data of mid-July 2012

volatility surface in Figure 15.3 on page 335, and also to the GARCH-parametrized surface in Figure 15.6 on page 351. The *Heston*-model captures the long-term skew quite well, but it fails to reproduce the steepness in the short-term smile. In particular the right wing is underestimated. This is typical for stochastic volatility models. The extreme short-term curvature and steepness is due to jump risk, which is not captured by those models. We will eventually encounter models that incorporate jumps, and we will learn what they add to the volatility surfaces in the next chapter. But before we do, let's talk about another stochastic volatility model, very popular with practitioners, because it allows easy fitting of the implied volatility smile.

16.7   Implied Volatility in the SABR-Model

The SABR-model (stochastic alpha-beta-rho) suggested by Hagan et al. (2002) is different from any other model we have encountered so far, because its output is an explicit expression for the implied volatility. This volatility has to be fed into the *Black–Scholes*-formula afterwards to determine the price of the option. You may have observed that we plot the volatility surface with respect to the log-ratio of the strike price of the option and the forward price of the underlying. The reason for this is simple: the bottom of the implied volatility valley, called the backbone, does not drift horizontally along the forward moneyness. Hence, the dynamics in the SABR-model are specified with respect to the forward price. Our usual geometric *Brown*ian motion under the risk-neutral measure Q is

$$dS_t = rS_t dt + \sigma S_t dW_t. \tag{16.105}$$

How does this change, if we observe the forward price $F_t = S_t e^{r(T-t)}$ instead? From Itô's lemma we have

$$
\begin{aligned}
dF_t &= rS_t \frac{\partial F}{\partial S} dt + \frac{\partial F}{\partial t} dt + \sigma S_t \frac{\partial F}{\partial S} dW_t + \frac{1}{2}\sigma^2 S_t^2 \frac{\partial^2 F}{\partial S^2} dt \\
&= rF_t dt - rF_t dt + \sigma F_t dW_t \\
&= \sigma F_t dW_t.
\end{aligned}
\tag{16.106}
$$

That is, the risk-neutral forward price is driftless. Hagan et al. (2002) studied a more general class of processes, called the CEV-model (constant elasticity of variance). In this model, the forward price has the dynamics

$$dF_t = \sigma_t F_t^\beta dW_{1,t} \qquad (16.107)$$

$$d\sigma_t = \alpha \sigma_t dW_{2,t}, \qquad (16.108)$$

with $0 \leq \beta \leq 1$ and $E[dW_1 dW_2] = \rho dt$, hence the name SABR-model, because the parameters are α, β, and ρ. Observe that the volatility in (16.108) is not mean reverting. Thus, it can explode and eventually become infinite. The justification for such a framework is that there is not much difference in the volatility smile characteristics, no matter which particular stochastic volatility model is used, and the SABR-model is the simplest of all. The whole point is not to describe the volatility dynamics most realistically, but to provide a simple and efficient framework to parametrize implied volatility for a given time to expiry.

In order to derive an expression for the implied volatility, Hagan et al. (2002) relied heavily on a technique called singular perturbation theory. Perturbation theory is a not completely rigorous branch of mathematics, widely used in physics. Often a problem is solvable under some convenient assumptions. In reality these assumptions may not be exactly true, but close to. If the proper problem can be formulated by adding or multiplying a small quantity ε into the idealized problem, then one can compute a perturbation series to solve the proper problem, too. Perturbation theory is well beyond the scope of this book. We can nevertheless gain some intuition about the basic principles. Assume y_0 is the solution of a known problem $f(x)$. What is the solution y to the problem $f(x + \varepsilon)$? Perturbation theory suggests that the solution can be represented as a *Taylor*-series

$$y = \sum_{n=0}^{\infty} \varepsilon^n y_n. \qquad (16.109)$$

The trick that makes this work is that *Taylor*-series are unique in every coefficient. Which means after plugging (16.109) into the problem, we can equate term by term in powers of ε and solve successively. This is best understood by looking at an example.

Example 16.1

The (positive) solution to the problem $y = \sqrt{1}$ is known to be $y_0 = 1$. What is the solution to the problem

$$y = \sqrt{1.1},$$

to the orders ε and ε^2, respectively?

Solution

First realize that we can rewrite the problem as

$$y = \sqrt{1 + \varepsilon},$$

where $\varepsilon = 0.1$ can be considered small compared to the unperturbed problem. Of course we can solve this by simply putting it into a calculator and reading off the result $y \approx 1.0488$. But we can do better. To order ε, our approximate solution is $y = y_0 + \varepsilon y_1$. Plugging this into the pervious equation yields

$$(y_0 + \varepsilon y_1)^2 = y_0^2 + 2\varepsilon y_0 y_1 + \varepsilon^2 y_1^2 = 1 + \varepsilon.$$

We can now order terms according to their power in ε, where the $O(\varepsilon^2)$ term is too small to be considered

$$O(\varepsilon^0) \quad \rightarrow \quad y_0^2 - 1 = 0$$
$$O(\varepsilon^1) \quad \rightarrow \quad 2y_0 y_1 - 1 = 0.$$

Form this, we can successively deduce that $y_0 = 1$ and $y_1 = \frac{1}{2}$. This is where the prior knowledge of y_0 comes in, it determines that the positive root has to be taken. To order ε, we thus obtain $y = 1 + \frac{\varepsilon}{2} = 1 + 0.05 = 1.05$.

The solution to order ε^2 is obtained analogously. It has the form $y = y_0 + \varepsilon y_1 + \varepsilon^2 y_2$. Plugging this solution into the original problem yields

$$(y_0 + \varepsilon y_1 + \varepsilon^2 y_2)^2 = 1 + \varepsilon.$$

Collecting all terms of order ε^2 results in the additional equation

$$O(\varepsilon^2) \quad \rightarrow \quad y_1^2 + 2y_0 y_2 = 0.$$

All lower order equations remain intact so we can refine the perturbation series term by term. The new equation yields $y_2 = -\frac{1}{8}$ and thus the $O(\varepsilon^2)$ solution becomes $y = 1 + \frac{\varepsilon}{2} - \frac{\varepsilon^2}{8} = 1 + 0.05 - 0.00125 = 1.04875$.

Perturbation theory is not a numerical method. Like a good burger, numerical methods make you happy until you learn what went into it. Perturbation theory is a method to obtain approximate analytical solutions. The degree of approximation is only limited by your willingness to compute another term of the series.

Hagan et al. (2002) assume that volatility itself, and the volatility of volatility are both small compared to the forward price. Thus, they substitute $\sigma_t \rightarrow \varepsilon \sigma_t$ and $\alpha \rightarrow \varepsilon \alpha$ in (16.107) and (16.108) to obtain

$$dF_t = \varepsilon \sigma_t F_t^\beta dW_{1,t} \tag{16.110}$$
$$d\sigma_t = \varepsilon \alpha \sigma_t dW_{2,t}, \tag{16.111}$$

with $\varepsilon = 1$. This immediately implies that in the unperturbed solution, the forward price F_t remains constant for all times t. The particular steps in deriving an expression for the implied volatility are very involved. Therefore, we state only the final result

$$\sigma_{\text{imp.}}(K, T) = \frac{\varepsilon \sigma_t}{(F_t K)^{\frac{1-\beta}{2}} \left(1 + \frac{(1-\beta)^2}{24} \log^2(F_t/K) + \frac{(1-\beta)^4}{1920} \log^4(F_t/K) + \cdots\right)} \cdot \frac{z}{\chi(z)}$$
$$\cdot \left(1 + \left(\frac{(1-\beta)^2}{24} \frac{\sigma_t^2}{(F_t K)^{1-\beta}} + \frac{1}{4} \frac{\beta \rho \alpha \sigma_t}{(F_t K)^{\frac{1-\beta}{2}}} + \frac{2 - 3\rho^2}{24} \alpha^2\right) \varepsilon^2 (T - t) + \cdots\right).$$

$$(16.112)$$

with

$$z = \frac{\alpha}{\sigma_t}(F_t K)^{\frac{1-\beta}{2}} \log(F_t/K) \quad \text{and} \quad \chi(z) = \log\left(\frac{\sqrt{1 - 2\rho z + z^2} + z - \rho}{1 - \rho}\right). \quad (16.113)$$

Note that the term in the first row of (16.112) is already exact to order ε^2, because the next term in the perturbation series is $O(\varepsilon^3)$. By the same argument, including this term makes the result exact to order ε^4. Typically, the corrections from this term are about 1%.

What is especially charming in the SABR-model is that the parameters control more or less isolated characteristics of the implied volatility. Let's for example analyze the role of the parameter β. To this end, let's compute the at-the-money implied volatility $\sigma_{\text{imp.}}(F_t, T)$. Here we run into a little bit of trouble, because z, as well as $\chi(z)$ approach zero, as $K \to F_t$. But with the help of l'Hôpital's rule, we have

$$\lim_{z \to 0} \frac{z}{\chi(z)} = \lim_{z \to 0} \frac{1}{\chi'(z)} = 1. \quad (16.114)$$

Quick calculation 16.16 Check that the last equality holds.

So after plugging back in $\varepsilon = 1$, we obtain

$$\sigma_{\text{imp.}}(F_t, T) = \frac{\sigma_t}{F_t^{1-\beta}} + O(\varepsilon^3). \quad (16.115)$$

This is the position of the backbone. Its height for a particular forward price F_t is determined by σ_t. If $\beta = 1$, as usual in our geometric *Brown*ian motion framework, the at-the-money implied volatility is given by σ_t. The backbone does not drift vertically, if F_t changes. For $\beta < 1$, the backbone also drifts vertically. To see this, observe that for $\sigma_s = \sigma_t$ and $F_s < F_t$

$$\sigma_{\text{imp.}}(F_s, T) > \sigma_{\text{imp.}}(F_t, T) \quad (16.116)$$

holds. We can thus deduce that β governs the drift behavior of the backbone, if the forward price F_t changes in time. Indeed the volatility smile and skew are largely unaffected by the choice of β. Because we are not interested in the dynamics of the implied volatility surface, but only in a snapshot, we choose $\beta = 1$ in the sequel. Further analysis reveals that the smile is largely controlled by α and the skew by the correlation coefficient ρ. Following our convenient notation, labeling today as time $t = 0$, we can state the simplified SABR-version

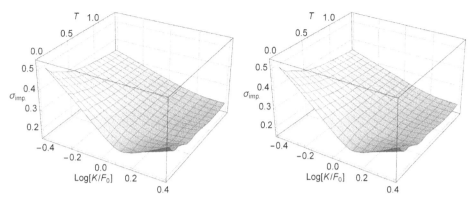

Fig. 16.4 **3D** Implied volatility surface generated by the SABR-model calibrated to DAX data of mid-July 2012

$$\sigma_{\text{imp.}}(K, T) = \frac{\sigma_0 z}{\chi(z)} \left(1 + \left(\frac{\rho \alpha \sigma_0}{4} + \frac{2 - 3\rho^2}{24} \alpha^2 \right) T \right) + O(\varepsilon^5), \tag{16.117}$$

with

$$z = \frac{\alpha}{\sigma_0} \log(F_0/K) \quad \text{and} \quad \chi(z) = \log \left(\frac{\sqrt{1 - 2\rho z + z^2} + z - \rho}{1 - \rho} \right). \tag{16.118}$$

What is very convenient about the SABR-model is that it is extraordinarily easy to calibrate to market data. This is due to the widely separated roles of the parameters. The price one has to pay is that the model can only be fitted to single slices in time to expiry. To obtain a representation of the whole implied volatility surface, one has to interpolate between the time slices appropriately. Figure 16.4 shows the result of this procedure for the DAX option data of Chapter 15. The surface is very similar to the one generated by the *Heston*-model, Figure 16.3 on page 373. In particular, the steepness of the smile for short-term contracts is underestimated. This is no surprise, because we have already learned that both the SABR-model and the *Heston*-model do not account for jump risk.

16.8   Further Reading

A very comprehensive source including the fundamental transform is Lewis (2000). A good summary of stochastic volatility is provided in Wilmott (2006c, chap. 51). Volatility surface issues of the *Heston*-model are discussed in Gatheral (2006, chap. 3). Besides the *Heston*- and SABR-model, there are several other prominent stochastic volatility models. An incomplete list is Hull and White (1987), Scott (1987), and Stein and Stein (1991). A stochastic model for implied volatility itself is provided in Schönbucher (1999).

16.9   Problems

16.1 Derive the extended *Black–Scholes*-equation for the *Heston*-model.

16.2 Show that the fair price of a European plain vanilla call option can be represented as

$$C_0(K, T) = e^{(b-r)T}S_0 - e^{-rT}K(I_1(v) + I_2(v)),$$

where $I_1(v)$ and $I_2(v)$ are the complex line integrals

$$I_1(v) = \frac{1}{2\pi} \int_{iv-\infty}^{iv+\infty} e^{-izk}\varphi_0(-z)\frac{i}{z}dz \quad \text{and} \quad I_2(v) = -\frac{1}{2\pi} \int_{iv-\infty}^{iv+\infty} e^{-izk}\varphi_0(-z)\frac{i}{z-i}dz,$$

evaluated along the contour $v \in (0, 1)$.

16.3 Shifting the integration contours to $v = 0$ and $v = 1$, respectively, the complex line integrals in Problem 16.2 become principal value integrals and pick up one half of the associated residue. The result is

$$I_1(v) = \frac{1}{2} + \frac{1}{\pi} \int_0^\infty \text{Re}\left[\frac{e^{iku}\varphi_0(u)}{iu}\right] du$$

$$I_2(v) = \frac{e^k}{2} - \frac{e^k}{\pi} \int_0^\infty \text{Re}\left[\frac{e^{iku}\varphi_0(u-i)}{iu}\right] du,$$

where again $k = \log(S_0/K) + bT$. Show that the call price can be expressed in a completely analogous form to the generalized *Black–Scholes*-formula.

16.4 Prove that the payoff function of a protective put position

$$w(x) = \max(e^x, K)$$

has no transformed payoff function $\hat{w}(z)$, regular in a connected strip $S_w = \{z = u + iv : v \in (\alpha, \beta)\}$.

16.5 Polynomials, orthogonal with respect to the weighting function $w(x) = 1$ in the interval $[-1, 1]$, are called the *Legendre*-polynomials. They are generated by

$$p_n(x) = \frac{1}{2^n n!} \frac{d^n}{dx^n}(x^2 - 1)^n.$$

Compute the *Legendre*-polynomials up to $N = 2$, as well as the associated quadrature points and weights.

16.6 Consider the SABR-model with $\beta = 1$. Show that the at-the-money smile for $F_0 = K \pm \delta$, with small δ, is symmetric. Use that δ is so small that $O(\delta^2)$ terms can be neglected.

17 Processes with Jumps

Inspecting for example the price processes of stocks, either on the microscopic level or on a macroscopic scale, it is hard to reject the clear evidence for the presence of jumps. As in the case of stochastic volatility, market completeness is destroyed by unhedgeable jump risks. But additionally, processes including jumps require a more sophisticated mathematical machinery, because the sample paths are no longer continuous.

17.1 Càdlàg Processes, Local-, and Semimartingales

The first major difference we face when introducing jump processes is that we can no longer rely on processes generating continuous sample paths. This may sound not very dramatic, but remember that Itô's lemma for example was based on the stochastic *Itô*-integral and therefore, on the continuous *Wiener*-process. Luckily, this important result can be extended to so-called càdlàg processes (French: "continue à droite, limite à gauche," right continuous with left limit). A càdlàg function $f : \mathcal{T} \to \mathbb{R}$ is defined by the properties

1. The left limit $f(t^-) = \lim\limits_{\varepsilon \to 0} f(t - \varepsilon)$ exists,

2. The right limit $f(t^+) = \lim\limits_{\varepsilon \to 0} f(t + \varepsilon)$ exists and equals $f(t)$,

(17.1)

for all $t \in \mathcal{T}$. This is the abstract description of the non-anticipating property we require from jump processes. We know such functions. For example, the distribution function of a discrete random variable is a càdlàg function. Every continuous function is a càdlàg function, but the converse is not true. The space of all càdlàg functions is called the *Skorokhod*-space. If we consider jump processes, then every possible state of the world $\omega \in \Omega$ generates a sample path in this class of functions. But there are other far reaching consequences.

To establish a complete theoretical framework including this wider class of sample paths, one needs the more general concept of semimartingales. A semimartingale is the sum of two processes, a càdlàg process of locally bounded variation, and a local martingale. The concept of local martingales is a purely continuous time issue. As proved by Kabanov (2008), in discrete time there is always an equivalent martingale measure that transforms the local martingale into a martingale. Local martingales are defined with the help of a localizing sequence of stopping times.

Theorem 17.1 (Local martingale) *An $\mathcal{F}_t$-adapted process X_t with $t \geq 0$ is a local martingale, if there exists a sequence of stopping times $\tau_n : \Omega \to [0, \infty)$, such that*

1. *the sequence τ_n is almost surely increasing, $P(\tau_n < \tau_{n+1}) = 1$,*
2. *the sequence τ_n diverges almost surely, $\lim_{n \to \infty} P(\tau_n < \infty) = 0$,*
3. *the stopped process*

$$Y_{t,n} = \begin{cases} X_t & \text{for } t < \tau_n \\ X_{\tau_n} & \text{for } t \geq \tau_n \end{cases}$$

is a martingale for every $n \in \mathbb{N}$.

Obviously, every martingale is also a local martingale, but the converse is not true. This can be seen from a simple example (cf. Iacus, 2011, sect. 3.17).

Example 17.1

Define the stopping time $\tau = \min\{t : W_t = -1\}$, which is the first time, the *Wiener*-process W_t crosses the lower bound -1. Consider the stopped process

$$Y_t = \begin{cases} W_t & \text{for } t < \tau \\ W_\tau & \text{for } t \geq \tau, \end{cases}$$

and rescale it, to obtain the new process

$$X_t = \begin{cases} Y_{\frac{t}{1-t}} & \text{for } 0 \leq t < 1 \\ -1 & \text{for } t \geq 1. \end{cases}$$

Is this new process X_t a martingale?

Solution

X_t is clearly not a martingale, because we have

$$E[X_t] = \begin{cases} 0 & \text{for } 0 \leq t < 1 \\ -1 & \text{for } t \geq 1. \end{cases}$$

But it is not hard to see that X_t is a local martingale with respect to the localizing sequence $\tau_n = \min\{t : X_t = n\}$.

Replacing martingales by semimartingales has some technical consequences. Without going into much detail, we generally cannot use equivalent martingale measures anymore, but equivalent local martingale measures, instead. The concept of no arbitrage is also modified slightly. It becomes the "no free lunch with vanishing risk" condition (NFLVR, Delbaen and Schachermayer, 1994). The good news is, those changes have absolutely minute consequences for all practical purposes; they merely generalize the background architecture of the financial market. Because the *Wiener*-process generates sample paths in the *Skorokhod*-space and every martingale is also a local martingale, everything we have done so far fits perfectly into this slightly modified framework. We will therefore continue to use the terms "martingale" and "no arbitrage" as before and skip the technical subtleties.

17.2   Simple and Compound *Poisson*-Process

The *Poisson*-process is one of the most important building blocks of the more general class of *Lévy*-processes. We will discuss those processes in quite some detail at a later time. For the moment, our objective is to understand the mechanics of pure jump processes. So let's ask, what kind of random variable is the random time τ, at which a jump occurs? Because we have required all processes to have the càdlàg property, we have $\{\tau \leq t\} \in \mathcal{F}_t$, and so the random jump time is a stopping time. But we can use a lot more intuition about the properties of τ.

Think of the microstructure of a stock exchange. A new price is quoted, if a sufficient number of orders can be executed at that price. Those orders usually come from different traders with unsynchronized order schedules. Thus, we have good reasons to believe that the random time until the next order comes in, has nothing to do with the time that has already passed. Obviously this argument carries over to the random time at which the next price is quoted. But every single quote of a new price is a jump event. Define the survival function

$$G(t) = P(\{\tau > t\}) \tag{17.2}$$

and observe that for $s \geq 0$, we have by the definition of conditional probability

$$P(\{\tau > s + t\} \cap \{\tau > t\}) = P(\{\tau > s + t\}|\{\tau > t\}) P(\{\tau > t\}). \tag{17.3}$$

It is quite clear that the left hand side is $P(\{\tau > s + t\})$. If our former assumption is correct and the probability for the next jump does not depend on the time passed since the last jump, the first probability on the right hand side of (17.3) has to be

$$P(\{\tau > t + s\}|\{\tau > t\}) = P(\{\tau > s\}). \tag{17.4}$$

To see this, recall that under our assumption the time t in (17.4) has to be arbitrary, so set it to $t = 0$.

Quick calculation 17.1   Use $P(\{\tau > 0\}) = 1$ to prove this statement.

Using our definition of the survival function (17.2), we have thus the functional equation

$$G(s + t) = G(s)G(t). \tag{17.5}$$

There is only one possible class of functions satisfying this relation, combined with the initial condition $G(0) = 1$,

$$G(t) = e^{-\lambda t}, \tag{17.6}$$

with $\lambda \geq 0$.

Quick calculation 17.2   Check that (17.6) satisfies (17.5).

Now using that the distribution function of τ has to be one minus the survival function, $F(t) = 1 - G(t)$, we finally obtain

$$P(\{\tau \leq t\}) = F(t) = 1 - e^{-\lambda t}. \tag{17.7}$$

This is obviously an exponential distribution. There is no other choice, if we agree on the jump times to be memoryless. Exponentially distributed random variables have a broad spectrum of applications. For example, phone calls in a service hotline are also assumed exponentially distributed. We can ask another question: What is the probability for exactly n jump events in the interval $[0, t]$? If τ_n is a cumulative sequence of independent copies of $\tau \sim \text{Exp}(\lambda)$, then there is a random variable N_t, with

$$P(N_t = n) = e^{-\lambda t} \frac{(\lambda t)^n}{n!}, \tag{17.8}$$

for all $n \in \mathbb{N}_0$ (cf. theorem 2.11 in Cont and Tankov, 2004, sect. 2.5). The associated process

$$N_t = \sum_{n=1}^{N} \theta(t - \tau_n), \tag{17.9}$$

where possibly $N = \infty$, is called a *Poisson*-process with intensity λ. The function $\theta(x)$ is again the *Heaviside-θ*-function. The *Poisson*-process is a pure counting process. It counts the number of jumps occurred until time t. *Poisson*-processes have two particularly useful properties. If $N_t \sim \text{Poi}(\lambda_1)$ and $M_t \sim \text{Poi}(\lambda_2)$ are independent processes, then $N_t + M_t \sim \text{Poi}(\lambda_1 + \lambda_2)$ holds.

Quick calculation 17.3   Prove this statement by computing the characteristic function, associated with the probability mass function (17.8).

Furthermore, if we know that exactly N jumps occurred in the interval $[0, t]$, then the jump times τ_n, with $n = 1, \ldots, N$, are uniformly distributed within $[0, t]$ (see theorem 2.9 in Cont and Tankov, 2004, sect. 2.5). This is very useful in simulation, because one only has to draw a number N from the appropriate *Poisson*-distribution and afterwards draw a sample of size N from a uniform distribution over $[0, t]$. The ordered sample represents the set of simulated jump times.

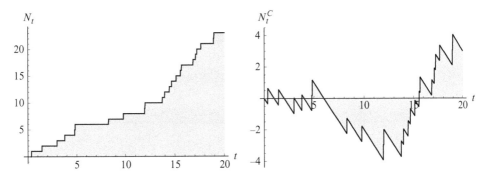

Fig. 17.1 Simple (left) and compensated (right) *Poisson*-process with intensity $\lambda = 1$

It is easy to compute the expectation value of the *Poisson*-process. Using (17.8), one obtains

$$E[N_t] = \sum_{n=0}^{\infty} n \cdot e^{-\lambda t} \frac{(\lambda t)^n}{n!} = e^{-\lambda t} \sum_{n=1}^{\infty} n \cdot \frac{(\lambda t)^n}{n!}$$
$$= \lambda t \cdot e^{-\lambda t} \sum_{n=1}^{\infty} \frac{(\lambda t)^{n-1}}{(n-1)!} = \lambda t \cdot e^{-\lambda t} \sum_{n=0}^{\infty} \cdot \frac{(\lambda t)^n}{n!} = \lambda t. \tag{17.10}$$

Subtracting the drift from the original *Poisson*-process yields the so-called compensated *Poisson*-process $N_t^C = N_t - \lambda t$. This process has zero expectation for all times t. Moreover, the compensated *Poisson*-process is a martingale. Figure 17.1 illustrates both processes with an intensity of $\lambda = 1$. This means that we are expecting to observe one jump per unit of time on average.

As mentioned before, the *Poisson*-process is a pure counting process. The consequence of this is that the jump size is fixed. Each single jump is a unit step. So the obvious question is: Can the *Poisson*-process be modified, such that jump sizes are random? The answer is yes and the process we obtain is called the compound *Poisson*-process. Let Y be a random variable, independent of N_t and with known distribution, and Y_n are independent copies of Y. Then we can define the compound *Poisson*-process

$$X_t = \sum_{n=1}^{N_t} Y_n. \tag{17.11}$$

Can we compute the expectation of this process? Yes, and it is quite simple using the conditioning argument $E[X_t] = E[E[X_t|N_t = n]]$, provided by the law of iterated expectations. The result is

$$E[X_t] = \sum_{n=0}^{\infty} n E[Y] \cdot P(N_t = n) = E[Y]E[N_t] = E[Y] \cdot \lambda t. \tag{17.12}$$

We might for example choose $Y \sim N(\mu, \sigma^2)$. Then the compensated compound *Poisson*-process is $X_t^C = X_t - \mu \lambda t$. The situation is illustrated in Figure 17.2 for $\mu = 1$ and $\sigma = 2$. It is easy to see that the jump sizes are now randomly distributed. They can even become negative, even though we still expect one unit step per time interval on average.

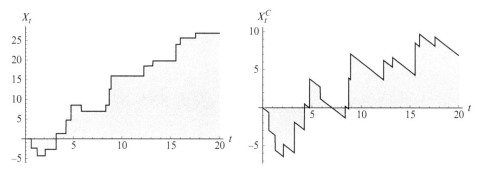

Fig. 17.2 Compound (left) and compensated compound (right) *Poisson*-process with intensity $\lambda = 1$ – Jumps are normally distributed with $\mu = 1$ and $\sigma = 2$

There is one more important issue we need to address with regard to the *Lévy–Khintchine*-representation, we will encounter shortly. This issue is the characteristic function of X_t. Luckily, the same conditioning argument still holds and one obtains

$$\varphi_X(t, u) = E[e^{iuX_t}] = E\left[E[e^{iunY}|N_t = n]\right] = E[\varphi_Y^{N_t}(u)]$$

$$= \sum_{n=0}^{\infty} \varphi_Y^n(u) e^{-\lambda t} \frac{(\lambda t)^n}{n!} = \sum_{n=0}^{\infty} e^{-\lambda t} \frac{(\varphi_Y(u)\lambda t)^n}{n!} = e^{\lambda t(\varphi_Y(u)-1)}. \tag{17.13}$$

If the probability density function of Y is $f(y)$, we can express the characteristic function of X_t as

$$\varphi_X(t, u) = \exp\left(\lambda t \int_{-\infty}^{\infty} (e^{iuy} - 1) f(y) dy\right). \tag{17.14}$$

Quick calculation 17.4 Convince yourself that the characteristic function of the compensated compound *Poisson*-process is given by $\varphi_{X^C}(t, u) = \exp\left(\lambda t \int_{-\infty}^{\infty} (e^{iuy} - 1 - iux) f(y) dy\right)$.

It seems that the compound *Poisson*-process is a good microstructure model frame for the price process. We had good reasons to assume that the times between two quotes are exponentially distributed, and the random jump size can be modeled by any appropriate distribution. How does this microstructure look on a macroscopic level? Because the expected intraday return is small, we abandon it for the moment, and thus $E[Y] = 0$. Let's only postulate that the variance of the jumps is $\text{Var}[Y] = \sigma^2$; we won't even specify the distribution of Y. What happens, if we scale the axes? Say, we multiply the time axis by a factor of α. Since we are mainly interested in the volatility, the drift is zero anyway, and we already learned that volatility is proportional to the square root of time, it seems intuitive to scale the spatial axis by a reciprocal factor of $\sqrt{\alpha}$. That is, we want to investigate the process $X_t^\alpha = \frac{1}{\sqrt{\alpha}} X_{\alpha t}$. It is easy to see that the characteristic function of this process is

$$\varphi_{X^\alpha}(t, u) = \varphi_X\left(\alpha t, \frac{u}{\sqrt{\alpha}}\right). \tag{17.15}$$

Quick calculation 17.5 Prove this statement.

Ultimately, we are interested in the limit $\alpha \to \infty$, to get an impression of the large scale behavior of X_t^α. So let's first manipulate the characteristic function a little bit

$$\begin{aligned} \varphi_{X^\alpha}(t, u) &= \exp\left(\lambda \alpha t \int_{-\infty}^{\infty} \left(e^{\frac{iuy}{\sqrt{\alpha}}} - 1\right) f(y) dy\right) \\ &= \exp\left(\lambda t \int_{-\infty}^{\infty} \left(iuy \sqrt{\alpha} - \frac{1}{2} u^2 y^2 + O(\alpha^{-1/2})\right) f(y) dy\right). \end{aligned} \tag{17.16}$$

In the limit, the $O(\alpha^{-1/2})$ term will vanish, and because the expectation value of Y is zero, we get

$$\lim_{\alpha \to \infty} \varphi_{X^\alpha}(t, u) = e^{-\frac{1}{2} u^2 \lambda \sigma^2 t}. \tag{17.17}$$

That should ring an enormous bell, because this is the characteristic function of a scaled *Wiener*-process. Therefore we obviously have

$$X_t^\alpha \xrightarrow{D} \sqrt{\lambda} \sigma W_t, \tag{17.18}$$

as $\alpha \to \infty$. This might be an explanation for the success of the *Brown*ian motion as stochastic model for the return process. But we can draw an additional conclusion. In times of market distress, it is likely that there is more activity, because investors want to protect or close some of their positions. If our compound *Poisson*-framework is at least roughly correct, we would expect the intensity λ to increase. According to (17.18) this adds to the volatility, which is exactly what is observed in the market. This is a smoking gun, pointing in the direction of GARCH- or stochastic volatility models.

The whole idea is illustrated in Figure 17.3. The original timescale of the process is one second. At this level the intensity $\lambda = 0.1$ means that we expect a new quote every ten seconds on average. Subsequently, the process was compressed to a natural scale of one minute, which means the scaling factor $\alpha = 60$ was chosen. On this timescale the process is already very similar to a *Brown*ian motion. So it seems the only jumps we have to worry about are those rare catastrophic events that occur from time to time on the macroscopic timescale.

17.3 GARCH-Models with Conditional Jump Dynamics

In 2002, Chan and Maheu introduced an ingenious family of GARCH-models, accounting for jumps with changing intensity. It is not surprising that they used a compound *Poisson*-process to model the additional jumps, because we have already

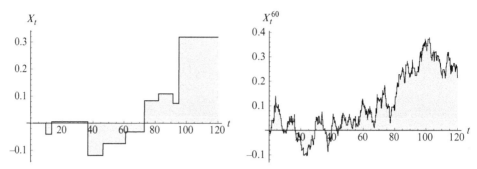

Fig. 17.3 Original (left) and scaled (right) compound *Poisson*-process with intensity $\lambda = 0.1$ – Jumps are normally distributed with zero expectation value and standard deviation $\sigma = 0.1$

seen that this specification is simple and sound. We will again only discuss the simplest member of the *Chan–Maheu*-family; extending the model to higher orders is straightforward. The basic model equations are

$$\Delta x_t = \mu_t + \sqrt{h_t} z_t + \sum_{n=0}^{N_t} Y_{n,t} \qquad (17.19)$$

$$h_t = \omega + \alpha \epsilon_{t-1}^2 + \beta h_{t-1} \qquad (17.20)$$

$$\lambda_t = \eta + \rho \lambda_{t-1} + \gamma \xi_{t-1}, \qquad (17.21)$$

where $z_t \sim N(0,1)$, $Y_{n,t}$ are independent copies of $Y \sim N(\theta, \delta^2)$, $N_t \sim \text{Poi}(\lambda_t)$, $\epsilon_t = \sqrt{h_t} z_t + \sum_{n=0}^{N_t} Y_{n,t}$, and

$$\xi_t = E[N_t | \mathcal{F}_t] - \lambda_t \qquad (17.22)$$

is an innovation.

Quick calculation 17.6 Show that if $E[\Delta x_t] = 0$, we must have $\mu_t = -\lambda_t \theta$.

Because the natural time interval in the GARCH-model is $\Delta t = 1$, the random variable N_t is the number of jumps in each unit time interval. Furthermore, the intensity of the compound *Poisson*-process has dynamics (17.21), and therefore we have $E[N_t | \mathcal{F}_{t-1}] = \lambda_t$.

Quick calculation 17.7 Confirm that $E[\xi_t | \mathcal{F}_{t-1}] = 0$.

Because we know the distribution of z_t and Y, we also know the conditional probability density function of Δx_t,

$$
\begin{aligned}
f(\Delta x_t | \mathcal{F}_{t-1}) &= \sum_{n=0}^{\infty} f(\Delta x_t | N_t = n, \mathcal{F}_{t-1}) \cdot P(N_t = n | \mathcal{F}_{t-1}) \\
&= \sum_{n=0}^{\infty} \frac{1}{\sqrt{2\pi(h_t + n\delta^2)}} \exp\left(-\frac{1}{2}\frac{(\Delta x_t - \mu_t - n\theta)^2}{h_t + n\delta^2}\right) \cdot e^{-\lambda_t}\frac{\lambda_t^n}{n!}.
\end{aligned}
\tag{17.23}
$$

Of course we have to truncate this series at a particular n, but that is not a problem. Because the natural time interval of a GARCH-model is one day, and the average number of large jumps over one day is very small,[1] we can truncate the series very early, say at $n = 10$. The probability density (17.23) is recognized as a *Gaussian* mixture density, where the weights are related to λ_t and the variances of the mixture components are related to h_t. Observe that ϵ_t contains both the fluctuations due to volatility and due to jumps. Thus, a large jump event does not only affect the conditional intensity, but also the conditional variance.

There is one subtle question we have not yet addressed: How is ξ_t computed? From the definition it is clear that it contains the conditional expectation

$$
E[N_t | \mathcal{F}_t] = \sum_{n=0}^{\infty} n \cdot P(N_t = n | \mathcal{F}_t).
\tag{17.24}
$$

But what does that mean? The probability $P(N_t = n | \mathcal{F}_t)$ is called the posterior probability for n jumps. It is the probability we assign to the state of the world in which n jumps occur, after we know everything else. In particular we know Δx_t, h_t, and λ_t, nevertheless we cannot obtain the posterior probability directly, but we can apply Bayes' rule to obtain

$$
P(N_t = n | \mathcal{F}_t) = \frac{f(\Delta x_t | N_t = n, \mathcal{F}_{t-1}) \cdot P(N_t = n | \mathcal{F}_{t-1})}{f(\Delta x_t | \mathcal{F}_{t-1})}.
\tag{17.25}
$$

Quick calculation 17.8   Use (17.23) to show that $P(N_t = n | \mathcal{F}_t)$ is indeed a probability.

You might wonder why there is a posterior probability for a large jump. If such a catastrophic event occurs shouldn't we know it? Not necessarily. The genuine jump distribution is a normal distribution. Even if a jump occurs, the jump size may be small just by chance. In this case it could prove difficult to separate the jump effect from ordinary fluctuations due to volatility. Furthermore, a small jump could neutralize the regular fluctuation by an opposite sign. Thus, it may very well be a problem to detect a jump, as long as it is not of catastrophic magnitude. We can use the posterior probability to get an idea of the likelihood that we encountered a jump event at a particular day. The probability for at least one jump at day t is given by

$$
P(N_t \geq 1 | \mathcal{F}_t) = 1 - P(N_t = 0 | \mathcal{F}_t).
\tag{17.26}
$$

---

[1] Usually, we expect to observe one large scale jump roughly in the order of magnitude of one year.

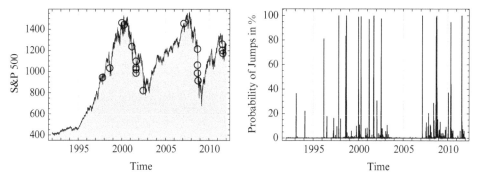

Fig. 17.4 Price process of the S&P 500 stock index (left) and filtered probability for at least one jump (right) – Jumps identified with probability greater or equal to 95% are indicated by circles

Thus, the *Chan–Maheu*-model provides us with the filtered probability for a jump event for free. And there is even more. By the law of iterated expectations, we get from (17.21)

$$E[\lambda_t] = \eta + \rho E[\lambda_{t-1}].\tag{17.27}$$

By now we know that this kind of recursion is typical for GARCH-models and after applying our geometric series trick, we obtain the stationary intensity

$$E[\lambda_t] = \lambda_\infty = \frac{\eta}{1-\rho}.\tag{17.28}$$

The *Chan–Maheu*-model was fitted to the S&P 500 stock index data, we encountered in Chapter 15. The posterior probabilities for at least one jump are illustrated in Figure 17.4 (right) together with the original price process (left). There is indeed roughly one jump in a year on average, if we assume that a posterior probability greater or equal to 95% is sufficient evidence for the presence of a jump. Those jumps are indicated by circles in Figure 17.4 left. The stationary intensity was estimated as $\hat{\lambda}_\infty \approx 2.2\%$. Taking into account that GARCH-models are calibrated in terms of trading days, we would eventually expect approximately five to six jumps per year. Obviously, only a small fraction of the jumps that occur has a noticeable impact, such that it can be detected by its posterior probability.

Unfortunately, it is far from trivial to relate a GARCH-model with conditional jump dynamics to an equivalent risk-neutral probability measure, so that it can be used for derivative pricing. Immediate calibration to plain vanilla option prices is usually impractical, because the valuation has to be conducted via Monte Carlo simulation.

17.4 Merton's Jump-Diffusion Model

In 1976, Robert Merton introduced an alternative model for the evolution of stock prices,

$$dS_t = \mu S_t dt + \sigma S_t dW_t + (e^{Y_t} - 1)S_t dN_t. \tag{17.29}$$

This equation needs some explanation. First of all, dN_t is the increment of a *Poisson*-process, and the random variable Y_t governs the jump dynamics with $Y_t = Y_n$ at $t = \tau_n$. The Y_ns are independent copies of the random variable $Y \sim N(\theta, \delta^2)$. But let's try to decipher this process step by step. To understand the increment dN_t, we will take a heuristical perspective. Remember how the *Poisson*-process is defined,

$$N_t = \sum_{n=1}^{N} \theta(t - \tau_n), \tag{17.30}$$

with the differences of the stopping times distributed as $\Delta\tau_n \sim \text{Exp}(\lambda)$. In the framework of generalized functions, we can write

$$dN_t = \sum_{n=1}^{N} \theta'(t - \tau_n)dt = \sum_{n=1}^{N} \delta(t - \tau_n)dt, \tag{17.31}$$

where $\delta(x)$ is again the *Dirac-δ*-function.[2] Of course, like the *Wiener*-increment, the *Poisson*-increment only makes sense, if interpreted as an integral

$$\int_t^{t+dt} dN_s = \sum_{n=1}^{N} \int_t^{t+dt} \delta(s - \tau_n)ds = \begin{cases} 1 & \text{with prob. } \lambda dt \\ 0 & \text{with prob. } 1 - \lambda dt. \end{cases} \tag{17.32}$$

In other words, $dN_t = 1$ only if there is a realization of any stopping time τ_n in the interval $[t, t + dt]$. Because the interval is so small, the probability of two jumps is $O(dt^2)$, and therefore zero. So let's see what Merton's model looks like, if we integrate over an infinitely small time interval

$$S_{t+dt} = S_t + \mu S_t \int_t^{t+dt} ds + \sigma S_t \int_t^{t+dt} dW_s + (e^{Y_t} - 1)S_t \int_t^{t+dt} dN_s$$
$$= S_t \cdot (1 - J_t) + e^{Y_t} S_t \cdot J_t + \mu S_t dt + \sigma S_t \sqrt{dt} Z_t, \tag{17.33}$$

where $Z_t \sim N(0, 1)$, and J_t is a *Bernoulli*-distributed random variable with $P(J_t = 1) = \lambda dt$ and $P(J_t = 0) = 1 - \lambda dt$. If for example Y_t were not random but fixed to a value of $Y_t = \log 0.9$, then every time a jump occurs, which means $J_t = 1$, the price of the underlying would be reduced to 90% of its former level.

To find a strong solution to (17.29), we need an extension of Itô's lemma, also valid for jump-diffusions. Such an extension can be found in Cont and Tankov (2004, proposition 8.14 in sect. 8.3)

---

[2] Do not confuse the expectation value $E[Y] = \theta$ and the variance $\text{Var}[Y] = \delta^2$ with the *Heaviside-θ*-function $\theta(x)$ and the *Dirac-δ*-function $\delta(x)$.

Theorem 17.2 (Itô's lemma for jump-diffusions) *Let X_t be a jump-diffusion process of the kind*

$$dX_t = f(X_t, t)dt + g(X_t, t)dW_t + h(X_t, Y_t, t)dN_t,$$

with deterministic or stochastic jumps Y_t. If $z(x, t)$ is a sufficiently smooth function, then the stochastic process $Z_t = z(X_t, t)$ is also a jump-diffusion and has the dynamics

$$dZ_t = \left(f(X_t, t)\frac{\partial z}{\partial x} + \frac{\partial z}{\partial t} + \frac{1}{2}g^2(X_t, t)\frac{\partial^2 z}{\partial x^2} \right) dt$$

$$+ g(X_t, t)\frac{\partial z}{\partial x}dW_t + \left(z(X_{t^-} + h(X_t, Y_t, t), t) - z(X_{t^-}, t) \right) dN_t,$$

where the partial derivatives are to be evaluated at $x = X_t$.

Using Theorem 17.2 together with our usual log-price transformation $x_t = \log S_t$, Merton's model (17.29) takes the form

$$dx_t = \left(\mu - \frac{1}{2}\sigma^2 \right) dt + \sigma dW_t + Y_t dN_t. \tag{17.34}$$

Quick calculation 17.9 Verify that the jump part of dx_t is indeed $Y_t dN_t$.

When integrating the last term on the right hand side, we get with the help of (17.31)

$$\int_0^t Y_s dN_s = \sum_{n=1}^N \int_0^t Y_s \delta(s - \tau_n)ds = \sum_{n=1}^{N_t} Y_n, \tag{17.35}$$

which is our old friend the compound *Poisson*-process. Thus, integrating the whole equation (17.34) we obtain

$$x_t = x_0 + \left(\mu - \frac{1}{2}\sigma^2 \right) t + \sigma W_t + \sum_{n=1}^{N_t} Y_n. \tag{17.36}$$

Exponentiating this expression yields the desired strong solution to (17.29)

$$S_t = S_0 e^{(\mu - \frac{1}{2}\sigma^2)t + \sigma W_t + \sum_{n=1}^{N_t} Y_n} = S_0 e^{(\mu - \frac{1}{2}\sigma^2)t + \sigma W_t} \prod_{n=1}^{N_t} e^{Y_n}. \tag{17.37}$$

Merton made a crucial assumption that opens the door to a tremendous shortcut. He assumed that the jumps are purely idiosyncratic events, which means they do not contribute to the systematic risk. But idiosyncratic risks should not be rewarded and thus, the risk-neutral measure Q is still found by applying the *Girsanov*-transformation, which means replacing μ by r. Under Q,

$$S_t = e^{-r(T-t)}E^Q[S_T|\mathcal{F}_t] \tag{17.38}$$

has to hold, which also means that we must have $E^Q[S_t] = S_0 e^{rt}$. So let's compute the expectation value of (17.37). To accomplish this task, we can use that the copies Y_n of

Y are independent and normally distributed, which means e^Y is log-normal. We thus obtain

$$
E\left[\prod_{n=1}^{N_t} e^{Y_n}\right] = E\left[E\left[e^{\sum_{k=1}^{n} Y_k}\big|N_t=n\right]\right] = \sum_{n=0}^{\infty} E[e^Y]^n \cdot P(N_t=n)
$$
$$
= \sum_{n=0}^{\infty} E[e^Y]^n \cdot e^{-\lambda t}\frac{(\lambda t)^n}{n!} = \exp\left(\lambda t(E[e^Y]-1)\right) = e^{\lambda k t},
$$
(17.39)

with $k = e^{\theta+\frac{1}{2}\delta^2} - 1$. Thus, under the risk-neutral measure Q, we have the strong solution

$$
S_t = S_0 e^{(r-\frac{1}{2}\sigma^2-\lambda k)t+\sigma W_t} \prod_{n=1}^{N_t} e^{Y_n}.
$$
(17.40)

With that knowledge, we can write the present value of a derivative, contingent on the underlying S, as discounted risk-neutral expectation, conditional on the usual information set and the number of jumps that may occur between now and the exercise date

$$
V(S_0,0) = e^{-rT} \sum_{n=0}^{\infty} \frac{e^{-\lambda T}(\lambda T)^n}{n!} E\left[V\left(S_0 e^{(r-\frac{1}{2}\sigma^2-\lambda k)T+n\theta+\sqrt{\sigma^2+\frac{n\delta^2}{T}}W_T}, T\right)\bigg|N_T=n\right]. \quad (17.41)
$$

Inventing the new variable $\sigma_n^2 = \sigma^2 + \frac{n\delta^2}{T}$, we can rewrite this as

$$
V(S_0,0) = e^{-rT} \sum_{n=0}^{\infty} \frac{e^{-\lambda T}(\lambda T)^n}{n!} E\left[V\left(S_0 e^{\left(r-\frac{1}{2}\sigma_n^2+\frac{n\delta^2}{2T}-\lambda k\right)T+n\theta+\sigma_n W_T}, T\right)\bigg|N_T=n\right]. \quad (17.42)
$$

Defining the new artificial interest rate $r_n = r + n\frac{\theta+\delta^2/2}{T} - \lambda k$, one finally obtains

$$
V(S_0,0) = \sum_{n=0}^{\infty} \frac{e^{-\tilde{\lambda}T}(\tilde{\lambda}T)^n}{n!} e^{-r_n T} E\left[V\left(S_0 e^{(r_n-\frac{1}{2}\sigma_n^2)T+\sigma_n W_T}, T\right)\bigg|N_T=n\right]
$$
$$
= \sum_{n=0}^{\infty} \frac{e^{-\tilde{\lambda}T}(\tilde{\lambda}T)^n}{n!} e^{-r_n T} E^{Q_n}[V(S_T,T)|N_t=n],
$$
(17.43)

with $k = e^{\theta+\frac{1}{2}\delta^2} - 1$, and $\tilde{\lambda} = \lambda e^{\theta+\frac{1}{2}\delta^2} = \lambda(1+k)$. By the measure Q_n, we simply indicate that the expectation is to be taken with respect to the modified interest rate r_n and volatility σ_n. Of course the change of measure does not induce a change in volatility and thus, Q_n is not to be understood as a new family of risk-neutral measures. The whole point is that we can valuate a contract under Merton's jump-diffusion process as weighted average of options under jump-free geometric *Brown*ian motions. We can summarize the formulas for European plain vanilla options as

$$
V_t(K,T,\lambda) = \sum_{n=0}^{\infty} \frac{e^{-\tilde{\lambda}(T-t)}\tilde{\lambda}^n(T-t)^n}{n!} V_{t,n}(K,T),
$$
(17.44)

with

$$k = e^{\theta + \frac{1}{2}\delta^2} - 1 \quad \text{and} \quad \tilde{\lambda} = \lambda(1 + k), \tag{17.45}$$

and the *Black–Scholes*-price $V_{t,n}(K, T)$ for a plain vanilla call or put option with modified interest rate and volatility

$$r_n = r + \frac{n(\theta + \frac{1}{2}\delta^2)}{T - t} - \lambda k \quad \text{and} \quad \sigma_n^2 = \sigma^2 + \frac{n\delta^2}{T - t}. \tag{17.46}$$

The series (17.44) converges rapidly, because usually λ is small and thus, one only needs to compute say the first 10 or 15 terms, depending on the remaining time to expiry.

What would have happened, if we did not take the shortcut? Our usual routine dictates that we have to set up a hedge-portfolio $\Pi = V - \Delta S$. Using Theorem 17.2, the change in this hedge-portfolio after appropriately regrouping terms is

$$d\Pi = \left(\frac{\partial V}{\partial t} + \frac{1}{2}\sigma^2 S^2 \frac{\partial^2 V}{\partial S^2} \right) dt + \left(\frac{\partial V}{\partial S} - \Delta \right)(\mu S dt + \sigma S dW)$$
$$+ \left(V(e^Y S, t) - V(S, t) - \Delta(e^Y - 1)S \right) dN. \tag{17.47}$$

Following Merton's argument, the dW-part is the only source of systematic risk, and the dN-part is the source of purely idiosyncratic risk. Thus, the systematic risk should be hedged away, because idiosyncratic risk has no market price. This can be achieved as usual by choosing $\Delta = \frac{\partial V}{\partial S}$. The result is

$$d\Pi = \left(\frac{\partial V}{\partial t} + \frac{1}{2}\sigma^2 S^2 \frac{\partial^2 V}{\partial S^2} \right) dt + \left(V(e^Y S, t) - V(S, t) - \frac{\partial V}{\partial S}(e^Y - 1)S \right) dN. \tag{17.48}$$

Because the remaining random fluctuations due to dN are meaningless with respect to the fair price of this hedge-portfolio, we must have

$$E[d\Pi] = r\Pi dt. \tag{17.49}$$

Considering $Y \sim N(\theta, \delta^2)$ and making some suitable rearrangements, one obtains the *Black–Scholes–Merton*-equation

$$\frac{\partial V}{\partial t} + (r - \lambda k)S\frac{\partial V}{\partial S} + \frac{1}{2}\sigma^2 S^2 \frac{\partial^2 V}{\partial S^2} - (r + \lambda)V + \lambda \int_{-\infty}^{\infty} V(e^y S, t)f(y)dy = 0, \tag{17.50}$$

where again $k = e^{\theta + \frac{1}{2}\delta^2} - 1$, and $f(y)$ is the normal probability density function

$$f(y) = \frac{1}{\sqrt{2\pi\delta^2}} e^{-\frac{1}{2}\left(\frac{y-\theta}{\delta}\right)^2}. \tag{17.51}$$

Equation (17.50) is called a partial integro-differential equation (PIDE). It can be solved and of course the solution is the one we already obtained in (17.44) to (17.46), even though we do not prove it here. Note that for $\lambda = 0$ the whole PIDE collapses to the usual *Black–Scholes*-PDE. For $\lambda > 0$, the integral-term makes this type of equation non-local, because it extends over the entire spatial direction. Such a non-local term has severe consequences for numerical schemes like the finite difference method of Chapter 14. Generally, one needs two grids, one for the PDE-part of the equation, and another for the integral-part. The good news is that jump-diffusion processes like (17.29) are easy to simulate via Monte Carlo. Thus, we have at least access to simple numerical valuation methods for a wide variety of European contracts.

17.5 Barrier Options and the Reflection Principle

There is a very efficient way to valuate barrier options via Monte Carlo simulation, when the dynamics of the underlying are modeled by a jump-diffusion process. The jump distribution has not necessarily to be log-normal as in the *Merton*-model, as long as the compound *Poisson*-structure is preserved. The method is based on the so-called reflection principle, which is a really beautiful piece of reasoning.

Key in understanding this principle and its implications is the situation illustrated in Figure 17.5. For simplicity, we conduct all calculations in the log-price space. Further, we assume for the moment that the barrier under consideration is an upper barrier $x_u = \log S_u > 0$ and that the model for the log-price process of the underlying is a plain *Wiener*-process. We will make the appropriate refinements later. The random time τ, when the *Wiener*-process hits the barrier for the first time is clearly a stopping time. If $\tau < T$, we can track an auxiliary path, reflected at the barrier, by multiplying all increments of the *Wiener*-process after $t = \tau$ by minus one. This auxiliary trajectory is indicated as a gray path in Figure 17.5. Because the distribution of the *Wiener*-increments is symmetric around the origin, the reflected path has exactly the same probability of occurrence as the original one. Of course the probability for a path to end up exactly at $W_T = w_T$ after crossing the barrier is zero. But the probability for

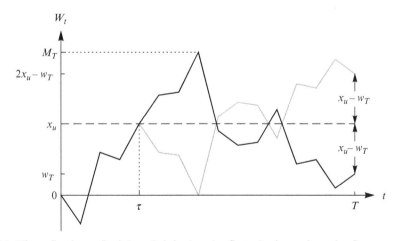

Fig. 17.5 The reflection principle – Original and reflected schematic path of a *Wiener*-process

$W_T \leq w_T$ is not zero and it equals the probability for $W_T \geq 2x_u - w_T$. We can thus state the important reflection equality

$$P(\{\tau \leq T\} \cap W_T \leq w_T) = P(W_T \geq 2x_u - w_T), \tag{17.52}$$

for $w_T \leq x_u$. If $W_T \geq 2x_u - w_T$, then of course $\tau \leq T$ has to be true, because the process must have crossed the barrier to end up at $2x_u - w_T$.

There is another random variable indicated in Figure 17.5: The maximum of the process W_t, between time $t = 0$ and $t = T$,

$$M_T = \max_{0 \leq t \leq T} W_t. \tag{17.53}$$

Observe that $M_T \geq x_u$ if and only if $\tau \leq T$. Thus, we can rewrite the reflection equality as

$$P(M_T \geq x_u \cap W_T \leq w_T) = P(W_T \geq 2x_u - w_T), \tag{17.54}$$

for $w_T \leq x_u$. This is enough information to deduce the joint distribution of M_T and W_T. Let $f(m, w)$ be the associated joint probability density function. Then we have

$$\int_m^\infty \int_{-\infty}^w f(x, y) dy dx = \frac{1}{\sqrt{2\pi T}} \int_{2m-w}^\infty e^{-\frac{1}{2}\frac{y^2}{T}} dy. \tag{17.55}$$

Differentiating this equation with respect to m yields

$$-\int_{-\infty}^w f(m, y) dy = -\frac{2}{\sqrt{2\pi T}} e^{-\frac{1}{2}\frac{(2m-w)^2}{T}}. \tag{17.56}$$

Finally, differentiating with respect to w and multiplying by minus one yields

$$f(m, w) = \frac{2(2m - w)}{T\sqrt{2\pi T}} e^{-\frac{1}{2}\frac{(2m-w)^2}{T}}. \tag{17.57}$$

The interesting question is, what is the probability of $M_T \leq x_u$, conditional on the information that $W_T = w_T$? In other words, how probable is it that a *Brown*ian bridge process with $B_0 = 0$ and $B_T = w_T \leq x_u$ has not crossed the upper barrier x_u? We can easily compute the probability density function of the maximum of the *Brown*ian bridge, by conditioning (17.57) on w,

$$\begin{aligned} f(m|w) &= \frac{f(m, w)}{f(w)} \\ &= \frac{2(2m - w)}{T\sqrt{2\pi T}} \sqrt{2\pi T} e^{-\frac{1}{2}\frac{(2m-w)^2}{T} + \frac{1}{2}\frac{w^2}{T}} \\ &= \frac{2(2m - w)}{T} e^{-\frac{2m(m-w)}{T}}. \end{aligned} \tag{17.58}$$

The desired probability is then obtained by integration over the conditional probability density for $w = w_T$

$$P(M_T \leq x_u|\mathcal{F}_{0 \to w_T}) = \int_{-\infty}^{x_u} f(m|w_T)dm = \int_{w_T}^{x_u} f(m|w_T)dm$$

$$= \left[-e^{-\frac{2m(m-w_T)}{T}}\right]_{w_T}^{x_u} = 1 - e^{-\frac{2x_u(x_u-w_T)}{T}}, \tag{17.59}$$

for $w_T \leq x_u$. Keeping in mind that $W_0 = 0$, it is easy to see that this probability only depends on the initial distance to the barrier $x_u = (x_u - 0)$, the final distance $(x_u - w_T)$, and the variance T. Indeed, repeating the whole derivation for the affine transformed process $X_t = x_0 + \mu t + \sigma W_t$, with $x_0 \leq x_u$ and $x_T \leq x_u$, yields

$$P(M_T \leq x_u|\mathcal{F}_{0 \to x_T}) = 1 - e^{-\frac{2(x_u-x_0)(x_u-x_T)}{\sigma^2 T}}. \tag{17.60}$$

Note that the drift μ does not enter the computation, because it is not relevant for the bridge process, if x_0 and x_T are fixed. The only situation we have not yet considered is what happens if $x_0 > x_u$ or $x_T > x_u$. In this case, the process has obviously crossed the barrier and the probability (17.60) should become zero. We can write the entire barrier probability as

$$P(M_T \leq x_u|\mathcal{F}_{0 \to x_T}) = \theta(x_u - x_0)\theta(x_u - x_T)\left(1 - e^{-\frac{2(x_u-x_0)(x_u-x_T)}{\sigma^2 T}}\right). \tag{17.61}$$

Quick calculation 17.10 What is the barrier probability for the minimum not to cross x_l?

How can we use the reflection principle to price a European barrier option when the underlying follows a jump-diffusion process? If we can write the risk-neutral expectation of a knockout option say with upper barrier in the form

$$V_0^\otimes(K, T, S_u, \lambda) = e^{-rT}E^Q\left[E[V(S_T, T)\theta(S_u - M_T)|\mathcal{F}_{0 \to S_T}]|\mathcal{F}_0\right]$$

$$= e^{-rT}E^Q\left[V(S_T, T) \cdot P(M_T \leq S_u|\mathcal{F}_{0 \to S_T})|\mathcal{F}_0\right], \tag{17.62}$$

then we are in business, because we can evaluate the inner expectation analytically and the outer one via Monte Carlo. Note that we have switched from log-prices x_t to ordinary prices S_t. We know that there are N_T jumps between $t = 0$ and $t = T$, occurring at random times τ_n. For given $N_T = N$ let's augment the sequence of stopping times by $\tau_0 = 0$ and $\tau_{N+1} = T$. In the interval $[\tau_n, \tau_{n+1})$, where no jumps occur, the price process of the underlying is a geometric Brownian bridge, connecting the initial value S_n at time τ_n, with the final value $F_n = S_{n+1}^-$ immediately before time τ_{n+1}. Of course F_N is the terminal price S_T. If $\mathcal{F}_{n \to F_n}$ is the σ-algebra generated by observing the bridge pair

(S_n, F_n), then the total probability for not crossing the barrier can be written as

$$P(M_T \le S_u | \mathcal{F}_{0 \to S_T}) = \prod_{n=0}^{N_T} P(M_{\Delta \tau_n} \le S_u | \mathcal{F}_{n \to F_n})$$

$$= \prod_{n=0}^{N_T} \theta(S_u - S_n)\theta(S_u - F_n)\left(1 - \left(\frac{S_n}{S_u}\right)^{\frac{2\log(S_u/F_n)}{\sigma^2 \Delta \tau_n}}\right), \quad (17.63)$$

with $\Delta \tau_n = \tau_{n+1} - \tau_n$.

Quick calculation 17.11 How does the last equation look for log-prices $x_t = \log S_t$?

We are now in a position to approximate the outer expectation value in (17.62) by an average over many replications of the payoff. To generate one replication, we only need to simulate the number of jumps N_T, the jump times τ_n, the jump sizes Y_n, and the final bridge values F_n, which are given by

$$F_n = S_n e^{(r - \frac{1}{2}\sigma^2)\Delta \tau_n + \sigma W_{\Delta \tau_n}}. \quad (17.64)$$

This is a very small number of random draws, $3N_T + 2$ to be precise. The computational burden is vanishingly low compared to simulating the whole trajectory. To see how it is done, let's look at an example.

Example 17.2

Consider a European style knockout call option, with lower barrier S_l, contingent on a foreign currency. Assume that the annual domestic interest rate r, the foreign interest rate r_f, and the volatility of the foreign currency σ is known. How can this option be valuated numerically, when the dynamics of the underlying are modeled by a jump-diffusion of the *Merton*-type, with intensity λ and jump distribution $Y \sim N(\theta, \delta^2)$?

Solution

The pseudo-code for valuating this contract is provided in Box 17.1. $U[0, T]$ is the uniform distribution on the interval $[0, T]$. The array $(u_1, \ldots, u_N)$ is a list of numbers, drawn from the uniform distribution $U[0, T]$ and the command $\texttt{Sort}[\ldots]$ arranges the components of a list in ascending order. The algorithm avoids some unnecessary computations by using $\texttt{If-then}$ gates.

The computations could have also been conducted in the log-price space, with $x_n = \log S_n$ and $\xi_n = \log F_n$. Then the probability for the minimum m_T not crossing the lower barrier $x_l = \log S_l$ would have been

$$P(m_T \ge x_l | \mathcal{F}_{0 \to x_T}) = \prod_{n=0}^{N_T} \theta(x_n - x_l)\theta(\xi_n - x_l)\left(1 - e^{\frac{-2(x_n - x_l)(\xi_n - x_l)}{\sigma^2 \Delta \tau_n}}\right). \quad (17.65)$$

Box 17.1 Pseudo-code for knock-out barrier option under jump-diffusion	

Set M ▷ Initialization

$b = r - r_f$ ▷ Cost-of-carry rate

$\tau_0 = 0$

For $m = 1$ to M ▷ Path replication

    Draw $N \sim \text{Poi}(\lambda T)$ ▷ Number of jumps

    $\tau_{N+1} = T$

    If $N > 0$ then

       Draw $(u_1, \ldots, u_N) \sim U[0, T]$

       $(\tau_1, \ldots, \tau_N) = \text{Sort}[(u_1, \ldots, u_N)]$ ▷ Jump times

    For $n = 0$ to N ▷ Bridge segments

       $\Delta\tau_n = \tau_{n+1} - \tau_n$

       Draw $z \sim N(0, 1)$

       $F_n = S_n \exp\left((b - \tfrac{1}{2}\sigma^2)\Delta\tau_n + \sigma\sqrt{\Delta\tau_n}\, z\right)$

       If $n < N$ then

          Draw $y \sim N(\theta, \delta^2)$ ▷ Logarithmic jump size

          $S_{n+1} = \exp(y) F_n$

    Next n

    $P = \prod_{n=0}^{N} \theta(S_n - S_l)\theta(F_n - S_l)\left(1 - (S_n/S_l)^{\frac{2\log(S_l/F_n)}{\sigma^2 \Delta\tau_n}}\right)$ ▷ Barrier probability

    $V_T^{(m)} = \max\left(F_N - K, 0\right) \cdot P$ ▷ Payoff function

Next m

$V_0 = \exp(-rT) \cdot 1/M \sum_{m=1}^{M} V_T^{(m)}$

Print V_0 ▷ Output

17.6   *Lévy*-Processes

Lévy-processes are named after the French mathematician Paul Pierre Lévy, who established major parts of the theoretical framework of stochastic processes. A *Lévy*-process L_t is defined by four properties:

$$
\begin{aligned}
&1. \ L_0 = 0, \\
&2. \ L_t \text{ has independent increments,} \\
&3. \ L_t - L_s \overset{D}{=} L_{t-s} \text{ for } 0 \leq s < t, \\
&4. \ \text{for } \varepsilon > 0, \ \lim_{\Delta t \to 0} P(|L_{t+\Delta t} - L_t| \geq \varepsilon) = 0.
\end{aligned}
\tag{17.66}
$$

The first two properties are identical to the *Wiener*-properties (13.2) on page 249. The third one is more general. Remember that for the *Wiener*-increment $W_t - W_s \sim N(0, t - s)$ holds. But this is also the distribution of W_{t-s} for $0 \leq s < t$. Hence, $W_t - W_s \overset{D}{=} W_{t-s}$, where the symbol $\overset{D}{=}$ means "equal in distribution." *Lévy*-processes are more general in that they are not restricted to normal distribution of their increments. The last property is called stochastic continuity. This is a subtle condition, because it does not imply that a *Lévy*-process has no jumps, but that the jump probability at any given time t is zero. This is because jump times are stopping times, and therefore continuously distributed random variables. Of course the single point $t \in \mathbb{R}_0^+$ must have zero probability. Thus, *Lévy*-processes can exhaust the jump repertoire of the càdlàg-class.

Lévy-processes have another important property called infinite divisibility. For $0 \leq s < t$, we can write $L_{t+s} = (L_{t+s} - L_s) + L_s$. Because of condition 2, both increments are independent and by condition 3, $(L_{t+s} - L_s) \overset{D}{=} L_t$. This implies that the characteristic function must satisfy

$$\varphi_L(t + s, u) = \varphi_L(t, u)\varphi_L(s, u). \tag{17.67}$$

We have already encountered such a functional equation in deriving the exponential distribution. There is only one possible solution to (17.67),

$$\varphi_L(t, u) = e^{t\psi(u)}, \tag{17.68}$$

where the function $\psi(u)$ is called the characteristic exponent. Since all the information of the distribution is contained in $\psi(u)$ and t is arbitrary, (17.68) tells us that we can divide the *Lévy*-process into arbitrary small independent increments, all with the same (scaled) distribution.

Quick calculation 17.12 Which process has characteristic exponent $\psi(u) = iu\mu - \frac{1}{2}u^2\sigma^2$?

The requirement (17.68) reveals severe limitations of the *Lévy*-class. For example the affine class *Heston*-process of Chapter 16 is clearly no *Lévy*-process. But we have already encountered lots of *Lévy*-processes. *Brown*ian motion is one, the compound *Poisson*-process is another. Merton's jump-diffusion process is also a *Lévy*-process. Jump-diffusions are actually a quite general class. Let's give them a name; call them *Lévy*-processes of type I.[3] The characteristic exponent of a general type I *Lévy*-process is

$$\psi(u) = iu\mu - \frac{1}{2}u^2\sigma^2 + \lambda \int_{-\infty}^{\infty} (e^{iux} - 1)f(x)dx. \tag{17.69}$$

We can clearly recognize each single component. The first one is a deterministic drift μ, the second one is a continuous random fluctuation due to a *Wiener*-process, scaled with σ, and the third one is a compound *Poisson*-process with intensity λ and jump distribution $F(x)$.[4] It is customary to modify the representation (17.69) in two ways. The first modification concerns the drift. Because the jump part of the process also

---

[3] These categories are due to Lewis (2002).

[4] We will switch variables for the jumps from Y to X, to avoid subsequent notational confusion.

induces a drift, one naturally wants to subtract this additional drift from the jump part, to make it a martingale. Thus, (17.69) becomes

$$\psi(u) = iu\tilde{\mu} - \frac{1}{2}u^2\sigma^2 + \lambda \int_{-\infty}^{\infty} (e^{iux} - 1 - iux)f(x)dx, \qquad (17.70)$$

with

$$\tilde{\mu} = \mu + \lambda \int_{-\infty}^{\infty} xf(x)dx. \qquad (17.71)$$

The second modification is necessary to also include the type II *Lévy*-processes later. It introduces the *Lévy*-measure

$$\nu(dx) = \lambda f(x)dx. \qquad (17.72)$$

This notation needs some comment. A measure takes as argument an interval, because intervals are the basic ingredients in the *Borel-σ-algebra*. But the notation is more than a technical reminder, it is an instruction for computing the measure of arbitrary intervals. Let's say, we have a not necessarily simple interval A. Its *Lévy*-measure is

$$\nu(A) = \int_A \nu(dx) = \int_A \lambda f(x)dx. \qquad (17.73)$$

This may very well include the sum of more than one integral over unconnected subintervals. On the other hand, it is easy to verify that $\nu(\mathbb{R}) = \lambda$. From this we can conclude that the *Lévy*-measure provides information about the intensity of jumps of a certain size in the unit time interval. Thus, knowing the *Lévy*-measure, we know everything about the characteristics of the jump process. This leads to our type I representation of the characteristic exponent

$$\psi(u) = iu\tilde{\mu} - \frac{1}{2}u^2\sigma^2 + \int_{-\infty}^{\infty} (e^{iux} - 1 - iux)\nu(dx), \qquad (17.74)$$

with the characteristic *Lévy*-triple $(\tilde{\mu}, \sigma^2, \nu(dx))$. Like a normal distribution that is determined by its mean and variance, a *Lévy*-process is completely determined by its *Lévy*-triple.

Processes of type I are also called finite activity processes, because the number of jumps in the unit time interval, and hence the *Lévy*-measure is finite. Type II processes are those with countably infinite jumps in the unit time interval, and thus $\nu(\mathbb{R}) = \infty$. It is immediately clear that our intuition of *Poisson*-intensity breaks down, because a parameter like λ becomes meaningless in this situation. Type II processes are also said to be of infinite activity. But there are two possible reasons for the *Lévy*-measure to become infinite. Either the jumps are too large, or there are too many small jumps. Luckily, it turns out that the number of large jumps is guaranteed to be finite, so that we can find a workaround. What does it mean that a jump is large and when is it too large? We can draw the line between small and large jumps completely arbitrarily.

A simple and widely used rule of thumb is to say a jump is large, if its absolute value is larger than one. We could have used any other absolute value, it does not make any difference. A process has too large jumps, if we have

$$\int_{\mathbb{R}\backslash(-1,1)} |x| \nu(dx) = \infty. \tag{17.75}$$

On the other hand, if there are too many small jumps, the problems are always due to divergence as $|x| \to 0$. We have therefore tremendous activity in the immediate vicinity of the origin. Unfortunately, the integral does not necessarily converge, if we give the small jumps a weight proportional to their absolute value as in (17.75), but if we choose x^2 as weighting function, we have always

$$\int_{-1}^{1} x^2 \nu(dx) < \infty. \tag{17.76}$$

It may not look that way, but this is the key to including all type II processes. Let's ask what the difficulty with those processes is in the first place. The whole problem lies within the integral of the characteristic exponent (17.74). For $|x| \to \infty$, the absolute value $|e^{iux} - 1 - iux|$ is of order $|x|$.

Quick calculation 17.13 Use Euler's identity to verify this statement.

Thus, because of (17.75), the corresponding integral does not exist. But $|e^{iux} - 1|$ is bounded for $|x| \to \infty$, and because there are only finitely many large jumps, we must have

$$\int_{\mathbb{R}\backslash(-1,1)} (e^{iux} - 1) \nu(dx) < \infty. \tag{17.77}$$

On the other hand, for $|x| \to 0$, the absolute value $|e^{iux} - 1 - iux|$ is of order $|x|^2$.

Quick calculation 17.14 Use *Taylor*-expansion to confirm this statement.

Thus, thanks to (17.76) we have

$$\int_{-1}^{1} (e^{iux} - 1 - iux) \nu(dx) < \infty. \tag{17.78}$$

We can therefore paste the interval pieces in the characteristic exponent together, to obtain an integral that always exists. The result is the important *Lévy–Khintchine*-representation

$$\psi(u) = iu\mu(h) - \frac{1}{2}u^2\sigma^2 + \int_{-\infty}^{\infty} (e^{iux} - 1 - iuh(x))\nu(dx), \tag{17.79}$$

with

$$h(x) = x\theta(1 - |x|) \quad \text{and} \quad \mu(h) = \mu + \int_{-\infty}^{\infty} h(x)\nu(dx). \tag{17.80}$$

The *Lévy–Khintchine*-representation includes all possible *Lévy*-processes, no matter if they are of finite or infinite activity and determines the process completely by the *Lévy*-triple $(\mu(h), \sigma^2, v(dx))$. The reason why this works is simply that the *Lévy*-measure satisfies

$$\int_{-\infty}^{\infty} \min(1, x^2) v(dx) < \infty. \tag{17.81}$$

Of course we are free to choose the truncation function $h(x) = 0$ or $h(x) = x$, if we are dealing with a type I process. In this case the representation reduces to (17.69) or (17.74), respectively.

To use *Lévy*-processes for derivative pricing, we assume that the return process is driven by such a process. In other words, we assume

$$S_t = S_0 e^{L_t}, \tag{17.82}$$

with known *Lévy*-triple. In complete analogy to stochastic volatility, we cannot hedge the jump risk and thus, we have to calibrate the model to observed prices of plain vanilla contracts. This is easily done with our standard formulas (16.29) and (16.34), if we know the conditional characteristic function of the Q-martingale process

$$e^{Y_t} = E^Q[e^{Y_{t+s}} | \mathcal{F}_t], \tag{17.83}$$

with $s \geq 0$ and $Y_0 = 0$, and the strip condition is satisfied. The process Y_t is easily found by taking our *Lévy*-process and adjusting the drift, such that $E^Q[e^{L_t}] = 1$ holds for all $0 \leq t \leq T$. Remember the definition of the conditional characteristic function

$$\varphi_t(u) = E^Q[e^{iuL_T} | \mathcal{F}_t] \tag{17.84}$$

and recognize that this means $\varphi_0(-i) = e^{T\psi(-i)} = 1$, or more compactly $\psi(-i) = 0$. The desired drift is therefore

$$\mu(h) = -\frac{1}{2}\sigma^2 - \int_{-\infty}^{\infty} (e^x - 1 - h(x)) v(dx). \tag{17.85}$$

Example 17.3

Consider the *Merton*-process, with logarithmic jump size $X \sim N(\theta, \delta^2)$. What is the drift adjustment for the truncation function $h(x) = 0$?

Solution

The *Lévy*-measure in this case is

$$v(dx) = \frac{\lambda}{\sqrt{2\pi\delta^2}} e^{-\frac{1}{2}\left(\frac{x-\theta}{\delta}\right)^2} dx.$$

Thus one obtains the drift adjustment

$$\mu(h) = -\frac{1}{2}\sigma^2 - \lambda\left(e^{\theta + \frac{1}{2}\delta^2} - 1\right),$$

where of course $\mu(h) = \mu$. The last term on the right hand side is precisely the drift adjustment we already saw in the *Black–Scholes–Merton*-PIDE (17.50).

······································

We can choose $h(x) = 0$ for all type I *Lévy*-processes, which simplifies matters considerably. To check the strip condition, we have to determine the strip of regularity S_Y. If this strip contains $z = 0$ and $z = -i$, then the process is an appropriate model. In the *Merton*-case, the generalized characteristic exponent of Y_t is

$$\psi(z) = iz\mu - \frac{1}{2}z^2\sigma^2 + \lambda\left(e^{iz\theta - \frac{1}{2}z^2\delta^2} - 1\right), \tag{17.86}$$

which is regular in the entire z-plane. We have thus an alternative method for pricing plain vanilla options under Merton's jump-diffusion model if we use $\varphi_0(u) = e^{T\psi(u)}$ with our drift adjusted characteristic exponent in (16.29) or (16.34), respectively.

17.7   Subordination of *Brown*ian motion

Subordination is a really fascinating and mind-boggling concept. In 1905, Albert Einstein turned our understanding of time upside down. He realized that the only resolution to the puzzle of a constant velocity of light in every inertial reference frame was that time had to proceed at different rates in every frame. Think of yourself as a passive observer at rest, maybe at a railroad station. The time you read off from your wristwatch is your coordinate time. Now you observe another person passing the platform in a train at high velocity. Because you have sharp vision, you can see her wristwatch through the window for a few seconds. Even if you wear identical watches, you should see hers ticking at a reduced rate. Of course the deviation is so small that you would never be able to really observe it, but the principle is, the faster a reference frame moves relative to your rest frame, the slower the rate of time in this frame, observed from your frame. If you find that mind-boggling, think about the following: The traveler is at rest in her own frame of reference inside the train compartment. From her perspective, you are moving relative to her with high velocity. Shouldn't she see your wristwatch slowed down, too?

The idea of subordination is precisely the same concept of time deformation. The investor only reads off the usual coordinate time t from her wristwatch, but in the market frame, we have the so-called business time τ, which can pass at a higher or slower rate, compared to the coordinate time t. If the market activity is high, there is fast movement in prices and business time slows down. If there is low activity and prices tend to move slowly, business time speeds up. What would the effect of such a time deformation be? If markets are highly active, we observe increased volatility. But perhaps this is only due to a compressed timescale relative to the business time. Maybe from inside the market frame, where the business timescale is the appropriate one, there is no increased volatility. You get the idea? A deformed business time process of this kind is called a subordination process, or subordinator for short. Which processes are useful as subordinators? Every *Lévy*-process qualifies, provided that it is increasing almost surely. This is another parallel to Einstein's theory of relativity. Business time can proceed infinitely slow if market activity is infinitely high, but it is not permitted to reverse direction. This requirement has a large impact on every component of the characteristic *Lévy*-triple. A subordinator is characterized by $(\eta, 0, \rho(dx))$, where $\eta \geq 0$, and the *Lévy*-measure $\rho(dx)$ assigns zero weight to all negative jumps. A subordinator has no *Brown*ian motion component, because the increments of the *Wiener*-process are normally distributed and thus, are not guaranteed to be positive. Subordinators are usually described by their moment-generating function

$$M(t, u) = E[e^{u\tau_t}] = e^{tl(u)}, \tag{17.87}$$

where

$$l(u) = u\eta + \int_0^\infty (e^{ux} - 1)\rho(dx) \tag{17.88}$$

is called the *Laplace*-exponent for all $u \leq 0$. The connection between characteristic function and moment-generating function is simply $\varphi(t, u) = M(t, iu)$. The really clever thing is that we have now immediate access to the characteristic function of the subordinated *Lévy*-process by

$$\varphi(t, u) = e^{tl(\psi(u))}. \tag{17.89}$$

Let's see if we can understand this result. Assume that the σ-algebra, generated by observing only the subordination process τ_t is $\mathcal{G}_t$. Then we can use a conditioning argument to create the following chain of equalities

$$\begin{aligned}\varphi(t, u) &= E[e^{iuL_\tau}] = E\left[E[e^{iuL_\tau}|\mathcal{G}_t]\right] \\ &= E[e^{\tau_t\psi(u)}] = e^{tl(\psi(u))}.\end{aligned} \tag{17.90}$$

What consequences has subordination for the return distribution of the underlying? Let's assume the log-price process is a subordinated *Brown*ian motion without drift,

$$dx_\tau = \sigma dW_\tau, \tag{17.91}$$

and the subordination process is independent of W_t. We can analyze the variance of this process

$$\begin{aligned}\text{Var}[x_\tau] &= \text{Var}[E[x_\tau|\mathcal{G}_t]] + E[\text{Var}[x_\tau|\mathcal{G}_t]] \\ &= 0 + \sigma^2 E[\tau_t].\end{aligned} \tag{17.92}$$

Quick calculation 17.15 Show that $E[x_\tau] = 0$ still holds.

That seems reasonable, because τ_t is a random variable. But things become more interesting if we consider the kurtosis. Remember that the kurtosis of a normally distributed random variable is always $K = 3$. The computation in this case is a little more involved but the final result is

$$K = 3\left(1 + \frac{\mathrm{Var}[\tau_t]}{E[\tau_t]^2}\right) > 3. \tag{17.93}$$

This is intriguing, because it seems to explain the excess kurtosis observed in financial return time series. Furthermore, a kurtosis of $K = 3$ looks like the deterministic limit, if $\mathrm{Var}[\tau_t]$ tends to zero. A good starting point; so let's look at a concrete subordination model next.

One of the most accessible subordinated models is the variance gamma process of Madan et al. (1998). The starting point is a subordinated *Brown*ian motion with drift. Because we need it anyway for pricing, let's take the exponential Q-martingale process

$$dY_\tau = -\frac{1}{2}\sigma^2 d\tau + \sigma dW_\tau. \tag{17.94}$$

The subordinator is a gamma process, independent of W_t, with drift $\eta = 0$ and *Lévy*-measure

$$\rho(dx) = \frac{\gamma e^{-\lambda x}}{x}dx, \tag{17.95}$$

for $x \geq 0$. Obviously the *Lévy*-density diverges for $x \to 0$; the process is of infinite activity. For a given time t, the marginal distribution of the process is a gamma distribution,[5] with expectation value

$$E[\tau_t] = \frac{\gamma t}{\lambda}. \tag{17.96}$$

Because the *Wiener*-process has the scaling property $\alpha W_t \overset{D}{=} W_{\alpha^2 t}$, it is sufficient to consider only subordinators with $E[\tau_t] = t$, which means, we can eliminate one parameter of the *Lévy*-density. So let's invent the new parameter κ and rewrite (17.95) as

$$\rho(dx) = \frac{e^{-\frac{x}{\kappa}}}{\kappa x}dx. \tag{17.97}$$

---

[5] The probability density function of a gamma distribution is

$$f(x) = \frac{(\lambda x)^\gamma e^{-\lambda x}}{x\Gamma(\gamma)}, \text{ with the gamma function } \Gamma(k) = \int_0^\infty y^{k-1}e^{-y}dy.$$

Now κ governs the magnitude of variation in the rate of business time. For $\kappa \to 0$, the *Lévy*-measure tends to zero and we have deterministic time. In order to compute the *Laplace*-exponent, we have to evaluate the nontrivial integral

$$l(u) = \int_0^\infty (e^{ux} - 1)\frac{e^{-\frac{x}{\kappa}}}{\kappa x}dx. \tag{17.98}$$

This is not an easy task at all. However, let's start by making the substitution $y = \frac{x}{\kappa}$. This change of variables does not affect the bounds of integration, but the increment becomes $dx = \kappa dy$. We get

$$l(u) = \int_0^\infty (e^{u\kappa y} - 1)\frac{e^{-y}}{\kappa y}dy = \frac{1}{\kappa}\sum_{n=1}^\infty \frac{(u\kappa)^n}{n!}\int_0^\infty y^{n-1}e^{-y}dy, \tag{17.99}$$

where we simply *Taylor*-expanded $e^{u\kappa y}$ and rearranged terms in the last step. The integral on the right hand side is the gamma function $\Gamma(n)$. Because this function is an extension of the factorial function, the relation $\Gamma(n) = (n-1)!$ holds for all positive integers $n \in \mathbb{N}$. Thus, replacing the integral on the right hand side of (17.99) by $(n-1)!$, we obtain

$$l(u) = \frac{1}{\kappa}\sum_{n=1}^\infty \frac{(u\kappa)^n}{n} = -\frac{1}{\kappa}\log(1 - u\kappa). \tag{17.100}$$

The last equality holds, because the sum in (17.100) is recognized as the *Taylor*-series of $-\log(1 - u\kappa)$ around $u = 0$. Using (17.89) it is now an easy task to compute the characteristic exponent of our subordinated *Brown*ian motion

$$\psi_{\text{sub.}}(u) = l(\psi(u)) = -\frac{1}{\kappa}\log\left(1 + \frac{1}{2}iu\sigma^2\kappa + \frac{1}{2}u^2\sigma^2\kappa\right). \tag{17.101}$$

Quick calculation 17.16 Use l'Hôpital's rule to compute $\lim_{\kappa\to 0}\psi_{\text{sub.}}(u)$.

It is easy to see that $\psi_{\text{sub.}}(-i) = 0$, which means that we do not need any drift adjustment. This is of course no surprise, because we chose the drift-compensated process Y_t in the first place for subordination. It remains to examine if the characteristic exponent satisfies the necessary strip condition. The generalized characteristic exponent is

$$\psi_{\text{sub.}}(z) = -\frac{1}{\kappa}\log\left(1 + \frac{1}{2}iz\sigma^2\kappa + \frac{1}{2}z^2\sigma^2\kappa\right). \tag{17.102}$$

This function is only regular, as long as the argument of the logarithm does not become zero. From Theorem 16.1 on page 357 we know that potential singularities are located on the imaginary axis. To track them down, we can set the argument equal to zero at $z = iv$,

$$1 - \frac{1}{2}v\sigma^2\kappa - \frac{1}{2}v^2\sigma^2\kappa \overset{!}{=} 0. \tag{17.103}$$

This is a simple quadratic equation and its solution is

$$v_{1/2} = -\frac{1}{2} \pm \sqrt{\frac{1}{4} + \frac{2}{\sigma^2 \kappa}}. \tag{17.104}$$

Because $0 < \kappa < \infty$, the strip of regularity is $\mathcal{S}_Y = \{z = u + iv : v \in (\alpha, \beta)\}$, with $\alpha < -1$ and $\beta > 0$. Thus, the process is appropriate for the whole range of κ.

Unfortunately, subordination is not the ultimate answer to all stylized facts observed in financial time series. We have seen that it generates heavy tails by excess kurtosis. But the variance gamma process is still a *Lévy*-process, which means it is infinitely divisible. Such processes cannot account appropriately for volatility clustering. Furthermore, most of the computations are exceedingly complicated and require sophisticated techniques far beyond the scope of this introduction. For example Madan et al. (1998) were able to derive an analytical formula for pricing vanilla options in the variance gamma model. But it can only be represented in terms of modified *Bessel*- and degenerate hypergeometric functions.

17.8   The *Esscher*-Transform

The *Esscher*-transform, also known as exponential tilting, is a very old idea (Esscher, 1932), introduced into the theory of derivative pricing by Gerber and Shiu (1994). As the *Girsanov*-transformation, the *Esscher*-transform generates a risk-neutral probability measure Q by changing the original one by a *Radon–Nikodym*-derivative. In case of the *Esscher*-transform this derivative is

$$\frac{dQ}{dP} = \frac{e^{-\gamma X}}{E[e^{-\gamma X}]}, \tag{17.105}$$

provided the expectation in the denominator exists.[6] It is easy to see that (17.105) is always positive and has unit expectation value under P. Thus, it satisfies all necessary requirements. But in incomplete markets there is a whole continuum of equivalent martingale measures. How does the *Esscher*-transform manage to single out a particular measure Q?

The story begins with an expected utility maximization problem. Suppose an agent holds one unit of an underlying S at time $t = 0$. If she plans to liquidate her position at time $t = T$, she can hedge against unfavorable outcomes by buying or selling a fraction η of a European style derivative, contingent on S. Her utility functional is then

$$U_\eta[S_T] = E\left[u\left(S_T + \eta(V(S_T, T) - e^{rT} V_0)\right)\right], \tag{17.106}$$

---

[6] It is also common to define the *Esscher*-transform with the parameter $\theta = -\gamma$. The notation we use here is due to a fundamental economic interpretation of the transformation.

where V_0 is today's price of the respective derivative. This price is fair, if the investor cannot increase terminal utility by entering a hedge-position. In other words, V_0 is a fair price, if $\eta = 0$ in the expected utility maximum. But that means

$$\frac{dU_\eta}{d\eta}\bigg|_{\eta=0} = 0. \tag{17.107}$$

This condition is sufficient, because $\frac{d^2 U_\eta}{d\eta^2} < 0$, if the utility function satisfies $u''(w) < 0$. This is precisely the case for a risk-averse agent. We can use condition (17.107) to solve for V_0,

$$V_0 = e^{-rT}\frac{E[V(S_T, T)u'(S_T)]}{E[u'(S_T)]}. \tag{17.108}$$

This is exactly how far this argument takes us without specifying the utility function. If the investor has constant relative risk aversion, which we assumed many times before, the utility function is

$$u(w) = \frac{w^{1-\gamma} - 1}{1 - \gamma}, \tag{17.109}$$

with relative risk aversion $\mathrm{RRA}(w) = \gamma$. In this case, the first derivative of the utility function is $u'(w) = w^{-\gamma}$ and (17.108) becomes

$$V_0 = e^{-rT}\frac{E[V(S_T, T)S_T^{-\gamma}]}{E[S_T^{-\gamma}]}. \tag{17.110}$$

Now consider two things. First, Equation (17.110) has to hold for every derivative, in particular for $V(S, t) = S$, and second, we have $S_t = S_0 e^{X_t}$, with $X_0 = 0$. X_t does not necessarily have to be a *Lévy*-process; the *Heston*-process is also perfectly fine. Putting those pieces together, one obtains

$$S_0 = e^{-rT}\frac{E[S_0 e^{(1-\gamma)X_T}]}{E[e^{-\gamma X_T}]}, \tag{17.111}$$

or by rearranging

$$\begin{aligned}
e^{rT} &= \int_{-\infty}^{\infty} \frac{e^{-\gamma x}}{E[e^{-\gamma X_T}]} e^x p(x, T)dx \\
&= \int_{-\infty}^{\infty} e^x q(x, T)dx = E^Q[e^{X_T}].
\end{aligned} \tag{17.112}$$

Since T was arbitrary this proves that the *Esscher*-transform singles out the risk-neutral probability measure Q, provided that the agent has constant relative risk aversion. Furthermore, the *Esscher*-parameter γ is precisely the relative risk aversion. We can summarize the transition from P to Q in terms of the respective probability density functions

$$q(x, t) = \frac{e^{-\gamma x}}{\int_{-\infty}^{\infty} e^{-\gamma y} p(y, t)dy} p(x, t). \tag{17.113}$$

A very useful trick worth keeping in mind is to recognize that $E[e^{-\gamma X}] = \varphi_X(i\gamma)$. Thus, we can compute the *Radon–Nikodym*-derivative very efficiently by

$$\frac{dQ}{dP} = \frac{e^{-\gamma X}}{\varphi_X(i\gamma)}. \tag{17.114}$$

To see the *Esscher*-transform in action, let's have another close look at Merton's jump-diffusion model. Originally, the jumps were considered purely idiosyncratic risks, but now we can do better. First observe that there are three separate sources of risk: The market risk, already completely hedged, the jump risk itself, and the risk induced by uncertainty of the jump size. Let's focus on the number of jumps for the moment. What happens, if we apply the *Esscher*-transform to a random variable $N \sim \text{Poi}(\lambda)$? The *Radon–Nikodym*-derivative according to (17.114) is

$$\frac{dQ}{dP} = e^{-\gamma N} e^{-\lambda(e^{-\gamma}-1)}. \tag{17.115}$$

Thus, the probability mass function becomes

$$Q(N=n) = e^{-\gamma n - \lambda e^{-\gamma}} \frac{\lambda^n}{n!} = e^{-\lambda e^{-\gamma}} \frac{(\lambda e^{-\gamma})^n}{n!}. \tag{17.116}$$

Under the risk-neutral measure Q, we have $N \sim \text{Poi}(\lambda e^{-\gamma})$. This makes perfect sense if you think it through. If the agent is risk-neutral in the first place, then $\gamma = 0$ and the intensity is unchanged. For a risk-averse investor, the intensity under Q is smaller than under the physical measure P. That is perfectly right; remember that the drift r under the risk-neutral measure is also smaller than the original drift μ. Now let's investigate the *Poisson*-increment dN_t under Q. With (17.116), we must have

$$\int_t^{t+dt} dN_s = \sum_{n=1}^N \int_t^{t+dt} \delta(s - \tau_n) ds = \begin{cases} 1 & \text{with prob. } \lambda e^{-\gamma} dt \\ 0 & \text{with prob. } 1 - \lambda e^{-\gamma} dt. \end{cases} \tag{17.117}$$

That is, we can write the expectation value $E^Q[dN_t] = \lambda e^{-\gamma} dt$. The *Merton*-PIDE on page 392 contains an expectation over the compound *Poisson*-increment $J(S, X, t) dN_t$, with

$$J(S, X, t) = V(e^X S, t) - V(S, t) - \frac{\partial V}{\partial S}(e^X - 1)S, \tag{17.118}$$

and $X \sim N(\theta, \delta^2)$, that was evaluated under the physical measure P. To find out how this expectation transforms, we use a little trick. Consider the process $d\tilde{N}_t$, defined by

$$\int_t^{t+dt} d\tilde{N}_s = \sum_{n=1}^N \int_t^{t+dt} e^{-\gamma}\delta(s - \tau_n) ds = \begin{cases} e^{-\gamma} & \text{with prob. } \lambda dt \\ 0 & \text{with prob. } 1 - \lambda dt. \end{cases} \tag{17.119}$$

It is immediately obvious that $E[d\tilde{N}_t] = E^Q[dN_t] = \lambda e^{-\gamma} dt$. Note that even though the expectations coincide, the process $\tilde{N}_t$ cannot be obtained from N_t by a change of probability measure. Such a change of measure must preserve all null sets, which means events or trajectories with zero probability under P must also have zero probability under Q. A *Poisson*-process assigns nonzero probabilities only to paths that occupy nonnegative integer values. On the other hand, the paths of $\tilde{N}_t$ occupy integer multiples of $e^{-\gamma}$. Nevertheless, from the resulting expectation, we can deduce what the change of measure has to be. So let's use the same intuition for the compound *Poisson*-increment in the *Merton*-model. In this case we have

$$E^Q[JdN] = \lambda \int_{-\infty}^{\infty} e^{-\gamma x} J(S, x, t) p(x) dx dt. \tag{17.120}$$

Multiplying and dividing the right hand side by $E[e^{-\gamma X}]$ yields

$$E^Q[JdN] = \lambda E[e^{-\gamma X}] \int_{-\infty}^{\infty} J(S, x, t) \frac{e^{-\gamma x}}{E[e^{-\gamma X}]} p(x) dx dt$$
$$= \lambda^Q \int_{-\infty}^{\infty} J(S, x, t) q(x) dx dt. \tag{17.121}$$

Obviously, the intensity, as well as the jump distribution itself is modified in going from P to Q. Let's first compute the expectation that multiplies λ,

$$E[e^{-\gamma X}] = \varphi_X(i\gamma) = e^{-\gamma\theta + \frac{1}{2}\gamma^2\delta^2}. \tag{17.122}$$

Therefore, we have $\lambda^Q = \lambda e^{-\gamma\theta + \frac{1}{2}\gamma^2\delta^2}$, and $q(x) = e^{-\gamma x + \gamma\theta - \frac{1}{2}\gamma^2\delta^2} p(x)$. To see what kind of distribution $Q(x)$ is, we can compute the characteristic function. The result is

$$E^Q[e^{iuX}] = e^{\gamma\theta - \frac{1}{2}\gamma^2\delta^2} E[e^{(iu-\gamma)X}]$$
$$= e^{iu(\theta - \gamma\delta^2) - \frac{1}{2}u^2\delta^2}. \tag{17.123}$$

Quick calculation 17.17 Confirm the last equality.

That is, the logarithmic jump distribution remains normal, but the expectation value is now $\theta^Q = \theta - \gamma\delta^2$. To summarize our findings, we have two modifications in going from the physical measure P to the risk-neutral measure Q, affecting the intensity and the expectation value of the jump size distribution,

$$\lambda^Q = \lambda e^{-\gamma\theta + \frac{1}{2}\gamma^2\delta^2} \quad \text{and} \quad \theta^Q = \theta - \gamma\delta^2. \tag{17.124}$$

Usually, the expected logarithmic jump size is negative, because jumps are mostly more or less catastrophic events. Thus under the risk-neutral probability measure, the investor considers an even higher jump intensity, with worse jumps on average. To complete our discussion, let's state the new *Merton*-PIDE, obtained by using the *Esscher*-transform to account for all parts of the jump risk

$$\frac{\partial V}{\partial t} + (r - \lambda^Q k^Q) S \frac{\partial V}{\partial S} + \frac{1}{2}\sigma^2 S^2 \frac{\partial^2 V}{\partial S^2} - (r + \lambda^Q) V + \lambda^Q \int_{-\infty}^{\infty} V(e^x S, t) g(x) dx = 0,$$
$$\tag{17.125}$$

with $k^Q = e^{\theta^Q + \frac{1}{2}\delta^2} - 1$ and the risk-neutral probability density function

$$g(x) = \frac{1}{\sqrt{2\pi\delta^2}} e^{-\frac{1}{2}\left(\frac{x-\theta^Q}{\delta}\right)^2}. \tag{17.126}$$

17.9   Combining Jumps and Stochastic Volatility

How do models based on jump processes perform in option pricing? At the beginning of this chapter, we have seen that many small *Poisson*-jumps on the microscopic level look like a *Brown*ian motion on a larger scale. But this analysis suggested also that the volatility may vary with time. So the question is, are jump models without stochastic volatility sufficient to generate realistic option prices? We have already made one important point: All jump models we have seen so far are geometric *Lévy*-processes. They have independent increments and can therefore not account for volatility clustering. To shed some light on their performance let's investigate what implied volatility surface they generate. Figure 17.6 illustrates the one resulting from calibration of the *Merton*-model to the DAX data of Chapter 15. Compare this one to the original surface in Figure 15.3 on page 335 and to the one generated by the *Heston*-model in Figure 16.3 on page 373. It is obvious that jumps add steepness to the short-term volatility smile. But clearly Merton's jump-diffusion does not do the trick alone. So let's see what we get, if we combine stochastic volatility with jumps.

A very straightforward approach to accomplish this task was suggested by Bates (1996). He simply combined Heston's stochastic volatility model with the log-normal structure of Merton's jump-diffusion. The model equations are

$$dS_t = \mu S_t dt + \sqrt{v_t} S_t dW_{1,t} + (e^{X_t} - 1)S_t dN_t \tag{17.127}$$

$$dv_t = \kappa(\theta - v_t)dt + \alpha\sqrt{v_t}dW_{2,t}, \tag{17.128}$$

where $E[dW_1 dW_2] = \rho dt$, and the jumps are completely independent from the *Wiener*-processes, with logarithmic jump size distribution $X \sim N(\eta, \delta^2)$. Since the parameter θ was already used in the volatility equation, the expected log-jump size is now η.

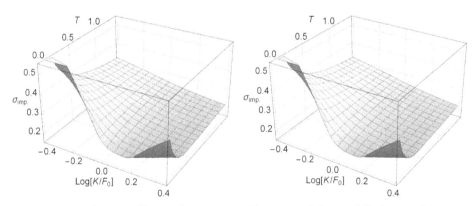

Fig. 17.6 3D Implied volatility surface generated by Merton's jump-diffusion model calibrated to DAX data of mid-July 2012

If you think it through carefully, you conclude that we have already done all the work necessary to implement this model for option pricing. We know the conditional characteristic function of the *Heston*-model, and we also know the drift compensated characteristic exponent of the jump part of the *Merton*-model. Because both parts of the model are independent from each other, the characteristic functions simply multiply and we obtain the new characteristic exponent

$$\psi(u) = \frac{A(0,u) + B(0,u)v_0}{T} - iu\lambda\left(e^{\eta + \frac{1}{2}\delta^2} - 1\right) + \lambda\left(e^{iu\eta - \frac{1}{2}u^2\delta^2} - 1\right), \qquad (17.129)$$

with $A(0,u)$ and $B(0,u)$ given by (16.84) to (16.86) on page 369. Because we already know that the *Heston*-part satisfies the martingale condition, it is easy to see that $\psi(-i) = 0$ holds. We have also already confirmed that the *Heston*-model satisfies the necessary strip condition. Because the generalized characteristic exponent of the *Merton*-model is regular in the entire z-plane, the intersection $S_Y = S_H \cap S_M$ also satisfies the strip condition, where S_H and S_M indicate the strips of regularity of the *Heston*- and *Merton*-part of the model, respectively. The conditional characteristic function of the exponential Q-martingale process Y_t is simply

$$\varphi_0(u) = e^{T\psi(u)}, \qquad (17.130)$$

where $\psi(u)$ is given by (17.129). This function is all we need to price European plain vanilla options with our standard formulas (16.29) and (16.34).

Figure 17.7 illustrates the implied volatility surface generated by the *Bates*-model, calibrated to our DAX option data sample. When comparing all attempts we have made so far to fit the interpolated surface in Figure 15.3 on page 335, the *Bates*-model is clearly the winner. But this extraordinary good fit comes at a price. It is exceedingly difficult to calibrate the model to market data. Usually, calibration is done by minimizing a possibly weighted sum of quadratic pricing errors. In case of the *Bates*-model, this problem is ill-posed. A workaround is to fit the *Heston*-part of the model to the long-term skew, and the jump part to the short-term smile, separately. Obviously,

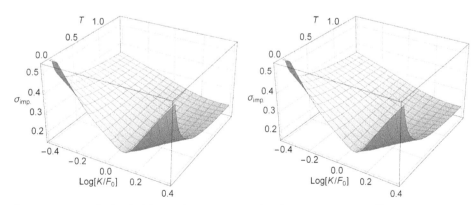

Fig. 17.7 **3D** Implied volatility surface generated by the *Bates*-model calibrated to DAX data of mid-July 2012

jump risks are only relevant in the short-term. The steepness in the volatility smile they induce decays rapidly into the long-term skew, we already know to be governed by the negative correlation between the geometric *Brown*ian motion and the stochastic volatility part. But clearly a complete option pricing model needs both stochastic volatility and jumps.

17.10   Further Reading

For the most general theoretical framework of the background architecture of financial markets see Delbaen and Schachermayer (1994, 2006). An excellent source, covering everything important about jump processes, is the book of Cont and Tankov (2004). For GARCH-models with jumps, see also the work of Duan et al. (2006a,b), and Christoffersen et al. (2009, 2012). An easy to handle jump-diffusion model with asymmetric jump distribution is the one of Kou (2002). More details on the reflection principle are provided in Shreve (2004b, sect. 3.7). Another subordinated *Brown*ian motion with explicit solution is the normal inverse *Gauss*ian process of Barndorff-Nielssen (1997, 1998). The most general class of equivalent martingale measures for jump-diffusions is derived in Colwell and Elliott (1993). The relation between the *Esscher*-transform and the minimal entropy measure is detailed in Hubalek and Sgarra (2006). A stochastic volatility model with jumps in returns and volatility is provided in Eraker et al. (2003).

17.11   Problems

17.1 Consider the random variable $N \sim \mathrm{Poi}(\lambda)$, which has expectation value $E[N] = \lambda$. Show that the variance is also $\mathrm{Var}[N] = \lambda$.

17.2 The double exponential jump-diffusion of Kou (2002) replaces the log-normal distributed jumps of the *Merton*-model, by *Laplace*-distributed ones, with probability density function

$$f(x) = \frac{1}{2\eta} e^{-\frac{|x-\kappa|}{\eta}},$$

and $0 < \eta < 1$. Show that the characteristic function is given by

$$\varphi_X(u) = \frac{e^{iu\kappa}}{1 + u^2\kappa^2}.$$

17.3 Analyze the characteristic exponent of the *Kou*-model of Problem 17.2. What is the proper drift adjustment to obtain the exponential Q-martingale Y_t and is the necessary strip condition satisfied?

17.4 Suppose x_u is an upper barrier. Use the reflection principle to prove that

$$f(t) = \frac{x_u}{t\sqrt{2\pi t}} e^{-\frac{x_u^2}{2t}},$$

with $t \geq 0$, is the probability density function of the stopping time τ, when the *Wiener*-process W_t hits the barrier x_u for the first time.

17.5 The normal inverse *Gauss*ian process is a subordinated *Brown*ian motion, where the subordinator is a process with drift $\eta = 0$, and *Lévy*-measure

$$\rho(dx) = \frac{1}{\sqrt{2\pi\kappa}} \frac{e^{-\frac{x}{2\kappa}}}{x^{\frac{3}{2}}} dx.$$

Prove that the *Laplace*-exponent is

$$l(u) = \frac{1}{\kappa} - \frac{1}{\kappa} \sqrt{1 - 2u\kappa}.$$

Use that for half-integers, the gamma function is $\Gamma(n - \frac{1}{2}) = 2^{1-n} \sqrt{\pi}(2n - 3)!!$ for $n \in \mathbb{N}$ and $(-1)!! = 1$, and that the *Taylor*-series

$$\sqrt{1 - 2u\kappa} = 1 - \sum_{n=1}^{\infty} \frac{(u\kappa)^n}{n!} (2n - 3)!!$$

holds.

17.6 Show that in the *Black–Scholes*-framework, the *Esscher*-transform of the *Wiener*-process W_t is equivalent to the *Girsanov*-transformation.

Part IV The Fixed-Income World

18 Basic Fixed-Income Instruments

We are now entering the fixed-income world, where nothing is really sure anymore. Until now, we have assumed that there is always the alternative of depositing a fixed amount of money in a bank account at a known risk-free interest rate. Interest rates in fixed-income markets are generally neither known, nor risk-free. To make things even worse, there is a whole family of interest rates, one for each tenor associated with a traded instrument. Thus, pricing fixed-income products can be a very delicate business.

18.1 Bonds and Forward Rate Agreements

The most elementary fixed-income instrument is the zero-coupon bond, or zero-bond for short. It behaves very much like the bank account we encountered in Chapter 11, with the exception that it has a fixed maturity time T. To be more precise, the zero-bond $B_0(t, T)$ is a claim to receive a known principal P at maturity T. As for the notation, the subscript 0 indicates that the bond is a zero-coupon bond, so we will drop it for coupon-bearing bonds. Furthermore, we use the same letter as for the bank account, but now we have two arguments, the present time t and the maturity time T. It is very helpful to develop a pictorial understanding for the sequence of cash flows, a bond represents. Figure 18.1 left shows the simple cash flow profile of our zero-bond.

The coupon-bearing bond $B(t, T)$, indicated in Figure 18.1 right, includes periodical coupon payments that are usually specified in percentage of the principal. The last coupon payment is due at maturity, together with the principal. The pictorial representation is so powerful, because we can simply add payments by adding the arrows that represent the cash flows. Usually the principal is something like $P = \$1000$ or $P = €1000$.

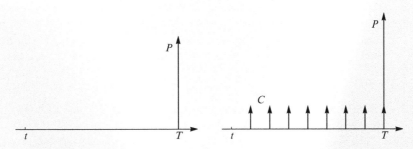

Fig. 18.1 Zero-coupon bond (left) and coupon-bearing bond (right)

Let us invent a standardized zero-coupon bond, called a discount bond $P(t, T)$, which is an ordinary zero-bond with a principal of one unit of the required currency, and thus

$$B_0(t, T) = P \cdot P(t, T). \tag{18.1}$$

The name $P(t, T)$ is only to remind us that the discount bond has unit principal, which means $P(T, T) = 1$. As we shall see, the mapping $T \mapsto P(t, T)$, sometimes called the discount curve, carries all the information required to price any standard instrument in the fixed-income world. For example, we can express every coupon-bearing bond as a portfolio of discount bonds with different maturities,

$$B(t, T) = C \sum_{n=1}^{N} P(t, T_n) + P \cdot P(t, T), \tag{18.2}$$

where of course $T_N = T$.

Quick calculation 18.1 Relate this formula to Figure 18.1 right.

This is a good place for a mild warning. Bond markets are subject to many strange conventions. One of them has to do with the coupon period. Let's standardize the coupon-bearing bond to a principal of $P = 1$, too. Then the coupon becomes $c = \frac{C}{P}$, which is a genuine percentage value. In the US market it is common to have semi-annual coupon payments, whereas in the Euro-area most bonds have annual coupon payments. When a coupon-bearing bond with semi-annual term structure is contracted to pay a coupon of 6%, this means that there is a cash flow of $c = 3\%$ every six months. If you find this confusing, wait until you learn more about day-count conventions.

Let's introduce rates. One dollar paid in a year is less valuable to the rational decision maker than one dollar paid today. This is true, even if there is no risk-free investment, because utility is higher, if the agent does not have to postpone consumption of the dollar until next year. In the bond-language this means that a particular interest rate has to be induced by the discount bond with maturity T,

$$P(t, T) = e^{-R(t,T)(T-t)}. \tag{18.3}$$

The so-called spot rate $R(t, T)$ is the current rate of return for a deposit between times t and T. In other words, this is the rate for the whole period $T - t$, as it stands today at time t. Let's agree on labeling such rates over whole periods with a capital letter. If we shrink the period smaller and smaller by taking the limit $T \to t$, we obtain what is called the short rate. This rate is valid only in the infinitely small interval $[t, t + dt]$. Such instantaneous rates are labeled by the corresponding small letter

$$\lim_{T \to t} R(t, T) = r(t). \tag{18.4}$$

Observe that the short rate has only one argument, because naturally there is no need to specify a period covered by this rate.

There is another instrument closely related to bonds, but inducing another rate. It is called a forward rate agreement (FRA). An FRA is a contract between two parties,

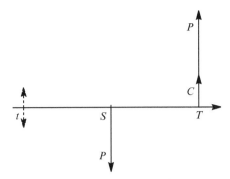

Fig. 18.2 Forward rate agreement (FRA) – Possible upfront payment indicated by dashed arrows

A and B. A pays a principal P to B at time S. At a later time $T > S$, B repays the principal plus a previously contracted coupon C. The cash flow structure of this contract is illustrated in Figure 18.2. Sometimes there is also an upfront payment, but not necessarily. Let's use our old trick and standardize the contract to a principal of $P = 1$. Then the new coupon c becomes a rate, but what kind of rate? Assume that the FRA is negotiated with zero upfront payment. Then we can decompose the cash flows into

$$\text{FRA}(t, S, T) = -P(t, S) + (1 + c)P(t, T) = 0. \qquad (18.5)$$

But from the pictorial representation it is immediately clear that $1 + c$ has to be the accumulation factor for a deposit between times S and T, as seen from today. That is

$$1 + c = e^{F(t,S,T)(T-S)}. \qquad (18.6)$$

The rate $F(t, S, T)$ is called the forward rate. It is the correct rate for compounding a deposit between times S and T, as it stands today. There is also an instantaneous version of the forward rate obtained in the limit $T \to S$,

$$\lim_{T \to S} F(t, S, T) = f(t, S), \qquad (18.7)$$

where we again used the small letter to indicate that the rate covers only the infinitely small period $[S, S + dS]$.

Quick calculation 18.2 Convince yourself that $f(t, t) = r(t)$ has to hold.

We can now finally express the value of a discount bond, and therefore the values of all other instruments we have seen so far, using the instantaneous forward rate,

$$P(t, T) = e^{-\int_t^T f(t,s)ds}. \qquad (18.8)$$

This is our most important valuation relation and therefore, knowledge of today's forward curve is indispensable. Generally, the mapping $t \mapsto f(t, s)$ is a random function,

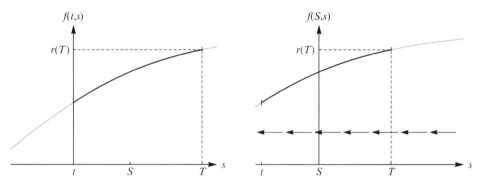

Fig. 18.3 Deterministic forward curve – The whole curve is shifted to the left as time proceeds

but we can specialize step by step to connect a few dots. First, assume that there is a deterministic term structure $T \mapsto R(t, T)$, which assigns different rates to deposits of different maturities, but which does not randomly change from day to day. In this case, the coupon rate in (18.6) has the slightly different interpretation

$$1 + c = e^{R(S,T)(T-S)} = \frac{1}{P(S, T)}, \tag{18.9}$$

where the last equality is due to (18.3). Using this relation in (18.5), we can conclude that the price of the forward starting discount bond is already determined by today's bond prices,

$$\frac{P(t, T)}{P(t, S)} = P(S, T). \tag{18.10}$$

Using representation (18.8), taking logarithms on both sides and multiplying by minus one, one obtains

$$\int_S^T f(t, s)ds = \int_S^T f(S, s)ds. \tag{18.11}$$

Finally, differentiating (18.11) with respect to T yields

$$f(t, T) = f(S, T) = r(T), \tag{18.12}$$

where the last equality holds because S is arbitrary and so we can as well choose $S = T$. What that means is that a deterministic forward curve is simply shifted horizontally as time goes by. The situation is illustrated in Figure 18.3. What happens, if the forward curve is not only deterministic, but completely flat? Obviously the spot rate no longer depends on the maturity time, and we have $r(T) = r$. This is sometimes called a flat term structure. We have implicitly assumed this situation until now. Therefore, derivative pricing theory as we have studied it before, is only correct in a world with a flat term structure. Fortunately, most derivatives are not very sensitive to violations of this assumption. Of course that changes dramatically, if we talk about interest rate derivatives.

18.2   LIBOR and Floating Rate Notes

The term fixed-income does not mean that the cash flows scheduled in a contract have to be fixed. Merely the periods of the payments are prespecified. There are many products with variable cash flows. Of course the contract parties have to agree on a reference, such that future payments can be determined by the future values of that reference. One of the most important references is the "London Interbank Offered Rate" (LIBOR) of the British Bankers' Association. The LIBOR is the rate at which financial institutions can borrow in the interbank market. LIBORs are quoted in percentage value for different maturities, usually from overnight to one year. Furthermore, they are not continuously compounded rates, but simple compounded ones. What does that mean? Assume $L(t, T)$ is the current LIBOR rate for a deposit of length $\Delta t = T - t$. Then the associated current price of a discount bond is

$$P(t, T) = \frac{1}{1 + \Delta t L(t, T)}. \tag{18.13}$$

Of course for small Δt, simple and continuous compounding are approximately identical

$$e^{\Delta t L(t,T)} = 1 + \Delta t L(t, T) + O(\Delta t^2), \tag{18.14}$$

but not quite. If the six month LIBOR is 4%, then the error is approximately 2 basis points (bps), where 100 bps = 1%. If the contracted volume is high, as it usually is in fixed-income markets, this can make a difference.

Let's investigate a floating rate note $B_{\text{fl.}}(t, T)$, which is a coupon-bearing bond, whose standardized coupons are reset to the appropriate LIBOR at the beginning of each cash flow period. Even though it is not necessary, we assume the term structure of cash flows equally spaced with $\Delta t = T_n - T_{n-1}$. Figure 18.4 top left illustrates the cash flow structure of the standardized contract. The first coupon rate is set to $c_1 = \Delta t L(t, T_1)$, right at initiation of the contract. This is of vital importance, as we shall see shortly. The second coupon rate is reset at time T_1 to $c_2 = \Delta t L(T_1, T_2)$. Of course this rate is not yet known, but it will be at time T_1. At maturity there is a coupon $c_N = \Delta t L(T_{N-1}, T)$, fixed at T_{N-1}, and the unit principal to be repaid. We have indicated floating rates by gray arrows, to emphasize that they are subject to a variable reference rate, in this case the LIBOR. What is the present value of this contract? Let's focus on the last cash flow at time T. It is composed of one unit of currency and the coupon payment c_N. We can treat these two cash flows as the principal

$$P_N = 1 + \Delta t L(T_{N-1}, T) \tag{18.15}$$

of a T_{N-1} zero-coupon bond $B_0(T_{N-1}, T) = P_N \cdot P(T_{N-1}, T)$. Using the value of the discount bond (18.13), this cash flow obviously has the time T_{N-1} value $B_0(T_{N-1}, T) = 1$.

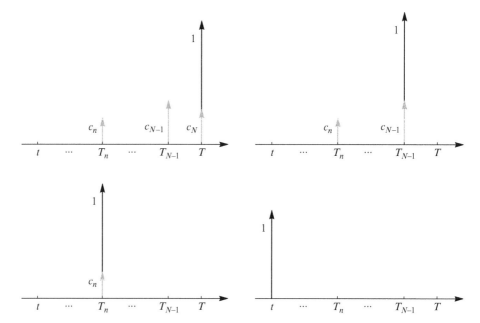

Fig. 18.4 Floating rate note – Cashflow successively shifted to former period

Quick calculation 18.3   Check that this statement is true.

Of course at T_{N-1} we have the additional coupon payment c_{N-1} and thus, the cash flows illustrated in the top row of Figure 18.4 have to have identical time t value. Observe that the last cash flow at time T has vanished in Figure 18.4 top right. We can apply the same chain of arguments to establish that the time T_{N-2} value of the principal $P_{N-1} = 1 + c_{N-1}$ is $B_0(T_{N-2}, T_{N-1}) = 1$. Let's define $t = T_0$ and $T = T_N$ for notational convenience. Then we have $B_0(T_{n-1}, T_n) = 1$ for every principal $P_n = 1 + c_n$ with $n = 1, \ldots, N$, as indicated in the bottom row of Figure 18.4. At time t, there is no further coupon payment and thus the surprisingly simple answer is

$$B_{\text{fl.}}(t, T) = 1. \tag{18.16}$$

At a later point, we will encounter contracts called swaps, which have a fixed and a floating leg of payments. But for the moment, let's discuss a few more basic properties of ordinary bonds.

18.3   Day-Count Conventions and Accrued Interest

The natural time period in finance is almost always one year. Interest rates, volatilities and so forth are usually provided as annualized quantities. The only exception we have seen are GARCH-models, which are based on daily intervals. The conversion problems arise, because every contracted time, like for example the maturity date T has the format

$d_T/m_T/y_T$, and not every month or year has the same amount of days. There are three popular conventions and every time you do computations with quoted prices, you have to check which one of the following is to be used:

Day-count conventions

- Actual/365:

$$T - t = \frac{\# \text{ days between } t \text{ and } T}{365},$$

- Actual/360:

$$T - t = \frac{\# \text{ days between } t \text{ and } T}{360},$$

- 30/360:

$$T - t = \frac{\min(d_T, 30) + (30 - d_t)^+}{360} + \frac{m_T - m_t - 1}{12} + y_T - y_t.$$

That looks worse than it actually is. Let's do an example to see how the computations work out in practice.

Example 18.1

Assume that a bond was issued at January 15, 2014 and its maturity date is October 15, 2015. What is the time to maturity computed with the three different day-count conventions?

Solution

For the first two conventions we have to count the actual number of days between t and T. For the specified dates, there are 638 calendar days in between. It is now easy to compute $T - t = 1.748$ years for Actual/365, and $T - t = 1.772$ years for Actual/360. In case of 30/360 one obtains

$$T - t = \frac{15 + (30 - 15)^+}{360} + \frac{10 - 1 - 1}{12} + 2015 - 2014$$

$$= \frac{1}{12} + \frac{8}{12} + 1 = 1.75 \text{ years.}$$

Until now, we have conveniently assumed that the bond is initiated at time t. But what happens, if the bond was already issued in the past, say at time T_0, and we want to know its present value? Obviously for $T_{k-1} < t \leq T_k$ with $k = 1, \ldots, N$, the standardized coupon-bearing bond must have the value

$$B(t, T) = c \sum_{n=k}^{N} P(t, T_n) + P(t, T). \tag{18.17}$$

The problem with this is that the value jumps at the coupon dates. In complete analogy to discrete dividend payments,

$$B(T_n^-, T) = B(T_n^+, T) + c \qquad (18.18)$$

has to hold for all $n = 1, \ldots, N$. The way we defined things, we have for the left limit

$$B(T_n^-, T) = \lim_{\varepsilon \to 0} B(T_n - \varepsilon, T) = B(T_n, T), \qquad (18.19)$$

which means the mapping $t \mapsto B(t, T)$ is a càglàd function. If you think it through, this clearly has to be, because the coupon-payment is a systematic and fully anticipated discontinuity in the price process of the bond. Therefore, it must be left continuous with right limit. The value in (18.17) is referred to as the "dirty price" of the bond. Unfortunately the dirty price is not the one quoted at the exchange. Instead, what is quoted is the so-called "clean price"

$$B_{\text{cl.}}(t, T) = B(t, T) - A_k(t), \qquad (18.20)$$

for $T_{k-1} < t \leq T_k$. The function $A_k(t)$ is called the accrued interest or the accrual factor and is defined by

$$A_k(t) = c \cdot \frac{t - T_{k-1}}{T_k - T_{k-1}}. \qquad (18.21)$$

The periods in the accrual factor have to be computed by the proper day-count convention to obtain the correct dirty prices from the quoted clean prices.

Example 18.2

A bond with principal $P = \$1000$ and semi-annual coupon payments of 4.5%, to be received at March 1 and September 1 of each year, respectively, is quoted with a clean price of $B_{\text{cl.}}(t, T) = \$1225.25$ at May 25. What is the correct dirty price when the 30/360 convention is to be used?

Solution

In order to compute the accrual factor, we need three components: The coupon, the difference $t - T_{k-1}$, and the coupon period $T_k - T_{k-1}$. Because our bond is not standardized and the coupon period is semi-annual, we have

$$C = \frac{0.045 \cdot 1000}{2} = \frac{45}{2} = \$22.5.$$

All differences are within one year and therefore we obtain

$$t - T_{k-1} = \frac{25 + (30 - 1)^+}{360} + \frac{5 - 3 - 1}{12} = \frac{7}{30} \text{ years,}$$

$$T_k - T_{k-1} = \frac{1 + (30 - 1)^+}{360} + \frac{9 - 3 - 1}{12} = \frac{1}{2} \text{ years.}$$

The accrual factor is thus

$$A_k(t) = \frac{45}{2} \cdot \frac{7}{15} = \$10.5,$$

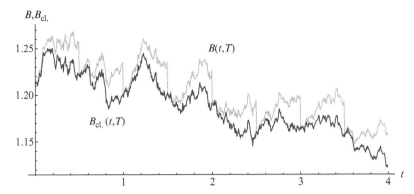

Fig. 18.5 Simulated clean (black) and dirty (gray) price process of a 10 year semi-annual coupon-bond

and therefore the correct dirty price is

$$B(t, T) = B_{\mathrm{cl.}}(t, T) + A_k(t) = \$1235.75.$$

Figure 18.5 illustrates both price processes for a bond with 10 years' time to maturity, unit principal, and semi-annual coupon payments. It can be easily seen that the dirty price drops down to the clean price immediately after the coupon is paid. Thus, the clean price is somewhat more regular, in that it has no foreseeable jumps.

18.4   Yield Measures and Yield Curve Construction

By now it should be clear that bonds can come in a vast variety of configurations and times to maturity. The natural question to ask is how to compare them? In other words, how much do we earn by holding a particular bond? This question is intimately related to the concept of yield. This concept itself comes in many variations. Let us explore two important representatives of the family of yield measures. Probably the simplest yield measure is the current yield (CY). It is defined as

$$CY = \frac{\text{annual coupon income}}{\text{clean price}}. \tag{18.22}$$

Example 18.3

Consider the coupon-bearing bond of Example 18.2. What is the current yield of this bond?

Solution

The annual coupon income of the bond is $45 and the clean price was quoted as $B_{cl.}(t, T) = \$1225.25$. Thus the current yield is

$$CY = \frac{45}{1225.25} \approx 3.67\%.$$

The current yield is obviously a very simple, but also crude measure. It does not take the coupon structure or the principal directly into account, but only indirectly in terms of the quoted price. Because the annual coupon income is constant, the current yield is only a snapshot at a particular instant of the lifetime of our bond and there is no way to tell, when this snapshot was taken. Furthermore, it is easy to see that we run into trouble if our bond is a zero-coupon bond.

A more elaborate yield measure is the yield to maturity (YTM). Unfortunately, the YTM is not so easy to define or to compute as the CY, except for zero-coupon bonds. The yield to maturity is the rate $y(t, T)$, that solves the pricing equation

$$B(t, T) = C \sum_{n=1}^{N} e^{-y(t,T)(T_n - t)} + P e^{-y(t,T)(T-t)}. \tag{18.23}$$

The YTM is also called the internal rate of return of the bond, for obvious reasons. This equation cannot be solved analytically, but only numerically. Fortunately, the problem is well posed, because the right hand side of (18.23) is a monotonic function of the internal rate of return $y(t, T)$. Altogether, this is a small price to pay for a yield measure that takes the whole structure of the respective bond into consideration.

Things become particularly easy, if we are interested in the YTM of a zero-coupon bond. We may without loss of generality take our discount bond. In this case, one immediately obtains

$$y(t, T) = -\frac{\log P(t, T)}{T - t}. \tag{18.24}$$

Quick calculation 18.4 Confirm this result with the help of (18.23).

You may wonder why we label the yield to maturity by a small letter, even though it seems not to be an instantaneous rate. The answer is, because it is not a spot rate either. It may look like a spot rate when computed for a zero-coupon bond. But as seen from Equation (18.23), it is a synthetic rate, at which all cash flows are discounted to match the observed price of the bond under consideration. That links the YTM inextricably to the particular bond for which it is computed. Thus, the second argument in $y(t, T)$ is misleading for coupon-bonds, because we can have two such contracts with identical

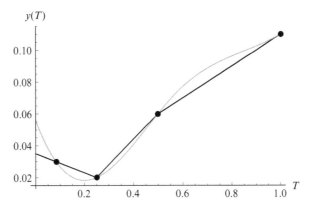

Fig. 18.6 Yield curve from US Treasury bonds of July 1, 2014 – Linear interpolation (black) and C^2 cubic spline (gray)

maturity date, but different coupon structure and therefore different yield to maturity. The somewhat awkward consequence of that was pointed out by Schaefer (1977): For different bonds there may be coupon payments occurring at the same time but discounted with different rates, whereas coupon payments of each particular bond occur at different times and are discounted with the same rate. This is precisely the opposite of our usual concept of rates. This problem has of course no relevance for zero-bonds.

If we restrict ourselves to zero-coupon bonds, we can plot the yield to maturity against the time to maturity, $T \mapsto y(t, T)$. Such a plot is called the yield curve or the term structure curve. For simplicity, let us set $t = 0$. The yields to maturity $y(0, T)$, extracted from a small set of US Treasury bonds of July 1, 2014 are indicated by dots in Figure 18.6. Unfortunately, there is only a finite number of bonds from which we can extract those yields and hence, for times to maturity in between, we have to interpolate. Strictly speaking, the yield curve is usually not extracted from bond prices, but from swap prices. Those contracts are far more liquid so that they determine the zero-bond prices. We will discuss this issue later. For the moment, let's call the interpolated yield curve $y(T)$. There is no correct method of interpolation and so the simplest thing we can do is to connect the dots with a straight line. This is also shown in Figure 18.6. As we will see shortly, we can also extract the forward curve from the yield curve, but this one will contain first derivatives of the yield curve. Here we run into a problem. The linearly interpolated yield curve is not differentiable at the maturity dates of the bonds we have used. This means that the forward curve will jump at those points. This is clearly not a favorable situation. If we can find an interpolating function with continuous first and second derivative, we are guaranteed to obtain a sufficiently smooth forward curve. This is the idea of spline interpolation, or more precisely of so-called C^2 cubic splines.

To understand spline interpolation, let's first take a look at linear interpolation from a different perspective. Linear interpolation means that we use a set of $N - 1$ different polynomials of degree one

$$y_n(T) = \sum_{k=0}^{1} a_{n,k}(T - T_n)^k, \qquad (18.25)$$

for $T_n \leq T \leq T_{n+1}$, to interpolate our N data points. We have therefore $2(N-1)$ coefficients $a_{n,k}$ we can tune, such that

$$y_n(T_n) = y(0, T_n) \quad \text{and} \quad y_n(T_{n+1}) = y(0, T_{n+1}), \tag{18.26}$$

for all $n = 1, \ldots, N-1$. This is exactly the number of equations we need to determine the coefficients. It is immediately obvious that we must have $a_{n,0} = y(0, T_n)$. Once we realize that, it is an easy task to deduce that

$$a_{n,1} = \frac{y(0, T_{n+1}) - y(0, T_n)}{T_{n+1} - T_n} \tag{18.27}$$

has to hold, and the linear interpolation problem is solved.

Quick calculation 18.5   Confirm the result for the coefficients $a_{n,1}$.

Note that in Figure 18.6 the interpolation function was extended to cover the interval $0 \leq T \leq T_1$. This is called extrapolation and was done by using the polynomial $y_1(T)$ outside its regular interval.

A natural C^2 cubic spline is a set of $N-1$ polynomials of third degree, defined analogously by

$$y_n(T) = \sum_{k=0}^{3} a_{n,k}(T - T_n)^k, \tag{18.28}$$

for $T_n \leq T \leq T_{n+1}$. We have now $4(N-1)$ coefficients $a_{n,k}$ and the following conditions:

1. $y_n(T_n) = y(0, T_n) \quad \text{and} \quad y_n(T_{n+1}) = y(0, T_{n+1})$,
2. $y_n'(T_{n+1}) = y_{n+1}'(T_{n+1}) \quad \text{and} \quad y_n''(T_{n+1}) = y_{n+1}''(T_{n+1})$, $\qquad$ (18.29)
3. $y_1''(T_1) = y_{N-1}''(T_N) = 0$,

for $n = 1, \ldots, N-1$. The first $2(N-1)$ conditions are the familiar ones, ensuring that the interpolation functions proceed right through the data points. In particular, we still have $a_{n,0} = y(0, T_n)$. The second set of conditions ensures that the first and second derivatives are continuous through the data points. There are $2(N-2)$ such continuity conditions. The third condition is called the natural boundary condition. It says that the function has no curvature at the start- and endpoint. There are other possible choices but the important fact is that this condition provides the last two restrictions, so that we have exactly $4(N-1)$ equations. It is no trivial task to solve for the remaining coefficients, but it can be done. The result is the smooth spline interpolation, indicated by a gray line in Figure 18.6. Extrapolation is again conducted by using $y_1(T)$ for $0 \leq T \leq T_1$. The C^2 cubic spline is by far not the most sophisticated spline interpolation method we can use, but it is a good starting point to understand the principle.

There is another common method for approximating the yield curve. One takes a smooth curve out of a parametric family with appropriate characteristics, and chooses the parameters such that the discretely observed yields are fitted as well as possible. Typically a quadratic objective function, containing the weighted squared errors,

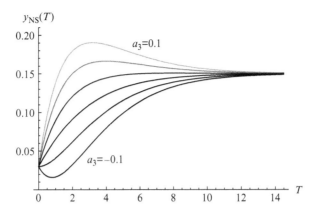

Fig. 18.7 *Nelson–Siegel*-curves with $a_1 = 0.15$, $a_2 = -0.12$, and $a_4 = 0.5$ – Third parameter varied from $a_3 = -0.1$ (black) to $a_3 = 0.1$ (gray)

is minimized to accomplish this task. An appropriate four parameter family was suggested by Nelson and Siegel (1987)

$$y_{NS}(T) = a_1 + (a_2 + a_3 T)e^{-a_4 T}. \tag{18.30}$$

A set of such curves is illustrated in Figure 18.7, for different values of a_3. Even though it might not look that way, the parameters of the *Nelson–Siegel*-curve determine its properties quite independently. For example the short rate is given by

$$y_{NS}(0) = a_1 + a_2, \tag{18.31}$$

whereas the long-term equilibrium yield is

$$\lim_{T \to \infty} y_{NS}(T) = a_1. \tag{18.32}$$

The parameter a_4 determines how strong the curve is pulled towards equilibrium, and only a_3 determines the essential shape of the curve. Essential shape means if the curve is humped or not, and if it is, in which direction. We have already seen one such hump in the US Treasury bond data in Figure 18.6. There is another commonly used extension to the *Nelson–Siegel*-family introduced by Svensson (1994)

$$y_{SV}(T) = a_1 + (a_2 + a_3 T)e^{-a_4 T} + a_5 Te^{-a_6 T}. \tag{18.33}$$

There are two more degrees of freedom in the *Svensson*-family, supporting even double humped shapes of the yield curve.

Comparing parametric curve fitting and spline interpolation, the advantage of the *Nelson–Siegel*- and *Svensson*-family is that there are very few global parameters to be calibrated and the derivative is also immediately available in terms of these parameters. Splines are constructed from many different piecewise polynomials that are pasted together at the available data points. The derivative of a spline is thus a piecewise function, too. On the other hand, splines need no fitting because they match every data point exactly. Table 18.1 summarizes the procedures used by several central banks, as reported in the technical documentation of the Bank for International Settlements (BIS, 2005).

Table 18.1 Yield curve estimation methods used by central banks 2005

Central bank	Method	Minimized error	Tax adj.	Maturity spectrum
Belgium	NS/SV	Weighted prices	No	Few days to 16 years
Canada	Spline	Weighted prices	Effectively[a]	3 months to 30 years
Finland	NS	Weighted prices	No	1 to 12 years
France	NS/SV	Weighted prices	No	Up to 10 years
Germany	SV	Yields	No	1 to 10 years
Italy	NS	Weighted prices	No	Up to 30 years
Japan	Spline	Prices	Effectively[b]	1 to 10 years
Norway	SV	Yields	No	Up to 10 years
Spain	SV	Weighted prices	Yes	Up to 10 years
Sweden	Spline/SV	Yields	No	Up to 10 years
Switzerland	SV	Yields	No	1 to 30 years
UK	Spline	Yields	No	Up to 30 years
USA	Spline	Weighted prices	No	Up to 1 year
USA	Spline	Prices	No	1 to 10 Years

[a] By excluding highly tax-distorted bonds.
[b] By price adjustments for short-term zero-coupon bonds.

18.5   Duration and Convexity

Let's return to ordinary coupon-bearing bonds. What happens to the value of the bond, if the yield to maturity changes? If the YTM is zero, the quoted value of the bond has to equal the nominal value (NV) of all future cash flows. That should be obvious by now, because with zero yield, there is no compounding of any kind. If we slowly start to dial up the YTM, the bond value has to decrease, until we reach a special yield y^*, where the value of the bond is precisely $B(t, T) = P$. In other words, the bond is quoted at par value. Observe that the value of the bond decreased from the nominal value of all future cash flows to the principal P, which is only one particular future cash flow. Because the bond price is a monotonic function of the yield, we can conclude that the price always decreases if the yield increases. The whole situation is illustrated in Figure 18.8. Duration is simply the derivative of the price-yield curve,

$$\text{Duration} = \frac{dB}{dy} = -C \sum_{n=1}^{N} (T_n - t)e^{-y(t,T)(T_n - t)} - (T - t)Pe^{-y(t,T)(T - t)}. \qquad (18.34)$$

Of course duration has to be negative, because the price-yield curve is downward sloping. Duration is very similar to the delta of an option, we encountered in Chapter 13. But why is this concept called duration? The answer is, because it has something to

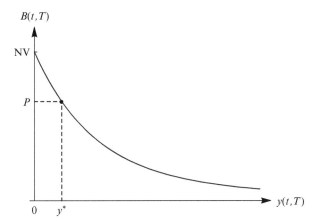

Fig. 18.8 Relation of YTM to value of the coupon-bearing bond – At y^* the bond is quoted at par value

do with the average time to maturity. To be more precise, the *Macaulay*-duration, defined by

$$Macaulay\text{-duration} = -\frac{1}{B(t, T)} \frac{dB}{dy},$$ (18.35)

is the average time to maturity. What does that mean? Suppose you have an ordinary coupon-bearing bond with principal P and given coupon structure. Now ask what time to maturity a zero-bond with the same yield and nominal value has to have, to match the price of the coupon-bond exactly? More formally, we are looking for a maturity date T^*, such that

$$B(t, T) = B_0(t, T^*) = \text{NV}\, e^{-y(t,T)(T^*-t)}$$ (18.36)

holds. To this end, take the derivative with respect to the yield,

$$\frac{dB}{dy} = -(T^* - t)\,\text{NV}\, e^{-y(t,T)(T^*-t)}.$$ (18.37)

Using the identity (18.36) and rearranging yields

$$-\frac{1}{B(t, T)} \frac{dB}{dy} = T^* - t.$$ (18.38)

But the left hand side is immediately identified as the *Macaulay*-duration, whereas the right hand side is what we called the average time to maturity. Using this concept, we are finally able to assign a meaningful quantity to the second argument of the coupon-bond yield, namely $y(t, T^*)$.

We can now map different coupon-bearing bonds in a yield-duration diagram as in Figure 18.9. What we would expect is that bonds with longer average time to maturity have higher internal yields. But this relation does not seem to hold exactly. Remember that each individual bond price reflects not only the risk of yield changes, but also

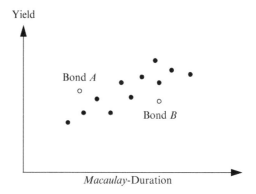

Fig. 18.9 Different bonds in a yield–duration diagram

liquidity risks, default risks, and so forth. Thus, two bonds with identical average time to maturity may very well differ considerably in their yield to maturity. In Figure 18.9, bond A has higher yield than bond B, but at the same time a much shorter average time to maturity. Thus, bond A seems more attractive than bond B from an investor's point of view. But keep in mind that the yield–duration diagram does not provide information about the true tenor and the coupon structure of the bonds. It may very well be the case that the actual time to maturity of bond A is longer than the one of bond B. Thus from the diagram, the investor cannot determine the time she is exposed to liquidity or default risks, if she is planning to hold the respective bond until maturity.

Convexity is a second order concept, similar to the gamma of an option. As in the case of duration, there are several measures of convexity. The simplest one is dollar convexity,

$$\text{Dollar convexity} = \frac{d^2 B}{dy^2} = C \sum_{n=1}^{N} (T_n - t)^2 e^{-y(t,T)(T_n - t)}$$
$$+ (T - t)^2 P e^{-y(t,T)(T-t)}.$$

(18.39)

That is, dollar convexity is the plain second derivative of the bond price with respect to the yield to maturity. The measure that is genuinely known as convexity, is the relative dollar convexity, or formally

$$\text{Convexity} = \frac{1}{B(t,T)} \frac{d^2 B}{dy^2}.$$

(18.40)

Quick calculation 18.6 Show that for a zero-coupon bond, convexity is the squared time to maturity.

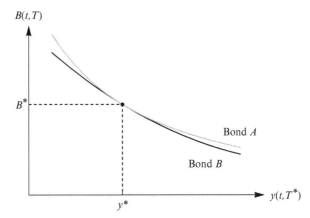

Fig. 18.10 Two bonds with identical price and yield to (average) maturity but different convexity

To be more precise, convexity measures the sensitivity of a bond with respect to parallel shifts in the yield curve. A parallel shift means that the yields for all maturities are shifted by the same amount. Look at the situation indicated in Figure 18.10. Bond A and bond B are identical in price and have the same internal yield and average time to maturity. But they are not identical securities. Bond A has a higher convexity than bond B. What happens, if the yield curve shifts in one or the other direction? If yields increase to $y > y^*$, the price of bond A is higher than the one of bond B. But the same holds in the opposite case $y < y^*$. Thus, under parallel shifts of the yield curve, we are better off with bond A, no matter in which direction the yield curve is shifted. Hence, if we have to choose between several bonds with identical prices, yields, and average times to maturity, we should choose the one with the largest convexity, if we expect primarily parallel yield curve shifts.

18.6   Forward Curve and Bootstrapping

We have already defined the instantaneous forward rate to be a function $f(t, s)$, such that the discount bond price is

$$P(t, T) = e^{- \int_t^T f(t,s)ds}. \tag{18.41}$$

Taking logarithms on both sides, multiplying by minus one and taking the derivative with respect to T, one obtains

$$f(t, T) = -\frac{\partial}{\partial T} \log P(t, T). \tag{18.42}$$

This is a very important formula, but it is usually of little practical use, because there is never a continuum of zero-bonds, such that taking the derivative makes any sense.

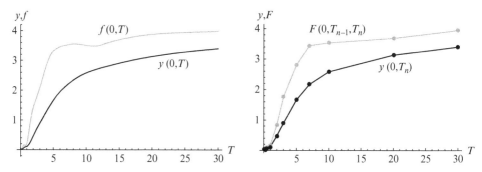

Fig. 18.11 Yield and forward curve from US Treasury bonds of July 1, 2014 in $\% - C^2$ cubic spline interpolation (left) and bootstrap (right)

Of course, we can use (18.42) in an approximate way by replacing the differential by a finite difference. This is essentially what is done by the bootstrap algorithm.[1] But let's first pursue an alternative avenue. We know by the definition of the yield to maturity that

$$P(t, T) = e^{-y(t,T)(T-t)} \tag{18.43}$$

has to hold. Thus, we can plug (18.43) into (18.42) to obtain the relation between the yield curve and the forward curve

$$f(t, T) = \frac{\partial}{\partial T}\big(y(t, T)(T - t)\big) = y(t, T) + \frac{\partial y}{\partial T}(T - t). \tag{18.44}$$

Since we have already learned how to obtain a smooth yield curve by spline interpolation or by fitting a parametric curve family, (18.44) provides a smooth forward curve. Figure 18.11 left illustrates the yield and forward curve obtained by cubic spline interpolation of the US Treasury bond data of July 2014. Both curves are perfectly smooth and allow for valuation of bonds with arbitrary time to maturity.

Another method very popular with practitioners is the so-called bootstrap. This method is based on the idea that the forward rate is constant between two given times to maturity. To see how it works, assume that we have normalized and arranged all available zero-bonds in increasing order of their times to maturity. For the first bond, we must have a rate $F(t, t, T_1)$, such that

$$P(t, T_1) = e^{-F(t,t,T_1)(T_1-t)} \tag{18.45}$$

holds. We can without further analysis conclude that $F(t, t, T_1) = y(t, T_1)$, because this is the definition of the YTM. But what about the second bond? We already know that

---

[1] In statistics the bootstrap procedure has a different meaning. It is a method to augment a small sample by redrawing random numbers from the sample realizations with the correct probability of occurrence.

$F(t, t, T_1)$ is the correct rate for compounding between t and T_1. But between T_1 and T_2 the yet unknown rate $F(t, T_1, T_2)$ has to be used

$$P(t, T_2) = e^{-F(t,t,T_1)(T_1-t)-F(t,T_1,T_2)(T_2-T_1)}. \tag{18.46}$$

Because of the exponential factors, we can rewrite (18.46) as

$$P(t, T_2) = e^{-F(t,t,T_1)(T_1-t)} e^{-F(t,T_1,T_2)(T_2-T_1)}$$
$$= P(t, T_1) \cdot e^{-F(t,T_1,T_2)(T_2-T_1)}. \tag{18.47}$$

Solving for $F(t, T_1, T_2)$ yields

$$F(t, T_1, T_2) = -\frac{\log P(t, T_2) - \log P(t, T_1)}{T_2 - T_1}. \tag{18.48}$$

Of course, the same argument carries over to all discount bonds $P(t, T_n)$ and the corresponding rates $F(t, T_{n-1}, T_n)$, for $n = 1, \ldots, N$. If we thus assume that $T_0 = t$, then the general bootstrap formula reads

$$F(t, T_{n-1}, T_n) = -\frac{\log P(t, T_n) - \log P(t, T_{n-1})}{T_n - T_{n-1}}. \tag{18.49}$$

Quick calculation 18.7   Verify that this is a finite difference approximation of (18.42).

Figure 18.11 right shows the result of the bootstrap procedure for the US Treasury bond data. Between times T_n, linear interpolation was used to fill the gaps. The bootstrap may not be the most elegant approach to extract the forward curve from observed bond prices, but it is simple and robust. This is why it is so popular with practitioners. An immediate consequence of (18.49) is

$$F(t, S, T) = \frac{1}{T-S} \int_S^T f(t, s) ds, \tag{18.50}$$

for arbitrary $t \le S < T$. That is, the forward rate for compounding over the time interval $[S, T]$ is the average instantaneous forward rate over the same interval.

Quick calculation 18.8   Prove this statement with the help of (18.42).

Fig. 18.12 Structure of a plain vanilla interest rate swap between parties A and B

18.7   Interest Rate Swaps

Interest rate swaps (IRS) are among the most liquidly traded derivatives in the entire financial market. As reported by the Bank for International Settlements (BIS, 2014, tab. 1), the global IRS market volume in June 2014 was about 421 trillion dollars. Thus, swaps are far more liquid than zero-coupon bonds, and in fact zero-bond prices are determined by the swap market. A plain vanilla interest rate swap is an agreement between two parties to exchange future interest payments on an identical principal. Either a sequence of fixed interest payments is exchanged for floating interest payments (payer swap), or floating is exchanged for fixed (receiver swap). The fixed and floating sides of the contract are called legs. The floating leg interest rates are usually pegged to the appropriate LIBOR. The schematic structure of an interest rate swap between two parties is illustrated in Figure 18.12. Keep in mind that the principal itself is not exchanged in a plain vanilla swap, only the interest payments.

Quick calculation 18.9 Is the contract in Figure 18.12 a payer or receiver swap from the perspective of A?

Let's first ask the question: Why should one enter such a contract? Assume we have two companies, A and B. Both companies can borrow in the financial market under the conditions specified in Table 18.2. The credit rating of A is higher than that of B and thus, A can borrow at a lower interest rate than B, both in fixed and floating interest markets. But the difference in the rates for A and B is not the same in the fixed and floating markets. A swap contract is a clever device to exploit comparative advantages, induced by the difference in Δ_{fix} and Δ_{fl}. Assume A would prefer floating interest rates and B would like to borrow at a fixed rate. In this case Table 18.2 tells us immediately that A has to pay LIBOR + 50 bps interest and B has a fixed rate of 7.2%. But there is a smarter and, more importantly, cheaper way of borrowing in the

Table 18.2 Financing conditions for A and B

Company	Fixed	Floating
A	6%	LIBOR + 50 bps (0.5%)
B	7.2%	LIBOR + 120 bps (1.2%)
	$\Delta_{fix} = 1.2\%$	$\Delta_{fl.} = 0.7\%$

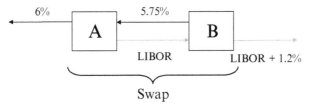

Fig. 18.13 Internal and external payments of companies A and B with interest rate swap

desired flavor. Imagine A borrows fixed and B floating. At the same time, they enter a mutual swap contract and internally exchange interest payments fixed for floating. The swap they contracted may be the one illustrated in Figure 18.13. First of all notice that the swap contract restores the original borrowing preferences. This is most easily seen for company B, which receives LIBOR from A and pays LIBOR to the market. Those cash flows cancel and all remaining payments are fixed. The funding costs for company A and B are summarized in Table 18.3. Obviously, when entering a swap contract, both companies can still borrow according to their preferences, but at lower rates. By contracting the suggested swap, the funding costs for both companies are 25 bps lower. This is exactly half the difference between Δ_{fix} and Δ_{fl}. Of course the swap contract does not necessarily have to split the comparative advantage equally. In reality, swaps are highly standardized derivatives, and each leg is offered independently by a financial intermediary. The intermediary takes the default risk of a potential counterparty and therefore, she takes a part of the comparative profit as risk compensation.

By now it should be obvious, why swaps are that attractive and liquidly traded. So let's take a closer look at the formal definition and pricing of an interest rate swap. A plain vanilla swap contract is determined by a fixed leg with a contracted rate κ, a reference for the floating leg, mostly LIBOR, and a tenor structure $T_0, \dots, T_N$. We make the slightly simplified assumption that the dates at which payments are exchanged are equally spaced with $\Delta t = T_n - T_{n-1}$ for $n = 1, \dots, N$. In practice this may not be entirely correct because of day-count conventions, but it is a very good approximation. If we assume that the swap contract is standardized to a unit principal, then at times T_n, the fixed leg pays $\Delta t \cdot \kappa$ and the floating leg pays $\Delta t \cdot L(T_{n-1}, T_n)$, for $n = 1, \dots, N$. For the pricing of a plain vanilla swap, it is vital that the floating rate to be paid at T_n is reset at

Table 18.3 Funding costs of A and B

Company	A		B
Without swap	LIBOR + 50 bps		7.2%
	6%		5.75%
With swap	$-$ 5.75%	$-$	LIBOR
	$+$ LIBOR	$+$	LIBOR + 1.2%
	LIBOR + 25 bps		6.95%

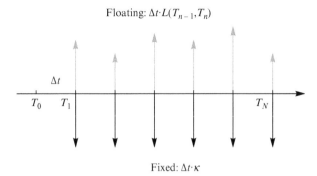

Fig. 18.14 Tenor structure of a plain vanilla payer interest rate swap

T_{n-1}. Thus, T_0 is the first reset date, which usually coincides with the starting date of the swap contract, whereas the first payments are exchanged at T_1. Figure 18.14 illustrates the structure of a typical payer interest rate swap. At time $t \leq T_0$, the price, say of a payer swap, should equal the present value of the floating leg minus the present value of the fixed leg. Obviously, the receiver swap has the same absolute value, but with the opposite sign, because both contracts are the opposite sides of the same agreement. So to price a swap, we merely have to compute the present value of both legs. Assume that we have extracted today's forward curve. Then the time t value of the fixed leg is obviously

$$\text{Fixed leg} = \Delta t \, \kappa \sum_{n=1}^{N} P(t, T_n). \tag{18.51}$$

To value the floating leg, we use a little trick. Let's add and subtract one dollar at time T_N, so that the overall cash flow is not affected. The situation is illustrated in Figure 18.15. This corresponds precisely to a long position in a time T_0 floating rate note $B_{\text{fl}}(T_0, T_N)$, and short one dollar to be paid at time T_N. We know from

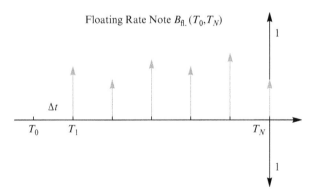

Fig. 18.15 Floating leg of an interest rate swap with one dollar added and subtracted at time T_N

(18.16) on page 422 that the time T_0 value of the floating rate note is one dollar. Thus, the present value of the floating leg has to be

$$\text{Floating leg} = P(t, T_0) - P(t, T_N). \tag{18.52}$$

With these results we can now easily price payer and receiver swaps. For example the receiver swap has time t value

$$\text{IRS}_R(t, \kappa) = \Delta t \, \kappa \sum_{n=1}^{N} P(t, T_n) - P(t, T_0) + P(t, T_N). \tag{18.53}$$

As already pointed out, the corresponding payer swap is worth $\text{IRS}_P(t, \kappa) = -\text{IRS}_R(t, \kappa)$.

In the sequel, suppose the swap is contracted today at $t = T_0$ in such a way that it can be entered from both sides with no upfront payment. The swap rate $\kappa = r_S$, which makes $\text{IRS}_P(T_0, r_S) = \text{IRS}_R(T_0, r_S) = 0$ is called the par rate of the swap. From (18.53) it is easily seen that the par rate is

$$r_S = \frac{1 - P(T_0, T_N)}{\Delta t \sum_{n=1}^{N} P(T_0, T_n)}. \tag{18.54}$$

Somehow this swap rate is made out of discount bonds, and so the natural question is, can we extract bond prices from a series of swap rates for different maturities? The answer is yes, and the procedure is again called bootstrapping. Suppose you observe the swap rate for entering a contract with maturity T_1 in the market, and call this rate $r_S(T_1)$. Setting $N = 1$ in (18.54) yields

$$r_S(T_1) = \frac{1 - P(T_0, T_1)}{\Delta t P(T_0, T_1)}. \tag{18.55}$$

This equation is easily solved for the bond price and one obtains

$$P(T_0, T_1) = \frac{1}{1 + \Delta t \, r_S(T_1)}. \tag{18.56}$$

Now assume you observe a second par rate, $r_S(T_2)$, for a swap contract maturing at T_2. We proceed as before and setting $N = 2$ in (18.54) gives us

$$r_S(T_2) = \frac{1 - P(T_0, T_2)}{\Delta t (P(T_0, T_1) + P(T_0, T_2))}. \tag{18.57}$$

It is now slightly more demanding to solve for $P(T_0, T_2)$, but not much. The result is

$$P(T_0, T_2) = \frac{1 - \Delta t \, r_S(T_2) P(T_0, T_1)}{1 + \Delta t \, r_S(T_2)}. \tag{18.58}$$

Quick calculation 18.10 Confirm the last equation.

Note that all quantities on the right hand side of (18.58) are known. The par rate $r_S(T_2)$ is observed in the market and the bond price $P(T_0, T_1)$ was already computed from $r_S(T_1)$. Continuing in this manner, one can solve (18.54) for general N and obtains

$$P(T_0, T_N) = \frac{1 - \Delta t \, r_S(T_N) \sum_{n=1}^{N-1} P(T_0, T_n)}{1 + \Delta t \, r_S(T_N)}. \tag{18.59}$$

When computed sequentially, all bond prices $P(T_0, T_n)$ on the right hand side of (18.59) are already known, and $r_S(T_N)$ is again observed in the market. Because swaps are that liquid, swap rates are easily available for a much greater collection of maturities than zero-coupon bonds. Thus, bond prices are largely determined by the swap market.

18.8   Further Reading

A very accessible introduction to the analysis of basic fixed-income products is Wilmott (2006a, chap. 13 & 14). A neat collection of additional yield measures is provided in Fabozzi (2007, chap. 6). A concise discussion of day-count conventions is found in Filipović (2009, sect. 2.5). The most common methods of yield curve construction are detailed in Andersen and Piterbarg (2010a, chap. 6). Measures of price sensitivity based on parallel shifts of the yield curve are extensively discussed in Tuckman (2002, chap. 6) and Sundaresan (2009, chap. 7). A swift formal introduction to interest rate swaps is given in Brigo and Mercurio (2007, sect. 1.5).

18.9   Problems

18.1 A consol is a perpetual bond that pays coupons forever, without repaying the principal. Consider a standardized consol, issued today at $t = 0$, with annual coupon payments c. Show that the relation

$$B(0, \infty) = \frac{c}{e^{y(0,T^*)} - 1}$$

between price and yield to (average) maturity holds.

18.2 Use the banking account as a numéraire to show that

$$e^{-\int_t^T f(t,s)ds} = E^Q\left[e^{-\int_t^T r(s)ds}\middle|\mathcal{F}_t\right]$$

has to hold.

18.3 Show that *Macaulay*-duration is a weighted average of times to maturity

$$\textit{Macaulay}\text{-duration} = \sum_{n=1}^{N} w_n(T_n - t),$$

where the weights w_n are the fractions of the present value of the bond, represented by the n-th cashflow.

18.4 Show that the bootstrap formula (18.49) on page 435 is equivalent to a finite difference approximation of (18.44), if the respective bonds are expressed in terms of their yield to maturity $y(t, T_n)$ and $y(t, T_{n-1})$.

18.5 Consider the financing conditions in Table 18.2 on page 436 for companies A and B. Assume that a financial intermediary C offers both companies a payer and a receiver swap to realize comparative advantages. C takes 20 bps of the comparative difference to insure herself against default of one counterparty. The rest is divided equally between A and B. Sketch the new situation as in Figure 18.13 and compare the funding costs for A and B.

19 Plain Vanilla Fixed-Income Derivatives

The major lesson we have learned so far is that knowledge of the forward curve, as it stands today, is enough to price any of the fixed-income instruments introduced until now. An option on such an instrument, expiring sometime in the future, requires knowledge of the forward curve as it will be at the time of expiry. This adds another level of sophistication to option pricing problems, and as we shall see, increases the complexity considerably.

19.1 The *T*-Forward Measure

Pricing derivatives on bonds or rates is largely a question of selecting a well suited numéraire and evaluating the conditional expectation of the claim in the associated equivalent martingale measure. We have done that many times before. To be more precise, we chose the bank account $B(t)$ as a numéraire, and the associated equivalent martingale measure was the risk-neutral measure Q. We thus obtained the martingale pricing relation

$$\frac{V_t}{B(t)} = E^Q\left[\frac{V_T}{B(T)}\middle|\mathcal{F}_t\right], \tag{19.1}$$

for an arbitrary *T*-claim V. It does not matter if V is a derivative or a genuine security. We have merely stated this relation in a slightly different form as

$$V_t = E^Q\left[\frac{B(t)}{B(T)}V_T\middle|\mathcal{F}_t\right] = E^Q\left[e^{-\int_t^T r(s)ds}V_T\middle|\mathcal{F}_t\right] \tag{19.2}$$

most of the time. If the interest rate $r(t)$ is deterministic, we can pull the discount factor out of the expectation and we are back in our familiar setting for security markets. Unfortunately, we are now in a stochastic interest rate world and furthermore, we have to assume that V also depends on r. This means, we cannot factor the last expectation value in (19.2), because there are covariance contributions between the discount factor and the payoff of the *T*-claim. There is a surprising twist to this problem. We can eliminate the covariance by choosing another numéraire. Recall that every traded asset with nonnegative price for all times t can be selected as a numéraire. So let's take the discount bond $P(t, T)$ and call the associated martingale measure the *T*-forward measure Q_T. One then obtains in complete analogy to (19.1)

$$\frac{V_t}{P(t, T)} = E^{Q_T}\left[\frac{V_T}{P(T, T)}\middle|\mathcal{F}_t\right]. \tag{19.3}$$

Recalling that $P(T, T) = 1$, we obtain

$$V_t = P(t, T)E^{Q_T}[V_T|\mathcal{F}_t].$$

(19.4)

Now the discount factor has moved out of the expectation. Of course there is a price to pay. We have to figure out the dynamics of V_t under the T-forward measure Q_T.

Let's start with a very simple quantity, the forward price. In a stochastic interest rate framework, the forward price F at time t of any T-claim V has to be

$$F_t = \frac{V_t}{P(t, T)}.$$

(19.5)

This can be easily verified by an arbitrage argument, taking into account that $P(T, T) = 1$, and therefore $F_T = V_T$. But this means that due to (19.4), F_t is a martingale under Q_T

$$F_t = E^{Q_T}[F_T|\mathcal{F}_t].$$

(19.6)

Since a martingale is driftless, we can immediately conclude that in a geometric *Brown*ian motion setup, the dynamics of F_t look like

$$dF_t = \sigma F_t dW_t$$

(19.7)

under Q_T. But what about the future price? We learned that future and forward prices coincide, as long as interest rates are deterministic. Now that we have entered the realm of stochastic interest rates, we should take a closer look at this. The future price $\hat{F}_t$ is a price quoted in the market, which makes entering a future contract on V at time t costless. It is immediately clear that $\hat{F}_T = V_T$ has to hold. The future contract is (nearly) continuously resettled, and therefore entering the contract with no upfront payment implies that

$$E^Q\left[\int_t^T e^{-\int_t^u r(s)ds} d\hat{F}_u \Big| \mathcal{F}_t\right] = 0$$

(19.8)

has to hold. Resettlement is done with the help of a margin account. Like the bank account, the margin account is a random process, but it has a very interesting property. Let $M(t)$ be the discounted value of the margin account. Then the following relation holds

$$M(t) = \int_0^t e^{-\int_0^u r(s)ds} d\hat{F}_u = E^Q\left[\int_0^T e^{-\int_0^u r(s)ds} d\hat{F}_u \Big| \mathcal{F}_t\right] = E^Q[M(T)|\mathcal{F}_t].$$

(19.9)

Quick calculation 19.1 Use (19.8) to prove the second equality.

The margin account only changes if the future price changes and hence, if $M(t)$ is a Q-martingale, so is $\hat{F}_t$. We thus conclude that

$$\hat{F}_t = E^Q[\hat{F}_T|\mathcal{F}_t]$$

(19.10)

has to hold. But because $\hat{F}_T = F_T = V_T$, future and forward prices cannot coincide. They are conditional expectations of the same quantity under different probability measures.

Let's analyze an S bond under the T-forward measure for $t \leq T < S$. To keep things simple, we choose the discount bond. Then we have

$$\frac{P(t, S)}{P(t, T)} = E^{Q_T}[P(T, S)|\mathcal{F}_t]. \tag{19.11}$$

Let us rewrite this expression in terms of the respective forward rates to obtain

$$e^{-\int_T^S f(t,s)ds} = E^{Q_T}\left[e^{-\int_T^S f(T,s)ds}\Big|\mathcal{F}_t\right]. \tag{19.12}$$

We might thus suspect that the forward rate itself, or at least one of them, is a Q_T-martingale. To elaborate this hypothesis, we need to learn something about the relation of the measures Q and Q_T. Remember that the *Girsanov*-theorem expressed the relation between the physical measure P and the risk-neutral measure Q with the help of the *Radon–Nikodym*-derivative $\frac{dQ}{dP}$. Thus, to switch between Q and Q_T, all we need is the appropriate *Radon–Nikodym*-derivative, which is easily recovered by replacing the numéraires,

$$\frac{dQ}{dQ_T}\Big|_{\mathcal{F}_t} = \frac{P(t, T)/P(T, T)}{B(t)/B(T)} = \frac{P(t, T)}{e^{-\int_t^T r(s)ds}}. \tag{19.13}$$

We have thus for an arbitrary T-claim V

$$E^Q\left[e^{-\int_t^T r(s)ds}V_T\Big|\mathcal{F}_t\right] = E^{Q_T}\left[e^{-\int_t^T r(s)ds}V_T\frac{dQ}{dQ_T}\Big|\mathcal{F}_t\right] = P(t, T)E^{Q_T}[V_T|\mathcal{F}_t]. \tag{19.14}$$

Let's now look at a very special T-claim,

$$-\frac{\partial P(t, T)}{\partial T} = E^Q\left[-\frac{\partial}{\partial T}e^{-\int_t^T r(s)ds}\Big|\mathcal{F}_t\right] = E^Q\left[e^{-\int_t^T r(s)ds}r(T)\Big|\mathcal{F}_t\right]. \tag{19.15}$$

Dividing both sides by $P(t, T)$, and using (19.13) to express the right hand side in the T-forward measure yields

$$-\frac{\partial \log P(t, T)}{\partial T} = E^{Q_T}[r(T)|\mathcal{F}_t]. \tag{19.16}$$

Quick calculation 19.2 Confirm this equation.

Now remember that the left hand side of (19.16) is the forward rate $f(t, T)$, and that $r(T) = f(T, T)$. It follows immediately that the forward rate

$$f(t, T) = E^{Q_T}[f(T, T)|\mathcal{F}_t] \tag{19.17}$$

is a Q_T-martingale.

19.2   The *Black*-76-Model

The pricing methodology in fixed-income derivative markets is largely built around Black's formula, also called the *Black*-76-model. Originally, it was designed to price options on futures in a deterministic interest rate world. So let's turn back the clock for a moment and assume a fixed interest rate r. The risk-neutral price process for an arbitrary non-dividend paying underlying is the geometric *Brown*ian motion

$$dS_t = r S_t dt + \sigma S_t dW_t. \qquad (19.18)$$

What is the dynamics of the forward price $F_t = e^{r(T-t)} S_t$? An application of Itô's lemma yields

$$dF_t = \sigma F_t dW_t. \qquad (19.19)$$

Quick calculation 19.3 Apply Itô's lemma to confirm this result.

That is, the forward price process is a Q-martingale. But that means the risk-neutral measure Q and the T-forward measure Q_T have to coincide. We can use the generalized version of the *Black–Scholes*-formula on page 269, set $b = 0$, and compute let's say the price of a European call option

$$C_t(K, T) = e^{-r(T-t)}(F_t \Phi(d_+) - K\Phi(d_-)), \qquad (19.20)$$

with $\Phi(x)$ again denoting the cumulative distribution function of a standard normal random variable X, and

$$d_{+/-} = \frac{\log(F_t/K) \pm \frac{1}{2}\sigma^2(T-t)}{\sigma \sqrt{T-t}}. \qquad (19.21)$$

In case of a fixed interest rate r, the price of a discount bond is $P(t, T) = e^{-r(T-t)}$, and therefore we can conclude that

$$E^{Q_T}[(F_T - K)^+ | \mathcal{F}_t] = F_t \Phi(d_+) - K\Phi(d_-), \qquad (19.22)$$

for the Q_T-martingale F_t. But the forward price is a Q_T-martingale whether or not interest rates are deterministic. Thus, in general the price of a plain vanilla European call option is

$$C_t(K, T) = P(t, T)(F_t \Phi(d_+) - K\Phi(d_-)). \qquad (19.23)$$

By completely analogous arguments, one obtains the price of the corresponding plain vanilla put option

$$P_t(K, T) = P(t, T)(K\Phi(-d_-) - F_t \Phi(-d_+)). \qquad (19.24)$$

Often interest rate sensitive products like bonds for example, need at least a deterministic term structure of volatility $\sigma(t)$. Take the simplest possible example, the discount bond. We know that its value approaches one for $t \to T$. This is also known as the pull to par phenomenon. But this means that the volatility of its dynamics has to vanish in that limit. To accommodate such requirements, we can express (19.21) in a slightly more general way

$$d_{+/-} = \frac{\log(F_t/K) \pm \frac{1}{2}\int_t^T \sigma^2(s)ds}{\sqrt{\int_t^T \sigma^2(s)ds}}. \tag{19.25}$$

Note that those formulas have to hold for every T-forward price, independently of the actual underlying.

Example 19.1

What is the fair price of a plain vanilla European call option, expiring at T, on a discount bond with maturity date S, with $t < T < S$?

Solution

The forward price of the S-bond is $F_t = \frac{P(t,S)}{P(t,T)}$. Of course this price is a Q_T-martingale and Black's formula immediately yields

$$C_t(K, T) = P(t, S)\Phi(d_+) - P(t, T)K\Phi(d_-),$$

with

$$d_{+/-} = \frac{\log\left(\frac{P(t,S)}{P(t,T)K}\right) \pm \frac{1}{2}\int_t^T \sigma_P^2(s)ds}{\sqrt{\int_t^T \sigma_P^2(s)ds}}.$$

Quick calculation 19.4   Compute $d_{+/-}$ for the bond volatility $\sigma_P(t) = \sigma \cdot (T - t)$.

Note that in the *Black*-76-model, call and put prices are uniquely determined, if the strike price K, the expiry date T, and the implied volatility

$$\sigma_{\text{imp.}} = \sqrt{\frac{1}{T - t}\int_t^T \sigma^2(s)ds} \tag{19.26}$$

are known, because the forward price can be observed in the market. It is thus customary to quote K, T, and $\sigma_{\text{imp.}}$ instead of the call or put price.

19.3   Caps and Floors

Caps/floors can be understood as payer/receiver interest rate swaps, where payments are only exchanged, if there is a net profit. As we shall see, there is a natural parity relation between caps, floors, and swaps. A cap can be decomposed into individual caplets. Assume we have $t < S < T$, where S is the reset date, and $\Delta t = T - S$. Then, the payoff of the T-caplet with unit principal is

$$\text{Cpl}_T(\kappa, T) = \Delta t(L(S, T) - \kappa)^+. \tag{19.27}$$

To determine the value of this caplet at time t, we have to analyze the dynamics of the LIBOR $L(S, T)$. To this end, define the forward LIBOR $L(t, S, T)$, using the relation (18.13) on page 421 between simple and continuous compounding

$$\frac{1}{1 + \Delta t L(t, S, T)} = e^{-\int_S^T f(t,s)ds} = \frac{P(t, T)}{P(t, S)}. \tag{19.28}$$

If we turn both sides of (19.28) upside down, we obtain

$$1 + \Delta t L(t, S, T) = \frac{P(t, S)}{P(t, T)}. \tag{19.29}$$

The right hand side of (19.29) is a Q_T-martingale, and so has to be the left hand side. The constant 1 is a trivial martingale under every measure and thus, $\Delta t L(t, S, T)$ must also be a Q_T-martingale

$$\Delta t L(t, S, T) = \Delta t E^{Q_T}[L(S, S, T)|\mathcal{F}_t]. \tag{19.30}$$

It is immediately obvious that the coefficient Δt cancels out of the equation, and from (19.28) it is easy to see that $L(S, S, T) = L(S, T)$ has to hold.

Quick calculation 19.5 Confirm this statement.

Summarizing our results, the forward LIBOR $L(t, S, T)$ is a martingale under the T-forward measure, and from (19.29) it is given by

$$L(t, S, T) = \frac{1}{\Delta t}\left(\frac{P(t, S)}{P(t, T)} - 1\right). \tag{19.31}$$

It is now a trivial exercise to compute the value of the T-caplet at time t, which is given by

$$\text{Cpl}_t(\kappa, T) = P(t, T)\Delta t(L(t, S, T)\Phi(d_+) - \kappa\Phi(d_-)), \tag{19.32}$$

with

$$d_{+/-} = \frac{\log\left(\frac{L(t,S,T)}{\kappa}\right) \pm \frac{1}{2}\int_t^S \sigma^2(s)ds}{\sqrt{\int_t^S \sigma^2(s)ds}}. \tag{19.33}$$

Usually, the caplet implied volatilities are quoted in the market, or to be a little more precise, they can be stripped from quoted cap volatilities. We will learn later how this works. The important point is that everything we need in order to compute the caplet price can be observed in the market. You may wonder, why the squared volatility in (19.33) is integrated only up to time S and not time T. This is because S is the reset date, which means the floating rate to be used for compounding between S and T is fixed at time S. Thus, a caplet is strictly speaking an option that expires at S, but pays off at the later time T.

A cap is a collection of caplets, based on a tenor structure like the one for swaps. Assume that interest payments are to be exchanged on a previously fixed schedule $T_0, \ldots, T_N$, where T_0 is only the first reset date for the floating reference rate, and $\Delta t = T_n - T_{n-1}$. Then it is immediately clear that the price of the cap at $t \leq T_0$ is

$$\mathrm{Cp}(t,\kappa) = \sum_{n=1}^N \mathrm{Cpl}_t(\kappa, T_n). \tag{19.34}$$

This formula looks not at all spectacular, but it relies heavily on the family of T_n-forward measures for $n = 1, \ldots, N$. To see this, let's rewrite (19.34) in a slightly different form

$$\mathrm{Cp}(t,\kappa) = \Delta t \sum_{n=1}^N P(t,T_n) E^{Q_n}\left[(L(T_{n-1},T_n) - \kappa)^+ | \mathcal{F}_t\right], \tag{19.35}$$

where $E^{Q_n}[\ldots]$ is the conditional expectation under the T_n-forward measure. It is a great advantage of the martingale pricing framework over the partial differential equation approach that we can freely manipulate the probability measure by changing the numéraire. In the field of fixed-income derivative pricing, this feature becomes very powerful.

For $t < S < T$ and $\Delta t = T - S$, the payoff of a T-floorlet is given by

$$\mathrm{Fll}_T(\kappa, T) = \Delta t(\kappa - L(S,T))^+. \tag{19.36}$$

This is immediately identified as the payoff of a put option on the LIBOR $L(S,T)$, with strike rate κ. We can now apply exactly the same chain of arguments to conclude that the price of the T-floorlet in Black's model has to be

$$\mathrm{Fll}_t(\kappa, T) = P(t,T)\Delta t(\kappa\Phi(-d_-) - L(t,S,T)\Phi(-d_+)), \tag{19.37}$$

with $d_{+/-}$ precisely as in (19.33). As in case of the cap, the floor is a collection of floorlets, based on a tenor structure $T_0, \ldots, T_N$. Thus, its fair price is

$$\mathrm{Fl}(t, \kappa) = \sum_{n=1}^{N} \mathrm{Fll}_t(\kappa, T_n). \tag{19.38}$$

Why should one wish to hold a cap or a floor? Imagine you have credit liabilities and interests are to be paid with reference to a floating rate, for example the respective LIBOR. Then you can "cap" the interest rate by buying a cap with the appropriate tenor structure and an exercise rate κ_{max}. If the LIBOR exceeds κ_{max} during the lifetime, the contract pays off the difference and you have effectively limited the maximum interest rate. Of course such an insurance does not come for free. But you can reduce the costs, if you are willing to pay interests at a rate of at least κ_{min}. Shorting a floor on the same tenor structure and strike rate κ_{min} generates proceeds from selling the contract. But now, the interest rate is effectively trapped between κ_{min} and κ_{max}. Such a position is called a collar. Let's raise an abstract question, independent of any background motivations. What would we get, if we held a collar with $\kappa_{min} = \kappa_{max} = \kappa$? If the appropriate LIBOR is greater than the strike rate κ, we would earn the difference from the cap. Otherwise we would have to pay the difference from the short position in the floor. But this payoff profile is exactly identical with the one of a payer interest rate swap. We have thus discovered the payer swap parity relation

$$\mathrm{Cp}(t, \kappa) - \mathrm{Fl}(t, \kappa) = \mathrm{IRS}_P(t, \kappa). \tag{19.39}$$

Quick calculation 19.6 State the receiver swap parity relation.

Caps and floors are easy to valuate, because they can be decomposed into caplets and floorlets, which can be priced with Black's formula. Such a decomposition property is not mandatory for interest rate derivatives and we will encounter an example where it is absent in the next section.

19.4 Swaptions and the Annuity Measure

A swaption is a contract that grants its holder the right, but not the obligation, to enter a swap contract at a fixed rate κ sometime in the future. Usually the expiry date of the option is the first reset date T_0 of the associated swap. A payer swaption has the payoff

$$\mathrm{Swpt}_P(T_0, \kappa) = \left(\Delta t \sum_{n=1}^{N} P(T_0, T_n)(L(T_0, T_{n-1}, T_n) - \kappa) \right)^+, \tag{19.40}$$

with our usual notation for the tenor structure. Now we run into a problem. This pay-off cannot be decomposed into a sum of individual payoffs, depending only on one forward LIBOR. Hence, we cannot apply our T_n-forward measure trick.

Let's try to rewrite the payoff function. Recall the definition of the par rate of a swap at $t = T_0$, (18.54) on page 439. For $t < T_0$ define the forward swap rate

$$r_S(t) = \frac{P(t, T_0) - P(t, T_N)}{\Delta t \sum_{n=1}^{N} P(t, T_n)}. \tag{19.41}$$

Quick calculation 19.7 Convince yourself that $r_S(T_0)$ is the original par rate.

The numerator of (19.41) is the present value of the floating leg of the swap and the denominator is called the annuity factor

$$A(t) = \Delta t \sum_{n=1}^{N} P(t, T_n). \tag{19.42}$$

If we reexpress the floating leg in terms of forward LIBOR, the forward swap rate becomes

$$r_S(t) = \frac{\Delta t \sum_{n=1}^{N} P(t, T_n) L(t, T_{n-1}, T_n)}{A(t)}. \tag{19.43}$$

Dividing and multiplying (19.40) by $A(T_0)$ allows us to express the swaption payoff in a very neat form

$$\text{Swpt}_P(T_0, \kappa) = A(T_0)(r_S(T_0) - \kappa)^+. \tag{19.44}$$

Quick calculation 19.8 Confirm the last equation.

The annuity factor (19.42) is a portfolio of traded assets and furthermore, it is guaranteed to be positive. Therefore, we can use it as a numéraire to obtain

$$\text{Swpt}_P(t, \kappa) = A(t) E^{Q_A} \left[(r_S(T_0) - \kappa)^+ | \mathcal{F}_t \right]. \tag{19.45}$$

Q_A is called the annuity measure or also the swap measure. From (19.43) it is easy to see that the forward swap rate is a martingale in the annuity measure,

$$r_S(t) = E^{Q_A}[r_S(T_0) | \mathcal{F}_t], \tag{19.46}$$

because the correct numerator is already part of the definition. But with $r_S(t)$ being a Q_A-martingale, we can again use Black's formula to price the payer swaption and the result is

$$\text{Swpt}_P(t, \kappa) = A(t)(r_S(t) \Phi(d_+) - \kappa \Phi(d_-)), \tag{19.47}$$

with

$$d_{+/-} = \frac{\log\left(\frac{r_S(t)}{\kappa}\right) \pm \frac{1}{2}\int_t^{T_0} \sigma^2(s)ds}{\sqrt{\int_t^{T_0} \sigma^2(s)ds}} \quad \text{and} \quad A(t) = \Delta t \sum_{n=1}^{N} P(t, T_n). \tag{19.48}$$

It is not a difficult task to guess what the price of a receiver swaption is. Obviously, the payoff of such a contract at expiry T_0 is

$$\text{Swpt}_R(T_0, \kappa) = A(T_0)(\kappa - r_S(T_0))^+. \tag{19.49}$$

This identifies the receiver swaption as a put option on the swap rate. We can thus apply all arguments again and obtain

$$\text{Swpt}_R(t, \kappa) = A(t)(\kappa\Phi(-d_-) - r_S(t)\Phi(-d_+)), \tag{19.50}$$

with $d_{+/-}$ and $A(t)$ as in (19.48). As in the cap market, implied volatilities for swaptions with different expiries and different tenors are quoted in the market. It is customary to encode the relevant information in the format $xYyY$, which means the swaption expires in x years and the underlying swap has a lifetime of y years. A 2Y5Y payer swaption is thus a call option with 2 years' time to expiry, on the par rate of a 5 years' swap contract. One can thus build a grid with implied volatility information for different tenors and expiries, and extract a volatility surface. There is a typical example of implied at-the-money (ATM) swaption volatility of May 16, 2000 that has become somewhat standard; see for example Brigo and Mercurio (2007, p. 288) or Filipović (2009, p. 24). The data is reproduced in Table 19.1. The resulting implied volatility surface, generated by spline interpolation, is illustrated in Figure 19.1.

There is another surprising application of swaptions. They allow for synthetic replication of a callable bond. A callable bond is a coupon-bearing bond, which allows the

Table 19.1 Implied ATM swaption volatility in % of May 16, 2000

xY/yY	1Y	2Y	3Y	4Y	5Y	6Y	7Y	8Y	9Y	10Y
1Y	16.4	15.8	14.6	13.8	13.3	12.9	12.6	12.3	12.0	11.7
2Y	17.7	15.6	14.1	13.1	12.7	12.4	12.2	11.9	11.7	11.4
3Y	17.6	15.5	13.9	12.7	12.3	12.1	11.9	11.7	11.5	11.3
4Y	16.9	14.6	12.9	11.9	11.6	11.4	11.3	11.1	11.0	10.8
5Y	15.8	13.9	12.4	11.5	11.1	10.9	10.8	10.7	10.5	10.4
7Y	14.5	12.9	11.6	10.8	10.4	10.3	10.1	9.9	9.8	9.6
10Y	13.5	11.5	10.4	9.8	9.4	9.3	9.1	8.8	8.6	8.4

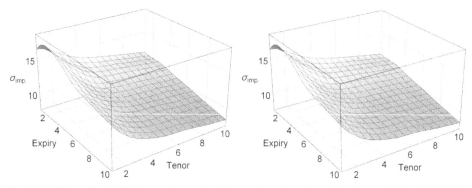

Fig. 19.1 **3D** Implied ATM swaption volatility surface based on the data of May 16, 2000

issuer to prematurely reimburse the principal and cease paying all further coupons. The way this works is best understood in an example.

Example 19.2

Suppose you have issued a coupon-bearing bond with 5 years' time to maturity and annual coupon payments at a rate of 6%. You want to reserve the right to reimburse the principal after 2 years to avoid further coupon payments, but you cannot change the original contract. How can the callable bond be replicated?

Solution

You can buy a 2Y3Y receiver swaption with the strike rate $\kappa = 6\%$. If you decide not to exercise, everything stays the same and you have not called the bond. If you exercise, the fixed leg cancels the coupon payments and you are stuck with the floating leg payments and the principal at the end of the contract. But notice that paying LIBOR on the principal due at the end of year 5 is effectively a floating rate note, and we know that this is equivalent to paying the principal at the end of year 2.

Quick calculation 19.9   Formulate the parity relation for a callable bond.

19.5   Eurodollar Futures

Eurodollar futures are standardized interest rate future contracts that are traded at the Chicago Mercantile Exchange (CME). Eurodollars are US dollar denominated deposits in institutions outside the United States. The CME interest rate future contracts are linked to the 3-months LIBOR. They are settled at a delivery price of

$$\hat{F}_T = 100 \cdot (1 - L(T, T + 1/4)), \tag{19.51}$$

Specific delivery dates are in March, June, September, and December. Define the 3-months LIBOR future $\hat{L}(t, T, T + 1/4)$ to be the rate induced by the quoted future price at time t,

$$\hat{F}_t = 100 \cdot (1 - \hat{L}(t, T, T + 1/4)). \tag{19.52}$$

Clearly, as t tends to T, the LIBOR future $\hat{L}(t, T, T + 1/4)$ approaches $\hat{L}(T, T, T + 1/4) = L(T, T + 1/4)$. What is a little bit confusing about Eurodollar futures is that the daily settlement is with respect to another price,

$$\tilde{F}_t = P \cdot \left(1 - \frac{1}{4}\hat{L}(t, T, T + 1/4)\right). \tag{19.53}$$

The principal is always $P = \$1$ million and thus, if there is a 1 bps (0.01%) increase in the LIBOR future, the CME contract buyer has to pay \$25 to the seller.

Quick calculation 19.10   Verify the last statement.

Because of the daily settlement, it is always costless to enter the future contract. We have seen before that the future price $\hat{F}_t$ is a Q-martingale. By the same arguments we used to show that the forward LIBOR $L(t, S, T)$ is a Q_T-martingale, we can prove that $\hat{L}(t, T, T + 1/4)$ is a Q-martingale. Since the factor 100 in (19.52) is constant and therefore a trivial martingale, we must have

$$-100 \cdot \hat{L}(t, T, T + 1/4) = -100 \cdot E^Q[\hat{L}(T, T, T + 1/4)|\mathcal{F}_t]. \tag{19.54}$$

Again, the factor -100 cancels out of the equation and leaves the desired result.

Quick calculation 19.11   Show that $\tilde{F}_t$ in (19.53) is also a Q-martingale.

19.6   Further Reading

A comprehensive introduction to the forward measure approach is provided in Cairns (2004, chap. 7). A nice collection of commonly used measures, including hybrid measures, is given in Andersen and Piterbarg (2010a, sect. 4.2). A detailed derivation of Black's formula, using the example of caplets, can be found in Brigo and Mercurio (2007, sect. 6.2). A very accessible introduction to plain vanilla interest rate derivatives is Joshi (2008, chap. 13). A vast collection of standard derivative instruments can be found in Andersen and Piterbarg (2010a, chap. 5). Eurodollar futures are discussed in Andersen and Piterbarg (2010a, sect. 5.4) and Filipović (2009, sect. 8.2). A background in trading and pricing forwards and futures is provided in Jarrow (2002, chap. 12) and Vellekoop (2010).

19.7   Problems

19.1 Suppose you have an expectation with respect to the T-forward measure, based on the information available at time $t < T$. You want to reexpress this expectation with respect to the S-forward measure for $S > T$,

$$V_t = P(t, T)E^{Q_T}[V_T|\mathcal{F}_t] = P(t, T)E^{Q_S}\left[V_T\frac{dQ_T}{dQ_S}\middle|\mathcal{F}_t\right].$$

Derive the *Radon–Nikodym*-derivative $\frac{dQ_T}{dQ_S}\big|_{\mathcal{F}_t}$ and write the solution for V_t.

19.2 Use an arbitrage argument, analogous to the one in Table 11.1 on page 212, to prove that in a stochastic interest rate world, the strike price of a forward contract $F_t(K, T)$ that can be entered costlessly at time $t = 0$ has to be

$$K = \frac{V_0}{P(0, T)},$$

which is the forward price of a non-dividend paying underlying V at $t = 0$.

19.3 Let today be time t. Suppose you want to price a plain vanilla option with expiry date T on a discount bond, maturing at S, within the *Black*-76-model, with $t < T < S$. Assume the bond volatility is given by

$$\sigma_P(t) = \sigma \sqrt{1 - e^{-(T-t)}}.$$

Compute the quantity $d_{+/-}$, required in Black's formula.

19.4 Use the definition of the forward LIBOR, (19.31) on page 447, to show that the present value of the floating leg of a plain vanilla interest rate swap is indeed

$$\text{Floating leg} = \Delta t \sum_{n=1}^{N} P(t, T_n)L(t, T_{n-1}, T_n).$$

19.5 Prove that the forward swap rate

$$r_S(t) = \frac{P(t, T_0) - P(t, T_N)}{\Delta t \sum_{n=1}^{N} P(t, T_n)}$$

can be understood as a weighted average of all forward LIBORs within the tenor of the swap.

Until now, we have traveled the paved road of standard instruments and derivatives that are very liquidly traded. In fact, we have been rewarded for this in terms of straightforward standard pricing formulas, with all necessary ingredients provided by the market. Leaving this road, we immediately find ourselves in a jungle of term structure models with very different advantages and shortcomings. What they all have in common is that none of them is universally optimal.

20.1 A Term Structure Toy Model

By now it should be very clear that the discount bond is a central element in pricing all sorts of claims. We have seen two different representations of its price,

$$P(t, T) = e^{-\int_t^T f(t,s)ds} = E^Q\left[e^{-\int_t^T r(s)ds}\Big|\mathcal{F}_t\right]. \tag{20.1}$$

In the preceding chapters, we mostly relied on the forward rate representation, and cleverly manipulated probability measures. But there are a few unanswered questions in this framework. For example, we are still not in a position to price a simple option on a coupon-bearing bond. We will temporarily leave this road and turn to the second equality in (20.1). To be a little more precise, we will specify particular dynamics for the short rate $r(t)$, in order to compute prices by evaluating the Q-expectation. Eventually, both frameworks will be reconciled in the seminal approach of Heath et al. (1992).

Term structure models come in many flavors with respect to the number of factors, their distributional properties, time-homogeneity of their parameters, and so forth. We will start with the simplest possible specification, which is merely a toy model. But we can learn a lot about the general setup by studying this simplified version. Suppose the stochastic interest rate process under the pricing measure Q is given by

$$dr(t) = \sigma_r dW(t). \tag{20.2}$$

We have now stated the time dependence in the *Wiener*-increment explicitly as a function argument to keep the notation consistent. At any later time $s > t$, the interest rate has changed and is given by

$$r(s) = r(t) + \sigma_r \int_t^s dW(u). \tag{20.3}$$

We can already identify this short rate model as *Gaussian*, because the *Itô*-integral is a normally distributed random variable. It is easy to verify that $E^Q[r(s)|\mathcal{F}_t] = r(t)$, and

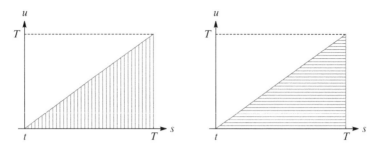

Fig. 20.1 Integration of a triangle – Order of integration switched between left and right figure

$\text{Var}[r(s)|\mathcal{F}_t] = \sigma_r^2(s - t)$. We can also determine the first shortcoming, common to all *Gaussian* models, namely that there is a nonzero probability for the interest rate to become negative. But let's ignore this problem for the moment. The quantity really needed, according to the right hand side of (20.1), is

$$- \int_t^T r(s)ds = -r(t) \int_t^T ds - \sigma_r \int_t^T \int_t^s dW(u)ds. \tag{20.4}$$

Even though the inner integral in the last term is stochastic, we are allowed to switch the order of integration due to a generalized version of Fubini's theorem that can be found in Filipović (2009, sect. 6.5). But something happens to the bounds of integration. Let's forget stochastic integration for a moment. Suppose you want to integrate over the area of the lower triangle inside a square with edge length $T - t$. If the inner integral is with respect to the vertical direction, as indicated in Figure 20.1 left, then the lower bound is t and the upper bound has to be variable. If we change the order of integration, the inner integral is with respect to the horizontal direction, as indicated in Figure 20.1 right. But now the upper bound has to be fixed at T and the lower bound has to vary. We can thus conclude that

$$\int_t^T \int_t^s du\,ds = \int_t^T \int_u^T ds\,du \tag{20.5}$$

holds. Even though the double integral in (20.4) does not represent a triangle in the usual sense, changing the bounds of integration works exactly the same, and we obtain

$$\int_t^T \int_t^s dW(u)ds = \int_t^T \int_u^T ds\,dW(u) = \int_t^T (T - u)dW(u). \tag{20.6}$$

A little algebra and cleaning up the notation shows that (20.4) now becomes

$$- \int_t^T r(s)ds = -r(t)(T - t) - \sigma_r \int_t^T (T - s)dW(s). \tag{20.7}$$

We can now see that the expression on the right hand side of (20.7) is a *Gaussian* random variable, with expectation

$$E^Q \left[- \int_t^T r(s)ds \,\middle|\, \mathcal{F}_t \right] = -r(t)(T - t), \tag{20.8}$$

and variance

$$\text{Var}\left[-\int_t^T r(s)ds\Big|\mathcal{F}_t\right]=\sigma_r^2\int_t^T (T-s)^2 ds=\frac{1}{3}\sigma_r^2(T-t)^3. \tag{20.9}$$

Recalling the expectation value of a log-normal distributed random variable, one obtains the explicit price for the discount bond

$$P(t,T)=E^Q\left[e^{-\int_t^T r(s)ds}\Big|\mathcal{F}_t\right]=e^{-r(t)(T-t)+\frac{1}{6}\sigma_r^2(T-t)^3}. \tag{20.10}$$

Applying Itô's lemma to (20.10), we can derive the dynamics of the discount bond price. One obtains

$$dP=\left(\frac{\partial P}{\partial t}+\frac{1}{2}\frac{\partial^2 P}{\partial r^2}\sigma_r^2\right)dt+\frac{\partial P}{\partial r}\sigma_r dW$$
$$=rPdt-\sigma_r(T-t)PdW. \tag{20.11}$$

Quick calculation 20.1 Verify the second equality.

There is much internal consistency demonstrated by this result. First of all, we are in the risk-neutral probability measure Q and therefore, every security should have the drift rate $r(t)$. Of course, because our interest rate model is *Gauss*ian, the bond price dynamics have to be log-normal, and everything works out in terms of a geometric *Brown*ian motion. But nevertheless, it is very reassuring that the drift comes out correctly. We can further deduce from (20.11) that the bond volatility is

$$\sigma_P(t)=-\sigma_r(T-t). \tag{20.12}$$

The minus sign has no particular meaning here, because the distribution of the *Wiener*-increment $dW(t)$ is symmetric. But more importantly, the pull to par requirement is satisfied. As $t\to T$, the bond volatility tends to zero.

So far nearly everything looks fine with our toy model, so where is the problem? Let's remember the definition of the yield to maturity

$$y(t,T)=-\frac{\log P(t,T)}{T-t}. \tag{20.13}$$

Using (20.10), the yield to maturity in this particular model is given by

$$y(t,T)=r(t)-\frac{1}{6}\sigma_r^2(T-t)^2. \tag{20.14}$$

Obviously, the mapping $T\mapsto y(t,T)$ is downward sloping with $\lim_{T\to\infty} y(t,T)=-\infty$. This is really bad news, because such a yield curve is definitely not observed in the market. We can furthermore extract the forward curve by

$$f(t,T)=-\frac{\partial}{\partial T}\log P(t,T)=r(t)-\frac{1}{2}\sigma_r^2(T-t)^2. \tag{20.15}$$

Quick calculation 20.2 Confirm this result by using $f(t,T)=y(t,T)+\frac{\partial y}{\partial T}(T-t)$.

The forward curve is also downward sloping, but more importantly, changes in $r(t)$ can only cause parallel shifts of the forward curve, but no structural changes like bending or twisting. This is the result of a shortcoming, common to all one-factor models, not particularly *Gauss*ian ones. In a one-factor short rate model, the movements of all points on the yield and forward curve are perfectly correlated. That matter is not open for debate, but the situation can be improved otherwise, by making the initial yield curve an input to the model. This is the idea of yield curve fitting due to Ho and Lee (1986).

20.2   Yield Curve Fitting

Imagine now that today is time $t = 0$, and you know the yield curve $y(0, T)$ in terms of an explicit, sufficiently smooth function of T. You want a model for the short rate that is able to reproduce all bond prices $P(0, T)$ you observe today, for every single T. Ho and Lee (1986) discovered that this goal can be achieved by simply injecting an auxiliary deterministic function $a(t)$ into the solution (20.3),

$$r(t) = r(0) + a(t) + \sigma_r \int_0^t dW(s), \tag{20.16}$$

with $a(0) = 0$. It is easy to see that this solution corresponds to the dynamic equation

$$dr(t) = \theta(t)dt + \sigma_r dW(t), \tag{20.17}$$

where $\theta(t) = \frac{da(t)}{dt}$ has to hold. But how should this auxiliary function $a(t)$ be chosen to generate the desired result? Let's make an educated guess,

$$a(t) = f(0, t) - r(0) + \frac{1}{2}\sigma_r^2 t^2. \tag{20.18}$$

Because the yield curve $y(0, T)$ is known and sufficiently smooth, so is the forward curve $f(0, T)$. But how does this definition of $a(t)$ help? From our discussion in the last section, we can conclude that

$$E^Q\left[e^{-\int_0^T r(t)dt}\Big|\mathcal{F}_0\right] = e^{-r(0)T + \frac{1}{6}\sigma_r^2 T^3} e^{-\int_0^T a(t)dt}. \tag{20.19}$$

Using (20.18) and $f(0, t) = -\frac{\partial}{\partial t}\log P(0, t)$, the integral in the last exponential becomes

$$-\int_0^T a(t)dt = \log P(0, T) + r(0)T - \frac{1}{6}\sigma_r^2 T^3. \tag{20.20}$$

Plugging this solution into (20.19), we indeed obtain

$$E^Q\left[e^{-\int_0^T r(t)dt}\Big|\mathcal{F}_0\right] = P(0, T). \tag{20.21}$$

That is, we managed to reconstruct the discount bond prices, observed today at $t = 0$. Furthermore, we can now deduce what the drift $\theta(t)$ in (20.17) has to be. Altogether we obtain

$$dr(t) = \left(\frac{\partial f(0, t)}{\partial t} + \sigma_r^2 t\right) dt + \sigma_r dW(t). \tag{20.22}$$

Reproducing the initial discount bond curve is unfortunately only the easy part. If we want to derive analytic expressions for bond options, we also have to derive the model induced price for a discount bond in the future, say $P(t, T)$ for $t > 0$. Let's again try an educated guess and show afterwards why it is correct. The price for the discount bond $P(t, T)$, induced by the model (20.22), is

$$P(t, T) = \frac{P(0, T)}{P(0, t)} e^{-\frac{1}{2}\sigma_r^2 t(T-t)^2} e^{-x(t)(T-t)}, \tag{20.23}$$

with $x(t)$ defined by

$$x(t) = r(t) - f(0, t) = \frac{1}{2}\sigma_r^2 t^2 + \sigma_r W(t). \tag{20.24}$$

The second equality results from plugging (20.18) into (20.16). Let's see, if we can prove (20.23). By definition we have

$$P(t, T) = E^Q\left[e^{-\int_t^T r(s)ds}\bigg|\mathcal{F}_t\right] = e^{-\int_t^T f(0,s)ds} E^Q\left[e^{-\int_t^T x(s)ds}\bigg|\mathcal{F}_t\right]. \tag{20.25}$$

The integral over the forward rate accounts for the factor $\frac{P(0,T)}{P(0,t)}$, so we only have to compute the conditional expectation involving $x(s)$. So let's first compute the integral

$$
\begin{aligned}
-\int_t^T x(s)ds &= -\frac{1}{2}\sigma_r^2 \int_t^T s^2 ds - \sigma_r \int_t^T \int_0^s dW(u)ds \\
&= -\frac{1}{6}\sigma_r^2(T^3 - t^3) - \sigma_r \int_t^T \int_0^t dW(u)ds - \sigma_r \int_t^T \int_t^s dW(u)ds \quad (20.26) \\
&= -\frac{1}{6}\sigma_r^2(T^3 - t^3) - \sigma_r W(t)(T - t) - \sigma_r \int_t^T (T - s)dW(s),
\end{aligned}
$$

where we again used Fubini's theorem to change the order of integration in the last line. From this calculation, it is clear that the integral is a *Gaussian* random variable. The expectation in (20.25) is therefore with respect to a log-normal random variable and one obtains

$$
\begin{aligned}
E^Q\left[e^{-\int_t^T x(s)ds}\bigg|\mathcal{F}_t\right] &= \exp\left(-\frac{1}{6}\sigma_r^2(T^3 - t^3) - \sigma_r W(t)(T - t) + \frac{1}{6}\sigma_r^2(T - t)^3\right) \\
&= \exp\left(-\frac{1}{2}\sigma_r^2(T^2 t - Tt^2) + \frac{1}{2}\sigma_r^2 t^2(T - t) - x(t)(T - t)\right) \\
&= \exp\left(-\frac{1}{2}\sigma_r^2 t(T^2 - 2Tt + t^2) - x(t)(T - t)\right) \\
&= \exp\left(-\frac{1}{2}\sigma_r^2 t(T - t)^2 - x(t)(T - t)\right),
\end{aligned}
\tag{20.27}
$$

which proves (20.23). The upshot of all these computations is that $x(t)$ is a normally distributed random variable and thus, we can derive *Black–Scholes*-like formulas to price European options on bonds, based on the short rate model (20.22). We will not push the analysis further at this point, because the shortcomings of the model still remain. In particular, we cannot hope to compute realistic option prices from it, regardless of whether we are able to derive analytic valuation formulas or not. Instead, let's move on to a more promising class of models.

20.3   Mean Reversion and the *Vasicek*-Model

What is observed in the market is that, unlike security prices, which seem to evolve geometrically, interest rates stay in a more or less fixed band. Furthermore, it looks as if they were pulled back to an equilibrium value. Of course this effect is not that clear from the charts, because there is a significant amount of random noise involved. Vasicek (1977) therefore used a mean reverting drift specification, first proposed by Uhlenbeck and Ornstein (1930), commonly known as the *Ornstein–Uhlenbeck*-process

$$dr(t) = \kappa(\theta - r(t))dt + \sigma_r dW(t). \tag{20.28}$$

There are two new elements involved in (20.28), the mean reversion level θ, and the mean reversion speed κ. We have already seen those elements in the stochastic volatility equation of the *Heston*-model (16.51) on page 365. The mean reversion level θ is the long-term rate to which $r(t)$ is pulled. The mean reversion speed κ governs the strength of this pull. For $\kappa = 0$ we are back in our toy model (20.2). So let's solve the *Ornstein–Uhlenbeck*-equation to determine the properties of the *Vasicek*-model. For $s > t$, consider the function $y(s) = e^{\kappa s} r(s)$, and apply Itô's lemma,

$$dy(s) = e^{\kappa s} \kappa \theta ds + e^{\kappa s} \sigma_r dW(s). \tag{20.29}$$

Quick calculation 20.3   Confirm this result.

This equation is easily integrated and one obtains

$$y(s) = y(t) + \kappa\theta \int_t^s e^{\kappa u} du + \sigma_r \int_t^s e^{\kappa u} dW(u). \tag{20.30}$$

Dividing both sides by $e^{\kappa s}$ and using a little bit of straightforward algebra yields

$$r(s) = \theta + (r(t) - \theta)e^{-\kappa(s-t)} + \sigma_r \int_t^s e^{-\kappa(s-u)} dW(u). \tag{20.31}$$

This is again clearly a *Gaussian* random variable, with $E^Q[r(s)|\mathcal{F}_t] = \theta + (r(t) - \theta)e^{-\kappa(s-t)}$, and conditional variance

$$\text{Var}[r(s)|\mathcal{F}_t] = \frac{\sigma_r^2}{2\kappa}(1 - e^{-2\kappa(s-t)}). \tag{20.32}$$

Quick calculation 20.4 Use *Itô*-isometry to compute $\text{Var}[r(s)|\mathcal{F}_t]$.

The *Vasicek*-model is also a *Gaussian* short rate model, but its long-term characteristics are very different from those of our toy model. In particular, we have

$$\lim_{s\to\infty} E^Q[r(s)] = \theta \quad \text{and} \quad \lim_{s\to\infty} \text{Var}[r(s)] = \frac{\sigma_r^2}{2\kappa}. \tag{20.33}$$

Most importantly, the variance tends to a finite constant in the long run. There is still a nonzero probability for the short rate to become negative, but it is usually small. In the long-term equilibrium this probability is

$$P(r(\infty) \leq 0) = 1 - \Phi\left(\frac{\sqrt{2\kappa}\theta}{\sigma_r}\right), \tag{20.34}$$

where $\Phi(x)$ is again the cumulative distribution function of a standard normally distributed random variable X.

Quick calculation 20.5 Prove equation (20.34).

In order to compute bond prices, we follow the same pattern as conducted in case of our toy example. In particular, we have

$$-\int_t^T r(s)ds = -\theta\int_t^T ds - (r(t) - \theta)\int_t^T e^{-\kappa(s-t)}ds - \sigma_r\int_t^T\int_t^s e^{-\kappa(s-u)}dW(u)ds$$
$$= -\theta(T - t) - (r(t) - \theta)\frac{1 - e^{-\kappa(T-t)}}{\kappa} + \frac{\sigma_r}{\kappa}\int_t^T(e^{-\kappa(T-s)} - 1)dW(s), \tag{20.35}$$

where we have switched the order of integration in the last integral. The left hand side of (20.35) is again a *Gaussian* random variable with conditional expectation value given by the first two terms on the right hand side. The variance is obtained with the help of *Itô*-isometry,

$$\text{Var}\left[-\int_t^T r(s)ds\bigg|\mathcal{F}_t\right] = \frac{\sigma_r^2}{\kappa^2}\int_t^T(e^{-\kappa(T-s)} - 1)^2 ds$$
$$= \frac{\sigma_r^2}{\kappa^2}\cdot\frac{-e^{-2\kappa(T-t)} + 4e^{-\kappa(T-t)} + 2\kappa(T - t) - 3}{2\kappa}. \tag{20.36}$$

As before, the discount bond price is the risk-neutral conditional expectation with respect to a log-normal random variable, and one obtains

$$
E^Q\left[e^{-\int_t^T r(s)ds}\Big|\mathcal{F}_t\right] = \exp\Bigg(-\theta(T-t) - (r(t)-\theta)\frac{1-e^{-\kappa(T-t)}}{\kappa}
$$

$$
+\frac{\sigma_r^2}{\kappa^2}\cdot\frac{-e^{-2\kappa(T-t)}+4e^{-\kappa(T-t)}+2\kappa(T-t)-3}{4\kappa}\Bigg). \tag{20.37}
$$

That is a very messy equation, so let's see if we can clean it up a little. Let's define the auxiliary functions

$$
A(t,T) = \left(\theta - \frac{\sigma_r^2}{2\kappa^2}\right)((T-t) - B(t,T)) + \frac{\sigma_r^2}{4\kappa}B(t,T)^2 \tag{20.38}
$$

$$
B(t,T) = \frac{1-e^{-\kappa(T-t)}}{\kappa}. \tag{20.39}
$$

With these functions, the discount bond price can be expressed very neatly as

$$
P(t,T) = e^{-A(t,T)-B(t,T)r(t)}. \tag{20.40}
$$

Quick calculation 20.6 Check that $A(T,T) = B(T,T) = 0$ holds.

That should ring an enormous bell. The *Vasicek*-model belongs to an affine term structure model class. We will learn more about this class later. It contains a number of term structure models, but not all of them. For the moment, let's continue with our analysis. The yield curve has the form

$$
y(t,T) = -\frac{\log P(t,T)}{T-t} = \frac{A(t,T) + B(t,T)r(t)}{T-t}. \tag{20.41}
$$

It is not difficult to see from (20.38) and (20.39) that in the limit $T \to \infty$, the yield to maturity tends to

$$
\lim_{T\to\infty} y(t,T) = \theta - \frac{\sigma_r^2}{2\kappa^2}. \tag{20.42}
$$

This is progress, because now the long-term yield tends to a fixed quantity, as observed in the market. Furthermore, some tedious but not difficult algebra shows that the yield curve can have three different shapes:

1. Increasing for $r(t) \le \theta - \dfrac{3\sigma_r^2}{4\kappa^2}$,

2. humped for $\theta - \dfrac{3\sigma_r^2}{4\kappa^2} < r(t) \le \theta$,   (20.43)

3. decreasing for $r(t) > \theta$.

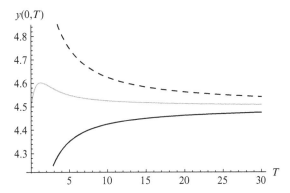

Fig. 20.2 Possible yield curve shapes in the *Vasicek*-model – Increasing (black), humped (gray), and decreasing (dashed)

Figure 20.2 illustrates the three possible shapes of the yield curve $y(0, T)$ in the *Vasicek*-model. You might already suspect that even though we made considerable progress, the *Vasicek*-model is still not capable of reproducing all yield curve shapes observed in the market. This assessment is correct, but we can use the same trick as in our toy model to improve the situation. Namely, we can introduce an auxiliary function $a(t)$ into the solution (20.31), and derive the required form of this function to match all observed discount bond prices. The result is the so-called *Hull–White*-extended *Vasicek*-model, and we will look into it shortly. In the meantime, let's concern ourselves with bond option pricing in the *Vasicek*-model.

20.4   Bond Option Pricing and the *Jamshidian*-Decomposition

Suppose today is time t, and we want to price a European plain vanilla option with expiry T on a discount bond with maturity S, for $t < T < S$. Even though it might not seem so, this is a very trivial exercise. From our T-forward measure trick, we computed the price of a call option with strike price K in Example 19.1 on page 446. Our result was

$$C_t(K, T) = P(t, S)\Phi(d_+) - P(t, T)K\Phi(d_-). \tag{20.44}$$

It is easy to see that from the same chain of arguments, the put price is

$$P_t(K, T) = P(t, T)K\Phi(-d_-) - P(t, S)\Phi(-d_+). \tag{20.45}$$

What we do not know is what the coefficients $d_{+/-}$ are in the *Vasicek*-model. More precisely, we do not know the volatility that goes into them. To figure that out, we can either undergo some very demanding computations (see for example Cairns, 2004, appendix B.1), or we can take a clever shortcut. We know that the squared volatility we are looking for is the variance of the logarithmic S-bond price at time T, conditional on the knowledge of $r(t)$. Because of the affine structure of the bond price (20.40), we obtain

$$\text{Var}[\log P(T, S)|\mathcal{F}_t] = B(T, S)^2 \cdot \frac{\sigma_r^2}{2\kappa}(1 - e^{-2\kappa(T-t)}).\tag{20.46}$$

The second factor on the right hand side is simply the conditional variance of $r(T)$ as in (20.32) on page 461.

Quick calculation 20.7 Verify the last equation.

We can thus immediately write the desired coefficients,

$$d_{+/-} = \frac{\log\left(\frac{P(t,S)}{P(t,T)K}\right) \pm \frac{1}{2}\sigma_V^2}{\sigma_V} \quad \text{with} \quad \sigma_V = \sigma_r \frac{1 - e^{-\kappa(S-T)}}{\kappa}\sqrt{\frac{1 - e^{-2\kappa(T-t)}}{2\kappa}}.\tag{20.47}$$

Let's now turn to a problem we were not able to address so far: The pricing of on option on a coupon-bearing bond.

To get an idea why it is so difficult to price a coupon bond option, let's assume that the bond pays coupons at a rate c on a unit principal, and that it has a swap-like tenor structure $T_0, \ldots, T_N$, with the first coupon payment at T_1. Then the payoff of a plain vanilla European call option, expiring at T_0, is

$$C_{T_0}(K, T_0) = \left(c\sum_{n=1}^{N} P(T_0, T_n) + P(T_0, T_N) - K\right)^+.\tag{20.48}$$

We cannot pull the individual discount bonds out of the payoff function, and thus we are in a similar situation as before, when we were trying to price a swaption. But this time, inventing a new probability measure does not do the trick. An ingenious solution to this problem was suggested by Jamshidian (1989), and is now known as the *Jamshidian*-decomposition. To make the important point clear, we have to modify our notation temporarily. The discount bond prices in (20.48) depend on the short rate $r(T_0) = r_0$. So let's indicate this dependence by writing $P(T_0, T_n, r_0)$ for $n = 1, \ldots, N$. Since the discount bond price is a strictly monotonic decreasing function of r_0, we can find a unique r^*, which solves the problem

$$c\sum_{n=1}^{N} P(T_0, T_n, r^*) + P(T_0, T_N, r^*) = K.\tag{20.49}$$

Of course this very special r^* has to be found by numerical root search. But that is a small price, because the problem is well posed and there is only one independent variable. The problem is indeed completely analogous to determining the yield to maturity of a coupon-bearing bond. Now define a sequence of synthetic strike prices

$$K_n = P(T_0, T_n, r^*),\tag{20.50}$$

such that due to (20.49)

$$c \sum_{n=1}^{N} K_n + K_N = K \tag{20.51}$$

holds. With these synthetic strikes, we can reexpress the payoff function (20.48) as

$$C_{T_0}(K, T_0) = \left(c \sum_{n=1}^{N} (P(T_0, T_n, r_0) - K_n) + (P(T_0, T_N, r_0) - K_N) \right)^+ . \tag{20.52}$$

The heart of this payoff function is a sequence of differences of the form $P(T_0, T_n, r_0) - P(T_0, T_n, r^*)$. Because of the monotonicity of the discount bond prices with respect to the short rate, all of these terms are either positive, if $r^* > r_0$, or they are all smaller than or equal to zero, for $r^* \leq r_0$. In consequence the maximum bracket becomes distributive and we can write

$$C_{T_0}(K, T_0) = c \sum_{n=1}^{N} (P(T_0, T_n) - K_n)^+ + (P(T_0, T_N) - K_N)^+ . \tag{20.53}$$

But this is merely the payoff of a portfolio of discount bond options, and we already know how to price them analytically. Of course the same trick works for put options, in fact the synthetic strike prices K_n are identical. Furthermore, the *Jamshidian*-decomposition is not limited to the *Vasicek*-model, it works for every one-factor term structure model. We finally state the general pricing formula for time $t < T_0$ for European plain vanilla bond options

$$V_t^B(K, T_0) = c \sum_{n=1}^{N} V_t^P(K_n, T_0) + V_t^P(K_N, T_0), \tag{20.54}$$

with the superscripts B and P referring to the ordinary and discount bond, respectively. The synthetic strikes K_n are precisely as in (20.50) for $n = 1, \ldots, N$.

Quick calculation 20.8 Which modifications have to be made, if the principal is not normalized?

20.5   Affine Term Structure Models

There have been many one-factor short rate models suggested over time; a small collection is reproduced in Table 20.1. Not all of them possess an affine term structure (ATS). Such a structure has the great advantage that discount bond prices can be computed

466   The Fixed-Income World

Table 20.1 Popular one-factor short rate models

Model	Dynamics	Dist.[a]	ATS
Ho and Lee (1986)	$dr_t = \theta(t)dt + \sigma dW_t$	N	Yes
Vasicek (1977)	$dr_t = \kappa(\theta - r_t)dt + \sigma dW_t$	N	Yes
Hull and White (1990)	$dr_t = \kappa(\theta(t) - r_t)dt + \sigma dW_t$	N	Yes
Cox et al. (CIR, 1985)	$dr_t = \kappa(\theta - r_t)dt + \sigma\sqrt{r_t}dW_t$	$\mathrm{NC}\chi^2$	Yes
Dothan (1978)	$dr_t = \theta r_t dt + \sigma r_t dW_t$	LN	No
Black et al. (BDT, 1990)	$d\log r_t = (\theta(t) + \frac{\sigma'(t)}{\sigma(t)}\log r_t)dt + \sigma(t)dW_t$	LN	No
Black and Karasinski (1991)	$d\log r_t = \kappa(t)(\theta(t) - \log r_t)dt + \sigma(t)dW_t$	LN	No

[a] The distribution of r_t is either normal (N), log-normal (LN), or non-central chi-squared ($\mathrm{NC}\chi^2$).

as soon as the functions $A(t, T)$ and $B(t, T)$ are known. What are the requirements for a short rate model to belong to the affine class? The answer is provided by the following theorem:

Theorem 20.1 (Affine term structure) *Suppose the short rate dynamics are governed by a general model of the form*

$$dr = \theta(r, t)dt + \sigma(r, t)dW.$$

This model has affine term structure, if and only if the squared diffusion and drift functions are of the form

$$\sigma(r, t)^2 = a(t) + \alpha(t)r \quad and \quad \theta(r, t) = b(t) + \beta(t)r,$$

for some smooth functions $a(t)$, $b(t)$, $\alpha(t)$, $\beta(t)$, and $A(t, T)$ and $B(t, T)$ satisfy the differential equation system

$$\frac{\partial}{\partial t}A(t, T) = \frac{1}{2}a(t)B(t, T)^2 - b(t)B(t, T),$$

$$\frac{\partial}{\partial t}B(t, T) = \frac{1}{2}\alpha(t)B(t, T)^2 - \beta(t)B(t, T) - 1,$$

for all $t < T$, with $A(T, T) = B(T, T) = 0$.

A proof of this theorem can be found in Filipović (2009, p. 84). Let's see, if we can figure out what the functions $A(t, T)$ and $B(t, T)$ are in the *Ho–Lee*-model (20.17) on page 458. We have obviously

$$a(t) = \sigma_r^2 \quad and \quad b(t) = \theta(t), \tag{20.55}$$

and the remaining functions $\alpha(t) = \beta(t) = 0$. That reduces the second differential equation to $\frac{\partial}{\partial t} B(t, T) = -1$, with the obvious solution

$$B(t, T) = T - t. \tag{20.56}$$

Quick calculation 20.9 Use $B(T, T) = 0$ to confirm this result.

Solving the first differential equation is a pure integration exercise. We have

$$A(t, T) = -\int_t^T dA(s, T) = -\frac{1}{2}\sigma_r^2 \int_t^T (T - s)^2 ds + \int_t^T \theta(s)(T - s)ds. \tag{20.57}$$

For a known yield curve $y(0, T)$, we know from (20.22) that

$$\theta(t) = \frac{\partial f(0, t)}{\partial t} + \sigma_r^2 t \tag{20.58}$$

holds. That makes (20.57)

$$A(t, T) = \frac{1}{2}\sigma_r^2 \left(2 \int_t^T s(T - s)ds - \int_t^T (T - s)^2 ds \right) + \int_t^T \frac{\partial f(0, s)}{\partial s}(T - s)ds$$

$$= \frac{1}{2}\sigma_r^2 t(T - t)^2 + \int_t^T \frac{\partial f(0, s)}{\partial s}(T - s)ds. \tag{20.59}$$

The easiest way to verify the second equality is to reverse engineer the integration procedure

$$t(T - t)^2 = -\left[s(T - s)^2 \right]_t^T = -\int_t^T \left(\frac{d}{ds} s(T - s)^2 \right) ds. \tag{20.60}$$

Computing the derivative in the integral exactly reproduces the bracket in (20.59). Let's now turn to the integral involving the derivative of the forward rate. This one can be computed using integration by parts,

$$\int_t^T \frac{\partial f(0, s)}{\partial s}(T - s)ds = f(0, s)(T - s)\Big|_t^T + \int_t^T f(0, s)ds$$

$$= -f(0, t)(T - t) + \int_t^T f(0, s)ds. \tag{20.61}$$

Summarizing our results, we have

$$A(t, T) = \frac{1}{2}\sigma_r^2 t(T - t)^2 - f(0, t)(T - t) + \int_t^T f(0, s)ds. \tag{20.62}$$

We can now express the discount bond price $P(t, T)$, calibrated to the yield curve $y(0, T)$ as

$$P(t, T) = e^{-A(t,T)-B(t,T)r(t)} = \frac{P(0, T)}{P(0, t)} e^{-\frac{1}{2}\sigma_r^2 t(T-t)^2} e^{-x(t)(T-t)}, \tag{20.63}$$

where we have again used the definition $x(t) = r(t) - f(0, t)$. But this is exactly Equation (20.23), we derived earlier. So obviously, our computations were correct; we only used the much more elegant ATS-framework.

Let's review two more standard one-factor short rate models, the *Hull–White*-extended *Vasicek*-model (Hull and White, 1990), and the *Cox–Ingersoll–Ross*-model (CIR, Cox et al., 1985). The first one is simply a yield curve fitted version of the original *Vasicek*-model,

$$dr(t) = \kappa(\theta(t) - r(t))dt + \sigma_r dW(t). \tag{20.64}$$

The *Hull–White*-version is still a *Gauss*ian short rate model and interest rates therefore can become negative. But it can now be calibrated to the initial yield curve $y(0, T)$. The required function has the form

$$\theta(t) = f(0, t) + \frac{1}{\kappa}\frac{\partial f(0, t)}{\partial t} + \frac{\sigma_r^2}{2\kappa^2}(1 - e^{-2\kappa t}). \tag{20.65}$$

The ATS-functions can be computed in the usual way and one obtains

$$A(t, T) = \frac{\sigma_r^2}{2\kappa^2}(B(t, T) - (T - t)) + \frac{\sigma_r^2}{4\kappa}B(t, T)^2 + \kappa\int_t^T \theta(s)B(s, T)ds \tag{20.66}$$

$$B(t, T) = \frac{1 - e^{-\kappa(T-t)}}{\kappa}. \tag{20.67}$$

Solving the integral in (20.66) is not an easy task, but it can be done. In this case, one may reexpress the function $A(t, T)$ as

$$A(t, T) = \int_t^T f(0, s)ds - f(0, t)B(t, T) + \frac{\sigma_r^2}{4\kappa}B(t, T)^2(1 - e^{-2\kappa t}). \tag{20.68}$$

A proof for the most general form of the mean reverting *Gauss*ian model can be found in Andersen and Piterbarg (2010b, p. 416). Of course the integral over the forward rate reproduces the characteristic discount bond ratio, and one obtains

$$P(t, T) = \frac{P(0, T)}{P(0, t)}\exp\left(-\frac{\sigma_r^2}{4\kappa}\left(\frac{1 - e^{-\kappa(T-t)}}{\kappa}\right)^2(1 - e^{-2\kappa t}) - x(t)\frac{1 - e^{-\kappa(T-t)}}{\kappa}\right), \tag{20.69}$$

where we have again used our definition $x(t) = r(t) - f(0, t)$.

The *Cox–Ingersoll–Ross*- or CIR-model for short is also a mean reverting specification, that looks very similar to the *Vasicek*-model at first sight,

$$dr(t) = \kappa(\theta - r(t))dt + \sigma_r\sqrt{r(t)}dW(t). \tag{20.70}$$

But both processes are actually very different on the theoretical level already. The *Vasicek*-dynamics are clearly driven by a scaled *Brown*ian motion, whereas the CIR-dynamics are linked to the class of squared *Bessel*-processes. If the stability condition $2\kappa\theta \geq \sigma_r^2$ is satisfied, the short rate remains positive almost surely, and the CIR-process has a stationary gamma distribution, with probability density function

$$f(r) = \frac{\beta^\alpha}{\Gamma(\alpha)} r^{\alpha-1} e^{-\beta r}, \tag{20.71}$$

with

$$\alpha = \frac{2\kappa\theta}{\sigma_r^2} \quad \text{and} \quad \beta = \frac{2\kappa}{\sigma_r^2}. \tag{20.72}$$

Moreover, the distribution of $r(s)$, conditional on the information $\mathcal{F}_t$ for $s > t$, is non-central χ^2, as proved by Feller (1951). After spending so much time with *Gauss*ian processes, these properties may appear rather exotic. Nevertheless, the CIR-model is a member of the ATS-class, and its affine functions (see for example Filipović, 2009, p. 87) are

$$A(t, T) = -\frac{2\kappa\theta}{\sigma_r^2} \log\left(\frac{\gamma e^{\frac{\gamma+\kappa}{2}(T-t)}}{e^{\gamma(T-t)} - 1} B(t, T) \right) \tag{20.73}$$

$$B(t, T) = \frac{2(e^{\gamma(T-t)} - 1)}{(\gamma + \kappa)(e^{\gamma(T-t)} - 1) + 2\gamma}, \tag{20.74}$$

with $\gamma = \sqrt{\kappa^2 + 2\sigma_r^2}$. The CIR-model can also be calibrated to a particular yield curve as shown by Hull and White (1990).

Although those models are a great deal more realistic than our initial toy model, they are at best appropriate in some particular situations. There are still rather severe shortcomings. To calibrate the model for example to observed caplet prices, we would need a more elaborate term structure of volatility. Furthermore, the one-factor paradigm limits our ability to model structural changes in the yield curve. This is a very tough restriction when dealing with products whose payoff function depends on the shape of the yield curve. Those problems can be remedied by considering multi-factor models with the necessary degrees of freedom. Unfortunately those models are nowhere near as tractable as the one-factor models we analyzed so far. We will eventually deal with multi-factor specifications, but we will do it in a modern framework to be introduced next.

20.6 The *Heath–Jarrow–Morton*-Framework

In 1992, Heath et al. introduced a general framework for interest rate models that caused a paradigm shift, which by no means came without resistance. The idea of the *Heath–Jarrow–Morton*- or HJM-framework for short, is not to ask how the short end of the forward curve evolves with time, but instead to identify the dynamics governing the evolution of the entire forward curve itself. This was a very bold attempt and they succeeded. Let's first try to catch the idea behind the HJM-derivation by once again using our short rate toy model

$$dr(t) = \sigma_r dW(t). \tag{20.75}$$

We have already determined the forward curve in (20.15) on page 457 to have the form

$$f(t, T) = r(t) - \frac{1}{2}\sigma_r^2 (T - t)^2. \tag{20.76}$$

Now let's apply Itô's lemma to compute the dynamics of the forward curve. This is a trivial task in our toy model and we obtain

$$df(t, T) = \sigma_r^2 (T - t)dt + \sigma_r dW(t). \tag{20.77}$$

Recognize that (20.77) indeed describes the dynamics of a whole curve. If we simulate the appropriate *Wiener*-increments, time t would progress, but for every arbitrary t^*, we can draw a curve with respect to the variable T for $t^* \leq T < \infty$.

It is often awkward to work in terms of maturity dates T, instead of time to maturity $\tau = T - t$. Therefore, one can use a slightly different form, called the *Musiela*-parametrization

$$f_M(t, \tau) = f(t, t + \tau). \tag{20.78}$$

Inspecting (20.78) closely, reveals that the maturity date T is now expressed as a function of t, which means $T = t + \tau$. Applying Itô's lemma and using the chain rule, the dynamics of $f_M(t, \tau)$ becomes

$$\begin{aligned}
df_M(t, \tau) &= \frac{\partial f_M}{\partial f} df(t, T) + \frac{\partial f_M}{\partial \tau} \frac{\partial \tau}{\partial T} \frac{\partial T}{\partial t} dt \\
&= df(t, T) + \frac{\partial f}{\partial T} dt,
\end{aligned} \tag{20.79}$$

where we used that $\frac{\partial T}{\partial t} = 1$. That is, the dynamics of our toy forward curve (20.77) under the *Musiela*-parametrization becomes

$$df_M(t, \tau) = \sigma_r dW(t). \tag{20.80}$$

Quick calculation 20.10 Use (20.76) to verify this result.

This result may seem even more awkward, but it is perfectly alright. In particular it does not mean that the forward curve $f_M(t, \tau)$ is flat, it only says that the curve changes for every time to maturity by the same amount. This is the true meaning of a parallel curve shift. To make this point perfectly clear, substitute $T = t + \tau$ in (20.76). The result is

$$f_M(t, \tau) = r(t) - \frac{1}{2}\sigma_r^2 \tau^2. \tag{20.81}$$

This equation depends on t only through the short rate $r(t)$. Thus, an application of Itô's lemma yields the trivial result

$$df_M(t, \tau) = dr(t). \tag{20.82}$$

Let's now turn to the real thing, the derivation of the HJM-framework. Suppose the general risk-neutral dynamics of the discount bond is given by

$$dP(t, T) = r(t)P(t, T)dt + \sigma_P(t, T)P(t, T)dW(t), \tag{20.83}$$

with the consistency condition $\sigma_P(T, T) = 0$. The drift under the risk-neutral measure Q has to be $r(t)$ for all securities in the market. There are some other requirements regarding the integrability of $\sigma_P(t, T)$, we will not discuss at this point, even though they are by no means mere technicalities. In fact, the problems they cause under certain conditions eventually led to the development of market models, which we will encounter in the next chapter. For the moment, we just assume everything is smooth and well behaved. The forward rate is linked to the discount bond price by

$$f(t, T) = -\frac{\partial}{\partial T} \log P(t, T). \tag{20.84}$$

So let's again apply Itô's lemma to determine the dynamics of the forward rate

$$df(t, T) = -\frac{\partial}{\partial T}\left(r(t) - \frac{1}{2}\sigma_P(t, T)^2\right)dt - \frac{\partial}{\partial T}\sigma_P(t, T)dW(t). \tag{20.85}$$

From this result we can already conclude that the forward rate volatility has to be

$$\sigma_f(t, T) = -\frac{\partial}{\partial T}\sigma_P(t, T). \tag{20.86}$$

Let's now examine the bracket in (20.85) a little bit closer. The derivative of the short rate $r(t)$ with respect to T vanishes, because the short rate does not depend on the maturity of the discount bond. Using (20.86), we can rewrite the T-derivative of the second term as

$$\begin{aligned}
\frac{\partial}{\partial T}\frac{1}{2}\sigma_P(t, T)^2 &= \sigma_P(t, T)\frac{\partial}{\partial T}\sigma_P(t, T) \\
&= \left(\frac{\partial}{\partial T}\sigma_P(t, T)\right)\int_t^T \frac{\partial}{\partial s}\sigma_P(t, s)ds \\
&= \sigma_f(t, T)\int_t^T \sigma_f(t, s)ds.
\end{aligned} \tag{20.87}$$

In the second step, we have used that $\sigma_P(t, t) = 0$ holds. We can thus write the celebrated HJM-condition for the risk-neutral forward rate dynamics

$$df(t, T) = \sigma_f(t, T)\int_t^T \sigma_f(t, s)ds\,dt + \sigma_f(t, T)dW(t). \tag{20.88}$$

The truly amazing thing about this equation is that even though the HJM-framework contains a multiverse of possible forward rate models, the dynamics of each of them are entirely governed by the specified volatility.

We have implicitly assumed that $\sigma_P(t, T)$ and therefore $\sigma_f(t, T)$ is deterministic, even though this restriction is not necessary for the HJM-condition to hold. It is sufficient to require $\sigma_P(t, T)$ regular enough for $\frac{P(t,T)}{B(t)}$ to be a square-integrable martingale, where $B(t)$ is our usual bank account. However, deterministic volatility leads to the very tractable class of *Gauss*ian HJM-models. But even within this class, we have to discuss an important subtlety, the so-called *Markov*-property. A *Markov*-process is special in that it stores all past information in the present state of the process itself. To see what that means, we can for example take the conditional expectation value. If X_t is a *Markov*-process, then we must have

$$E[X_t|\mathcal{F}_s] = f(X_s), \tag{20.89}$$

for $t \geq s$ and a suitable function $f: \mathbb{R} \to \mathbb{R}$. Of course an analogous property holds for the entire conditional distribution, not only for the expectation value. But from the expectation we can deduce that a martingale is even more special than a *Markov*-process, in that it requires $f(x) = x$. We have used *Markov*-processes dozens of times, without even mentioning it. So why discuss them now? The *Itô*-process, which is the foundation of almost all dynamic processes we have discussed in this book, is a *Markov*-process. If we want to use specifications of this type any further, we have to understand under which conditions the HJM-framework breeds *Markov*ian models. To this end, let's investigate the short rate in the HJM-framework. Using $r(t) = f(t, t)$ and integrating (20.88) yields

$$r(t) = f(0, t) + \int_0^t \sigma_f(u, t) \int_u^t \sigma_f(u, s) ds du + \int_0^t \sigma_f(u, t) dW(u). \tag{20.90}$$

The delicate term in this equation is the last one on the right hand side. So let's give it a name to analyze it a little further,

$$X_t = \int_0^t \sigma_f(u, t) dW(u). \tag{20.91}$$

First of all, think of the volatility $\sigma_f(u, t)$ as a family of functions with independent variable u, and the particular member of the family indicated by t.

Quick calculation 20.11 Show that X_t is not a martingale.

If we compute the expectation of X_t, conditional on the information at time $s < t$, we obtain

$$E^Q[X_t|\mathcal{F}_s] = \int_0^s \sigma_f(u, t) dW(u) \neq f(X_s). \tag{20.92}$$

The volatility function in (20.92) is simply from the wrong family. The random variable X_s contains the volatility function $\sigma_f(u, s)$, which means the s-member of the family, not the t-member. This seems hopeless, but it is not. All that is necessary to manufacture *Markov*ian dynamics is a particular condition on the volatility function. If $\sigma_f(u, t)$ has the form

$$\sigma_f(u, t) = g(u)h(t), \tag{20.93}$$

then the resulting HJM-model generates a *Markov*ian short rate process. Let's see if we can prove this statement. With the condition (20.93), our process X_t becomes

$$X_t = h(t) \int_0^t g(u)dW(u). \tag{20.94}$$

So let's see if the *Markov*ian condition is now satisfied. Again computing the conditional expectation yields

$$E[X_t|\mathcal{F}_s] = h(t) \int_0^s g(u)dW(u) = \frac{h(t)}{h(s)} X_s. \tag{20.95}$$

That is, the right hand side of (20.95) is clearly a function of X_s and hence X_t is a *Markov*-process.

Quick calculation 20.12   Verify that $\sigma_f(t, T) = \sigma e^{-\kappa(T-t)}$ generates a *Markov*ian model.

Most of the commonly used short rate models have a HJM-representation, but not all of them. The way HJM-modeling works is a kind of reverse engineering principle. One fixes the forward volatility structure and then determines the properties of the resulting model. Let's demonstrate this principle within the simplest possible specification

$$\sigma_f(t, T) = \sigma. \tag{20.96}$$

Using (20.88), the forward rate dynamics are easily computed,

$$df(t, T) = \sigma^2(T - t)dt + \sigma dW(t). \tag{20.97}$$

Since (20.96) clearly induces a *Markov*ian structure, choose for example $g(t) = \sigma$ and $h(T) = 1$, we should be able to derive conventional short rate dynamics. Let's first integrate (20.97) to see what the forward rate eventually looks like

$$\begin{aligned} f(t, T) &= f(0, T) + \sigma^2 \int_0^t (T - s)ds + \sigma \int_0^t dW(s) \\ &= f(0, T) - \frac{1}{2}\sigma^2(T - t)^2 + \frac{1}{2}\sigma^2 T^2 + \sigma W(t). \end{aligned} \tag{20.98}$$

Recall that the short rate and the forward rate are related through $r(t) = f(t, t)$. Therefore, we must have

$$\begin{aligned} dr(t) &= df(t, T)\Big|_{T=t} + \frac{\partial f(t, T)}{\partial T}\Big|_{T=t} dt \\ &= \sigma dW(t) + \left(\frac{\partial f(0, t)}{\partial t} + \sigma^2 t\right) dt, \end{aligned} \tag{20.99}$$

which is exactly the *Ho–Lee*-specification. What we can learn from this maybe surprising result is that HJM-models are automatically calibrated to the initial yield curve. There is nothing we have to do to force the issue. By choosing the volatility specification

$$\sigma_f(t, T) = \sigma e^{-\kappa(T-t)}, \tag{20.100}$$

one obtains the *Hull–White*-extended *Vasicek*-model (for a general proof see Andersen and Piterbarg, 2010a, p. 188).

Staying within the class of *Gaus*sian HJM-models has another advantage. We know that the forward rate $f(t, T)$ is a Q_T-martingale, with $f(T, T) = r(T)$. On the other hand, we know that the future rate is a Q-martingale. Therefore, the connection between forward and future rates in the *Gaus*sian HJM-framework has to be

$$E^{Q_T}[r(T)|\mathcal{F}_t] = E^Q[r(T)|\mathcal{F}_t] - \int_t^T \sigma_f(u, T) \int_u^T \sigma_f(u, s)dsdu. \quad (20.101)$$

The last term on the right hand side is called the **convexity adjustment**. We can see from (20.101) that the future rate is always greater than the forward rate, which confirms the heuristic argument about daily settlement, we introduced earlier. Furthermore, we can now understand, why for deterministic term structure both rates coincide. This is simply because the volatility vanishes. And finally, it is now very clear that the convexity adjustment is model dependent. It changes with the volatility specification we use. If we take for example $\sigma_f(t, T) = \sigma$, then the convexity adjustment is

$$\text{Convexity adjustment} = \frac{1}{2}\sigma^2(T - t)^2. \quad (20.102)$$

Quick calculation 20.13 Verify this result.

Let's finally state the HJM-equation in terms of the time to maturity $\tau = T - t$, using the *Musiela*-parametrization. We already know that the dynamics of $f_M(t, \tau)$ has the form

$$df_M(t, \tau) = df(t, T) + \frac{\partial f}{\partial T}dt. \quad (20.103)$$

Using the chain rule on the partial derivative, we have

$$\frac{\partial f}{\partial T} = \frac{\partial f_M}{\partial \tau}\frac{\partial \tau}{\partial T} = \frac{\partial f_M}{\partial \tau}, \quad (20.104)$$

because $\frac{\partial \tau}{\partial T} = 1$. Defining the corresponding volatility function

$$\sigma_M(t, \tau) = \sigma_f(t, t + \tau), \quad (20.105)$$

we can express the HJM-equation in terms of the *Musiela*-parametrization

$$df_M(t, \tau) = \frac{\partial f_M(t, \tau)}{\partial \tau}dt + \sigma_M(t, \tau)\int_0^\tau \sigma_M(t, s)dsdt + \sigma_M(t, \tau)dW(t). \quad (20.106)$$

This is far more convenient to use in practice, because all rates quoted in the market are with respect to a fixed tenor, not a date. Figure 20.3 illustrates a simulated evolution of the *Musiela*-parametrized forward curve, based on the volatility structure (20.100).

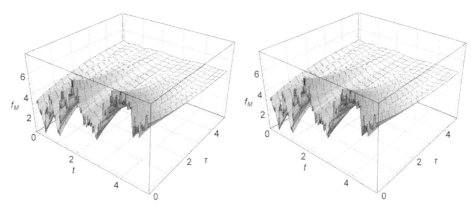

Fig. 20.3 📐 Simulated forward rate surface under *Musiela*-parametrization

Figure 20.4 shows the dynamics in three different τ-slices. It is not hard to see that if the short rate drops, the rates for all larger tenors decrease, too, even though by a smaller amount. The same is true for rising short rates. As mentioned earlier, this is the result of using a one-factor model. The changes in the forward curve for different tenors are all perfectly correlated. This is of course not what we are observing in the market. Thus, we have to talk about choosing a realistic HJM-model and calibrating it to historical market data.

20.7   Multi-Factor HJM and Historical Volatility

We are now entering the world of multi-factor term structure models, and we will do it inside the most general HJM-framework. We have already learned that the properties of a specific HJM-model solely depend on the choice of the volatility function. We have therefore to answer two questions. First, how many factors should we take into

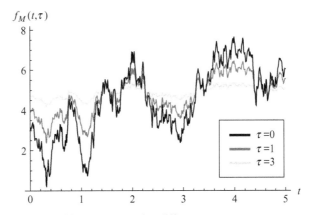

Fig. 20.4 Time evolution of forward rates for different tenors

account? And second, which volatility structure is appropriate for the particular factors? At this point, the discussion may seem pretty abstract. Therefore, let us first state the multi-factor version of the HJM-equation

$$df(t, T) = \sum_{q=1}^{Q} \sigma_q(t, T) \int_t^T \sigma_q(t, s) ds dt + \sum_{q=1}^{Q} \sigma_q(t, T) dW_q(t), \qquad (20.107)$$

with mutually uncorrelated *Wiener*-increments $dW_q(t)$, for $q = 1, \ldots, Q$. It is straightforward to state those dynamics under the *Musiela*-parametrization

$$df_M(t, \tau) = \frac{\partial f_M(t, \tau)}{\partial \tau} dt + \sum_{q=1}^{Q} \sigma_q(t, \tau) \int_0^\tau \sigma_q(t, s) ds dt + \sum_{q=1}^{Q} \sigma_q(t, \tau) dW_q(t), \quad (20.108)$$

where we have omitted the subscript M of the volatility functions, to simplify the notation. To require that all *Wiener*-increments are uncorrelated is the connection to classical factor analysis. Because $dW(t)$ is normally distributed, uncorrelated means independent. That is, the forward rate is driven by Q orthogonal random factors. So let's see, how we get our hands on those factors.

To analyze the structure of the forward rate volatility, yield curve data for Treasury bonds from 2010 to the end of 2014, recorded by the US Department of the Treasury, was used. The times to maturity τ_n are 1, 2, 3, 5, 7, 10, 20, and 30 years. From this data, the forward rates $f(t, \tau_n)$ were computed using (18.44) on page 434, with the differential approximated by a forward difference. The variance in the change of the forward rate for a particular time to maturity τ_n according to (20.108) is

$$\mathrm{Var}[df_M(t, \tau_n)] = \sum_{q=1}^{Q} \sigma_q(t, \tau_n)^2 dt. \qquad (20.109)$$

The important quantity is the scaling factor dt. Of course we cannot observe arbitrary small changes in the forward curve, and thus we have to approximate $df_M(t, \tau_n)$ by $\Delta f_M(t, \tau_n)$ and dt by Δt. In this case, daily data was used, and therefore $\Delta t = \frac{1}{252}$. Let $\hat{S}$ be the N-dimensional empirical covariance matrix, estimated from the forward rate difference data $\Delta f_M(t, \tau_n)$ for $n = 1, \ldots, N$. Then the correct estimator for the annualized covariance matrix of the observed rates is

$$\hat{\Sigma} = \frac{1}{\Delta t} \hat{S}. \qquad (20.110)$$

The matrix $\hat{\Sigma}$ is symmetric and positive definite, and therefore we have a complete set of positive eigenvalues and orthogonal eigenvectors. Hence, we can apply the spectral decomposition

$$\hat{\Sigma} = V \Lambda V' = \sum_{n=1}^{N} \lambda_n |v_n\rangle\langle v_n|, \qquad (20.111)$$

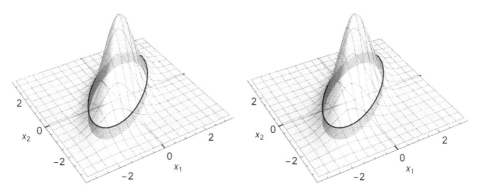

Fig. 20.5 **3D** Bivariate standard normal density function with correlation $\rho = 0.7$ and covariance ellipse

where $|v_n\rangle$ is the n-th normalized eigenvector, which means the n-th column of V. That is, we have decomposed the estimated covariance matrix into a sum of N outer products. If the eigenvalues are ordered along their magnitude, $\lambda_n > \lambda_{n+1}$, the contribution from additional terms in the sum becomes smaller and smaller. In statistics this is called principal component analysis. What really happened is that we have rotated the axes such that they coincide with the half-axes of the covariance ellipsoid. This coordinate transformation is illustrated in Figures 20.5 and 20.6 for the two-dimensional case. We can extract the desired factor volatilities immediately at the observed maturities τ_n by

$$\sigma_q(t, \tau_n) = \sqrt{\lambda_q} v_{nq}. \tag{20.112}$$

Those volatilities are indicated by points, squares, and triangles in Figure 20.7 right, for the first three principal components. We have of course to interpolate between the observed maturities. This was done with quadratic splines in the present example. A similar analysis can also be found in Rebonato (2000, sect. 3.1) and Wilmott (2006b, sect. 37.13). They, however, used historical data of the time before the sovereign dept crisis and their first three principal components looked slightly different. In fact, the first one was nearly a perfect straight line, the second one was also nearly straight, but

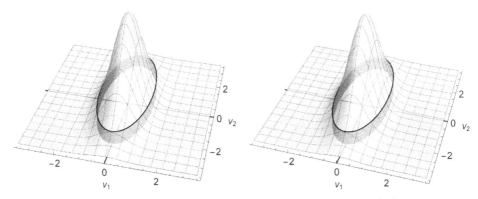

Fig. 20.6 **3D** Density function of Figure 20.5 with rotated axes due to principal component analysis

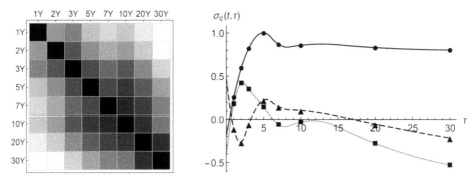

Fig. 20.7 Correlation matrix for different times to maturity (left) and first three principal components of the volatility structure (right) – First component (black), second one (gray), and third one (dashed)

with a slope, and the third one had a roughly parabolic shape. This result had a very nice interpretation for the first factor to cause parallel shifts in the yield curve, the second one to affect its slope, and the third one to introduce curvature. These nice shapes are not that striking in our example, but they are still partly recognizable. The correlation structure between the different rates, is indicated schematically in Figure 20.7 left. A correlation of one is represented by a black square, whereas smaller correlations are indicated by the respective gray levels. There is an anomaly in the correlation structure of the 1Y-bond. It seems that it is more strongly correlated with the 3Y-bond than it is with the 2Y-bond. We usually would expect the correlation to be a decreasing function of the difference in time to maturity. There is no logical explanation for this anomaly, as we shall see in the next chapter, except that unconstrained estimated correlation matrices are prone to such artifacts. We will talk about alternative parametric estimation methods that avoid those anomalies, when dealing with market models. For the moment we leave everything as it is and proceed with our analysis.

The question is now, how many factors should we use to represent the entire covariance structure reasonably well? This one can be answered conveniently. The matrix Λ in (20.111) is obviously the covariance matrix of a complete set of N random factors F_n. Because they are orthogonal, there are no covariance terms and we have

$$\mathrm{Var}\left[\sum_{n=1}^{N} F_n\right] = \sum_{n=1}^{N} \lambda_n = \langle 1|\lambda\rangle. \tag{20.113}$$

If we do not include all factors, but say just $Q < N$, then the relative proportion of variance explained by the Q factors is

$$\text{Variance explained} = \frac{1}{\langle 1|\lambda\rangle} \sum_{q=1}^{Q} \lambda_q. \tag{20.114}$$

In our present example, including only the first factor explains 80.3% of the total variance. Adding the second factor accounts for 91.8%. The first three factors altogether

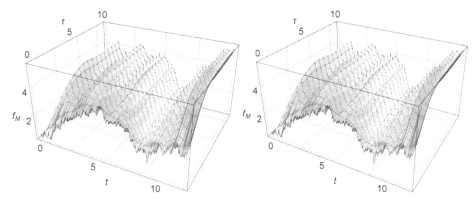

Fig. 20.8 3D Simulated forward rate surface for the historically calibrated 3-factor HJM-model

explain 95.4% of the total variance. Explaining 95% of the total variance is usually considered sufficient, and thus we have to include only three factors.

We are now in a position to simulate the entire forward rate surface, as we have done before. We know the volatility functions in terms of quadratic splines, which means piecewise second order polynomials, that are easily integrated. The result of such a simulation run is illustrated in Figure 20.8. Unlike the *Vasicek*-surface, where the movements of all points on the forward curve were perfectly correlated, the different rates are now decoupled to a certain degree. The result is that the forward curve can bend and twist over time, and can take various different shapes, as seen in Figure 20.9 right, where the surface is sliced several times parallel to the τ-direction. The left illustration in Figure 20.9 shows three different slices parallel to the t-direction, which means the time evolution of forward rates with different times to maturity. Although there is considerable correlation, it is not perfect. Furthermore, it is very clear that the mapping $t \mapsto f_M(t, \tau)$ is a stochastic process for all τ, whereas the mapping $\tau \mapsto f_M(t, \tau)$ is

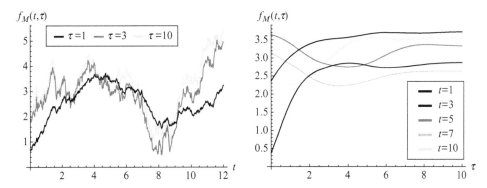

Fig. 20.9 Time evolution of forward rates for different times to maturity (left) and several forward curves at different points in time (right)

a smooth function for all t. A mild warning is advisable here. Even though it is customary to quote and plot rates in percentage values, the true rates and also their volatilities have to be scaled properly. Otherwise, the drift of the forward rate is boosted by a factor of 10^4, whereas the diffusion term only contributes with a factor of 10^2.

Quick calculation 20.14 Verify this statement by reviewing (20.107) on page 476.

It remains to discuss, how the HJM-model, based on the historical volatility structure, can be used to price non-vanilla contracts. The bad news is pricing has to be done via Monte Carlo simulation, so let's focus on European contracts. In this case an arbitrary claim V, expiring at time T can be valued today by

$$V(t, T) = E^Q\left[e^{-\int_t^T r(s)ds} V(T, T)\big|\mathcal{F}_t\right]. \tag{20.115}$$

We will eventually again approximate this expectation value by an average value over many simulated forward curve scenarios. There are two elements inside the expectation that depend on the forward rate, the contract V itself, and the discount factor, containing the short rate. Chances are that knowledge of the future forward curve $f_M(T, \tau)$ is sufficient to know the payoff $V(T, T)$, unless V is a second order contract or it has some forward starting features. In this case we would simply simulate the forward curve further into the future, until all necessary information is available. But the discount factor is also a function of the forward curve. To see this, let's rewrite it in a slightly different form

$$e^{-\int_t^T r(s)ds} = e^{-\int_t^T f(s,s)ds} = e^{-\int_t^T f_M(s,0)ds}. \tag{20.116}$$

That is, discounting is with respect to the zeroth slice in the τ-direction. The best way to see how it works is to look at an example. Let's revisit the bond valuation problem from Example 19.1 on page 446.

Example 20.1

What steps are necessary to price a plain vanilla European call option, expiring at T, on a discount bond with maturity date S, with $t < T < S$ in the HJM-framework?

Solution
Take the following steps:

1. Choose a volatility function $\sigma_q(t, \tau)$ for all included factors $q = 1, \ldots, Q$.
2. Extract the latest forward curve $f_M(t, \tau)$ from market data.
3. Simulate the forward curve until time T to obtain $f_M(T, \tau)$.
4. Evaluate the payoff function

$$V^{(n)}(T, T) = \left(e^{-\int_0^{S-T} f_M(T,\tau)d\tau} - K\right)^+.$$

5. Discount the payoff using the short rate

$$V^{(n)}(t, T) = e^{-\int_t^T f_M(s,0)ds} V^{(n)}(T, T).$$

6. Repeat steps 3 to 5 a large number N of times and compute the average

$$V(t, T) \approx \frac{1}{N} \sum_{n=1}^N V^{(n)}(t, T).$$

This list is generic for all similar pricing problems.

We can see from Example 20.1 that the intermediate forward rates $f_M(s, \tau)$ for $t < s < T$ and $\tau > 0$ do not have to be stored, with the exception of the short rate $f_M(s, 0)$. This usually eases the computational burden considerably.

20.8   Further Reading

An impressive collection of one- and multi-factor short rate models can be found in Andersen and Piterbarg (2010b), Brigo and Mercurio (2007), and also Rebonato (2000). The pros and cons of yield curve fitting are discussed in Wilmott (2006b, chap. 31). Jump-extended short rate models can be found in Nawalkha et al. (2007, chap. 5–7). For the derivation and technical details of the HJM-framework, see the original work of Heath et al. (1992), and also Filipović (2009, chap. 6). Consistency requirements are discussed very thoroughly in Filipović (2001). A detailed discussion of possible convexity adjustments can be found in Deutsch (2002, sect. 15.5). Continuous time *Markov*-processes are treated very thoroughly in Aït-Sahalia et al. (2010).

20.9   Problems

20.1 Derive the discount bond volatility $\sigma_P(t, T)$ in the *Vasicek*-model and verify that $\sigma_P(T, T) = 0$ holds.

20.2 Suppose pricing is conducted with a one-factor short rate model. Use the *Jamshidian*-decomposition to compute the generic price of a receiver swaption, expiring at T_0, with tenor structure $t < T_0, \ldots, T_N$ and $\Delta t = T_n - T_{n-1}$.

20.3 Consider the short rate model

$$dr(t) = e^{-\theta t} dt + \sigma_r dW(t).$$

Show that this model is a member of the affine term structure class and derive the ATS-functions $A(t, T)$ and $B(t, T)$.

20.4 Show that the GARCH(1,1)-process x_t, defined by

$$x_t = \sqrt{h_t} z_t$$
$$h_t = \omega + \alpha x_{t-1}^2 + \beta h_{t-1},$$

with independent and identically distributed innovations $z_t \sim N(0,1)$, is not a *Markov*-process.

20.5 Compute the convexity adjustment in the *Hull–White*-extended *Vasicek*-model.

20.6 In fitting the historical volatility structure of the HJM-factors, quadratic splines were used. Suppose there are N observations $\sigma(t, \tau_n)$, for $n = 1, \ldots, N$. Show that all spline coefficients can be computed, if the data points are matched exactly, the condition

$$\sigma'_n(\tau_{n+1}) = \sigma'_{n+1}(\tau_{n+1})$$

holds, and the first spline is only a linear function.

The LIBOR Market Model

As the market for plain vanilla interest rate derivatives is dominated by the *Black*-76-model, the market for non-vanilla contracts is ruled today by so-called market models. To qualify this statement it has to be emphasized that this market is divided into cap- and floor-like derivatives, and those based on swaps. Unfortunately, these market segments are not compatible under the respective LIBOR or swap market model. Thus, not all questions are finally answered yet.

21.1 The Transition from HJM to Market Models

There are two major problems with the HJM-framework. The first one is that HJM is based on a continuum of infinitesimal rates that cannot be observed. This problem is not that severe; we have already seen how HJM-models can circumvent this obstacle by interpolating observed rates. The second problem is a real disaster: The HJM-framework is completely incompatible with log-normal specifications. Let's do a somewhat heuristic computation to see how severe this problem really is.[1] Suppose we choose the geometric volatility specification

$$\sigma_f(t, T) = \sigma f(t, T). \tag{21.1}$$

Now $\sigma_f(t, T)$ is no longer deterministic, because $f(t, T)$ is random. With this choice, the forward rate dynamics in the HJM-framework becomes

$$df(t, T) = \sigma^2 f(t, T) \int_t^T f(t, s) ds dt + \sigma f(t, T) dW(t). \tag{21.2}$$

This looks harmless, but as we will see soon, those dynamics are highly explosive in the shortest amount of time. Let's pretend for the moment that a solution to (21.2) exists and try to find it. The first step is to determine the dynamics of $\log f(t, T)$. To this end, we use again Itô's lemma to obtain

$$d\log f(t, T) = \left(\sigma^2 \int_t^T f(t, s) ds - \frac{1}{2} \sigma^2 \right) dt + \sigma dW(t). \tag{21.3}$$

---

[1] A very similar calculation can be found in Filipović (2009, sect. 6.4.1).

This equation can be integrated and afterwards exponentiated, as we have done several times before. The result is

$$f(t, T) = f(0, T) \exp\left(\sigma^2 \int_0^t \int_u^T f(u, s) ds du - \frac{1}{2}\sigma^2 t + \sigma W(t)\right). \qquad (21.4)$$

To simplify matters, assume that the initial forward curve is flat, $f(0, T) = r(0)$, and take the derivative of (21.4) with respect to T,

$$\frac{\partial}{\partial T} f(t, T) = f(t, T)\sigma^2 \int_0^t f(u, T) du = \frac{\sigma^2}{2} \frac{\partial}{\partial t} \left(\int_0^t f(u, T) du\right)^2. \qquad (21.5)$$

Now integrate both sides with respect to t from 0 to ε and interchange the order of integration and differentiation on the left hand side to obtain

$$\frac{\partial}{\partial T} \int_0^\varepsilon f(u, T) du = \frac{\sigma^2}{2} \left(\int_0^\varepsilon f(u, T) du\right)^2. \qquad (21.6)$$

It might not be obvious, but for every random path $\omega \in \Omega$, this is a family of ordinary differential equations. To enhance clarity, define

$$X_\varepsilon(T) = \int_0^\varepsilon f(u, T) du, \qquad (21.7)$$

and rewrite (21.6) as

$$\frac{\partial}{\partial T} X_\varepsilon(T) = \frac{\sigma^2}{2} X_\varepsilon(T)^2. \qquad (21.8)$$

The solution to this differential equation is not that hard to guess. For $T \geq \varepsilon$ it is given by

$$X_\varepsilon(T) = \frac{X_\varepsilon(\varepsilon)}{1 - \frac{\sigma^2}{2} X_\varepsilon(\varepsilon)(T - \varepsilon)}. \qquad (21.9)$$

Quick calculation 21.1 Differentiate this equation to prove the claim.

Again, for every path $\omega \in \Omega$, there is a very special maturity time $T^* = \varepsilon + \frac{2}{\sigma^2 X_\varepsilon(\varepsilon)}$. If T tends to T^*, we have

$$\lim_{T \to T^*} X_\varepsilon(T) = \infty. \qquad (21.10)$$

But $X_\varepsilon(T)$ integrates the instantaneous forward rate between $t = 0$ and $t = \varepsilon$. That means the forward rate itself is unbounded almost surely. There is no way to escape this conclusion, even though our argument was not entirely rigorous. It is impossible to reconcile HJM-models and log-normal dynamics. Surprisingly, combining a discrete forward rate with log-normal dynamics is not a problem. This is the idea of market models.

Assume, we have a fixed tenor structure $t < T_0, \ldots, T_N$, with $\Delta t = T_n - T_{n-1}$. From the definition of the forward LIBOR (19.29) on page 447 we have

$$1 + \Delta t L(t, T_{n-1}, T_n) = \frac{P(t, T_{n-1})}{P(t, T_n)}. \tag{21.11}$$

This notation is somewhat bulky and in what follows, we need to preserve an unobstructed view on the structurally important things. So let's write more compactly

$$L(t, T_{n-1}, T_n) = L_n(t) \quad \text{and} \quad P(t, T_n) = P_n(t). \tag{21.12}$$

With this new efficient notation, (21.11) becomes

$$1 + \Delta t L_n(t) = \frac{P_{n-1}(t)}{P_n(t)}. \tag{21.13}$$

We will occasionally even suppress the time argument to simplify things further. The approach of Brace et al. (1997) and also Jamshidian (1997) was to describe a particular forward LIBOR by a geometric *Brown*ian motion

$$dL_n = \mu_n L_n dt + \sigma_n L_n dW_n, \tag{21.14}$$

with some bounded volatility function $\sigma_n(t)$. This equation looks very innocent, but it is more like an iceberg, hiding its true extent from the spectator. First of all, the drift $\mu_n(t)$ could contain all kinds of deterministic and stochastic influences, yet to be determined. Because $L_n(t)$ is not a traded asset, we cannot postulate that its drift under the risk-neutral measure Q is $r(t)$. Furthermore, we know from (21.13) that $L_n(t)$ is related to $P_n(t)$ and also to $P_{n-1}(t)$. But because $P_{n-1}(t)$ is connected with $P_{n-2}(t)$ via $L_{n-1}(t)$ and so forth, we have to conclude that the risk-neutral dynamics for the discount bond has to look something like

$$dP_n = r P_n dt + P_n \sum_{k=1}^{n} a_{n,k} dW_k, \tag{21.15}$$

with the set of yet unknown, and hopefully bounded functions $a_{n,k}(t)$. We further have to assume that the random shocks are highly correlated, $E[dW_n dW_k] = \rho_{nk} dt$. So the situation seems irresolvable, but it is not. From (21.13) we have

$$P_{n-1}(t) = (1 + \Delta t L_n(t)) P_n(t), \tag{21.16}$$

so application of Itô's lemma yields

$$dP_{n-1} = (1 + \Delta t L_n) dP_n + \Delta t P_n dL_n + \Delta t \sigma_n L_n P_n \left(\sum_{k=1}^{n} a_{n,k} \rho_{nk} \right) dt. \tag{21.17}$$

There are three sorts of terms in this equation that have to match separately: terms involving dW_n, terms involving dW_k for $k = 1, \ldots, n-1$, and those terms involving dt. So let's see what we can learn by equating them. First, look at the dW_n-terms,

$$0 = (1 + \Delta t L_n) P_n a_{n,n} dW_n + \Delta t P_n \sigma_n L_n dW_n \quad \Leftrightarrow \quad a_{n,n} = -\frac{\sigma_n \Delta t L_n}{1 + \Delta t L_n}. \tag{21.18}$$

We were allowed to divide through by the *Wiener*-increments, because $dW_n \neq 0$ almost surely. Next, consider the dW_k-terms for $k = 1, \ldots, n-1$,

$$P_{n-1} a_{n-1,k} dW_k = (1 + \Delta t L_n) P_n a_{n,k} dW_k \quad \Leftrightarrow \quad a_{n,k} = a_{n-1,k}. \tag{21.19}$$

Quick calculation 21.2   Check this result by using (21.16).

What (21.19) says is that the function $a_{n,k}(t)$ actually does not depend on n. Equation (21.16) still holds under the shift $n \to (n-1)$, and then (21.19) would yield $a_{n-1,k} = a_{n-2,k}$ and so on. But because we know $a_{k,k}$ from (21.18), we can conclude that

$$a_{n,k} = -\frac{\sigma_k \Delta t L_k}{1 + \Delta t L_k}. \tag{21.20}$$

We can furthermore see that there is no problem with boundedness, because obviously

$$\lim_{L_k \to \infty} a_{n,k} = -\sigma_k < \infty \tag{21.21}$$

for $n = 1, \ldots, N$, because $\sigma_k(t)$ is bounded. Finally, equating the dt-terms yields

$$r P_{n-1} dt = (1 + \Delta t L_n) r P_n dt + \Delta t P_n \mu_n L_n dt + \Delta t \sigma_n L_n P_n \left(\sum_{k=1}^{n} a_{n,k} \rho_{nk} \right) dt \tag{21.22}$$

A lot of terms cancel in this expression and one finally obtains

$$\mu_n = -\sigma_n \sum_{k=1}^{n} a_{n,k} \rho_{nk} = \sigma_n \sum_{k=1}^{n} \frac{\Delta t L_k}{1 + \Delta t L_k} \sigma_k \rho_{nk}. \tag{21.23}$$

Quick calculation 21.3   Confirm this result.

Putting all the pieces together, we can write the risk-neutral dynamics of the discrete forward LIBOR $L_n(t)$ as

$$dL_n = \left(\sum_{k=1}^{n} \frac{\Delta t L_k}{1 + \Delta t L_k} \rho_{nk} \sigma_k \right) \sigma_n L_n dt + \sigma_n L_n dW_n. \tag{21.24}$$

It is easily seen that we have no problem with boundedness or explosive behavior anymore. These types of models are called LIBOR market models (LMM) or log-normal forward LIBOR models (LFM). Think of (21.24) as a discrete version of the HJM-framework.

We followed here the very elegant derivation of Paul Wilmott (2006b, sect. 37.16) that hides one important fact. Since there is no instantaneous short rate, we can no longer use our usual bank account as a numéraire. However, there exists a discretely rebalanced analogue $B_d(t)$, which is effectively a rolling certificate of deposit. It works in the following way: At $t = 0$, $B_d(t)$ starts with one unit of currency, precisely as the usual bank account $B(t)$. But this amount is instantly invested in a T_0-bond. At time $t = T_0$, the bond is cashed out and the proceeds are immediately reinvested in a T_1-bond, and so on. The resulting measure is often referred to as the spot LIBOR measure Q_B. The only real difference is that discounting inside the tenor occurs discretely with a factor

$$\frac{P_n(t)}{P_0(t)} = \prod_{k=1}^{n} \frac{1}{1 + \Delta t L_k(t)}. \tag{21.25}$$

Quick calculation 21.4 Prove the equality by writing $\frac{P_n(t)}{P_0(t)}$ as a telescoping product.

So if we simulate the LMM dynamics under Q_B, every payoff occurring at times T_n has to be discounted to its present value at T_0 with such a factor.

Unfortunately, there are situations, where other equivalent martingale measures are more appropriate for pricing particular derivative contracts contingent on the LIBOR. By changing the measure, the LMM changes its appearance. So we have to develop a machinery to convert the LIBOR market model through different measures.

21.2 The Change-of-Numéraire Toolkit

Applying the LIBOR market model to pricing problems, where the underlying has a tenor structure, like for example options on coupon-bearing bonds or swaps, means that we have to evolve a whole vector of rates

$$|dL\rangle = \begin{pmatrix} dL_1 \\ \vdots \\ dL_N \end{pmatrix}. \tag{21.26}$$

There is also a vector of correlated *Wiener*-increments $|dW\rangle$, with $E[|dW\rangle\langle dW|] = R dt$, where R is the correlation matrix. The question we have to answer is how these increments transform if we change the numéraire. The solution is provided by the following theorem that can be found in Brigo and Mercurio (2007, p. 33).

Theorem 21.1 (Change of numéraire) *Assume there are two numéraire assets S and U, with dynamics*

$$dS = (\ldots)dt + \langle \sigma_S | dW^U \rangle$$
$$dU = (\ldots)dt + \langle \sigma_U | dW^U \rangle$$

under the probability measure Q_U, with $E[|dW\rangle\langle dW|] = Rdt$. A change of measure from Q_U to Q_S results in the transformation

$$|dW^S\rangle = |dW^U\rangle - R\left(\frac{|\sigma_S\rangle}{S} - \frac{|\sigma_U\rangle}{U}\right)dt,$$

with invariant correlation matrix R under every measure.

The proof is an application of a generalized version of the *Girsanov*-theorem and the stochastic *Leibnitz*-rule, and can also be found in Brigo and Mercurio (2007, p. 33). Let's look at a simple example.

Example 21.1

The risk-neutral dynamics of a non dividend paying stock S in the *Black–Scholes*-model is

$$dS_t = rS_t dt + \sigma S_t dW_t^Q.$$

What does the dynamics look like, if S itself is taken as the numéraire asset?

Solution

The probability measure Q is induced by the risk-free bank account $B(t)$, with dynamics

$$dB(t) = rB(t)dt.$$

Thus, the resulting transformation of the *Brown*ian motion is

$$dW_t^S = dW_t^Q - \sigma dt.$$

Because there was only one *Wiener*-increment involved, the correlation is $\rho = 1$. Plugging this result into the original dynamics yields

$$dS_t = (r + \sigma^2)S_t dt + \sigma S_t dW_t^S.$$

Brigo and Mercurio invented another incredibly useful device, the DC-operator. DC is an abbreviation for (vector) "diffusion coefficient." Suppose an arbitrary process X_t has dynamics

$$dX = (\ldots)dt + \langle \sigma | dW \rangle, \tag{21.27}$$

with N-dimensional *Brown*ian motion vector $|dW\rangle$, then the way DC acts on X_t is

$$\text{DC } X_t = \sum_{n=1}^{N} \sigma_n(X_t, t)|e_n\rangle = |\sigma\rangle, \tag{21.28}$$

where $|e_n\rangle$ is the n-th orthonormal basis vector.[2] Operating for example on the n-th forward LIBOR (21.24) yields

$$\text{DC } L_n(t) = \sigma_n(t)L_n(t)|e_n\rangle. \tag{21.29}$$

That is a vector with $N - 1$ zeros and only the n-th slot occupied. With the DC-operator, we can write the change-of-numéraire transformation of Theorem 21.1 as

$$|dW^S\rangle = |dW^U\rangle - R\left(\frac{\text{DC } S}{S} - \frac{\text{DC } U}{U}\right)dt. \tag{21.30}$$

The DC-operator has a lot of useful properties. Looking at the definition (21.28), we can immediately conclude that the DC-operator is linear, that is

$$\text{DC } aX_t = a\,\text{DC } X_t \quad \text{and} \quad \text{DC}\,(X_t + Y_t) = \text{DC } X_t + \text{DC } Y_t \tag{21.31}$$

holds for arbitrary random processes X_t and Y_t, and $a \in \mathbb{R}$. Furthermore, for a deterministic function $g(t)$, we have

$$\text{DC } g(t) = |0\rangle. \tag{21.32}$$

Last but not least, applying Itô's lemma to the generic dynamics (21.27), one obtains

$$d\log X = (\dots)dt + \frac{1}{X}\langle\sigma|dW\rangle. \tag{21.33}$$

From this we can conclude that

$$\frac{\text{DC } X_t}{X_t} = \text{DC }\log X_t \tag{21.34}$$

has to hold. We can therefore write the change-of-numéraire transformation in its most compact and useful form

$$|dW^S\rangle = |dW^U\rangle - R(\text{DC }\log(S/U))dt. \tag{21.35}$$

Quick calculation 21.5 Use linearity of the DC-operator to prove (21.35).

---

[2] Originally, Brigo and Mercurio (2007, sect. 2.3.1) defined the DC-operator to map onto a co-vector. Our definition is solely a matter of convenience.

As a first application of our change-of-numéraire toolkit, let's compute the dynamics of the forward LIBOR $L_N(t)$ under the T_N-forward measure Q_N, also called the terminal measure. This is one of the most widely used pricing measures, because the numéraire bond is guaranteed to be alive until the end of the tenor. Because we are interested only in the dynamics of $L_N(t)$ at the moment, we have to premultiply our transformation rule with the co-vector $\langle e_N |$,

$$\langle e_N | dW^{Q_N} \rangle = \langle e_N | dW^Q \rangle - \langle e_N | R(\mathrm{DC} \log P_N) dt. \tag{21.36}$$

From the dynamics of P_N, (21.15), and (21.20), we can conclude that

$$\mathrm{DC} \log P_N = |a\rangle \quad \text{with} \quad a_n = -\frac{\Delta t L_n}{1 + \Delta t L_n} \sigma_n. \tag{21.37}$$

That makes the desired transformation

$$dW_N^{Q_N} = dW_N^Q - \langle e_N | R |a\rangle dt = dW_N^Q + \sum_{k=1}^{N} \frac{\Delta t L_k}{1 + \Delta t L_k} \rho_{Nk} \sigma_k dt. \tag{21.38}$$

Changing measures in (21.24) on page 486 according to this transformation rule yields

$$dL_N = \sigma_N L_N dW_N, \tag{21.39}$$

under the terminal measure Q_N. That is a perfectly correct result, because we have already proved that the forward LIBOR $L(t, S, T)$ with $t \leq S < T$ is a Q_T-martingale.

When evolving the N-dimensional random vector $|dL\rangle$ under the terminal measure Q_N, the last component $L_N(t)$ is a martingale, but all other components $L_n(t)$ for $n = 1, \ldots, N - 1$ are not. So what are their dynamics? Let's use our toolkit. We know that the numéraire of the terminal measure is $P_N(t)$. And we know further that $L_n(t)$ is a martingale under the T_n-forward measure, induced by the numériare $P_n(T)$. Thus, we have

$$dW_n^{Q_N} = dW_n^{Q_n} - \langle e_n | R(\mathrm{DC} \log(P_N/P_n)) dt. \tag{21.40}$$

Observe that the log-ratio of the two bonds can be expressed as

$$\begin{aligned} \log\left(\frac{P_N(t)}{P_n(t)}\right) &= \log\left(\frac{P_N(t)}{P_{N-1}(t)} \frac{P_{N-1}(t)}{P_{N-2}(t)} \cdots \frac{P_{n+1}(t)}{P_n(t)}\right) \\ &= \log\left(\frac{1}{1 + \Delta t L_N(t)} \frac{1}{1 + \Delta t L_{N-1}(t)} \cdots \frac{1}{1 + \Delta t L_{n+1}(t)}\right) \\ &= -\log\left(\prod_{k=n+1}^{N} (1 + \Delta t L_k(t))\right) = -\sum_{k=n+1}^{N} \log(1 + \Delta t L_k(t)). \end{aligned} \tag{21.41}$$

Because of the linearity of the DC-operator, we have

$$\begin{aligned} \mathrm{DC} \log(P_N/P_n) &= -\sum_{k=n+1}^{N} \mathrm{DC} \log(1 + \Delta t L_k) = -\sum_{k=n+1}^{N} \frac{\mathrm{DC}(1 + \Delta t L_k)}{1 + \Delta t L_k} \\ &= -\sum_{k=n+1}^{N} \frac{\Delta t \, \mathrm{DC} \, L_k}{1 + \Delta t L_k} = -\sum_{k=n+1}^{N} \frac{\sigma_k \Delta t L_k}{1 + \Delta t L_k} |e_k\rangle. \end{aligned} \tag{21.42}$$

Therefore, the transformation we are looking for is

$$dW_n^{Q_N} = dW_n^{Q_n} + \langle e_n | R \sum_{k=n+1}^{N} \frac{\sigma_k \Delta t L_k}{1 + \Delta t L_k} | e_k \rangle dt$$

$$= dW_n^{Q_n} + \sum_{k=n+1}^{N} \frac{\Delta t L_k}{1 + \Delta t L_k} \rho_{nk} \sigma_k dt. \tag{21.43}$$

Thus, the dynamics of $L_n(t)$ under the Q_N-forward measure is

$$dL_n = - \left(\sum_{k=n+1}^{N} \frac{\Delta t L_k}{1 + \Delta t L_k} \rho_{nk} \sigma_k \right) \sigma_n L_n dt + \sigma_n L_n dW_n. \tag{21.44}$$

For pricing purposes it is often more convenient to write this equation in the original form (21.14), with the drift function

$$\mu_n(t) = - \sum_{k=n+1}^{N} \frac{\Delta t L_k(t)}{1 + \Delta t L_k(t)} \rho_{nk} \sigma_n(t) \sigma_k(t). \tag{21.45}$$

This drift is of course only correct, if we look at the dynamics of $L_n(t)$ under the terminal measure Q_N.

Keep in mind that our ability to price contracts consistently, depends on the specification of the volatility structure and the instantaneous correlation matrix. There are some pitfalls to be avoided, as we shall see next.

21.3   Calibration to Caplet Volatilities

Inspecting the drift (21.45), there is a term, representing the instantaneous covariance between different forward LIBORs,

$$\text{Cov}[L_n(t), L_k(t)] = \rho_{nk} \sigma_n(t) \sigma_k(t). \tag{21.46}$$

We have therefore to determine the instantaneous correlation coefficients ρ_{nk}, and appropriate volatility functions $\sigma_n(t)$ for all n. We will deal with correlations later; let's focus on the volatility functions for the moment. Here is what we observe in the market. For an arbitrary forward LIBOR $L(t, S, T)$, with $t < S < T$, volatility is small for $t \to S$. Volatility is also small, if S is much larger than t, which means there is plenty of time left, until the forward LIBOR becomes effective. But for $S - t$ approximately two or three years, volatility is considerably larger. What makes this phenomenon a stylized fact is that it seems to be true for every date S. The reason why volatility behaves that way is not entirely resolved yet, but Rebonato (2004, p. 672) gives a sound financial justification for the humped volatility curve. His argument aims at the particular trading dynamics of different forward and future contracts. For short maturities those contracts are linked to short-term deposit rates, which are strongly influenced by decisions of monetary authorities like central banks. Central banks always try to keep their actions predictable and to avoid surprises, and thus, there is not much volatility in the short-term rates. In the long term, rates are dominated by market expectations about long-term inflation. Because central banks align their monetary policy along appropriate inflation targets, there is again very little volatility in the long-term rates. The rates in between are more flexible, because they are not sort of pinned down at one end.

Returning to our usual tenor grid $t < T_0, \ldots, T_N$, we can therefore infer that the volatility function is at least partly time homogeneous

$$\sigma_n(t) = g_n h(T_{n-1} - t), \tag{21.47}$$

with $g_n \in \mathbb{R}^+$, and a suitable function $h: \mathbb{R} \to \mathbb{R}$, yet to be determined. Because the volatility is usually single humped, it is customary to choose a curve of the *Nelson–Siegel* family,

$$h(x) = a_1 + (a_2 + a_3 x)e^{-a_4 x}. \tag{21.48}$$

This choice has several advantages. First of all, $\sigma_n^2(t)$ is analytically integrable, which is a desirable property with regard to calibration and pricing. More generally, the integral

$$\int_t^T h(T_n - s)h(T_k - s)ds \tag{21.49}$$

can be solved analytically.[3] Furthermore, $\sigma_n(t)$ can be calibrated exactly to implied caplet volatilities provided by the market. There is only one problem: Usually caplet prices are not quoted, instead we can observe cap prices with different tenor structures and maturities. In the US cap market it is customary to use three-months rates, $\Delta t = 0.25$, whereas in European markets semi-annual rates are used, $\Delta t = 0.5$. It is easy to strip caplet prices from observed cap prices, because we know that a cap is just a basket of caplets. Suppose that T_0 is the first reset date. Then the T_1-cap is obviously a caplet, because there is only one caplet contained in it. Therefore, we have

$$\mathrm{Cpl}_t(\kappa, T_1) = \mathrm{Cp}_1(t, \kappa). \tag{21.50}$$

But knowing the price of the T_1-caplet, we can immediately compute the price of the T_2-caplet

$$\mathrm{Cpl}_t(\kappa, T_2) = \mathrm{Cp}_2(t, \kappa) - \mathrm{Cpl}_t(\kappa, T_1), \tag{21.51}$$

---

[3] The solution is

$$\int_t^T h(T_n - s)h(T_k - s)ds = a_1^2(T-t) + bc\left(\frac{a_2^2}{2a_4} + \frac{a_3^2}{4a_4^3}\right) + a_2 a_3 b\left(\frac{c}{2a_4^2} + \frac{c(T_k+T_n) - 2(Te^{2a_4 T} - te^{2a_4 t})}{2a_4}\right)$$

$$+ a_3^2 b\left(\frac{c(T_k + T_n) - 2(Te^{2a_4 T} - te^{2a_4 t})}{4a_4^2} + \frac{cT_k T_n - (T_k + T_n - T)Te^{2a_4 T} + (T_k + T_n - t)te^{2a_4 t}}{2a_4}\right)$$

$$+ \frac{a_1 a_2 b(d_k + d_n)}{a_4} + a_1 a_3 b\left(\frac{d_k + d_n}{a_4^2} + \frac{d_n T_k + d_k T_n - (Te^{a_4 T} - te^{a_4 t})(e^{a_4 T_k} + e^{a_4 T_n})}{a_4}\right).$$

with $b = e^{-a_4(T_k+T_n)}$, $c = e^{2a_4 T} - e^{2a_4 t}$, and $d_{k/n} = e^{a_4(T_{k/n}+T)} - e^{a_4(T_{k/n}+t)}$.

and so forth. Generally, we get the price of the T_n-caplet from the caplets with shorter maturity and the T_n-cap as

$$\text{Cpl}_t(\kappa, T_n) = \text{Cp}_n(t, \kappa) - \sum_{k=1}^{n-1} \text{Cpl}_t(\kappa, T_k). \tag{21.52}$$

But the sum on the right hand side is the T_{n-1}-cap. Thus we get a really simple relation between cap and caplet prices

$$\text{Cpl}_t(\kappa, T_n) = \text{Cp}_n(t, \kappa) - \text{Cp}_{n-1}(t, \kappa). \tag{21.53}$$

It is now an easy task to compute the implied caplet volatilities by numerically inverting Black's formula, provided we know the required forward LIBORs and discount bond prices.

There are, however, some potential intricacies. First of all, it is common practice not to quote cap prices directly, but implied cap volatilities instead. The subtlety in this becomes apparent, if we temporarily extend our notation to make implied volatility a variable

$$\text{Cp}_N(t, \kappa, \sigma_{\text{imp.}}) = \sum_{n=1}^{N} \text{Cpl}_t(\kappa, T_n, \sigma_{\text{imp.}}). \tag{21.54}$$

That is, the implied cap volatility is only one number to be fed into the *Black*-76-formula for every caplet. But implied caplet volatilities are different for each caplet. We have therefore a kind of total implied volatility. The good news is, formula (21.53) still works, but we have to compute the cap prices first, and then reverse engineer the resulting caplet price, to solve for the implied caplet volatility. We cannot strip implied volatilities directly, as if they were prices.

The reason to choose caplets to calibrate the volatility functions is simple: There are no correlations involved. That is, we can split the task of determining the covariance structure of different forward LIBORs into volatility calibration and estimation of a correlation matrix. Usually at-the-money caps are used to strip the required caplet prices and implied volatilities, and this is another subtlety. A cap is said to be at the money, if the strike rate is

$$\kappa = r_S(t), \tag{21.55}$$

with the appropriate forward swap rate $r_S(t)$, as in (19.43) on page 450.

Quick calculation 21.6 Prove that the prices of ATM caps and floors coincide.

Because the swap curve is not flat, different swap tenors have different forward swap rates and thus, the ATM-strike changes. But as we have discussed in depth for ordinary derivatives, implied volatility usually has smile or skew. Since we have not accounted for that in our volatility function, the result of our calibration is inextricably linked to the strike rates of the caps we used. In analyzing the implied volatility in the *Black–Scholes*-model, we found that the forward ATM-strike is the really fundamental reference for the volatility smile. Thus, using at-the-money caps seems to be the right choice here. More advanced volatility structures incorporate smiles and skews, for example using the SABR-model.

Now that we have discussed some details of stripping implied caplet volatilities, let's assume that all the work is done and we have a nice list $\sigma_{\text{imp},n}$ for $n = 1, \ldots, N$. We now have to actually calibrate the volatility functions to the numbers on our list. This can be done very efficiently in a two-step procedure. The first step is to calibrate the *Nelson–Siegel*-parameters by minimizing the mean square error with respect to the implied variances

$$\text{MSE} = \frac{1}{N} \sum_{n=1}^{N} \left(\sigma_{\text{imp},n}^2 - \frac{1}{T_n - t} \int_t^{T_{n-1}} h(T_{n-1} - s)^2 ds \right)^2. \tag{21.56}$$

The resulting parameters $a_1^*, \ldots, a_4^*$ will not induce an exact match with the observed implied variances, but the mean square error should become reasonably small. To achieve perfect alignment, we come back in a second step and choose the numbers g_n, such that

$$\sigma_{\text{imp},n}^2 = \frac{g_n^2}{T_n - t} \int_t^{T_{n-1}} h^*(T_{n-1} - s)^2 ds \tag{21.57}$$

holds for all n. This procedure offers a nice interpretation. The function $h^*(x)$ represents the fundamental time homogeneous volatility structure, whereas the individual parameters g_n indicate (hopefully) small idiosyncratic deviations from the homogeneous structure. If all went well, we should have $g_n \approx 1$ for $n = 1, \ldots, N$. If some g_ns deviate considerably from unity, we have to think about another parametric form of $h(x)$, or we have to add additional degrees of freedom by generalizing the whole volatility function.

The upshot of this analysis is that we can calibrate the time homogeneous volatility structure separately from the correlation structure, using implied caplet volatilities. If we want to price contracts that are cap-like, we already have all we need and furthermore, we can finetune our volatility functions to match the observed caplet prices exactly. If we want to price swap-like contracts, we have to take the next step and that is calibrating the correlation structure.

21.4   Parametric Correlation Matrices

It is extraordinarily difficult to construct a robust estimate of the instantaneous correlation matrix of a set of different rates. We have already faced problems with anomalies when trying to estimate correlations from historical data within the HJM-framework. Even if we assume that instantaneous correlations do not vary much over time, there are still two primary reasons why estimation is so difficult. The first one is statistical in nature. Correlation estimates have an asymptotic standard error of order one over the square root of the sample size. But because there are $\frac{N(N-1)}{2}$ individual correlation coefficients in an $N \times N$ correlation matrix, we cannot expect the entire matrix to be estimated reliably, based on a sample of moderate length. But the longer the sample, the higher the risk that correlations have changed over time. So this is an unpleasant perspective. The second problem is a theoretical one and it is called terminal decorrelation. It is best understood by looking at a rather extreme example.

Example 21.2

Suppose there are two stochastic processes, X_t and Y_t, with dynamics

$$dX(t) = \sigma_X(t)dW(t) \quad \text{and} \quad dY(t) = \sigma_Y(t)dW(t),$$

each one driven by the *Brown*ian motion $W(t)$. Further assume that the volatility functions are given by

$$\sigma_X(t) = \theta\left(\frac{1}{2} - t\right) \quad \text{and} \quad \sigma_Y(t) = \theta\left(t - \frac{1}{2}\right),$$

where $\theta(x)$ is the *Heaviside-θ*-function. What is the correlation of $X(1)$ with $Y(1)$?

Solution

First of all observe that the instantaneous correlation between $X(t)$ and $Y(t)$ is one, because both processes are driven by the same *Brown*ian motion. The terminal correlation is[4]

$$\text{Cov}[X(1), Y(1)] = E[X(1)Y(1)] = \int_0^1 \sigma_X(t)\sigma_Y(t)dt = 0,$$

because the area under the product of the two *Heaviside-θ*-functions is zero.

Both processes are completely decorrelated by the shape of the volatility functions. As mentioned before this is a rather extreme example, but the lesson to be learned is that terminal correlation is influenced by the shape of the volatility functions. In fact, in Example 21.2, there is no way of extracting any correlation information from $X(1)$ and $Y(1)$. This leaves us with two possible choices: Either relying on time series data to estimate correlations historically and dealing with empirical issues, or calibrating correlations to appropriate market instruments and facing the decorrelation problem. Which way to go is largely a matter of taste, so let's not pursue this question any further.

---

[4] The second equality is true, because for $\mathcal{F}_t$-adapted square-integrable processes $\sigma_X(t)$ and $\sigma_Y(t)$

$$E\left[\int_0^T \sigma_X(t)dW_X(t) \int_0^T \sigma_Y(t)dW_Y(t)\right] = E\left[\int_0^T \sigma_X(t)\sigma_Y(t)\rho dt\right]$$

holds, with instantaneous correlation ρ of the *Brown*ian motions. This is a generalization of the *Itô*-isometry. In the present example, there is only one driving *Brown*ian motion and thus, the correlation is $\rho = 1$.

Instead, let's see what we can do to enhance robustness of the whole correlation matrix, independent of the estimation or calibration problem.

Our best chance to make an estimate of the correlation matrix more robust is to reduce the number of free parameters, by making the individual correlation coefficients functions of a smaller set of parameters. We have to consider some important properties of correlation matrices that should be preserved, like symmetry and positive definiteness. Thus, there are some limits on what we are allowed to do. Let's see if we can build some intuition about the general form of a parametrized correlation matrix, still satisfying the desired conditions. Joshi (2008, p. 336) makes a very intuitive point about the general structure of correlations. The argument is the following: Consider three contiguous forward LIBORs, for simplicity take the first three, and suppose that every movement in $L_1(t)$ that is uncorrelated with $L_2(t)$ is also uncorrelated with $L_3(t)$. This is a very reasonable assumption, because we would not expect that there are triggers that affect $L_1(t)$ and $L_3(t)$, but not $L_2(t)$. There is a way to express this situation, using three independent *Brown*ian motions,

$$dL_1 = \mu_1 L_1 dt + \sigma_1 L_1 \left(\sqrt{1 - \rho_{12}^2} dW_1 + \rho_{12} dW_2 \right) \tag{21.58}$$

$$dL_2 = \mu_2 L_2 dt + \sigma_2 L_2 dW_2 \tag{21.59}$$

$$dL_3 = \mu_3 L_3 dt + \sigma_3 L_3 \left(\sqrt{1 - \rho_{23}^2} dW_3 + \rho_{23} dW_2 \right). \tag{21.60}$$

It is easy to see that the instantaneous correlation between $L_1(t)$ and $L_3(t)$ is channeled solely through $dW_2(t)$ and one obtains

$$\rho_{13} = \rho_{12} \rho_{23}. \tag{21.61}$$

Quick calculation 21.7 Show that $\text{Cov}[dL_1, dL_3] = \sigma_1 L_1 \sigma_3 L_3 \rho_{12} \rho_{23} dt$.

All maturities T_n of the forward rates in our usual tenor structure are separated by a year fraction Δt. What (21.61) tells us is that correlation is a function of the separation between rates, such that we have the functional equation

$$\rho(2\Delta t) = \rho(\Delta t)\rho(\Delta t). \tag{21.62}$$

As we already learned in Chapter 17, there is only one function satisfying this condition, the exponential. But we have a few more things on the list that have to be considered. For example, the correlation matrix has to be symmetric. That means only the absolute value of the separation counts. Furthermore, correlations are not allowed to exceed unity. Taking these additional conditions into account, there is only one possible correlation function

$$\rho_{nk} = e^{-\beta \Delta t |n-k|}, \tag{21.63}$$

with the free parameter $\beta \in \mathbb{R}^+$. This choice indeed guarantees an admissible correlation matrix. Furthermore, no matter how large the matrix is, there is only one parameter to be calibrated. Even though this parametrization is extremely simple, it provides a decent approximation with $\beta \approx 0.1$ in most practical applications.

The correlation function (21.63) can be refined to provide additional degrees of freedom, or to match empirical observations closer, respectively. Observe that the correlation in the present functional form tends to zero, if the rates are separated by a large number of year fractions. If we assume that correlation does never decay completely, but instead a certain basis correlation ρ_∞ always remains, then similar arguments lead to the form

$$\rho_{nk} = \rho_\infty + (1 - \rho_\infty)e^{-\beta\Delta t|n-k|}, \tag{21.64}$$

with $0 \le \rho_\infty < 1$. A correlation matrix based on this correlation function is also guaranteed to be admissible. But now there are two parameters that can be used for calibration. Obviously, (21.63) is a special case of (21.64), with $\rho_\infty = 0$.

An empirical observation is that the correlation between contiguous long-term rates is stronger than the one between short-term rates with identical separation. You can check that for the correlation matrix in Figure 20.7 left on page 478. That means, when moving along the sub-diagonals of the correlation matrix from "north-west" to "south-east," correlations should increase. Rebonato (1999) suggested a generalization of (21.64) to account for this fact, namely to make β a function of "position" in the correlation matrix. In the original approach there were some problems with positive definiteness of the resulting correlation matrix, but an improved formulation can be found in Rebonato (2004, p. 691)

$$\rho_{nk} = \rho_\infty + (1 - \rho_\infty)e^{-\beta_{nk}\Delta t|n-k|} \quad \text{with} \quad \beta_{nk} = \beta_0 e^{-\gamma\Delta t \min(n,k)}, \tag{21.65}$$

and $\beta_0, \gamma \in \mathbb{R}^+$. This three parameter representation also generates an admissible correlation matrix that has all stylized features, observed in the market. Figure 21.1 is a schematic illustration of a correlation matrix using the *Rebonato*-parametrization. Alternatively, the instantaneous correlation surface can be computed using a continuous version of Equation (21.65),

$$\rho(T_n, T_k) = \rho_\infty + (1 - \rho_\infty)e^{-\beta(T_n, T_k)|T_n - T_k|} \quad \text{with} \quad \beta(T_n, T_k) = \beta_0 e^{-\gamma\min(T_n, T_k)}. \tag{21.66}$$

The resulting surface is illustrated in Figure 21.2. From this illustration it becomes very clear that correlations of neighboring rates become much stronger if the maturity dates are far in the future.

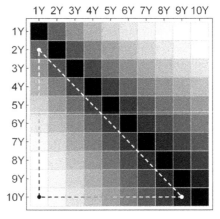

Fig. 21.1 Parametrized correlation matrix with lower triangular pivot points

21.5   Calibrating Correlations and the Swap Market Model

Let's go back to the LIBOR market model (21.24) on page 486 and apply Itô's lemma to obtain the logarithmic dynamics under Q_B

$$d\log L_n = \left(\sum_{k=1}^{n} \frac{\Delta t L_k}{1 + \Delta t L_k} \rho_{nk}\sigma_k - \frac{1}{2}\sigma_n \right)\sigma_n dt + \sigma_n dW_n. \tag{21.67}$$

Because variances and correlations are unaffected by *Girsanov*-transformations, we can conclude that the covariance between changes in different logarithmic rates is

$$\mathrm{Cov}[d\log L_n, d\log L_k] = \sigma_n\sigma_k\rho_{nk}dt \tag{21.68}$$

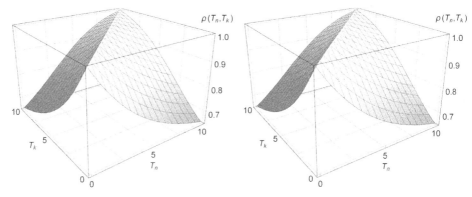

Fig. 21.2 ⓷Ⓓ Smooth parametric correlation surface with parameters $\rho_\infty = 0.6$, $\beta_0 = 0.2$, and $\gamma = 0.2$

under every measure. That is, we can estimate the covariance matrix $\hat{\Sigma}$ from time series data of the changes in the logarithmic rates $\Delta \log L_n$. The estimated correlation matrix $\hat{R}$ is obtained by computing the matrix elements

$$\hat{\rho}_{nk} = \frac{\hat{\sigma}_{nk}}{\sqrt{\hat{\sigma}_{nn}\hat{\sigma}_{kk}}}. \qquad (21.69)$$

Call R_P the parametrized correlation matrix, whatever parametrization is used. The most obvious thing to do now is to choose the parameters such that some distance measure between $\hat{R}$ and R_P is minimized. The measure almost always used is the *Frobenius*-norm $\|\cdot\|_F$. For an arbitrary $N \times K$ matrix A, the *Frobenius*-norm is defined as

$$\|A\|_F = \sqrt{\sum_{n=1}^{N}\sum_{k=1}^{K}|a_{nk}|^2}. \qquad (21.70)$$

Minimizing $\|\hat{R} - R_P\|_F$ is thus nothing more than a quadratic optimization problem that can be solved numerically. While this approach is pretty straightforward, there is another method, tailored to Rebonato's three-parameter form (21.65), called pivot matrices.

The idea of this second, very elegant approach is to identify key entries in the estimated correlation matrix and to represent these entries exactly in the parametric approximation. All entries in between follow from the theoretical structure of the matrix. Such key entries are called pivot points. Consequently the resulting parametrized version of the matrix is often called the associated pivot matrix. The pivot points for our estimated correlation matrix are $\hat{\rho}_{21}$, $\hat{\rho}_{N1}$, and $\hat{\rho}_{N(N-1)}$. Those points are indicated in Figure 21.1. They mark the lower sub-diagonal triangle of the correlation matrix. If you think about it, all the knowledge we used to give R_P a reasonable structure, is represented by those three pivot points. Of course, we could have chosen the upper super-diagonal triangle as well, because the correlation matrix is symmetric. The question is now, how do we determine the parameters ρ_∞, β_0, and γ? Let's take a look at the first two pivot points. In order to have $\hat{\rho}_{21} = \rho_{21}$ and $\hat{\rho}_{N1} = \rho_{N1}$, we must have

$$\hat{\rho}_{21} = \rho_\infty + (1 - \rho_\infty)\exp(-\beta_0 e^{-\gamma \Delta t}\Delta t) \qquad (21.71)$$

$$\hat{\rho}_{N1} = \rho_\infty + (1 - \rho_\infty)\exp(-\beta_0 e^{-\gamma \Delta t}\Delta t(N - 1)). \qquad (21.72)$$

From this, it is easy to deduce the condition

$$\frac{\hat{\rho}_{N1} - \rho_\infty}{1 - \rho_\infty} = \left(\frac{\hat{\rho}_{21} - \rho_\infty}{1 - \rho_\infty}\right)^{N-1}, \qquad (21.73)$$

which can be easily solved numerically for ρ_∞. Having determined ρ_∞, the rest is straightforward algebra. The third required coefficient is

$$\hat{\rho}_{N(N-1)} = \rho_\infty + (1 - \rho_\infty)\exp(-\beta_0 e^{-\gamma \Delta t(N-1)}\Delta t). \qquad (21.74)$$

Now the remaining parameters become

$$\gamma = \frac{\log\log\left(\frac{\hat{\rho}_{21}-\rho_\infty}{1-\rho_\infty}\right) - \log\log\left(\frac{\hat{\rho}_{N(N-1)}-\rho_\infty}{1-\rho_\infty}\right)}{\Delta t(N-2)} \quad \text{and} \quad \beta_0 = -\frac{e^{\gamma\Delta t}}{\Delta t}\log\left(\frac{\hat{\rho}_{21}-\rho_\infty}{1-\rho_\infty}\right).$$

$$(21.75)$$

Quick calculation 21.8 Check this result.

The only problem with the pivot method is that Equation (21.73) may have several real roots which qualify as asymptotic correlation. In this case it is likely that the first positive root smaller than $\hat{\rho}_{N1}$ is the right one, because for large N, ρ_{N1} should tend to ρ_∞ from above.

As mentioned earlier, it is largely a matter of taste whether to extract the correlation matrix from historical data, or to calibrate it to observed market instruments. To give a balanced picture, we now turn to the second alternative. The instruments used here for calibrating the correlation matrix are swaptions, because they are liquidly traded and their at-the-money implied volatility is usually quoted. Pricing swaptions with market models is similar to pricing caplets and floorlets. The difference is that in the latter case, we have assumed the forward LIBOR to be log-normal distributed, and we will now assume the same for the forward swap rate. Consequently, this branch of market models is referred to as swap market models (SMM). Recall from (19.43) on page 450 that the forward swap rate can be written as

$$r_S(t) = \frac{\Delta t \sum_{n=1}^{N} P_n(t)L_n(t)}{A(t)},$$

$$(21.76)$$

with the annuity factor

$$A(t) = \Delta t \sum_{n=1}^{N} P_n(t).$$

$$(21.77)$$

But (21.76) is a weighted sum of forward LIBORs that can be written alternatively as

$$r_S(t) = \sum_{n=1}^{N} w_n(t)L_n(t) \quad \text{with} \quad w_n(t) = \frac{P_n(t)}{\sum_{k=1}^{N} P_k(t)}.$$

$$(21.78)$$

The great advantage of this representation is that the weights $w_n(t)$ usually do not vary much over time and one obtains very good approximations for the dynamics of $r_S(t)$ by freezing the weights at their initial values. To see how this approximation works, recall that the forward swap rate is a martingale under the annuity measure

Q_A. So what we need in order to compute swaption prices is the volatility associated with the logarithmic dynamics $d \log r_S(t)$. To this end, let's first go back to the definition of the DC-operator. Under the general dynamics (21.27) for the process X_t on page 488, we had DC $X_t = |\sigma\rangle$. We now wish to define the adjoint operator $\mathrm{DC}^\dagger$, such that $\mathrm{DC}^\dagger X_t = \langle \sigma|$. It is easy to see that this definition implies

$$\mathrm{DC}^\dagger X_t = \sum_{n=1}^{N} \langle e_n | \sigma_n(X_t, t), \tag{21.79}$$

and therefore

$$dX = (\ldots)dt + \mathrm{DC}^\dagger X | dW \rangle \tag{21.80}$$

holds. Now we are in a position to express the desired volatility with the help of the adjoint DC-operator,

$$d \log r_S = (\ldots)dt + \mathrm{DC}^\dagger \log r_S | dW \rangle. \tag{21.81}$$

We only have to determine what $\mathrm{DC}^\dagger \log r_S(t)$ is. Because from (21.78) we have $r_s(t) = \langle w(t)|L(t)\rangle$, we can use the properties of the DC-operator, which also hold for the adjoint version, to write

$$\mathrm{DC}^\dagger \log r_S = \frac{\mathrm{DC}^\dagger r_S}{r_S} = \frac{\mathrm{DC}^\dagger \sum_{n=1}^{N} w_n L_n}{\langle w|L\rangle} = \frac{\sum_{n=1}^{N} w_n \mathrm{DC}^\dagger L_n}{\sum_{k=1}^{N} w_k L_k}. \tag{21.82}$$

From the LIBOR market model we can immediately read off that $\mathrm{DC}^\dagger L_n = \langle e_n | \sigma_n L_n$ holds, and we thus obtain

$$\mathrm{DC}^\dagger \log r_S(t) = \sum_{n=1}^{N} \langle e_n | v_n(t) \sigma_n(t) \quad \text{with} \quad v_n(t) = \frac{w_n(t) L_n(t)}{\sum_{k=1}^{N} w_k(t) L_k(t)}. \tag{21.83}$$

Quick calculation 21.9 Prove that $v_n(t) = \frac{P_{n-1}(t) - P_n(t)}{P_0(t) - P_N(t)}$ holds.

We can now finally reexpress (21.81), to identify the desired volatility,

$$d \log r_S = (\ldots)dt + \sum_{n=1}^{N} v_n \sigma_n dW_n. \tag{21.84}$$

Rebonato (2000, sect. 1.3 & 1.5) extended the freezing argument for $w_n(t)$ to $v_n(t)$ to obtain an approximation for the variance of $\log r_S(T_0)$, which is the required quantity to be fed into Black's formula. One obtains

$$\mathrm{Var}[\log r_S(T_0)] \approx \langle v(t)|\Sigma|v(t)\rangle \quad \text{with} \quad \sigma_{nk} = \rho_{nk} \int_{t}^{T_0} \sigma_n(s)\sigma_k(s)ds. \tag{21.85}$$

The volatility functions $\sigma_n(t) = g_n h(T_{n-1} - t)$ are those calibrated to market prices of at-the-money caplets, with the individual coefficients preferably set to $g_n = 1$ for

$n = 1, \ldots, N$. The correlation coefficients are computed with one of the three suggested parametric forms (21.63) to (21.65). The respective parameters can now be calibrated easily to implied ATM swaption volatilities, because we have for swaptions with our usual tenor structure

$$\sigma_{\text{imp.}} \approx \sqrt{\frac{\langle v|\Sigma|v\rangle}{T_0 - t}}, \tag{21.86}$$

with

$$v_n = \frac{P_{n-1}(t) - P_n(t)}{P_0(t) - P_N(t)} \quad \text{and} \quad \sigma_{nk} = \rho_{nk} \int_t^{T_0} \sigma_n(s)\sigma_k(s)ds. \tag{21.87}$$

The only problem with this approach is that the LMM and the SMM are inherently incompatible. From (21.78) we have that the forward swap rate is a weighted sum of forward LIBORs. But if forward LIBORs are log-normal distributed, the sum of forward LIBORs cannot be log-normal distributed at the same time. However, this is mainly a theoretical problem, in practice the distribution seems to be very close to log-normal.

21.6   Pricing Exotics in the LMM

We have already covered many necessary tools for pricing non-vanilla contracts within market models. Let's now put in some structure and tie up some loose ends. We can decompose the whole pricing process into four phases:

Phase 1: Identification
Identify the payoff function $V(T_0, T_0)$ of the claim and the associated tenor structure $t < T_0, \ldots, T_N$ of the underlying payments, with $\Delta t = T_n - T_{n-1}$.

Phase 2: Calibration
Calibrate volatility functions and instantaneous correlations to market instruments and/or historical observations. If the contract is cap-like, correlations are not required and the observed ATM caplet volatilities can be matched exactly. If the contract is swap-like, assume time homogeneous volatility functions and calibrate a parametric correlation matrix to historical data or implied ATM swaption volatilities.

Phase 3: Computation
Choose a suitable numéraire, usually but not necessarily a discount bond $P_k(t)$, that makes the present value

$$\begin{aligned}
V(t, T_0) &= P_k(t)E^{Q_k}\left[\frac{V(T_0, T_0)}{P_k(T_0)}\bigg|\mathcal{F}_t\right] \\
&= P_k(t)E^{Q_k}\left[V(T_0, T_0)\prod_{n=1}^{k}(1 + \Delta t L_n(T_0))\bigg|\mathcal{F}_t\right].
\end{aligned} \tag{21.88}$$

Compute the drifts of the forward LIBORs under Q_k using the change-of-numéraire toolkit and the DC-operator.

Phase 4: Simulation

Run a Monte Carlo simulation of the forward LIBORs $L_n(t)$ with a large number M of replications to approximate the conditional expectation in (21.88) by the average value

$$V(t, T_0) \approx P_k(t) \frac{1}{M} \sum_{m=1}^{M} \left(V^{(m)}(T_0, T_0) \prod_{n=1}^{k} (1 + \Delta t L_n^{(m)}(T_0)) \right). \tag{21.89}$$

If necessary, use appropriate techniques to improve Monte Carlo precision in order to speed up the simulation process.

Quick calculation 21.10 Prove the second equality in (21.88).

To see how the process works, at least schematically, let's look at a very simple example.

Example 21.3

Suppose we want to price an exotic T_0-claim, with T_0 far in the future, contingent on some nonlinear function of a large sequence of equispaced future payments occuring at $T_1, \ldots, T_N$. The payoff is fully determined at time T_0 and there are no early exercise features. What can be said about the four phases of pricing?

Solution

Phase 1: Since the tenor structure of the underlying payments is obvious, we merely have to identify how these payments depend on the LIBORs in order to compute the payoff function explicitly.

Phase 2: Since the payoff is a nonlinear function of the payments, which means we generally will not be able to decompose it into caplets or floorlets, we have to calibrate volatility functions and the correlation matrix.

Phase 3: Because the payoff can be computed as a simple conditional expectation at time T_0, we can use $P_0(t)$ as a numéraire. This choice has the advantage that $P_0(T_0) = 1$, but the drawback that none of the forward LIBORs $L_n(t)$ is a martingale.

Phase 4: Since T_0 is far in the future and there is a large number of forward rates to be simulated, improvement techniques should be used to speed up the simulation.

In the sequel, we will concentrate on phases 3 and 4 of Example 21.3 to elaborate on the simulation aspect. First of all, let's compute the drift of the forward LIBORs under Q_0. From the change-of-numéraire formalism, we have

$$dW_n^{Q_0} = dW_n^{Q_n} - \langle e_n | R(\text{DC} \log(P_0/P_n)) dt. \tag{21.90}$$

From the properties of the DC-operator we obtain in complete analogy to (21.42) on page 490

$$\text{DC} \log(P_0/P_n) = \sum_{k=1}^{n} \text{DC} \log(1 + \Delta t L_k) = \sum_{k=1}^{n} \frac{\sigma_k \Delta t L_k}{1 + \Delta t L_k} |e_k\rangle. \tag{21.91}$$

Quick calculation 21.11 Confirm the first equality.

Therefore, the dynamics of the forward LIBOR $L_n(t)$ under the T_0-forward measure becomes

$$dL_n = \left(\sum_{k=1}^{n} \frac{\Delta t L_k}{1 + \Delta t L_k} \rho_{nk} \sigma_k \right) \sigma_n L_n dt + \sigma_n L_n dW_n. \tag{21.92}$$

Now apply Itô's lemma to find the logarithmic dynamics of the n-th forward LIBOR. One obtains

$$d \log L_n = \left(\sum_{k=1}^{n} \frac{\Delta t L_k}{1 + \Delta t L_k} \rho_{nk} \sigma_k \right) \sigma_n dt - \frac{1}{2} \sigma_n^2 dt + \sigma_n dW_n. \tag{21.93}$$

There is good news and bad news about this equation. The good news is, as we have seen earlier for geometric *Brown*ian motions, that the diffusion term is no longer random. The bad news is that one of the drift terms is state dependent. This means that integrating (21.93) is not that simple. Let's see if we can find a good approximation that permits analytical integration. To this end, notice that the first drift term is small, compared to the second one, because it involves factors of $\Delta t L_k(t)$, which are usually expressed in percentage. Moreover, if $L_k(t)$ varies over time, this is only a small perturbation in the overall drift of the process. As a first approximation, we can therefore freeze the forward LIBORs at their time t values. We then obtain the solution

$$\log L_n(T_0) \approx \log L_n(t) + \sum_{k=1}^{n} \frac{\Delta t L_k(t)}{1 + \Delta t L_k(t)} \rho_{nk} \int_t^{T_0} \sigma_n(s)\sigma_k(s)ds$$
$$- \frac{1}{2} \int_t^{T_0} \sigma_n^2(s)ds + \int_t^{T_0} \sigma_n(s)dW_n(s). \tag{21.94}$$

But even this solution is not so innocent as it seems. The *Wiener*-increments are instantaneously correlated, so that we cannot simply draw random numbers. To simulate the forward LIBORs efficiently, define the covariance matrix Σ and populate it with

$$\sigma_{nk} = \rho_{nk} \int_t^{T_0} \sigma_n(s)\sigma_k(s)ds. \tag{21.95}$$

Furthermore, let S be the *Cholesky*-root, such that $\Sigma = SS'$. If we now define the overall integrated approximate drift

$$\mu_n = \sum_{k=1}^{n} \frac{\Delta t L_k(t)}{1 + \Delta t L_k(t)} \langle e_k | \Sigma | e_n \rangle - \frac{1}{2} \langle e_n | \Sigma | e_n \rangle, \qquad (21.96)$$

we obtain the strong solution

$$\log L_n(T_0) \approx \log L_n(t) + \mu_n + \sqrt{T_0 - t} \langle e_n | S | z \rangle, \qquad (21.97)$$

where $|z\rangle$ is a N-dimensional random vector of uncorrelated standard normally distributed random variables $Z_n \sim N(0, 1)$. But that means, we can simulate the whole vector of logarithmic forward LIBORs at once,

$$|\log L(T_0)\rangle \approx |\log L(t)\rangle + |\mu\rangle + \sqrt{T_0 - t}\, S | z \rangle. \qquad (21.98)$$

This is a very fast and efficient way to simulate the dynamics of the forward LIBORs. Unfortunately, the approximation is not good enough, if the time to expiry $T_0 - t$ is large. Large here means considerably longer than one year. In this case, we have to improve the scheme.

Since the expiry date T_0 in Example 21.3 is far in the future, we will now introduce an easy and very efficient trick to improve the approximation (21.98), see also Joshi (2008, sect. 14.6). What if our first approximation is only say a test, to see where we end up roughly? We could use this first prediction to enhance the precision of our actual solution. This principle is called "predictor-corrector" method. It works as follows: Since we have now an estimate where our logarithmic forward LIBORs end up, we can shift the freezing point from the left border t to the midpoint $\frac{1}{2}(t + T_0)$. In integration this is called the trapezoidal rule. That means after our predictor run, we take the results for $L_n(T_0)$ and compute the drift correction

$$\hat{\mu}_n = \frac{1}{2} \sum_{k=1}^{n} \left(\frac{\Delta t L_k(T_0)}{1 + \Delta t L_k(T_0)} - \frac{\Delta t L_k(t)}{1 + \Delta t L_k(t)} \right) \langle e_k | \Sigma | e_n \rangle. \qquad (21.99)$$

Afterwards, we come back to correct our solution

$$|\log \hat{L}(T_0)\rangle = |\log L(T_0)\rangle + |\hat{\mu}\rangle, \qquad (21.100)$$

hence the name predictor-corrector.

Quick calculation 21.12 Show that the corrected solution $\log \hat{L}_n(T_0)$ contains indeed a drift function, frozen at the midpoint between t and T_0.

The improvement accomplished with this small and computationally cheap trick is fantastic. For reasonable rates and volatilities this approximation holds well for time steps of about ten years. Furthermore, it is very straightforward to implement.

The extraordinary success of the market models is due to some very desirable properties realized in those kinds of models. We have seen that the LMM can be calibrated to observed market instruments easily. It is compatible with the *Black*-76-model, where the HJM-framework failed. Its state variables are discrete rates that can be simulated quite efficiently. Last but not least, it can be extended to account for volatility smile and skew, but this is clearly the realm of advanced fixed-income modeling.

21.7   Further Reading

There are some very comprehensive books about the LIBOR market model, like the ones of Gatarek et al. (2006) and Rebonato (2002). The link between LMM and HJM is established rigorously in the original work of Brace et al. (1997), and also in Filipović (2001, sect. 5.6). The change-of-numéraire toolkit and the DC-operator is due to Brigo and Mercurio (2007, sect. 2.3). Calibration algorithms for caps, floors, and swaptions are described in much detail, in Gatarek et al. (2006, part II). Further calibration techniques can be found in Brigo and Mercurio (2007, chap. 7). An extended analysis of the approximations involved in swaption pricing is provided in Brigo and Mercurio (2007, chap. 8). A nice and accessible guide to pricing exotics in the LMM is Joshi (2008, chap. 14). Further improvement techniques for Monte Carlo simulation can be found in Andersen and Piterbarg (2010b, sect. 14.6). For incorporation of volatility smiles and skews, see the book of Rebonato et al. (2009) and also Brigo and Mercurio (2007, part IV).

21.8   Problems

21.1 Suppose that the tenor structure $T_{-1}, T_0, \ldots, T_N$ is equispaced, with $\Delta t = T_n - T_{n-1}$ and $T_{-1} = 0$. For $0 \le t \le T_N$, the discretely rebalanced bank account $B_d(t)$ has present value

$$B_d(t) = X_t P_{N_t}(t),$$

with

$$X_t = \prod_{n=0}^{N_t} \frac{1}{P_n(T_{n-1})} \quad \text{and} \quad N_t = \sum_{n=0}^{N-1} \theta(t - T_n),$$

where $\theta(x)$ is again the *Heaviside-θ*-function. Use Theorem 17.2 on page 390 to prove that X_t has the dynamics

$$dX_t = \left(\frac{1}{P(t, t + \Delta t)} - 1 \right) X_t dN_t.$$

21.2 Show that $B_d(t)$ as defined in Problem 21.1 is almost surely a continuous process.

21.3 Use the change-of-numéraire toolkit and the DC-operator to derive the drift of the n-th forward LIBOR under the spot LIBOR measure Q_B, for an arbitrary time $0 \le t < T_{n-1}$. Keep in mind that the process X_t in the definition of $B_d(t)$ in Problem 21.1 is almost surely constant.

21.4 Consider a hypothetical contract called a "reversing pair" by Joshi (2008, p. 319), which consists of a long position in a forward rate agreement, running from T_0 to T_1, and a short position in another FRA, spanning T_1 to T_2. Suppose the reversing pair pays off at time T_2. Under which measure should this contract be priced and why?

Complex Analysis

Complex numbers are rarely an issue in economics, if it all, then in time series analysis. This appendix covers some of the basics, used in the main part of the book, and maybe a little bit more. The interested reader can consult any standard text book on complex analysis for additional background information. Some really good introductions, like the book of George Cain (1999), are freely available on the Internet.

A.1 Introduction to Complex Numbers

Complex numbers extend the real axis to a complex plane, where the complex axis is orthogonal to the real axis; see Figure A.1 left. Thus, every element of the complex numbers $z \in \mathbb{C}$ has a real part $\text{Re}[z] = x$ and an imaginary (complex) part $\text{Im}[z] = y$, with $x, y \in \mathbb{R}$. The complex numbers are represented as

$$z = x + iy, \qquad (A.1)$$

where i is the complex unit with the peculiar property $i^2 = -1$. But for the moment let i simply label the complex direction. Every complex number has a secret twin, called the complex conjugate number,

$$z^* = x - iy. \qquad (A.2)$$

The complex conjugate is always obtained by changing the sign of the imaginary part of a complex number.

Quick calculation A.1 Verify that the real and imaginary part of a complex number is obtained by $\text{Re}[z] = \frac{1}{2}(z + z^*)$ and $\text{Im}[z] = \frac{1}{2i}(z - z^*)$.

Addition and subtraction of complex numbers is straightforward and precisely what you would expect

$$z_1 \pm z_2 = x_1 \pm x_2 + i(y_1 \pm y_2). \qquad (A.3)$$

However, multiplication and division is a little bit more intricate. To multiply two complex numbers, you have to compute the product and to use the fact that $i^2 = -1$.

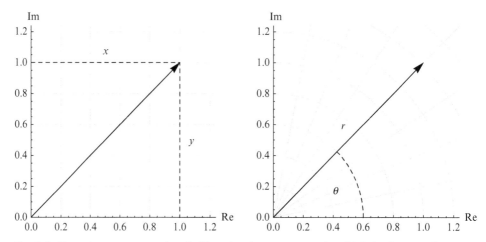

Fig. A.1 Cartesian representation (left) and polar representation (right) of a complex number $z = x + iy$

The product of two complex numbers is thus

$$z_1 \cdot z_2 = (x_1 + iy_1) \cdot (x_2 + iy_2)$$
$$= x_1 x_2 - y_1 y_2 + i(x_1 y_2 + x_2 y_1). \tag{A.4}$$

Quick calculation A.2 Show that $z_1^* \cdot z_2^* = (z_1 \cdot z_2)^*$.

Division is even more bulky. Following the recipe to the letter one obtains

$$\frac{z_1}{z_2} = \frac{x_1 + iy_1}{x_2 + iy_2} = \frac{x_1 + iy_1}{x_2 + iy_2} \cdot \frac{x_2 - iy_2}{x_2 - iy_2}$$
$$= \frac{x_1 x_2 + y_1 y_2}{x_2^2 + y_2^2} + i \frac{x_2 y_1 - x_1 y_2}{x_2^2 + y_2^2}. \tag{A.5}$$

There is a far more elegant way to multiply and divide complex numbers, based on an alternative representation. Define the coordinate transformation

$$x = r \cos\theta \tag{A.6}$$
$$y = r \sin\theta. \tag{A.7}$$

From the identity $\cos^2\theta + \sin^2\theta = 1$, we obtain by adding the squares of (A.6) and (A.7)

$$r = \sqrt{x^2 + y^2}. \tag{A.8}$$

The radius r is also called the absolute value or the modulus of the complex number, $r = |z|$.

Quick calculation A.3 Show that $r^2 = |z|^2 = z^* z$ holds.

Dividing (A.7) by (A.6) and recalling that $\frac{\sin\theta}{\cos\theta} = \tan\theta$ yields[1]

$$\theta = \tan^{-1}\left(\frac{y}{x}\right). \tag{A.9}$$

The angle θ is called the argument of the complex number, $\theta = \arg z$. Note that the range of the new variables is different, $r \in \mathbb{R}_0^+$ and $\theta \in [0, 2\pi)$. We can thus write the complex number z as

$$z = r(\cos\theta + i\sin\theta). \tag{A.10}$$

Figure A.1 right illustrates the complex number $z = 1 + i$ in polar coordinates. An extremely important identity can be derived by assuming $r = 1$ and expanding z in a *Taylor*-series around $\theta_0 = 0$,

$$\begin{aligned}
z &= \cos\theta + i\sin\theta \\
&= 1 - \frac{\theta^2}{2!} + \frac{\theta^4}{4!} - \cdots + i\theta - i\frac{\theta^3}{3!} + i\frac{\theta^5}{5!} - \cdots \\
&= 1 + i\theta + \frac{(i\theta)^2}{2!} + \frac{(i\theta)^3}{3!} + \frac{(i\theta)^4}{4!} + \frac{(i\theta)^5}{5!} + \cdots
\end{aligned} \tag{A.11}$$

Recognize this series? It is the *Taylor*-series of an exponential. We thus obtain the famous *Euler*-identity

$$e^{i\theta} = \cos\theta + i\sin\theta. \tag{A.12}$$

We can now represent the complex number z in its most useful polar form

$$z = re^{i\theta}. \tag{A.13}$$

Why is this form so efficient? Let's multiply two complex numbers, but now do it in the polar form. One obtains

$$z_1 z_2 = r_1 r_2 e^{i(\theta_1 + \theta_2)}. \tag{A.14}$$

You see how easy this is? The radii get multiplied, whereas the angles are simply added. Figure A.2 illustrates the process. It is straightforward to deduce how division of complex numbers is accomplished in the polar coordinate representation. One simply obtains

$$\frac{z_1}{z_2} = \frac{r_1}{r_2} e^{i(\theta_1 - \theta_2)}. \tag{A.15}$$

---

[1] Strictly speaking, this is not entirely general. Because the tangent has multiple branches, the inverse function has to be defined such that it keeps track of the quadrant. This version is often called atan$_2$ and is defined by

$$\text{atan}_2(x, y) = 2\tan^{-1}\left(\frac{y}{\sqrt{x^2 + y^2} + x}\right).$$

The result is in the range $(-\pi, \pi]$ and can be shifted to the interval $[0, 2\pi)$ by adding 2π, whenever $y < 0$.

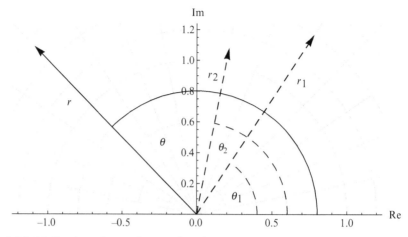

Fig. A.2 Multiplication of complex numbers in polar coordinates

Let's talk briefly about another application of the polar representation. Focus for the moment on complex numbers with modulus $|z| = 1$. Then the polar representation becomes $z = e^{i\theta}$, which is sometimes also called a pure phase. You might have learned that an n-th order polynomial has exactly n (complex) roots. Look at the polynomial equation

$$z^n - 1 = 0 \quad \Leftrightarrow \quad e^{in\theta} = 1. \tag{A.16}$$

In order for this equation to be satisfied, the exponent has to vanish. This happens at all angles θ_k, for which $n\theta$ is an integer multiple of 2π, because for $k \in \mathbb{Z}$

$$1 = e^0 = e^{i2\pi k}. \tag{A.17}$$

Quick calculation A.4 Use the *Euler*-identity to confirm (A.17).

Example A.1

Take $n = 4$ in equation (A.16). What are the roots of the polynomial?

Solution

We have four angles, $\theta_0 = 0$, $\theta_1 = \frac{\pi}{2}$, $\theta_2 = \pi$, and $\theta_3 = \frac{3\pi}{2}$, for which 4θ is an integer multiple of 2π. We have thus the four roots $z_0 = 1$, $z_1 = i$, $z_2 = -1$, and $z_3 = -i$.

Quick calculation A.5 Show that i^i is a real number. Use that i has an exponential representation.

A.2   Complex Functions and Derivatives

There are actually two kinds of complex functions, we will distinguish by a slight abuse of terminology. We will call $\gamma : \mathbb{R} \to \mathbb{C}$, with

$$\gamma(t) = x(t) + iy(t) \tag{A.18}$$

a complex valued function. There is nothing new about such an object, because $x(t)$ and $y(t)$ are real functions. We have already seen such a complex valued function. Think of the complex valued exponential,

$$\gamma(t) = \cos t + i \sin t = e^{it}. \tag{A.19}$$

A complex valued function has a derivative, if both parts $x(t)$ and $y(t)$ are differentiable. The result is

$$\gamma'(t) = x'(t) + iy'(t), \tag{A.20}$$

where we have used the prime notation to indicate the derivative with respect to the argument of the function. Everything you ever learned in calculus still holds. Let's check that on our complex valued exponential (A.19)

$$\gamma'(t) = -\sin t + i \cos t = i(\cos t + i \sin t) = ie^{it}. \tag{A.21}$$

Complex valued functions are important in parametrizing complex curves. For the moments let's keep it that way and move on to complex functions.

A genuine complex function $f : \mathbb{C} \to \mathbb{C}$ can be represented as

$$f(z) = u(x, y) + iv(x, y), \tag{A.22}$$

with real functions $u(x, y)$ and $v(x, y)$. For example the function $f(z) = z^*$ is a particularly simple complex function, with $u(x, y) = x$ and $v(x, y) = -y$. One can also have polynomials in z and all kinds of other functions.

Example A.2

Consider the real functions $u(x, y) = e^x \cos y$ and $v(x, y) = e^x \sin y$. What complex function is obtained from them?

Solution
Plugging the functions into (A.22) one obtains

$$f(z) = e^x(\cos y + i \sin y) = e^{x+iy} = e^z,$$

which is the complex exponential.

The issue of derivatives of complex functions is a little more involved than in the real case. The definition follows the familiar limit concept

$$f'(z) = \lim_{\Delta z \to 0} \frac{f(z + \Delta z) - f(z)}{\Delta z},$$ (A.23)

but now there is a large variety of directions from which we can approach that limit. To illustrate this point, take the very simple function $f(z) = z^*$. Let's try to compute the derivative by taking the limit from the real direction. In this case $\Delta z = \Delta x$ holds, and

$$\lim_{\Delta z \to 0} = \frac{(x + \Delta x - iy) - (x - iy)}{\Delta x} = \frac{\Delta x}{\Delta x} = 1.$$ (A.24)

Now take the orthogonal direction along the imaginary axis, which means $\Delta z = i\Delta y$. Then one obtains

$$\lim_{\Delta z \to 0} = \frac{(x - iy - i\Delta y) - (x - iy)}{i\Delta y} = \frac{-i\Delta y}{i\Delta y} = -1.$$ (A.25)

We have two different limits, if we approach the limit point from two different directions. Thus, we have to conclude that $f(z) = z^*$ is not differentiable. This immediately implies the need for a criterion for complex functions to have a derivative at a particular point z_0. Such a criterion exists. If the complex function $f(z)$ has continuous partial derivatives at $z_0 = x_0 + iy_0$, obeying the *Cauchy–Riemann*-equations

$$\frac{\partial u}{\partial x}(x_0, y_0) = \frac{\partial v}{\partial y}(x_0, y_0) \quad \text{and} \quad \frac{\partial u}{\partial y}(x_0, y_0) = -\frac{\partial v}{\partial x}(x_0, y_0),$$ (A.26)

then there exists a derivative $f'(z)$ at $z = z_0$.

Quick calculation A.6   Which *Cauchy–Riemann*-equation was violated for $f(z) = z^*$?

Now let's ask, what this derivative is exactly, provided it exists. To this end, calculate the total differential of the complex function $f(z_0)$ and use the *Cauchy–Riemann*-equations to obtain

$$\begin{aligned} df(z_0) &= \frac{\partial u}{\partial x}dx + \frac{\partial u}{\partial y}dy + i\frac{\partial v}{\partial x}dx + i\frac{\partial v}{\partial y}dy \\ &= \frac{\partial u}{\partial x}dx - \frac{\partial v}{\partial x}dy + i\frac{\partial v}{\partial x}dx + i\frac{\partial u}{\partial x}dy \\ &= \frac{\partial u}{\partial x}(dx + idy) + i\frac{\partial v}{\partial x}(dx + idy). \end{aligned}$$ (A.27)

Of course, we could have substituted the *Cauchy–Riemann*-equations the other way around as well. Because $dx + idy = dz$, we have

$$\begin{aligned} f'(z_0) = \frac{df(z_0)}{dz} &= \frac{\partial u}{\partial x}(x_0, y_0) + i\frac{\partial v}{\partial x}(x_0, y_0) \\ &= \frac{\partial v}{\partial y}(x_0, y_0) - i\frac{\partial u}{\partial y}(x_0, y_0). \end{aligned}$$ (A.28)

If $f(z)$ is differentiable at all points inside the open disk

$$D_r = \{z \in \mathbb{C} : |z - z_0| < r \text{ for } r > 0\}, \tag{A.29}$$

then $f(z)$ is called **analytic** (or holomorphic) at $z = z_0$. Actually, an analytic function is infinitely differentiable at $z = z_0$. If $f(z)$ is analytic at all points in $\mathbb{C}$, then it is called an **entire** function. Polynomials of arbitrary order in z are examples of entire functions. Of course this implies that the complex exponential

$$e^z = \sum_{n=0}^{\infty} c_n z^n \tag{A.30}$$

with $c_n = \frac{1}{n!}$ is also an entire function. The coefficients of complex polynomials are allowed to be complex themselves. Thus, using the coefficients $c_n = \frac{i^n}{n!}$ in the sum (A.30) proves that e^{iz} is also an entire function. Based on that insight, we can deduce that complex trigonometric functions are also entire functions, because we have for example

$$\sin z = \frac{e^{iz} - e^{-iz}}{2i}, \tag{A.31}$$

by the *Euler*-identity (A.12).

Quick calculation A.7   How is $\cos z$ represented in terms of complex exponentials?

If a complex function is differentiable, all results from real calculus still hold with the replacement $x \to z$. That includes also the product, quotient, and chain rule of differentiation.

A.3   Complex Integration

Complex integration is substantially richer than real integration. In particular there are amazing results, like Cauchy's integral formula, that have no equivalent in real analysis. But let's start modestly with complex valued functions. For a function $\gamma : \mathbb{R} \to \mathbb{C}$, the integral is defined simply by

$$\int_\alpha^\beta \gamma(t) dt = \int_\alpha^\beta x(t) dt + i \int_\alpha^\beta y(t) dt. \tag{A.32}$$

For a complex function, the situation is quite different. If $f : \mathbb{C} \to \mathbb{C}$, and a and b are complex numbers, then we have to say along which path the integral $\int_a^b f(z) dz$ has to be evaluated. Figure A.3 left illustrates the situation. Let the curve C denote the path from a to b. If we can find a smooth function $\gamma : [\alpha, \beta] \to C$, with $\gamma(\alpha) = a$ and $\gamma(\beta) = b$, then we succeeded in parametrizing the path C. All we have to do then is add up all the infinitesimal line segments, like in Figure A.3 right, to obtain

$$\int_C f(z) dz = \int_\alpha^\beta f(\gamma(t)) d\gamma(t) = \int_\alpha^\beta f(\gamma(t)) \gamma'(t) dt. \tag{A.33}$$

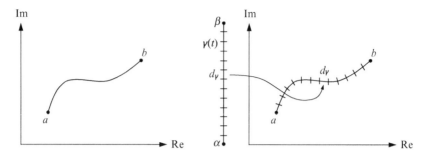

Fig. A.3 Complex integration – Curve from a to b (left) and parametrization (right)

The last equality is justified, because we assumed $\gamma(t)$ to be smooth. Let's take a look at an example.

Example A.3

Consider the complex function

$$f(z) = x - 2y^2 - ixy,$$

to be evaluated between $a = 0$ and $b = 1 + i$ along a parabolic path. The curve C is thus parametrized by

$$\gamma(t) = t + it^2,$$

with $\alpha = 0$ and $\beta = 1$. What is the value of this integral?

Solution

Using (A.33) one obtains

$$\int_C f(z)dz = \int_0^1 (t - 2t^4 - it^3)(1 + i2t)dt$$

$$= \int_0^1 tdt + i\int_0^1 2t^2 - t^3 - 4t^5 dt$$

$$= \frac{1}{2} - \frac{i}{4}.$$

Quick calculation A.8 Show that the integral equals $\frac{1}{6} - \frac{i}{2}$, when calculated along the straight line $\gamma(t) = t + it$.

Note that we have not excluded the case where $a = b$. In this case, we are dealing with a closed curve and we have to specify an orientation. Unless otherwise stated, we always assume a counterclockwise orientation.

Let's talk a little bit about antiderivatives. If $\gamma(t)$ is our usual smooth complex valued function and $F(z)$ is a complex function, differentiable at $\gamma(t)$, then we can write

$$\frac{d}{dt}F(\gamma(t)) = \frac{\partial u}{\partial x}\frac{dx}{dt} + \frac{\partial u}{\partial y}\frac{dy}{dt} + i\left(\frac{\partial v}{\partial x}\frac{dx}{dt} + \frac{\partial v}{\partial y}\frac{dy}{dt}\right). \tag{A.34}$$

Applying the *Cauchy–Riemann*-equations (A.26) on this, one obtains

$$\begin{aligned}
\frac{d}{dt}F(\gamma(t)) &= \frac{\partial u}{\partial x}\frac{dx}{dt} - \frac{\partial v}{\partial x}\frac{dy}{dt} + i\left(\frac{\partial v}{\partial x}\frac{dx}{dt} + \frac{\partial u}{\partial x}\frac{dy}{dt}\right)\\
&= \left(\frac{\partial u}{\partial x} + i\frac{\partial v}{\partial x}\right)\left(\frac{dx}{dt} + i\frac{dy}{dt}\right)\\
&= F'(\gamma(t))\gamma'(t).
\end{aligned} \tag{A.35}$$

If the complex function $f(z)$ has an antiderivative, such that $F'(z) = f(z)$, then we have for the complex integral

$$\int_\alpha^\beta f(\gamma(t))\gamma'(t)dt = \int_\alpha^\beta dF(\gamma(t)) = \int_a^b dF(z) = F(b) - F(a). \tag{A.36}$$

Every dependence on a particular path has vanished. If $f(z)$ has an antiderivative, then the complex integral is path independent. The converse is also true. Furthermore, such an integral around a closed loop $a = b$ has to be zero. But under which conditions can we expect a function to have an antiderivative? The answer to that question is provided by Cauchy's theorem.

Theorem A.1 (*Cauchy–Goursat*) *Let the complex function $f : D \to \mathbb{C}$ be analytic on the simply connected open subset $D \subseteq \mathbb{C}$. Then for any closed curve C in D,*

$$\oint_C f(z)dz = 0$$

holds.

Simply connected means in a manner of speaking that the patch $D \subseteq \mathbb{C}$ has no "holes" in it. If there are holes, then the integral along a closed curve, enclosing one or more of them, does not vanish. But if two curves C_1 and C_2 can be transformed into each other continuously, then the *Cauchy*-theorem implies that

$$\oint_{C_1} f(z)dz = \oint_{C_2} f(z)dz. \tag{A.37}$$

Two such curves C_1 and C_2 are called **homotopic**. Figure A.4 left shows three different closed curves. C_1 and C_2 are homotopic to each other but not to C_3.

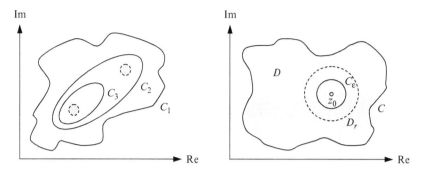

Fig. A.4 Homotopy in a region with two holes (left) and derivation of Cauchy's integral formula (right)

We can now see that Theorem A.1 is a special case of (A.37), where the curve C is homotopically contracted to a point. There is another quite remarkable theorem by Cauchy.

Theorem A.2 (Cauchy's integral formula) *Suppose a region $D \subset \mathbb{C}$ is bounded by a curve C, and the complex function $f(z)$ is analytic on and inside the boundary. Let z_0 be an interior point of D, then*

$$f(z_0) = \frac{1}{2\pi i} \oint_C \frac{f(z)}{z - z_0} dz$$

is the value of $f(z)$ at $z = z_0$.

Let's first try to understand why Theorem A.2 is true and afterwards discuss its implications. Our first step is to evaluate the integral

$$\int_C \frac{1}{z - z_0} dz \tag{A.38}$$

along a closed circle C_ε in D, centered at z_0 with radius $\varepsilon > 0$. Such a circle is parametrized by $\gamma_\varepsilon : [0, 2\pi] \to C_\varepsilon$, with

$$\gamma_\varepsilon(t) = z_0 + \varepsilon e^{it}. \tag{A.39}$$

Following the usual routine, one obtains

$$\oint_{C_\varepsilon} \frac{1}{z - z_0} dz = \int_0^{2\pi} \frac{i\varepsilon e^{it}}{\varepsilon e^{it}} dt = i \int_0^{2\pi} dt = 2\pi i. \tag{A.40}$$

Observe that the function $\frac{f(z)}{z - z_0}$ has a singularity at $z = z_0$, but it is analytic in the region between C_ε and C. Furthermore, C_ε and C are homotopic with respect to $\frac{f(z)}{z - z_0}$, because they both enclose the only singularity at $z = z_0$. We can thus manipulate Cauchy's integral formula in the following way

$$\oint_C \frac{f(z)}{z - z_0} dz - 2\pi i f(z_0) = \oint_{C_\varepsilon} \frac{f(z)}{z - z_0} dz - f(z_0) \oint_{C_\varepsilon} \frac{1}{z - z_0} dz$$
$$= \oint_{C_\varepsilon} \frac{f(z) - f(z_0)}{z - z_0} dz. \tag{A.41}$$

Again following our usual routine, we can simplify this expression by plugging in the parametrization

$$\oint_{C_\varepsilon} \frac{f(z) - f(z_0)}{z - z_0} dz = \int_0^{2\pi} \frac{f(\gamma_\varepsilon(t)) - f(z_0)}{\gamma_\varepsilon(t) - z_0} \gamma'_\varepsilon(t) dt$$
$$= i \int_0^{2\pi} f(z_0 + \varepsilon e^{it}) - f(z_0) dt. \tag{A.42}$$

Now recall that $f(z)$ is analytic at $z = z_0$, which also means that it has a *Taylor*-series, converging to the point $z \in D_r$, where D_r is the open disk with radius r, centered at z_0; see (A.29) on page 515. The whole situation is indicated in Figure A.4 right. Choosing $\varepsilon < r$, the series can be evaluated, and one obtains

$$i \int_0^{2\pi} f(z_0 + \varepsilon e^{it}) - f(z_0) dt = i \sum_{n=1}^\infty \frac{\varepsilon^n}{n!} f^{(n)}(z_0) \int_0^{2\pi} e^{int} dt$$
$$= \sum_{n=1}^\infty \frac{\varepsilon^n}{n \cdot n!} f^{(n)}(z_0)(e^{i2\pi n} - 1) = 0, \tag{A.43}$$

because $e^{i2\pi n} = 1$ for all $n \in \mathbb{N}$. Thus Theorem A.2 has to be correct. The amazing consequence of this theorem is that if you know the value of a function on the boundary of a region, then you know the value of that function at all points within the enclosed region. Think about it, the entire information contained in the region is somehow preserved on the boundary. There is really no analogue in real analysis and such a thing would be very peculiar. Imagine if the customs officer could tell exactly what is inside your suitcase, only from inspecting its exterior shell.

A.4 The Residue Theorem

If the complex function $f(z)$ is analytic at $z = z_0$, we know that for all $z \in D_r$ the *Taylor*-series

$$f(z) = \sum_{n=0}^\infty c_n(z - z_0)^n, \tag{A.44}$$

with $c_n = \frac{1}{n!} f^{(n)}(z_0)$ exists. But from Theorem A.2, we also know $f(z_0)$ for any closed curve C in D_r. Computing the n-th derivative with respect to z_0 yields

$$f^{(n)}(z_0) = \frac{n!}{2\pi i} \oint_C \frac{f(z)}{(z - z_0)^{n+1}} dz, \tag{A.45}$$

which generalizes Cauchy's integral formula. We can see now that the n-th coefficient in the *Taylor*-series (A.44) is

$$c_n = \frac{1}{2\pi i} \oint_C \frac{f(w)}{(w-z_0)^{n+1}} dw, \qquad (A.46)$$

where the name of the integration variable was changed to avoid confusion.

Quick calculation A.9 Check that (A.45) is correct.

Theorem A.3 (*Laurent*-series) *Let $f(z)$ be analytic on the annulus $A_{r,R}$, defined by*

$$A_{r,R} = \{z \in \mathbb{C} : r < |z-z_0| < R \text{ for } r \geq 0\}.$$

Then $f(z)$ can be represented by the Laurent-series

$$f(z) = \sum_{n=-\infty}^{\infty} c_n(z-z_0)^n,$$

with coefficients

$$c_n = \frac{1}{2\pi i} \oint_{C_\odot} \frac{f(w)}{(w-z_0)^{n+1}} dw,$$

for every $z \in A_{r,R}$. $C_\odot$ is any simple closed curve C in $A_{r,R}$ that encloses z_0.

Note that in Theorem A.3 neither $r = 0$, nor $R = \infty$ is excluded. Now it's time to talk about singularities and their connection to *Laurent*-series.

A singularity z_0 is called **isolated**, if there exists a disk D_r, in which $f(z)$ is analytic at all points $z \in D_r$, except for z_0. This means, there are no other singularities present in the neighborhood of z_0. One can think of other singularities that are not isolated. Consider for example the complex logarithm

$$\log z = \log|z| + i \arg z = \log r + i\theta. \qquad (A.47)$$

Obviously, this function is not unique, because of the periodicity of θ. Therefore, one defines a principal branch, separated from other branches by a **branch cut**, which is a kind of continuous singularity. For the complex logarithm, the branch cut is usually chosen along the negative real axis. It is also the reason why the integral over $\frac{1}{z}$ along the circle C_ε does not vanish; $\frac{1}{z}$ has the domain $A_{0,\infty}$ and we would expect $\log z$ to be its antiderivative, such that

$$\oint_C \frac{1}{z} dz = \int_a^b d\log z = \log b - \log a. \qquad (A.48)$$

But $\log z$ has the domain $\mathbb{C} \setminus \mathbb{R}_0^-$. Is that really a problem? Yes it is, because we can choose the initial/endpoint on a closed curve freely. If we integrate along C_ε and choose $a = b = -\varepsilon$, then we are obviously stranded. Thus, $\frac{1}{z}$ has generally no antiderivative, at least not on its entire domain, and the integral enclosing $z = 0$ does not vanish. Let's return to the more pleasant isolated singularities. Such a singularity is called

- **removable**, if the *Laurent*-series has no coefficients c_n with $n < 0$ (that is, the *Laurent*-series is in fact a *Taylor*-series),
- **pole** of order n, if the smallest nonzero coefficient of the *Laurent*-series is c_{-n},
- **essential**, if the *Laurent*-series has infinitely many coefficients c_n, with $n < 0$.

Let's look at an example to understand the different kinds of singularities better.

Example A.4

The three complex functions

$$f(z) = \frac{\sin z}{z}, \quad g(z) = \frac{1}{z^2} \quad \text{and} \quad h(z) = e^{\frac{1}{z}}$$

all have isolated singularities at $z = 0$. What particular kind of singularity is present?

Solution

The singularity in $f(z)$ is removable, because the expansion

$$f(z) = \frac{1}{z} \sum_{n=0}^{\infty} \frac{(-1)^n}{(2n+1)!} z^{2n+1} = \sum_{n=0}^{\infty} \frac{(-1)^n}{(2n+1)!} z^{2n}$$

is a *Taylor*-series. $g(z)$ is already a *Laurent*-series with only one nonzero coefficient,

$$c_{-2} = 1.$$

Thus, the singularity is a second order pole. Expanding $h(z)$ into a power series yields

$$h(z) = \sum_{n=0}^{\infty} \frac{1}{n!} z^{-n} = \sum_{n=-\infty}^{0} \frac{1}{(-n)!} z^n.$$

Hence, the *Laurent*-series has infinitely many nonzero coefficients c_{-n} and the singularity is essential.

The residue of a complex function $f(z)$ at $z = z_0$ is the first negative coefficient of the *Laurent*-series of $f(z)$,

$$\operatorname*{Res}_{z=z_0} f = c_{-1}. \tag{A.49}$$

You might wonder what is so special about this coefficient that it deserves its own name. Suppose z_0 is an isolated singularity of $f(z)$, and $A_{0,R}$ is the domain of the *Laurent*-series of $f(z)$ at $z = z_0$, for some $R > 0$. Then we have the surprising result

$$\oint_{C_\circ} f(z)dz = \oint_{C_\circ} \sum_{n=-\infty}^{\infty} c_n(z-z_0)^n dz = \sum_{n=-\infty}^{\infty} c_n \oint_{C_\circ} (z-z_0)^n dz = 2\pi i c_{-1}. \tag{A.50}$$

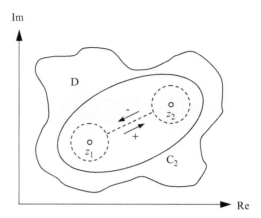

Fig. A.5 Residue theorem – C_2 is homotopic to curves around the singularities and traverse paths

That looks like a miracle. Let's see what has happened. For all $n \geq 0$ the function $(z - z_0)^n$ is simply a polynomial. Polynomials are entire functions and thus, the integral has to vanish by Cauchy's theorem. For $n \leq -2$, $(z - z_0)^n$ has an antiderivative on $A_{0,\infty}$, and thus the integral along the closed curve $C_\ominus$ has to be zero. The only integral left is the one over $(z - z_0)^{-1}$. But we already calculated this integral in (A.40) to be $2\pi i$.

In certain cases there are more pleasant ways to calculate the residue than by computing the magic coefficient of the *Laurent*-series. We will come back to that issue later. For the moment, let's state the residue theorem.

Theorem A.4 (Cauchy's residue theorem) *Let $D \subseteq \mathbb{C}$ be a simply connected region and $f(z)$ be analytic on D, except for finitely many isolated singularities $z = z_k$. If C_K is a simple closed curve in $D \setminus \{z_k\}$, enclosing precisely K singularities, then*

$$\oint_{C_K} f(z)dz = 2\pi i \sum_{k=1}^{K} \operatorname*{Res}_{z=z_k} f$$

holds.

In understanding the sum on the right hand side, we have to contemplate on the meaning of the term simple closed curve. By that we mean a closed loop that is not twisted, and has our usual counterclockwise orientation. Take the case where $K = 2$ and look at Figure A.5. The curve C_2 is homotopic to the dashed dumbbell-shaped curve around the two singularities with the traversing connection in both directions. We can move these traverse parts of the curve as close together as we like. But the path integral contribution from the segment connecting the circles around z_1 and z_2 is canceled exactly by the contribution from the segment joining the circles around z_2 and z_1, because the direction and hence the sign is exactly opposite. Orientation counts. The residue theorem generalizes the initial integral theorem A.1 by Cauchy. In the case $K = 0$, there is no singularity and the integral along C_0 is zero.

Poles are a very common type of singularity, and they permit an easy computation of the residue. Recall that if a function $f(z)$ has a pole of degree n at $z = z_0$, then the coefficient c_{-n} is the smallest nonzero coefficient in the *Laurent*-series of $f(z)$. In this situation, we can just as well define a new function

$$g(z) = (z - z_0)^n f(z) = \sum_{k=0}^{\infty} c_{k-n}(z - z_0)^k. \tag{A.51}$$

But (A.51) is obviously a *Taylor*-series, and we know what the coefficients are. In fact, we can immediately read off that for $k = n - 1$, the residue

$$\operatorname*{Res}_{z=z_0} f = c_{-1} = \frac{g^{(n-1)}(z_0)}{(n-1)!} \tag{A.52}$$

is obtained. This is a very straightforward recipe for computing the residue. Let's look at a final example.

Example A.5

Consider the complex function

$$f(z) = \frac{e^z}{z^2(z^2 + 1)}.$$

What are the residues?

Solution

First of all, $f(z)$ has three isolated singularities at $z = 0$ and at $z = \pm i$. The latter is easy to see by expanding the second factor in the denominator into $z^2 + 1 = (z + i)(z - i)$. All three are poles, because we can specify a function $g_k(z)$ that has no singularity at $z = z_k$. Let's start with the pole $z_1 = 0$. This one is second order, because the function

$$g_1(z) = z^2 f(z) = \frac{e^z}{z^2 + 1}$$

is well defined at $z = 0$. Because the pole is second order, the residue involves the first order derivative

$$g_1'(z) = \frac{(z^2 + 1)e^z - 2ze^z}{(z^2 + 1)^2}.$$

The residue of $f(z)$ at $z = 0$ is thus

$$\operatorname*{Res}_{z=0} f = g_1'(0) = 1.$$

In the next step, compute the residue at the pole $z_2 = i$. This one is first order and one obtains

$$g_2(z) = (z - i)f(z) = \frac{e^z}{z^2(z + i)},$$

which is well defined at $z = i$. In fact, because the pole is first order, the residue involves the function itself,

$$\operatorname*{Res}_{z=i} f = g_2(i) = -\frac{e^i}{2i}.$$

The residue at the third pole $z_3 = -i$ is computed in exact analogy to the former and one obtains

$$\operatorname*{Res}_{z=-i} f = g_3(-i) = \frac{e^{-i}}{2i}.$$

Quick calculation A.10   Verify that integrating the complex function of Example A.5 along a simple closed curve C_3, enclosing all three singularities, yields $\oint_{C_3} f(z)dz = 2\pi i(1 - \sin 1)$.

Solutions to Problems

B.1   Solutions to Problems in Chapter 2

Problem 2.1

The obvious choice for the sample space is $\Omega = \{1, 2, 3\}$. Because Ω is finite, a suitable σ-algebra is the power set

$$\mathcal{F} = \{\emptyset, \{1\}, \{2\}, \{3\}, \{1, 2\}, \{1, 3\}, \{2, 3\}, \Omega\}.$$

Because the wheel is fair, the probabilities assigned to the elementary events are

$$P(\{\omega\}) = \begin{cases} \frac{1}{4} & \text{for } \omega \leq 2 \\ \frac{1}{2} & \text{for } \omega = 3. \end{cases}$$

Because all elementary events are distinct, the probability of an arbitrary event $A \in \mathcal{F}$ is

$$P(A) = \sum_{a=1}^{\#A} P(\{\omega_a\}).$$

The triplet $(\Omega, \mathcal{F}, P)$ is thus the required probability space.

Problem 2.2

The natural filtration after one turn with outcome $A = \{2\}$ is

$$\mathcal{F}_1 = \{\emptyset, \{2\}, \{1, 3\}, \Omega\},$$

which is obviously smaller than $\mathcal{F} = 2^\Omega$. Remember that $\mathcal{F}_1$ is the smallest possible σ-algebra containing the observed event A.

Problem 2.3

Choose the sample space $\Omega = \{\omega_1, \ldots, \omega_6\}$ and $X(\omega_n) = n$. First consider the unconditional expectation value

$$E[X] = \sum_{n=1}^{6} n f(n) = \frac{1}{6} \sum_{n=1}^{6} n = \frac{7}{2}.$$

This result was obtained by using the unconditional probability mass function for the fair die, which equals $f(n) = P(X = n) = \frac{1}{6}$ for $n = 1, \ldots, 6$. Next, consider the probability mass function conditioned on event A of throwing an even number

$$f(n|A) = P(X = n|A) = \frac{P(\{\omega_n\} \cap A)}{P(A)} = \begin{cases} \frac{1}{3} & \text{for } n \text{ even,} \\ 0 & \text{for } n \text{ odd.} \end{cases}$$

Computing the conditional expectation yields

$$E[X|A] = \sum_{n=1}^{6} nf(n|A) = \frac{1}{3}\sum_{k=1}^{3} 2k + 0\sum_{k=1}^{3}(2k-1) = 4,$$

which is clearly greater than the unconditional expectation.

Problem 2.4

Again choose the same setup as in the solution to Problem 2.3 and realize that the probability mass function of X, conditional on A^C is

$$f(n|A^C) = \begin{cases} 0 & \text{for } n \text{ even,} \\ \frac{1}{3} & \text{for } n \text{ odd.} \end{cases}$$

An analogous calculation yields the conditional expectation

$$E[X|A^C] = \sum_{n=1}^{6} nf(n|A^C) = 3.$$

Therefore, the unconditional expectation has to equal

$$E[E[X|A]] = E[X|A]P(A) + E[X|A^C]P(A^C) = \frac{1}{2}(4+3) = \frac{7}{2},$$

which is of course true.

Problem 2.5

Recall that the increments of the *Wiener*-process are normally distributed, $W_{t-s} \sim N(0, t-s)$. Further, use the moment structure (2.31) of normally distributed random variables to express the fourth moment of the *Wiener*-increment

$$M_4 = E[(W(t) - W(s))^4] = 3(t-s)^2.$$

Observe that the numbers $a = 4$, $b = 1$, and $c = 3$ satisfy the required condition. Thus the *Wiener*-process has continuous paths with probability one.

Problem 2.6

Let $g(x)$ be the unknown probability mass/density function of X and condition on N,

$$g(x) = \sum_{N=0}^{\infty} g(x|N)f(N).$$

We do not know the conditional distribution any more than the unconditional one, but for the conditional characteristic function of X,

$$E[e^{iuX}|N] = \varphi_n^N(u)$$

has to hold, because all X_n are independent and identically distributed. Putting the pieces together we obtain

$$\varphi(u) = E[e^{iuX}] = \sum_{N=0}^{\infty} E[e^{iuX}|N]f(N)$$

$$= e^{-\lambda} \sum_{N=0}^{\infty} \varphi_n^N(u)\frac{\lambda^N}{N!} = e^{-\lambda} \sum_{N=0}^{\infty} \frac{(\lambda\varphi_n(u))^N}{N!}$$

$$= e^{-\lambda + \lambda\varphi_n(u)},$$

which is already the desired result. In the final step we used the *Taylor*-series expansion of the exponential $e^x = \sum_{k=0}^{\infty} \frac{x^k}{k!}$.

B.2 Solutions to Problems in Chapter 3

Problem 3.1
Using the universal identity $\cosh^2 \phi - \sinh^2 \phi = 1$, one obtains the new coordinates as functions of the old ones

$$\rho = \sqrt{a_1^2 - a_2^2} \quad \text{and} \quad \phi = \tanh^{-1}\left(\frac{a_2}{a_1}\right).$$

The first coordinate is obtained by subtracting the square of a_2 from the square of a_1, the second one by dividing a_2 by a_1. It is now obvious how scaling affects the hyperbolic coordinates

$$\alpha|a\rangle = \begin{pmatrix} \alpha\, a_1 \\ \alpha\, a_2 \end{pmatrix} = \begin{pmatrix} \alpha\rho \\ \phi \end{pmatrix}.$$

Problem 3.2
With the definition of the identity operator $I|a\rangle = |a\rangle$ we can build the following chain:

$$\sum_{n=1}^{N} |e_n\rangle\langle e_n|a\rangle = \sum_{n=1}^{N} a_n|e_n\rangle = |a\rangle.$$

Hence, we can conclude that

$$\sum_{n=1}^{N} |e_n\rangle\langle e_n| = I.$$

Problem 3.3
The claim follows immediately from the coordinate representation of an arbitrary matrix $M \in \mathbb{R}^{2\times2}$,

$$M = \begin{pmatrix} m_{11} & m_{12} \\ m_{21} & m_{22} \end{pmatrix} = m_{11}\begin{pmatrix} 1 & 0 \\ 0 & 0 \end{pmatrix} + m_{12}\begin{pmatrix} 0 & 1 \\ 0 & 0 \end{pmatrix} + m_{21}\begin{pmatrix} 0 & 0 \\ 1 & 0 \end{pmatrix} + m_{22}\begin{pmatrix} 0 & 0 \\ 0 & 1 \end{pmatrix}$$

$$= \sum_{k=1}^{2}\sum_{n=1}^{2} m_{kn}|e_k\rangle\langle e_n|.$$

Problem 3.4

The first thing to do is to calculate the inner product:

$$\langle \psi_k | \psi_n \rangle = \frac{1}{2\pi} \int_0^{2\pi} e^{-ikx} e^{inx} dx = \frac{1}{2\pi} \int_0^{2\pi} e^{ix(n-k)} dx$$

$$= \frac{e^{ix(n-k)}}{i2\pi(n-k)} \bigg|_0^{2\pi} = \frac{e^{i2\pi(n-k)} - 1}{i2\pi(n-k)}.$$

It is not that bad. Let's call the integer $n - k = \Delta$ and apply Euler's formula to the complex exponential

$$\frac{\cos(2\pi\Delta) + i\sin(2\pi\Delta) - 1}{i2\pi\Delta} = \frac{\sin(2\pi\Delta)}{2\pi\Delta}.$$

We have used here that $\cos(2\pi\Delta) = 1$ for every integer Δ. We are nearly done. Note that the result on the right hand side is zero for all $\Delta \neq 0$, because $\sin(2\pi\Delta) = 0$ for all integers. That takes care of orthogonality. The only slight difficulty emerges for $\Delta = 0$, because numerator and denominator become zero. But in this case, we can use l'Hôpital's rule to obtain

$$\lim_{\Delta \to 0} \frac{\sin(2\pi\Delta)}{2\pi\Delta} = \lim_{\Delta \to 0} \frac{2\pi\cos(2\pi\Delta)}{2\pi} = 1.$$

Thus, we have proved orthonormality of the *Fourier*-functions.

Problem 3.5

Use the eigenvalue decomposition and the permutation-property of the trace:

$$\text{tr}[M] = \text{tr}[V\Lambda V^{-1}] = \text{tr}[\Lambda V^{-1} V] = \text{tr}[\Lambda] = \sum_{n=1}^{N} \lambda_n.$$

Problem 3.6

First observe that the exponential of a diagonal matrix is a diagonal matrix of exponentials,

$$e^\Lambda = \sum_{k=0}^{\infty} \frac{\Lambda^k}{k!} = \sum_{k=0}^{\infty} \begin{pmatrix} \frac{\lambda_1^k}{k!} & \cdots & 0 \\ \vdots & \ddots & \vdots \\ 0 & \cdots & \frac{\lambda_N^k}{k!} \end{pmatrix} = \begin{pmatrix} \sum_{k=0}^{\infty} \frac{\lambda_1^k}{k!} & \cdots & 0 \\ \vdots & \ddots & \vdots \\ 0 & \cdots & \sum_{k=0}^{\infty} \frac{\lambda_N^k}{k!} \end{pmatrix} = \begin{pmatrix} e^{\lambda_1} & \cdots & 0 \\ \vdots & \ddots & \vdots \\ 0 & \cdots & e^{\lambda_N} \end{pmatrix}.$$

Next, expand the original matrix in a *Taylor*-series and use the eigenvalue decomposition,

$$e^M = \sum_{k=0}^{\infty} \frac{M^k}{k!} = I + M + \frac{1}{2} M^2 + \frac{1}{6} M^3 + \cdots$$

$$= I + V\Lambda V^{-1} + \frac{1}{2} V\Lambda V^{-1} V\Lambda V^{-1} + \frac{1}{6} V\Lambda V^{-1} V\Lambda V^{-1} V\Lambda V^{-1} + \cdots$$

$$= VV^{-1} + V\Lambda V^{-1} + \frac{1}{2} V\Lambda^2 V^{-1} + \frac{1}{6} V\Lambda^3 V^{-1} + \cdots$$

$$= V \sum_{k=0}^{\infty} \frac{\Lambda^k}{k!} V^{-1} = Ve^\Lambda V^{-1}.$$

This concludes the proof.

Problem 3.7

Minimizing $F = \langle \epsilon | \epsilon \rangle$ is a convex optimization problem and thus all we have to do is to calculate the derivative and set it equal to zero,

$$\frac{\delta F}{\delta \langle \beta |} = -2X'(|y\rangle - X|\beta\rangle) \stackrel{!}{=} 0.$$

Note that $-X'$ is the chain rule term from differentiating with respect to $\langle \beta |$. Slightly rearranging yields

$$X'X|\beta\rangle = X'|y\rangle \,\big|\, \rightarrow \cdot (X'X)^{-1} \quad \Leftrightarrow \quad |\beta\rangle = (X'X)^{-1}X'|y\rangle,$$

which is the desired estimator. We have implicitly assumed that $X'X$ is invertible. This is the case, as long as there are at least as many observations as parameters to be estimated. In other words, X is not allowed to have more columns than rows.

Problem 3.8

The variance of Y is obtained by carrying out the matrix/vector multiplication

$$\mathrm{Var}[\,Y\,] = \langle 1 | \Sigma | 1 \rangle = \sigma_1^2 + 2\sigma_{12} + \sigma_2^2.$$

This corresponds to the variance of a sum of not necessarily uncorrelated random variables

$$\mathrm{Var}[X_1 + X_2] = \mathrm{Var}[X_1] + 2\mathrm{Cov}[X_1, X_2] + \mathrm{Var}[X_2].$$

B.3   Solutions to Problems in Chapter 4

Problem 4.1

Because each coin flip is independent of the previous one, the probabilities multiply. Therefore, the probability for the first heads in the n-th toss is $p_n = p \cdot (1 - p)^{n-1}$. For a fair coin we have $p = \frac{1}{2}$ and thus, the probability is $p_n = \left(\frac{1}{2}\right)^n$. The expectation value is the sum of all possible gains, weighted with their probabilities

$$E[W] = \sum_{n=1}^{\infty} w_n p_n = \sum_{n=1}^{\infty} 2^{n-1} \frac{1}{2^n} = \frac{1}{2} \sum_{n=1}^{\infty} 1 = \infty.$$

Problem 4.2

Calculate the expected utility of the St. Petersburg game

$$E[u(W)] = \sum_{n=1}^{\infty} \log(2^{n-1}) \frac{1}{2^n} = \log 2 \sum_{n=1}^{\infty} \frac{n-1}{2^n} = \log 2 \cdot \frac{1}{2} \sum_{n=0}^{\infty} \frac{n}{2^n} = \log 2.$$

It is immediately obvious that $w^* = \$2$.

Problem 4.3

Look at the possible outcomes. If the loss event occurs, your wealth is $w - l$, but you might have insured a fraction of your wealth at a price of $p\eta$, and now you are entitled to an indemnity η. That makes it $w - l + (1 - p)\eta$. If the loss event does not occur, you still have $w - p\eta$, because you nevertheless had to pay the insurance premium. So the expected utility functional is

$$U[L] = p \cdot u(w - l + (1 - p)\eta) + (1 - p) \cdot u(w - p\eta).$$

The next step is to differentiate with respect to η

$$\frac{\partial U}{\partial \eta} = p(1 - p) \cdot u'(w - l + (1 - p)\eta) - p(1 - p) \cdot u'(w - p\eta) \stackrel{!}{=} 0,$$

and after equating to zero, one obtains

$$u'(w - l + (1 - p)\eta^*) = u'(w - p\eta^*).$$

Because of risk aversion, the second derivative of u is negative. That means u' is strictly monotonic decreasing and $u'(w_1) = u'(w_2)$ can only be true, if $w_1 = w_2$. Equating the arguments and rearranging yields

$$\eta^* = l.$$

You would insure only the loss fraction of your wealth at an actuarial fair price. Observe that this statement is very strong, because it is independent of your individual utility function.

Problem 4.4
Recall that the central moment of a probability distribution is defined as

$$M_k = E[(W - E[W])^k].$$

Taylor-expanding Bell's risk aversion term yields

$$E\left[e^{-a(W - E[W])}\right] = 1 - aE[W - E[W]] + \frac{1}{2}a^2 E[(W - E[W])^2] - \cdots$$

$$= 1 + \sum_{k=2}^{\infty} \frac{(-a)^k}{k!} M_k.$$

The first central moment of course vanishes.

Problem 4.5
Rewrite the HARA-utility as exponential and *Taylor*-expand,

$$u(w) = \frac{e^{(1-\gamma)\log w} - 1}{1 - \gamma} = \frac{1 + (1 - \gamma)\log w + \frac{1}{2}(1 - \gamma)^2 \log^2 w + \cdots - 1}{1 - \gamma}.$$

Now do the cancelations and take the limit,

$$\lim_{\gamma \to 1} u(w) = \lim_{\gamma \to 1} \log w + \frac{1}{2}(1 - \gamma)\log^2 w + \cdots = \log w.$$

Problem 4.6

First, compute expected utility in terms of μ and σ^2,

$$
\begin{aligned}
U[L] &= -E[(\eta - W)^2] = -E[(\eta - \mu - W + \mu)^2] \\
&= -E[(\eta - \mu)^2] + 2E[(\eta - \mu)(W - \mu)] - E[(W - \mu)^2] \\
&= -(\eta - \mu)^2 - \sigma^2.
\end{aligned}
$$

Now, for $\mu < \eta$ one obtains

$$
\frac{\partial U}{\partial \mu} = 2(\eta - \mu) > 0 \quad \text{and} \quad \frac{\partial U}{\partial \sigma^2} = -1 < 0.
$$

Problem 4.7

The first order conditions with respect to c_1 and c_2 are

$$
\frac{\partial \mathcal{L}}{\partial c_1} = \frac{1}{2}\sqrt{\frac{c_2}{c_1}} - \lambda \overset{!}{=} 0 \quad \text{and} \quad \frac{\partial \mathcal{L}}{\partial c_2} = \frac{1}{2}\sqrt{\frac{c_1}{c_2}} - 2\lambda \overset{!}{=} 0.
$$

Solving for λ yields the necessary quantity relation $c_2^* = \frac{1}{2}c_1^*$. The remaining first order condition

$$
\frac{\partial \mathcal{L}}{\partial \lambda} = w - c_1 - 2c_2 \overset{!}{=} 0
$$

reproduces the budget constraint and using the quantity relation one obtains $c_1^* = \frac{w}{2}$ and $c_2^* = \frac{w}{4}$. Plugging this result into the utility function yields

$$
u(c_1^*, c_2^*) = \sqrt{\frac{w}{2} \cdot \frac{w}{4}} = \frac{w}{\sqrt{8}},
$$

which is the desired result.

B.4   Solutions to Problems in Chapter 5

Problem 5.1

In an arbitrage free market, the price of an arbitrary security is given by

$$
s_n = \langle \psi | d_n \rangle = \sum_{\omega=1}^{\Omega} \psi_\omega d_{\omega n}.
$$

From the first order conditions, we have

$$
\psi_\omega = \frac{\partial U / \partial c_\omega}{\partial U / \partial c_0} = e^{-\rho T} p_\omega \frac{u'(c_\omega)}{u'(c_0)}.
$$

Thus, the fair price can be written as

$$
s_n = \sum_{\omega=1}^{\Omega} e^{-\rho T} \frac{u'(c_\omega)}{u'(c_0)} d_{\omega n} p_\omega = E[M d_n],
$$

which is the desired expectation with respect to the product of d_n with the stochastic discount factor M.

Problem 5.2
This one is obvious. Using the SDF-representation one obtains

$$\frac{1}{1+r} = \langle \psi | 1 \rangle = E[M \cdot 1] = E[M].$$

Problem 5.3
From Problem 5.1 we have the SDF-representation

$$s_n = E[Md_n].$$

With help of the covariance formula, this can be expanded into

$$s_n = E[M]E[d_n] + \text{Cov}[M, d_n] = \frac{1}{1+r}E[d_n] + \text{Cov}[M, d_n],$$

where we have used the statement to be verified in Problem 5.2.

Problem 5.4
The first and second payoff vector are linearly independent. Thus, the market is complete. Call the cyclical permutations of $\langle s |$

$$\langle s_1 | = \begin{pmatrix} 1 & 2 & 3 \end{pmatrix}, \quad \langle s_2 | = \begin{pmatrix} 2 & 3 & 1 \end{pmatrix}, \quad \text{and} \quad \langle s_3 | = \begin{pmatrix} 3 & 1 & 2 \end{pmatrix}.$$

We have to check each state price form $\langle \psi_k |$, induced by

$$\langle \psi_k | = \langle s_k | D'(DD')^{-1},$$

for $k = 1, 2, 3$ separately. To this end, first calculate the D-products, because they do not depend on k:

$$DD' = \begin{pmatrix} 1 & 2 & 3 \\ 1 & 1 & 4 \end{pmatrix} \begin{pmatrix} 1 & 1 \\ 2 & 1 \\ 3 & 4 \end{pmatrix} = \begin{pmatrix} 14 & 15 \\ 15 & 18 \end{pmatrix}$$

$$(DD')^{-1} = \frac{1}{14 \cdot 18 - 15^2} \begin{pmatrix} 18 & -15 \\ -15 & 14 \end{pmatrix} = \frac{1}{27} \begin{pmatrix} 18 & -15 \\ -15 & 14 \end{pmatrix}$$

$$D'(DD')^{-1} = \frac{1}{27} \begin{pmatrix} 1 & 1 \\ 2 & 1 \\ 3 & 4 \end{pmatrix} \begin{pmatrix} 18 & -15 \\ -15 & 14 \end{pmatrix} = \frac{1}{27} \begin{pmatrix} 3 & -1 \\ 21 & -16 \\ -6 & 11 \end{pmatrix}.$$

Now calculate the state price forms $\langle \psi_k |$,

$$\langle \psi_1 | = \frac{1}{27} \begin{pmatrix} 1 & 2 & 3 \end{pmatrix} \begin{pmatrix} 3 & -1 \\ 21 & -16 \\ -6 & 11 \end{pmatrix} = \begin{pmatrix} 1 & 0 \end{pmatrix}$$

$$\langle \psi_2 | = \frac{1}{27} \begin{pmatrix} 2 & 3 & 1 \end{pmatrix} \begin{pmatrix} 3 & -1 \\ 21 & -16 \\ -6 & 11 \end{pmatrix} = \begin{pmatrix} \frac{7}{3} & -\frac{13}{9} \end{pmatrix}$$

$$\langle \psi_3 | = \frac{1}{27} \begin{pmatrix} 3 & 1 & 2 \end{pmatrix} \begin{pmatrix} 3 & -1 \\ 21 & -16 \\ -6 & 11 \end{pmatrix} = \begin{pmatrix} \frac{2}{3} & \frac{1}{9} \end{pmatrix}.$$

The state price form has to be strictly positive in order to prevent arbitrage opportunities. Therefore, only $\langle\psi_3|$ is a valid candidate. It remains to check whether or not it solves the original problem (5.12),

$$\langle\psi_3|D = \left(\tfrac{2}{3}\ \tfrac{1}{9}\right)\begin{pmatrix}1 & 2 & 3\\ 1 & 1 & 4\end{pmatrix} = \left(\tfrac{7}{9}\ \tfrac{13}{9}\ \tfrac{22}{9}\right) \neq \langle s_3|.$$

Thus, no cyclical permutation of the security price form $\langle s|$ determines an arbitrage free market.

Problem 5.5

In order to compute the risk-neutral probability measure, you can always first compute the state price form and subsequently extract the qs. However, there is a smarter way to do it. We know that the relation

$$S_0 = \frac{1}{1+r} E^Q[S_1]$$

has to hold. This equation can be written in its concrete form, to determine the risk-neutral probability q,

$$10 = \frac{4}{5}(15 \cdot q + 5 \cdot (1-q)) = \frac{4}{5}(10q + 5) = 8q + 4.$$

It is immediately obvious that $q = \tfrac{3}{4}$ solves the equation, that is $1 - q = \tfrac{1}{4}$. We can now use the power of the equivalent martingale approach to compute

$$C_0 = \frac{1}{1+r} E^Q[C_1] = \frac{4}{5}\left(2 \cdot \frac{3}{4} + 0 \cdot \frac{1}{4}\right) = \frac{6}{5}.$$

Problem 5.6

First recognize that the state dependent payoff of the call option is

$$C_1(\omega) = \begin{cases} 2 & \text{if } \omega = \uparrow \\ 0 & \text{if } \omega = \downarrow. \end{cases}$$

Hence, the payoff of the whole portfolio has to be

$$\Pi_1(\omega) = \begin{cases} 3 - 2 = 1 & \text{if } \omega = \uparrow \\ 1 - 0 = 1 & \text{if } \omega = \downarrow. \end{cases}$$

But this is a perfect replication of a zero-coupon bond. Because there are no arbitrage opportunities, we can conclude that the price of this replicating portfolio has to equal the price of a zero-coupon bond at all times. We therefore have

$$\Pi_0 = \frac{1}{1+r}.$$

Now, making the last equation concrete,

$$\frac{4}{5} = \frac{1}{5} \cdot 10 - C_0 = 2 - C_0,$$

we see that $C_0 = \frac{6}{5}$ solves the equation. But this is exactly the same result as in Problem 5.5. This is no coincidence; we have just seen the duality of replication and equivalent martingale measures at work.

B.5   Solutions to Problems in Chapter 6

Problem 6.1

The solution is trivial, if you consider saving as an investment with risk-free return $r = 0$. Equation (6.65) immediately yields the desired result. You can however proceed in the standard way and locate an arbitrary portfolio on the capital market line by

$$U_1[R_0] = w_0 \cdot 0 + \langle \mu | w \rangle - \frac{1}{2} \langle w | \Sigma | w \rangle,$$

and use $w_0 = 1 - \langle 1 | w \rangle$. The first order condition of this problem is

$$\frac{\delta U_1}{\delta \langle w |} = |\mu\rangle - \Sigma |w\rangle \overset{!}{=} |0\rangle.$$

Solving this equation and considering the normalization condition for $w_0 = 0$ in the second step, provides the answer

$$|w_{MP}\rangle = \frac{\Sigma^{-1}|\mu\rangle}{\langle 1 | \Sigma^{-1} | \mu \rangle}.$$

Problem 6.2

The simplified *von Neumann–Morgenstern*-utility functional for $\alpha = 1$ is

$$U_1[R_P] = (1 - \lambda) \cdot 0 + \lambda \mu_{MP} - \frac{1}{2}\lambda^2 \sigma_{MP}^2.$$

This is easily maximized with respect to λ and one obtains

$$\lambda^* = \frac{\mu_{MP}}{\sigma_{MP}^2}.$$

For λ^* to become one, the expected return on the market portfolio has to be $\mu_{MP} = \sigma_{MP}^2$. Once again, this result could have been obtained from (6.70), for $r = 0$ and $\alpha = 1$.

Problem 6.3

The situation is illustrated in Figure B.1. There is no longer a unique market portfolio. As long as the agent holds a fraction of the riskless security, she will combine it with tangential portfolio TP$_1$. If her risk aversion decreases, she moves onto the efficient frontier between TP$_1$ and TP$_2$. If her risk aversion decreases even more, she sells the riskless security short, paying a rate r^b, and buys more of TP$_2$. Thus, the capital market line becomes a curve that has a nonlinear segment between the two tangential portfolios.

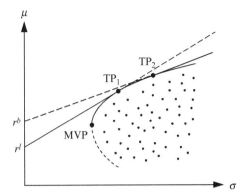

Fig. B.1 Different risk-free rates of return for borrowing and lending – Capital market curve and tangential portfolios

Problem 6.4

The expected return and standard deviation of the portfolio, the agent holds is

$$\mu_P = (1 - \lambda)r + \lambda\mu_{MP} \quad \text{and} \quad \sigma_P = \lambda\sigma_{MP}.$$

Next, consider what it means that she is willing to accept a nominal loss with 2.5% probability. Formally we can write this statement as

$$P(R_P \leq 0) = 2.5\%.$$

But from the symmetry of normal distributions around the mean, we also know that

$$P(R_P \leq \mu_P - 2\sigma_P) = 2.5\%.$$

Hence, we can identify terms and obtain an equation in λ,

$$0 = (1 - \lambda)r + \lambda\mu_{MP} - 2\lambda\sigma_{MP},$$

which is easily solved. One obtains the desired proportion

$$\lambda = \frac{r}{2\sigma_{MP} - (\mu_{MP} - r)}.$$

Problem 6.5

The first thing to recognize is that both funds are uncorrelated. That simplifies matters substantially. We have

$$\Sigma = \begin{pmatrix} \sigma_B^2 & 0 \\ 0 & \sigma_S^2 \end{pmatrix} \quad \Rightarrow \quad \Sigma^{-1} = \begin{pmatrix} \frac{1}{\sigma_B^2} & 0 \\ 0 & \frac{1}{\sigma_S^2} \end{pmatrix}.$$

The next step is to calculate the vector of not normalized weights

$$|w^*\rangle = \begin{pmatrix} \frac{1}{\sigma_B^2} & 0 \\ 0 & \frac{1}{\sigma_S^2} \end{pmatrix}\begin{pmatrix} \mu_B - r \\ \mu_S - r \end{pmatrix} = \begin{pmatrix} \frac{\mu_B - r}{\sigma_B^2} \\ \frac{\mu_S - r}{\sigma_S^2} \end{pmatrix}.$$

Now calculate the normalizing factor

$$\langle 1 | w^* \rangle = \frac{\mu_B - r}{\sigma_B^2} + \frac{\mu_S - r}{\sigma_S^2} = \frac{\sigma_S^2(\mu_B - r) + \sigma_B^2(\mu_S - r)}{\sigma_B^2 \sigma_S^2}.$$

Putting all the pieces together, one obtains the MP-weights

$$w_B^* = \frac{\sigma_S^2(\mu_B - r)}{\sigma_S^2(\mu_B - r) + \sigma_B^2(\mu_S - r)} \quad \text{and} \quad w_S^* = \frac{\sigma_B^2(\mu_S - r)}{\sigma_S^2(\mu_B - r) + \sigma_B^2(\mu_S - r)}.$$

B.6 Solutions to Problems in Chapter 7

Problem 7.1

Iterating $\hat{\beta}_k$ backwards in time, one obtains

$$\hat{\beta}_k = \frac{1}{3}\hat{\beta}_{k-1} + \frac{2}{3}$$

$$= \left(\frac{1}{3}\right)^2 \hat{\beta}_{k-2} + \frac{2}{3}\left(1 + \frac{1}{3}\right)$$

$$= \left(\frac{1}{3}\right)^k \hat{\beta}_0 + \frac{2}{3}\sum_{n=0}^{k-1}\left(\frac{1}{3}\right)^n.$$

Using the geometric series representation, the summation term can be written as

$$\frac{2}{3}\sum_{n=0}^{k-1}\left(\frac{1}{3}\right)^n = \frac{2}{3} \cdot \frac{1 - \left(\frac{1}{3}\right)^k}{1 - \frac{1}{3}} = 1 - \left(\frac{1}{3}\right)^k.$$

Combining both expressions, one obtains

$$\hat{\beta}_k = 1 + \left(\frac{1}{3}\right)^k (\hat{\beta}_0 - 1),$$

which is the desired result.

Problem 7.2

To calculate the half life of the deviation of $\hat{\beta}_0$ from $\beta_{MP} = 1$, make the following ansatz

$$(\hat{\beta}_k - 1) = \frac{1}{2}(\hat{\beta}_0 - 1).$$

Plugging in the solution to Problem 7.1, one obtains

$$\left(\frac{1}{3}\right)^k = \frac{1}{2}.$$

A few simple algebraic manipulations yield

$$k = \frac{\log 2}{\log 3}.$$

Problem 7.3

In order to synchronize monthly and yearly periods, the half life of the β-deviation has to coincide. In complete analogy to Problem 7.1, one obtains for the general model

$$\hat{\beta}_k = 1 + \lambda^k(\hat{\beta}_0 - 1).$$

The half life in the general case is

$$k = -\frac{\log 2}{\log \lambda}.$$

In order to preserve the term structure of the yearly model, the condition

$$-\frac{\log 2}{\log \lambda} = 12\frac{\log 2}{\log 3}$$

has to hold. Solving for λ, one obtains

$$\lambda = \sqrt[12]{\frac{1}{3}}.$$

Problem 7.4

Use the representation (7.44) on page 131

$$|\hat{\beta}\rangle = |\beta\rangle + (X'X)^{-1}X'|\epsilon\rangle,$$

and condition on the σ-algebra $\mathcal{R}_T$, generated by the historical realizations x_t up to time T. The variance decomposition then yields

$$\begin{aligned}\text{Var}[|\hat{\beta}\rangle] &= \text{Var}[|\beta\rangle] + E[\sigma_\epsilon^2(X'X)^{-1}]\\ &= 0 + \sigma_\epsilon^2 E[(X'X)^{-1}].\end{aligned}$$

The first term on the right hand side vanishes, because the true but unknown parameter vector $|\beta\rangle$ is not a random variable. The second term follows from $\text{Var}[|\epsilon\rangle] = \sigma_\epsilon^2 I$. Note that $E[(X'X)^{-1}]$ is the expectation value of a highly nonlinear function of the random variables X_t for $t = 1, \ldots, T$, which generally cannot be computed analytically.

Problem 7.5

The coefficients of the multiple regression model are determined by least-squares estimation. At time t, the empirical observation is

$$r_{P,t} - r = \alpha + \beta_1(r_{\text{MP},t} - r) + \beta_2\text{SMB}_{P,t} + \beta_3\text{HML}_{P,t} + \epsilon_{P,t}.$$

Substituting $\alpha = \lambda_0 - r(\lambda_2 + \lambda_3)$ and relabeling $\beta_q \to \lambda_q$ for $q = 1, 2, 3$ yields

$$r_{P,t} - r = \lambda_0 + \lambda_1(r_{\text{MP},t} - r) + \lambda_2(\text{SMB}_{P,t} - r) + \lambda_3(\text{HML}_{P,t} - r) + \epsilon_{P,t},$$

which is precisely the time t observation of a three-factor APT-model with factors R_{MP}, SMB_P, and HML_P.

Problem 7.6

The first step is to single out one particular row n of the factor model, describing the returns of say security S,

$$R_S = R_0 - R_0\langle\lambda_S|1\rangle + \langle\lambda_S|F\rangle + \epsilon_S$$
$$= R_0 + \langle\lambda_S|(|F\rangle - R_0|1\rangle) + \epsilon_S.$$

Taking unconditional expectations on both sides and writing out the inner product yields

$$\mu_S = r + \langle\lambda_S|(|\mu_F\rangle - r|1\rangle)$$

$$= r + \sum_{q=1}^{Q}\lambda_{S,q}(\mu_{F_q} - r),$$

which is the desired result.

B.7   Solutions to Problems in Chapter 8

Problem 8.1

To simplify the notation, write $E[R] = \mu$ and $\text{Var}[R] = \sigma^2$. One then obtains for the moments of the portfolio P in the CAPM-framework

$$\mu_P = r + \beta_p(\mu_{MP} - r) \quad \text{and} \quad \sigma_P^2 = \beta_P^2\sigma_{MP}^2 + \sigma_\epsilon^2.$$

Recall that in the CAPM $\beta_P = \frac{\text{Cov}[R_P,R_{MP}]}{\text{Var}[R_{MP}]}$, and thus $\beta_{MP} = 1$ holds, to obtain the numerator of the information ratio

$$E[R_P - R_{MP}] = (\beta_P - 1)(\mu_{MP} - r).$$

For the denominator, one obtains

$$\text{Var}[R_P - R_{MP}] = \beta_P^2\sigma_{MP}^2 + \sigma_\epsilon^2 - 2\beta_P\sigma_{MP}^2 + \sigma_{MP}^2$$
$$= (\beta_P^2 - 2\beta_P + 1)\sigma_{MP}^2 + \sigma_\epsilon^2$$
$$= (\beta_P - 1)^2\sigma_{MP}^2 + \sigma_\epsilon^2$$
$$\geq (\beta_P - 1)^2\sigma_{MP}^2.$$

Putting these components together, the following relation holds

$$\text{IR}_P = \frac{E[R_P - R_{MP}]}{\sqrt{\text{Var}[R_P - R_{MP}]}} \leq \frac{\mu_{MP} - r}{\sigma_{MP}} = \text{SR}_{MP},$$

which had to be shown.

Problem 8.2

Considering the possible deposition of the fraction $1 - \pi$ in a bank account, the time T wealth becomes

$$w_T = w_0\prod_{t=1}^{T}(1 + \pi r_{P,t} + (1 - \pi)r).$$

Arguments completely analogous to those in (8.7) to (8.10) indicate that the long-term average growth rate is

$$\log g_\infty = E[\log(1 + \pi R_P + (1 - \pi)R_0)].$$

Again, *Taylor*-expanding around $R_P = R_0 = 0$ to second order and neglecting all $O(\varepsilon^2)$-terms yields

$$\log g_\infty \approx \pi\mu_P + (1 - \pi)r - \frac{1}{2}\pi^2\sigma_P^2.$$

Taking the derivative with respect to π and setting equal to zero, one obtains the desired result

$$\pi^* = \frac{\mu_P - r}{\sigma_P^2}.$$

Problem 8.3

The first equivalence is easy to show just by plugging in the definition

$$|\mu_{KF}\rangle = |\mu\rangle + K|\eta\rangle = |\mu\rangle + \Sigma P'(P\Sigma P' + \Omega)^{-1}(|v\rangle - P|\mu\rangle) = |\mu_{BL}\rangle.$$

In the second part, use that $\Gamma = P\Sigma P' + \Omega = \Gamma'$ is symmetric and plug in

$$\Sigma_{KF} = \Sigma - K\Gamma K' = \Sigma - \Sigma P'\Gamma^{-1}\Gamma\Gamma^{-1}P\Sigma = \Sigma - \Sigma P'(P\Sigma P' + \Omega)^{-1}P\Sigma = \Sigma_{BL}.$$

Problem 8.4

Note that for $\Omega = 0$ and invertible P, the inverse variance of $|V\rangle$ can be written as $\mathrm{Var}[|V\rangle]^{-1} = (\Sigma P')^{-1}P^{-1}$. The posterior expectation now becomes

$$|\mu_{BL}\rangle = |\mu\rangle + \Sigma P'(\Sigma P')^{-1}P^{-1}(|v\rangle - P|\mu\rangle) = |\mu\rangle + P^{-1}|v\rangle - |\mu\rangle = P^{-1}|v\rangle.$$

The same trick applies to the posterior covariance

$$\Sigma_{BL} = \Sigma - \Sigma P'(\Sigma P')^{-1}P^{-1}P\Sigma = \Sigma - \Sigma = 0.$$

For the pick-matrix P to be invertible, it has to be a square matrix. This means, there have to be exactly as many views as securities under consideration. Furthermore, P has to have full rank, or in other words, all forms contained in P have to be linearly independent. Thus, there has to be exactly one view for every return, absolute or relative.

B.8   Solutions to Problems in Chapter 9

Problem 9.1

Using the required properties, one can write

$$\sum_{k=0}^{\infty} 2^k = 1 + \sum_{k=1}^{\infty} 2^k = 1 + 2\sum_{k=1}^{\infty} 2^{k-1} = 1 + 2\sum_{k=0}^{\infty} 2^k.$$

From this expression it is clear that

$$\sum_{k=0}^{\infty} 2^k = -1$$

solves the equation.

Problem 9.2
If the stochastic discount factors are conditionally uncorrelated, the first expectation term on the right hand side factorizes,

$$E\left[\prod_{n=1}^{k} M_{t+n}\Big|\mathcal{F}_t\right] = \prod_{n=1}^{k} E[M_{t+n}|\mathcal{F}_t] = \prod_{n=1}^{k} \frac{1}{R^*_{0,t+n}},$$

where $R^*_{0,t+n}$ is the risk-free gross return at time $t + n$, based on time t information. The original formula can thus be written as

$$S_t = \sum_{k=1}^{\infty} \frac{E[D_{t+k}|\mathcal{F}_t]}{\prod_{n=1}^{k} R^*_{0,t+n}} + \sum_{k=1}^{\infty} \mathrm{Cov}\left[\prod_{n=1}^{k} M_{t+n}, D_{t+k}\Big|\mathcal{F}_t\right].$$

Problem 9.3
The CARA-class of utility functions is represented by the family

$$u(c) = -e^{-\alpha c}.$$

Under the usual *von Neumann–Morgenstern*-utility functional, the SDF is defined as

$$M_T = e^{-\rho T}\frac{u'(C_T)}{u'(c_0)},$$

with $u'(c) = -\alpha u(c)$. The initial claim follows immediately.

Problem 9.4
For the utility function $u(c) = \sqrt{c}$, the inverse function is $u^{-1}(z) = z^2$. Together with the parameter value $\alpha = \frac{1}{2}$ one obtains

$$U[C_t] = \left(\sqrt{c_0} + e^{-\rho t}E[\sqrt{C_t}]\right)^2$$
$$= c_0 + 2\sqrt{c_0}e^{-\rho t}E[\sqrt{C_t}] + e^{-2\rho t}E[\sqrt{C_t}]^2.$$

From the derivative with respect to c_0

$$\frac{\partial U}{\partial c_0} = 1 + e^{-\rho t}\frac{E[\sqrt{C_t}]}{\sqrt{c_0}},$$

it can already be seen that temporally mixed terms occur. Thus, the functional is not time separable.

Problem 9.5

We have from (9.105) that

$$r_t = \rho + \gamma(g + (1 - \phi)(\bar{s} - s_{t-1})) - \frac{1}{2}\gamma^2\sigma_\epsilon^2(1 + \lambda(s_{t-1}))^2$$

has to hold. Using the new steady state surplus consumption ratio in the sensitivity function one obtains

$$r_t = \rho + \gamma(g + (1 - \phi)(\bar{s} - s_{t-1})) - \frac{1}{2}\gamma^2\sigma_\epsilon^2\frac{1 + 2(\bar{s} - s_{t-1})}{\sigma_\epsilon^2\gamma}\left(1 - \phi - \frac{B}{\gamma}\right).$$

This expression is still identical with (9.105), apart from the $\frac{B}{\gamma}$ term in parenthesis. Factoring this term out yields

$$r_t = r + \frac{1}{2}B(1 + 2(\bar{s} - s_{t-1})) = r_0 + B(\bar{s} - s_{t-1}),$$

with $r_0 = r + \frac{1}{2}B$, and r as in (9.105).

B.9   Solutions to Problems in Chapter 10

Problem 10.1

The fallacy boils down to the definition of conditional probability. If one defines the events

$$A = \text{``Linda is a bank teller''}$$

and

$$B = \text{``Linda is active in the feminist movement,''}$$

then the first alternative is event A and the second one is $A \cap B$. From the definition of conditional probability

$$P(A \cap B) = P(B \cap A) = P(B|A)P(A),$$

and the fact that $P(B|A) \leq 1$, it follows immediately that

$$P(A \cap B) \not> P(A)$$

has to hold.

Problem 10.2

The necessary conditions for a function to be an admissible probability weighting function are $w(0) = 0$, $w(1) = 1$, and $w'(p) \geq 0$. It is immediately clear from the definition of $w(p)$ that

$$w(1) = e^0 = 1 \quad \text{and} \quad \lim_{p \to 0} w(p) = \lim_{q \to \infty} e^{-q} = 0$$

holds, with $q = (-\log p)^\gamma$. Computing the derivative of $w(p)$, one obtains

$$w'(p) = \frac{\gamma w(p)}{p(-\log p)^{1-\gamma}} \geq 0,$$

Table B.1 Distribution functions of gambles A and B

	$x < 12$	$12 \leq x < 14$	$14 \leq x < 90$	$90 \leq x < 96$	$x \geq 96$
$F_A(x)$	0	0.05	0.1	0.1	1
$F_B(x)$	0	0.1	0.1	0.15	1

which satisfies the final condition. To see this, recognize that the numerator is non-negative, because $w(p)$ is an exponential, and the denominator is nonnegative, because $0 \leq p \leq 1$ holds.

Problem 10.3
For $w(p)$ to have a concave-convex S-shape, it has to cross the $45°$ (identity) line precisely one time, and has to approach $p = 1$ from below. To see that it indeed crosses the identity line only once, consider the condition

$$e^{-(-\log p)^\gamma} \overset{!}{=} p.$$

This equation is obviously satisfied for $p = 0$, $p = 1$, and $p = e^{-1}$. From the derivative of $w(p)$, it is clear that the numerator tends to $\gamma > 0$, if p approaches one from below, whereas the denominator tends to zero. Thus, one obtains

$$\lim_{p \to 1} w'(p) = \infty,$$

which means that $w(p)$ approaches $p = 1$ from below. Hence, $w(p)$ has to be S-shaped with concave curvature for $p \leq e^{-1}$ and convex curvature for $p \geq e^{-1}$.

Problem 10.4
Gamble A stochastically dominates gamble B to first order, because

$$F_A(x) \leq F_B(x),$$

with strict inequality for some x, see Table B.1.

Problem 10.5
Let the probability space of a fair coin flip experiment be $(\Omega, \mathcal{F}, P)$, with $\Omega = \{H, T\}$, $\mathcal{F} = 2^\Omega$, and the probability measure

$$P(A) = \begin{cases} 0 & \text{for } A = \emptyset \\ 1 & \text{for } A = \Omega \\ \frac{1}{2} & \text{otherwise.} \end{cases}$$

Now, define the random variables X and Y for example as

$$X(\omega) = \begin{cases} 2 & \text{for } \omega = H \\ 0 & \text{for } \omega = T \end{cases} \quad \text{and} \quad Y(\omega) = \begin{cases} 0 & \text{for } \omega = H \\ 1 & \text{for } \omega = T. \end{cases}$$

Table B.2 Distribution functions of X and Y

	$x < 0$	$0 \leq x < 1$	$1 \leq x < 2$	$x \geq 2$
$F_X(x)$	0	1/2	1/2	1
$F_Y(x)$	0	1/2	1	1

It is easy to see that $X(H) > Y(H)$, but $X(T) < Y(T)$ and thus, no state dominance relation exists. But reviewing the distribution functions of X and Y in Table B.2, it is obvious that X dominates Y stochastically to first order.

B.10   Solutions to Problems in Chapter 11

Problem 11.1

The arbitrage portfolio for the forward contract on a dividend paying stock is given in Table B.3. Initially the fraction e^{-qT} of the stock has to be shorted. From the value of the arbitrage portfolio at $t = T$, we immediately see that

$$K = e^{(r-q)T} S_0$$

is the desired delivery price.

Problem 11.2

Figure B.2 illustrates the payoff function of a binary call and a binary put option

$$C_T^B(S_T) = \theta(S_T - K) \quad \text{and} \quad P_T^B(S_T) = \theta(K - S_T),$$

where $\theta(x)$ is the *Heaviside-θ-function* defined by

$$\theta(x) = \begin{cases} 1 & \text{if } x \geq 0 \\ 0 & \text{if } x < 0. \end{cases}$$

Observe that with this definition, both options pay one unit of currency at expiry, if $S_T = K$. But since this event occurs with zero probability, everything holds almost surely.

Table B.3 Forward dividend arbitrage portfolio

Position	Value at $t = 0$	Value at $t = T$
Forward	0	$S_T - K$
Stock	$-e^{-qT} S_0$	$-S_T$
Bank account	$e^{-qT} S_0$	$e^{(r-q)T} S_0$
Total sum	$e^{-qT} S_0 - e^{-qT} S_0 = 0$	$e^{(r-q)T} S_0 - K = 0$

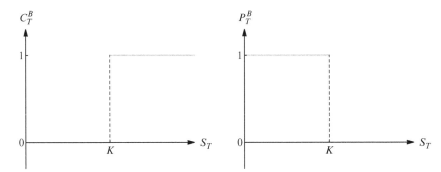

Fig. B.2 Payoff function of a binary call option (left) and a binary put option (right) from the holder's perspective (long position)

Problem 11.3
Figure B.3 summarizes the payoff generated by adding a long position in a binary call and a long position in a binary put. Obviously, the following relation holds at expiry

$$C_T^B + P_T^B = 1 = e^{-rT}B(T).$$

But shorting a cash position of $e^{-rT}B(T)$, in addition to the long position in both binaries, creates a portfolio with zero value. This means we can establish a parity relation. Reversing time to an arbitrary instant t results in the binary put-call parity

$$C_t^B + P_t^B = e^{-rT}B(t) = e^{-r(T-t)}.$$

Problem 11.4
For $S_T = K_1$ all calls have zero payoff, therefore we have to focus only on the right limit. For $S_T = K_3$ the payoff is

$$\Pi_T = (K_3 - K_1) - a(K_3 - K_2) + 0 \overset{!}{=} 0.$$

Trivial algebraic manipulations yield the desired value of a,

$$a^* = \frac{K_3 - K_1}{K_3 - K_2}.$$

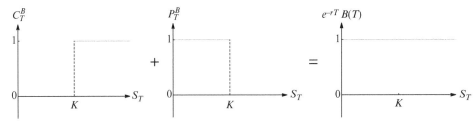

Fig. B.3 Sum of the payoff functions of a binary call and a binary put with identical exercise price K and expiry date T

Problem 11.5

Again for $S_T \leq K_1$ all calls have zero payoffs, and thus only the behavior of the position at $S_T \geq K_3$ matters. At $S_T = K_3$ we operate under the same conditions as in Problem 11.4 and thus, the coefficient a should again be chosen

$$a^* = \frac{K_3 - K_1}{K_3 - K_2}.$$

For $S_T > K_3$, the payoff of the generalized butterfly position should not depend on S_T anymore. We have therefore

$$\left. \frac{\partial \Pi_T}{\partial S_T} \right|_{S_T > K_3} = S_T(1 - a^* + b) \overset{!}{=} 0.$$

It is immediately clear that the bracket has to vanish, because $S_T > K_3 > 0$ by definition. Thus one obtains

$$b^* = a^* - 1 = \frac{K_2 - K_1}{K_3 - K_2}.$$

Problem 11.6

Combining both positions one obtains the portfolio

$$\Pi_t = -(C_t(K, T) + P_t(K, T)) + e^{rt}(C_0 + P_0).$$

This is immediately identified as a short straddle position. The investor has written a put and a call option with identical exercise price and time to expiry at $t = 0$. The premium for both options was deposited in the bank account to earn interest. If the underlying ends up at K at expiry, the investor maximizes her profit from the position. If on the other hand the underlying ends up significantly above or below the exercise price, the investor faces obligations from one or the other option contract.

Problem 11.7

Again establish the overall position, held by the investor

$$\Pi_t = 2S_t - (C_t(K, T) - P_t(K, T)) + e^{rt}(C_0 - P_0)$$
$$= 2S_t - F_t(K, T) + e^{rt}F_0.$$

Note that the price of the forward contract at $t = 0$ is not necessarily zero, because we did not insist on the exercise price to be $K = e^{rT}S_0$. Thus, the payoff of the entire position is

$$\Pi_T = 2S_T - (S_T - K) + e^{rT}(S_0 - e^{-rT}K)$$
$$= S_T + e^{rT}S_0.$$

B.11   Solutions to Problems in Chapter 12

Problem 12.1

First of all, because the risk-free interest rate is zero, there is no need to worry about discounting. Next, the hedge-portfolio at every vertex of the tree is given by

$$\Pi_t^{(n)} = P_t^{(n)} - \Delta_t^{(n)} S_t^{(n)},$$

where $\Delta_t^{(n)}$ is the individual hedge-ratio of every vertex, defined by

$$\Delta_t^{(n)} = \frac{P_{t+1}^{(n+1)} - P_{t+1}^{(n)}}{S_{t+1}^{(n+1)} - S_{t+1}^{(n)}}.$$

Because the portfolio $\Pi_t^{(n)}$ is designed to hedge against random fluctuations, its value has to be the same for both successive branches. One obtains for the first two Δs

$$\Delta_1^{(1)} = \frac{0 - 6}{121 - 99} = -\frac{3}{11}$$

$$\Delta_1^{(0)} = \frac{6 - 24}{99 - 81} = -1.$$

With these hedge-ratios, one can assemble the associated hedge-portfolios

$$\Pi_1^{(1)} = P_1^{(1)} + \frac{3}{11} \cdot 110 = \begin{cases} 0 + \frac{3}{11} \cdot 121 = 33 & \text{if } \omega_1 = \uparrow \\ 6 + \frac{3}{11} \cdot 99 = 33 & \text{if } \omega_1 = \downarrow \end{cases}$$

$$\Pi_1^{(0)} = P_1^{(0)} + 90 = \begin{cases} 6 + 99 = 105 & \text{if } \omega_1 = \uparrow \\ 81 + 24 = 105 & \text{if } \omega_1 = \downarrow. \end{cases}$$

Solving these equations is easy and the result is $P_1^{(1)} = 3$ and $P_1^{(0)} = 15$. Using these put prices, one obtains the new hedge-ratio Δ_0,

$$\Delta_0 = \frac{3 - 15}{110 - 90} = -\frac{3}{5},$$

and the associated hedge-portfolio

$$\Pi_0 = P_0 + \frac{3}{5} \cdot 100 = \begin{cases} 3 + \frac{3}{5} \cdot 110 = 69 & \text{if } \omega_0 = \uparrow \\ 15 + \frac{3}{5} \cdot 90 = 69 & \text{if } \omega_0 = \downarrow. \end{cases}$$

Solving this equation, one obtains the final result $P_0 = 9$. Figure B.4 summarizes the entire computation.

Problem 12.2

The general formula for pricing a European binary put option in the binomial model is

$$P_0^B(K, T) = \frac{1}{(1 + r\Delta t)^T} \sum_{n=0}^{a-1} \mathcal{B}_n(q, T).$$

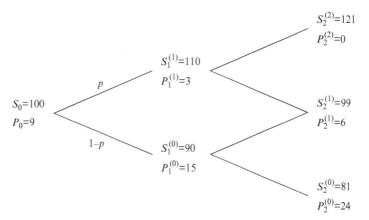

Fig. B.4 Binomial tree for European plain vanilla put option

From the setting in Example 12.2 one obtains

$$P_0^B(105, 2) = \frac{1}{(1 + 0.05)^2} \cdot \left(\binom{2}{0} 0.25^2 + \binom{2}{1} 0.75 \cdot 0.25 \right)$$

$$= 0.907 \cdot (0.0625 + 0.375) = 0.40.$$

Considering the traditional discrete compounding in the binomial model, the binary put-call parity can be written as

$$C_0^B(K, T) + P_0^B(K, T) = \frac{1}{(1 + r\Delta t)^T}.$$

Plugging in the already computed binary call value and the discounting factor yields

$$P_0^B(105, 2) = 0.907 - 0.51 \approx 0.4,$$

which perfectly coincides with the earlier result.

Problem 12.3
The set based definition of the stopped σ-algebra is somewhat bulky, thus one should proceed with the constructive method. From Figure 12.11 it is obvious that the process is stopped at the events $X_1^{(0)}$, $X_2^{(2)}$, and $X_2^{(1)}$. These events have the pre-images

$$A_1 = \{(\downarrow, \uparrow), (\downarrow, \downarrow)\}, \quad A_2\{(\uparrow, \uparrow)\}, \quad \text{and} \quad A_3\{(\uparrow, \downarrow)\}.$$

The stopped σ-algebra is the one generated by these events, $\mathcal{F}_\tau = \sigma(A_1, A_2, A_3)$. Adding all complements and unions required by the definition of a σ-algebra, we get

$$\mathcal{F}_\tau = \{\emptyset, \{(\uparrow, \uparrow)\}, \{(\uparrow, \downarrow)\}, \{(\uparrow, \uparrow), (\uparrow, \downarrow)\}, \{(\downarrow, \uparrow), (\downarrow, \downarrow)\},$$
$$\{(\uparrow, \downarrow), (\downarrow, \uparrow), (\downarrow, \downarrow)\}, \{(\uparrow, \uparrow), (\downarrow, \uparrow), (\downarrow, \downarrow)\}, \Omega\}.$$

Problem 12.4
Obviously, for $t < s$ the process is never stopped, and thus $\{\tau \leq t\} = \emptyset$. For $t \geq s$, the process is stopped with certainty, which means no matter which event has happened, the process has been stopped at every single one. Therefore, $\{\tau \leq t\} = \Omega$ has to hold.

Problem 12.5

For this one, it is more convenient to stick to the set based definition of the stopped σ-algebra

$$\mathcal{F}_\tau = \{A \in \mathcal{F} : A \cap \{\tau \leq t\} \in \mathcal{F}_t \text{ for all } t \in \mathcal{T}\}.$$

Start by dividing the problem into three phases, $0 \leq t < s$, $t = s$, and $s < t \leq T$:

- In the first phase, one clearly has $\{\tau \leq t\} = \emptyset$, as detailed in the solution to Problem 12.4. But every possible event $A \in \mathcal{F}$ that is intersected with the empty set yields the empty set, $A \cap \emptyset = \emptyset$, which is of course always in the σ-algebra $\mathcal{F}_t$. Thus, phase one contributes the entire σ-algebra $\mathcal{F}$.

- In phase two, one has $t = s$ and hence $\{\tau \leq t\} = \Omega$. But any event A intersected with Ω is again A. Thus, phase two contributes all sets $A \in \mathcal{F}_s$, which is of course $\mathcal{F}_s$.

- In the final phase with $t > s$, the stopping event is still $\{\tau \leq t\} = \Omega$, and thus by an identical argument, the contribution from phase three is $\mathcal{F}_t$.

The desired stopped σ-algebra $\mathcal{F}_\tau$ is the collection of sets, which are contained in all contributions. For $0 < s < t$, one obtains from the three phases

$$\mathcal{F} \supset \mathcal{F}_s \subset \mathcal{F}_t,$$

which indicates that $\mathcal{F}_s$ is the desired smallest collection of sets.

Problem 12.6

In computing the n-th vertex in time slice t, one has to consider the barrier condition, as well as the American exercise right. Thus, the computation rule is

$$C_{t-1}^{(n)} = \begin{cases} \max\left(\frac{1}{1+r\Delta t} \cdot \left(q \cdot C_t^{(n+1)} + (1-q) \cdot C_t^{(n)}\right), (S_{t-1}^{(n)} - K)^+\right) & \text{if } S_{t-1}^{(n)} < S_u \\ 0 & \text{if } S_{t-1}^{(n)} \geq S_u. \end{cases}$$

Figure B.5 illustrates the entire binomial tree. Note that the contract is indeed exercised early at vertex $C_2^{(2)}$. Intuitively, this can be understood, because there is a substantial risk of hitting the barrier in the next step.

Problem 12.7

From the martingale pricing principle it follows that

$$S_t = \frac{1}{1 + r\Delta t}\left(q \cdot e^{\sigma\sqrt{\Delta t}} S_t + (1-q) \cdot e^{-\sigma\sqrt{\Delta t}} S_t\right)$$

has to hold. *Taylor*-expanding the exponential yields

$$e^{\pm\sigma\sqrt{\Delta t}} = 1 \pm \sigma\sqrt{\Delta t} + \frac{1}{2}\sigma^2\Delta t + O(\Delta t^{3/2}),$$

where the higher order terms are to be neglected. Plugging this expansion into the martingale condition and rearranging yields

$$q = \frac{r\Delta t + \sigma\sqrt{\Delta t} - \frac{1}{2}\sigma^2\Delta t}{2\sigma\sqrt{\Delta t}} = \frac{1}{2} + \frac{r - \frac{1}{2}\sigma^2}{2\sigma}\sqrt{\Delta t},$$

which completes the proof.

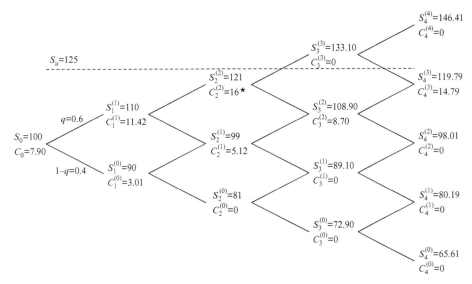

Fig. B.5 Binomial tree for American knockout barrier call option – Early exercise indicated by a star

B.12   Solutions to Problems in Chapter 13

Problem 13.1
The dynamic process usually assumed for the underlying S is the geometric *Brown*ian motion

$$dS_t = \mu S_t dt + \sigma S_t dW_t.$$

Using Itô's lemma with respect to the forward price $F_t = e^{r(T_F - t)} S_t$ yields

$$dF = \left(\mu S \frac{\partial F}{\partial S} + \frac{\partial F}{\partial t} + \frac{1}{2}\sigma^2 S^2 \frac{\partial^2 F}{\partial S^2} \right) dt + \sigma S \frac{\partial F}{\partial S} dW.$$

It is easily seen that the second partial derivative is $\frac{\partial^2 F}{\partial S^2} = 0$. One thus obtains

$$dF = (\mu F - rF)dt + \sigma F dW,$$

which is already the desired result.

Problem 13.2
The starting point is the *Black–Scholes*-equation with volatility $\sigma = 0$,

$$\frac{\partial V}{\partial t} + rB\frac{\partial V}{\partial B} - rV = 0.$$

The first step is to make the substitution $V(B, t) = e^{-r(T-t)} U(B, t)$. That makes the partial derivatives

$$\frac{\partial V}{\partial t} = rV + e^{-r(T-t)}\frac{\partial U}{\partial t} \quad \text{and} \quad \frac{\partial V}{\partial B} = e^{-r(T-t)}\frac{\partial U}{\partial B}.$$

The result after multiplying with $e^{r(T-t)}$ is

$$\frac{\partial U}{\partial t} + rB\frac{\partial U}{\partial B} = 0.$$

Now define $x = \log B$. This leaves the partial derivative with respect to t unchanged, but the B-derivative becomes

$$\frac{\partial U}{\partial B} = \frac{\partial U}{\partial x}\frac{\partial x}{\partial B} = \frac{\partial U}{\partial x} \cdot \frac{1}{B}.$$

Putting all the pieces together, one obtains the transport equation

$$\frac{\partial U}{\partial t} + r\frac{\partial U}{\partial x} = 0.$$

Problem 13.3

The fair price for a plain vanilla binary call option is

$$C_t^B(K, T) = e^{-r(T-t)}\Phi(d) \quad \text{with} \quad d = \frac{\log(S_t/K) + (r - \frac{1}{2}\sigma^2)(T-t)}{\sigma\sqrt{T-t}}.$$

Computing the derivative of the binary call price with respect to S yields

$$\Delta_C^B = \frac{\partial C^B}{\partial S} = \frac{e^{-r(T-t)}\phi(d)}{S_t\sigma\sqrt{T-t}},$$

where as usual $\phi(z) = \frac{1}{\sqrt{2\pi}}e^{-\frac{1}{2}z^2}$. Because the fair price of the corresponding put can be written as

$$P_t^B(K, T) = e^{-r(T-t)}(1 - \Phi(d)),$$

the delta of the binary put follows immediately

$$\Delta_P^B = -\Delta_C^B = -\frac{e^{-r(T-t)}\phi(d)}{S_t\sigma\sqrt{T-t}}.$$

Problem 13.4

First analyze the impact on the quantities $d_{+/-}$. To this end, define the modified exercise price

$$X = \frac{e^{2b(T-t)}S_t^2}{K}.$$

Then one obtains

$$-d_{+/-}^X = \frac{\log(X/S_t) - (b \pm \frac{1}{2}\sigma^2)(T-t)}{\sigma\sqrt{T-t}}$$

$$= \frac{\log(S_t/K) + 2b(T-t) - (b \pm \frac{1}{2}\sigma^2)(T-t)}{\sigma\sqrt{T-t}}$$

$$= \frac{\log(S_t/K) + (b \mp \frac{1}{2}\sigma^2)(T-t)}{\sigma\sqrt{T-t}} = d_{-/+}.$$

Now start with the right hand side of the symmetry relation and substitute

$$\frac{K}{e^{b(T-t)}S_t}P_t(X, T) = -e^{-r(T-t)}K\Phi(d_-) + e^{(b-r)(T-t)}S_t\Phi(d_+) = C_t(K, T).$$

Thus, the European put-call symmetry holds.

Problem 13.5
Vanna can either be computed as the derivative of the option delta, with respect to volatility, or as the derivative of the option vega, with respect to the price of the underlying. Since vega is the same for plain vanilla puts and calls, so is vanna. Let's choose the vega avenue

$$\frac{\partial V}{\partial S} = \frac{\partial}{\partial S}aS_t\sqrt{T-t}\,\phi(d_+),$$

where again $a = e^{(b-r)(T-t)}$. There are two derivative terms to be computed, because d_+ is also a function of S. As usual, $\phi(z)$ represents the standard normal probability density function, and thus

$$\frac{\partial}{\partial S}\frac{1}{\sqrt{2\pi}}e^{-\frac{1}{2}d_+^2} = -d_+\frac{\partial d_+}{\partial S}\cdot\frac{1}{\sqrt{2\pi}}e^{-\frac{1}{2}d_+^2} = -\frac{d_+}{S_t\sigma\sqrt{T-t}}\cdot\phi(d_+).$$

Hence, the derivative of vega with respect to S is

$$\frac{\partial V}{\partial S} = a\sqrt{T-t}\,\phi(d_+)\left(1 - \frac{d_+}{\sigma\sqrt{T-t}}\right) = \frac{a\phi(d_+)}{\sigma}\left(\sigma\sqrt{T-t} - d_+\right).$$

Using the fact that $d_+ - \sigma\sqrt{T-t} = d_-$, the final form of vanna is

$$\text{vanna} = \frac{\partial^2 V}{\partial S\partial\sigma} = -\frac{e^{(b-r)(T-t)}d_-\,\phi(d_+)}{\sigma}.$$

Problem 13.6
The liabilities can be represented as a long position in the debt and a short plain vanilla put, contingent on the firm value. Accounting for the time value of money, the position is

$$B_0(t, T) = e^{-r(T-t)}D - P_t(D, T).$$

In the *Black–Scholes*-framework, the fair price of a European plain vanilla put option is

$$P_t(D, T) = -V_t\Phi(-d_1) + e^{-r(T-t)}D\Phi(-d_2),$$

with

$$d_{1/2} = \frac{\log(V_t/D) + (r \pm \frac{1}{2}\sigma_V^2)(T-t)}{\sigma_V\sqrt{T-t}}.$$

Therefore, the fair price of the liabilities has to be

$$B_0(t, T) = V_t\Phi(-d_1) + e^{-r(T-t)}D(1 - \Phi(-d_2))$$
$$= V_t\Phi(-d_1) + e^{-r(T-t)}D\Phi(d_2),$$

where again the relation $\Phi(x) = 1 - \Phi(-x)$ was used.

B.13   Solutions to Problems in Chapter 14

Problem 14.1

To prove that the scheme is still explicit, one has to move the $rV_{m+1}^{(n)}$-term to the left hand side and divide by $1 + r\Delta\tau$

$$V_{m+1}^{(n)} = \frac{1}{1 + r\Delta\tau}\left(V_m^{(n)} + \Delta\tau bn\Delta S \cdot \Delta_m^{(n)} + \frac{1}{2}\Delta\tau\sigma^2 n^2 \Delta S^2 \cdot \Gamma_m^{(n)}\right).$$

Remember that in switching from t to τ, the flow of time was reversed. Thus, the right hand side is immediately identified as a discounted expectation value for $V_{m+1}^{(n)}$, depending on $V_m^{(n+1)}$, $V_m^{(n)}$, and $V_m^{(n-1)}$. Sorting out the terms contained in $\Delta_m^{(n)}$ and $\Gamma_m^{(n)}$ with respect to the spatial points in time slice m, one obtains

$$V_{m+1}^{(n)} = \frac{1}{1 + r\Delta\tau}\sum_{k=-1}^{1} q_k V_m^{(n+k)},$$

with

$$q_{\pm 1} = \frac{\Delta\tau}{2}(\sigma^2 n^2 \pm bn) \quad \text{and} \quad q_0 = 1 - \Delta\tau\sigma^2 n^2.$$

It is easily checked that the sum of the weights is one, which implies that they induce a trinomial risk-neutral probability measure Q. But in order to do so, there is a second requirement, namely that all weights q_k are nonnegative. To ensure that, the parameters have to satisfy two conditions,

$$q_0 \geq 0 \Rightarrow \Delta\tau\sigma^2 n^2 \leq 1 \quad \text{and} \quad q_{-1} \geq 0 \Rightarrow \sigma^2 n \geq b.$$

The first one is the stability condition (14.23), and the second is the additional one, as claimed before.

Problem 14.2

Obviously the time derivative is not affected by the substitution $S = S^\alpha$. The first partial derivative with respect to S becomes

$$\frac{\partial V}{\partial S} = \frac{\partial V}{\partial S}\frac{\partial S}{\partial S} = \frac{\partial V}{\partial S}\cdot \alpha S^{\alpha-1} = \frac{\partial V}{\partial S}\cdot \alpha\frac{S}{S}.$$

For the second partial derivative with respect to S, one obtains

$$\frac{\partial^2 V}{\partial S^2} = \frac{\partial}{\partial S}\left(\frac{\partial V}{\partial S}\cdot \alpha S^{\alpha-1}\right) = \frac{\partial^2 V}{\partial S^2}\cdot \alpha^2 S^{2\alpha-2} + \frac{\partial V}{\partial S}\cdot \alpha(\alpha-1)S^{\alpha-2}$$

$$= \frac{\partial^2 V}{\partial S^2}\cdot \alpha^2\frac{S^2}{S^2} + \frac{\partial V}{\partial S}\cdot \alpha(\alpha-1)\frac{S}{S^2}.$$

Putting all the pieces together, the *Black–Scholes*-equation reads

$$\frac{\partial V}{\partial t} + \left(b\alpha + \frac{1}{2}\sigma^2\alpha(\alpha-1)\right)S\frac{\partial V}{\partial S} + \frac{1}{2}\sigma^2\alpha^2 S^2\frac{\partial^2 V}{\partial S^2} - rV = 0.$$

It is now immediately clear that this has the form of the original *Black–Scholes*-PDE, with the adjusted quantities

$$b_{\text{adj.}} = \alpha\left(b + \frac{1}{2}\sigma^2(\alpha - 1)\right) \quad \text{and} \quad \sigma_{\text{adj.}} = \alpha\sigma.$$

Problem 14.3

Using the definition of the probability current, the *Fokker–Planck*-equation takes the simple form

$$\frac{\partial p}{\partial t} + \frac{\partial F}{\partial S} = 0.$$

The meaning of this equation is that the gain and loss in probability mass and the in- and outflow of probability mass through the boundaries $S = 0$ and $S = \infty$ have to coincide. Because $p(S, t)$ is a rapidly decreasing function, integrating the second term on the left hand side yields

$$\int_0^\infty \frac{\partial}{\partial S} F(S, t)dS = \int_0^\infty dF(S, t) = F(S, t)\Big|_{S=0}^{S=\infty} = 0.$$

Hence, there is no flux of probability mass through the boundaries at any time and thus, the probability mass is conserved.

Problem 14.4

The first claim is easy to prove, using the properties of the δ-function,

$$\hat{h} = \frac{1}{N}\sum_{n=1}^N h(x^{(n)}) = \frac{1}{N}\sum_{n=1}^N \int h(x)\delta(x - x^{(n)})dx = \int h(x)\hat{f}(x)dx.$$

The second property follows also immediately from integration with the δ-function,

$$E[\hat{f}(x)] = \frac{1}{N}\sum_{n=1}^N \int \delta(x - y)f(y)dy = \frac{1}{N}\sum_{n=1}^N f(x) = f(x),$$

which concludes the proof.

Problem 14.5

To show that $\hat{h}$ is unbiased, one has to compute its expectation with respect to $g(x)$,

$$E^G[\hat{h}] = \sum_{n=1}^N E^G[w_n h(X)] = \sum_{n=1}^N \int \frac{f(x)}{N \cdot g(x)} h(x)g(x)dx$$

$$= \frac{1}{N}\sum_{n=1}^N \int h(x)f(x)dx = \frac{1}{N}\sum_{n=1}^N E[h(X)] = E[h(X)].$$

Thus, the expectation of $\hat{h}$ is still unchanged, but its variance can be reduced considerably, if $g(x)$ is chosen in a clever way.

Problem 14.6

Differentiating the exponentially weighted average $\bar{S}_t$ with respect to t yields the differential equation

$$\frac{d\bar{S}_t}{dt} = \lambda(S_t - \bar{S}_t).$$

Obviously, λ governs the adjustment speed of the average value $\bar{S}$. If λ is very small, there is nearly no change in the average value and one obtains

$$\lim_{\lambda \to 0} \bar{S}_t = S_0.$$

If both sides of the differential equation are divided by λ, then the left hand side approaches zero for large values of λ. Thus, we have

$$\lim_{\lambda \to \infty} \bar{S}_t = S_t,$$

which means that the adjustment is instantaneous.

Problem 14.7

There are two exceptional aspects of this Asian option: the exponential averaging and the knockout condition. The latter is simple to implement, see Box B.1; the former is a little tricky. To update the exponentially weighted average, the differential equation

---

Box B.1 Pseudo-code for floating strike exponential arithmetic Asian call

Set N, M	▷ Initialization
$b = 0$	▷ Cost-of-carry rate
$\bar{S}_0 = S_0$	▷ Zeroth average
$\Delta t = T/M$	
$m^* = \text{Int}\,(M/2)$	▷ Knockout time

For $n = 1$ to N	▷ Path replication
$\quad$ For $m = 1$ to M	▷ Path discretization
$\quad\quad$ Draw $z \sim N(0, 1)$	▷ Random number generation
$\quad\quad S_m = S_{m-1} \exp\left((b - \frac{1}{2}\sigma^2)\Delta t + \sigma\sqrt{\Delta t}\,z\right)$	
$\quad\quad \bar{S}_m = (\bar{S}_{m-1} + \lambda\Delta t\, S_m)/(1 + \lambda\Delta t)$	▷ Exponential average
$\quad$ Next m	
$\quad V_T^{(n)} = \max\,(S_M - \bar{S}_M, 0)$	▷ Payoff function
$\quad$ If $S_{m^*} \le \bar{S}_{m^*}$ then $V_T^{(n)} = 0$	▷ Knockout condition
Next n	

$V_0 = \exp\,(-rT) \cdot 1/N \sum_{n=1}^{N} V_T^{(n)}$	
Print V_0	▷ Output

for $\bar{S}_t$ has to be discretized

$$\frac{\Delta \bar{S}_t}{\Delta t} = \lambda(S_t - \bar{S}_t).$$

This can be accomplished by using a forward or backward difference. In this case the backward difference $\Delta\bar{S}_t = \bar{S}_t - \bar{S}_{t-\Delta t}$ is chosen, because we want $\bar{S}_t$ to be a function of S_t and $\bar{S}_{t-\Delta t}$. Plugging in this difference and rearranging yields

$$\bar{S}_t = \frac{\bar{S}_{t-\Delta t} + \lambda\Delta t\, S_t}{1 + \lambda\Delta t}.$$

It is easily checked that the limiting properties of the weight factor for $\lambda \to 0$ and $\lambda \to \infty$ are preserved. The complete pseudo-code is provided in Box B.1.

B.14   Solutions to Problems in Chapter 15

Problem 15.1
The first step is to solve the differential equation for the actual variance. Because σ_∞^2 is a constant, we can write

$$\frac{d\sigma^2(t)}{dt} = \frac{d}{dt}(\sigma^2(t) - \sigma_\infty^2) = -\lambda(\sigma^2(t) - \sigma_\infty^2).$$

This is an ordinary differential equation in the difference $\sigma^2(t) - \sigma_\infty^2$, whose solution is already known,

$$\sigma^2(t) = \sigma_\infty^2 + e^{-\lambda t}(\sigma_0^2 - \sigma_\infty^2).$$

From (15.5) we know that implied volatility is given by

$$\sigma_{\text{imp.}}(T) = \sqrt{\frac{1}{T}\int_0^T \sigma^2(t)dt}.$$

Thus, we have to compute the integral over the actual variance from $t=0$ to $t=T$,

$$\int_0^T \sigma^2(t)dt = \sigma_\infty^2 \int_0^T dt + (\sigma_0^2 - \sigma_\infty^2)\int_0^T e^{-\lambda t}dt$$

$$= \sigma_\infty^2 T - \frac{\sigma_0^2 - \sigma_\infty^2}{\lambda}(e^{-\lambda T} - 1).$$

Plugging this expression into the implied volatility formula yields

$$\sigma_{\text{imp.}}(T) = \sqrt{\sigma_\infty^2 + \frac{1 - e^{-\lambda T}}{\lambda T}(\sigma_0^2 - \sigma_\infty^2)}.$$

Problem 15.2
The limit $T \to \infty$ is easy to check. The exponential tends to zero and the second term under the square root vanishes. One thus obtains

$$\lim_{T\to\infty} \sigma_{\text{imp.}}(T) = \sqrt{\sigma_\infty^2} = \sigma_\infty,$$

which is of course perfectly consistent. To analyze the limit $T \to 0$ one can use the rule of l'Hôpital to determine the limit of the ratio under the square root,

$$\lim_{T \to 0} \frac{1 - e^{-\lambda T}}{\lambda T} = \lim_{T \to 0} \frac{\lambda e^{-\lambda T}}{\lambda} = 1.$$

Hence, the implied volatility becomes

$$\lim_{T \to 0} \sigma_{\text{imp.}}(T) = \sqrt{\sigma_0^2} = \sigma_0,$$

which is also perfectly consistent.

Problem 15.3

Because kurtosis is defined as $K = M_4/h_\infty^2$, and the stationary variance is known by (15.11) on page 330 to be

$$h_\infty = \frac{\omega}{1 - \alpha - \beta},$$

one has to compute the fourth moment of the stationary distribution. Arguments, completely analogous to (15.12) yield

$$M_4 = E[\epsilon_t^4] = 3E[h_t^2] = 3E\left[(\omega + \alpha\epsilon_{t-1}^2 + \beta h_{t-1})^2\right]$$

$$= 3\omega^2 + 6\omega E[\alpha z_{t-1}^2 + \beta]E[h_{t-1}] + 3E\left[(\alpha z_{t-1}^2 + \beta)^2\right]E[h_{t-1}^2]$$

$$= 3\omega^2 + 6\omega(\alpha + \beta)E[h_{t-1}] + (3\alpha^2 + 2\alpha\beta + \beta^2) \cdot 3E[h_{t-1}^2]$$

$$= 3\omega^2 + 6\omega^2 \frac{\alpha + \beta}{1 - \alpha - \beta} + (3\alpha^2 + 2\alpha\beta + \beta^2)E[\epsilon_{t-1}^4].$$

Because M_4 is a moment of the stationary distribution, the stationary variance $E[h_{t-1}] = h_\infty$ was used. For the same reason $M_4 = E[\epsilon_t^4] = E[\epsilon_{t-1}^4]$ has to hold, and one obtains

$$M_4 = \frac{3\omega^2 \left(1 + \frac{2(\alpha+\beta)}{1-\alpha-\beta}\right)}{1 - 3\alpha^2 - 2\alpha\beta - \beta^2}$$

$$= \frac{\omega^2}{(1 - \alpha - \beta)^2} \cdot 3 \frac{(1 - \alpha - \beta)(1 + \alpha + \beta)}{1 - 2\alpha^2 - (\alpha + \beta)^2}.$$

Realizing that the first term on the right hand side is h_∞^2, it is immediately clear that the kurtosis is

$$K = 3 \frac{1 - (\alpha + \beta)^2}{1 - 2\alpha^2 - (\alpha + \beta)^2}.$$

Problem 15.4

First note that $E[\epsilon_t] = 0$, and thus $\text{Cov}[\Delta x_{t+1}, \epsilon_t] = E[\Delta x_{t+1}\epsilon_t]$. Plugging in the GARCH-in-mean equation one obtains

$$\text{Cov}[\Delta x_{t+1}, \epsilon_t] = E[(\mu + \lambda h_{t+1} + \epsilon_{t+1})\epsilon_t]$$

$$= \lambda E\left[(\omega + \alpha(\epsilon_t - \gamma)^2 + \beta h_t)\epsilon_t\right]$$

$$= \lambda \alpha E[\epsilon_t^3 - 2\gamma\epsilon_t^2 + \gamma^2\epsilon_t]$$

$$= -2\lambda\alpha\gamma E[h_t].$$

But $E[h_t] = h_\infty > 0$ is the stationary variance. That means tomorrow's logarithmic returns are negatively correlated with today's random shocks, and thus Δx_t is clearly not a noise process.

Problem 15.5
By the same argument as in the *Duan*-model, under the locally risk-neutral measure, the logarithmic return dynamics has to be given by

$$\Delta x_t = r - \frac{1}{2} h_t + \sqrt{h_t} z_t^Q.$$

That means $\lambda^Q = -\frac{1}{2}$ has to hold. But for this equation to coincide with the original one for the logarithmic returns, we also have to require $z_t^Q = z_t + (\lambda + \frac{1}{2}) \sqrt{h_t}$. Switching from z_t to z_t^Q also affects the variance equation. To compensate the effect, the modification $\gamma^Q = \gamma + \lambda + \frac{1}{2}$ is necessary. Now, the model is algebraically equivalent under both measures, P and Q.

B.15   Solutions to Problems in Chapter 16

Problem 16.1
The *Heston*-model has the particular form

$$dS_t = \mu S_t dt + \sqrt{v_t} S_t dW_{1,t}$$
$$dv_t = \kappa(\theta - v_t)dt + \alpha \sqrt{v_t} dW_{2,t},$$

with $E[dW_1 dW_2] = \rho dt$. Hence, the drift of the variance equation is $f(S, v, t) = \kappa(\theta - v)$ and the diffusion is $g(S, v, t) = \alpha \sqrt{v}$. Applying Itô's lemma yields

$$dV = \frac{\partial V}{\partial S} dS + \frac{\partial V}{\partial v} dv + \frac{\partial V}{\partial t} dt + \frac{1}{2} \left(v S^2 \frac{\partial^2 V}{\partial S^2} + 2\rho \alpha v S \frac{\partial^2 V}{\partial S \partial v} + \alpha^2 v \frac{\partial^2 V}{\partial v} \right) dt.$$

The next step is to set up the hedge-portfolio $\Pi = V - \Delta_1 S - \Delta_2 V_a$, where V_a is again any traded auxiliary contract. The change in Π is given by

$$d\Pi = dV - \Delta_1 dS - \Delta_2 dV_a = r\Pi dt.$$

Because the right hand side of this equation is not stochastic, Δ_1 and Δ_2 have to be chosen such that any random influence is eliminated. The appropriate condition for this is

$$\left(\frac{\partial V}{\partial S} - \Delta_1 - \Delta_2 \frac{\partial V_a}{\partial S} \right) dS + \left(\frac{\partial V}{\partial v} - \Delta_2 \frac{\partial V_a}{\partial v} \right) dv = 0.$$

Therefore, one obtains the hedge-ratios

$$\Delta_1 = \frac{\partial V}{\partial S} - \Delta_2 \frac{\partial V_a}{\partial S} \quad \text{and} \quad \Delta_2 = \frac{\partial V}{\partial v} \Big/ \frac{\partial V_a}{\partial v}.$$

The change in the hedge-portfolio thus becomes

$$d\Pi = \frac{\partial V}{\partial t} dt + \frac{1}{2}\left(\ldots\right) dt - \Delta_2 \frac{\partial V_a}{\partial t} dt - \frac{\Delta_2}{2}\left(\ldots\right)_a dt$$

$$= rV dt - rS \frac{\partial V}{\partial S} dt + \Delta_2 rS \frac{\partial V_a}{\partial S} dt - \Delta_2 r V_a dt.$$

Equating the first and second row and rearranging terms yields

$$\frac{\frac{\partial V}{\partial t} + rS\frac{\partial V}{\partial S} + \frac{1}{2}vS^2\frac{\partial^2 V}{\partial S^2} + \rho\alpha vS\frac{\partial^2 V}{\partial S\partial v} + \frac{1}{2}\alpha^2 v\frac{\partial^2 V}{\partial v^2} - rV}{\frac{\partial V}{\partial v}}$$

$$= \frac{\frac{\partial V_a}{\partial t} + rS\frac{\partial V_a}{\partial S} + \frac{1}{2}vS^2\frac{\partial^2 V_a}{\partial S^2} + \rho\alpha vS\frac{\partial^2 V_a}{\partial S\partial v} + \frac{1}{2}\alpha^2 v\frac{\partial^2 V_a}{\partial v^2} - rV_a}{\frac{\partial V_a}{\partial v}}.$$

Both sides are again separate functions of V and V_a and therefore, we can replace the right hand side by a function $h(S, v, t)$. This function can be rewritten as

$$h(S, v, t) = \lambda(S, v, t) \cdot \alpha \sqrt{v} - \kappa(\theta - v)$$
$$= \lambda v - \kappa(\theta - v),$$

where the drift, diffusion, and the risk premium of the *Heston*-model was plugged in. Collecting terms, one obtains

$$\frac{\partial V}{\partial t} + rS\frac{\partial V}{\partial S} + (\kappa(\theta - v) - \lambda v)\frac{\partial V}{\partial v} + \frac{1}{2}vS^2\frac{\partial^2 V}{\partial S^2} + \rho\alpha vS\frac{\partial^2 V}{\partial S\partial v} + \frac{1}{2}\alpha^2 v\frac{\partial^2 V}{\partial v^2} - rV = 0,$$

which is the desired extended *Black–Scholes*-equation.

Problem 16.2
Adding both integrals, one obtains

$$I_1(v) + I_2(v) = \frac{1}{2\pi} \int_{iv-\infty}^{iv+\infty} e^{-izk}\varphi_0(-z)\left(\frac{i}{z} - \frac{i}{z-i}\right) dz$$

$$= \frac{1}{2\pi} \int_{iv-\infty}^{iv+\infty} e^{-izk}\varphi_0(-z)\frac{1}{z^2 - iz} dz.$$

Plugging this result back into the call price formula yields

$$C_0(K, T) = e^{(b-r)T}S_0 - \frac{e^{-rT}K}{2\pi} \int_{iv-\infty}^{iv+\infty} \frac{e^{-izk}\varphi_0(-z)}{z^2 - iz} dz, \quad v \in (0, 1),$$

which is precisely (16.28) on page 361.

Problem 16.3
Using that $e^{-rT}K \cdot e^k = e^{(b-r)T}S_0$, it is straightforward to deduce that the call price can be expressed as

$$C_0(K, T) = e^{(b-r)T}S_0\Pi_- - e^{-rT}K\Pi_+,$$

with

$$\Pi_{+/-} = \frac{1}{2} + \frac{1}{\pi}\int_0^\infty \mathrm{Re}\left[\frac{e^{iku}\varphi_0\left(u - \frac{i}{2} \pm \frac{i}{2}\right)}{iu}\right] du.$$

This is also the form originally derived by Heston (1993).

Problem 16.4

First observe that the payoff function $w(x)$ can be written as

$$w(x) = \max(e^x, K) = (e^x - K)^+ + K.$$

One then obtains the transformed payoff function

$$
\begin{aligned}
\hat{w}(z) &= \int_{-\infty}^{\infty} e^{izx}(e^x - K)^+ dx + \int_{-\infty}^{\infty} e^{izx} K dx \\
&= \int_{\log K}^{\infty} e^{izx}(e^x - K) dx + \int_{-\infty}^{\infty} e^{izx} K dx \\
&= \int_{\log K}^{\infty} e^{(iz+1)x} dx + \int_{-\infty}^{\log K} e^{izx} K dx \\
&= \left[\frac{e^{(iz+1)x}}{iz + 1} \right]_{\log K}^{\infty} + \left[K \frac{e^{izx}}{iz} \right]_{-\infty}^{\log K}.
\end{aligned}
$$

The upper limit in the first term only exists for $\mathrm{Im}[z] > 1$, whereas the lower limit in the second term requires $\mathrm{Im}[z] < 0$. Both cannot be satisfied at the same time and thus $S_w = \emptyset$.

Problem 16.5

Computing the *Legendre*-polynomials is straightforward using the *Rodrigues*-formula,

$$p_0(x) = 1, \quad p_1(x) = x, \quad \text{and} \quad p_2(x) = \frac{1}{2}(3x^2 - 1).$$

The quadrature points are the zeros of $p_2(x)$, obtained by

$$\frac{1}{2}(3x^2 - 1) \overset{!}{=} 0 \quad \Rightarrow \quad x_{1/2} = \pm \frac{1}{\sqrt{3}}.$$

From (16.93) on page 370, the conditions for the weights are

$$w_1 + w_2 = 2 \quad \text{and} \quad \frac{1}{\sqrt{3}} w_1 - \frac{1}{\sqrt{3}} w_2 = 0.$$

It is easy to see that those conditions are satisfied for $w_1 = w_2 = 1$.

Problem 16.6

For $F_0 = K \pm \delta$, the auxiliary variable z becomes

$$z = \frac{\alpha}{\sigma_0} \log\left(1 \pm \frac{\delta}{K}\right) = \pm \frac{\alpha\delta}{\sigma_0 K},$$

where the logarithm was expanded in a *Taylor*-series and $O(\delta^2)$ terms were neglected. Thus, the auxiliary quantity z is of order δ. Next compute the function $\chi(z)$ and only keep $O(z)$ terms,

$$\chi(z) = \log\left(\frac{\sqrt{1-2\rho z}+z-\rho}{1-\rho}\right) = \log\left(\frac{1-\rho z+z-\rho}{1-\rho}\right)$$

$$= \log\left(\frac{(1-\rho)(1+z)}{1-\rho}\right) = \log(1+z) = z.$$

The square root and the logarithm were again *Taylor*-expanded and $O(z^2)$ terms were neglected. Plugging the result $\chi(z) = z$ into the SABR-model (16.117), one obtains

$$\sigma_{\text{imp.}}(K,T) = \sigma_0\left(1+\left(\frac{\rho\alpha\sigma_0}{4}+\frac{2-3\rho^2}{24}\alpha^2\right)T\right),$$

which is simply a number. In particular, there is no indication of the sign of δ and hence, the smile has to be symmetric.

B.16   Solutions to Problems in Chapter 17

Problem 17.1
First recall that $\text{Var}[N] = E[N^2] - E[N]^2$. For $E[N^2]$, the following chain of equalities holds

$$E[N^2] = \sum_{n=0}^{\infty} n^2\frac{\lambda^n}{n!}e^{-\lambda} = \lambda e^{-\lambda}\sum_{n=1}^{\infty} n\frac{\lambda^{n-1}}{(n-1)!}$$

$$= \lambda e^{-\lambda}\left(\sum_{n=1}^{\infty}(n-1)\frac{\lambda^{n-1}}{(n-1)!} + \sum_{n=1}^{\infty}\frac{\lambda^{n-1}}{(n-1)!}\right)$$

$$= \lambda e^{-\lambda}\left(\lambda\sum_{n=2}^{\infty}\frac{\lambda^{n-2}}{(n-2)!} + \sum_{n=1}^{\infty}\frac{\lambda^{n-1}}{(n-1)!}\right)$$

$$= \lambda e^{-\lambda}\left(\lambda\sum_{n=0}^{\infty}\frac{\lambda^n}{n!} + \sum_{n=0}^{\infty}\frac{\lambda^n}{n!}\right) = \lambda e^{-\lambda}(\lambda e^{\lambda}+e^{\lambda})$$

$$= \lambda^2 + \lambda.$$

Considering the initial formula for the variance, one obtains

$$\text{Var}[N] = \lambda^2 + \lambda - \lambda^2 = \lambda,$$

which is the desired result.

Problem 17.2
The *Laplace*-density can be written without absolute value in the exponent as

$$f(x) = \frac{1}{2\eta}\begin{cases} e^{\frac{x-\kappa}{\eta}} & \text{for } x \le \kappa \\ e^{-\frac{x-\kappa}{\eta}} & \text{for } x > \kappa. \end{cases}$$

Thus, the *Fourier*-integral of the characteristic function can be split up and one obtains

$$
\begin{aligned}
\varphi_X(u) &= \int_{-\infty}^{\kappa} e^{iux} f(x)dx + \int_{\kappa}^{\infty} e^{iux} f(x)dx \\
&= \frac{e^{-\frac{\kappa}{\eta}}}{2\eta} \int_{-\infty}^{\kappa} e^{(iu+\frac{1}{\eta})x} dx + \frac{e^{\frac{\kappa}{\eta}}}{2\eta} \int_{-\infty}^{\kappa} e^{(iu-\frac{1}{\eta})x} dx \\
&= \frac{e^{-\frac{\kappa}{\eta}}}{2\eta} \left[\frac{e^{(iu+\frac{1}{\eta})x}}{iu + \frac{1}{\eta}} \right]_{x=-\infty}^{x=\kappa} + \frac{e^{\frac{\kappa}{\eta}}}{2\eta} \left[\frac{e^{(iu-\frac{1}{\eta})x}}{iu - \frac{1}{\eta}} \right]_{x=\kappa}^{x=\infty} \\
&= \frac{e^{iu\kappa}}{2\eta(iu + \frac{1}{\eta})} - \frac{e^{iu\kappa}}{2\eta(iu - \frac{1}{\eta})} = \frac{e^{iu\kappa}}{2} \left(\frac{1}{1 + iu\eta} + \frac{1}{1 - iu\eta} \right) \\
&= \frac{e^{iu\kappa}}{2} \cdot \frac{2}{(1 + iu\eta)(1 - iu\eta)} = \frac{e^{iu\kappa}}{1 + u^2\eta^2}.
\end{aligned}
$$

Problem 17.3

With the characteristic function $\varphi_X(u)$ of the logarithmic jump size distribution, computed in the solution to Problem 17.2, the characteristic exponent of the *Kou*-model has the form

$$
\psi(u) = iu\mu - \frac{1}{2}u^2\sigma^2 + \lambda\left(\frac{e^{iu\kappa}}{1 + u^2\eta^2} - 1 \right),
$$

for $0 < \eta < 1$. The desired drift correction μ is found by computing $\psi(-i) \overset{!}{=} 0$. One obtains

$$
\mu = -\frac{1}{2}\sigma^2 - \lambda\left(\frac{e^{\kappa}}{1 - \eta^2} - 1 \right).
$$

The next step is to locate possible singularities in the generalized characteristic exponent of Y_t,

$$
\psi(z) = iz\mu - \frac{1}{2}z^2\sigma^2 + \lambda\left(\frac{e^{iz\kappa}}{1 + z^2\eta^2} - 1 \right).
$$

Such singularities can only be found on the imaginary axis. In this case it is easy to see that they are located at $z = \pm\frac{i}{\eta}$. Because of the restriction $0 < \eta < 1$, the strip of regularity is $S_Y = \{z = u + iv : v \in (\alpha, \beta)\}$, with $\alpha < -1$ and $\beta > 0$. Thus, the required strip condition is satisfied.

Problem 17.4

Key to the proof is the reflection equality (17.52) on page 394

$$
P(\{\tau \le T\} \cap W_T \le w_T) = P(W_T \ge 2x_u - w_T).
$$

Start by setting $T = t$ and $w_T = x_u$. Then the reflection equality becomes

$$
P(\{\tau \le t\} \cap W_t \le x_u) = P(W_t \ge x_u).
$$

On the other hand, if $W_t > x_u$, then the process must have crossed the barrier in the past, and thus

$$
P(\{\tau \le t\} \cap W_t > x_u) = P(W_t > x_u)
$$

has to hold. Recalling that $P(W_t = x_u) = 0$, and therefore $P(W_t > x_u) = P(W_t \geq x_u)$, one can add the last two equations to obtain

$$P(\{\tau \leq t\}) = P(\{\tau \leq t\} \cap W_T \leq x_u) + P(\{\tau \leq t\} \cap W_t > x_u) = 2P(W_t \geq x_u).$$

The distribution of W_t is normal, with zero expectation and variance t. Thus, one obtains

$$P(\{\tau \leq t\}) = 2 \int_{x_u}^{\infty} \frac{1}{\sqrt{2\pi t}} e^{-\frac{x^2}{2t}} dx.$$

Make a change of variables $z = \frac{x}{\sqrt{t}}$. Then the increment becomes $dx = \sqrt{t}dz$ and the probability is

$$P(\{\tau \leq t\}) = 2 \int_{\frac{x_u}{\sqrt{t}}}^{\infty} \frac{1}{\sqrt{2\pi}} e^{-\frac{z^2}{2}} dz.$$

Computing the derivative with respect to t yields the desired probability density function

$$f(t) = \frac{x_u}{t\sqrt{2\pi t}} e^{-\frac{x_u^2}{2t}},$$

for $t \geq 0$.

Problem 17.5

The *Laplace*-exponent is computed by

$$l(u) = \int_0^{\infty} (e^{ux} - 1) \frac{1}{\sqrt{2\pi\kappa}} \frac{e^{-\frac{x}{2\kappa}}}{x^{\frac{3}{2}}} dx.$$

Make the substitution $y = \frac{x}{2\kappa}$. Then the increment is $dx = 2\kappa dy$ and the integral becomes

$$l(u) = \int_0^{\infty} (e^{2u\kappa y} - 1) \frac{1}{2\kappa\sqrt{\pi}} \frac{e^{-y}}{y^{\frac{3}{2}}} dy$$

$$= \frac{1}{2\kappa\sqrt{\pi}} \sum_{n=1}^{\infty} \frac{2^n (u\kappa)^n}{n!} \int_0^{\infty} y^{n-\frac{3}{2}} e^{-y} dy$$

$$= \frac{1}{2\kappa\sqrt{\pi}} \sum_{n=1}^{\infty} \frac{2^n (u\kappa)^n}{n!} \Gamma\left(n - \frac{1}{2}\right).$$

Using now that $\Gamma(n - \frac{1}{2}) = 2^{1-n}\sqrt{\pi}(2n-3)!!$, one obtains

$$l(u) = \frac{1}{\kappa} \sum_{n=1}^{\infty} \frac{(u\kappa)^n}{n!} (2n-3)!!$$

$$= \frac{1}{\kappa} - \frac{1}{\kappa}\left(1 - \sum_{n=1}^{\infty} \frac{(u\kappa)^n}{n!} (2n-3)!!\right).$$

But the term in parenthesis is the *Taylor*-series of $\sqrt{1 - 2u\kappa}$, and hence the result is

$$l(u) = \frac{1}{\kappa} - \frac{1}{\kappa}\sqrt{1 - 2u\kappa}.$$

Problem 17.6

Under the *Esscher*-transform, the *Radon–Nikodym*-derivative of the *Wiener*-process W_t is

$$\left.\frac{dQ}{dP}\right|_{\mathcal{F}_t} = \frac{e^{-\gamma W_t}}{E[e^{-\gamma W_t}]}.$$

The expectation value can again be computed using the characteristic function of the *Wiener*-process,

$$E[e^{-\gamma W_t}] = \varphi_W(t, i\gamma) = e^{\frac{1}{2}\gamma^2 t}.$$

Thus, the *Radon–Nikodym*-derivative is

$$\left.\frac{dQ}{dP}\right|_{\mathcal{F}_t} = e^{-\gamma W_t - \frac{1}{2}\gamma^2 t}.$$

The *Girsanov*-transformation provides the *Radon–Nikodym*-derivative

$$\left.\frac{dQ}{dP}\right|_{\mathcal{F}_t} = e^{-\int_0^t \lambda_s dW_s - \frac{1}{2}\int_0^t \lambda_s^2 ds}.$$

In the *Black–Scholes*-framework, the risk premium is $\lambda = \frac{\mu - r}{\sigma}$, which does not depend on time. Thus, by executing the integrals and setting $\lambda = \gamma$, both transformations coincide.

B.17   Solutions to Problems in Chapter 18

Problem 18.1

All future cashflows of the consol can be expressed as

$$B(0, \infty) = c \sum_{n=1}^{\infty} e^{-y(0, T^*) \cdot n} = c \left(\sum_{n=0}^{\infty} \left(e^{-y(0, T^*)} \right)^n - 1 \right).$$

Because $e^{-y(0, T^*)} < 1$, the sum on the right hand side is a convergent geometric series,

$$\sum_{n=0}^{\infty} \left(e^{-y(0, T^*)} \right)^n = \frac{1}{1 - e^{-y(0, T^*)}}.$$

Plugging this result in, one obtains

$$B(0, \infty) = c \left(\frac{1}{1 - e^{-y(0, T^*)}} - 1 \right) = c \cdot \frac{e^{-y(0, T^*)}}{1 - e^{-y(0, T^*)}}.$$

Multiplying and dividing by $e^{y(0, T^*)}$ yields

$$B(0, \infty) = \frac{c}{e^{y(0, T^*)} - 1},$$

which is the desired result.

Problem 18.2

First recall that the exponential integral over the forward rate is precisely the price of a discount bond,

$$P(t, T) = e^{-\int_t^T f(t,s)ds}.$$

If such a bond is equipped with the banking account

$$B(t) = e^{\int_0^t r(s)ds}$$

as a numéraire, the ratio has to be a Q-martingale

$$\frac{P(t, T)}{B(t)} = E^Q\left[\frac{P(T, T)}{B(T)}\bigg|\mathcal{F}_t\right],$$

where Q is again the risk-neutral probability measure. Using that $P(T, T) = 1$ and rearranging yields

$$P(t, T) = E^Q\left[e^{-\int_t^T r(s)ds}\bigg|\mathcal{F}_t\right].$$

But this result closes the circle, because there are now two equalities for $P(t, T)$.

Problem 18.3

Let's organize the tenor of the bond such that at $t = T_n$ the cashflow C_n is due, no matter if this payment is merely a coupon or a coupon plus principal. The value of the bond is then

$$B(t, T) = \sum_{n=1}^N C_n e^{-y(t,T^*)(T_n-t)}.$$

The *Macaulay*-duration is then computed as

$$\textit{Macaulay}\text{-duration} = \frac{1}{B(t, T)} \sum_{n=1}^N (T_n - t)C_n e^{-y(t,T^*)(T_n-t)}.$$

Defining the weight

$$w_n = \frac{C_n e^{-y(t,T^*)(T_n-t)}}{\sum_{k=1}^N C_k e^{-y(t,T^*)(T_k-t)}},$$

this can be rewritten in the desired form

$$\textit{Macaulay}\text{-duration} = \sum_{n=1}^N w_n(T_n - t).$$

Hence, the term average time to maturity refers indeed to a weighted average of individual times to maturity.

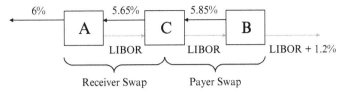

Fig. B.6 Payer and receiver interest rate swap contracted between A, B, and C

Problem 18.4

For simplicity, assume that $t = 0$. Plugging in the yields, the bootstrap formula (18.49) becomes

$$F(0, T_{n-1}, T_n) = \frac{y(0, T_n)T_n - y(0, T_{n-1})T_{n-1}}{T_n - T_{n-1}}.$$

Adding and subtracting $y(0, T_n)$, this can be written as

$$F(0, T_{n-1}, T_n) = y(0, T_n) + \frac{y(0, T_n)T_n - y(0, T_{n-1})T_{n-1} - y(0, T_n)(T_n - T_{n-1})}{T_n - T_{n-1}}$$

$$= y(0, T_n) + \frac{y(0, T_n) - y(0, T_{n-1})}{T_n - T_{n-1}}T_{n-1} = y(0, T_n) + \frac{\Delta y(0, T_n)}{\Delta T_n}T_{n-1},$$

which is a discrete version of (18.44).

Problem 18.5

The situation between companies A and B, and the financial intermediary C is illustrated in Figure B.6. Obviously, the floating leg is unchanged and the profit margin of C is generated solely from the difference in the fixed legs of the swap contracts. This does not necessarily have to be the case, but it is the simplest alternative. The new funding costs for A and B, together with the profit margin of the intermediary C, are given in Table B.4. As desired, C takes 20 bps of the comparative difference and the rest is divided equally between A and B, resulting in a 15 bps comparative advantage for both companies.

Table B.4 Funding costs of A & B and profit margin of C

Company	A	B	C
Without swap	LIBOR + 50 bps	7.2%	–
	6%	5.85%	
With swap	– 5.65%	– LIBOR	– LIBOR + 5.65%
	+ LIBOR	+ LIBOR + 1.2%	+ LIBOR + 5.85%
	LIBOR + 35 bps	7.05%	20 bps

B.18 Solutions to Problems in Chapter 19

Problem 19.1

Under the S-forward measure, the ratio $\frac{V_t}{P(t,S)}$ has to be a Q_S-martingale,

$$\frac{V_t}{P(t,S)} = E^{Q_S}\left[\frac{V_T}{P(T,S)}\middle|\mathcal{F}_t\right].$$

Comparing this equation with the original one with respect to the T-forward measure, one can immediately conclude that the *Radon–Nikodym*-derivative has to be

$$\frac{dQ_T}{dQ_S}\bigg|_{\mathcal{F}_t} = \frac{P(t,S)/P(T,S)}{P(t,T)/P(T,T)} = \frac{P(t,S)}{P(t,T)P(T,S)}.$$

Plugging this expression into the right hand side of the original equation yields

$$V_t = P(t,S)E^{Q_S}\left[\frac{V_T}{P(T,S)}\middle|\mathcal{F}_t\right].$$

Problem 19.2

Suppose at time $t = 0$ you enter a forward contract on the underlying V, with expiry time T. By definition $F_0(K,T) = 0$, which means there is no upfront payment. At the same time take a short position in one unit of the underlying at the price V_0. Use the proceeds to buy the quantity $\frac{V_0}{P(0,T)}$ of a T-maturity discount bond. This operation is also costless; the associated arbitrage portfolio is given in Table B.5. The initial position at $t = 0$ has zero value, and hence the value of the final position at $t = T$ has to be zero, too. Otherwise an arbitrage opportunity would be present. Adding up the individual values at $t = T$,

$$K = \frac{V_0}{P(0,T)}$$

has to hold, which is the desired forward price of V.

Table B.5 Forward arbitrage portfolio

Position	Value at $t = 0$	Value at $t = T$
Forward	0	$V_T - K$
Underlying	$-V_0$	$-V_T$
Discount bond	$\frac{V_0}{P(0,T)} \cdot P(0,T)$	$\frac{V_0}{P(0,T)} \cdot 1$
Total sum	$V_0 - V_0 = 0$	$\frac{V_0}{P(0,T)} - K = 0$

Problem 19.3

From Example 19.1 on page 446 it is known that the quantity $d_{+/-}$ has the form

$$d_{+/-} = \frac{\log\left(\frac{P(t,S)}{P(t,T)K}\right) \pm \frac{1}{2}\int_t^T \sigma_P^2(s)\,ds}{\sqrt{\int_t^T \sigma_P^2(s)\,ds}}.$$

The only challenge is to compute the integrals for $\sigma_P(t) = \sigma\sqrt{1 - e^{-(T-t)}}$. By straight-forward calculus one obtains

$$\sigma^2 \int_t^T 1 - e^{-(T-s)}\,ds = \sigma^2 \left[s - e^{-(T-s)}\right]_t^T = \sigma^2(T - t + e^{-(T-t)} - 1).$$

The desired quantity is thus

$$d_{+/-} = \frac{\log\left(\frac{P(t,S)}{P(t,T)K}\right) \pm \frac{1}{2}\sigma^2(T - t + e^{-(T-t)} - 1)}{\sigma\sqrt{T - t + e^{-(T-t)} - 1}}.$$

Problem 19.4

The definition of the forward LIBOR is

$$L(t, S, T) = \frac{1}{\Delta t}\left(\frac{P(t, S)}{P(t, T)} - 1\right).$$

Plugging this expression into the original equation yields

$$\text{Floating leg} = \Delta t \sum_{n=1}^N P(t, T_n) \cdot \frac{1}{\Delta t}\frac{P(t, T_{n-1}) - P(t, T_n)}{P(t, T_n)}$$

$$= \sum_{n=1}^N P(t, T_{n-1}) - P(t, T_n)$$

$$= P(t, T_0) - P(t, T_N),$$

which is precisely the present value (18.52). The last equation holds, because the sum in the second line is a telescoping series.

Problem 19.5

Using the forward LIBOR representation of Problem 19.4 for the floating leg, the forward swap rate can be written as

$$r_S(t) = \frac{\Delta t \sum_{n=1}^N P(t, T_n)L(t, T_{n-1}, T_n)}{\Delta t \sum_{k=1}^N P(t, T_k)}.$$

It is immediately clear that this is the weighted sum

$$r_S(t) = \sum_{n=1}^n w_n L(t, T_{n-1}, T_n) \quad \text{with} \quad w_n = \frac{P(t, T_n)}{\sum_{k=1}^N P(t, T_k)}.$$

Because $w_n > 0$ for $n = 1, \ldots, N$ and $\sum_{n=1}^N w_n = 1$, it is indeed a weighted average of forward LIBORs. This representation is extremely useful, because usually the weights do not vary much over time and can thus be treated approximately constant.

B.19   Solutions to Problems in Chapter 20

Problem 20.1
The *Vasicek*-model has the affine term structure

$$P(t, T) = e^{-A(t,T)-B(t,T)r(t)} \quad \text{with} \quad B(t, T) = \frac{1 - e^{-\kappa(T-t)}}{\kappa}.$$

The discount bond price dynamics can be derived by applying Itô's lemma,

$$dP = \left(\frac{\partial P}{\partial r} \kappa(\theta - r) + \frac{\partial P}{\partial t} + \frac{1}{2} \frac{\partial^2 P}{\partial r^2} \sigma_r^2 \right) dt + \frac{\partial P}{\partial r} \sigma_r dW$$

$$= \left(\dots \right) dt - \sigma_r B(t, T) P dW.$$

From this result, one can immediately conclude that the desired bond volatility is

$$\sigma_P(t, T) = -\sigma_r \frac{1 - e^{-\kappa(T-t)}}{\kappa}.$$

It is furthermore obvious that the condition $\sigma_P(T, T) = 0$ is satisfied, because $e^0 = 1$.

Problem 20.2
The payoff of a receiver swaption with strike rate κ is either positive, if the receiver swap has positive value, or zero. Using (18.53) on page 437, this can be written as

$$\text{Swpt}_R(T_0, \kappa) = \left(\Delta t \kappa \sum_{n=1}^{N} P(T_0, T_n, r_0) - 1 + P(T_0, T_N, r_0) \right)^+,$$

where the dependence of the discount bond prices on the short rate $r(T_0) = r_0$ was stated explicitly. As in case of the coupon-bearing bond, one can determine a particular rate r^* by numerical root search, such that

$$\Delta t \kappa \sum_{n=1}^{N} P(T_0, T_n, r^*) + P(T_0, T_N, r^*) = 1$$

holds. The next step is to define the strike prices

$$K_n = P(T_0, T_n, r^*),$$

and to observe that the swaption payoff can now be expressed as

$$\text{Swpt}_R(T_0, \kappa) = \left(\Delta t \kappa \sum_{n=1}^{N} (P(T_0, T_n) - K_n) + (P(T_0, T_N) - K_N) \right)^+.$$

Realizing that each difference in this payoff becomes positive simultaneously if and only if $r^* > r_0$, the maximum bracket becomes distributive again and one obtains

$$\text{Swpt}_R(T_0, \kappa) = \Delta t \kappa \sum_{n=1}^{N} (P(T_0, T_n) - K_n)^+ + (P(T_0, T_N) - K_N)^+.$$

But the remaining brackets are the payoffs of call options on discount bonds and thus, the generic value of a receiver swaption at time t has to be

$$\text{Swpt}_R(t,\kappa) = \Delta t\, \kappa \sum_{n=1}^{N} C_t^P(K_n, T_n) + C_t^P(K_N, T_N),$$

with the superscript P again referring to the discount bond. This is by the way identical to a call option on a coupon-bearing bond, with coupon rate $c = \Delta t\, \kappa$ and strike price $K = 1$, see (20.54) on page 465.

Problem 20.3

Clearly the model belongs to the affine class, because the drift and squared diffusion are affine functions of $r(t)$. In particular using Theorem 20.1 on page 466, one obtains

$$a(t) = \sigma_r^2 \quad \text{and} \quad b(t) = e^{-\theta t},$$

whereas $\alpha(t) = \beta(t) = 0$. This immediately implies $\frac{\partial}{\partial t} B(t,T) = -1$, and considering the terminal condition $B(T,T) = 0$, one obtains the trivial solution

$$B(t,T) = T - t.$$

Thus, the condition for $A(t,T)$ becomes

$$\frac{\partial}{\partial t} A(t,T) = \frac{1}{2}\sigma_r^2 (T-t)^2 - e^{-\theta t}(T-t).$$

This equation can be integrated immediately and one obtains

$$A(t,T) = -\int_t^T dA(s,T) = -\frac{1}{6}\sigma_r^2 (T-t)^3 + \int_t^T e^{-\theta s}(T-s)ds.$$

The remaining integral on the right hand side is not that trivial to solve, but using integration by parts one obtains

$$\int_t^T e^{-\theta s}(T-s)ds = T \int_t^T e^{-\theta s}ds - \int_t^T s e^{-\theta s}ds$$

$$= T \int_t^T e^{-\theta s}ds + \frac{s e^{-\theta s}}{\theta}\Big|_t^T - \frac{1}{\theta}\int_t^T e^{-\theta s}ds$$

$$= -\left(T - \frac{1}{\theta}\right)\frac{e^{-\theta T} - e^{-\theta t}}{\theta} + \frac{T}{\theta}e^{-\theta T} - \frac{t}{\theta}e^{-\theta t}$$

$$= \frac{1}{\theta}e^{-\theta t}\left(T - t - \frac{1}{\theta}\right) + \frac{1}{\theta^2}e^{-\theta T}.$$

Putting all the pieces together, the solution for $A(t,T)$ is

$$A(t,T) = -\frac{1}{6}\sigma_r^2 (T-t)^3 + \frac{1}{\theta}e^{-\theta t}\left(T - t - \frac{1}{\theta}\right) + \frac{1}{\theta^2}e^{-\theta T}.$$

Problem 20.4

The easiest way to see that the *Markov*-property fails for x_t, is to consider the conditional variance

$$\text{Var}[x_{t+1}|\mathcal{F}_t] = E[h_{t+1}|\mathcal{F}_t]E[z_{t+1}^2] = \omega + \alpha x_t^2 + \beta h_t = f(x_t, h_t).$$

This cannot be a *Markov*-process, because the conditional variance is a function of x_t and h_t. In fact the joint process (x_t, h_t) is *Markov*ian.

Problem 20.5

The forward rate volatility function in the *Hull–White*-extended *Vasicek*-model is known from (20.100) on page 471

$$\sigma_f(t, T) = \sigma_r e^{-\kappa(T-t)}.$$

The convexity adjustment can then be computed as

$$\text{Conv. Adj.} = \int_t^T \sigma_f(u, T) \int_u^T \sigma_f(u, s)dsdu = \sigma_r^2 \int_t^T e^{-\kappa(T-u)} \int_u^T e^{-\kappa(s-u)}dsdu$$

$$= \frac{\sigma_r^2}{\kappa} \int_t^T e^{-\kappa(T-u)}(1 - e^{-\kappa(T-u)})du = \frac{\sigma_r^2}{\kappa}\left(\frac{1 - e^{-\kappa(T-t)}}{\kappa} - \frac{1 - e^{-2\kappa(T-t)}}{2\kappa}\right)$$

$$= \frac{\sigma_r^2}{2\kappa^2}(1 - 2e^{-\kappa(T-t)} + e^{-2\kappa(T-t)}) = \frac{\sigma_r^2}{2\kappa^2}(1 - e^{-\kappa(T-t)})^2.$$

As anticipated, the convexity adjustment is always positive, that is future rates are always greater than forward rates.

Problem 20.6

A quadratic spline is a set of second degree polynomials

$$\sigma_n(\tau) = \sum_{k=0}^{2} a_{n,k}(\tau - \tau_n)^k = a_{n,0} + a_{n,1}(\tau - \tau_n) + a_{n,2}(\tau - \tau_n)^2,$$

for $n = 1, \ldots, N - 1$. There is a total of $3(N - 1)$ unknown coefficients to be determined. Because all starting points have to be matched,

$$\sigma_n(\tau_n) = a_{n,0} = \sigma(t, \tau_n)$$

has to hold. That fixes the first $N - 1$ coefficients. The endpoints of every spline also have to match the observations, and thus

$$\sigma_n(\tau_{n+1}) = a_{n,0} + a_{n,1}(\tau_{n+1} - \tau_n) + a_{n,2}(\tau_{n+1} - \tau_n)^2 = \sigma(t, \tau_{n+1})$$

has to hold, too. Because of the linearity of the first spline, which means $a_{1,2} = 0$, this also determines $a_{1,1}$. That accounts for $N + 1$ coefficients. From the derivative condition $\sigma_n'(\tau_{n+1}) = \sigma_{n+1}'(\tau_{n+1})$, one obtains

$$a_{n,1} + 2a_{n,2}(\tau_{n+1} - \tau_n) = a_{n+1,1}.$$

Solving for $a_{n,2}$ and plugging the result into the previous equation yields the sequential formula

$$a_{n+1,1} = 2\frac{\sigma(t, \tau_{n+1}) - a_{n,0}}{\tau_{n+1} - \tau_n} - a_{n,1},$$

determining the $N - 2$ coefficients $a_{n,1}$ for $n = 2, \ldots, N - 1$. The remaining $N - 2$ coefficients $a_{n,2}$ can now be deduced from the endpoint condition, because everything else is known. This accounts for all $3(N - 1)$ coefficients, as desired.

B.20   Solutions to Problems in Chapter 21

Problem 21.1

The claim is proved by solving the stochastic differential equation in X_t. Using Itô's lemma for jump-diffusions, the dynamics of $\log X_t$ is

$$d\log X_t = \left(\log\left(\frac{X_{t^-}}{P(t, t + \Delta t)}\right) - \log X_{t^-}\right)dN_t$$
$$= -\log P(t, t + \Delta t)dN_t,$$

with the increment of the counting process

$$dN_t = \sum_{n=0}^{N-1} \delta(t - T_n)dt.$$

This equation can be integrated immediately and one obtains

$$\log X_t = \log X_0 - \sum_{n=0}^{N-1} \int_0^t \log P(s, s + \Delta t)\delta(s - T_n)ds$$
$$= -\sum_{n=0}^{N_t} \log P(T_{n-1}, T_n),$$

where $X_0 = \frac{1}{P(0, T_0)}$ was used. Exponentiating both sides yields the desired result

$$X_t = \prod_{n=0}^{N_t} \frac{1}{P_n(T_{n-1})}.$$

Problem 21.2

Notice that the stopping times T_n in the counting process N_t are deterministic and therefore the jumps in X_t are foreseeable. When approaching a jump time T_k from the left, we have

$$\lim_{t \to T_k^-} B_d(t) = \prod_{n=0}^{k} \frac{1}{P_n(T_{n-1})},$$

because $P_k(T_k^-) = 1$. Approaching T_k from the right, we have

$$\lim_{t \to T_k^+} B_d(t) = \prod_{n=0}^{k+1} \frac{P_{k+1}(T_k)}{P_n(T_{n-1})} = \prod_{n=0}^{k} \frac{1}{P_n(T_{n-1})} = \lim_{t \to T_k^-} B_d(t),$$

which means, there is no jump in $B_d(t)$ at T_k. Because $P_n(t)$ is almost surely continuous for all n, so is $B_d(t)$.

Problem 21.3

From the change-of-numéraire toolkit, we have for the *Wiener*-increment of $dL_n(t)$

$$dW_n^{Q_B} = dW_n^{Q_n} - \langle e_n | R(\mathrm{DC} \log(B_d/P_n)) \rangle dt.$$

A closer analysis of the DC-operator term yields

$$\mathrm{DC} \log(B_d/P_n) = \mathrm{DC} \log(XP_{N_t}/P_n) = \mathrm{DC} \log X + \mathrm{DC} \log(P_{N_t}/P_n).$$

Since X_t is constant almost surely, $\log X_t$ is just a number and the associated DC-term vanishes. All that is left is

$$\mathrm{DC} \log(P_{N_t}/P_n) = \mathrm{DC} \log\left(\frac{P_{N_t}}{P_{N_t+1}} \frac{P_{N_t+1}}{P_{N_t+2}} \cdots \frac{P_{n-1}}{P_n}\right) = \mathrm{DC} \log\left(\prod_{k=N_t+1}^{n} (1 + \Delta t L_k)\right)$$

$$= \sum_{k=N_t+1}^{n} \mathrm{DC} \log(1 + \Delta t L_k) = \sum_{k=N_t+1}^{n} \frac{\mathrm{DC}(1 + \Delta t L_k)}{1 + \Delta t L_k}$$

$$= \sum_{k=N_t+1}^{n} \frac{\Delta t \, \mathrm{DC} \, L_k}{1 + \Delta t L_k} = \sum_{k=N_t+1}^{n} \frac{\sigma_k \Delta t L_k}{1 + \Delta t L_k} |e_k\rangle,$$

where again linearity of the DC-operator was used. The desired change-of-numéraire transformation is thus

$$dW_n^{Q_B} = dW_n^{Q_n} - \sum_{k=N_t+1}^{n} \frac{\Delta t L_k}{1 + \Delta t L_k} \rho_{nk} \sigma_k dt.$$

Under every measure, $dL_n(t)$ has diffusion $\sigma_n(t)L_n(t)$ and therefore the drift under the spot LIBOR measure Q_B has to be

$$\mu_n(t) = \sum_{k=N_t+1}^{n} \frac{\Delta t L_k(t)}{1 + \Delta t L_k(t)} \rho_{nk} \sigma_n(t) \sigma_k(t).$$

The fact that only "surviving" rates $L_k(t)$ for $k > N_t$ contribute is perfectly right, because all rates for $k \le N_t$ have already realized and therefore their volatilities are zero. But for $\sigma_k(t) = 0$, the associated term in the sum vanishes.

Problem 21.4

The reversing pair should be priced under the terminal measure Q_2 for two reasons. First of all, two forward LIBORs $L_1(t)$ and $L_2(t)$ have to be simulated, and the terminal measure makes the dynamics of one of them, namely $dL_2(t)$, driftless. Furthermore, the payoff has to be discounted, because it occurs delayed at T_2. Under the terminal measure, the numéraire and the discount factor cancel and one obtains

$$V(t, T_0) = P_2(t) E^{Q_2}\left[P_2(T_0)V(T_0, T_0) \prod_{n=1}^{2}(1 + \Delta t L_n(T_0)) \middle| \mathcal{F}_t\right]$$

$$= P_2(t) E^{Q_2}[V(T_0, T_0)|\mathcal{F}_t].$$

REFERENCES

Abel, A. B. 1990. Asset Prices under Habit Formation and Catching up with the Joneses. *American Economic Review*, 80, 38–42.

Abramowitz, M. and Stegun, I. A. 1970. *Handbook of Mathematical Functions*. New York: Dover Publications.

Ackert, L. F. and Deaves, R. 2010. *Behavioral Finance: Psychology, Decision-Making, and Markets*. Mason, Ohio: South-Western Cengage Learning.

Aït-Sahalia, Y., Hansen, L. P., and Scheinkman, J. A. 2010. Operator Methods for Continuous-Time Markov Processes. Pages 1–66 of: Aït-Sahalia, Y. and Hansen, L. P. (eds.), *Handbook of Financial Econometrics – Volume 1*. Amsterdam: North-Holland.

Albrecher, H., Mayer, P., Schoutens, W., and Tistaert, J. 2007. The Little Heston Trap. *Wilmott Magazine*, 6(1), 83–92.

Allais, M. 1953. Le comportement de l'homme rationnel devant le risque: critique des postulats et axiomes de l'école Américaine. *Econometrica*, 21(4), 503–546.

Almgren, R. and Chriss, N. 2006. Optimal Portfolios from Ordering Information. *Journal of Risk*, 9(1), 1–47.

Andersen, L. B. G. and Piterbarg, V. V. 2010a. *Interest Rate Modelling – Volume 1: Foundations and Vanilla Models*. London: Atlantic Financial Press.

Andersen, L. B. G. and Piterbarg, V. V. 2010b. *Interest Rate Modelling – Volume 2: Term Structure Models*. London: Atlantic Financial Press.

Arnold, L. 1974. *Stochastic Differential Equations. Theory and Application*. New Jersey: Wiley-Interscience.

Arrow, K. J. 1965. The Theory of Risk Aversion. Chapter 3, pages 90–109 of: *Aspects of the Theory of Risk Bearing*. Helsinki: Yrjö Jahnsson Foundation. Reprinted in: *Essays in the Theory of Risk-Bearing*. Chicago: Markham Publishing Co., 1971.

Arrow, K. J. and Debreu, G. 1954. Existence of an Equilibrium for a Competitive Economy. *Econometrica*, 2, 265–290.

Baaquie, B. E. 2004. *Quantum Finance: Path Integrals and Hamiltonians for Options and Interest Rates*. Cambridge University Press.

Bachelier, L. 1900. *Théorie de la Spéculation*. Ph.D. thesis, Sorbonne, Paris.

Bakshi, G. S. and Chen, Z. 1996. The Spirit of Capitalism and Stock Market Prices. *American Economic Review*, 86(1), 133–157.

Barberis, N. and Thaler, R. H. 2005. A Survey of Behavioral Finance. Chapter 1, pages 1–75 of: Thaler, R. H. (ed.), *Advances in Behavioral Finance*, vol. II. Princeton University Press.

Barberis, N., Shleifer, A., and Vishny, R. 1998. A Model of Investor Sentiment. *Journal of Financial Economics*, 49, 307–343.

Barndorff-Nielssen, O. E. 1997. Normal Inverse Gaussian Distributions and Stochastic Volatility Modelling. *Scandinavian Journal of Statistics*, 24, 1–13.

Barndorff-Nielssen, O. E. 1998. Processes of Normal Inverse Gaussian Type. *Finance and Stochastics*, 2(1), 41–68.

Bates, D. 1996. Jumps and Stochastic Volatility: The Exchange Rate Processes Implicit in Deutschemark Opions. *Review of Financial Studies*, 9, 69–107.

Bell, D. E. 1988. One-Switch Utility Functions and a Measure of Risk. *Management Science*, 34(2), 1416–1424.

Bellman, R. 1954. The Theory of Dynamic Programming. *Bulletin of the American Mathematical Society*, 60(6), 503–516.

Bellman, R. 1957. *Dynamic Programming*. Princeton University Press.

Benartzi, S. and Thaler, R. H. 1995. Myopic Loss Aversion and the Equity Premium Puzzle. *Quarterly Journal of Economics*, 110(1), 73–92.

Bernardo, J. M. and Smith, A. F. M. 2000. *Bayesian Theory*. New York, Chichester, Brisbane: John Wiley & Sons.

Billingsley, P. 1995. *Probability and Measure*. 3rd edn. New York, Chichester, Brisbane: John Wiley & Sons.

Bingham, N. H. and Kiesel, R. 2004. *Risk-Neutral Valuation*. 2nd edn. London, Berlin, Heidelberg: Springer.

Birnbaum, M. H. and Navarrete, J. B. 1998. Testing Descriptive Utility Theories: Violations of Stochastic Dominance and Cumulative Independence. *Journal of Risk and Uncertainty*, 17, 49–78.

BIS 2005. *Zero-Coupon Yield Curves: Technical Documentation*. Bank for International Settlements, Monetary and Economic Department, Basel, Switzerland. BIS Papers No. 25.

BIS 2014. *Statistical Release: OTC Derivatives Statistics at End-June 2014*. Bank for International Settlements, Monetary and Economic Department, Basel, Switzerland. Available at www.BIS.org.

Black, F. 1976. The Pricing of Commodity Contracts. *Journal of Financial Economics*, 3, 167–179.

Black, F. and Karasinski, P. 1991. Bond and Option Pricing when Short Rates are Lognormal. *Financial Analysts Journal*, 47(4), 52–59.

Black, F. and Litterman, R. 1992. Global Portfolio Optimization. *Financial Analysts Journal*, 48(5), 28–43.

Black, F. and Scholes, M. 1973. The Pricing of Options and Corporate Liabilities. *Journal of Political Economy*, 81, 637–654.

Black, F. Derman, E., and Toy, W. 1990. A One-Factor Model of Interest Rates and Its Application to Treasury Bond Options. *Financial Analysts Journal*, 46(1), 33–39.

Blanchard, O. J. 1979. Speculative Bubbles, Crashes and Rational Expectations. *Economics Letters*, 3(4), 387–389.

Bollerslev, T. 1986. Generalized Autoregressive Conditional Heteroskedasticity. *Journal of Econometrics*, 31(3), 307–327.

Brace, A., Gatarek, D., and Musiela, M. 1997. The Market Model of Interest Rate Dynamics. *Mathematical Finance*, 7(2), 127–147.

Breeden, D. and Litzenberger, R. 1978. Prices of State-Contingent Claims Implicit in Option Prices. *Journal of Business*, 51, 621–651.

Brigo, D. and Mercurio, F. 2007. *Inerest Rate Models: Theory and Practice*. 2nd edn. Berlin, Heidelberg, New York: Springer.

Brockwell, P. J. and Davis, R. A. 2006. *Time Series: Theory and Methods*. 2nd edn. Berlin, Heidelberg, New York: Springer.

Cain, G. 1999. *Complex Analysis*. Available at www.FreeScience.info.

Cairns, A. J. G. 2004. *Interest Rate Models: An Introduction*. Princeton University Press.

Campbell, J. Y. and Cochrane, J. H. 1999. By Force of Habit: A Consumption-Based Explanation of Aggregate Stock Market Behavior. *Journal of Political Economy*, 107(2), 205–251.

Campbell, J. Y. and Cochrane, J. H. 2000. Explaining the Poor Performance of Consumption-Based Asset Pricing Models. *Journal of Finance*, 55(6), 2863–2878.

Capinski, M. and Zastawniak, T. 2003. *Mathematics for Finance: An Introduction to Financial Engineering*. Berlin, Heidelberg, New York: Springer.

Carr, P. P. and Madan, D. P. 1999. Option Valuation Using the Fast Fourier Transform. *Journal of Computational Finance*, 2(4), 61–73.

Casscells, W., Schoenberger, A., and Grayboys, T. B. 1978. Interpretation by Physicians of Clinical Laboratory Results. *New England Journal of Medicine*, 299, 999–1001.

Chan, W. H. and Maheu, J. M. 2002. Conditional Jump Dynamics in Stock Market Returns. *Journal of Business & Economic Statistics*, 20(3), 377–389.

Chiang, A. C. and Wainwright, K. 2004. *Fundamental Methods of Mathematical Economics*. 4th edn. New York, Chicago, San Francisco: McGraw-Hill.

Christoffersen, P., Jacobs, K., and Ornthanalai, C. 2009. *Exploring Time-Varying Jump Intensities: Evidence from S&P 500 Returns and Options*. Tech. rept. 2009s-34. Cirano.

Christoffersen, P., Jacobs, K., and Ornthanalai, C. 2012. *GARCH Option Valuation: Theory and Evidence*. Tech. rept. 2012-50. Creates.

Cochrane, J. H. 2005. *Asset Pricing*. Princeton University Press.

Colwell, D. B. and Elliott, R. J. 1993. Discontinuous Asset Prices and Non-Attainable Contingent Claims. *Mathematical Finance*, 3(3), 295–308.

Constantinides, G. M. 1982. Intertemporal Asset Pricing with Heterogeneous Consumers and without Demand Aggregation. *Journal of Business*, 55(2), 253–267.

Constantinides, G. M. 1990. Habit Formation: A Resolution of the Equity Premium Puzzle. *Journal of Political Economy*, 98(3), 519–543.

Constantinides, G. M. and Duffie, D. 1996. Asset Pricing with Heterogeneous Consumers. *Journal of Political Economy*, 104(2), 219–240.

Cont, R. and Tankov, P. 2004. *Financial Modelling with Jump Processes*. Boca Raton, London, New York: Chapman & Hall/CRC Press Company.

Conze, A. and Viswanathan. 1991. Path Dependent Options: The Case of Lookback Options. *Journal of Finance*, 46(5), 1893–1907.

Cox, A. 2010. Arbitrage Bounds. Pages 53–61 of: Cont, R. (ed.), *Encyclopedia of Quantitative Finance*. Chichester, West Sussex: John Wiley & Sons.

Cox, J. C., Ross, S. A., and Rubinstein, M. 1979. Option Pricing: A Simplified Approach. *Journal of Financial Economics*, 7, 229–263.

Cox, J. C., Ingersoll, J. E., and Ross, S. A. 1981. The Relation Between Forward Prices and Future Prices. *Journal of Financial Economics*, 9, 321–346.

Cox, J. C., Ingersoll, J. E., and Ross, S. A. 1985. A Theory of the Term Structure of Interest Rate. *Econometrica*, 53, 385–407.

Crank, J. and Nicolson, P. 1996. A Practical Method for Numerical Evaluation of Solutions of Partial Differential Equations of the Heat-Conduction Type. *Advances in Computational Mathematics*, 6, 207–226. Reprint.

Cuthbertson, K. and Nitzsche, D. 2004. *Quantitative Financial Economics: Stocks, Bonds and Foreign Exchange*. 2nd edn. Chichester, West Sussex: John Wiley & Sons.

Daniel, K. D., Hirshleifer, D., and Subrahmanyam, A. 2001. Overconfidence, Arbitrage, and Equilibrium Asset Pricing. *Journal of Finance*, 56(3), 921–965.

De Giorgi, E. G. and Hens, T. 2006. Making Prospect Theory Fit for Finance. *Financial Markets and Portfolio Management*, 20, 339–360.

De Giorgi, E. G., Hens, T., and Levy, H. 2011. *CAPM Equilibria with Prospect Theory Preferences*. Social Science Research Network (SSRN): 420184.

Delbaen, F. and Schachermayer, W. 1994. A General Version of the Fundamental Theorem of Asset Pricing. *Mathematische Annalen*, 300, 463–520.

Delbaen, F. and Schachermayer, W. 2006. *The Mathematics of Arbitrage*. Berlin, Heidelberg: Springer.

Derman, E. and Kani, I. 1998. Stochastic Implied Trees: Arbitrage Pricing with Stochastic Term and Strike Structure of Volatility. *International Journal of Theoretical and Applied Finance*, 1, 61–110.

Deutsch, H.-P. 2002. *Derivatives and Internal Models*. 2nd edn. Basingstoke, New York: Palgrave.

Dothan, L. U. 1978. On the Term Structure of Interest Rates. *Journal of Financial Economics*, 6(1), 59–69.

Duan, J.-C. 1995. The GARCH Option Pricing Model. *Mathematical Finance*, 5(1), 13–23.

Duan, J.-C., Ritchken, P., and Sun, Z. 2006a. Approximating GARCH-Jump Models, Jump-Diffusion Processes and Option Pricing. *Mathematical Finance*, 16(1), 21–52.

Duan, J.-C., Ritchken, P., and Sun, Z. 2006b. *Jump Starting GARCH: Pricing and Hedging Options with Jumps in Returns and Volatilities*. Tech. rept. 06-19. Federal Reserve Bank of Cleveland.

Duffie, D. 2001. *Dynamic Asset Pricing Theory*. 3rd edn. Princeton University Press.

Duffie, D. 2003. Intertemporal Asset Pricing Theory. Chapter 11, pages 641–742 of: Constantinides, G. M., Harris, M., and Stulz, R.M. (eds.), *Handbook of the Economics of Finance*, vol. 1B. Amsterdam, Boston, Heidelberg: North-Holland.

Dumas, B., Fleming, J., and Whaley, R. E. 1998. Implied Volatility Functions: Empirical Tests. *Journal of Finance*, 53, 2059–2106.

Dupire, B. 1994. Pricing with a Smile. *Risk*, 7, 18–20.

Dybvig, P. H. and Ross, S. A. 2003. Arbitrage, State Prices and Portfolio Theory. Chapter 10, pages 606–637 of: Constantinides, G.M., Harris, M., and Stulz, R.M. (eds.), *Handbook of the Economics of Finance*, vol. 1B. Amsterdam, Boston, Heidelberg: North-Holland.

Ekstrand, C. 2011. *Financial Derivatives Modeling*. Berlin, Heidelberg, New York: Springer.

Elliott, R. J. and Kopp, P. E. 2005. *Mathematics of Financial Markets*. 2nd edn. Berlin, Heidelberg, New York: Springer.

Ellsberg, D. 1961. Risk, Ambiguity, and the Savage Axioms. *Quarterly Journal of Economics*, 75(4), 643–669.

Elton, E. J., Gruber, M. J., Brown, S. J., and Goetzmann, W. N. 2010. *Modern Portfolio Theory and Investment Analysis*. 8th edn. New York, London, Toronto: John Wiley & Sons.

Engle, R. F. 1982. Autoregressive Conditional Heteroskedasticity with Estimates of the Variance of United Kingdom Inflation. *Econometrica*, 50, 987–1008.

Engle, R. F. 1990. Discussion: Stock Market Volatility and the Crash of '87. *Review of Financial Studies*, 3, 103–106.

Engle, R. F. 2001. GARCH 101: The Use of ARCH/GARCH Models in Applied Econometrics. *Journal of Econometric Perspectives*, 14(4), 157–168.

Engle, R. F. and Ng, V. 1993. Measuring and Testing the Impact of News on Volatility. *Journal of Finance*, 43, 1749–1778.

Epps, T. W. 1993. Characteristic Functions and their Empirical Counterparts: Geometrical Interpretations and Applications to Statistical Inference. *American Statistician*, 47, 33–38.

Epstein, L. G. and Zin, S. E. 1989. Substitution, Risk Aversion and the Temporal Behavior of Consumption Growth and Asset Returns: A Theoretical Framework. *Econometrica*, 57(4), 937–969.

Epstein, L. G. and Zin, S. E. 1991. Substitution, Risk Aversion and the Temporal Behavior of Consumption Growth and Asset Returns: An Empirical Analysis. *Journal of Political Economy*, 99(2), 263–286.

Eraker, B., Johannes, M., and Polson, N. 2003. The Impact of Jumps in Volatility and Returns. *Journal of Finance*, 58(3), 1269–1300.

Esscher, F. 1932. On the Probability Function in the Collective Theory of Risk. *Skandinavisk Aktuarietidskrift*, 15, 175–195.

Estrada, J. 2005. *Finance in a Nutshell*. London, New York, Toronto: Prentice Hall.

Evans, L. C. 2010. *Partial Differential Equations*. 2nd edn. Graduate Studies in Mathematics, vol. 19. Providence: American Mathematical Society.

Fabozzi, F. J. 2007. *Fixed Income Analysis*. 2nd edn. Hoboken, New Jersey: John Wiley & Sons.

Fabozzi, F. J., Gupta, F., and Markowitz, H. M. 2002. The Legacy of Modern Portfolio Theory. *Journal of Investing*, 11(3), 7–22.

Fama, E. F. 1970. Efficient Capital Markets: A Review of Theory and Empirical Work. *Journal of Finance*, 25(2), 383–417.

Fama, E. F. and French, K. R. 1993. Common Risk Factors in the Returns on Stocks and Bonds. *Journal of Financial Economics*, 33, 3–56.

Fama, E. F. and French, K. R. 1996. Multifactor Explanations of Asset Pricing Anomalies. *Journal of Finance*, 51(1), 55–84.

Farin, G. and Hansford, D. 2005. *Practical Linear Algebra: A Geometry Toolbox*. Wellesley, Massachusetts: A. K. Peters.

Feller, W. 1951. Two Singular Diffusion Problems. *Annals of Mathematics*, 54, 173–182.

Filipović, D. 2001. *Consistency Problems for Heath-Jarrow-Morton Interest Rate Models*. Heidelberg, London, New York: Springer.

Filipović, D. 2009. *Term-Structure Models*. Heidelberg, London, New York: Springer.

Föllmer, H. and Schied, A. 2011. *Stochastic Finance: An Introduction in Discrete Time*. 3rd edn. Berlin, New York: De Gruyter.

Froot, K. A. and Dabora, E. M. 1999. How Are Stock Prices Affected by the Location of Trade? *Journal of Financial Economics*, 53, 189–216.

Froot, K. A. and Obstfeld, M. 1991. Intrinsic Bubbles: The Case of Stock Prices. *American Economic Review*, 81(5), 1189–1214.

Gatarek, D., Bachert, P., and Maksymiuk, R. 2006. *The LIBOR Market Model in Practice*. Chichester, New York: John Wiley & Sons.

Gatfaoui, H. 2010. Capital Asset Pricing Model. Pages 241–249 of: Cont, R. (ed.), *Encyclopedia of Quantiatative Finance*. New York: John Wiley & Sons.

Gatheral, J. 2006. *The Volatility Surface: A Practitioner's Guide*. New Jersey: John Wiley & Sons.

Gerber, H. U. and Shiu, E. S. W. 1994. Option Pricing by Esscher Transforms. *Transactions of Society of Actuaries*, 46, 99–140.

Glasserman, P. 2010. *Monte Carlo Methods in Financial Engineering*. Berlin, Heidelberg, New York: Springer.

Goldman, M. B., Sosin, H. B., and Gatto, M. A. 1979. Path Dependent Options: "Buy at the Low, Sell at the High." *Jounral of Finance*, 34(5), 1111–1127.

Gordon, M. J. 1959. Dividends, Earnings, and Stock Prices. *Review of Economics and Statistics*, 41(2), 99–105.

Gradshteyn, I. S. and Ryzhik, I. M. 2007. *Table of Integrals, Series, and Products*. 7th edn. Amsterdam, Boston, Heidelberg: Academic Press.

Greene, W. H. 2003. *Econometric Analysis*. 5th edn. New Jersey: Prentice-Hall.

Grinblatt, M. and Han, B. 2005. Prospect Theory, Mental Accounting, and Momentum. *Journal of Financial Economics*, 78, 311–339.

Hagan, P. S., Kumar, D., Lesniewski, A. S., and Woodward, D. E. 2002. Managing Smile Risk. *Wilmott Magazine*, September, 84–108.

Hansen, L. P. and Jagannathan, R. 1991. Implications of Security Market Data for Models of Dynamic Economies. *Journal of Political Economy*, 99(2), 225–262.

Harrison, J. M. and Kreps, D. M. 1979. Martingales and Arbitrage in Multiperiod Securities Markets. *Journal of Economic Theory*, 20, 381–408.

Harrison, J. M. and Pliska, S. R. 1981. Martingales and Stochastic Integrals in the Theory of Continuous Trading. *Stochastic Processes and their Applications*, 11, 215–260.

Haug, E. G. 2007. *The Complete Guide to Option Pricing Formulas*. 2nd edn. New York, Chicago, San Francisco: McGraw-Hill.

Heath, D., Jarrow, R., and Morton, A. 1992. Bond Pricing and the Term Structure of Interest Rates: A New Methodology for Contingent Claims Valuation. *Econometrica*, 60(1), 77–105.

Hens, T. and Rieger, M. O. 2010. *Financial Economics: A Concise Interduction to Classical and Behavioral Finance*. Berlin, Heidelberg, New York: Springer.

Heston, S. L. 1993. A Closed-Form Solution for Options with Stochastic Volatility with Applications to Bonds and Currency Options. *Review of Financial Studies*, 6(2), 327–343.

Heston, S. L. and Nandi, S. 1997. *A Closed-Form GARCH Option Pricing Model*. Tech. rept. 97-9. Federal Reserve Bank of Atlanta.

Heston, S. L. and Nandi, S. 2000. A Closed-Form GARCH Option Valuation Model. *Review of Financial Studies*, 13(3), 585–625.

Ho, T. S. Y. and Lee, S.-B. 1986. Term Structure Movements and Pricing Interest Rate Contingent Claims. *Journal of Finance*, 41(5), 1011–1029.

Hoggard, T., Whalley, A. E., and Wilmott, P. 1994. Hedging Option Portfolios in the Presence of Transaction Costs. *Advances in Futures and Options Research*, 7, 21–35.

Hubalek, F. and Sgarra, C. 2006. Esscher Transforms and the Minimal Entropy Martingale Measure for Exponential Lévy Models. *Quantitative Finance*, 6(2), 125–145.

Huberman, G. 1982. A Simple Approach to Arbitrage Pricing Theory. *Journal of Economic Theory*, 28(1), 183–191.

Hull, J. and White, A. 1987. The Pricing of Options on Assets with Stochastic Volatilities. *Journal of Finance*, 42(2), 281–300.

Hull, J. and White, A. 1990. Pricing Interest-Rate-Derivative Securities. *Review of Financial Studies*, 3(4), 573–592.

Hull, J. C. 2009. *Options, Futures, and other Derivatives*. 7th edn. New Jersey: Prentice Hall.

Hull, J. C. 2012. *Risk Management and Financial Institutions*. 3rd edn. New Jersey: John Wiley & Sons.

Iacus, S. M. 2011. *Option Pricing and Estimation of Financial Models with R*. West Sussex, New York, San Francisco: John Wiley & Sons.

Ingersoll, J. E. 1987. *Theory of Financial Decision Making*. Lanham, Maryland: Rowman & Littlefield Publishers.

Jamshidian, F. 1989. An Exact Bond Option Formula. *Journal of Finance*, 44(1), 205–209.

Jamshidian, F. 1997. LIBOR and Swap Market Models and Measures. *Finance and Stochastics*, 1, 293–330.

Janssen, J., Manca, R., and Volpe, E. 2009. *Mathematical Finance: Deterministic and Stochastic Models*. New York, London: John Wiley & Sons.

Jarrow, A. R. 2002. *Modeling Fixed-Income Securities and Interest Rate Options*. 2nd edn. Stanford University Press.

Jegadeesh, N. and Titman, S. 1993. Returns to Buying Winners and Selling Losers: Implications for Stock Market Efficiency. *Journal of Finance*, 48(1), 65–91.

Jensen, M. C. 1968. The Performance of Mutual Funds in the Period 1945–1964. *Journal of Finance*, 23(2), 389–416.

Johansen, A., Ledoit, O., and Sornette, D. 2000. Crashes as Critical Points. *International Journal of Theoretical and Applied Finance*, 3(2), 219–255.

Joshi, M. S. 2008. *The Concepts and Practice of Mathematical Finance*. 2nd edn. Cambridge University Press.

Kabanov, Y. 2008. In Discrete Time a Local Martingale is a Martingale under an Equivalent Probability Measure. *Finance and Stochastics*, 12(3), 293–297.

Kabanov, Y. M. and Kramkov, D. O. 1998. Asymptotic Arbitrage in Large Financial Markets. *Finance and Stochastics*, 2, 143–172.

Kahneman, D. and Tversky, A. 1979. Prospect Theory: An Analysis of Decision under Risk. *Econometrica*, 47(2), 263–291.

Kahneman, D. and Tversky, A. 1981. The Framing of Decisions and the Psychology of Choice. *Science*, 211(4481), 453–458.

Kahneman, D. and Tversky, A. 1992. Advances in Prospect Theory: Cumulative Representation of Uncertainty. *Journal of Risk and Uncertainty*, 5(4), 297–323.

Kan, R. and Smith, D. R. 2008. The Distribution of the Sample Minimum-Variance Frontier. *Management Science*, 54(7), 1364–1380.

Keller-Ressel, M. and Teichmann, J. 2009. *A Remark on Gatheral's "Most-Likely Path Approximation" of Implied Volatility*. Tech. rept. TU Berlin.

Kelly, J. L. 1956. A New Interpretation of Information Rate. *Bell Systems Technical Journal*, 35, 917–926.

Kemna, A. G. Z. and Vorst, A. C. F. 1990. A Pricing Method for Options Based on Average Asset Values. *Journal of Banking and Finance*, 14, 113–129.

Kostrikin, A. I. and Manin, Y. I. 1997. *Linear Algebra and Geometry*. Amsterdam: Overseas Publisher Association.

Kou, S. G. 2002. A Jump-Diffusion Model for Option Pricing. *Management Science*, 48(8), 1086–1101.

Lee, R. W. 2004. Implied Volatility: Statics, Dynamics, and Probabilistic Interpretation. Chapter 11, pages 241–268 of: Baeza-Yates, R., Glaz, J., Gzyl, H., Hüsler, J., and Palacios, J. L. (eds.), *Recent Advances in Applied Probability*. Berlin, Heidelberg, New York: Springer.

Leland, H. E. 1985. Option Pricing and Replication with Transaction Costs. *Journal of Finance*, 40(5), 1283–1301.

Lengwiler, Y. 2004. *Microfoundations of Financial Economics: An Introduction to General Equilibrium Asset Pricing*. Princeton University Press.

LeRoy, S. F. and Porter, R. D. 1981. The Present-value Relation: Tests Based on Implied Variance Bounds. *Econometrica*, 49, 55–574.

Lewis, A. 2000. *Option Valuation under Stochastic Volatility*. Newport Beach, California: Finance Press.

Lewis, A. 2001. *A Simple Option Formula for General Jump-Diffusion and Other Exponential Levy Processes*. Social Science Research Network (SSRN): 282110.

Lewis, A. 2002. Fear of Jumps. *Wilmott Magazine*, December 2002, 60–67.

Lighthill, M. J. 1980. *Introduction to Fourier Analysis and Generalised Functions*. Cambridge University Press.

Lintner, J. 1965. The Valuation of Risk Assets and the Selection of Risky Investments in Stock Portfolios and Capital Budgets. *Review of Economics and Statistics*, 47(1), 13–37.

Longstaff, F. A. and Schwartz, E. S. 2001. Valuing American Options by Simulation: A Simple Least-Squares Approach. *Review of Financial Studies*, 14, 113–148.

Lukacs, E. 1970. *Characteristic Functions*. 2nd edn. London: Charles Griffin & Co.

Machina, M. J. 1982. Expected Utility Analysis without the Independence Axiom. *Econometrica*, 50, 277–323.

Madan, D. B., Carr, P. P., and Chang, E. C. 1998. The Variance Gamma Process and Option Pricing. *European Finance Review*, 2, 79–105.

Magnus, J. R. and Neudecker, H. 2007. *Matrix Differential Calculus with Applications in Statistics and Econometrics*. 3rd edn. New York, Brisbane, Toronto: John Wiley & Sons.

Mardia, K. V., Kent, J. T., and Bibby, J. M. 2003. *Multivariate Analysis*. New York, London: Academic Press.

Markowitz, H. 1952. Portfolio Selection. *Journal of Finance*, 7, 77–91.

Markowitz, H. 1959. *Portfolio Selection: Efficient Diversification of Investments*. New York, London: John Wiley & Sons, Chapman & Hall.

Mazzoni, T. 2015. A GARCH Parametrization of the Volatility Surface. *Journal of Derivatives*, 23(1), 9–24.

McNeil, A. J., Frey, R., and Embrechts, P. 2005. *Quantitative Risk Management*. Princeton University Press.

Mehra, R. and Prescott, E. C. 1985. The Equity Premium: A Puzzle. *Journal of Monetary Economics*, 15, 145–161.

Mejlbro. 2009. *Linear Algebra*. bookboon.com.

Merton, R.C. 1973. The Theory of Rational Option Pricing. *Bell Journal of Economics and Management Science*, 4, 141–183.

Merton, R. C. 1974. On the Pricing of Corporate Dept: The Risk Structure of Interest Rates. *Journal of Finance*, 29(2), 449–470.

Merton, R. C. 1976. Option Pricing when Underlying Stock Returns are Discontinuous. *Journal of Financial Economics*, 3, 125–144.

Meucci, A. 2006. Beyond Black-Litterman in Practice. *Risk*, 19, 114–119.

Meucci, A. 2009. Enhancing the Black-Litterman and Related Approaches: Views and Stress-Test on Risk Factors. *Journal of Asset Management*, 10(2), 89–96.

Meucci, A. 2010a. Black-Litterman Approach. Pages 196–198 of: Cont, R. (ed.), *Encyclopedia of Quantitative Finance*. Chichester, West Sussex: John Wiley & Sons.

Meucci, A. 2010b. *The Black-Litterman Approach: Original Model and Extensions*. Social Science Research Network (SSRN): 1117574.

Misner, C. W., Thorne, K. S., and Wheeler, J. A. 1973. *Gravitation*. New York: W. H. Freeman and Company.

Mossin, J. 1966. Equilibrium in a Capital Asset Market. *Econometrica*, 34(4), 768–783.

Nawalkha, S. K., Beliaeva, N. A., and Soto, G. M. 2007. *Dynamic Term Structure Modeling*. Hoboken, New Jersey: John Wiley & Sons.

Neftci, S. N. 2000. *An Introduction to the Mathematics of Financial Derivatives*. 2nd edn. Amsterdam, Boston, London, New York: Academic Press.

Nelson, C. R. and Siegel, A. F. 1987. Parsimonious Modeling of Yield Curves. *Journal of Business*, 60(4), 473–489.

Pratt, J. W. 1964. Risk Aversion in the Small and in the Large. *Econometrica*, 32(1), 122–136.

Prelec, D. 1998. The Probability Weighting Function. *Econometrica*, 66(3), 497–527.

Qian, E. and Gorman, S. 2001. Conditional Distribution in Portfolio Theory. *Financial Analyst Journal*, 57, 44–51.

Quiggin, J. 1982. A Theory of Anticipated Utility. *Journal of Economic Behavior and Organization*, 3, 225–243.

Rabin, M. 2000. Risk Aversion and Expected-Utility Theory: A Calibration Theorem. *Econometrica*, 68(5), 1281–1292.

Rebonato, R. 1999. On the Simultaneous Calibration of Multifactor Lognormal Interest Rate Models to Black Volatilities and to the Correlation Matrix. *Journal of Computational Finance*, 2(4), 5–27.

Rebonato, R. 2000. *Interest-Rate Option Models*. 2nd edn. Chichester, New York: John Wiley & Sons.

Rebonato, R. 2002. *Modern Pricing of Interest-Rate Derivatives: The LIBOR Market Model and Beyond*. Princeton University Press.

Rebonato, R. 2004. *Volatility and Correlation*. 2nd edn. Chichester, New York: John Wiley & Sons.

Rebonato, R., McKay, K., and White, R. 2009. *The SABR/LIBOR Market Model: Pricing, Calibration and Hedging for Complex Interest-Rate Derivatives*. Chichester, New York: John Wiley & Sons.

Reghai, A. 2015. *Quantitative Finance: Back to Basic Principles*. Basingstoke, New York: Palgrave Macmillan.

Resnik, M. D. 1987. *Choices: An Introduction to Decision Theory*. University of Minnesota Press.

Rieger, M. O. and Wang, M. 2006. Cumulative Prospect Theory and the St. Petersburg Paradox. *Economic Theory*, 28, 665–679.

Roger, P. 2010. *Probability for Finance*. Available at www.bookboon.com.

Roll, R. and Ross, S. A. 1980. An Empirical Investigation of the Arbitrage Pricing Theory. *Journal of Finance*, 35(5), 1073–1103.

Ross, S. A. 1976. The Arbitrage Theory of Capital Asset Pricing. *Journal of Economic Theory*, 13, 341–360.

Ross, S. M. 2010. *A First Course in Probability*. 8th edn. New York, London: Pearson Prentice Hall.

Rouwenhorst, K. G. 1998. International Momentum Strategies. *Journal of Finance*, 53(1), 267–284.

Rudin, W. 1976. *Principles of Mathematical Analysis*. 3rd edn. New York: McGraw-Hill.

Rudin, W. 1991. *Functional Analysis*. 2nd edn. New York: McGraw-Hill.

Samuelson, P. A. 1963. Risk and Uncertainty: A Fallacy of Large Numbers. *Scientia*, 98(4), 108–113.

Schaefer, S. M. 1977. The Problem with Redemption Yields. *Financial Analysts Journal*, 33(4), 59–67.

Schönbucher, P. J. 1999. A Market Model for Stochastic Implied Volatility. *Philosophical Transactions of the Royal Society A*, 357(1758), 2071–2092.

Scott, L. O. 1987. Option Pricing when the Variance Changes Randomly: Theory, Estimation, and an Application. *Journal of Financial and Quantitative Analysis*, 22, 419–438.

Sharpe, W. F. 1964. Capital Asset Prices: A Theory of Market Equilibrium under Conditions of Risk. *Journal of Finance*, 19(3), 425–442.

Sharpe, W. F. 1966. Mutual Fund Performance. *Journal of Business*, 39(1), 119–138.

Shiller, R. J. 1981. Do Stock Prices Move Too Much to be Justified by Subsequent Changes in Dividends? *American Economic Review*, 71(3), 421–436.

Shiryaev, A. N. 1996. *Probability*. 2nd edn. Berlin, Heidelberg, New York: Springer.

Shiryaev, A. N. 1999. *Essentials of Stochastic Finance: Facts, Models, Theory*. Singapore, New Jersey, London, Hong Kong: World Scientific.

Shreve, S. E. 2004a. *Stochastic Calculus for Finance I: The Binomial Asset Pricing Model*. Berlin, Heidelberg, New York: Springer.

Shreve, S. E. 2004b. *Stochastic Calculus for Finance II: Continuous-Time Models*. Berlin, Heidelberg, New York: Springer.

Sornette, D. 2003. *Why Stock Markets Crash: Critical Events in Complex Financial Systems*. Princeton University Press.

Stein, E. M. and Stein, J. C. 1991. Stock Price Distribution with Stochastic Volatility: An Analytic Approach. *Review of Financial Studies*, 4, 727–752.

Stoer, J. and Bulirsch, R. 1993. *Introduction to Numerical Analysis*. 2nd edn. New York, Berlin, Heidelberg: Springer.

Sundaresan, S. 2009. *Fixed Income Markets and Their Derivatives*. 3rd edn. Boston, Heidelberg, New York: Academic Press.

Svensson, L. E. O. 1994. *Estimating and Interpreting Forward Interest Rates: Sweden 1992–1994*. Tech. rept. 114. Washington, DC: International Monetary Fund.

Tobin, J. 1958. Liquidity Preference as Behavior Towards Risk. *Review of Economic Studies*, 67, 65–86.

Treynor, J. L. 1966. How to Rate Management Investment Funds. *Harvard Business Review*, 43, 63–75.

Tuckman, B. 2002. *Fixed Income Securities: Tools for Today's Markets*. 2nd edn. Hoboken, New Jersey: John Wiley & Sons.

Tversky, A. and Kahneman, D. 1983. Extensional Versus Intuitive Reasoning: The Conjunction Fallacy in Probability Judgment. *Psychological Review*, 90(4), 293–315.

Tversky, A. and Kahneman, D. 1991. Loss Aversion in Riskless Choice: A Reference Dependent Model. *Quarterly Journal of Economics*, 106(4), 1039–1061.

Uhlenbeck, G. E. and Ornstein, L. S. 1930. On the Theory of the Brownian Motion. *Physical Review*, 36, 823–841.

van der Kamp, R. 2009. Local Volatility Modelling. M.Phil. thesis, University of Twente, Enschede, The Netherlands.

Vasicek, O. 1977. An Equilibrium Characterization of the Term Structure. *Journal of Financial Economics*, 5, 177–188.

Vellekoop, M. 2010. Forwards and Futures. Pages 773–778 of: Cont, R. (ed.), *Encyclopedia of Quantitative Finance*. Chichester, West Sussex: John Wiley & Sons.

von Neumann, J. and Morgenstern, O. 1953. *Theory of Games and Economic Behavior*. 3rd edn. Princeton Univerity Press.

Wakker, P. and Tversky, A. 1993. An Axiomatization of Cumulative Prospect Theory. *Journal of Risk and Uncertainty*, 7(7), 147–176.

Weil, P. 1992. Equilibrium Asset Prices with Undiversifiable Labor Income Risk. *Journal of Economic Dynamics and Control*, 16, 769–790.

Wilmott, P. 2006a. *Paul Wilmott on Quantitative Finance: Volume 1*. 2nd edn. West Sussex, New York, San Francisco: John Wiley & Sons.

Wilmott, P. 2006b. *Paul Wilmott on Quantitative Finance: Volume 2*. 2nd edn. West Sussex, New York, San Francisco: John Wiley & Sons.

Wilmott, P. 2006c. *Paul Wilmott on Quantitative Finance: Volume 3*. 2nd edn. West Sussex, New York, San Francisco: John Wiley & Sons.

Yaari, M. E. 1987. The Dual Theory of Choice Under Risk. *Econometrica*, 55(1), 95–115.

INDEX

For EU product safety concerns, contact us at Calle de José Abascal, 56–1°, 28003 Madrid, Spain or eugpsr@cambridge.org.

www.ingramcontent.com/pod-product-compliance
Ingram Content Group UK Ltd.
Pitfield, Milton Keynes, MK11 3LW, UK
UKHW012201180425
457623UK00020B/348